Google® Power Tools Bible

Google® Power Tools Bible

Ted Coombs
Roderico DeLeon

BICENTENNIAL
1807
WILEY
2007
BICENTENNIAL

Wiley Publishing, Inc.

Google® Power Tools Bible

Published by
Wiley Publishing, Inc.
10475 Crosspoint Boulevard
Indianapolis, IN 46256
www.wiley.com

Copyright © 2007 by Wiley Publishing, Inc., Indianapolis, Indiana

Published simultaneously in Canada

ISBN: 978-0-470-09712-0

Manufactured in the United States of America

10 9 8 7 6 5 4 3 2 1

For general information on our other products and services or to obtain technical support, please contact our Customer Care Department within the U.S. at (800) 762-2974, outside the U.S. at (317) 572-3993 or fax (317) 572-4002.

Library of Congress Control Number: 2006939604

About the Authors

Ted Coombs has written many books on computer programming, networking, and Internet applications, including *Setting Up an Internet Site For Dummies*. He works in the area of computer forensics. He also heads the effort of documenting world history at wikihistory.org. He lives and works in both Hawaii and the Netherlands.

Roderico DeLeon has authored several books on computer technology, networking and Internet applications, and a video game guide. He presently works as a computer applications and forensics consultant in Mexico City. His passion is tourism. When not in Mexico City, he travels the world while running the xtremetours.com travel site.

*To Ocean, Sebastian, Diego and Ana Paula; may
Google help you toward a better future.*

Credits

Acquisitions Editor
Courtney Allen

Project Editors
Tim Borek
Gwenette Gaddis Goshert

Technical Editor
Lee Musick

Copy Editor
Kim Heusel

Editorial Manager
Robyn Siesky

Business Manager
Amy Knies

**Vice President and Executive Group
Publisher**
Richard Swadley

Vice President and Executive Publisher
Bob Ipsen

Vice President and Publisher
Barry Pruett

Project Coordinator
Adrienne Martinez

Graphics and Production Specialists
Claudia Bell
Denny Hager
Barbara Moore
Heather Pope
Amanda Spagnuolo

Quality Control Technicians
John Greenough
Christine Pingleton

Proofreading and Indexing
Techbooks

Wiley Bicentennial Logo
Richard J. Pacifico

Contents

Contents

Contents

Contents

Contents

Contents

Part IV: Google-izing Your Computer

Chapter 29: Messaging with Google 409

Contents

Contents

Contents

Contents

Preface

Google Power Tools Bible gives everyone — whether a computer guru trying to figure out how Google can help with their business, or the average person at home who uses Google to do Web searches but would like to know more about what other things Google provides — an in-depth look at the products and services Google offers to date. Learn about services like Gmail, Google Talk, Google Desktop, or how to make money with Google AdSense. This book helps business owners by guiding them through the many services Google offers business, whether it's advertising on the Web, or integrating satellite images of the Earth into business processes. More than anything, this book helps you discover things about Google that will entertain you, simplify your life, and make your Internet experience more efficient.

How To Use This Book

The book is divided into the following parts:

- **Part I: Navigating Google Information** — Finding things on the Internet is what Google does best. The chapters in this part help you navigate the many services Google offers for finding Web pages, images, videos, news, scholarly articles, maps, and products. In addition to Web searching, this part covers Google Earth, configuring Google Desktop, portfolio management with Google Finance, and selling just about anything through Google Base.

- **Part II: Communicating Google Style** — Google provides a number of great programs for communicating and sharing information. This part shows you how to setup and use Gmail for your e-mail, Google Talk for instant messaging, and Picasa for editing and sharing pictures. Learn to communicate with others using Google Groups and Blogger, or share your daily schedule using Google Calendar.

- **Part III: Going Mobile** — You're not stuck to your desk with Google. When you're on the go, find out where it is you're going using Google Mobile Maps. Chapters in this part also help you get the most from your mobile Web surfing experience and find just about any information you need using SMS text messaging. You also learn about creating mobile Web resources.

- **Part IV: Google-izing Your Computer** — Installing and using the Google Pack applications help you get the most out of your computer. This part also covers the efficiency-increasing Google Toolbar and Firefox extensions as well as creating 3D models using Google's SketchUp.

- **Part V: Google and the Enterprise** — The chapters in this part help businesses of all sizes, from sole proprietorships to large corporations learn how to market themselves using Google AdWords. Also learn how to make money by hosting Google ads on your Web pages and blogs. Make good business decisions regarding online resources by using Google Analytics and Google Trends. Use Google enterprise applications to expand business desktops and discover how you can use Google Maps in your business processes. When you need extra Google power, you can always add Google hardware.

■ **Part VI: Exploring Google Innovation** — Find out about what's coming next at Google. See what is developing in the Google labs and try the newest Google applications while they are being developed.

Using the Book's Icons

The following margin icons are used to help you get the most out of this book:

NOTE   Notes highlight useful information that you should take into consideration.

TIP   Tips provide an additional bit of advice that will make a particular feature quicker or easier to use.

CAUTION   Cautions warn you of a potential problem before you make a mistake.

CROSS-REF   Watch for the Cross-Reference icon to learn where in another chapter you can go to find more information on a particular feature.

ON the WEB   Watch for the Web Reference icon to learn where on the Internet you can go to find more information on a particular feature.

Acknowledgments

We would first like to thank authors Donna Baker, Craig Long, and Adrian Solomon for their invaluable assistance in completing this book. This was truly a global effort with Roderico in Mexico, Ted in the Netherlands, Donna in Canada, Craig in Hawaii, and Adrian in Romania. Thanks also to Tim Borek and Courtney Allen at Wiley for your support in the creation of this book. A big thanks to Matt Wagner at Fresh Books for managing the whole process, and congratulations on your new baby. Thanks to the entire van den Berg family in Utrecht, Netherlands, Thijs and Lorenzo for putting up with us while writing this book. Finally, thanks to all the wonderful developers at Google who have created some great products and services.

Introduction

This book is a "bible," which, if you use Google's glossary, you find out comes from the ancient Greek word *byblos,* or "papyrus." Ancient Greek and Egyptian papyrus texts provide information to us even today, and using Google you can find that information written thousands of years ago. But Google is about more than simply searching the Web. See the world in a different way using Google Earth, or find your way throughout the world using Google Maps. Tell others how you feel about the world using Blogger or how you feel about them using Google Talk. While chatting with friends, look up movie times, find information about your favorite books, go shopping with Froogle, and entertain yourself watching Google Video.

In a time when our lives are filled with sound bites, it's difficult to know if the information the media blasts at us minute by minute is fair and balanced. Google News aggregates media in an impartial and apolitical manner. The stories themselves may be biased, but when you can read all the stories, you can create that balance for yourself and form your own opinion. Google News is also a great feature to install on your Google Desktop, which creates a great environment for hosting information applications, reading your Gmail, and adding "gadgets" for fun and profit. Google Finance provides access to financial information and helps you manage your financial portfolio.

On the way to making your first, second, or tenth million? Let people know about your business by showing up in searches relevant to your business. With Google AdWords, you can advertise to people in Google searches and on partner Web sites. Need a little help on your way to that first million? Become part of the Google network and host Google ads on your Web page and earn money. It's gratifying to wake up in the morning and see how many people visited your Web pages each night while you slept, and how many people clicked ads, sending money your way.

Google isn't just about enhancing your personal life. There are business software and hardware solutions that can give your enterprise a competitive information edge. Gain an even greater edge through Google's Open software development, which allows for easy access to Google services through the use of application programming interfaces (APIs) and software development kits (SDKs).

What's more, Google is fun. Last night I left my brother-in-law's house after showing him Google Trends. All I heard as he waved, never taking his eyes off the screen, was "Oh wow! Look at this!" That's exactly how I feel about all of the Google services, tools, and technologies. *"Oh wow! Look at this!"*

Part I

Navigating Google Information

Chapter 1

Searching the Web

Web searching has become a part of the day-to-day life of any person who has a computer. Searches vary from words, phrases, products, people, images, and many other forms. Today, when you want to know something you simply do a Web search. There are many search engines but none, according to `searchengineshowdown.com`, quite as large due to Google's inclusion of file types such as PDF, DOC and PS, not indexed by other search engines. What makes Google so powerful is not just the sheer number of files it has indexed, but the tools that make arriving at the answer to your question simple and straightforward.

This chapter helps you learn to better form your queries and introduce you to the basic Google search. Even the basic Google search is powerful and gives you an amazing amount of control over how you view your results and how to best focus your search so that you arrive quickly and easily at the results you seek.

Forming the Basic Query

The most basic Google search is performed by navigating to the Google home page at `www.google.com`, typing a search term into the Google Search box (shown in Figure 1.1), and pressing Enter. Before you can say Google, your results appear for you to peruse.

Your search results appear with a short description of the resulting page and a link to navigate to it. Clicking the link causes you to navigate away from Google to the page. To return to Google, click the Back button in your browser. This is often represented as a left-facing arrow icon.

FIGURE 1.1

Type a search term and press Enter to find out almost anything.

Keywords

The search terms you type on the Google home page are called *keywords*. When typing keywords, there are a few things to remember. More keywords narrow your search, but too many may cause you to be too specific and miss the information you are looking for. Google pays attention to whether the keywords are singular or plural and also searches based on the order of your keywords. For example, if you search on the two keywords town and dog in that order you will get results that start off with links to dogtown.com, a skateboard company. But the second link is to a pet shop. Change the order to dog and then town and the results change. Now at least the first 15 or so results refer specifically to Dogtown skateboarding.

Google also uses something known as *stemming*. This means that Google automatically looks for variations of a keyword. For example, if type the search text **cloning your cat**, Google also looks for clone cat (see www.savingsandclone.com).

TIP
   Don't use the word *and* as a keyword. Google will ignore it. Google automatically looks for all of your keywords within a page. The most relevant page will contain all or most of the keywords.

Occasionally you will want to create phrases out of your keywords. This is particularly useful when searching on names. To create a phrase, enclose a group of words in quotes like this: "dog town". If you try this search you will see that it gives you different results from the previous two searches on those terms. If you search on the terms John and Smith, Google looks for pages that contain the name John and the name Smith, not necessarily in the same name. The resulting Web page may have the names John Anderson and Joan Smith. Putting the name John Smith in quotes like this — "John Smith" — forces Google to search for that phrase specifically.

Querying the results

One thing Google is good at is giving you as many possible results for your query as possible. This is good in that Google is thorough and bad in that too many results could mean that the result you are really looking for is lost in the weeds. Google gives you the opportunity to do a second search but only through the results of the previous search.

Let's say you have searched on dog breeds. The results are innumerable (actually just over 11 million). This is far too many pages to search manually. At this point you have two options: Go back and form a more specific query, or search through the 11 million results to narrow the number. At the bottom of the results page you will see a link, <u>Search within results</u>. Clicking this link will cause a new Search within results search box to appear. Enter a new search term. Continuing this example, try typing **"fox terrier"**. Even though this example returns 780,000 results, they are more specific to the dog breed fox terrier. Unfortunately you cannot continue searching through your results a second time. If there are still too many results and not specific enough you will have to go back and form a better query. Knowing how Google does is job can help you form better queries.

How Google Searches the Web

To get the best out of Google it helps to know a little bit about how Google goes about searching the Web. This will help you create better queries and understand the results you are seeing and why they are ordered the way they are. Google ranks the results of a search by using "traditional" factors such as the URL (Web page address such as `www.google.com`), *meta tags* (invisible pieces of information about a Web page added by a Web page author), keywords (search terms), and its own patented technology called PageRank.

Google follows four steps to complete the search:

- Finds all the pages that match the keywords on the page.
- Ranks the pages using "traditional" factors (URL, meta tags, and keyword frequency).
- Calculates the relevancy of the link text. How related are the keywords to what appears in the link?
- Google displays the results using PageRank to determine the result order.

Google employs search bots (Web crawlers), which are special programs that search through Web pages, evaluating the pages based on certain criteria and creating an index that allows for rapid search results.

Traditional factors

There is certain information within a Web page that Web crawlers look at to analyze where a page should fall within the results of a search. The term for this is *relevancy*. Pages in a search engine most often appear in the results based on the most relevant pages first. There are several factors in determining the degree of relevancy a page might have. Some of these are obvious, such as the keywords appearing within the text of the Web page. Other, less obvious, factors are involved in determining the relevancy of the page. These include meta tags, descriptive tags, and link text.

Meta tags

Meta tags refer to information that is placed within the header of a Web page that is not visible to the person viewing the page. The information in these tags, which is stored in name/value pairs, is passed to search bots or Web crawlers like the ones Google uses. The information stored in these tags often includes keywords and descriptions of the page that the Web page author would like to associate with the page.

Even though Google does not give these tags much weight, it still looks for keywords in them. There are many types of meta tags but the two most commonly used for assisting in PageRank are the `<DESCRIPTION>` tag and the `<KEYWORD>` tag. The `<DESCRIPTION>` tag includes a text string describing the contents of the page. This is the description used by Google and other search engines to describe the page to Web searchers. The `<KEYWORD>` tag contains a comma-delimited list of keywords the Web page author feels are important in finding the Web page. This includes terms that may not be found within the actual text of the page. For example, an e-commerce site might include keywords such as *hefty man* in the `<KEYWORD>` tag but not include this term in the actual text viewed on the Web site. Someone then searching for hefty man clothing may then find this page. Where, without this keyword the page may not have been included in their search results. Other HTML tags, such as `<TITLE>`, `<H1>`, and `<H2>` are also searched by Google's Web crawler for keywords.

The link text

The URL, or link text, has always been important in determining a page's relevance. When the URL of a Web page contains the keyword it will be considered much more relevant by Google than a page that may contain the keywords within the text but not within the link text. For example, when you search for the word *house* using Google, the first five results have the word *house* in their URLs as shown in Figure 1.2.

FIGURE 1.2

When search terms appear in the URL, they are considered more relevant.

CROSS-REF   The Web browser shown in Figure 1.2 displays the Google Toolbar. See Chapter 31 to learn more about downloading and installing the Google Toolbar. Another factor Google takes into account when considering page relevancy is the frequency with which the keyword appears on the Web page. The more times the word you are searching for appears within the Web page the higher the relevancy of that page.

PageRank

PageRank was created at Stanford University in 1985 as part of a research project studying a new kind of search engine. The project was developed by Larry Page and Sergey Brin. They created a functional search prototype that they called Google. Shortly after creating the PageRank technology Larry and Sergey founded Google, Inc., making use of the PageRank technology as a key element in its new Web search software.

If you search for PageRank on Google, you find the following description:

PageRank relies on the uniquely democratic nature of the web by using its vast link structure as an indicator of an individual page's value. In essence, Google interprets a link from page A to page B as a vote, by page A, for page B. But, Google looks at more than the sheer volume of votes, or links a page receives; it also analyzes the page that casts the vote. Votes cast by pages that are themselves "important" weigh more heavily and help to make other pages "important."

The PageRank that a Web page receives is determined by the number of links that are pointing to the page. So each link is basically a vote but since Google is not a democratic country, not all votes are equal. Some votes are more important and have greater value. PageRank gives a little more value to the votes on pages that are themselves listed higher in the PageRank.

NOTE   **Some votes can count against you. Webmasters, in order to increase their PageRank, add their pages to link farms. These are locations on the Internet that will add links to your page. Google punishes this behavior by removing the page from the Google index.**

Of most importance to PageRank is the link to a Web page. The type of Web sites that link to a page will most determine the PageRank. For example, when there is a Web page that talks about Labradors (breed of dogs) and the American Kennel Club (`www.akc.org`) has a link to that page, this link is given greater weight than perhaps a link from a personal Web page. This is because the AKC Web page is specifically about dogs and breeds and is likely to have a very high PageRank of its own.

More About Keywords and Queries

Now that you know a little bit more about how Google searches through Web pages, determines relevancy, and PageRank, it's time to understand a little bit more about the most fundamental part of doing a Web search, the *keyword*.

A keyword is a significant or descriptive word that defines the topic on which you are searching. In other words, keywords define the core of your search. To best find content on the Web you must use the most efficient keywords. Using more keywords narrows your search but doesn't necessarily make it more efficient. You are limited to using a maximum of ten keywords. When you narrow your search, fewer search results are returned, but you may make the search so narrow that you miss what you were looking for. It is sometimes better to group keywords into a search phrase, as described in the first part of this chapter or by creating a search expression.

Introducing search expressions

A *search expression* is a set of keywords and operators such as *and, or, +,* and *–*. Using search expressions can often help you narrow your search most effectively. Here is a sneak peak at the more detailed discussion in Chapter 2. Use the + sign before any word to tell Google that this word must be in the results. This can be particularly important because Google often leaves out common words that it considers unimportant to the meaning or context. Common words such as who, what, when, where, and how are often ignored when included as keywords. When a common word must be considered, precede it with the plus sign like this: **+how +now brown cow.**

Without the plus signs, Google may have ignored the keywords *how* and *now.*

TIP   **You can forget about capitalizing words. Google ignores all capitalization.**

Another useful way to affect the way Google understands keywords is to tell Google what to ignore. Precede keywords that you specifically don't want to see in your results with a – (minus sign). For example, if you are searching on old *M.A.S.H.* TV shows and using the keyword *potter,* and don't want to see an endless stream of pages about Harry Potter, you can precede the word *harry* with a minus sign like this: **–harry potter mash tv**.

Whether using the + or – sign to affect how Google handles your keywords, make certain there is a space before either of these characters when following another keyword.

The query

Type your keywords into the Google Search box as shown in Figure 1.3. You can begin your search by pressing Enter or by clicking Search.

> **TIP** Don't be afraid to get extra help by clicking the Search Tips link at the bottom of each Google results page.

Google Search boxes have become ubiquitous. They are everywhere. Google has given the ability to include its search box on any Web page that wants to have one. You don't necessarily have to be on the Google home page to perform your query. Be advised that many of the Google Search boxes that appear on other sites have the ability of searching the entire Web or just that site. Normally, the Web page informs you of any search limitations.

> **WARNING** Google searches are not secure. Never enter personal or financial information into a Google Search box, particularly one that is on a page other than the Google home page.

FIGURE 1.3

Type your search term into the Google Search box.

The missing word query

Earlier in this chapter you learned how to create a phrase by enclosing keywords within quotes. Another useful tool is the * (missing word wildcard), which is used only within phrases. This is particular great when you are searching for things like song lyrics and can't remember all the words. For instance, "If you could * my mind love" as a search phrase will return the words from the Gordon Lightfoot song that begins, "If you could read my mind love."

Using the missing word wildcard is also great when you need answers. Here is an example: "the circumference of the Earth is * miles" returns "the circumference of the Earth is 24901.55 miles in the first result." Of course, you could have typed the phrase "the circumference of the Earth is" without the wildcard and the word miles and you might receive different results including the circumference in kilometers or feet. It is a little-used feature but can help you narrow your search.

One last useful feature of the missing word wildcard is that Google does not count this wildcard when calculating whether or not you have exceeded the ten-keyword limit. You might find it useful when too many search terms have become a problem.

The Search Results Page

Once you click the Google Search button, Google launches a new page displaying the results of your search. The first thing you notice in the results page is the number of results Google found in response to your query. For example, if you searched on *dogs,* the page tells you that it is displaying the first 10 results of about 183 million links for dogs. Next to the number of results there is a link to read the definition of dog. To the right of the definition link Google tells you how long it took to perform the search. Perhaps this is bragging rights but I can see no real purpose for this metric.

Search results

Each search result displays the name of the Web page, a short description of the page contents, the link you will navigate if you choose that result (the Web page address), the size of the page, the cached version of the page, and another link called Similar Pages.

Occasionally you may click a link attempting to see one of the results and find that it no longer exists, or that the information on the page has changed since Google last indexed it and the information you are interested in no longer appears on the page. Google keeps a snapshot of the indexed page in a cache (historical storage space) on the Google servers. The cached version of the page is what Google uses to set the PageRank for your query. Use the Cached link when you are unable to access the page containing the information in which you are interested. When the cached link is missing it's because Google has either not yet indexed the page or the owner of the page requested that the page's content not be cached. This often happens with commercial content for which the owner of the Web page expects you to pay.

When you see results that are indented, this means that Google has found your keywords within other pages from the same Web site. Remember your results will not necessarily appear on the site's home page. Clicking the links in the indented results help you jump to different pages within this Web site. You may not find exactly what you are looking for on the page that contains your keywords. You may want to navigate to other pages in the resulting Web site. Navigating through the site can often be challenging. Some Web sites don't provide a menu or simple mechanism for navigating the site. In those cases it is often easiest to start at the site's home page. After navigating to the resulting Web page, look at the URL in the address bar of your Web browser. Copy only the domain name portion, for example, `www.google.com`, and forget everything that appears after the .com, .org, or whatever suffix might appear in the domain name. Paste this back into the address bar of your Web browser and press Enter. That should take you to the site's home page.

Oops

When you receive the result that states: Your search – keyword list – did not match any results, it means that your keywords or phrases matched no Web pages within the Google index. That doesn't mean they don't exist, they have just not been indexed by Google's Web crawlers. Here are three good suggestions:

- Make sure all words are spelled correctly.
- Try different keywords.
- Try more general keywords.

Google is really good about catching misspelled words. Unless the keyword is very obscure, Google usually suggests an alternate spelling. Trying different keywords or more general keywords is probably your answer. If you are have used quotes to create an exact phrase, try doing the search without the quotes.

On to the next one

By default Google displays ten results per page. You learn how to adjust that later in this chapter. Once you review all the results in the page you can continue on to the next page by clicking several different things at the bottom of the results page. You can click the blue right arrow at the end of the word *Goooooooooogle*. You can click the <u>Next</u> link beneath that. Last, you can click a specific page number to go directly to a specific page. Ten pages are there initially to choose from. When there are more than ten pages of results, which is often the case, navigating to some page forward causes Google to show you the next ten pages after that. For example, navigating to page 10 causes Google to list pages 1 through 19. Once you navigate away from the first page, a <u>Previous</u> link appears to allow you to navigate backward through the result pages.

Sponsored links

When viewing the results you will notice that on the right side of the page there are *sponsored links*. These links are paid for by companies so you can see them when you search on a specific topic. Some sponsored links may also appear above the other results, and appear with a shaded background to call attention to them. Google also labels them as sponsored links (see Figure 1.4).

FIGURE 1.4

Sponsored links appear as the first results and to the right side of the results page.

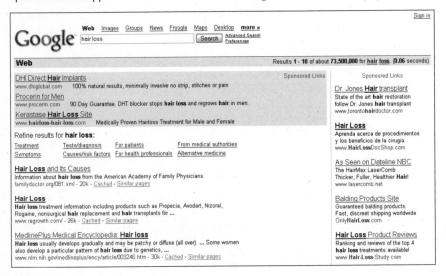

Results that assist you

Depending on the keywords you type, Google may present the results in various ways. For example, if you search for golden retriever the results page begins by showing you three images of golden retriever puppies. A similar thing happens when you search on orchids: You are shown three images of orchids.

If you search for a place like Los Angeles or Tampa, the first result is a link to a map of that location. You are then asked if you want to refine your search and look for: dining guides, attractions, lodging guides, shopping, suggested itineraries, and tour and day trips.

Google includes a spell-check feature. When Google thinks you might have misspelled a word, an alternate suggestion is displayed as the first result. If you type **goldon retreiver** as the keywords in the Google Search box the results show a legend "Did you mean:" and then a link to <u>golden retriever</u>, which is the corrected spelling. If you decide that Google is right in its assumption that the keyword(s) is misspelled, you can click the link and the search is performed again with the correct spelling. A new results page appears.

It makes no difference what your search topic is, Google displays within the first links of the results page the links that will help you continue your search.

Using the I'm Feeling Lucky Button

The I'm Feeling Lucky feature is one of Google's unique attributes. What this feature does is bypass the search results page and takes you directly to the first Web page that Google returns from your query.

For example: When you type **golden retriever** and click I'm Feeling Lucky, Google points your browser to the American Kennel Club's Golden Retriever page, where you find information about this breed.

 **Use the I'm Feeling Lucky button only for very specific topic searches.**

You can find the I'm Feeling Lucky button on Google's home page. You can also find it when using the Google Toolbar by clicking the little down arrow next to the keyword search box to open the drop-down menu. You can then select I'm Feeling Lucky, as shown in Figure 1.5. The browser navigates to the Web page that most closely matches your keyword search.

FIGURE 1.5

Select I'm Feeling Lucky from the drop-down menu on Google's Toolbar.

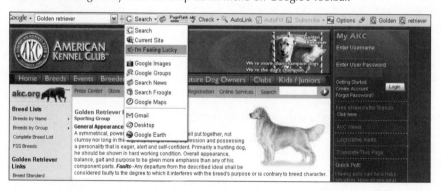

Getting the Right Pages

Getting to the right page will be influenced by which keywords you select or your search expression. Because Google returns results that match any of the keywords in your query, a good search expression with the right keywords will help you focus your search.

There are four questions you should ask yourself before doing your search. If you keep the answers to these questions in mind when you search, the results will be much closer to those you were looking for:

- What are you looking for? Conceptualize your search by finding the right keywords or create the right search expression.
- Do your keywords have synonyms or related terms? If so, you might want to think about using them.
- Does your search expression have the correct syntax and use the right search operators?
- After your search, were the results relevant to your query? If not, go back and try refining your keywords and search expression in step 3.

Additional features that can assist you in focusing your search are the ability to search similar pages and restricting your search to a single site.

- **Similar Pages:** Google displays a link under each search result called Similar Pages. This link takes you to pages that are relevant to your search result and most like that particular result.
- **Site Search:** You can restrict your search to a single site or domain. Type your keywords, then type the word **site:**, making certain to include a colon, followed by the site address — for example, **firefox site:mozilla.com**.

Setting Search Preferences

There are five global preferences you can change. These include

- Interface Language
- Search Language
- Safe Search Filtering
- Number of Results
- Results Window

If you go to the Google main page (`www.google.com`) you see three links next to the box where you type the search expression. One of these is the Preferences link. Clicking this link takes you to a page where you can modify the way Google delivers its search results.

 **Changing your preferences will apply to all Google services.**

Setting languages

The first preference, Interface Language, allows you to select from among the 119 different languages of which Google is capable to display tips and messages. All Google pages will be displayed in the language you select, not including Google search results.

CROSS-REF   See Chapter 23 to learn more about setting language preferences in Google.

The Search Language preference allows you to choose which language Google uses to perform its Web page search. Results will include Web pages written in your selected language. There are two options: You can search for pages written in any language, or you can search only for pages written in the languages you select. You are provided with a list of 31 languages, and you can select as many as you want. Click the checkbox next to the language to select it. Google recommends choosing the first option: Search for pages written in any language. This is recommended because when you do your search you will get more results. If you only choose a few or a single language only, Google will not search the whole World Wide Web; it searches only the pages written in the specified language or languages.

Setting filter options

SafeSearch Filtering filters adult sites containing explicit sexual content. There are three SafeSearch options:

- **Use strict filtering:** This eliminates search results with explicit images and explicit textual content.
- **Use moderate filtering:** This filters only explicit images. This is the default setting for Google.
- **Do not filter my search result:** No filtering takes place.

SafeSearch filtering its not 100 percent accurate but it does a very good job. Chapter 4 contains much more information about SafeSearch.

Result number setting

When searches return a large number of results it can be time consuming to continue paging through the results. Instead of using the default number of ten results per page you can choose to customize the results page by choosing a larger number of results per page. To change the number of results that Google displays use the Number of results preference setting. You may choose to see 10, 20, 30, 50, or even 100 results for page by selecting from the drop-down list.

 The more results you choose, the longer it takes the results to load into your browser.

Opening a new results window

The last preference is Results Window. By selecting this option you can choose to view search results in a new browser window. Every time you do a search and click on a search result link a new browser window opens on your computer displaying the results of your search. This is particularly handy if you want to compare or view many results at the same time.

Another option to seeing your results displayed in a new window is after you perform your Google search, you have the option of opening each result in a new window by holding the Ctrl key and clicking the link with your mouse. On a Macintosh this is the Option key.

Prefetching

Prefetching is a special feature of Mozilla and Firefox browsers. Similar to I'm Feeling Lucky, Prefetching bets that what you are looking for is in the first Web page. With Prefetching set in your browser, Google begins downloading the first Web page that appears on the Google search results page. This increases efficiency as the first page is already loaded and ready to display rather than waiting for it to load after clicking the link in the search results.

CAUTION If you have this feature turned on in your browsers, you may end up with cookies from Web pages you have never visited along with additional pages in your Firefox or Mozilla caches. If these pages contain images, they will be saved in your Temporary Internet files.

Summary

Google is much more than simply a search engine. It is an information resource. Still, what makes Google what it is, is the ability to search the Web and get the answers you are looking for. In this chapter you learned about searching with keywords and phrases, received an introduction to search expressions, and learned just how Google comes up with its results.

Searching Google and getting to the answers is a bit of an art, but luckily all arts can be learned through practice. This first look at Google searching may have seemed simple. That's because searching with Google is simple. There are ways to create complex queries. The next chapter goes into greater detail in describing how to create a search expression and using the advanced search features of Google.

Chapter 2

Focusing Your Web Search

Most of the time, the simple Google search helps you find the Web content you need. There will be other occasions, however, where your search is too broad and you need to narrow, or focus, your search. Focusing your search results in fewer matches, hopefully limiting the number of Web pages you need to explore in order to arrive at just the right information. Focusing your search can be accomplished using search operators — special Google commands that tell the search engine how to limit the search — using the Google Advanced Search, and using topic-specific searches. You can also search within your results, further narrowing the results.

Search Operators

Search operators are special words and symbols, sometimes followed by a colon, which when accompanying search terms, instruct the Google search engine how to focus the search.

In most cases, Google search operators, like Google search terms, are not case sensitive. In other words, the search term *pumpernickel* and *PuMperNickEl* return the same results. There are a few exceptions, and this chapter notes when search operators are case sensitive.

When terms are absolutely required in the search results you can precede the search term with the plus sign +. It is important be certain that there is a space before the + sign. For example, if you set a search term of blue +moon, the term moon must be in the results.

> **TIP** When used with numbers, the + sign is used in addition calculations.

IN THIS CHAPTER

Track packages, define words and find specialized information

Learn to perform Special queries on cached pages or similar pages

Search Google News, Google Groups, and Froogle

Focus your search using the Advanced Search

Narrow your search by finding results in a previous search

Create powerful search phrases by combining search terms with *operators*. Operators are special words or symbols used to create search phrases by combining search terms, or instructing Google how to act on them.

- **AND:** Queries where the terms contain an *AND* return results that contain all the terms. The *AND* operator is not required because Google automatically looks for all terms in the query. For example, **Blue Moon** is the same as **Blue AND Moon**.

- **OR:** When you use the *OR* operator between two words or phrases either term or phrase may be included. Say you are searching on planets, and you don't need all the planet names to appear on a single page. You can search on **Mercury OR Earth OR Saturn OR Venus OR Jupiter OR Pluto OR Mars OR Uranus OR Neptune**. The *OR* here is capitalized for emphasis; this operator is not case sensitive. You can further limit this search by using the *AND* operator and including the term planet.

- **"":** To create a search phrase, enclose the entire phrase in double quotes: "*search term*". You must use double quotes; single quotes do not work to create a phrase. A good example of when phrasing is useful is searching on names. Searching the name Jane Smith, for example, returns results where a page contains both the name Jane and the name Smith, but not necessarily the same person. Jane Jones and Tommy Smith on the same page are valid results. Therefore, enclosing "**Jane Smith**" in quotes ensures that you only receive results where the name Jane Smith is included on the page.

- **-:** The minus sign tells the search engine that the keyword that follows it must not be included in the results. This is useful in cases where you know which words or phrases will best limit your search by being excluded. For example, if you are searching on the name Mickey and you want all results with the word Mouse excluded, you can precede the word Mouse with a minus sign like this: **-Mouse**.

- **~:** A seldom-used but very powerful operator is the tilde symbol. This operator causes the Google search engine to return synonyms (words that have the same meaning). For example, a search on **end of the ~earth** returns pages with **end of the world** and **end of the universe** in addition to pages containing the phrase **end of the earth**.

Got Info?

Google includes the ability to recognize special kinds of information and performs a search returning very specific information. Google can distinguish when the information entered as a search is an address or a vehicle ID number or a phone number. When one of these types of information is encountered, special handling of that information gives you more than simply Web page results.

Special Number Searches

Instead of remembering hundreds of different Web page resources for looking up important numbers, such as finding telephone number area codes or to track shipping of packages, you can simply type those numbers into the Google search and the first result is normally the Web page containing the result you are looking for.

Track Packages

One of the most common reasons to visit the Web page of shipping companies or the U.S. Postal Service is track packages that you send or that others send to you. A shortcut, particularly if you have the Google search box installed in your Web browser, is to type the tracking number. Google is smart enough to figure out what type of number it is, find the right shipping Web site, perform the query, and post the result. Currently, Google finds tracking numbers from the following shippers:

- United Parcel Service (UPS)
- Federal Express (FedEx)
- U.S. Postal Service (USPS)

Information about your car

Typing a vehicle identification number (VIN) into a Google search returns a CARFAX record search result. Clicking the link causes you to navigate to the CARFAX Web site where you can see the following information:

- VIN
- Year/Make/Model
- Body style
- Engine type
- Manufacturer's location
- Number of CARFAX search results

CARFAX is a commercial service that returns information about a vehicle that has become part of the public record. This information includes the odometer readings, accident records, theft records, salvage, and more. CARFAX charges a fee to retrieve this additional information.

Q&A

When you are tired of reading through hundreds of Web pages to find the answer to a straightforward question you can use the Google Q&A. Using this feature is almost transparent when doing a Google search. The results you receive depend largely on how you form your question. Type **capital of Hawaii** into the Google search text box.

The first result displays the name of the capital, in this case Honolulu, and on the following line (as shown in Figure 2.1) displays the source that Google used to find the information.

FIGURE 2.1

Q&A presents simple answers to direct questions.

Definitions

There are many online dictionaries and encyclopedias. Google offers something just a little different and a little more powerful. Using the Google operator **define:** gives much more than your average dictionary, including related phrases you can search on by clicking the link, definitions, and their sources, as shown in Figure 2.2.

FIGURE 2.2

Get more than a dictionary definition with the *define:* operator.

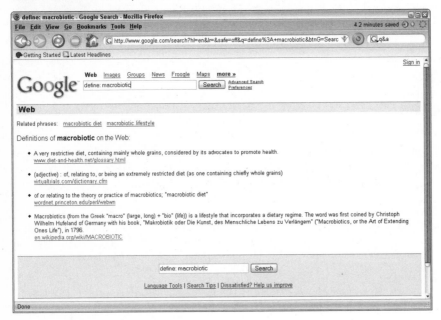

Define

The keyword *define*, placed before a word or phrase, returns a definition but does not return the level of information returned by using the *define:* operator. Google returns a definition, the source of the definition, and then lists results that include the definition of the word you are trying to define. Try **define** with and without a colon to see which one provides you the result you want.

What is

When you want to ask a specific question such as the population of a specific state or country you can precede your query with the phrase *what is*. For example, "What is the population of Idaho".

This query returns a result based on the type of question you ask. This example first returns books that include the requested information. The second result is a Google Q&A result. These are followed by normal Google Web page results.

Range of Numbers

One of the best ways to focus searches that involve numbers is to use the pound sign (#) operator. Enclose your range of numbers between two pound signs (#) and separate the numbers in the range by using two periods (..). This type of search is best used in addition to keywords. You can search on a wide variety of number ranges. Here is an example of a useful search: *digital camera #$100..$500#*.

This example query results in Web pages that list digital cameras between the price of $100 and $500. You can use this number range to find other things such as hours of operation, real estate within a certain price range, or equipment within a range of specifications.

Look for Books

Preceding your query with the word *books* causes your first Google result to be a link to a new page that contains a list of books that contain your query terms. Using a colon after the word *books* does not change your query. The result appears as a link that reads Book results for **book *search term.*** Clicking this link lists your book search results, usually preceded by an icon of the books' cover art.

> **TIP**
>
> When searching for author names it is best to enclose them in quotes. This improves the focus your query.

Navigating to the detail about the book often allows you to preview the book. Occasionally, the content of the book is restricted, which prevents you from reviewing sample content. You can also:

- Learn more about the book
- Read the table of contents
- View the title page
- Peruse the index
- See the copyright information

Google also lists places you can buy the book.

> **CROSS-REF**
>
> For more details on using Google to find books, see Chapter 6.

Site Searching

The *site:* operator allows you to limit searches to a particular Web site (domain). To search within a specific site, type the name of the Web site in the Google search text box with the *site:* operator like this: **site:www.cnn.com**.

You can also eliminate certain Web sites from your search. This is useful when a particular Web site clutters your search results. An example of this would be to eliminate all responses from the Open Source encyclopedia, Wikipedia. Eliminate those results from your search by typing **-site:www.wikipedia.org panda bears**.

This results in a search of all Web sites containing the words *panda* and *bears* but eliminates any pages from Wikipedia.org.

Using the *site:* operator followed by a single word finds all occurrences of that word in the site's URL. For example, when searching for ATA Airlines you can type this: **site:ata**.

This search returns ata.com as well as ata.org and any other URL containing *ata*. This is not a normal use of this operator. Consider using the *inurl:* operator discussed later in this chapter.

Limit Search File Types

Most of the search results Google returns are HTML and PDF documents. For other types of documents, such as Microsoft Word or Excel files available over the Web, consider limiting your results with the *filetypes:* operator. Using this operator makes it possible to limit your results to particular file types. The supported file types include:

- PDF
- PS
- DOC
- XLS
- PPT
- RTF

To create a search that limits the files that are returned to a particular file type, type the following along with your search terms: *search terms* **filetype:***type*.

You are limited to specifying a single file type. You cannot include an additional *filetype:* operator in your query. You cannot add additional file types to this operator, either. To find different file types, run a new query specifying the different file type along with the *filetype:* operator.

Find Links to a Page

It is possible to find Web pages that are related to a particular Web page by following backward all the people who have linked to a particular Web page from their own Web page. This is a great way to find related or similar pages.

When you are the author of the Web page, using the *link:* operator is also a very useful way to find out how many people have provided a link to your site and who they are. Use the *link:* operator to create queries that include only pages that have linked to the Web page you specify with the operator like this: **link:***webpageURL*.

For example, to find all web pages linked to www.whitehouse.gov, type **link:www.whitehouse.gov** in the Google query text box.

 You can include search terms other than the Web page URL. Google returns results focused with your additional search terms.

To see an interesting graphic version of this type of reverse link finding, visit www.touchgraph.com/TGGoogleBrowser.html.

This Web site, by TouchGraph LLC, displays a graphic diagram of all links to a page in its GoogleBrowser software. You must enable Java in your Web browser to view this page.

Let your fingers do the walking

There are many phone directories on the Internet. None of them provides the services offered by Google, which makes finding phone numbers and address information simple, particularly if you have the Google toolbar installed in your Web browser. The simplest way to find telephone directory information is to type a person's name and any identifying location information such as city and state into the Google search text box. If Google has this entry in its phone directory, a special result appears with a small phone icon next to it.

In addition to typing a phone number and hoping that Google recognizes it as such you can let Google know that your search is specifically for a phone number by using one of the phone book operators:

- **phonebook:** Searches residential and business listings
- **rphonebook:** Searches only residential listings
- **bphonebook:** Searches only business listings

Use of the *phonebook:* operator may result in the display of fewer results. When a combination of business and residential listings both contain your search term, a fewer number of results appears for each, business or residential, with a link to see more results in each category.

 The *phonebook:* operator is case sensitive. Typing Phonebook: will not work properly.

You can further focus your Google PhoneBook search by using either the *bphonebook:* operator to search only for business listings or the *rphonebook:* operator to search only through the residential listings.

Movie guide

Looking for information about a movie? Precede the name of the movie with the Google operator *movie:*, and if the movie is playing in theaters you will see the rating (displayed in number of stars), the length of the movie in minutes, the MPAA rating and a description of the movie genre. You will also see a listing of online reviews. If you are in the U.S., you are also prompted to type your ZIP Code to see the places and times you can view the movie in your area. Google remembers your ZIP Code for future searches.

When the movie is no longer playing in theaters you can still read all of the movie reviews. Each review has the number of stars displayed next to it to making a quick glance at how the movie was rated simple.

Financial information

A quick and easy way to retrieve important financial information about publicly traded stock is to use Google. Use the *Stocks:* operator followed by a valid stock symbol to retrieve a summary of stock information, as seen in Figure 2.3.

Figure 2.4 shows that there are links to additional financial information from several other online resources such as Google Finance, Yahoo Finance, MSN Money, MarketWatch, CNN Money and Reuters. Displayed with this information you will find the current stock quotes along with the day's trading graph.

Weather, whether you like it or not

Weather forecasts for any place in the United States can be viewed directly in your Google search results using the weather operator. Simply type **weather** followed by a place name to see the weather for that location. Large cities, like Los Angeles, do not require a state, but many states have cities with the same name. In those cases you need to include the state. Figure 2.4 shows the five-day forecast for Hilo, Hawaii. As an aside, this is the five-day forecast for Hilo, no matter what time of year you search.

FIGURE 2.3

Stock summary information is retrieved using the *Stocks:* operator.

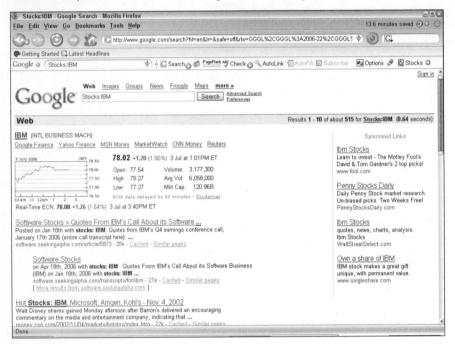

FIGURE 2.4

See the five-day weather forecast using Google.

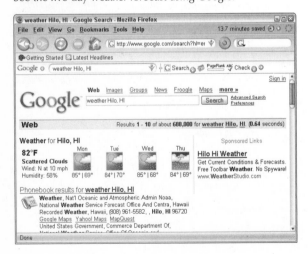

 Using the word weather with a colon (*weather:*) works identically to using weather without the colon.

Special queries

Special Google operators allow you to gain special access to Web information, such as old versions of Web pages stored by Google in its cache, or Web site descriptions. Use the cache:, info:, and related: operators to view this special Google information.

View past versions of Web pages

Occasionally, the information you are searching for no longer appears on the Internet. This can happen for any number of reasons. For example, the Web site may no longer exist, or the author has changed the contents of the Web page. When your search displays information that no longer appears in the page pointed to by the link you can view the version of the Web page last indexed by Google and saved in its cache by using the *cache:* operator. Precede the URL of a Web site with the *cache:* operator (for example, type **cache: www.oldwebpage.com**) and you are automatically shown the cached version of the page, even if a newer version exists on the Web.

Using the *cache:* operator is the same as using the cache link often displayed in the Google search results. There are times when no version of the page exists in cache. In this event, using the *cache:* operator has no effect; no results are returned.

Find similar pages

In the event that finding pages containing search terms does not locate the information you're looking for, you can use the *related:* operator to find Web pages similar to another may meet your need. Find the Web page that has information similar to the type you are looking for and type that into your Google search text box preceded with the *related:* operator like this: **related:www.science.org**.

This lists all the Web pages and their descriptions that contain similar content to the one you typed. Google uses keywords in the text to determine similarity.

 Make sure you type the URL of a valid Web page or Google thinks that the word related is a search term and finds Web pages containing the word related and the address or search terms you typed.

Once you find a Web page that contains the type of information you are searching for, try running the related query again with the address of that page. It may give you more of the results for which you are looking.

Google Web page information

Find all the information Google has about a Web page all in one place. Precede the Web site URL with the info: operator to view the following:

- A Web site description and link to the site
- A link to the Google cached version
- Web pages that are similar to the one you entered
- Web pages that link to the one you entered
- Web pages that are linked from the one you entered
- Web pages that contain the URL or name of the Web site you entered

This information is available using individual operators. This is a great shortcut to all the information about a Web page. This also keeps you from needing to remember all the individual operator names for finding this information. Info: is easy to remember.

Locate search words in certain places

It may not be enough to have your search terms appear somewhere in a Web page. For example, if you know part of a URL but do not remember the entire Web site address, you can search for it within the address only. There may be other times where you want to search for a term in only the title of the page. These terms look for search terms in only the places specified by the operator. A complete list of the Google search location operators appears in Table 2.1.

TABLE 2.1

Search Location Operators

Operator	Description
allinanchor:	The anchor is the text you click when you click on a hyperlink. This is the descriptive text, not the URL. The *allinanchor:* operator finds <u>all</u> the search terms you typed within the anchor text.
inanchor:	Use the *inanchor:* operator when you want to include a search on a single term within the anchor text as part of a larger search. This is normally used along with search terms that search the entire Web site contents.
allintext:	The *allintext:* operator finds all your search terms in the text of the Web page. It ignores the search terms in any other part of the page such as the title, anchor text, or URL.
intext:	Search the text of a Web page for a single term as part of a larger search that includes search terms that may appear elsewhere within the page.
allintitle:	The *allintitle:* operator allows you to find Web pages where all of your search terms must appear in the title of the Web page. The title of the Web page is the title text created by the Web page developer and normally appears in the top border of your Web browser.
intitle:	Use the *intitle:* operator when a single term must appear in the title, while your other search terms can appear elsewhere in the Web page.
allinurl:	When you want your results to include only Web pages where your search terms all appear in the URL (Web page address) use the *allinurl:* operator. This is a very restrictive search. Be careful with the number of search terms you include.
inurl:	Use the *inurl:* operator to find Web pages that have a single search term in the URL while all other search terms can appear in other places within the Web page.

Special Google searches

There are Google services such as News, Froogle, and Google Groups that contain a great deal of specialized information. You can perform special searches just through these services. Some of these searches require you to visit the specific Google service, all of which are discussed in greater detail throughout the rest of this book.

Search Google News

`News.google.com` is a great resource for world and local news. You can search Google News using two special operators, *location:* and *source:*.

CROSS-REF Chapter 14 provides detailed information about using Google News.

- **location:** Include this operator in a query and Google automatically searches Google News for items from the location you specify. For example, *location:Los Angeles* finds news articles that mention this city.
- **source:** Use this operator to specify the news source you want articles from: for example, *hurricanes source:cnn*.

You can use these operators in a Google search text box, and Google knows to search Google News only. If you are already viewing the Google News site, you can use them in a query within the news site.

Search for the best prices using Froogle

Froogle is an online shopping guide discussed in more detail in Chapter 8. You can use the *store:* operator to specify in what store you want to search for prices. Unlike the location: operator that directs searches to Google News, the store: operator does not redirect the search to Froogle. You must be searching the Froogle site to use this operator (`froogle.google.com`).

Here is an example of how to use the *store:* operator. Specify the name of the store you want to search for product information. This must be a store that Froogle searches. For example, a query on televisions might look like this: *television source:Sears. Television source:Best Buy* will not return Froogle results. Vendors must request that Google include their product information within Froogle. When your favorite retailer does not appear in the Froogle results, contact them and request that they add themselves to the Froogle index.

Searching Google Groups

Google Groups provides access to the Internet Usenet news groups. Unlike Google News, Usenet news is an e-mail archived messaging service and does not really provide news. Instead, Usenet has messages organized into tens of thousands of topics. The *author:*, *group:*, and *insubject:* operators allow you to search Usenet messages through Google Groups. You must be on the Google Groups site to use these search operators (`groups.google.com`). Use these operators like this:

- **author:** Finds messages authored by the name you specify. It is best to enclose full names in quotes. Example: *author:smith*. This finds posts by anyone with the name Smith.
- **group:** Specifies a particular Usenet newsgroup name to focus your search within a single group. Example: *group:alt.sci.geography*. This finds posts in the alt.sci.geography group.
- **insubject:** Locates messages with a particular keyword in the subject line using this operator. Example: *insubject:rhesus*. This finds posts where the word rhesus is found within the subject line of the post.

CROSS-REF See Chapter 22 for more information about Google Groups.

You can use any combination of these operators and search terms to focus your search. For example, use the author: operator with the group: operator to locate messages posted by a specific person within a particular group.

Advanced Search

The Google Advanced Search page makes your life simpler by providing a user interface to create complex searches without having to know the Google operators. It also provides search functionality not available through the operators such as occurrences and usage rights.

Access the Advanced Search page by clicking the Advanced Search link to the right of the search text box. The result is shown in Figure 2.5.

FIGURE 2.5

The Advanced Search page provides additional search capability.

Standard Advanced Search page

The top portion of the Advanced Search page has search features outlined with a blue border signifying a group of similar search capabilities. This outlined portion of the page is not specifically labeled but contains abilities similar to those described earlier in this chapter.

The first group of search criteria has a darker background and essentially mimics the functionality you can achieve with the Google search operators.

Search terms entered in the textbox labeled *with **all** the words* finds Web pages that contain every search term you typed in the text box. The terms may appear anywhere in the text of the page, the title of the page, or meta tags, which are discussed in Chapter 1.

You can search on a phrase by typing the entire phrase in the text box labeled with the *exact phrase* and clicking Google Search. When typing phrases in this text box it is not necessary to enclose the phrase in quotes.

Occasionally, you may need to find Web pages using search terms that may not contain all the words, but at least one of the terms must appear in the page. Type the list of terms in the textbox labeled *with at least one of the words*. An example of how you might use this search feature is to find information about some of your favorite sports teams. You can type a list of the team names in this text box and your results will include links to pages with information about at least one of the teams. Of course, the result can contain more than one of the terms, but must include at least one. It is not necessary to separate the terms with a comma.

Excluding results that contain certain words is very useful for narrowing your search. A good example is narrowing your search for information about Leonardo DaVinci where you may not want results that point to pages that discuss Dan Brown's book, *The DaVinci Code*. This search feature is normally used in conjunction with one or more of the other search parameters discussed previously. For example, you may type the search term DaVinci in the text box labeled *with **all** the words*. Then type **code** in the **without** *the words* text box. The results list pages that discuss DaVinci but probably do not include pages that discuss *The DaVinci Code*.

The Results drop-down list next to the Google Search button allows you to format your search results. You can specify how many search results you want displayed per page. The default is 10, or you can also specify 20, 30, 50, or 100 results per page.

You can further narrow your search by specifying the language of the Web page. This feature does not translate Web pages for you but returns pages only in the language you specify. Select a language from the Language drop-down list. The default is set to return results in any language.

NOTE Choosing a language that is not supported by your computer returns results that appear with all question marks like this: ??????????? ???????.

A number of document types can be delivered through the World Wide Web in addition to the standard Web page. These include

- Adobe Acrobat (PDF)
- Adobe PostScript (PS)
- Microsoft Word (DOC)
- Microsoft Excel (XLS)
- Microsoft PowerPoint (PPT)
- Rich Text Format (RTF)

You have a choice of specifying that your results be one of these document types or excluding a document type from your results. You can find this selection labeled File Format. Whether you limit document types or exclude them, you can only select one type.

First, select whether you want documents only of a particular type by selecting Only from the drop-down list. Exclude document types by selecting Don't return results of the file format, then select the format type from the drop-down list. The default value is any format. Notice that specifying a file type without also typing a search term returns no results.

The Date criteria allow you to retrieve results that have been updated within the last year, the last six months, or the last three months. By default, results are not filtered by when the Web page was last updated. Narrow your search to Web pages updated more recently by selecting from the Date drop-down list. Like File Format, the Date criteria require a search term.

The Numeric Range criteria allow you to further limit your searches based on a range of numbers. Return Web pages containing numbers between ? and ?. You can select a range of numbers without typing a search term. For example, selecting a range between 1 and 20 returns a large number of results that may not be very meaningful. You can achieve more meaningful results if you use the Numeric Range criteria along with other criteria, such as a search term. For example, Figure 2.6 displays a query where the search term temperature is typed in the *with **all** the words* text box. The phrase vacation spots and the numeric range of 77 and 90 return a list of Web pages that contain vacation spots with a temperature between 77 and 90. This would be the same as typing the following search manually using operators: **allinanchor: temperature "vacation spots" 77..89**.

FIGURE 2.6

Combining search criteria narrows your search.

The Occurrences criteria allow you to specify where your search terms appear in the Web page. The choices are

- anywhere in the page (default)
- in the title of the page
- in the text of the page
- in the URL of the page
- in links to the page

The Occurrences criteria are excellent if you have some idea of where your results might appear. For example, when you want to search for results that only appear on the CNN news pages, you might specify CNN as the search term and select in the URL of the page from the Occurrences drop-down list. The title of the page is the text that appears in the top border of your Web browser when visiting a page. The text of the page is any text, both visible and invisible to the person viewing the page. Invisible text might include the text that accompanies images in the HTML ALT tag, or the HTML meta tags discussed in Chapter 1. The URL of the page is the address you type or click on to retrieve a page from the Web, and links to the page include links that appear in other Web sites that link to the page you may be interested in finding.

You can search for documents within a single Web site domain name. The Domain criteria allow you to limit your searches to a single domain or to exclude that domain from your search. A domain is the portion of the URL that specifies the specific location on the Internet — for example, google.com is a domain, cnn.com is a domain, whitehouse.gov is a domain.

You can elect to receive results that are filtered by how you intend to use the content. The Usage Rights criteria setting allows you to select the appropriate result filter. You can keep the default setting of *not filtered by license* or select one of the following from the drop-down list:

- free to use or share
- free to use or share, even commercially
- free to use, share, or modify
- free to use, share ,or modify, even commercially

The SafeSearch criteria allow you to have your results filtered from text and graphics that contain explicit adult content. SafeSearch is covered in more detail in Chapter 4.

Page-specific search

There are two search criteria in the group labeled Page-Specific Search. Both of these criteria require you to already have a specific Web page in mind. These two search criteria help you find pages related to the initial page. These two criteria stand alone and are not related to any of the other search criteria in the Advanced Search page.

The Similar search allows you to type the address of a Web page and find all pages similar to the one you are viewing based on the textual content of the page. For example, typing **www.science.org** returns pages with similar science, technology, and forensic content. Because the results are not related to other types of search, the <u>Search within results</u> link does not appear at the bottom of the results page.

Links allows you to create a list of each Web page linked to the one you specify in your search. This is particularly important to commercial Web sites hoping that many other sites will link to theirs. Now, it's simple to find out who is linking to any Web site. Like the previous search, you cannot search within the results.

Topic-specific search

Google has many topic-specific searches. These allow you to search for Web pages that list very specific information. The Advanced Search page lists only eight of them:

- Google Book Search
- Google Scholar
- Apple Macintosh
- BSD Unix
- Linux
- Microsoft
- U.S. Government
- Universities

Each of these topic-specific searches is covered in greater detail throughout this book. The topic-specific searches are not interrelated to the search criteria discussed earlier in this chapter.

Narrowing Your Search

There are times when Google returns far too many results to search by hand. You can go back and create a more focused search by using the Advanced Search page or by using search operators, or you can simply type new search terms that only search within the results of a Google search.

Following a standard Google search, the Search within results link appears at the bottom of the results page. Clicking this link launches a new search page listing the number of results from your previous search, as shown in Figure 2.7.

FIGURE 2.7

Type new search terms to search within results.

Do not type the search terms you used previously when searching within the results; this does not help to further focus your results. Think of new terms that might help limit the results. For example, in the example shown in Figure 2.7, the number of results for the search term *fox terrier* is 4,080,000. Typing the new term **Peruvian long hair** limits the results to 73,000 (Figure 2.8).

FIGURE 2.8

The new query is performed including terms you used in the original search, narrowing the results.

You may notice that when viewing the results of your new search, your original search terms are included in the text box where you type Google search terms. Google simply performs the search a second time and includes the new search terms. You achieve these same results if you type the same search terms the first time.

Using Search within results saves you a little bit of time by not requiring you to remember or type the original search terms. Try using some of the operators discussed in this chapter when searching within results. This helps you achieve the greatest amount of focus for your search.

Summary

For many people, Google search is simply the word or phrase typed into a Google search text box. The power of Google searching far exceeds this simple capability. This chapter showed how you can:

- Build focused queries using search operators
- Perform special number searches
- Look up the definition of words
- Find specialized information such as movie guides, financial information and the weather
- Perform specialized queries to find similar or past versions of pages
- Search through Google services such as Google News, Froogle and Google Groups
- Perform advanced page-specific and topic-specific searches

Chapter 3

Topic Searching

Google has created special topic areas to help focus your searches. At the moment, the number of topics is still small, but we expect it to grow over time. When you do a Google search using these special topic areas, your query is limited to just that topic, which highly refines your search.

Topic Searches

Google has simplified the process of finding information in complex areas such as the U.S. government, university Web sites, and topics on the Web where it may be difficult to narrow your search using a normal Web search. For example, Linux, Mac, and Windows are commonly used operating systems. These terms appear on many Web pages not directly related to information about those technologies. For example, they are commonly listed in software requirements. In response, Google has created special searches just for those technologies and difficult search areas.

Google U.S. Government Search

The number of U.S. Government Web pages is staggering. Finding U.S. government information can be difficult. Google makes this simpler by limiting the number of Web pages you may have to look through to find your information by creating a U.S. Government topic search, as shown in Figure 3.1. To take advantage of this enhanced search capability, point your Web browser to www .google.com/ig/usgov.

You will find that the topics listed on the Google U.S. Government Search page include many topics you might not expect to find on a U.S. Government Search page. They are included so you can use this as a type of "Home" page loaded by your Web browser by default.

FIGURE 3.1

Locate U.S. government information using the U.S. Government Search.

The topics within the U.S. Government Topic Search page have both an _edit_ link and an **X** to remove the topic. Click the _edit_ link to set special customizing features. In each of the topics described throughout this chapter, the special edit features are covered in more detail.

Weather

If you are wondering about the weather in the nation's capital or anywhere else in the country, you can have the weather appear as a topic on this page. You can easily customize what city weather is shown on your page by clicking the _edit_ link.

The _edit_ link features include

- **_C _F:** Allowing you to switch the temperature display between Celsius and Fahrenheit.
- **Country/Region:** Select a country or region from the drop-down list.
- **Add a city:** Type a city, state, or Zip code in this text box and click Add.

Click Save to save your changes or click the _cancel_ link to cancel editing and return to the previous settings.

Additional sections

Most of the other sections are created from news postings. Each of these sections can be removed by clicking the small X across from the section title. The _edit_ link feature allows you to customize how many items are listed in the section. Select a number between 1 and 9; the default is 3. Click Save. New sections can be added by clicking the _Add content_ link at the top left of the page. (See the section "Add Content" for more information.) The default sections include:

- American Forces Information Service
- White House News
- Government Executive

- Google News
- Washington Post

Add Content

Clicking the <u>Add content</u> link, shown in the upper-left corner of Figure 3.1, launches a new menu located to the left of the page (see Figure 3.2).

FIGURE 3.2
_____

Add Content allows you to customize your U.S. Government Search page.

Clicking the Add Content link displays this menu.

Each of the sections listed in the menu on the left side of the page is expandable. When the right-facing arrow appears, click the arrow and additional menu items appear, and the arrow changes to a downward-facing arrow. When the sections are expanded, the menu items appear with a small add>> button. Clicking add>> causes that item to appear in the page and the menu on the left to disappear.

The sections include

- **My Stuff:** Google Tips, Bookmarks, Gmail, and Stockmarket
- **Government:** White House, Defense and International Relations, Environment, Health, Science & Technology, which includes NASA, DOE, FERC and CERT news, Business, Education & Employment
- **News:** Includes a long list of government-related news sources including Google News.
- **Business:** Financial news sources such as CNN Money and Forbes
- **Technology:** A number of government-related technology news and information sites including publications such as Federal Computer Week, Government Computer News, Government Technology News and more.
- **Sports:** Sports sources such as CBS Sportsline and Sports Illustrated

- **Lifestyle:** Includes information from *People* magazine
- **Fun:** Several fun information sites including "How To" of the Day from wikihow.com, Reuters Oddly Enough, Word of the Day, Ziff Davis 1UP
- **Create a Section:** Make your own sections by including RSS feeds and topic searches. A search box is included to simplify this process.

Advanced Search

The Advanced Search features allow you to use all the same advanced features discussed in Chapter 2 except that in the Advanced Search page, you can choose to search only government Web sites, or choose to search the entire Web by clicking the associated search button located in the upper-right portion of the search page.

Special computer topic searches

Searching for information on operating systems and computer companies through Google can be a difficult task because the names of the operating systems and computer are used on millions of Web pages discussing software products that operate on these operating systems or computers. To make finding information about these important topics easier, Google has created special topic search areas for them.

Linux search

Linux is the open-source operating system first created by Linus Torvalds in 1991 by programming an operating system kernel based on the popular and powerful Unix operating system. Linux, Unix, Linux...Get it? This kernel was released under the Gnu open-source license making expansion of this operating system by programmers, believing in open source, not only possible, but a mission.

Point your Web browser to `www.google.com/linux` to learn more about Linux, or to search for Linux-related information, use the special Google topic search shown in Figure 3.3.

FIGURE 3.3

Find Linux-related information in the Linux topic search.

BSD search

BSD, the short name for Berkeley Unix, is a variant of Unix version 6 released by Bell Telephone Laboratories in 1975.

Today's Internet communications are based largely on BSD TCP/IP and BIND communications technology. For more information about BSD history, these technologies, or anything related to BSD, use Google's special topic search (see Figure 3.4) and point your Web browser to `www.google.com/bsd`.

FIGURE 3.4

Find BSD-related information using the BSD topic search.

Apple Macintosh search

The brainchild of Apple's Steve Jobs, the Macintosh computer was first announced in a single television commercial running on a single station in 1983. This computer became the biggest advancement in home computing and became the standard computer in schools throughout the United States. For more information about the amazing history of this computer revolution search the Google special topic area shown in Figure 3.5 and found at `www.google.com/mac.html`.

 There is no Advanced Search on the Apple Macintosh topic search page.

Microsoft search

It's difficult to think of computers without thinking of Microsoft and Bill Gates. The history of the Intel-based personal computer is closely linked to the history of its first operating system, DOS, MS-DOS, and later the graphic Windows operating system. For more information about Microsoft, Windows, Office, or the many other things Microsoft is involved in, visit `www.google.com/microsoft.html`.

The special Google topic search area for Microsoft-related topics is shown in Figure 3.6.

 There is no Advanced Search on the Microsoft topic search page.

FIGURE 3.5

Search for Apple Macintosh-related information in the Apple Macintosh topic search.

FIGURE 3.6

Search for Microsoft-related information in the Microsoft topic search.

Public Service Search

Google offers a special service to nonprofit organizations and nonprofit educational institutions. It will index your site and provide you a special search box for your Web site so people can do a Google search just through your site. This is a little similar to the service offered to universities (see the next section) except that Google maintains the University search box on its site, rather than the Public Service search service, where the nonprofit or school hosts the search box on its site.

This is actually the same result someone would achieve by using the Advanced Web search features and limiting the domain to just your Web site. Providing this as a search box on your site makes searching your site much easier for those visiting your site.

 **To use Google's Public Service Search, your organization must qualify as nonprofit according to IRS rules governing 501(c)(3) organizations and nonprofit educational institutions.**

Register your organization. When you complete registration, the following message appears:

Your registration is now complete. Thank you for signing up for our Public Service Search program.

To use customized Public Service Search, you must create a search form on your webpage. Feel free to use the HTML we provide as a starting point.

Please remember that after your customizations have been submitted, it can take up to two hours for them to be pushed out to our servers.

NOTE **If you or your organization does not qualify for the Public Service Search but you'd still like to host a Google Search box on your site where the search results are customized to the look and feel of your site, try Google Free at** www.google.com/searchcode.html.

When you register, you have the choice of selecting the type of search service that appears on your site. You can choose to allow searches of your site only, or you can also elect to allow people to search the Web. To limit searches to your site only, select that option on the Search Optimizations page. Customizing your search page is one of the first steps in setting up your Public Service Search.

When you customize the Public Service Search, the results page includes your organization's logo and is formatted to look and feel like your Web page, although the results are actually hosted on the Google server. The URL of the results page is www.google.com/u/organizationname.

University Search

Google has links to search most of the U.S. university Web sites and many from around the world. The ability to search a single university site, rather than using the Web search, clearly reduces the number of results you may need to review in finding the information you are looking for. Visit www.google.com/universities.html to see a list, as shown in Figure 3.7.

The university sites listed in Google do not link directly to the university Web sites, but instead to a search box that allows you to search just one university for information. This focuses your search when hunting for information at a particular university.

Searching on a topic using the University Search box may provide you information on admissions, faculty members, classes, papers available online, library resources, online catalogs, and any other types of information or resources the University Web site maintains online. Universities often host student Web pages as well.

The Advanced Search features are the same as those for searching the Web using Google's Advanced Web Search. See Chapter 2 for more information on using these advanced search features.

To add your university's Web site, visit www.google.com/options/mycampus.html.

FIGURE 3.7

Choose a university Web site from the list.

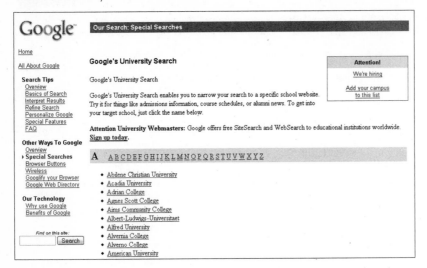

Google News Archive

When you search through Google news you get links to many of the very latest news articles. But sometimes you need historical information rather than the current news. Google provides a special search page just to search the Google News Archive. You can find this search site at: `http://news.google.com/archivesearch`.

You can search the news archive as you would search through Google News (see Chapter 14). You can also click the Show Timeline button. When you search the archive, the search results appear on the right; in the column to the left you see links to specific time periods. The articles are listed in chronological order. Clicking these links limits your search results to just those time periods, and the articles are listed by year.

In the search results page, you can toggle between the Show timeline view and the Search articles view by clicking the links in the upper-right portion of the page. In the Search articles view, you can also limit the results to a particular news source. The news sources are listed on the left as links.

The Advanced Archive Search allows you to focus your search through the archive by searching on keywords, as with any search, but also allows you to limit your search by publication date, the language of the article, the source of the article, and if you want to search pay-per-view articles, you can search by price of the article.

Summary

Finding information on the Web is not always easy, even using Google's Web search. Therefore, Google has made it simpler by organizing some of the information into special topics. This certainly makes finding information within the multitude of U.S. government Web pages easier, and the same for tough-to-search topics such as Microsoft, Apple Macintosh, Linux, and BSD.

In addition to these special topic searches Google provides special site search services for nonprofits, schools, and universities. These services assist the Web searcher by providing searches through a specific domain and help the organization by customizing the results to feel like they are part of the organization's Web site.

The Google News Archive search is a special topic search that allows you to search for historical information through the many news articles indexed and included in the archive. But, if words are not enough for you, the next chapter shows you how to use Google's Image search.

Chapter 4

Discovering Images on the Web

T he World Wide Web has always included images. Even before the creation of Mosaic, the first graphic Web browser, you could download and view images from the Web. Today, images are a normal part of the user experience when surfing the Web. The collection of images on the Internet today is truly innumerable. Google has a direct interface to images found on the Internet that are included in Google's index of Web pages.

Whether you want an image to display on your desktop, create a greeting card for a friend, add graphics to a school or business report, or any other reason, the best method for finding images is using Google's Image Search. This chapter helps you quickly learn how to find the image you are looking for using the simple interface or the advanced search features. You also learn how to virtually eliminate sexually explicit images from your search results. Finally, this chapter gives you an idea of what rights you have when using an image you download from the Internet.

Searching for Images

Begin your image search by navigating from the Google home page to the Google Image Search page by clicking the Images link above the search text box. The Google page reloads and is ready for you to type your search terms (see Figure 4.1).

How Google finds images

Successfully finding the images you are looking for requires that you understand how Google searches for images on the Web. Because images are graphics, they do not contain searchable information. Even if the image appears to have text, this text is stored in a graphic format that search engines are not capable of understanding. Therefore, Google searches on any text it can find that might relate to the image you want to find. The search includes image filenames and the HTML <alt> tag description.

FIGURE 4.1

Click on the Images link to begin searching for images.

Image filenames are the actual names given to the graphic by the people who published the image on the Internet. For example, a picture of someone's pet might be sammy-poodle.jpg. A search on the word *poodle* would definitely find this image.

Web page authors can choose to store additional text with their images. This practice started when Internet bandwidth was limited, causing images to load very slowly. People browsing the Web often chose to turn off the loading of images in their browser so that Web pages would load faster. In place of the image, alternate (ALT) text would appear. This text also appears before an image loads into a Web page. You may see this text while you wait for an image to appear in your Web browser. Google then relies only on the image filename to locate images based on your search term.

NOTE   ALT text is optional and may not be included in a Web page.

Google also searches the text of a Web page to see if there are images that match the terms for which you have searched.

TIP   Images returned by finding the search terms on a Web page rather than the image filename or ALT text are not always very relevant. Sometimes it helps to visit the Web page of such an image just to see if there are other images on the Web page that may be more relevant to your search. It does help find Web pages that may have related images. For example, a search on Yorkshire terriers may find Web pages about Yorkshire terriers, but the images may be named Fido.jpg, Sammy.jpg, and Fluffy.jpg.

Creating your search term

Finding the image you want among the millions of images stored on the Internet depends on how well you create your search. Too many words in the search terms may limit the search in such a way that you don't find the image you're looking for. Or, the search may give you unexpected results. Typing just a few words can mean far too many results to search through. It often takes experimentation to find the right balance. For example, let's say you are looking for images of Yorkshire terriers, a small dog breed. In particular, you want an image of a brown, toy variety. In the search text box you type *brown toy Yorkshire terrier*, as shown in Figure 4.2.

FIGURE 4.2

Search terms are typed in the Image Search text box.

The search terms, *brown, toy, Yorkshire,* and *terrier* return about 366 images. But, the images that are returned are not what you might expect. Looking at Figure 4.3 you can see that the first two images are of handbags, and the rest of the images in the search results have more to do with jewelry and other gift items.

FIGURE 4.3

Typing too many terms can give you unexpected search results.

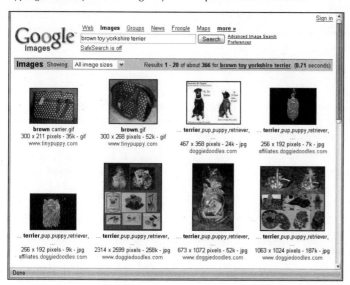

Scrolling through the results in the Google Image Search it becomes apparent that the search did not result in images of small brown Yorkshire terriers. The next attempt includes fewer search terms, simply *Yorkshire terrier.*

 Search terms are not case-sensitive. You can type your search terms in lower-, upper-, or mixed case and it will not affect your search results.

The results of the Image Search using only two keywords are shown in Figure 4.4. These results include images of small Yorkshire terriers. Even though it seems a little counterintuitive, by limiting the number of keywords, you have actually narrowed your search.

FIGURE 4.4

Sometimes, typing fewer keywords can help narrow your search.

Create phrases to help limit your searches. Phrases are typed with quotes around them. For example, "Yorkshire terrier" is a phrase that limits your searches to only results containing that exact phrase. So, an image labeled *terrier-Yorkshire* would not match, but it keeps your searches from returning images of Yorkshire pudding.

CROSS-REF For more information about limiting searches with operational characters, see Chapter 2.

Viewing the Images

Once you type a search term in the text box on the Image Search page, press Enter or click Search. Be patient while Google compiles and displays the results.

The results of your image search are displayed as thumbnails, as shown in Figure 4.4. To view an image as something other than a thumbnail, click on the thumbnail in the results page, or click on the URL address displayed below the image's description. Clicking either the thumbnail or the URL takes you to the Web page where the image is published.

The page that is displayed (see Figure 4.5) contains a top frame, where a slightly larger thumbnail than the one in the search results appears, and a lower frame, where the Web page displays the image as it was published.

FIGURE 4.5

Click the thumbnail to view a full-size image.

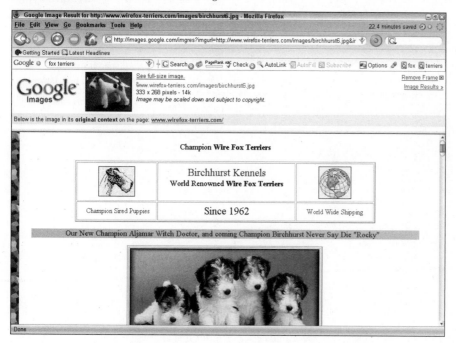

The top frame is branded with the Google Images logo. It displays a thumbnail that you can click to view the full-size image by itself on a Web page. The Web page that displays the full-size image will not have a frame or navigational controls. To navigate back to the previous page you need to use your browser's Back button.

Also displayed in the top frame is the URL of the Web page labeled as the **original context**. Clicking that link launches the Web page containing the image without the top frame. Again, if you want to navigate back to the Google results after clicking the original context URL, use your browser's Back button. Another way to view the Web page in its original context is by clicking the Remove Frame link or the X next to the link on the upper-right corner of the top frame. This takes you to the Web page containing the image.

TIP Clicking links with the right mouse button allows you to select the option to open the link in a new window. This allows you to keep your Google Search results in the original window.

To return to the Image results page click the Image Results link on the right-hand side of the top frame to navigate back to the Google page that displayed your search results as thumbnail images.

 Clicking links within the Web page will not remove the top frame. To remove the top frame, either click the original context link or the Remove Frame link.

On a computer that runs Windows, to save, copy, or send an image in e-mail you can right-click on the image and select one of the menu choices from the pop-up menu. On a Macintosh, you Control-click on the image and use the context menu that appears to copy and paste. If your Mac has a two-button mouse try, right-clicking. When saving images for future use, be aware that many images on the Internet are protected by copyright. Please read the section "A Bit About Copyright" later in this chapter before using images you find through Google's Image Search.

Advanced Image Search

Experimenting with typing the right search terms is one way to achieve your desired search results. A more direct way is to use the Google Advanced Image Search page. Launch the Advanced Image Search page by clicking the Advanced Image Search link next to the Search Images button (see Figure 4.1). You can also launch the Advanced Image Search page from within a results page, as shown in Figure 4.4.

The Advanced Image Search allows you to find results based on the following criteria:

- Refined search words and phrases
- Image file sizes
- Image file types
- Image coloration
- Web site address or domain
- SafeSearch filtering criteria

Finding results

In the Find Results section of the Advanced Image Search page (see Figure 4.6), there are several ways to filter your search. You can use a single search filter, or you can improve your search by using a combination of filters.

In the related to **all** of the words text box, you can type search terms that appear anywhere and in any order within the text searched by Google. For example, you can type the terms *furry* and *pest*, and they might appear within the ALT text of the image.

In the related to the **exact phrase** text box, you can type entire phrases that must appear as you have typed them, such as *grizzly bear*. Any results must have the words *grizzly* and *bear* appearing as the phrase *grizzly bear*. This has the same effect as putting quotes around your phrase in the simple search.

When you use the related to **any** of the words filter, you can list several search terms and if any of them match the text related to an image, that page appears in your results.

Limit the scope of your search by telling Google which words you do not want to match in your results. Perhaps you are interested in images of grizzly bears, particularly the ones that are pests in national parks, but not interested in bears that inhabit Yosemite National Park. In this example you may want to type the word *Yosemite* in the **not related** to the words text box.

Additional Search Filters

You can limit the size of files that appear in your result. There are several reasons why you might want to limit the file sizes. You may be looking for an image of a particular size or quality either for print reproduction, use on your own Web page, or perhaps you want only small images to make download times quicker. The choices for file sizes are small, medium, large, or any size, which is the default.

Another way to filter your search is by specifying the image file type. Only certain image types are viewable using a Web browser, therefore the possible file types are already limited. Google allows you to limit the file types to JPG, GIF, or PNG. If you want to learn more about each of these image file types, type **graphic file types explained** into a Google Web search.

There are times you may want to find only full-color images and other times when you want black-and-white or grayscale images. Select which image color type you want in the Coloration drop-down list, or use the default, which returns images of any color type.

FIGURE 4.6

Filter your results using the Advanced Image Search page.

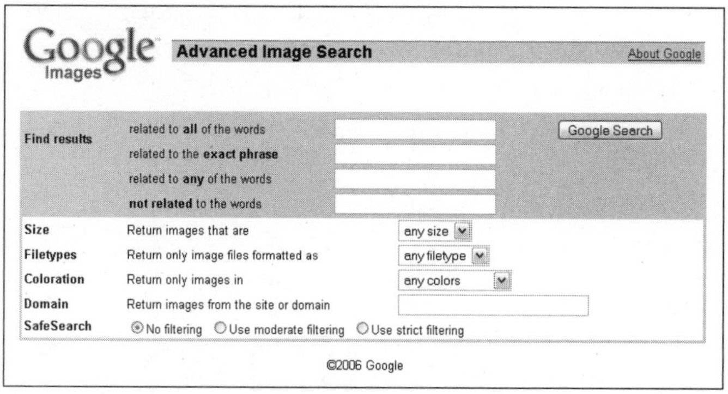

The Domain text box allows you to limit your search to particular Web sites or Web pages. A domain is a particular Internet site. Each site might contain many Web pages, e-mail addresses, and FTP sites, and may be running many other applications. You can limit your search to a particular domain, such as searching for images on NASA.gov. To limit your search to images found on the NASA domain, type *nasa.gov* in the Domain text box.

Safe Search

Google understands that its users may want to exclude adult-oriented images from their image search results. A feature known as SafeSearch is provided that uses advanced search algorithms to eliminate most of the adult content. Of course, as Google admits, no attempt at eliminating adult content is going to be completely effective. Google uses a combination of techniques to eliminate adult content in search results, whether searching the Web or searching the Internet for graphic images.

CAUTION   **Parents should be aware that SafeSearch is not a parental control feature. It has no password protection and is easily selected or deselected by people performing searches. It is a feature designed to eliminate adult content by choice.**

Google uses the following mechanisms to prevent adult sexual content from ending up in your search results:

- Keyword filtering
- Phrase checking
- Open Directory category matching
- Direct input from Google users

 SafeSearch can filter both explicit images as well as explicit text.

Web sites that have deceptive practices, such as using commonly misspelled URLs (Web site addresses) are not allowed in the search results. Deceiving users and tricking them to come to your site expecting one thing but finding another, is a practice known as *cloaking*. Cloaking can be achieved by registering and using a deceptive domain name and also by using deceptive keywords so that search engines like Google's register the site in their search engine. It is also possible to send one version of a Web page to a search engine, while sending a completely different version to the user who requests the page. If this happens to you, please report it to Google at `http://www.google.com/contact/spamreport.html`.

Setting SafeSearch

Setting the SafeSearch feature is simple. The SafeSearch options are located in the Advanced Search page of either the text or image search page. The text search allows you to turn SafeSearch on and off by selecting either the No Filtering or Filter using SafeSearch option.

SafeSearch has three selections when searching on images, as shown in Figure 4.5. Select one of the following three SafeSearch filtering levels:

- **No filtering:** This option allows you to search with no SafeSearch filters applied.
- **Use Moderate Filtering:** This option allows you to see Google search results with sexually explicit images eliminated from the results, while allowing results containing sexually explicit words or phrases to appear in the results.
- **Use Strict Filtering:** This option attempts to eliminate search results from Web pages that contain either sexually explicit images or sexually explicit words and phrases or both.

For example, a search on the word *playboy* without filtering returns images of a sexually explicit nature. Searching with **Use Moderate Filtering** selected removes images that contain complete nudity. Selecting **Use Strict Filtering** allows no images to appear from this example search.

CROSS-REF   If you set SafeSearch levels in your Google Global Preferences you can always choose to override them. Learn more in Chapter 2.

A final word about SafeSearch

There is currently no perfect technology for removing unwanted material from search results. Google does its best to make its search engine Family Safe but makes no promises of perfection. Part of the problem faced by people using the SafeSearch feature is that many Web sites are incorrectly removed from the search results.

Sites removed from search results based on key words might relate to medical, health improvement, news reports or other site that may use a word in a non-sexually explicit manner, but still be filtered based on words or phrases.

The SafeSearch technology is largely based on text search. This type of search is also limited by which languages the search checks. Google text searches for offensive material in English, French, Italian, German, Dutch, or Portuguese, based on which language preference you select.

A Bit about Copyright

The Internet is filled with millions of images, many of which have been indexed by Google's Web crawler. The world's images are at your fingertips, but be aware that even though you can view the images Google displays, Google does not offer you any rights to use that image.

What is copyright

Governments provide certain rights over the manner in which an idea or information is expressed. Copyright protection covers works such as books, photos, musical works, sound recordings, paintings, software, and designs, but only for a limited time. Copyright is then legal protection for authors and artisans to keep others from copying or using their work without their explicit permission.

Copyright protection is automatically granted whenever something copyrightable is created, whether it is officially registered with the copyright office or not. Once you create something, such as a photo, you are the copyright holder, unless you give those rights to someone else, such as an employer. A copyright holder has the privilege of granting or not granting the right to copy something or if it is a musical or sound recording, the right to play it.

Copyright is protected by both civil and criminal law. Copyright holders can sue someone they believe has infringed on their copyright. In other words, the work was used or copied without permission. Depending on the financial loss and how many copies of the work were created, the person who infringed the copyright may be guilty of a felony.

The bottom line here is that things people create are protected and you must get permission to use other people's creations. The idea that you can use it for nonprofit purposes freely is not true. No matter how you use it, you need to get permission.

Getting permission

It is always safest to assume that anything you find on the Internet, such as images and Web page content is copyright protected. Before you can use all or part of the work you find, ask for written permission from the owner of the copyright. It's best not to believe that you can use an original work and not get permission. For example, my grandson has a picture of himself on his Web page wearing a surf helmet and a great smile. One day, I was helping a friend find a dentist locally, and I was stunned to find my grandson's smiling face staring back at me as part of a dentist locator service Web page. I admit that the likelihood that I would come across that image was remote, but there are organizations that actively search out people violating their copyright.

Who to ask

An original work, as just described, does not have to be registered with the government before it is protected by copyright law. It is protected immediately upon creation. The author, unless commissioned or hired to do the work, is automatically the copyright holder for the original work. When more than one person works on an original work, they are considered co-owners of the copyright.

Sometimes Web pages have a copyright notice, including the year of copyright. Copyright notices will have the word **copyright** or the copyright symbol (c). Remember, Web pages do not have to have a copyright notice to be protected by copyright; they are protected automatically. A good first place to look for the name of the copyright holder is to look for either a copyright notice or a link to legal information. Some professional Web pages have an entire page dedicated to stating their legal protections.

When you can't find the name of the copyright holder, such as on a personal Web page, for example, look for the name of the Web page creator. Sometimes this simply appears as a link to the Webmaster, the author of the Web page. In the event that no author information exists on the page, there is one other way you can sometimes find the author, and that is through tracking down the owner of the domain name. You can usually find out the name and sometimes the contact information for domain owners by using the Whois application and most domain registrars like GoDaddy.com. Find the Whois link, and type the domain name of the Web site for which you would like the owner's name.

How to ask

When you know the name of the person or organization that holds the copyright to an image, it is best to send a letter documenting your request. Clearly identify the image with a description, and name of the image file. To find the name of the image file you can right-click on the image displayed in your Web browser and choose Properties from the pop-up menu. The filename is usually displayed. In some cases, the filename is masked, and you must describe the image and the URL of the Web page on which you found it. It's best to simply copy and paste the URL from the address bar in your Web browser.

You can sometimes send an e-mail to the copyright holder, and use the e-mail response as proof of permission. If you are going to use the image for anything other than personal reasons — for example, if you are going to use the image in a book — it is best to have the copyright holder send you a release form. There are sample release forms you can use as a template. Use Google to search on keywords *sample copyright release*.

In addition to finding people yourself and negotiating the copyright release, there are also commercial services available that will handle this on your behalf. One of those services can be found at www.copyright.com.

Images in the public domain

Creations such as art, music, drama, and inventions to which no one claims a copyright are held in the *public domain*. These creations are considered a part of our common cultural heritage and may be used freely by anyone for any reason. For example, many of the images available from the archives of the presidential libraries are public domain.

CROSS-REF Once you find the image you want to use and obtain permission to use it, consider using Google's Picasa program to edit the image. Learn more about using Picasa to edit images in Chapter 21.

When researching whether an item of interest is in the public domain, do not confuse it with works offered for free, or *open source* creations. Open source is covered in more detail in the next section. An author, creator, or inventor may offer his or her work for free while still maintaining the copyright. Offering a work for free does not place it in the public domain. One distinction is that works offered for free may have limits placed on its use. For example, images offered for free but held under copyright may be excluded from use for the promotion of adult or sexual content.

You can find hundreds of sites on the Internet that offer public domain images, either exclusively or as part of their gallery of images. There are many U.S. government Web sites that contain public domain images. For example you might start here: http://www.firstgov.gov/Topics/Graphics.shtml.

Even on the firstgov.gov site there is a warning that even though the images can be freely used, many of them are covered under a license.

Open source images

Open Source is a philosophy about how intellectual property should be made available to others. Inventions, creations, images, and other intellectual property released as Open Source are covered under a special license agreement. The most common of these is called the GNU public license (www.gnu.org). When the movement first started, it was the exclusive domain of software developers who believed that source code should be made freely available to others to use, and to create derivative works. Later, many other forms of intellectual property were made available as Open Source. Here is one Web site you can access to find open source images: http://openphoto.net/.

You can find additional resource for Open Source images by doing a search in Google on **open source images**.

Summary

A picture is worth a thousand words. It's probably more like tens or hundreds of thousands of words when you consider the file size of many graphics on the Internet. They are an important part of what has made the World Wide Web what it is today. Prior to the graphic Web browser, the World Wide Web was just one more interesting Internet application along with so many others. Google has provided a unique way to search for images. No other search engine has this type of search, and certainly not with the capabilities, using the Google Advanced Image Search, for finding just the right image.

Understanding the way in which images are distributed is very important. You need to know whether the image you've found can be copied. Most organizations allow you to use their copyrighted photos if you pay a license fee. There are many others that are public domain or offered under the guidelines and licensing of Open Source.

Chapter 5

Hunting for Videos

I f you are bored watching cable TV and need entertainment, try Google Video. It's a fun place to find videos on practically any topic. Google Video hosts free amateur videos, free funny clips, or previews for some of your favorite TV shows and digital movies. After you watch the previews to longer productions, Google makes it easy to purchase them to watch any time you want.

Video Categories

To begin your video adventure at Google Video point your Web browser to video.google.com. Visiting this page launches the Google Video search page, as shown in Figure 5.1. Notice along the top of the page, just beneath the search box, there are links to the various video categories. They include:

- ■ Top 100
- ■ Comedy
- ■ Music videos
- ■ Movies
- ■ Sports
- ■ Animation
- ■ TV shows
- ■ Google Picks

Links to the top 100 rated videos are displayed in the Top 100 category along with a user rating and the number of people who rated the video. Google bases the rating on how many people watched a video the previous day. On the Top 100 page, you can also click the link at the top to see the top Movers & Shakers. Clicking this link allows you to see the list of videos that are popular today and most likely to end up in the next day's Top 100.

IN THIS CHAPTER

Find videos to watch by category and featured lists

Play selected videos on the Web

Tell others about videos you see on Google video

Learn to download and use the Google Video Player

Purchase videos for viewing

Upload and share your video with others

Manage your videos and add transcripts

FIGURE 5.1

Search for all types of videos from the Google Video page.

Click on the Comedy category to see humorous videos, including several animated comedy previews where the longer, complete videos are for sale. You may need to click through several pages to find the video you are looking for. You can narrow your search using different methods explained in the next section.

The Music videos category contains primarily previews to longer music videos that you can purchase for viewing through Google videos. The Sports category contains many videos of amazing feats along with video highlights of your favorite sports. The Movies category is a little different from the rest, providing trailers to movies currently in the theater. You can also search for local show times. The Animation category allows you to see previews to animated movies, but you can also search on free videos to see stock footage and amateur creations. TV shows category displays previews for TV shows and segments where complete versions are largely available for purchase.

The Google Picks category provides links to the best videos according to the folks at Google. There are normally some excellent choices available for your free viewing pleasure.

Selecting videos

When selecting from the thousands of available videos, it helps to be able to select based on criteria. After all, Google's strength is allowing you to find what you're looking for quickly and easily. The same is true for most of the categories in Google Video.

Sort the videos in a category by price, duration, and the type of search. Select from the drop-downs found in the blue bar above the videos. From the Price drop-down you can select All prices, Free only, or For sale only. From the Duration drop-down you can choose to see videos that are Short (< 4 min), Medium (4-20 min), and Long (>20 min). You can also sort by Relevance, Date, and Title.

You can sort videos in the Music videos, Sports, Animation, TV shows, and Google Picks. The sorting option is not currently available in the other categories.

Featured Videos

In addition to the categories listed earlier, the selections on Google Video are also organized into featured video sections found on the Google Video home page. You can see the top featured videos in a number of different areas. Some of the featured areas are the same as the categories. Videos can also be selected from the most popular, those that are featured, and featured on AOL. This is simply one more way Google helps you find what you're looking for and improve your browsing experience.

The feature lists include the following types of videos:

- Popular
- Featured
- Featured on AOL
- Comedy
- Music
- Movie Trailers
- TV Shows
- Sports
- Education

Each group of featured videos is available using an RSS feed. This allows you to use a news feed reader to keep up to date on current videos. You might also want to try Google Reader, Google's Web-based news reader.

CROSS-REF Chapter 14 has detailed information on setting up and using a news feed reader. For more about Google Reader, check out Chapter 39.

Playing the Video

So far, this chapter has discussed the organization of videos on the Google Video site and how to find what you're looking for. Now it's time to find out what you can do once you find a video you want to watch. Once you select the video you want to see, click on the image associated with the video. A new page launches and the video begins loading in your Web browser. At first, you see a black area on the screen where the video eventually begins playing, and the message "buffering..." appears as the video loads. The time it takes for the video to load depends on your computer, your Internet connection, and the length of the video.

TIP For best video viewing, you should have a broadband connection to the Internet. While it is possible to watch the videos over a dial-up connection, load times may be long depending on the duration of the video.

Choose a format

Many people are predicting a time when we won't have computers as we know them now, large things that sit on our desktops serving only as a "computer." Many people are already using their phones or small handheld devices such as the iPod and PlayStation PSP. With Google Video, you are not restricted to viewing videos on your computer. You have a choice of three formats in which you can download video:

- Windows/Mac
- Video iPod
- Sony PSP

To download, select one of the formats from the drop-down list next to the Download button. Once you select a format, click Download to begin transferring the video. You should refer to your documentation for information about transferring a video to your handheld device once it downloads to your computer.

Buffering saves time

For longer videos or slower Internet connections, you don't have to wait for the entire video to load before you can start playing it on your computer. The video begins playing when enough of it downloads to begin playing, hopefully uninterrupted, as the rest of the video continues to download. This is a process called *buffering*. You can watch the progress of the video download in comparison to the speed at which the video is playing by watching the status bar of the video player software. You can see in Figure 5.2 that the partially filled bar shows buffering progress while the arrow slider tracks the video play progress.

FIGURE 5.2

Track buffering and video play at the same time.

The video display page

The Web page that displays the video contains quite a bit of information and functionality. First, it contains the name of the video. Right beneath the name is a list of stars with a blue background where you can provide your feedback for future viewers of the video. You can rate a video by clicking stars from 1 (Poor) to 5 (Excellent!). You can see an average rating next to yours and the number of people who rated the video.

The video information also includes the name of the person — usually a screen name — of the person who uploaded the video along with the date it was uploaded and the length of the video in minutes and seconds.

In addition to the categories and featured categories discussed earlier, Google has more detailed categories you can browse. Next to the Browse: label you see a number of categories shown as links. These are detailed categories created by other users in which this video falls. This allows you to view other videos similar to this one based on one or more of the detailed user-created categories.

You can also add your own label to create a category in which you think this video best fits. You may go back later to see that other videos have been added to your category. To create your own label, type a new label by clicking on the Add label link. A text box appears where you can type your label, then click Add label. A response pops up under the text box that tells you the label is saved.

Using the Playlist

The Playlist provides useful functions and information about the video. For example, clicking the <u>Details</u> link presents a sequence of images from the video. If you click different images, the progress bar beneath the video advances to a different time within the video. This works in the same way as a DVD menu that allows you to start from different scenes in a movie.

When you want Google Video to act like a video jukebox, you can configure Google to continuously play the next video as though you had manually clicked the <u>Next video</u> link. Find the Continuous Feedback On or Off configuration setting. Click On to begin continuous play. Stop continuous play by clicking Off.

Click the <u>From user</u> link to see a list of any other videos on the Google site by the same user that posted the video you are viewing. A list of videos appears if the user has posted any other videos.

Clicking the <u>Related</u> link shows you other videos that Google believes are similar or related to the video you are viewing. Clicking on one of the related videos takes you to the detail page of a different video. Use your browser's Back button to return to the video you were viewing previously.

The <u>Comments</u> link loads user comments and reviews. You can write your own comments about the video and rate it in number of stars. Simply click on the stars until the number of them you would like to appear are highlighted. Type your name or alias and then type your comment. Click Publish to post your comment for others to see.

You can navigate to the next or previous video by clicking either the <u>Previous</u> or <u>Next video</u> links.

Let others know

Once you see a video, you may want to let others know about it. When you view videos in Google's Top 100 you can send e-mail and blog posts to let others know how to view the video and what you thought of it.

Send a blog post

You can send a post to one of a number of different blog sites about the video. You can post to MySpace, Blogger, LiveJournal, or TypePad by selecting the site you want to post to, as shown in Figure 5.3. You can send a link to the video by clicking the <u>Embed HTML</u> link. The HTML necessary to access this video is automatically embedded in the text box below. You can copy and paste that HTML link into your own Web page to present that video from your own Web page.

E-mail this video

You can choose to send an e-mail notification with a link to the video to others. They receive an e-mail message telling them that their friend has sent them the following Google video. You can type your own customized message to accompany the notification. You aren't sending the entire video in e-mail, only a link to it, so don't worry that you are sending a huge file.

FIGURE 5.3

Select which blog site you want to log in to, and add your username and password.

Google Video Player

When you want more control over your video viewing experience, use the Google Video Player. Many people use Windows Media Player; Google Video Player works in much the same way but is created specifically for reading the proprietary Google Video file format. When you want to view the Google videos using other than the Web interface you must use the Google Video Player, other multimedia players will not read the Google format.

Download the Google Video Player by clicking the link on the Google Video page or by navigating to one of these URLs and manually downloading the Google Video Player.

Windows users download from: `http://video.google.com/playerdownload`; Macintosh users download from: `http://video.google.com/playerdownload_mac.html`.

Once you install the Google Video Player you can use it to watch videos from the Google Video site. When you find a video you want to watch using the Google Video Player, click Download. This launches the Google Video Player, and the video begins playing automatically.

When you click Download, you are not actually downloading the video. You will still need to be connected to the Internet because even though you are using something other than the Web page to view them, the videos are not stored on your computer. Instead, you download a small file that tells the Google Video Player where to find and begin streaming the video. When you want to load a video you have already "downloaded," choose File ⇨ Open from the menu. A Google Video directory is created on your hard drive, and this is where the small information GVI files are stored. Select one and the video loads and plays.

Control the play of the video using the Rewind, Play, and Fast–Forward arrow buttons. When the video plays, the Play button changes to a Pause button. Clicking the Pause button changes the button back into the Play button and resumes playing the video.

Control the volume using the small volume slider next to the buttons. Typing a search request into the Search videos box on the player launches the Google Video page and starts your query.

With Google Video player you can browse through the scenes of the video. Clicking the thumbnail index button to the right of the search box, as displayed in Figure 5.4, presents you with small thumbnail still images taken from the video. It works a little like a scene index on a DVD. Each thumbnail is time indexed, and clicking on the thumbnail takes you to that part of the video, as shown in Figure 5.5.

FIGURE 5.4

Use the Google Video Player instead of a Web browser.

Unlike other video players, you can skip to a portion of a video that is not downloaded yet, and Google begins downloading that portion of the video. The Google Video Player uses the most advanced download features, and even continues interrupted downloads automatically.

Like other video players, you can watch videos in small- or full-screen mode. Switch to full-screen mode by clicking the small screen icon. To return to normal size (no longer in full-screen mode), press Esc.

You can also choose to view your video in original, half size, and double size by selecting the associated entry in the View menu. This menu also has entries for playing the video in a loop and for showing the thumbnail time index.

FIGURE 5.5

Click a thumbnail to play the video at a specific location.

Set the Google Video preferences by selecting Preferences from the File menu. In the Google Video preferences, you can choose to set:

- The directory where Google stores the Video Information files.
- Rendering method: DirectX and OpenGL. DirectX is the default.
- Connection settings if your computer is behind a firewall and requires proxy settings. If you are at work, you may need to see your system administrator for proxy settings.

Purchasing Videos

There are many free videos you can watch on the Google Video Web site. In addition to the free videos, many are trailers or teasers meant to entice you to buy the complete video. Notice in Figure 5.6 that each of the *NCIS* TV show episodes has a price associated with it. The trailer for the episode lasts less than a minute, and then you are asked to pay to see the entire episode. There are many other videos that also charge. In most cases, you need to pay if you want to see music videos in their entirety, for example.

To buy the video, first watch the trailer. This puts you on the page with the video's details. If the video is for sale, you can click Buy High Quality and follow these steps:

1. Sign in to your Google account.
2. Type your credit card information.
3. Confirm your order.
4. View the video.

A small GVP file is downloaded to your computer. This is not the video itself. Instead, it contains download instructions for the Google Video Player. Before you can view your video you need to have an Internet connection and Google Video Player installed.

The price of the video is listed in bold in the video description.

Once you purchase a video, Google keeps track of it for you. When you want to see a list of the videos you have purchased, you must first sign in to your Google account. Once you log in, along the top of the page next to your Google username, you can click the Purchased Videos link (see Figure 5.7). Clicking this link displays a list of your purchased videos. From this page you can view the receipt or choose to view the video at any point in the future. Click the name of the video, which appears as a link. This takes you to the video's information page. The page looks different now because it does not ask you to purchase the video. Instead, the page tells you that you have already purchased the video. View the video again by clicking Download.

See a list of your purchased videos so you can watch them again.

Sharing Your Video

You can upload your own video to Google Video. This allows you to view your own video on Google and share it with friends, family, business associates, anyone you want.

You must first be logged into your Google account before uploading a video. Once you log in, upload your video. It must be saved in one of the following formats:

- AVI
- MPEG
- QuickTime
- Real
- Windows Media

Begin uploading the video from this Google Video page at `video.google.com/videouploadform`.

Select a title for your video. Try to select a title that best describes what a user might expect to see. Titles like "My Video" are not going to interest anyone in watching what you're taking the time to upload. Type a description of the video, but don't get too wordy. People scrolling through the videos have a short attention span. Try to get right to the point — for example, "A rabbit attacks my doberman." Of course, you can be as specific as you want in the description. Take a look at some of the descriptions others use in order to get an idea of the best way to describe your video.

Select a category for the video you're uploading. Choose from 38 genres from Action and Adventure to Western by selecting one from the Genres drop-down list. Don't worry about getting exactly the right one; you can select up to three categories, and you can change it later.

Agree to the terms and conditions, and click Upload video to start the upload.

Do not close the Web page while your video is uploading or your upload could be canceled. When the upload is complete the Web page notifies you that the video successfully uploaded (see Figure 5.8).

FIGURE 5.8

Watch your video once it is successfully uploaded.

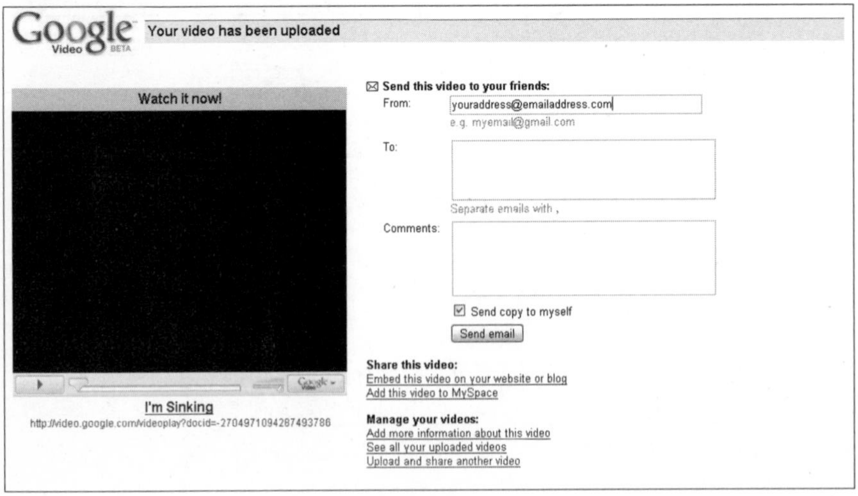

Once you upload the video to Google, you can share your video with others. Clicking the <u>Embed this video in your website or blog</u> link causes a text box to appear filled with HTML code. You need to copy this code into your Web page, your MySpace.com profile, or blog so others can view your video. Simply copy and paste this code into your Web page editor or into MySpace.com, as shown in Figure 5.9.

 **TIP** You can upload videos directly to MySpace.com if you'd rather not link to the video you've uploaded to Google Video.

FIGURE 5.9

Copy and paste the HTML right into your MySpace.com blog.

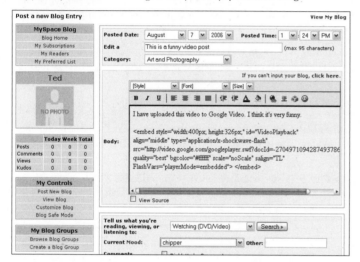

Managing Uploaded Videos

Once you upload one or more videos, you can choose to manage the information (*metadata*), such as the video title, production company, genre, and your Web site URL, displayed on the Google Video page alongside your video. To access the video management page, click the <u>Uploaded Videos</u> link at the top of the Google Video page. This only appears when you log in to Google.

The management page of the Google Video Upload program lists all your uploaded videos. If you have recently uploaded a video and it does not appear in the list, try clicking the <u>Refresh Videos</u> link located beneath the table listing of videos.

Edit video information

When you upload the video you can add some fundamental information. Editing the information actually allows you to add more details than you are able to add when you first upload the video. For example, you can add additional genres where at first you could only select one. Additional information you can add about this video includes:

- Change the video title or description.
- You will additionally be asked to certify by checking a box that the video is not pornographic.

- If you know the name of the production company that made the video you can add it to the form.
- On the Add/Edit Video Information page you can select up to three genres for your video.
- Add a link to your Web site.
- Add the names of the people you want to credit. To add additional credits click the Add link.

Setting the Advanced Options

Clicking the Advanced Options link drops down an additional set of features within the video information edit page. Most important, this is where you get to charge others to view the video.

CAUTION Pay attention to the laws regarding copyright, particularly if you charge money to have others view the video you upload. Free viewing can still be unlawful, but easier to forgive than if you charge a fee.

If you want your video to be viewed freely without charge, select the Free Video radio button. Additionally, if you want to allow users to download the video, as opposed to viewing on the Google Video Web page only, select the Allow users to download this video checkbox.

If your video can be purchased, select the Purchasable Video option. You have two options for charging: First, select the Purchase price checkbox and type a price after the USD$ label. USD$ stands for United States dollars. The format is *dd.cc*, with *dd* being dollars and *cc* being cents. If you select the Allow copying to iPod and other devices option, users will be able to download the video to handheld devices, but this defeats all copy protection.

The other option is to charge a Day-Pass price. People who pay can view the video for 24 hours after paying the Day-Pass price. You cannot delete any live videos after people have paid to view that video. To select this option, click the Day-Pass checkbox and type a price.

It's important to offer a free preview of your video if you want people to purchase it. The default preview length is 30 seconds. You can choose to show a preview from the beginning of the video or start at a particular time within the video. Type the Start time and End time of the preview. For example, if your start time is 22 seconds and you want your preview to last 30 seconds, the end time should be 52 seconds.

If you want to allow others to display your video on their Web sites, select the Embedded Video checkbox. Last, you can select areas where your video will not be shown. This is particularly important if your video contains something that is culturally sensitive. To choose countries to exclude, select the Select countries where the video won't be shown option. Then select the countries from the list box. To select more than one country press and hold the Ctrl key while clicking selections with your mouse.

When you finish editing your options, click Save Video Information>>.

Add a transcript

You can easily add a transcript for your video. You can upload a transcript, edit a transcript, or create one from scratch. Click the Edit Captions/Subtitles link in the Actions column of the table listing your uploaded videos, as shown in Figure 5.10.

Each time you edit your video, someone at Google reviews the edits to make certain that they comply with the Google guidelines.

FIGURE 5.10

Edit, delete videos, or add transcripts and subtitles after a video has been uploaded.

Creating Video Transcripts

Adding a transcript can be a time-consuming process but can help others find your video. Google searches on text and by providing the transcript Google is able to search on the text of the video transcript.

The transcript must follow the spoken words in the video according to the timing of when they are spoken in the video. Therefore, it is necessary to include the time, relative to the beginning of the video, before and after the spoken words in a text file. The time must be displayed in the following form: HH:MM:SS.mmm, where HH is hours from 00 to 24, MM is minutes from 00 to 59, SS is seconds from 00 to 59, and mmm is milliseconds from 000 to 999 and separated from the seconds by a decimal point, not a colon. Here is an example:

```
00:00:08.000
[James] Hi there.
00:00:08.000
[Judy] Great to see you.
9:54:54.000
```

Although the time must be displayed using this particular method, the format of the text you provide is completely up to you. The names in the example were set off by brackets to make the text easier to read. You can type your transcript directly in the text box provided by Google or create it in a text editor. The text editor must provide UTF-8-encoded output. Windows Notepad works just fine. When you finish adding your transcript to Google click Save Transcript.

Summary

Google Video is incredibly entertaining. It was difficult to finish writing this chapter as we stopped to watch all the videos. There is something for everyone — adults, students, and children. Google makes certain that Google Video is family-friendly.

Like all other Google resources, Google Video is designed to allow people to find exactly what they are looking for. The Google Video Web site is organized by categories and featured lists. You can also find related videos by user-created labels and by other videos a user may have uploaded. You can also pay to watch videos, like old TV episodes, any time of the day or night.

Watching the videos that others have uploaded is only half the fun; you can upload your own videos for others to watch. If you create the video or own the content, you can even charge others to view it, a nice way to make a little extra cash. Once you upload videos, you can manage them through Google's Uploader program, which allows you to create great entertainment or educational resources.

Chapter 6

Searching through Books

It may seem unusual that one of Google's key search areas is for books, one of its few non-digital-oriented search technologies. It's going to be a very long time before we see the end of paper books. Google's Book search allows you to discover books that you'd like to purchase or obtain. Once you "discover" a book you can buy it online, or use Google's library catalog system discussed later in this chapter.

It was actually the Google Book project that formed the foundation of Google in the very beginning. While creating software to help index digitized books while working as researchers on the Stanford Digital Library Technologies Project Google founders, Larry Page and Sergey Brin, created a crawler named BackRub. It was the work they did on BackRub that formed the foundation of Google's PageRank system, the core of the Google search technology.

Google Book Search is NOT a bookstore, and Google does not make money if you purchase books through its search pages. This is important to know so that you can be assured that the search results you view are not biased to allow for greater book sales. You may find contextual ads placed on some of the book pages by permission of the publisher. Clicking on these ads is how Google pays its employees.

IN THIS CHAPTER

Find books using Google Book Search

Use the Advanced Search features to focus your book search

Discover detailed information about books that interest you

Read entire books in the public domain

Librarians learn to use Google Book Search in your library

Learn about the Google Books Partner Program

Searching for Books

Google obtains books from authors and publishers in order to scan them and make portions of the books available online, and allow for searches through the text. Google also maintains partnerships with libraries. Some of the book types scanned by Google include

- Fiction
- Non-fiction
- Reference

- Textbooks
- Children's books
- Scientific
- Medical and Legal

To access Google Book Search, navigate to `books.google.com` or from the main Google page click the more>> link. Click Books in the pop-up menu that appears, as shown in Figure 6.1.

FIGURE 6.1

Click the more>> link to navigate to the Google Books page.

Begin your search by typing search terms into the Google Book Search search box. Your search terms can include the author's name, part of the author's name, all or part of the book title, or text that might be found in the book. Press Enter or click Search Books after typing your search terms.

A list of books appears. A small thumbnail image of the book cover may appear next to the snippet of information about each book. The book information contains the following:

- The book title as a clickable link
- The author's name
- Subject category
- Publication year
- A small bit of the text
- Any of these optional features — Table of Contents, Index, and About this book

Selecting the view

Google Book Search allows you to search for books based on whether the book is fully available through Google. The search choices are All books and Full view books. Books that are fully viewable are in the public domain, the copyright has expired, or the publisher has asked Google to make the entire book available through Google.

Select your view by selecting the radio button beneath the Google Book Search box. Selecting All books enables you to see what type of view is available for that book. The view choices are:

- **Snippet View:** Extremely brief cutaway view of the book.
- **Limited Preview:** Normally contains the Table of Contents or the Index, or About the book, or some combination of these.
- **No preview available:** You are not able to preview any portion of the book.
- **Full view:** Entire book is available for viewing.

When you select Full view, only books with their entire contents available for viewing appear in your results.

 While you search on books, Google associates identifying information such as your Google account name with your page views. This enforces the copyright limit not to invade your privacy.

Advanced Book Search

When you need extra assistance in finding a book, you can choose to use the Google Advanced Book Search page. Click the <u>Advanced Book Search</u> link next to the search box on the Google Book Search main page. This launches the Advanced Book Search page, as shown in Figure 6.2.

FIGURE 6.2

The Advanced Book Search page assists you in narrowing your search.

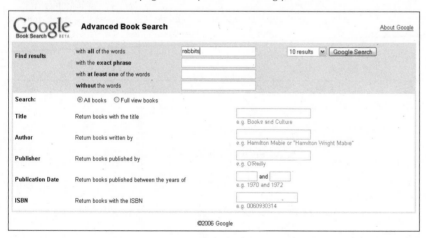

The first portion of the Advanced Search Page helps you narrow your search with keywords and phrases. The Find results section allows you to do the following:

- **Find results with *all* the words:** All keywords typed must be in the result.
- **Find results with the *exact phrase*:** The keywords you type are treated as a phrase.
- **Find results with at *least one* of the words:** Each keyword is treated separately, and the result need only contain one of the keywords if you type more than one in this field.
- **Find results *without* the words:** Limits the search by making certain that your results do not contain the word or words typed in this field.

The same view selection that is available from the main Google Book Search box is also available in the Advanced Book Search page. Choose between All books and Full view books by selecting the appropriate radio button.

The next five advanced search fields deal with book information such as title and International Standard Book Number (ISBN) rather than the text of the book. This is a simple way to limit your book search when you know the author, the title of the book, the publisher, the range of years in which the book was published, or the ISBN of the book. Type the requested information in the following fields to further limit your search:

- **Return books with the title:** Type all or part of the book title.
- **Return books written by:** Type all or part of the author's name.
- **Return books published by:** Type the name of the publisher. Depending on the publisher this can return a large number of results without adding further search criteria.
- **Return books published between the years of:** Provide a range of dates in which the book was published.
- **Return books with the ISBN:** If you type the exact ISBN, a single book result should appear.

You can optionally choose how many results you want to appear on each page by selecting from the drop-down list in the top right of the page next to the Google Search button. The default is 10 results per page, but you can select 10, 20, 30, 50, or 100 results per page.

To begin your search, click Google Search.

Viewing the book detail

Your search results, provided that they find books with your search criteria, appear as a list of books. To view the book detail, click the title of the book, which appears as a clickable link. The book's detailed information appears as shown in Figure 6.3. In this example, *Alice in Wonderland* by Lewis Carroll is selected.

FIGURE 6.3

The book detail page allows you to view the preview and more information about the book.

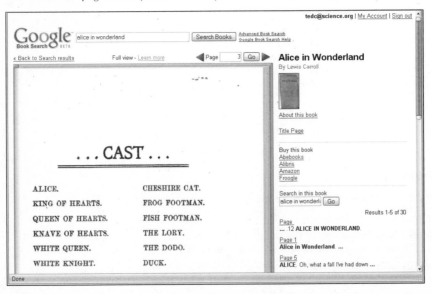

Essential information, such as the book's title, author, and when available, a scan of the cover, is displayed. The book cover and title pages normally appear as clickable thumbnails. Clicking the thumbnail displays a much larger view of either the cover or title page. The book detail in Figure 6.3 displays only the title page of this 1897 work.

In addition to the About this book link shown in Figure 6.3, some books have a More about this book link displayed in the column on the right. Clicking this link displays a synopsis of the book, a link to a Web search for reviews on the book, a link to other Web pages related to the title, and detailed bibliographic information. This information contains details not shown normally in the detail page. These are details such as whether the book is paperback or hardcover, the dimensions, and the total number of pages.

Purchase the book

The next section of the detail page provides a list of places you can buy the book online. To purchase the physical book, click one of the links in this section. Clicking the Froogle link displays a list of vendors with comparative pricing. Remember, Google Book Search is not a bookstore and makes no money when you purchase the book.

Search within the book

Google maintains the entire text of the book in its archive. Even when the entire book is not available for viewing, you can still search through the book for keywords. Type a keyword or phrase in the Search in this book search box and click the **Go** button.

The results of your search within the book are displayed for you in the column below the search box. Each result displays the line of text containing your keyword or phrase and the page number is listed above as a clickable link. When copyright restrictions apply you will be limited to the number of pages of the book you are able to view. Therefore, select the page for viewing carefully. Google keeps track!

Previewing the book

There are two primary ways to preview the book. One is to view the pages that Google selects for you to preview, and the second is to perform a keyword search through the text and view specific pages of interest to you.

The scanned text of the book appears in the viewer on the left side of the book's detail page. You may need to use the scroll bar in your Web browser to view the entire page. You can then "turn the page" by clicking the left and right blue arrow keys above and below the right corners of the page (refer back to Figure 6.3). The current page number is displayed between the arrows. Viewing the next page increments the counter of total number of viewable pages when copyright restrictions are in place.

In some cases, certain pages are restricted by the publisher and cannot be viewed as part of the preview. Additionally, certain images are restricted through copyright and the publisher may not have the right to display the image within Google Book Search. In this event, the image is replaced with the note Copyrighted Image.

Reading the entire book

In much the same way as you watch videos, which is described in Chapter 5, once you find a book and read through the preview, some publishers allow you to purchase access to the full content of the book online. Similar to how Google does not allow you to copy an entire video, the contents of the books remain on the Google site. This means that in order to read the book you must have Internet access. This copy protection mechanism allows you to read the book whenever you want. Just log in to your Google account and begin reading. The interface is easy to use, as shown previously in Figure 6.3.

NOTE As of the publishing date of this book, the online reading of purchased books was not available.

Some books are available to be read in their entirety when either the copyright has expired or when the book is in the public domain (see the next section). To read the entire book, use the blue page number arrows above and below the book pages as you would when previewing a limited sampling of a book. You may also type a specific page number and click Go. This page number feature does not appear in works with limited previews.

Books in the public domain

Some books are written for the common good of the people and are never copyrighted. Additionally, copyrights eventually expire. These works, along with books written for the common good, are considered in the *public domain*. For example, this chapter uses *Alice in Wonderland*, which was written by Lewis Carroll in 1897. The copyright on this work expired long ago and the book is now considered to be in the public domain. By the way, if you've seen the movie, try reading the book. It's fun.

Google researchers have been working for years with organizations and libraries around the world to speed up the scanning of public domain books to make them available in digital format. The goal is not to replace printed books but to form a foundation of information that inspires new books, protecting the copyright of authors. When a copyright expires (current law says that happens with books 70 years after the death of the author), the books enter the public domain. Some of the organizations working to digitize the world's public domain written word are:

- The Gutenberg Project (www.gutenberg.com)
- Universal Library (www.ul.cs.cmu.edu/html)
- Million Book Project (www.archive.org/details/millionbooks)
- American Memory (http://memory.loc.gov/ammem/index.html)

If you know of a public domain work not included in the Google Book search you should let Google know. Also, if you see a book in the Google Book search that is incorrectly labeled as public domain or not in the public domain, let Google know by sending e-mail to: books-feedback@google.com.

NOTE The rules for public domain differ from country to country. Before you use works from another country, check local copyright laws.

Find it in a library

When the Find this book in a library link appears in the book detail you can click it and Google takes you to the OCLC Worldcat (world catalog). Type your ZIP code in the OCLC catalog to find the book in a library near your home or office.

Using AutoLink

When you have the Google Toolbar installed and you visit a Web page that contains an ISBN (this could be any Web page), the AutoLink button changes to Show Book Info. Clicking Show Book Info on the toolbar changes all the ISBNs to links. Google determines where that link sends the user when clicked. It may be to the OCLC system or it may be to an online bookstore.

Google Librarian Center

To better support the efforts of librarians, Google has created the Google Librarian Center found at `www.google.com/librariancenter`. Google feels that its mission is one similar to that of a librarian and wants to partner with librarians in attaining the common goal of access to the information stored in the world's written word.

The Google Librarian Center allows librarians to join an e-mail list to enable them to keep up to date with the latest news and features offered by Google. You can also read an archive of the *Google Librarian Newsletter* by clicking the Newsletter Archive link on the left side of the page.

To help library patrons use Google more effectively, Google has made downloadable teaching tools for librarians. Click the Tools link on the left side of the Librarian Center Web page and download the teaching tools for use within your library.

Read the Tips of the Trade page to learn innovative and effective uses of Google from librarians around the world who are participating in the Google Tips of the Trade campaign. Click the Tips of the Trade link to navigate to this page. If you are a librarian, you may want to participate by sharing your own stories or ideas.

Join the Partner Program

Google is partnering with authors and publishers to build its content for Google Book Search. Google is primarily looking for publishers who have books it wants to appear in the Google Book Search. Google also wants to partner with people who have self-published their books and with authors who currently own the copyright to their books.

Friends, authors, publishers: Send me your books

Publishers have incentive to join the Google Partner Program. It's a free way to promote book sales. People who do searches will find books, read the preview, and hopefully click a link to one of the online bookstores and immediately buy the book.

This is a great way for people find books in which they have an interest. More and more online bookstores allow readers to browse a few pages of the books, see the table of contents, and in some cases view the index of the book just as they do when browsing for books in a physical bookstore. Even though Google is not a bookstore, Google Book Search offers the same features and drives book sales.

Authors are not left out of the partner program. Google is looking for authors who have self-published their books. Additionally, when books go out of print, the copyright, once held by the publisher, normally returns to the author. At this time, the author may choose to work with Google by submitting the book. It might also be a great time to write a second edition of the book and self-publish it using Google to help market the book.

Another thing authors can do is to contact their publishers and convince them to send their books to Google for scanning. It's important that authors take an active part in the marketing process.

Participate in the Partner Program

Becoming a part of the Partner Program is simple. Just follow these steps:

1. Click the Join Now link on the left side of many of the Google Book Search Help pages. Google collects some basic information from you. It first needs to know if you are the person who owns the rights to the books.

2. Click the Function drop-down list to tell Google if you are an author, a publisher, a book distributor, publishing service, or other (see Figure 6.4).

FIGURE 6.4

Click the Join Now link to access this form and join the Partner Program.

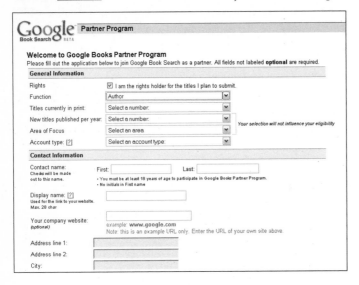

3. Respond to the remaining General Information fields as in step 2.
4. Type your full name, mailing address, e-mail address, and telephone number in the field under "Contact Information." When you complete the form, Google sends you an e-mail message.
5. Check your e-mail inbox and respond to the Google message by clicking the link in the e-mail message. You are not automatically enrolled in the program. Your application is reviewed by the Google Books staff, and you are notified of the decision.

Using Author Resources

Authors who are allowed to participate as partners because they have self-published or own the copyright to their books may open a Google Books account. In this way, they can manage book sales by reading detailed reports of things like:

- **Page views:** How many people visited the Google Books Search Web page that features your book.
- **Ad clicks:** How many people clicked on an ad placed within the book.
- **Buy this Book clicks:** How many people chose to click on the Buy this Book link to purchase the book. This does not indicate they completed the purchase, only that they clicked the link.

Google essentially has three ways of obtaining books to be scanned: when publishers send books, when authors send books, and the Google Library Project, where books in libraries are being scanned and presented only with limited bibliographic information so the copyright is not violated. If you are an author with a Google Books account and you find that one of your books has been scanned as part of the Library Project, you can have it included in your Google Books account.

Authors participating in the Partner Program can send a list of books they do not want scanned as part of the Library Program. Authors who are not part of the program can still submit a list of books they want avoided by the Library Program. They simply need to submit additional information about themselves.

Participate in Google's Library Project

If you know of a library with a special collection that is currently not part of the Google search, ask your librarian to send an e-mail to: books-support@google.com. If you are the person in charge of a library collection, send Google the following information:

- The name or title of the collection
- The size of the collection in number of works or archived items
- Description of the unique or specialized content
- How much of the collection is already digitized
- Languages used within the collection

For additional information about this process and what libraries are currently involved, visit: http://books.google.com/googlebooks/library.html.

Summary

Book searching is at the very heart of what formed Google in the first place. Google has worked with many of the book-digitizing projects to create an amazing online digital book resource. You can participate and use these resources simply as a person interested in finding a book or possibly buying a book, or as a publisher, author, or librarian. The search features for finding books are powerful. You may even find the answer you are looking for simply by doing keyword searches through the book itself.

Publishers and authors can promote their books by participating in the Google Books Partner Program. Google can scan your books and make them available for preview or purchase through several online bookstores. Although Google is not a bookstore, it makes shopping for books simple and powerful, very similar to the Google Catalog discussed in the next chapter.

Chapter 7

Searching Google Catalogs

I t may not be as fun, or as creatively useful as the old Sears catalog, but Google has created a streamlined and common way you can search the catalogs of many online vendors. This way you don't have to figure out where and how to navigate through the many kinds of online catalogs. You can do all your searching in a single place.

Google has scanned catalogs from partner vendors. You can see the vendor's full-color catalog online in an easy-to-browse format. You can navigate to the vendor's home page and have the catalog right at your fingertips. You can also use some of the other Google shopping tools such as Froogle to comparison shop by switching back and forth between Froogle and Google Catalogs. You may find vendors that you never knew existed have exactly what you're looking for.

Browsing through catalogs gives you an entirely different experience than many e-commerce sites that try to get you to the page where you click the Buy button. Catalogs make you familiar with a company's entire line of products. You may find companion products or models that are superior to the product you had in mind. You might just enjoy browsing catalogs without the intention of buying anything. For example, many hobbyists browse catalogs to keep up with the latest gadgets and things of interest.

IN THIS CHAPTER

Learn to search through online Catalogs

Advanced searching through the catalogs

Navigating catalogs with Google's special interface

Get your catalog online with Google Catalogs

Search or Browse Catalogs

Start searching through Google Catalogs by navigating to http://catalogs .google.com. This launches a Web page that serves as a portal to hundreds of online catalogs (see Figure 7.1). Find the category of item you are searching for among the 16 links, or use the search box at the top of the page. Using the search box may speed up your search by letting you type the name of the item you want to purchase, or it may slow you down by returning items in categories not related to the item you want. You will have to try your search; if you need to browse the catalogs, you may find that more effective and possibly more fun.

Browsing the catalogs

The interface for browsing catalogs is simple. Click one of the major catalogs from the main Google Catalogs page. For example, clicking the Computers link displays vertical columns. The right column contains thumbnails of catalogs and brief descriptive information, such as the catalog name, when it was published and direct link to the vendor's homepage.

The left column displays the category selected, and the previous level above and below any subcategories. In the example of clicking on the Computers category, the previous level is All Categories and the subcategories are Software, Systems & Accessories, and Windows. You can choose to browse through all the related catalogs in the right pane or select a subcategory to further focus your search. You can see in the upper-right corner of the page how many catalogs Google found for the category you selected.

Google Catalogs makes it simple to find what you're looking for in online catalogs.

Using the search box

Typing search terms in the Catalog search box is similar to any other Google search. Type the name of the item, the brand, or category of item you are searching for, and a list of catalogs appears, as shown in Figure 7.2. In the example shown in this figure, the search term **golf clubs** is typed. A list of catalogs, with the cover of the catalog displayed on the left, appears in the search results.

The search results include the name of the catalog, when it was published, a description of the catalog and a link that allows you to see more results that include your search term within the catalog. Clicking this link gives you a list of the pages that contain your search term. Figure 7.3 shows the results page from within the catalog. Notice also in Figure 7.3 that you can search just within the catalog by typing your search terms into the search box in the column on the left of the results page.

For ease of purchasing, included in the left column of the catalog detail page is the telephone number and link to the vendor's Web page. There is more about buying from a catalog later in this chapter.

FIGURE 7.2

Searching on a category of item presents many catalogs to search.

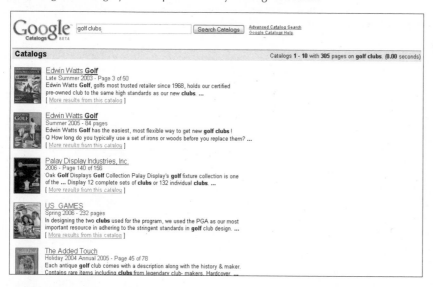

FIGURE 7.3

Find your results within the catalog.

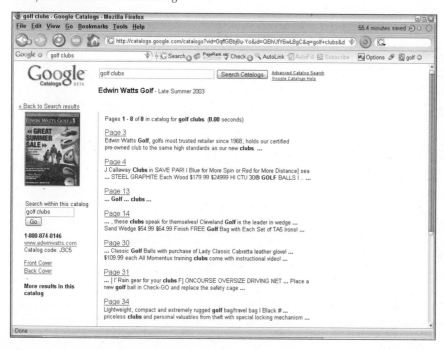

Viewing the catalog

When you find the catalog you want to browse through, it is displayed using the Web-based, Google Catalog Interface. The catalog interface includes a scanned view of the catalog in the center of your screen and links in the left column to scans of both the front and back cover of the catalog. You aren't restricted to this view of the catalog. Google's catalog interface provides four different views:

- **Multi-page view:** This view allows you to see many pages of the catalog at the same time in thumbnail view. The thumbnail is large enough so that you may be able to use this view to quickly locate the item you are looking for within the catalog. Each page appears as a link so simply clicking on the thumbnail launches that page in Normal view.
- **Two page view:** View two pages at the same time. This view is useful when reviewing a lot of information about a single item or comparing many different items.
- **Normal page view:** This is the default view and displays a single page of the catalog.
- **Zoom view:** When the catalog is a little too small to see, you need not go out and get laser eye surgery. Select Zoom view and see the catalog page just a little larger than the normal view.

Change among these four views by selecting from the icons that appear in the box labeled View: that appears above the upper-left corner of the catalog page shown in your browser window. It may be necessary, depending on your computer's display settings, to use the left and right window scroll bars to see the entire scanned page. This is particularly true when using Zoom view.

While viewing the catalog, you will notice that your keywords or phrases found within the catalog are highlighted in yellow. This helps you quickly locate the item you searched for. Also, if you do not find the item, the items highlighted in yellow may help you figure out how to better focus your search using the Advanced Search features discussed later in this chapter.

The vendor may choose not to have Google scan certain pages in its catalog. This decision may be made for any number of reasons. The page is still "in" the catalog: You just can't view it. Instead, an image stating "Image not available" appears in its place.

Changing pages

Navigate through the catalog by using the blue, left, and right arrow keys found above the upper-right corner of the catalog. The current page number or numbers are displayed between the arrows. The number of pages that increment or decrement changes depending on the view that is set. The Normal and Zoom setting change to either the previous or next page. The others change two or more pages at a time depending on the setting.

 Click the Back to Search results link to go back to your initial results, listing individual catalogs, not results within a single catalog.

Advanced Catalog Search

To access the Advanced Catalog Search, click the link next to the search box found near the top of nearly any Google Catalog page. When you click the Advanced Catalog Search link from a result page, your search terms appear automatically in the Advanced Catalog Search page in the "with **all** the words" box.

Setting the advanced search settings is similar to any other Google Web search. You can focus your search terms, as shown in Figure 7.4, by limiting your search to search results matching all your search terms, with an exact phrase, with at least one of the words within a list of words, or by limiting the search by excluding pages with a specified term or phrase.

Focus your searches to find the right catalog.

Unlike other Google searches, the advanced search features allow you to search for a specific catalog title — for example, The Sports Authority. In the Return catalogs with the title box, type all or part of the name of the vendor who publishes the catalog. If you type part of a name, you may get more than one catalog with vendors that have similar names. For example, typing **Sports** will give you 1,340 results, of which The Sports Authority is only one. When you know the exact name of the vendor, you may also want to enclose the name of the vendor in quotes to better focus your search.

You can choose to focus your search by selecting a category for your search. These categories are similar to the ones listed on the main Google Catalogs page. Select one of the 16 different categories from the drop-down list. You can choose one. If you need to search on multiple categories, you may need to perform more one than one search, changing the catalog category each time.

The last advanced search criterion allows you to specify whether you want to see only recent catalogs or all catalogs by the different vendors. Of course, specifying all catalogs increases the potential number of search results but may show you old and out-of-date catalogs.

Buying From a Catalog

There is currently no way to purchase items in the various catalogs using a Google interface like the one used to purchase videos. In the event that you find the item you want to purchase, you need to contact the vendor either by calling the phone number provided on each of the Google catalog results pages for the vendor or by visiting the vendor's Web site. That link is also provided on each of the catalog results. See Figure 7.5 for the location of the vendor information.

NOTE Clicking on the vendor's homepage link causes you to navigate away from the Google Catalogs pages. Use your browser's Back button to return to your search results or you can right-click and choose Open Link in New Window, or simply Shift+click on the link.

Remember that items and prices within the catalog may have changed. Don't depend on the prices you find in the catalogs to make your final decision. You may even decide to use Google's Froogle application before purchasing to find and compare prices.

CROSS-REF You can learn more about Froogle in Chapter 8.

FIGURE 7.5

Call the vendor or visit its Web page to order products.

Telephone number and home page link

In some cases, when ordering online you can refer to the optional catalog code listed in the left pane when speaking with a customer service representative. When this is available it will help you know that you are shopping from the most current catalog and the customer service representative may be able to refer to specific page numbers if he or she knows exactly what catalog you are shopping from. Generally, each item within the catalog will also have an item number making ordering or referring to an item much simpler.

Merchant Information

Google is looking for a few good catalogs. Actually, it's looking for many good catalogs and wants to partner with vendors to host their catalogs for free. The requirements for submitting a catalog include the following:

- The catalog must be from a U.S.-based company.
- The prices for each item must be printed in the catalog.
- The catalog must be designed to assist people with making immediate purchases.
- Items for sale must be legal in all 50 states.

When selecting catalogs to scan, Google may reject catalogs that are of an unusual size. This includes oversized catalogs or small, pocket-sized catalogs. Because of Google's viewing interface, the catalog must also be oriented in portrait view, not the landscape view often used in automobile catalogs.

For now, at least, Google is not accepting catalogs in the following categories:

- Non-U.S. catalogs
- Travel brochures
- Travel guides
- Course catalogs from schools or private educational organizations
- Manufacturing data sheets (single-page, sometimes printed both sides, informational sheet)

Before you can send Google your catalogs to be scanned, you must first sign up at `services.google.com/catalogs/application` and be approved as a vendor. Signing up is easy and consists largely of typing your company's contact information and agreeing to the terms and conditions. Once your entry is accepted, you are sent by e-mail a specific address to which you should send your catalogs to be scanned.

If you are already a merchant with a catalog in Google Catalogs you may want to manage which catalog people see. To update your catalog with Google, simply send the new catalog to the special address Google provided when you became a vendor. If you've lost this address, you can always contact Google's catalog services team at the e-mail address `catalogs-merchants@google.com`. You can also write to catalog services at this e-mail address if you want to remove your catalog or change the description displayed with your catalog.

For more information, go to the Google Catalog Help page at `http://catalogs.google.com/intl/en/googlecatalogs/help.html`.

You may be wondering what Google gets out of hosting other people's catalogs for free if it doesn't take a percentage of the sale. Google, with its catalog-hosting service, forms relationships with vendors that will eventually use Google's other merchant services such as Google AdWords and all the other services discussed in Part V of this book.

Summary

This chapter taught you how to search for and find items within a vendor catalog on the Google Catalog site. You can find catalogs by browsing or searching for catalogs using the familiar Google search box. Once you find a catalog, you can browse through it page by page or do keyword searches through the catalog itself, taking you right to the page that displays the items you're interested in purchasing or simply interested in knowing more about.

If you are a vendor or merchant, Google lets you put your catalog online for free. If you meet the requirements you can use the power of Google to display your catalog online. Not only is this useful for small- to medium-sized businesses, but for larger companies as well. People use Google to find things, and having people find your product and buy it is probably why you are in business.

Several times in this chapter, we mention Froogle as a perfect companion to the Google Catalogs. Learn more about shopping with Froogle in the next chapter and see that it's true that Google Catalogs is a great companion to Froogle.

Chapter 8

Shopping as a Sport

One of the biggest uses of the Internet, after communications, is shopping. More people shop online today than ever before, and it's not hard to believe that someday shopping online will surpass shopping in brick and mortar stores. Of course, it's hard to pass up the air conditioning of the local mall on a hot day. Even with the temptation of cool air on a hot day, Google has made the online shopping experience even more fun and more powerful by creating a tool that allows you to comparison shop for products based on price and features. Chapter 7 showed you how easy it is to view catalogs online. Comparison shop with Google's Froogle and there is no need to ever leave the house again. You can do all your shopping online.

Experiencing Froogle

Froogle is a shopping search engine that uses Google's search technology for one very specific task: locating sellers that offer the item you are interested in purchasing and pointing you directly to the place where you can buy it. Froogle not only gets you quickly to the right vendor but also helps you find the best price among many vendors selling exactly the same product.

There are two ways that Froogle obtains the information it displays about the products. First, sellers add the information about their products, taking advantage of Froogle's free service. Second, Froogle uses Google's powerful search technology to crawl the Web in order to identify vendors for a specific product.

> **NOTE** You can't buy products from Froogle. Froogle is not a store. It is a service that assists you in finding the right vendor for the product in which you have an interest.

IN THIS CHAPTER

Experience a new kind of shopping with Froogle

Navigating the Froogle Results page

Find products fast with Smart Search

Learn comparative shopping

All about Ratings & Reviews

Creating My Shopping List

The Meaning of Froogle!

Froogle is a play on words — a combination of *Google* and *frugal*. If you type **define:frugal** in Google's Web page search box, the result page appears with two definitions:

- *Economical: avoiding waste*
- *A horse that survives well on minimum food rations*

Because Froogle is not about horses, you can forget about the second definition and focus on the first one. Avoiding waste is what Froogle truly does best. This service not only helps you find a store that has the product you want, it also allows you to compare prices among vendors and choose the best option for you. The best price is not always the best option. You may know about quality issues with certain products or vendors that affect your decisions about which products to purchase or where to purchase them. To assist you with this, Froogle offers product and vendor reviews. In this way, Froogle not only helps you save time and money by quickly locating vendors that sell the products you are looking for, it also helps you find the best products based on customer reviews.

Froogle's home page offers its own definition:

Froo-gle (fru'gal) n. Smart shopping through Google

Use the definition you want and definitely use Froogle to help you with your shopping.

The advantages of searching for products on Froogle are:

- Froogle searches for products in your locale. It tells you the store that has the product close to you and/or the online store where you can purchase your product.
- Froogle takes advantage of Google's search technology to find all types of products.
- Through advanced search technology, Google rapidly finds what you are looking for.
- The results are presented to you in an unbiased way. Google does not accept money to put products on the top of searches. They are placed in the order you see them based on Google's PageRank technology.

Introducing the Froogle home page

There are several ways you can get to the Froogle home page. The most direct is to type **www.froogle.com** into your Web browser's address bar. If you are used to using the addressing scheme for many of the other Google services, you may prefer to type **froogle.google.com**. Both addresses take you to the same place.

Another way to end up on the Froogle home page is to first go to Google's home page (`www.google.com`) and click the <u>More</u> link. In the pop-up menu that appears, click Froogle to launch the Froogle home page.

Don't be confused by its appearance. Froogle's home page looks very similar to Google's home page (see Figure 8.1). The same colors and options appear above the search box (<u>Web</u>, <u>Images</u>, <u>Video</u>, <u>News</u>, <u>Maps</u>, and <u>More >></u>).

FIGURE 8.1

Froogle's home page looks similar to Google's home page.

Next to the Search Froogle button are three links: <u>Advanced Froogle Search</u>, <u>Preferences</u>, and <u>Froogle Help</u>. You learn more about Advanced Froogle Search later in this chapter. The <u>Preferences</u> link takes you to the same preferences found for Google search. These are general preferences and do not provide any customizing attributes specifically for Froogle. Clicking the <u>Froogle Help</u> link presents information about Froogle, including a FAQ (Frequently Asked Questions) section and other links that help you better use Froogle.

In the middle of Froogle's home page, you see about 25 links to products on which other people have recently searched using Froogle and found products. Clicking any of these links takes you to the results page for that product.

Froogle has a feature called the Froogle Shopping List. Using your Google account, you can add products to your personalized shopping list for easy and fast access to product information at a later time. You can also share your list with friends and family, perhaps during the holiday shopping season. To start your shopping list, you can find a link to Froogle Shopping List on Froogle's home page in the top-right corner.

CROSS-REF See the section "My Shopping List" more about Froogle Shopping List later in this chapter.

In addition to those already mentioned, you'll find four other links on Froogle's home page:

- **Google Home:** Takes you to Google Search home page.
- **Information for Sellers:** If you are a merchant, this link takes you to where you can learn more about how Froogle helps you sell your products.
- **Froogle Tour:** Links to the Find it on Froogle page, a quick reference to how Froogle works.
- **About Google:** Links to Google's About page, where you can learn more about Google.

Increasing your sales with Froogle

As a product merchant you will want to take advantage of the Froogle Services. Even when your customers know who you are and what you sell, Froogle still has a lot to offer. It makes little difference whether you are an online merchant or if you have a physical store, if you sell one product or hundreds, taking advantage of Google search technology through Froogle helps customers better find your products. The Froogle service is free and your store does not need to have its own Web site.

Here is a quick guide and an example of how to get started selling your products through Froogle.

1. From the Froogle home page click the <u>Information for Sellers</u> link. This launches the Sell with Google page, also known as Google Base.

2. Optionally elect the type of product you sell from the dropdown list.

3. Click either Post one at a time or Bulk upload.

4. The page that launches is called Google Base. Here you can post all types of content and have it show up on Google searches; in this case, also in Froogle.

5. You need a Google Account because you will need to sign in. Click the <u>Sign in</u> link.

6. When prompted, type your e-mail and password, and click Sign in.

7. You have now logged in to the Google Base page. The first time you log in, you are asked to fill in your display name, a description of your business, and if you have one, the URL to your Web page. Make certain to select the checkbox if your pages contain information or images unsuitable for children. When you complete this information, click Next. Here you can see all the items you have active or inactive on Google Base. Instead of typing the name of each of your products, upload them in bulk from this page. Choose an existing item type from the drop-down list, or create a custom type (see Figure 8.2). Then click Next.

FIGURE 8.2

Select an item type or create one of your own.

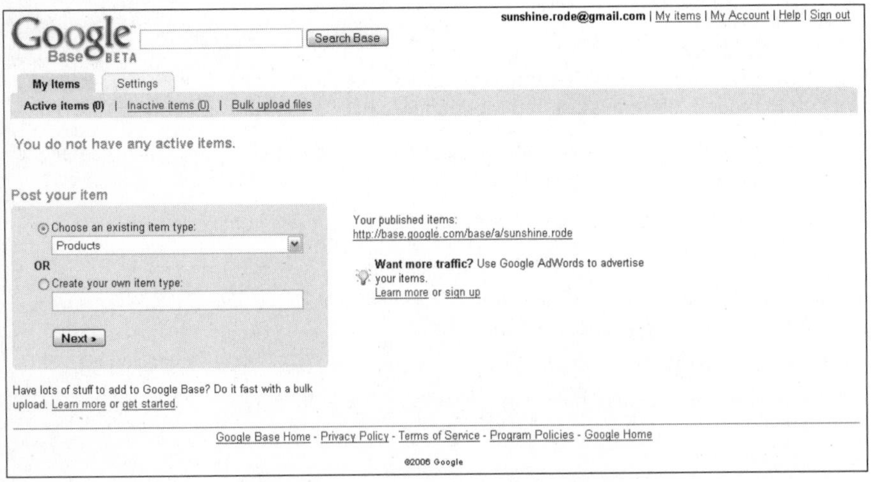

8. Type the information describing your product (see Figure 8.3). Enter information such as price, unit price type, quantity you are selling, if applicable, the product type, condition, and product brand.

9. You can also upload pictures and files related to your products by adding them into the shaded portion of the page. Upload files of the following types: PDF, DOC, PPT, XLS, TXT, ASCII, HTML, RTF, XML, and WPD.

10. Add attributes describing your product by adding attribute names, and then the values. An example of an attribute might be *vehicle weight* and an example value would be *1 ton*. Add additional attributes by clicking the Add another attribute link.

11. Add a detailed description of your product in the Description box. Use the rich text editing controls to format your text.

12. Edit the Contact, Payment and Location and delivery information. If you are an AdWords customer, edit this section to add keywords regarding this product.

13. Type the number of days this ad will run. The maximum length is 30 days.

14. Preview your item (Figure 8.4). If you are not happy with the information you typed for your product, you can click Edit. When you are ready to release the information, click Publish.

FIGURE 8.3

Enter all the information about your product.

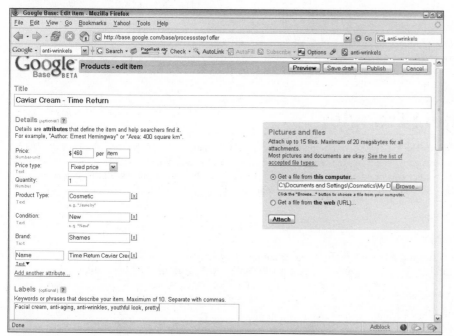

FIGURE 8.4

Preview your product advertisement.

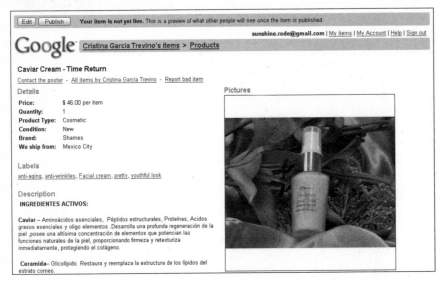

When you finish publishing your item, Froogle returns you to the Google Base My Items page. You see your product listed, and the Status area should read "Published ... searchable soon." That is how, with the click of a mouse, your product advertisement is made available to the world.

Searching Froogle

You may find using the Froogle search helps you locate just the right product. The true power of Froogle is experienced by analyzing the Froogle search results. Performing a product search can be as simple as typing the name of a product and pressing Enter. Even the advanced search features are not all that complicated. In most cases you can easily find the product you are searching for by using either the simple or advanced search features.

Simple searching

Performing a basic product search with Froogle is simple. Type the product name in the search box and click Search Froogle. To achieve the best search results, type a combination of the following:

- Name of the product
- Model number
- Manufacturer

Similar to Google Web search, clicking Search Froogle or pressing Enter after typing product information into the search box launches the Froogle results page. Consider logging into your Google account before searching Froogle so you can use Froogle features such as the ability to save your shopping list and review your search history.

Advanced searching

To better focus your search you can use the Froogle Advanced Search. From Froogle's home page or any Froogle results page click the Advanced Froogle Search link located to the right of the search box.

Froogle Advanced Search really helps you narrow the number of products listed in the search results and configures the display of the Froogle results page for customized and easier viewing. Figure 8.5 shows the Froogle Advanced Search page.

FIGURE 8.5

Use the Froogle Advanced Search page to narrow your product search.

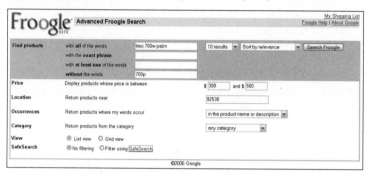

Froogle divides the Advanced Search into seven configurable categories. Setting one or more of the attributes in each of these categories allows you to better focus your product search. When you have finished configuring these categories, click Search Froogle.

Find products

The "Find products" section is where you can configure one or more of the search types to best narrow a search on the name of the product. The search types you can configure are:

- **With *all* the words:** This search type looks for sites containing all the search terms you enter in this box. For example, when you are looking for cell phones you might type **Treo 700w Palm** (product name, model number, and manufacturer).

- **With the *exact phrase*:** Looks for search phrases within a product site. For example: typing **Treo 700w Palm** will give you different results than by typing **Palm 700w Treo**.

- **With *at least one* of the words:** Shows you results with product descriptions that contain at least one of the keywords.

- **Without the words:** Limit your results to product descriptions that do not contain the terms entered here. For example: When you are looking for the Treo 700w not the Treo 700p, so you can type **700p** in the last box and the results will exclude descriptions of 700p products.

This Customize the number of search results in the **Find products** category section. The choices are 10, 20, 30, 50, or 100 results per result page. Make your selection from the drop-down list.

One of the important and sometimes overlooked search configurations is the ability to sort your product description results, making it easier to find what you consider important. Sort your results by one of the following:

- Relevance
- Price (high to low, or low to high)
- Product rating
- Sellers' rating

Price

You can select a price range for your product results. Having Froogle show you the results within a high and low price limit is useful for a couple of reasons. First, when you search for a product that also has accessories for sale, the accessories are usually priced lower than the actual product. By setting a lower limit price in your search you can avoid seeing results that include the lower-priced accessories, most of which will also contain the product name. For example, your result might be: "Power plug for Big Blend Food Muncher." Use price ranges to exclude items such as a product's replacement power plug.

The second reason price ranges are useful has to do with specifying the upper limit. This is useful for finding products within your shopping budget.

Location

Typing location information, such as your city name or your Zip code, allows Froogle to display results that are sold in stores located near you. When Froogle can not find products sold in a store close to you, it displays results as though you had not specified a location.

Occurrences

The Occurrences selection allows you to tell Froogle where in the product description you expect to find your search term. Select the occurrences from the drop-down list box. The choices include: in the product name and description, only in the product name, or only in the description. These options are very restrictive when it comes to narrowing your search.

 **When Froogle fails to return search results after specifying an occurrence, consider removing this restriction.**

Category

When you know the type of product category in which your search should occur, select one of the predefined categories from this drop-down list. The categories include: Apparel & Accessories; Arts & Entertainment; Auto & Vehicles; Baby; Books, Music & Video; Business & Industry; Computers; Electronics; Flowers; Food & Gourmet; Health & Personal Care; Home & Garden; Office; Sports & Outdoor; and Toys & Games.

View

The View option does not narrow your search. Instead, this option customizes the way your results are displayed. Select either the List view (default view), displaying product descriptions in a simple list or the Grid view option (see Figure 8.6), where viewing product comparisons is easier.

FIGURE 8.6

The Grid view on a results page makes it simpler to perform product comparisons.

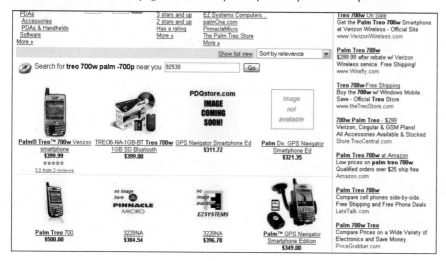

SafeSearch

Configure SafeSearch to filter adult content from the product results. Just a reminder: Google's filtering technology is not perfect but does its best to eliminate adult text and images from your results.

The Search Result Page

Froogle differs from the normal Google Web search because Web search results merely act as a jumping-off point to the information you are looking for. With Froogle, the results page may contain the information you are looking for, and the fact that you can click to purchase or visit the vendor's home page is less important than the results of a Web search.

Knowing your way around the results page can help you get the answers you need. The search result page is divided into four distinct areas (see Figure 8.7):

- Smart Search Features
- Sponsored Links
- Search results
- Bottom and navigation links

Most of the Froogle Smart Search features are located in the top section of the search result page. In this area, you can use these self-customizing search features to refine your search. Learn more about the Froogle Smart Search features in the "Smart Search" section of this chapter.

FIGURE 8.7

The Froogle results page is divided into different, useful sections.

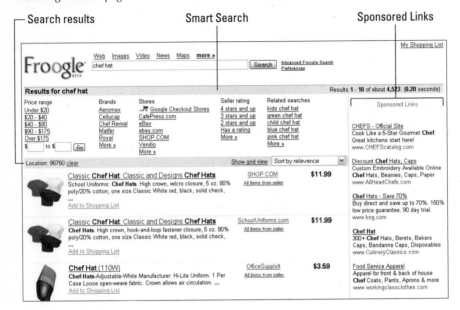

Sponsored Links are special links for which companies, or individuals, pay Google to have their products and services advertised. Sponsored links are designed to be related to your search and therefore may not appear in every result page. The number of sponsored links may also vary depending on the product you have specified in your search. When the sponsored links appear, they are located on the right side of the search results page.

By default, you see up to ten search results per page. You can customize the number of results displayed per page by changing your Froogle preferences. Additionally, the number of results per page can vary depending on whether you have selected to view the results in the List view or Grid view format.

In the List view, each result displays the following information:

- The product name as a link to the site advertising the product
- A brief description of the product
- Optional ratings of the product
- Optional links to product reviews
- An <u>Add to Shopping List</u> link
- The name of the store or site that sells the product. If the store has a rating you see its rating and the number of customers participating in the rating.
- The product price

Between the top section, containing the Smart Search features, and the search results are three options located on a blue separator bar. The first option allows you to enter or clear your location. The information in this option changes the order in which results are displayed. Google attempts to display products for sale close to your location when you have typed a Zip code. When you want to locate stores that carry products close to you, type your Zip code.

The second option allows you to switch between Grid and List views of the results by clicking the link to the right side of the bar. The link changes depending on which view you are currently using.

The third option is one of the most useful of the Froogle options. Choose to sort the product description results based on the following criteria:

- **Relevance:** How relevant is the product to your keyword search?
- **Price:** Low to high, or high to low. This is very important for finding the lowest-priced product or for finding products of a certain quality based on price. It also allows you to easily shop for the right vendor based on price.
- **Sort by product rating:** This lets you know what others think of the product.
- **Sort by vendor rating:** This information is important when purchasing from companies or people you've never heard of before.

Following the results, and located at the bottom of the page, are navigation buttons and links. When the product you are looking for is very popular you see links to navigate to more results by continuing to the next page of results. In this case, Click Next or click on a specific page number to change pages. When you are on a page other than the first page you can also move back by clicking Previous. There is an additional Froogle search box located at the bottom of the page. This search box does not have links to the Advanced Search, but it operates in the same manner as the search box located at the top of the page.

Smart Search

Smart Search is what Google calls the combination of Froogle features that assist you in finding products easier and faster by further allowing you to focus your search. Even though you won't find a Smart Search label on the Froogle results page, understand all the ways Google helps you find products and you'll agree that this is a smart way to search.

The Smart Search focusing process starts with the setting the Froogle preferences. To begin, you can set the display language, create a search filter, and configure the number of results displayed in the Froogle results page. Set these Froogle preferences by clicking the <u>Preferences</u> link next to the Froogle search box.

The bulk of Smart Search functionality becomes available after you search for a product. On the search results page, you'll see a section located beneath the Froogle logo you won't find in a normal Google Web search. This special Froogle section begins by displaying the name of the product for which a search is performed and on the same line, the number of results that are found, and not as important, the time it took Google to find these results. Figure 8.8 shows the various sections of the Froogle results page that make up the Smart Search functionality.

The special Smart Search categories intelligently configure themselves based on the type of product for which you've searched. Different categories are displayed for further focusing your search. The most common categories are Price, Sellers ratings, Related searches, and Stores. Another category that you will often see is Brand. The Brand category appears when the product you searched for includes this type of information. Another important category that you will see, when Smart Search thinks it's appropriate, is Or refine by.... This category displays additional categories such as Stores, Capacity, Watts, Frequency, Volts, and other very specific categories you can use to further focus your product search.

FIGURE 8.8

Froogle displays different categories to assist in focusing your search.

The content within the categories also changes depending on your search. For example, when you search on *USB memory*, Froogle displays five different links beneath the Price category. There are also boxes allowing you to type a price range with a Go button, as shown in Figure 8.8. When you change products and search for *speakers*, you see four links with price ranges that appear far different from those displayed for the *USB memory* search. The only feature that remains the same between these searches is the ability to type a price range and click Go.

Rating and Reviews

Froogle does not actually rate the stores or products. Froogle gets its product ratings information from other merchant sites such as shopping.com, designtechnica.com, pricegrabber.com, and others. Sellers are rated by customers. Sellers and products can be rated from 0 to 5 stars, with 5 stars meaning Excellent and 0 meaning Poor.

Not all the sellers or products are rated. When they do have ratings, the product ratings appear on the left, beneath the product, while the vendor ratings appear beneath the vendor name.

Seller ratings

When a seller is reviewed and rated you see the stars displayed beneath the seller name along with the number of customers that reviewed and rated them.

To see the comments about the seller and why it obtained its rating, click on the stars or the number of sellers rating link. Froogle takes you to a page where you can read customer comments, as shown in Figure 8.9.

When reviewing the rating, you'll find the seller's name highlighted on the left side of the page, under Froogle's logo. Shown in a box located beneath the seller's name, is the rating (in stars), also, a numeric version of the rating, and a total of how many reviews were averaged to achieve this rating.

The left side of the page is informational and a way to browse through the comments. The Show section displays information about the reviews. You can click the <u>Positive reviews</u> link to read positive comments left by people about the seller. There are also links to Neutral reviews and Negative reviews. The number of reviews in each category is posted next to each link.

You can search for a term or keyword in all the reviews by typing the keyword in the search box and then clicking Go. For example, when you want to search to see if there is anything wrong with the service or item, type *wrong* in the box and click Go. If any reviews contain the word *wrong,* those reviews appear on the results page.

Occasionally, you find an <u>All items from vendor</u> link located below the store name. Clicking this link takes you to a new Froogle page that displays all the items this vendor has registered with Froogle.

Another section located on the left side of the store review page is called Frequently mentioned terms. These terms are the ones that appear frequently within the reviews. This feature is useful in order to see what people are saying frequently about this store.

NOTE Some sites add terms at the end of their review such as customer support, customer service, see all ratings, and rating by online, so these terms will appear in the Froogle Frequently mentioned terms.

FIGURE 8.9

Froogle's review page for eToys

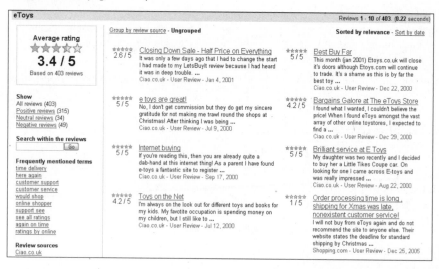

The Review sources section allows you to see all the sites that Froogle uses to display the store rating. On the right side of the page you can read reviews for the store written by customers. Froogle displays the first ten reviews (if the store has that many). If it has more than ten reviews you can click Next at the bottom of the page to see the next ten. You can sort the reviews by date by clicking the <u>Sort by date</u> link.

Product ratings

Froogle's product rating page works in a manner similar to the seller rating page. After clicking on the stars or on the numeric rating the review page launches. You will find the box located beneath the Froogle logo that displays the product rating. There are four features located on the left side of the review page. These include:

- Show
- Search within the review
- Frequently mentioned terms
- Review sources

Read the customer reviews located in the center of the review page. You may find yourself interested in a particular review source. You can group the reviews by source by clicking the Group by review source link.

My Shopping List

In each of the Froogle pages you will find the My Shopping List link located in the top right-hand corner of the page. You need a Google account to use this feature. If you don't have a Google account, you can create one from the Froogle My Shopping List home page.

The Froogle My Shopping List feature is useful for all online shoppers. This feature is for true shoppers. When you consider purchasing a product but are not ready to buy it yet, My Shopping List keeps track of those products. You can add notes to the products or create a wish list to send to your family and friends so they know what to get you!

One important thing to know is that you can keep your shopping list private but still send your wish list to everyone. Because maintaining a shopping list requires that you log into your Google account, you can access your list from any Internet-connected computer.

Manage your shopping list by sorting the list items by price, by the date you added the item to the list, or in convenient alphabetical order.

Once you sign in to your Google account the My Shopping List page opens (see Figure 8.9). Find shopping list navigations links located on the left side of the page. They are divided into the following four parts:

- **View:** You can view My Shopping List or My Wish List.
- **Sort by:** Sort your list by Date added, Price: low to high, Price: high to low, and Title.
- **Search for other items:** Type the product name you want to search on Froogle.
- **Find a Wish List:** Type the e-mail address of your friends and family to see their wish lists.

To add an item to My Shopping List, log in to your Google account and follow these steps:

1. Go to Froogle's home page (www.froogle.com).
2. Type the product name, and click Search.
3. When you find the product you want to add, click the Add to Shopping List link located on the search results page next to the product description.

NOTE You can add products to My Shopping List only when Froogle is displaying results in the List View.

After clicking the Add to Shopping List link, Froogle launches the My Shopping List page and the item you added will then appear. On the right side of the page you see a product image (if one is available). You also see the product name (with a link to the store where you can purchase it) and beneath that, the price, the store name, and a brief description of the product, as shown in Figure 8.10.

You can add a personal note to the product by clicking the edit link next to Notes. Type your note, and then click Save. Your notes are visible in your wish list as well. To add items to your Wish List, select the In Wish List checkbox.

FIGURE 8.10

Keep track of your shopping items in the My Shopping List page.

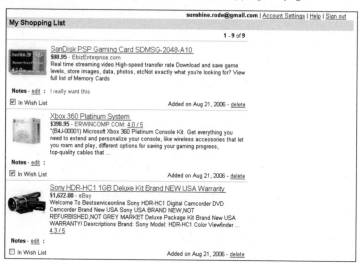

To help you better manage your list, keeping it current, you can see the date you added products to your list. To delete a product from the shopping list click the Delete link.

You can add as many products as you want, but you are only able to view ten items at one time.

Summary

Froogle makes comparison shopping simple. Find the product you are looking for simply using the powerful Froogle search features. In addition to finding products, you can read reviews of the products and the vendors that sell them.

Froogle lets you find products being sold by both online sellers as well as physical stores. Typing your ZIP code allows Froogle to find stores with your desired product close to your home.

When you find products but are not quite ready to by them, or possibly hope that others will buy them for you, add them to My Shopping List and make sure to send others your Wish List. Shopping and browsing online can be a fun experience when it's made this simple. You can continue your browsing fun by browsing through Google's Directories, which are discussed in the next chapter.

Chapter 9

Making Use of Directories

Google Directory (http://directory.google.com) is a completely different view of the Web than you might be used to experiencing through Google. In addition to using Google's powerful search technology, searching can be done manually by the user. To facilitate this type of browsing, Google Directory organizes the World Wide Web by topic into categories.

Google Directory is based on the open source project called DMOZ or, for people who don't speak acronym, Open Directory Project. The primary difference between experiencing the Web through directories and by simply performing Google searches and surfing through the results is that directories — and in particular this one — are edited by humans. While dependent upon someone else's opinion of what may or may not be relevant to a topic, it manages to cut out most of the non-relevant information that tends to overwhelm someone searching the Web.

Google Directory is not a clone of the DMOZ directory. Instead, Google applies its PageRank technology to the information submitted by the DMOZ editors. This ensures that results are organized by order of importance. Even in a human-edited directory with more than 1.5 million entries, it's easy for the result you are looking for end up lost in the weeds. PageRank ensures that the most relevant and most important pages appear first.

Google Directory information also forms an information base for Google's standard Web search. When additional information exists in the Google Directory for a Web page, Google displays this information as part of its normal Web search.

Using Directories

Google Directory is broken into topics and categories. On the main Google Directory page (shown in Figure 9.1), the 16 primary topics are listed as links. Beneath each topic is a list of the first few categories. Click the topic link to view all the categories for each topic.

103

FIGURE 9.1

Select a topic and view directory results ordered using PageRank technology.

Category

Topic

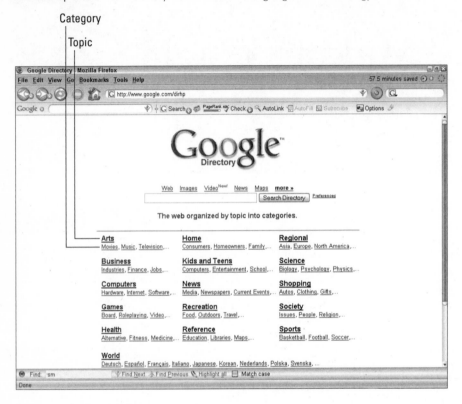

There are two primary ways of locating information within the Google Directory, performing a search, and browsing through the categories. The most expedient is the one Google users are all accustomed to: doing a Google search. The main pages, and all of the other category pages, contain a Google search box at the top of the page. Beneath the search box are two choices. The first radio button selection limits your search to the Google Directory topic or category you are currently viewing. The other selection tells Google to perform a traditional Web search.

 There are no advanced search features for the Google Directory search.

Searching the Directory

Performing a search using the Google Directory search is similar to performing a Web search. You cannot, however, use the Google search operators. Simply type the keywords or phrases (enclosed in quotes) and click the Search Directory button. The advantage of doing your search using Google Directory rather than a traditional Web search is that you can focus your search on very specific categories.

The results of a search through the Google Directory are very familiar. They are almost identical to the results you would expect to see from a traditional Web search. The primary difference is that when viewing the results you see the category displayed beneath the result title link. Displaying the category is useful for two reasons: You know whether the search is relevant based on the category in which it is found, and more importantly you can click the category, displayed as a link, to view all listings within the category.

 **The directory search may result in sponsored links appearing in the right column of your search results.**

Category browsing

Select a topic from the main Google Directory page, and you can begin navigating through the categories within that topic. The first page of category information lists the categories and any related categories. Related categories are those that are similar but appear within other topics. For example, when selecting the Arts topic, the categories organized within that topic appear in columns. Beneath those columns you see a section labeled "Related category." In this example, the related category is Arts & Entertainment within the Business topic.

Each category (shown in Figure 9.2) is followed by a number representing the number of directory entries in that category. This is one indicator about the popularity of that particular category. The extremely popular categories are listed in bold type.

FIGURE 9.2

Categories are listed in alphabetical order.

As with other Web directories, the categories are initially listed in alphabetical order. It is also customary to display the number of entries in each category. That is where the similarity stops.

Within many of the categories you find subcategories. These smaller categories assist you in focusing your search where possible by creating very specific categories in which to search. Here is an example:

The Science topic contains 30 subcategories. One of those categories is called Search Engines. Clicking on the Search Engines category displays one additional subcategory, Math Publications. This last category contains entries related to mathematical and scientific publications that discuss search engines. By navigating through the hierarchy of categories, you can focus your search to a very specific area.

To return to the previous category, or page of results, you click your browser's Back button. Unlike the Google Web search results, you are shown many more results on a single page.

NOTE   In the English language version of the Google Directory, you can quickly navigate to the top of the category hierarchy by clicking the <u>Go to Directory Home</u> link located above the blue bar on the right side of the page.

Categories by letter

Some categories — for example, Science — that have far more subcategories than the 30 that are displayed, allow you to display subcategories beginning with a specific letter. For example, if you are searching for paleobotany you would select the letter P, as shown in Figure 9.3.

FIGURE 9.3

Subcategories can often be selected by the first letter of the subcategory.

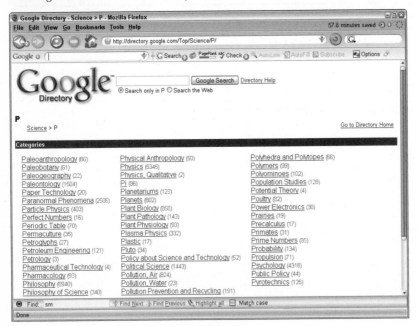

Not all categories allow you to search by letter. This option appears in categories that have a significant number of subcategories. Myths and Folktales is a category that allows you to search by letter. Clicking the letter G displays an additional eight subcategories including

- Ghost Stories
- Gilgamesh
- Graffiti
- Greek Gods and Goddesses
- Greek Myths
- Green Man
- Grimm Brothers

Selecting one of these categories may or may not offer you additional subcategories. For example, Gods and Goddesses provides an additional three subcategories: Heroes, Muses, and Olympians.

Ordering Results

Google Directory orders the Web sites listed in each category in its patented PageRank order. The advantage of ordering the results already edited by a human being in such a fashion is that while the page may be relevant, all the other factors that affect whether you can expect a page to be relevant to your search are not included by the human editor. Knowing how many other sites link to a page, or whether the URL contains the keywords, and how many people regularly visit the site are all important factors in presenting results in a Google-like manner.

Comparing the Open Directory Project category listing to Google's Directory, you find many similarities. The hierarchy of categories and subcategories is very similar. Even the entries in each category are similar, although not always exactly the same. The primary difference between the two directories is how the pages are ordered. The DMOZ results are ordered alphabetically. Google Directory results are ordered in PageRank order.

Changing the result order

If you prefer to see your results in alphabetical order, perhaps making it easier to find a page by name, Google lets you reorder the results in alphabetical order. Click the <u>View in alphabetical order</u> link in the green bar above the results labeled Web pages.

Switch between alphabetical and PageRank order by clicking the links in the bar above the results. The link, after it has been clicked and your results are reordered, changes to text that tells you that you are viewing the results in a particular order.

 Changing the result order will not affect any searches you perform using the Google Directory search. The results of a search are always in PageRank order.

Visual page rank

When viewing Web page listings in the Google Directory in PageRank order Google displays a small green bar to the left of the entry. This green bar displays the importance of a site as measured by the PageRank software. As the darker green bar extends farther to the right the page is more important. This is useful when determining if pages, even though one is listed before another, may be of nearly equal importance based on the Google PageRank formula.

> **NOTE** Google does not accept money to increase rankings within the Google Directory and therefore does not show bias among pages. Google does not evaluate the importance of a Web page, but rather determines its importance based on how others use, link to, or organize the content.

The small green bars disappear when you order the page alphabetically. It's not really certain why this provides a good measure of importance while still allowing the users to view the entries in alphabetical order.

Open Directory Project

The goal of the Open Directory Project is to create the most comprehensive human-reviewed directory of Web pages. It is a project originally begun by and continues to be managed by Netscape. You may remember that the Netscape logo was once a dinosaur named Mozilla. Many of Netscape's projects and products have thus born that name, and this project is no exception. At the beginning of the chapter it was explained that the acronym for the Open Directory Project is DMOZ. That certainly doesn't stand for Open Directory Project in any language. What it does stand for is `directory.mozilla.org`, the original name for the project at Netscape.

You will probably notice the distinct similarity between the Open Directory Project page and the Google Directory page. This is by design. The Google Directory is based on the Open Directory Project and relies on the volunteer editors to supply content to the Google Directory.

The Open Directory Project makes its content available through a special license known as an *open content license*. The license that governs the Open Directory Project at `www.dmoz.org` gives you the right to use, reproduce, modify, and create derivative works from the Open Directory. You can find the license here: (`http://dmoz.org/license.html`).

Submitting a Site

Because Google takes advantage of the more than 20,000 volunteer editors and the millions of links already in the Open Directory Project, you will not be submitting a Web site to Google. Rather, you submit your site to the Open Directory Project. Here are the steps you should follow:

1. Begin by searching the Open Directory Project's directory at `www.dmoz.org` for the site you want to submit. This helps avoid duplication.

2. Navigate through the directories to find what you believe is the proper category for the site you are submitting. Navigating through the directories is very similar to navigating through the Google Directory. When locating a category, make sure that there is a Suggest URL or Update URL link at the bottom of the page. If these links do not appear, this category does not accept submissions.

3. Click the Suggest URL link in the proposed category.

4. Fill in the Suggest URL form. Your descriptions should be clear, concise, and not sound like a late-night, used-car advertisement. Unclear or clearly promotional descriptions may delay your entry or keep it out of the directory altogether.

DMOZ

The project was originated by two Sun Microsystems engineers named Rich Skrenta and Bob Truel. Later, other Sun employees joined with Skrenta and Truel to found Gnuhoo. After complaints by people in the industry, comparing Gnuhoo with the spirit of the Gnu open source software project, it was renamed Newhoo. The early goal of the project was to create a competing directory to the Yahoo! directory using volunteer labor.

In October 1998, Newhoo was purchased by Netscape and renamed the Open Directory Project. Netscape later became an AOL Time Warner company. That's why when you visit the DMOZ page you may notice the logo In partnership with AOL Search.

The Open Directory Project is a Netscape volunteer project.

Once you send your submission, an Open Directory Project volunteer editor reviews it. Be warned that this is not a speedy process. These editors are tasked with reviewing a multitude of submissions. Don't get impatient and submit again and again. That only upsets the editors and may be cause for banning you from the Open Directory Project site.

Assuming that your submission is accepted and included in the directory it is eventually included within the Google Directory as it updates its entries from the Open Directory Project's content.

Discovering the World Topic

The World topic contains entries in languages other than English. Clicking the World link from the main Google Directory page (www.google.com/dirhp) shows a listing of 76 different languages. As with other categories, those that have a significant number of entries appear in bold.

Selecting a language provides a topic listing similar to the one on the main Google Directory page, only that it is written in the language you select from the category list. You will also notice that all the descriptions and links on the page have also switched to the same language. The World topic does not appear in the alternate language versions.

> **NOTE** Viewing some languages requires that you first update your computer with the appropriate language character set. Alternatively, Google may display question marks where unsupported character sets appear.

The advantage of using the World topic to search for entries in other languages is that these are not English translations of pages in other languages, but rather remain in their original language allowing those searching to perform searches in their native languages.

Some of the language categories do not have the same number of topics. Topics are only displayed when content exists within those topics in that language.

Summary

The Google Directory provides an alternate way to view and search the Web. Using the Open Content of the Open Directory Project (DMOZ), Google has uses its PageRank technology to enhance the way results are presented when searching the directory. With millions of entries and hundreds of categories you can quickly focus your search.

When you view results you can view them in the traditional Google PageRank order or alphabetical order as you might find them in other directories, such as DMOZ. You can become a part of the DMOZ project by submitting sites to the human-edited directory. If you feel inclined, you can also volunteer to become an editor. There are currently over 20,000 people editing this content.

The Google Directory does not limit its content to English entries. You can view the Directory in one of many languages and search through pages in only that language. The Google Directory, while an older paradigm for organizing Web content, still fulfills an important function, and information from this directory is incorporated into the normal Google Web search when extra information about a topic is available.

Chapter 10

Keeping in Touch with E-Mail Alerts

In this day and age, finding time to read the newspaper, watch the news, or listen to the radio is difficult. Still, it's important to keep track of the news, information found on the Web, or posted in the Usenet News groups. Even when you have time to read the newspaper or news Web site in the morning, keeping abreast of the news throughout the day can be difficult. Google has developed E-mail Alerts for anyone that needs to stay on top of the latest news or events happening around them. Because most people now read their e-mail throughout the day, getting special news alerts in your e-mail is a great way to stay abreast of changing information.

What is a Google E-Mail Alert?

E-mail alerts are saved topic searches through Google News, Google Groups, or the Web on topics you choose. When those searches meet a threshold of relevance, an alert is sent to your e-mail account letting you know about the information that triggered the alert.

By signing up for Google E-mail Alerts, Google sends information and news directly to you by e-mail. You decide the topic of the E-mail Alert and how often you want Google to send it. There are four types of Google E-mail Alerts:

- **News:** Every time your selected topic makes it into the top ten news articles through your saved Google News search, you receive the alert.
- **Web:** When the top 20 search results for your Web topic search change, a Google E-mail Alert is sent to you.
- **News and Web:** This is a combination of News and Web alerts. When your topic search results in hits from either of these two lists, you will you receive an e-mail alert.
- **Groups:** When you subscribe to a Google group, you can add an alert so that you get an e-mail when there is a new post to that group.

CROSS-REF To learn more about Google News, see Chapter 14.

If you're like most people, you get a lot of e-mail, some of it from people you know and some from people you wish would not send you e-mail. However, with the amount of e-mail most people get, sensitivity to the number of e-mail messages you receive has grown. You can choose how often you want Google to send you an alert by selecting one of these options:

- **Once a day:** Each day Google sends you an e-mail when your topic triggers an alert sometime throughout the day.

- **As-it-happens:** Google sends you the alert immediately each time your topic triggers the alert.

- **Once a week:** You receive a single weekly e-mail from Google combining all the alerts that have accumulated throughout the week.

Signing Up for Alerts

Signing up for alerts is simple. Having a Google Account in order to sign up for Google Alerts is not necessary, but recommended. You can manage your Google E-mail alerts easier using your Google account as well as take advantage of the other features that Google offers.

Having a Google Account is useful for using many of the Google applications, not just Google Alerts. It's highly recommended that you sign up for your own Google Account. They are free and it's easy to sign up. Point your browser to `www.google.com/accounts/ManageAccount`. This link takes you to the Google Accounts home page where you can create and also later access your account once it's set up.

Another way to sign up for a Google Account is by going to the Google home page (`www.google.com`) and clicking on the Sign-in link in the top-right corner of the page. Clicking this link takes you to the Google Accounts page. Click the Create an account now link located on the right side of the page and below the question "Don't have a Google Account?" You are then asked to provide the following information:

- **Your current e-mail address:** Use the e-mail address you want your Google Account linked with.

- **Choose a password:** You must type a password that is a minimum of six characters. Next to the box where you type the password you see a rating of your password's security.

- **Re-enter password:** Retype the password you typed in the previous step exactly the same.

- **Remember me on this computer:** When you check this box, Google will not ask you for your password again (unless you erase the cookie file).

- **Enable Personalize Search:** Another advanced feature of Google that keeps track of your searches launched from any Google page (Web pages, books, news). By keeping track, Google uses this information to recommend future searches and displays the results based on all your past searches.

- **Location:** Choose your location from the drop-down list.

- **Word Verification:** Type the graphic characters you see displayed in the box. Google uses this feature for protection from spammers.

■ **Terms of service:** You must accept the terms of service in order to create an account. To read the terms of service click the link to Google's Privacy Policy. Accept the terms of service and privacy policy by clicking I accept Create my Account.

Google must verify your e-mail address before your account becomes active and does so by sending you an e-mail to the address you typed while signing up. You receive an e-mail with the subject: Google Email Verification. This e-mail message contains a link to verify your e-mail address and complete your Google account signup.

When you click the link or copy and paste the link into a Web browser, a Web page opens where you will see the message: Email Address Verified. You are ready to use your Google account.

Log in to your account by clicking the Click here to manage your account profile link or click the Sign-in link in the top-right corner of the Google home page.

Your Google Account page contains several sections including Personal information, My Services, and when entered, Default payment method and Default shipping address..

Click the Edit link beside Personal Information, as shown in Figure 10.1, to change your name, nickname, e-mail address, home country and time zone. Click the Change password link to change your password. Additionally, you can change your security question by clicking the Change security question link.

TIP It is good computer security practice to regularly change your password. Make them at least six characters long. Use upper and lower case characters and include numbers for maximum security.

FIGURE 10-1

All the information you add is optional.

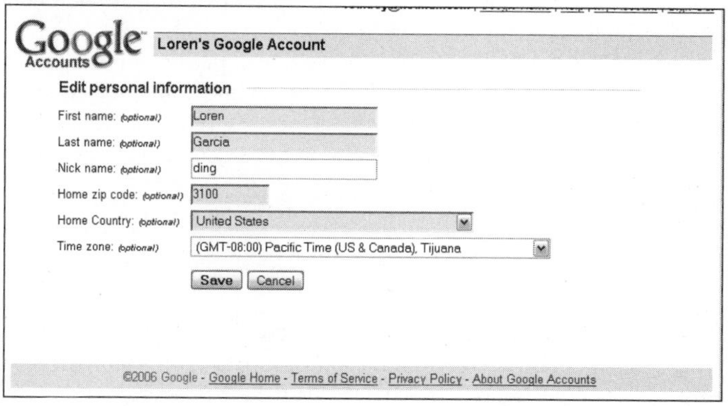

My Services displays the Google services for which you have signed up. When you click the Edit link found next to "My services" on your Google Account page, you are taken to the Edit services page, where you can choose to delete some of the services you've signed up for or choose to delete your entire Google account.

Signing Up for Alerts

Once you've signed up for a Google Account You can sign up for Google alerts directly from your Google Account page or from the Google Alerts home page. To create an alert, follow these steps:

1. Look for the <u>Alerts</u> link in the Try something new section to create new alerts, and when you already have alerts, click the <u>Alert</u> link in the My Services section. You can also create or add alerts from Google E-mail Alert accounts. Go to the Google Alerts home page by clicking the <u>More</u> link on the Google home page, then click Even More, then Alerts. If you are not signed into your Google account automatically, type your user name and password, and click the Sign in button.

2. From the **Manage your Alerts** page you can create a new alert and see a list of alerts previously created by you. Enter search terms in the **Search terms** box. Select a search term as though you were doing a Google search in a normal Google search box.

3. Select the Google services you would like to search in order to receive an alert from the **Type** selection list. Choose: News, Blogs, Web, Groups, or to search all of them, Comprehensive.

4. Select how often you want to receive the alert by choosing a frequency from the **How often** selection list.

5. Click Create Alert.

Once you complete this brief process you begin receiving alerts according to the schedule you specified.

 Begin by choosing to receive the alert "as it happens." If you receive too many alert e-mail messages, you can modify the alert frequency.

News Alert

When you create a Google News Alert, you can be sure you will be up-to-date with the latest news in the topic of your choice. Google continuously searches thousands of news sources to compile the top stories on its Google News page. Google searches more than 4,500 news sources using the search terms specified in your alert. When Google finds your search terms located in one of the top ten news stories, you receive a News Alert.

The News Alert is a great way to stay connected to the news without having to repeatedly scan the news on your own. Because Google Alerts creates an alert each time your topic of interest makes the news and sends it to you in an e-mail, based on the frequency specified in the alert, you never have to worry about missing this information.

Alerts can be created for a wide variety of topics, including sports news, financial news, and general news for a specific country or region. Creating alerts to search for very specific information can get a little tricky. For assistance in creating complex alerts use Google Advanced Search to create the perfect alert.

Creating an Advanced Google Alert

Create an alert to be notified when specific information about a particular topic is posted on the Internet in a news article, in a Google Group, or on the Web. Create advance Google Alerts to focus your search, and thereby receiving exactly the information you want as an alert. The process is very similar to performing advanced searches through any of the other Google services, such as the Google Web search. The following is an example of creating an advanced News Alert. You can follow similar steps for creating Web and Group Alerts.

Here are the steps for creating the example Advanced News Alert shown in Figure 10.2:

1. Click the <u>Advanced news search</u> link found on the Google News page (`http://news.google.com`).

2. In the "Find results" area, type **Barry Bonds** in the *with **all** the words* box.

3. Type **home run** in the *with the exact phrase* box.

4. In the *with at least one of these words* box, type **hits, record**.

5. In the *without the words box*, type **trainer**.

6. In the *News source* box type **MLB.com, San Francisco Chronicle, Reuters, CNN**.

7. In the Location box, type **U.S.**

8. The last two boxes, Occurrences and Date are not important for you to create your alert so leave them unchanged.

9. Click Google Search.

10. After completing step 9, you will be on the search results page. The search box contains a search string created from the information you specified when completing the Advanced News search page. Copy the search string found in the Google News search box. The example in the above steps creates a search string that looks like this: "Barry Bonds "home run" hits, OR record -trainer source:MLB.com, San Francisco Chronicle, Reuters, cnn location:usa".

11. Go to your Alerts home page. The Google News search results page will have a link to My Account located in the upper right corner of the page.

12. In the Search terms box on the Create a Google Alert page, paste the search string copied from step 10.

13. Select a service to search from the Type selection list. For this example, select *News*.

14. Choose a frequency from the How often selection list. For this example, choose *as-it-happens*.

15. Click Create Alert.

FIGURE 10.2

Use Advanced News Search to narrow your search, creating better News Alerts.

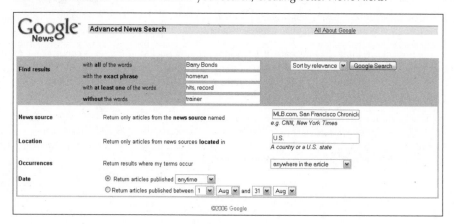

In this example you have created an Advanced News Alert. The following table (Table 10.1) shows the string taken from the News page divided into different parts and a description of what it does.

TABLE 10.1

Analyzing the Example Search String

String	Function
Barry Bonds	Tells Google you are looking for information about Barry Bonds.
"home run"	Google will search for the exact phrase *home run*. The main topic of interest is home runs hit by Barry Bonds.
hits or record	In this alert you are interested in knowing when Barry hits another home run and if he breaks another record.
trainer	Exclude alerts about Barry Bonds' trainer. Each time news breaks about Barry Bonds you will not receive an alert when the article includes anything about his trainer.
source:MLB.com, San Francisco Chronicle, Reuters, CNN	You have told Google to find news from these sources.
Location:U.S.	This specifies that only news generated in the U.S. will trigger the alert.

It's a good idea to use Advanced Alerts when you find yourself receiving e-mail not related to the exact topic you were hoping to be alerted about.

Groups Alerts

Google Groups contains information published through Usenet news groups on the Internet. Google Groups is one interface to that system and tracking information in some of these groups can prove to be very important. Many of the Google Groups contain important technical and business information. Searches through Google Groups can support research performed using Google Finance (`http://finance.google.com`).

CROSS-REF Find more information about Google Finance in Chapter 16.

When you follow the postings in more than a single news group, keeping track of these posts can become a complex and time-consuming task. Thanks to Google's technology and Google Alerts, tracking the information posted in Google Groups becomes easier. Similar to Google News Alerts, you can receive an alert each time something is posted to the groups you specify that match your topic search.

To create a Google Group alert, navigate to the Google Alerts page. On the Manage your Alerts page, type a search term. For the Type, select *Groups*. Select how often you want to receive the alert and click Create Alert. The new alert then appears in the list of alerts displayed in the Your Google Alerts section of the page. From this section you can choose to edit the alert or delete it completely.

Managing Alerts

When you receive Google Alerts in e-mail you are given the option of deleting the alert directly from the e-mail message by clicking the link provided in the e-mail. Without a Google Account, the only way to manage alerts is to delete them and create new ones.

A more efficient way of managing your Google Alerts is to sign into your Google Account and choose the Manage link next to the Alerts link found in the My Services section of your Google Account home page.

The Google Alert Manage your Alerts page is divided into two sections: Create a Google Alert and Your Google Alerts. In these two sections you can choose to create new alerts of any type, edit them, and delete them. Remember that deleting an alert cancels the alert, and you no longer receive alerts from deleted alerts.

Manage alerts you've created previously in the Your Google Alerts section. The alerts are displayed in a table with the following three columns:

- **Search terms:** Contains which keywords and phrases you used to create the Google Alert
- **Type:** Specifies the source of the information used to trigger the alert
- **How often:** Specifies the frequency with which you receive the alert

To the left of the alert information are two links: one to edit the alert and the other link to delete the alert.

You can change your alerts by clicking the edit link. After clicking this link the three columns (Search terms, Type, and How often) change so that they can be edited. You can add, delete, or change the Search terms, and select a different type and change how often you receive alerts. Figure 10.3 shows you an alert in edit mode.

When you finish editing the alert, click Save. To leave it unchanged click Cancel.

FIGURE 10.3

You can edit one alert at a time.

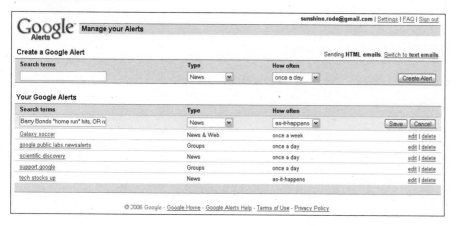

> **TIP**   By default, you receive all Google Alerts in HTML form. You can switch to text e-mail by
> clicking the <u>switch to text emails</u> link located in the upper-right side of the page. There is no
> way to change an individual alert from HTML to text e-mail. You must change all your alerts from one type
> to the other.

Summary

E-mail Alerts are a great way to keep track of changing information found in the news, the Web, and in Google Groups. Creating an alert is simple but creating a focused alert takes a little bit of work, but is made simpler by using the Advanced Search pages in each of the different information sources to create more focused search strings. Once you've created an alert, you can manage the alert from your Google Account or simply delete it.

Chapter 11

Personalizing Google Desktop

Google offers software that you can download to your computer and use to perform searches through your files and folders on your personal computer. Google Desktop is a free software program that not only gives you the power of Google on your own hard drive but also allows you to have fun with its plug-ins and gadgets.

Google Desktop Features

Google Desktop gives you the ability to search your computer for information stored there such as e-mail, Web pages you have visited, chats, and other files such as music, video, and word processing documents. Searching your desktop is just as simple as using Google to search the Web. Your search results appear using the same interface used to display Google Web search results. Google's search technology employs a flexible, quick, and accurate indexing system that allows you to find your files wherever they exist on your computer.

You can customize your Desktop search results so that future searches provide more of what you're looking for and fewer of the files you aren't interested in seeing appear in your search results. By deleting files from your search results, the next time you do a similar search you won't see them. Erasing files from the search results only erases them from the Google index. The actual file is not erased.

Adding small programs known as Gadgets and Plug-ins to Google Desktop can be fun, not only because of the games you can play, but many of them can provide important information and services. The number of Gadgets and Plug-ins grows almost every day.

With the interaction of Google Desktop with Gadgets and Plug-ins, Google Desktop can personalize the content for your Google home page. Depending on the Gadgets and/or Plug-ins you install, Google recommends new Gadgets and shows you content based on the topics on which you normally search.

Installing and Using Google Desktop

To download Google Desktop, point your Web browser to www.google.com. Click the more>> link; from the pop-up menu that appears click even more>>. This launches the More Google products Web page. In the Search category of products locate the Desktop link and click it to display the Google Desktop page. You can also navigate directly to the Google Desktop page by navigating to http://desktop.google.com/.

On the Google Desktop page, you see a button called Agree and Download. You also see some of the Gadgets and Plug-Ins that Google offers. To download Google Desktop, click Agree and Download.

After clicking the button, a File Download–Security Warning window may appear. You can click Run to install the program after it downloads, click Save to place the program on your computer to install later, or Cancel to abandon the download. Because this program simply installs Google Desktop you won't need it after the installation has completed, so it's fine to select the Run option or choose to save it to your hard drive in case you need to start the download over again. Some people find it useful to save the installer programs.

Google Desktop may have to close some of the programs that are running on your computer. When a window appears telling you to close the programs, first save your work in any open files, then click Yes. Google Desktop continues to install on your computer.

Once Google Desktop finishes installing, a browser window opens with some of the Google Desktop preferences and features. On this initial preference page you can do the following:

- Choose to create a Google Account or Sign-in to your current account after completing the preference selection process.

- If you have a Gmail account you can select to index and search your Gmail messages.

- Some of the Gadgets and Plug-ins have information, settings, or preferences that you can select to save in your Google Account. To save this information in your Google Account select "Backup my gadget content in my Google Account." Selecting this means, for example, you can access your To Do list or Scratch Pad notes from any computer after logging into your Google Account.

- Select Google to be your default search engine.

Once you complete setting the preferences, click "Set preferences and continue."

Setting Google Desktop preferences

The installation of Google Desktop continues after completing the preference process. Your browser loads a new page where you are given the option to personalize your Google home page. It is not important to set all these options during installation. All of these options can be changed later. While this new Web page is loading, Google Desktop starts. Once it loads, a panel, or sidebar, appears on the right of your screen. You learn more about panels and the sidebar later in this chapter. You also notice some of the Google Gadgets on your desktop. By default, the Analog Clock and Media Player Remote appear on your desktop. Another element that you see is the Google Gadget Tips, which displays tips on managing your Desktop Gadgets. Either choose to personalize your Google home page or click "No, don't personalize my homepage" and continue the installation. Remember, you can personalize your Google home page at another time.

Continuing to the next installation Web page, the preferences allow you to enable the Google Advanced Features. These features allow Google to collect information about your search habits, which enables Google to better provide content on your Google home page or your Desktop sidebar. Additionally, other data, such as crash reports, are sent to Google to improve Google Desktop. Because no personal identifying information is sent to Google and this option improves the software, select the Enable Advanced Features option button.

The last page in the installation process is the Google Desktop home page. Google Desktop starts indexing your computer every time your computer begins to idle. The first time that you index your information, the Google Desktop home page tells you how much was indexed on your computer. After the first indexing, the message is not displayed again.

Searching the Desktop

Once you install the Google Desktop software you can search for files, e-mail, Web history, and chat sessions on your computer. In addition to searching for files, you can also begin using the Google Gadgets and Plug-ins installed on your computer.

The easiest way to start using the Desktop search is by going to Google's home page. Click the Desktop link, and you are ready to begin your search. The search page is exactly like the one you saw as you finished installing the Google Desktop software.

Begin the search through the files on your hard drive from this search page. From this page you can also go to Google Desktop preferences, Advanced search, Browse timeline, and also see the Index Status, Privacy, and About Google Desktop.

Type search terms and phrases in the search box and press Enter. The results window displays all your search results. You can scroll through your results, or to assist you in finding just the right result, Google Desktop organizes the results by the type of file in which they are found.

Narrowing your search

Your Desktop search results are divided into six major file types: All, emails, files, web history, chats, and other. Clicking any of these links that appear along the top bar of the search results page refines your search to that particular file type. The number that appears next to each file type tells you how many of those file types were found.

Clicking emails displays results found in any of the following programs: Outlook, Outlook Express, Thunderbird, Mozilla Mail, Netscape Mail, and Gmail (only if you chose to include Gmail in your index). By default, the results are sorted by date. Therefore, you will see the most recent e-mail you received containing the keyword you specified as a search term. You also have the option of viewing e-mail messages from or to a specific e-mail address or person. Only after clicking the emails link two drop-down lists appear near the top of the page containing the names of the people from which e-mail was either received or sent appearing in your results. Select addresses from one or both lists to further focus your search through e-mail messages.

Google Desktop also searches for file types including:

- Text documents (.txt)
- Microsoft Office documents (.doc, .ppt, .xls)
- Adobe Acrobat documents (.pdf)
- Web files (.html)
- Images (.jpg, .gif, .png, .bmp)
- Audio (wave, .mp3, .acc)
- Video (.wmv, .mpg, .avi)

Google's Home Page

Like the difference between the new Coke and Classic Coke, there are two ways to view the Google home page. The first is called Classic Home. This is the page you normally see when you visit www.google.com. Basically, it contains a search box and a button. The second is your personalized home page containing information of your design. You can switch between the two by clicking the link at the top of the Google page. To switch to your personalized home page you must be logged in to your Google account.

Whenever you want to personalize your Google home page, point your browser to www.google.com/ig. The information that Google Desktop sends to Google about the way you interact with the software, the Gadgets, and the content on your sidebar, is used to personalize your home page. If you are not satisfied with the content that Google selects for you, feel free to change the content.

When you first see your Google home page (www.google.com/ig) it contains six panels: Google Calendar, New York Times home page, How-to of the Day, Top Stories, Date & Time, and Weather (you must type your ZIP code the first time to see your local weather).

The first time you open the page, you see a Make it your own link under the search box. This link takes you to Configure your homepage. From here you can add or delete content and configure the panels that appear on the page. When you click the Make it your own link, a box appears with 16 different topics to choose from, as shown in Figure 11-1. There are hundreds of content plug-ins you can add to your Google home page. To see all the available content plug-ins click The entire collection link.

Google divides the homepage content plug-ins into seven main categories. These are: News, Tools, Communication, Fun & Games, Finance, Sports, Lifestyle and Technology. There are two additional categories: Popular that contains a selection of the most popular content plug-ins, and New stuff where you can find the newest content plug-ins for your homepage.

Choose as many content plug-ins as you want for your homepage.

> **NOTE** If you don't see the <u>Make it your own</u> link, there's another link in the left top corner of the page called <u>Add content>></u>.

Once you select to add content, you navigate to the page listing all of the content plug-ins (www.google.com/ig/directory). To learn more about each content plug-in, click its link or picture. To add a content plug-in to your home page, click the Add it now button located beneath each plug-in. When you finish adding content plug-ins, click the <u><<Back to homepage</u> link located at the top-left corner of the page.

You can rearrange the content panels in your Google home page by clicking on the content title bars and dragging them to their new position on the page.

The content plug-ins come in all sizes and colors, and their contents vary. You can edit some of the content plug-ins from their panels by clicking the <u>Edit</u> link. Depending on the plug-in, you are presented with different options. Sometimes you change the colors or size of the plug-in. In some cases, you aren't presented with an <u>Edit</u> link.

To remove a panel from your home page, click the X in the top-right corner of the panel you want to delete.

If you have not already done so, when you finish adding and editing your home page, sign in to your Google account so you can save your home page. Google saves your home page configuration in the form of a cookie. If that cookie is erased or expires you must configure the home page again. Saving the home page configuration to your Google account gives you access to your customized view from any computer after logging in to your account. You can sign in to your account from the link on the top-right corner of the home page.

You can refine your search to any of these types of files by file types from the list. Once you've selected a file type click Go. The search results page displays only results where the search terms are found in the file type you've selected.

When you visit Web pages, most Web browsers maintain a copy of the pages you visit in cache. The Web history searches these temporary Web *cache* files. When Google Desktop finds matches to your keyword, the results page displays them along with the date the page was visited.

Google Desktop also searches chat transcripts from programs such as MSN Messenger, AOL Instant Messenger, Trillian, and Google Talk. Chat transcripts, unless you tell your chat software you want your chat history saved, tend to be more temporary.

Clicking the <u>other file types</u> link returns file results found in your contacts, calendar, tasks, journals, and notes entries.

Advanced desktop searching

Clicking the <u>Advanced Search</u> link, located on the main Desktop Search page, launches a new page allowing you to choose which type of files you want to search, or select All to include all file types in the index. Some of the file types have additional advanced search options. Some of the search options common to all of the file types are: Has the words, Doesn't have, Date within (search for files within a specific date range), and Show results from. (When you have more than one computer on your account using Desktop search, you can specify which computer or computers you want to search.) Figure 11.1 shows you the Advanced Desktop search page.

The supplementary advanced search options change with the group you select to search. Table 11.1 shows the group name and the extra advanced options for each group.

FIGURE 11.1

Focus your Desktop search by configuring the Search Options.

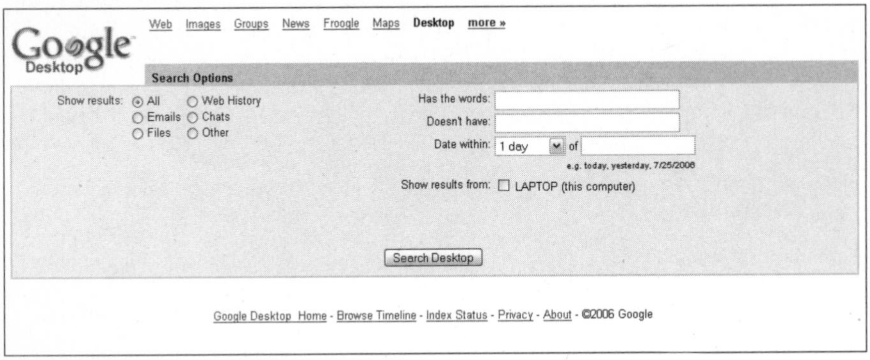

TABLE 11.1

Advanced Search Options

Group name	Additional Advanced Search Options	Description
Chats	None	
Emails	To:	
From:	To whom the e-mail was sent.	
	Who the e-mail was sent from.	
Files	Enter type:	
In the location:		
Include subfolders	From the drop-down list there are different options: Text, Word, Excel, PowerPoint, PDF, Music, Images, Video, and Enter other type (the extension of the files you want to search for).	
	You can browse the computer and choose a specific folder you want to look in for the file.	
	Check box if you want to include subfolders in your search.	
Other	Other types	Look for Contacts, Appointments, Tasks, Notes, and Journal Files.
Web History	In the Site	Search for a specific domain name.

Browsing the Timeline

When you click the <u>Browse Timeline</u> link from the bottom of either the main search page or the results page, a new page displays the last files that were accessed, used, or created on your computer. Figure 12.2 shows an example of how a Timeline page appears. A date and time stamp of the exact time the file was last accessed appears before each filename, which is displayed as a link. On the right-hand side of the page is a small calendar. Each day appears as a link. When you click on a specific day (you can click only days in the past) the results page displays the results of the file search for files last accessed on the day you specify by clicking the calendar. This is particularly useful if you have an idea of when the file, e-mail, or chat was stored on your computer.

In addition, you can define your Timeline search by specifying the file type group as discussed in the last section. There is also a <u>Remove events</u> link where you can choose to remove events (but not the files) from the index that Google creates from the files on your computer. Once you remove the file from the index it no longer appears in any of your search results.

FIGURE 11.2

See your results in last accessed date order.

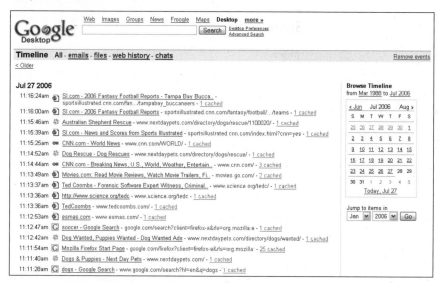

Tracking the Index Status

The <u>Index Status</u> link launches a Web page that displays information about your desktop indexing status, as shown in Figure 11.3. You see the percentage of files indexed and the approximate time it will take the program to complete indexing the files. Normally, indexing only occurs when the computer is idle. The indexing status is displayed for: Total searchable items, Emails, Chats, Web history, and Files with the number of files indexed displayed to the right of the file type. You will also see the file dates of the newest files in the index.

Display the current indexing status or choose to <u>Index now</u>.

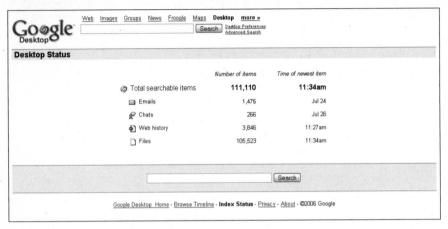

You can choose to index the computer now by clicking the <u>Index now</u> link. Just as the Web page warns you, this operation uses many of your computer's resources and may slow your computer's performance while the index is taking place.

Understanding Google Desktop Privacy

The <u>Privacy</u> link contains a page where Google lets you know that it takes your privacy seriously. You are, after all, giving a search engine company access to your private files. It is Google's intention to make your Desktop search as simple as a Web search, and in some cases your Desktop search results are mixed with those of a Web search. Be assured that Google does not give access to your files to anyone else. Neither the files nor the results are available through the Web.

Read the privacy policy at `http://desktop.google.com/privacypolicy.html`.

You may find additional answers by reading the Google Desktop Privacy FAQ at `http://desktop.google.com/privacyfaq.html`.

CAUTION Anyone who has access to your computer will also have access to Google's desktop search. He or she will be able to browse your files, see your Web history, and read your chats. If others have access to your computer you may want to remove private files from the Google Desktop index or lock the Desktop search, which is explained later in this chapter.

The last link on Google's desktop search page is <u>About</u>. The <u>About</u> link takes you to a page that has information about the types of files that Google indexes on your computer. The About page also contains links to Plug-ins, Getting Started (more information about learning to use Google's desktop search), Online Help, Privacy, and how to uninstall Google Desktop. You might also be interested in knowing what version of Google Desktop you currently have installed on your computer. From time to time it's a good idea to make sure you have the latest version. The version number is displayed at the bottom of the About page.

Managing Panels

The way Google Desktop appears on your computer is quite versatile. It can sit as a sidebar, which takes up quite a bit of screen real estate, or be nothing more than a notification icon. Here are the four ways Google Desktop software can appear on your computer:

- Notification icon
- Deskbar
- Floating deskbar
- Sidebar

Notification icon

Google Desktop's notification icon is primarily a status icon. When the icon appears, it means that Google Desktop software is working. Figure 11.4 shows the Google Desktop icon, which in this example is the second icon to the left of the Windows clock. It may appear in a different place within the taskbar icons on your computer.

NOTE The notification area or system tray is part of the Windows taskbar on your desktop. When your taskbar is oriented horizontally, the icon is located on the right end of the taskbar. When your taskbar is oriented vertically it appears at the bottom of the taskbar. The desktop icon appears in the area where you can see the Windows clock and other status and event notification icons.

FIGURE 11.4

Google Desktop's notification icon

Notification icon

When you choose not to display the Google Desktop search box in the display preferences, the Google Desktop icon is the only way you can choose to perform a desktop query without first opening a Web browser.

To open the Google Desktop query window right-click the Google Desktop icon in the taskbar. Click Search Desktop in the pop-up menu that appears (see Figure 11.5).

As you can see in Figure 11.5, the Google Desktop pop-up menu also has options that you can select to launch Web pages such as Preferences and About. One of the important options available from this menu is Index. There are three indexing menu options:

- **Pause Indexing:** Google stops indexing your computer by default for 15 minutes. When you select this option a balloon notification appears that tells you about the pause, and the icon changes color to gray, and becomes unavailable. The indexing menu also changes. You no longer see the Pause Indexing option as it changes to Resume Indexing and an additional option, Pause for 15 more minutes. Once Indexing starts again, another balloon notification appears, and the icon changes to its normal colors.

- **Re-Index:** This option causes Google Desktop to reindex your whole computer. This may take a few hours the first time Google indexes your computer. In subsequent indexes, it begins indexing every time your computer is idle for more than 30 seconds.

- **Index Status:** Selecting this option opens a browser window that displays your computer's indexing status.

FIGURE 11.5

You can always right-click the Google Desktop icon to open this menu.

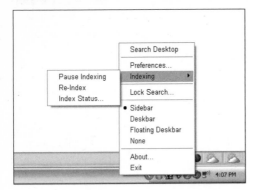

Locking your Google Desktop search

If your computer is used by several people or is located in a place where others may have physical access to it, it's a good idea to protect your private information. The information is still available for someone accessing your computer who is determined to find it. That's why Google Desktop search comes with a lock.

The Lock Search option locks the Google Desktop Search so that a password is required before a search can be performed. When you access the Google Desktop Search page a message something like "Google Desktop Search is locked. To begin enter the Windows password for *COMPUTERNAME\username*" appears. Your computer name and username appear in this message. To unlock and begin using the Desktop Search, type the username (it may already be entered for you) and the password you use to log into your computer. Figure 11.6 shows the Google Desktop Search page when the search feature is locked.

FIGURE 11.6

Limit access to your private information by locking the Google Desktop Search.

Once you type the correct password and click Unlock Desktop, the page reloads and the Desktop Search page functions normally.

Selecting display options on the fly

The Desktop icon menu also you to configure the way Google Desktop Search appears on your computer. The configurable display options are: Sidebar, Deskbar, Floating deskbar, and None.

Selecting Exit closes Google Desktop Search. After exiting you need to restart Google Desktop before you can perform a Desktop search. Closing Google Desktop also removes the Desktop option from the selections on the Google Search page.

Deskbar

Google Deskbar is a search box that appears on the right side of the taskbar (see Figure 11.7). This search box is used for performing Google Web searches. Simply type keywords or phrases and press Enter and a Google results page appears in your Web browser.

NOTE By default, all the Google Search boxes that appear on your desktop, whether as a sidebar, deskbar, or floating deskbar, search the Web. You can change the default search type for all search box types in the Google Desktop Search preferences.

FIGURE 11.7

The Google Deskbar appears in the Windows taskbar.

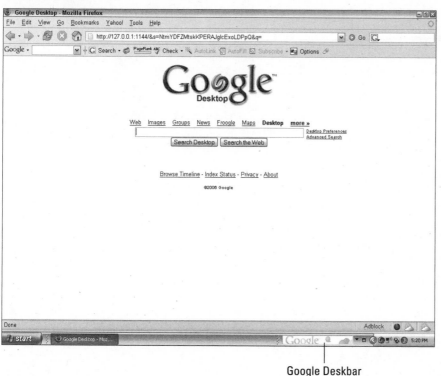

Google Deskbar

When you begin typing a keyword in the search box, a pop-up appears above the search box displaying the results of a search through files on your local computer. Google calls this *Quick Find*. Quick Find shows you the results of your search as you type. You can turn Quick Find on or off and select the number of results that are displayed in the Google Desktop Preferences page. Quick Find displays only results of the Google Desktop Search through files indexed on your computer, not Web search results. Along the top of the Quick Find box you see the number of results for the keyword that Quick Find found on your desktop. If you click that number a page displaying the Desktop search results appears. When you find what you looking for in the Quick Find box, click on the result.

Along the bottom of the Quick Find box are two additional options:

- **Search More:** With this option you can choose to Search Google Earth, Search Maps, Search Froogle, Search News, Search Groups, Search Images, or go to the I'm Feeling Lucky page result and Search Desktop.

- **Search Web:** This option enables Google to search the Web as though you had pressed Enter after typing your search terms.

Clicking the black arrow next to the Deskbar search box gives you a menu similar to the one you get when right-clicking the Desktop icon. One exception is that where the Search Desktop and the Exit options would be, you now have a Close option. When you click Close, the Deskbar box closes but Google Desktop Search remains active. The Google Desktop Search icon remains visible in the system tray.

As you can see in Figure 11.8, there is a small window icon next to the black arrow. When you click that window icon, the Deskbar disappears and Google Desktop Search converts to a sidebar.

Floating Deskbar

The Floating Deskbar is similar to the Deskbar. The only difference is that you can drag the Floating Deskbar box all over your screen and drop it wherever it is most convenient for you. To drag the Floating Deskbar box, click over the left side of the Floating Deskbar, and drag the Deskbar to a new location. Figure 11.8 shows the Floating Deskbar in the middle of the screen.

Sidebar

The Google Sidebar provides the richest functionality of any of the Google Desktop bars. The Google Sidebar, because of the plug-ins and gadgets, could easily become one of the most important and easy-to-use tools on your computer. The Sidebar serves as a container for other programs. It can be located on either side of your screen.

Plug-ins and gadgets

A Plug-in is a small piece of software that enhances a larger software program. In other words, it complements or gives new functionality to the main program. In Google Desktop, plug-ins add functionality to the search features. Using plug-ins enables you to perform advanced searches. For example, Google Desktop Extreme Plug-in adds functionality to make searches faster and more productive. Another example is the Google Desktop Extra Images Plug-in. This handy plug-in searches for more than 90 different types of images on your computer.

Defining gadgets is a little more difficult. A gadget is also software, but in this case, it has its own functions that may be similar or different from the functions provided by the main program. Gadgets, as a rule, do not provide additional search functionality. A Google gadget is a small program that depends on Google Desktop to run. For example, the Google Analog Clock gadget displays the time and date on your desktop. It cannot run unless Google Desktop is already running.

FIGURE 11.8

Locate the Floating Deskbar anywhere on your desktop.

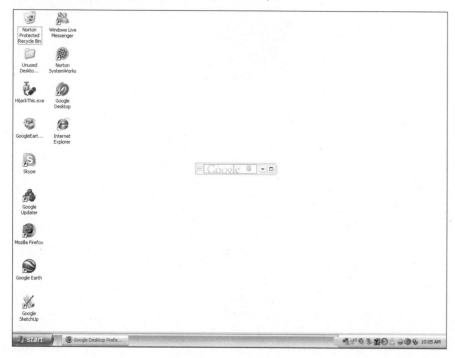

When you first launch the Sidebar, it opens with the following default gadgets (see Figure 11.9):

Each of the gadgets has a down arrow that launches a gadget configuration menu. Most gadgets have the following options: Expand (if the gadget is collapsed) or Collapse (when the gadget is expanded), About, Undock from Sidebar, and Remove. Different gadgets have different menu options.

All the gadgets on the Sidebar have a double arrow called Toggle Expanded View. Depending where your sidebar is located on your screen, the double arrow points to the opposite side. In Figure 11.9, the Sidebar is shown docked on the left side so the double arrows are pointing to the right. When you click these double arrows, the gadget expands and displays more of the gadgets' features and information.

CROSS-REF To learn more about installing Google Plug-ins and Gadgets and also about some of the other plug-ins and gadgets available, see Chapter 30.

Email

This gadget retrieves your e-mail. It primarily works with Gmail but also works with several other mail programs. The menu has a selection called Options where you will find a link to set up e-mail indexing or configure Gmail on the Desktop Search preference software. An additional option allows you to filter e-mail that you don't want the Sidebar to show. You can filter e-mail according to From, To, Subject, Has the words, and Does not have.

FIGURE 11.9

Some of the gadgets undock from the Sidebar and can be moved around the screen.

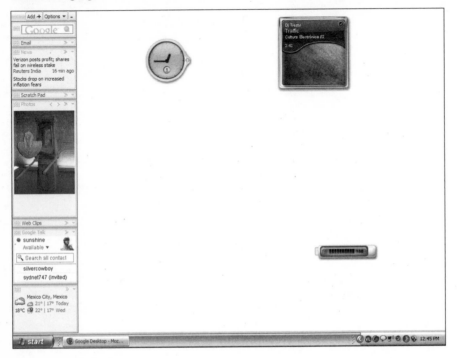

News

Google uses sources like *Forbes*, *Reuters*, *BusinessWeek*, SI.com, *CNN International*, *PC World*, *ZDNet*, and others to bring you the latest news from around the world. With this news gadget you see the story name, the source of the story, and how long ago the story was released. On the Menu button, you can find options that allow you to select news editions from 25 different countries.

Scratch Pad

The Scratch Pad is a very useful gadget. It allows you to write anything you want at any time, like a note creator. You can copy and paste text from the Web, chats, e-mail, Word documents and anything else because the Scratch Pad is available on the Sidebar at all times. Everything you type on the Scratch Pad is saved until you decide what to do with it. From the Menu button you can Save to File and Clear the Scratch Pad when you no longer need the text.

Photos

The Sidebar will display pictures from your computer, changing the image regularly, depending on your preference settings. By default, the Sidebar loads pictures from the My Documents\My Pictures folder. Clicking on the image causes it to expand displaying the file name, the image, and its location on your hard drive. You can remove the picture from the Sidebar and it will no longer be displayed. It is only removed from the Google index, not your computer.

Navigate through the photos using the Sidebar by clicking on the arrows located above the image, Choose the previous photo or move to the next image. When you select **Expand View** on this gadget, the main image appears in the middle, the three previously displayed images appear on top, and the three upcoming images appear beneath the main image. The **Menu** button has the following options: Photos on My Computer, Photos Online, and Slideshow Speed. In the Photos on My Computer option, you can select the folders that contain the images you want the Sidebar to display. From the Photos Online option, choose an online source such as RSS, Atom feeds, or regular URLs to display photos. To configure the time delay between images, click Slideshow Speed and set the value. The value is in seconds and can be set between the minimum of 1 second and the maximum of 9,999 seconds.

Web Clips

The Web Clips gadget is a Google News Reader in gadget form. This gadget displays updated news clips sent to you through Atom or RSS feeds. Generally the feeds are updated every 30 seconds. The Menu button has options to Find Web Clips to Add. You can also Edit your Current Web Clips and configure the number of clips you want the Sidebar to show for each site. When you have selected the option to have the Web Clips gadget automatically add feeds, each time you visit a Web page offering a feed, that feed is added. You can also choose to turn this feature off. The Web Clips gadget can be undocked from the Sidebar and placed anywhere on your desktop.

Google Talk

The Google Talk gadget for the Sidebar works like the regular Google Talk software except that it's attached to the Sidebar.

 To learn more about Google Talk, see Chapter 27.

Weather

The Weather gadget shows you the current weather conditions, the current weather, and tomorrow's forecast. The Menu button allows you to configure the display of weather from 25 countries, right in your Sidebar. The Weather gadget is limited to displaying the weather from 10 different cities. You can also choose between having the temperature displayed in Fahrenheit or Celsius.

Adding Gadgets

While your mouse hovers above any part of the Sidebar, three buttons appear above the Google search box. The Add button, allows you to add more gadgets. The Options button allows you to add additional gadgets and also configure the gadgets you already have installed. You can select to have the Sidebar appear on top of everything (the Sidebar will remain open). But, when you choose Auto-hide, the sidebar collapses to either the right or the left side of your screen depending on where you have it docked. You can configure the docking location. To cause a hidden sidebar to reappear, move your mouse over the edge of the screen where the sidebar is normally displayed. You can change the Font Size to Larger or Smaller than the Default size.

TIP Use either the Windows+G or Ctrl+Alt+G keyboard shortcut to jump into the search box when Google Desktop is displayed in Deskbar, Floating Deskbar, or Sidebar mode.

Quick Search Box

The Google Desktop search box can be displayed on your computer as a *Quick Search Box*. The Quick Search Box must first be enabled in the Google Desktop Preferences page. When Quick Search Box is enabled, press Ctrl twice and a search box displays in the middle of your screen. The Quick Search Box works in the same manner as other Google search boxes. When you begin typing, Quick Find answers appear automatically. You have the option of searching the Web or searching while using: Search Desktop, I'm Feeling lucky, Search Images, Search Groups, Search News, Search Froogle, Search Maps, or Google Earth.

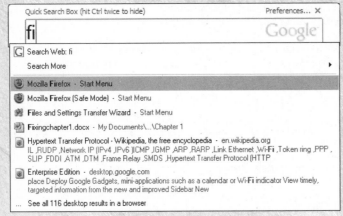

Quick Search Box appears in the middle of the screen with all search options.

When you press Ctrl twice again, the Quick Search Box disappears.

Preferences for Google Desktop

Personalize Google Desktop using the Preferences. No matter how Google Desktop is displayed on your computer, you can always find a menu option or a link that allows you to configure the Desktop Preferences. On the Google bars, launch Preferences from the Option menu button. On the Web browser's Google bar, click the <u>Preference</u> link on the right side of the search box. Each of these launches the Preferences page.

Preferences are divided in four groups:

- Local Indexing
- Google Account Features
- Display
- Other

Local Indexing

Google Desktop indexes your files and information to make it easy to find answers when you perform a desktop search. Select which types of files you want Google to index on your computer. Local Indexing options allow you to select file types by clicking the option boxes next to the desired file types. Selecting a file type causes Google Desktop to index files of that type.

File types that Google Desktop will index include: Email, Chats, Web history, Media files, Text and other files, Word, Excel, PowerPoint, PDF, Contacts, Calendar, Tasks, Notes, Journal, and Zip Files.

Secure Files

There are two other file types indexed by Google Desktop: Password-protected Office documents (Word, Excel) and Secure pages (HTTPS) in Web history. Password-protected Office documents are Office documents you have previously password protected. Secure pages (HTTPS) are Web pages, for example, a bank page or e-commerce checkout page where you type your credit card number, or other pages containing sensitive information. For security reasons it's better not to have Google Desktop index HTTPS pages.

Chat Files

Index chat conversations from many of the popular chat programs. This includes Trillian, an instant messenger that is configured to communicate with services such as MSN Messenger, AOL Messenger, Yahoo Messenger, and ICQ. Google Desktop adds chats from these programs to its index. When you have Trillian installed and you want to have its files indexed, select the option to add Trillian to the index found in the **Indexing Plug-ins** section on the Preferences page.

Selecting folders and files to index

The Search These Locations preference allows you to select files, folders, or drives on the network that Google Desktop has not indexed. By default, Google desktop indexes the all the drives on your computer, even external drives, but does not index files, folders, or drives located on other computers shared across a network.

In the Don't Search These Items preference, you can select which files, folders, or Web sites not to index. Type the Web site address in the box and click Add URL, or click the <u>Add file or folder to exclude</u> link and browse your computer for that file or folder.

Google Desktop can encrypt your index and cache using the Windows Encrypted File System. When you encrypt your index and cache the information is only viewable on your local desktop.

CAUTION Encrypting the index reduces the performance of Google Desktop because of the requirement to encrypt and decrypt the information.

You can only encrypt indexes stored on the New Technology File System (NTFS) and not File Allocation Table (FAT) file systems.

Encrypting the index disables the Search Across Computers feature within Google Desktop.

Searching Across Computers

Searching across computers is easy. All you need is a Google Account to have this feature configured on your Google Desktop preferences page. On the Preferences page, select the **Google Account Features** tab. Select **Search Across Computers** to activate the remote searching option. You are asked to type the name of the computer where Google Desktop is installed. In future Desktop search results, this computer name is how you will identify the files that are located on this computer within searches across multiple computers. You may also configure which file types are searchable, whether on your local computer or remote computers.

Once the feature is active, perform a search as you would any other Google Search. Simply type the keyword or phrase in the search box and click **Search Desktop**.

The search results page is almost identical to the Desktop Search results page. The difference is that when Google finds a file located on another computer, you see the name of the computer, in parentheses, on which the file is located. This appears to the right of the link to the file. As the following figure shows, doing a search for *backgammon* on this network, the first three results came back from a computer called LEU. The rest of the results on the result page came from the local computer.

The first three results came from a remote computer named LEU.

When you select Disable Indexing any new word-processor documents, chats, Web history, and other files that Google Desktop indexes, new files of these types placed on your hard drive will no longer be included in the index, and therefore, will not appear in subsequent searches.

When you perform a desktop search, the results page displays an option to delete items. When your preference is set to Remove Deleted Items, and you choose to delete files displayed in the results, the files are removed from the index and will not appear in future searches of your desktop. The files are not removed from your computer, only the Google Desktop index.

Google accounts and features

Using a Google account to save your Google Desktop preferences enables you to access the Google Desktop gadgets on other computers in the same manner as they are installed on your primary computer. There are three Desktop preferences you can set in your Google Account:

- **Gmail:** Configure indexing of your Gmail account. Indexing your e-mail allows you to easily search for information stored in e-mail messages using Google Desktop search.

- **Save my Google Gadgets Content and Settings:** The settings and information for your gadgets are saved in your Google account. When you access the Google Desktop on another computer your gadgets will operate using previously set preferences. For example, you can access a note that you saved using the Scratch Pad on your computer at home from a remote computer. Also your stocks, to-do list, news, and other saved items are available remotely.

- **Search Across Computers:** Google can index more than one more computer and assign those computers to your account. Google securely transfers your index into Google Desktop Servers so you can search these locations from any computer using your Google account. When **Search Across Computers** is enabled, additional preferences become available. You can change the name that appears on your computer and on other computers. You can also configure which file types are searchable between computers.

 Only files accessed after you turn on Search Across Computers are accessible to your other computers via search. Your previously indexed files are not accessible.

Display Preferences

In the display group of preferences, you can set preferences for the following:

- **Search Box:** Select how to display Google Desktop on your computer. The options are Sidebar, Deskbar, Floating Deskbar, and None.

- **Quick Search Box:** Enables or disables Quick Search Box. You can also have the Quick Search Box appear all the time on the desktop behind any open windows.

- **Default Search Type:** Choose which type of search your Google Desktop boxes perform when you press Enter. Choose among Search the Web, Search Desktop, I'm Feeling lucky, Search Images, Search Groups, Search News, Search Froogle, Search Maps, and Change on Each Search.

- **Taskbar Gadgets Button:** You have the option to set how Google appears in your computer taskbar — icon and text, icon only — to have easy access to your gadgets. You can choose not to have anything displayed.

- **Quick Find:** Enable or disable Quick Find and set how Quick Find interacts with your search. The preferences you can set are: Search text inside documents and e-mail messages (it will look for your keyword or phrase within documents and e-mails) and Show spelling correction (Quick Find has a built-in spelling check to help you with your search). Also, select how many results Quick Find returns (from 1 to 10). There are two other options that you can select. When you press Enter after typing text in the search box, you can have Google Desktop either do a search (the default) or open a program or file that Quick Find located. For example, when you select Launch Programs/Files, by default, when you type **minesweeper** and press Enter, the Minesweeper game opens. If you select Search, by default, when you press Enter Google performs a search on *minesweeper*.

- **Number of Results:** Sets how many results per page you want Google to display. Choose from 10, 20, 30, 50, or 100.

- **Google Integration:** If you want Google to show your Desktop Search results even when doing a Web search, select this option.

Setting the Advanced Features

There is a single Advanced Features preference option. Find it located beneath the <u>Other</u> link. When you enable Advanced Features, you send information to Google about how you are using Google Desktop, what other programs you use, and which Web pages you visit. Google uses this information to personalize your Sidebar (for example, your News) and also to improve Google Deskbar with new features.

Google Desktop sends only non-personal data. This means that information such as your bank account number or credit card numbers are never sent to Google. You can feel safe having this feature enabled. To learn more about Google Privacy and Protection policy see `http://desktop.google.com/en/privacypolicy.html`.

Summary

In this chapter, you learned to install and configure the Google Desktop. This powerful tool indexes the files found on your computer, or other computers located across a network.

The Google Desktop software also serves as a container for other small programs called gadgets and plug-ins. These useful programs provide functionality that ranges from displaying an analog desktop clock to gathering information using RSS and Atom feeds. Google Gadgets are covered in much greater detail in Chapter 29.

Managing how Google Desktop indexes the files on your computer can bring about peace of mind while allowing quick access to the important information stored on your computer. As hard drives become larger and the number of applications increase, information can be more difficult to find as it is often stored in hundreds of formats and located in thousands of places. Google excels at finding distributed information. Finding your files is almost as useful as finding your way using Google Maps, covered in the next chapter.

Chapter 12

Exploring Google Maps

IN THIS CHAPTER

Learn to use the Google
Map Interfaces

Search for local business

Let Google Map give you
driving directions

Get more visibility by adding
your business

Learn how you can go farther
with Google Maps

Google Maps (maps.google.com) uses Google's powerful search technology to power many map-based services. Dynamic, interactive maps allow you to scroll to new map areas without waiting for the entire map to refresh. Google Maps simplifies getting directions, finding businesses, and obtaining satellite views of the Earth using either your mouse or keyboard. The map information can even be accessed with many mobile devices. Google Maps utilizes a combination of JavaScript and XML commonly referred to as Ajax, for faster screen loading and user customization.

Much of the data Google Maps uses to calculate these routes comes from a geographic information system provider called Navteq. Its digital map database is used by businesses for a variety of things including fleet management and GPS navigation. Navteq was recently selected as the primary map data provider for the U.S. government.

Because Google Maps uses this satellite data to plot your route, these directions are far more useful than those you might plot using a traditional paper map. One-way streets or Do Not Enter signs are already accounted for, and this information can be updated much faster digitally and more frequently than traditional paper maps. Similarly, information about new roads, road closures, and new construction is already included in your Google Maps directions.

Navigating the Google Maps Interface

The first time you visit Google Maps (http://maps.google.com), you see the familiar Google search box at the top of the page and a map of the entire continental United States with Search the map, Find businesses, and Get directions links (see Figure 12.1). You can change the map that loads on startup to a view of your home city or anywhere else you like.

FIGURE 12.1

Use Google Maps to find your way, find businesses and community resources.

Figure 12.2 shows you how to navigate the map interface. Three buttons at the top right within the map allow you to change the view from Map to Satellite or Hybrid with a mouse click. Buttons to maneuver around beyond the viewable region of the map appear in the upper left. Click any of these controls with your mouse to move in the indicated direction.

A pane in the lower right-hand corner of the map shows a rectangle representing the area the map includes in a field approximately nine times larger than that. Click and drag this rectangle in any direction within the larger field to see adjacent areas. Additional links on this page allow you to save locations, add or edit your business, or access Maps Help with a mouse click. Finally, a distance scale appears in the lower-left corner of the map; it adjusts itself automatically depending on the degree to which the map is zoomed in or out with distance displayed in U.S. Customary and Metric units.

Finding locations with the Search box

From the Google Maps home page, type an address into the Search box to find and display a map for that location. Any of the following formats work:

- **City, State.** For example, *Portsmouth, NH.*
- **City Country.** For example, *Moscow Russia.*
- **Number Street City State.** For example, *874 Elm Street Alexandria Virginia.*
- **Zip Code/Postal Code.** For example, *96720.*

Latitude and longitude coordinates in either decimal or DMS (Degrees/Minutes/Seconds) format also work. Commas are not necessary. More general searches such as *pizza,* or *office supplies,* or *schools* place lettered balloons on the map at the location of those search items and generate a list of links with names, phone numbers, and addresses for the corresponding locations. Use the Search box to do a keyword search for the location of businesses even if the keyword does not appear in the name of that business. Similarly, type a telephone number and Google Maps places a numbered balloon at the corresponding location on your map.

Using different views

The Google Maps page defaults to the Map view. Click Satellite in the upper right-hand corner of the map to change the view of the map to a scalable satellite or aerial image of the corresponding location (see Figure 12.2). Click Hybrid and Google Maps superimposes an image of streets and landmarks and their names over the satellite image (Figure 12.3).

FIGURE 12.2

Google displays a high-resolution satellite photo of the area you select to map.

Click arrow to "move" the map.   Click a button to change views.

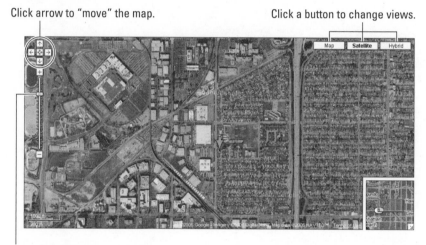

Drag the slider to zoom in and out.

FIGURE 12.3

In Hybrid view, street names are superimposed over the top of the satellite photo of the area you map.

Portions of the image in Hybrid view may appear obscured. In some situations Google has blurred regions of the image for security reasons.

Panning with arrow buttons

For mouse users, Google has incorporated an intuitive suite of control buttons. The map includes five clickable buttons arranged in a cross in the upper-left corner. Click the buttons with the single directional arrows to pan to areas adjacent to the map. Click the center button of these directional arrows and return to the previous view of the map. You can do this with the keyboard as well. Press and hold the arrow keys on the keyboard to pan incrementally in the corresponding direction. Use the following keyboard keys to move in greater increments:

- **Page Up.** North
- **Page Down.** South
- **End.** East
- **Home.** West

Page Up shifts the view in the viewport up (north) so that the northernmost portion, or the preceding view, is now the southernmost. To see a map of the region just south of your current view, press Page Down. The Home and End keys allow you to pan left and right in the same fashion.

Controlling magnification

Beneath the panning buttons sits a slider control with + and – buttons above and below it. Click + to zoom in for a closer view with greater detail. Click – to zoom out and see more of the surrounding area. The +/– keys on the keyboard produce the same result.

To zoom in or out in larger increments, click and drag the rectangular handle of the ladder-like slider control in the desired direction, + or –. Notice that each degree of zoom either doubles or halves the coverage of the previous view. The distance scale automatically updates with each step you move, either in or out.

 If your mouse has a scroll wheel, it also serves as a zoom tool. Scroll up to zoom in; scroll down to zoom out.

 Double-click anywhere on the map to zoom in. Double-right-click to zoom out.

Dragging maps to new locations

Click anywhere on the map and drag it in any direction for an even faster way to see adjacent areas. The standard arrow-shaped mouse pointer changes to a small hand that appears above the map. Clicking the left mouse button changes the mouse pointer to a grasped hand, letting you know that it has "grabbed" the map. While holding down the mouse button, you can move the map in the direction you move your mouse

 Depending on the speed of your Internet connection, it may take a moment to update the map as you expose new map areas, particularly in the more graphic-intensive satellite view.

See your map coverage area

The inset pane in the lower right-hand corner of the map has a blue rectangle showing the area the map covers, as well as the adjacent area surrounding this region (see Figure 12.3). This adjacent area is roughly equivalent to the area of the map you are viewing zoomed out approximately 250 percent. Click the rectangle in this box and drag it in any direction for yet another way to view the areas bordering the map. Click the arrow button in the lower-right corner of this box to toggle this feature off and on. Zooming into and out of the map, changing coverage area, is simple. See Table 12.1 for a list of shortcuts you can use to zoom in and out of the map.

TABLE 12.1	
	Zoom Shortcuts

To zoom in	Click and drag the slider up.
	Click the + sign at the top of the slider control.
	Use the – key on your keyboard.
	Double-click within the map.
	Scroll wheel up.
To zoom out	Click and drag the slider down.
	Click the – sign at the top of the slider control.
	Use the – key on your keyboard.
	Double-right-click within the map.
	Scroll wheel down.

Searching for Local Businesses

Google Maps makes the process of finding a particular business by searching on the business name or type of business, such as a pizza restaurant, or gas station, in any area very easy. Just type the name of the business and the city or zip code, and Google Maps searches for the map and produces a results list of businesses matching your search. You can also type *pizza*, or other keyword identifying a business and Google will find related businesses.

The location of these businesses is plotted on your map with small orange location balloons, called *DOT icons,* cross-referenced by letter to the results list of matching businesses. The results list includes the address and telephone number of those businesses. If you don't know the name of the business, type a keyword like **cleaners** or **hardware stores** in the Search box. Google Maps returns a list of appropriate matches for you to select from. Once you have a map for your desired location, refine your search by typing additional keywords, for example: **24 hours** or **foreign**. Google Maps adds or removes results and the corresponding DOT icons located within your particular map view.

When you choose a DOT icon on the map and click on it, two things occur. An information balloon (Figure 12.4) appears over your selected location and the name is highlighted with a gray box in the results list to the left. You can make the information balloon appear by clicking the link for that business in the result list as well.

NOTE Switching to Satellite or Hybrid views can return an aerial view of the business or building you are looking for.

The information balloon contains the name, phone number, and address of the selected business as well as links for directions to its location from yours, or an option to plot a course using that location as your starting point (read more in Getting Directions). Additionally, a link appears to upload these directions to your cell phone or other mobile device. Often, a link to that company's Web site is displayed. Click the small x (Close button) to make the information balloon disappear, or choose another location balloon or entry in the results list. Click any unlabeled section of the map to remove the info balloon.

FIGURE 12.4

Find business locations marked with DOT markers.

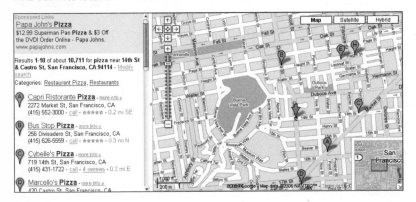

Click the send to phone link in the information balloon, and another balloon appears. Type your phone number and select your provider from the drop-down list, and Google Maps sends the information balloon data to your mobile device. This is a very efficient way to copy your directions and bring them along on the way to your objective.

NOTE Information balloons may have multiple folder tabs such as an address tab or a details tab. Click on these additional tabs for more information such as user reviews and rankings or payment options.

Getting Driving Directions

Google Maps provides more than one method for plotting a course to your destination. If you have followed the steps in the preceding section and already have an information balloon, you are practically there. Try this:

1. Click the to here link in the information balloon. Google Maps prompts you for a starting address.

2. Type your starting address as completely as possible (street number, city, state) in the Start Address box and then click Go (or press Enter). Google Maps refreshes the map, charting a course from your start point to your destination. New DOT icons appear with a green start (or play) icon marking your start address and an orange stop icon at your destination.

   On the left side of the screen, as shown in Figure 12.5, step-by-step instructions appear outlining each turn you will make and the distance traveled on each road. These steps are numbered. Click on the number for an intersection and another information balloon appears at that portion of the route. The balloon reveals another small inset map of just that portion of the route. You can zoom in or out of this map using the +/– buttons, or, like the main map, switch to Satellite or Hybrid views. Click the Start address or End address links to get the inset map for your start and end points. Click the Reverse directions link to rechart a course from your destination to your start point. All the route steps are updated.

FIGURE 12.5

Follow the simple directions on the left or use the map guide to navigate between locations.

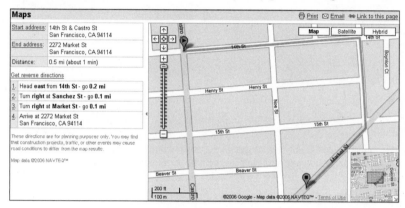

Get quick directions

To generate directions using Google Maps' single search box convenience, type your start and end points separated by to; for example, type **flint michigan to dallas tx** in the Search box, and Google Maps produces the appropriate maps and instructions.

Click the Get directions link and a second search box appears, representing the end points of your trip. If you have already loaded a specific map, one of these search boxes will already be filled in for you. Fill in the other box, click the Get Directions button (*not* the Get directions link) and let Google Maps chart your course.

Saving waypoints

You may find it useful to save a particular map as your start location. Here's how:

1. Click the Search the map link to find your home street, hotel, or workplace. C
2. Click the Make this my default location link. On all subsequent visits to Google Maps, this map appears *and* this address is the default starting point in the Get Directions feature, eliminating the need to type this starting point (for example, your home address) each time. You can change this default any time by repeating these steps.

NOTE When you go to http://maps.google.com, your saved default address/location appears in the upper-left corner of the screen. Click the Clear link to restore the Google Maps default start page.

Put Your Business on the Map

Although Google Maps uses a variety of sources to collect and display business information like telephone directories and Web search results, it is possible that information about your business is missing, inaccurate, out of date, or incomplete. In fact, you may occasionally see an <u>unverified listing- Report incorrect data</u> link in a given address information balloon. On the left side of the Google Maps home page is a list of example searches, and beneath this is the <u>Business Owners: Add/Edit Your Business</u> link. Click this link and find links for the following:

- <u>Login to your Google Account</u>
- <u>Create a Google Account</u>
- <u>Local Business Center</u>
- <u>Create, Edit, or Suspend your listing</u>
- <u>Add a coupon to your Google Maps Listing</u>

These services are free, but you must have a Google account or a Gmail account to use them. Setting up an account is free as well, although additional services, such as being listed as a sponsored link or creating local business ads have associated fees and require a Google account.

 At time of this book's printing, only businesses in the United States, Canada, the United Kingdom, China, and Japan can currently create local business ads.

Adding business information

Once you create an account and/or log in, you are rerouted to the Google Local Business Center. Follow these steps to include your business in Google maps:

1. Type your business name and address in the appropriate text boxes (see Figure 12.6).

2. Click Continue to add more specific options such as a description of your business, telephone numbers, hours of operation, and more. Optional text boxes allow you to type your Web site URL or e-mail address.

3. Click Continue again to select a category to aid Google in generating relevant search results for people who may try to find your business or one like it, or click Continue again for options to see a list of all available categories.

4. Select a category or recommend one for consideration by Google. Select up to five categories by choosing them from the list of categories and clicking **Add to List**.

5. Click the Continue button, taking you to a page where you can preview your business listing. You will then need to verify your listing. Select either to receive a phone call or a post card and click **Continue**, nearly completing the process.

Verifying your business listing

Once you add your business information, preview and accept your listing, Google provides you with a PIN. This number is used to verify your listing and to update it in the future. Next, Google calls your business number (either immediately or in five minutes) and an automated system asks you to enter the PIN on your phone keypad. You also have the option to verify your listing by mail, with a verification postcard being sent to your business address. Google seems to know if you list a cell phone number for your business phone and then requires verification by mail.

FIGURE 12.6

Enter your business information to create a listing.

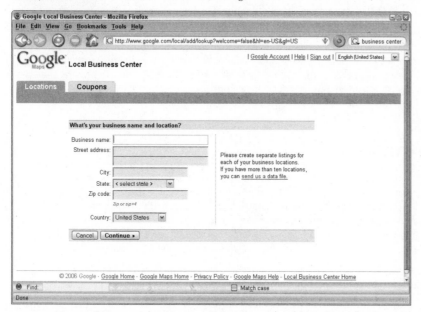

If you choose the mail option or are required to verify by mail, your mailing address must be a physical location where you can receive mail. Post office boxes are not accepted.

Now that you have verified your listing, the automated voice system alerts you that your listing should appear in about four weeks.

Creating coupons

Once your business listing is approved, you can return to the Local Business Center (www.google.com/local/add/login) and, after signing in to your account, click the Coupons tab, create a coupon that will appear on the business details page of your listing in Google Maps. A list of editorial guidelines and recommendations, and disclaimers appears in Google Maps Help section such as:

```
Please note that if you wish to limit coupon use to one per customer
you must include this in your coupon text. We cannot restrict the
number of times a customer can print your coupon.
```

About sponsored links

Sponsored links appear at the top of the search results listing. These sites pay a fee and then place a bid for certain keywords. Google uses a complicated algorithm to determine which of the sponsored links appear for a given search and in what order. While the process for obtaining a sponsored link is not terribly difficult, the fee structure gets a bit complex as the hosts of these links must bid in an auction for certain keywords (words that a Google user might type into a search box to find a particular product). Whoever bids the highest for a particular keyword gets, if not a higher position in the sponsored list ranking, at least a heavier weighting in the Google search algorithm. Sponsors pay only when their ads appear above a given search results list, and then only if their links are clicked. However, they don't pay the amount they bid to use that particular keyword. They pay one cent higher than the next highest bidder committed for that same keyword, a figure the sponsor does not know in advance.

Because the number of possible clicks on a sponsored link in a given time period is potentially huge, and because the sponsor does not know precisely what rate a given keyword is going for on a particular day (one cent more than the next highest bid), the cost for these links might be staggering. To give the sponsors some degree of control over their advertising budgets Google provides a number of ways to control the cost, such as only paying for x number of clicks, or a certain dollar figure per day.

Going Further

Web developers, programmers, hackers, and gamers not affiliated with Google are hard at work reverse-engineering and reintegrating Google Maps to help push this fascinating tool to its limits. Google has even released its own set of programmer tools called the Google Maps API (application programming interface). If you have a Google account, sign up to receive an API key and agree to the terms of service, you can embed Google Maps into your own Web site or make dynamic overlays to place over Google Maps to create your own routes and pathways that automatically scale and adjust as you zoom or drag your map.

Link your own photos or videos to points of the map to create your own interactive tour, with events triggered as the viewer clicks on the corresponding point on the map. Or, create your own animated map that pans or zooms to predetermined locations. The Google Maps API contains tools to create your own custom map icons. You can even create your own controls for users to explore your map.

A *geocoder* feature is included with the Google Maps API. Use it to generate longitude and latitude coordinates from points on the map. Even though Google Maps does not incorporate this feature on its site, you can improvise it:

1. Search for the location for which you want coordinates.
2. Get the desired location as close to the center of the map as possible.
3. Click the Link to this page link above the upper-right corner of the map.

The address bar in your Web browser changes to something like `http://www.google.com/maps?f=q&hl=en&q=space+needle&ie=UTF8&z=12&ll=47.624446,-122.349586&spn=0.104359,0.346069&om=1&iwloc=A`.

Click Fraud

Google, along with federal authorities and government watchdog groups are paying close attention to an online scam known as *click-fraud*. By clicking a competitor's sponsored link, a user generates a fee for that competitor. It is alleged that unethical individuals are doing this repeatedly, or going so far as to hire teams of people, sometimes in other countries, to generate these bogus charges. Computers can be programmed to click certain links, automatically racking up huge fees for the sponsor. Google's chief financial officer has referred to click-fraud as the biggest threat facing the Internet economy.

In this example, the latitude is 47.624446. The longitude is −122.349586. While this is a fairly quick and easy way to pinpoint a single spot, the Google Maps API allows you to enter a string of addresses or locations and geocode them all at once.

By integrating information from other Web sites, developers have greatly expanded the functionality of Google Maps. One popular site takes housing information from craigslist.org to chart the location of homes available on a Google Map. By incorporating FDIC bank office data, another site is able to show you the nearest branch of your bank regardless of where you are in the United States. Sites with dynamic weather maps, updating crime statistics, potential mates, recent earthquakes, even a site showing the locations of the biggest election donors, already exist to inform and entertain you. A user in San Jose has a map of gas prices in that city, constantly updated by visitors to his site looking for the cheapest fuel. By providing end users the tools to link dynamic free data feeds or their own research to Google Maps a new way of viewing the country is under development on the Web.

Summary

With its simple, intuitive interface combined with Google's powerful search capabilities, Google Maps has made the mundane and cumbersome details of getting from point A to point B, or finding a decent place to eat at 3 a.m. fast, efficient, and fun. The ability to click and drag around the field of view and zoom in and out with the flick of the scroll wheel provides a refreshing update to one of oldest navigational tools. The speed at which a destination can be located, a route plotted, and that information sent to your mobile device is almost dizzying, but hours can be lost idly playing with the tools and switching back and forth to hybrid and aerial views because it's so simple yet engaging.

Despite the ease of getting your business information to appear on Google Maps, it is probably unnecessary, as Google's search technology has undoubtedly already included it, waiting for you to add your unique marketing flourish. But even with all this power at your fingertips, developers are constantly striving to add another degree of utility to this tool suite.

Switching to the Satellite view can give some notion of terrain, and overlaying a route or location icon adds a sense that you are navigating a real space. Drop shadows on the DOT icons and information balloons enhance this effect. But ultimately, you are still manipulating static two-dimensional images. While it might not be more practical, wouldn't it be a bit more fun to explore the planet in three dimensions? Why can't Google render buildings as they rise above the landscape instead of just flat 2-D aerial views? See how Google has addressed this question in the next chapter.

Chapter 13

Exploring the World with Google Earth

It is not often in life that access to a completely new kind of information enters our lives, and changes them forever. This is what Google Earth has done for many people around the world. Google Earth provides simple, powerful, and rapid access to the entire Earth via satellite imagery, some of it captured in such high resolution that you can clearly see the shadows of the people on the ground and even make out the make and model of cars parked in front of houses.

The Google Earth images are being used for quite a number of different applications. Now, when you get driving directions you can see more than artistically drawn map, you can actually see landmarks, large trees, you can even see what buildings look like from above. Amazing fly-throughs have been created for large events, like air shows, to show people what the events look like, and where certain displays are located. Annotated Google Earth maps provide location information for businesses, national parks, clubs and World Heritage Sites.

IN THIS CHAPTER

Search and view locations in Google Earth

Mark the places you've seen with placemarks

Use Google Earth navigation tools to take guided tours of the earth

Add polygons and paths to your satellite images

Select the right version of Google Earth for your personal or business needs

Obtaining the Google Earth Software

Unlike many of Google's applications, this one requires you to download and install a client application. The Google Earth client, when launched, communicates with the Google Earth servers to retrieve satellite imagery. To get started, download the free version. Point your browser to http://earth.google.com.

Before you head to the Web site you should read through the next section to find out about the different versions that are available.

Choosing a Version

Google Earth has several different versions, from the free version to the enterprise version. This chapter helps you with some information to make the best choice on a version. Each has different features, but all use the same satellite imagery.

Click the Get Google Earth link in the upper-right portion of the Google Earth Web page. After you install it on your computer you are ready to begin seeing the Earth from a new perspective — from outer space.

The most important thing to remember when selecting a version of Google Earth, particularly one that costs money, is that the satellite images in all the versions are identical. Only the capabilities of the software vary.

Google Earth Free

The free version of Google Earth has almost all the power you'll ever need to entertain and amuse yourself and others for hours. This version is for personal use only but still has very few limitations on its functionality. When you need Google Earth for business purposes, check out Google Earth Pro.

The free version of Google Earth lets you search, locate fly-through, save, and print locations all around the globe.

Google Earth Plus

The Plus license can be had for a very nominal fee. The added features include the ability to print at higher resolution. You can also create and add paths and polygons, as discussed earlier in this chapter. You can import up to 100 different address points from Comma Separated Value (CSV) files. I used this to map the Starbucks Coffee locations in a ten-square-block-area in my hometown (wink). Of greater importance is the ability to import GPS data. If you own a GPS device, you can import the data from your GPS and map locations, paths, trips you've taken, property lines, and any other place you can think to use your GPS. You can now integrate the power of GPS with the terabytes of satellite imagery at Google.

Google Earth Pro

Upgrading to Google Earth Pro is more expensive than Google Earth Plus but as a business tool, it falls in the category of not very expensive. The Plus version gives you faster image load times, but the Pro version gives you the fastest load time. While it has lots of extra features, the main reason to upgrade to the Pro version is that you can use it for business purposes, while the free and Plus versions are for personal use only.

One of the cool features offered by the Pro version is the ability to export movies of your tours and fly-throughs. They are exported in compressed format, which is easy to send along to others. You can make great sales and training tools with this feature.

Of particular interest to many businesses is the ability of Google Earth Pro to import data from Geographic Information Systems (GIS). For example, you can import demographic data that has been coded for GIS applications.

The location import feature handles up to 2,500 locations compared to the 100 locations supported by the Plus version.

Google Earth Enterprise

Google Earth Enterprise is the ultimate business client server software and hardware solutions for mapping and satellite imaging solutions. Google Earth Fusion program is part of Google Earth Enterprise and allows you to integrate your business data, GIS data, terrain, and data point information into a single application.

There are two levels of Enterprise functionality. The Pro version consists of a massively scalable Google Earth Enterprise server that streams data to Google Earth Enterprise Client software. Use this hardware and software combination to host and integrate all your own data with terabytes of geodata and the power of Google Earth. The LT version allows you to host your own data layers locally while fusing it with the basemap data hosted by Google.

Welcome to the Earth

When you first launch the Google Earth client, or simply Google Earth, you are shown an impressive zoom-in from outer space onto the Earth and shown a view (see Figure 13.1) of the continental United States.

When Google Earth first loads, you are shown the default view.

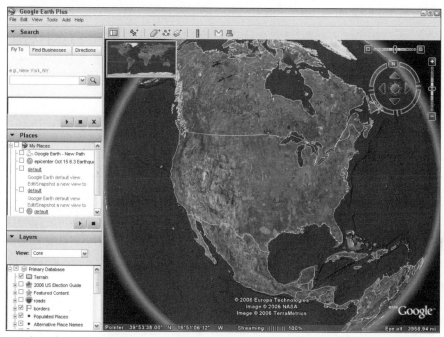

Google Earth image © Google Inc. used with permission.

This is the default view shown each time you load Google Earth. You can change the default location, and that is covered later in the chapter. Of course, you must be connected to the Internet to use Google Earth, and it's highly recommended that you be connected over a fast connection, rather than dial-up. You can still use Google Earth over dial-up — it just takes a bit of time to transfer the large image files to your computer.

Navigating Google Earth

Before you begin exploring the Earth, a good place to start is with Google Earth. The better you know how to use this fun tool the easier it will be to explore the rest of the planet.

The Search panel

In the upper-left corner of the Google Earth window are three tabs, each containing search boxes to help you locate points on the Earth. The three tabs are:

- **Fly to:** Type a physical address or latitude and longitude coordinates.
- **Find Businesses:** Two search boxes appear; type the name or type of business in the top box and the location in the bottom box.
- **Directions:** Two search boxes appear; type a beginning location in the top box and a destination in the bottom box.

After you type the information in the search box or boxes click the search button (the magnifying glass next to the search box) to have Google find your requested locations. In the event that a pop-up message appears that tells that your search returned no results, first check your spelling. If everything looks okay, then Google cannot find the location as you described it. Try a more general location, such as the street name without the number, or simply the name of a town.

When you type the location correctly, Google Earth begins panning to your location and, when it finds it, zooms partially in on the location.

X marks the spot

Google Earth gives you the ability to mark the places you "visit" with special marks, making it easier to return to the same places in the future. Each time you mark a location by adding a special icon known as a *placemark*, a reference to it is saved in the Places panel. The Places panel appears below the Search panel.

Creating a placemark

You may want to organize your placemarks, making them easier to find. Before you begin creating the placemark, select a folder from the Places panel on the left, or choose to create a new folder in the panel.

TIP Quickly create a new folder by selecting Folder from the Add menu or by pressing Ctrl+Shift+N.

To create a placemark, select Placemark from the Add menu or click the small pushpin icon in the toolbar above the display. This launches the New placemark window (see Figure 13.2). Get started by typing a meaningful name for the new placemark. For example, if you are marking the location of your favorite restaurant, a good name for the placemark might be the name of the restaurant.

Type a description for the placemark in the Description box found in the Description tab. Adding a description is optional but when you are marking the location of your favorite fishing spot, you can describe which types of fish you can catch in this location or describe the monsters you caught there in the past.

Select an icon for your placemark. Clicking the pushpin button next to the place name launches a window of icons to choose from. There is a large selection; or you can click Add Custom Icon along the bottom of this window to include your own custom icon. You can also elect to have no icon by clicking No Icon, also found along the bottom of the window.

After you save your placemark, it appears over the satellite image. It also appears in the Places panel, along with the icon you select. You can check a single or multiple places in the list then click the Play button below. Google Earth will display each place in a 'tour', slideshow style. By double-clicking on a place, Google Earth displays the location in the map.

FIGURE 13.2

Fill in this form to create a new placemark.

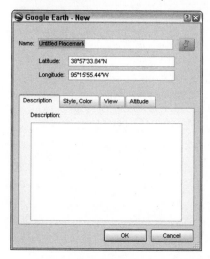

Customizing a placemark

To customize your placemark select it in the Places panel so that it is highlighted (not simply checked). Select Properties from the Edit menu and the Edit Placemark window appears, as shown in Figure 13.2. Or you can right-click the placemark and select Properties from the menu.

Select a color for the text label and icon by first selecting the Style, Color tab. Set the color for the label (the text that appears next to the placemark) by clicking the small color box and selecting a new color from the palette that appears. You can also change the color of your icons by clicking the color box in the Icons section. Change the scale (size) of both the label text and the icon by clicking either the Scale button and moving the slider or typing a scale value.

Opacity is the ability to see through something. When something is 100 percent opaque you cannot see through it. 0 percent might be something like clear glass. You can change the level of opacity for both the icon and the label. In heavily marked areas, it helps to have more important labels and icons at 100 percent, with less important labels at some lower opacity so they do not completely block the more important placemarks.

Moving a placemark

You can move a placemark in several ways. The easiest, but least accurate, way is to launch the Edit window. You notice that a yellow rectangle appears around the placemark. You can then click inside the yellow rectangle and drag it to its new location.

Another way to change the placemark location is by resetting the latitude and longitude settings. Click the View tab in the placemark Edit window. Click the Location tab and type new coordinates.

Try locking the placemark in the center of your view and moving the Earth under it. This is great for moving the placemark long distances. In the Location tab, select Center Placemark in View. This locks the placemark in the center. You are then free to move the Earth.

By default, all the locations are on the ground. But, you can put placemarks at different altitudes, either relative to the ground, or from sea level (absolute). You can optionally have Google Earth draw a line from the placemark to the ground making it easier to see when the image is tilted. Without the image tilted, you really can't tell if a placemark is attached to the ground or in midair.

> **TIP** Creating placemarks with very high altitudes is one way to mark satellites in geosynchronous orbit.

The Places panel also includes default view, the one that appears when you launch Google Earth, you can easily change the default location by first navigating to the point on the Earth, and setting the altitude, tilt, and direction you want to see as your default. Find default in the list of places. Right-click on the entry and choose Snapshot view from the menu. This sets the values in the saved location to those you are currently viewing. From that point on, each time you load Google Earth you navigate to this new place. You can change it as often as you want.

The Places panel also includes a sightseeing selection that, when expanded, displays a number of preconfigured locations you can visit. If you are new to Google Earth, this can be a fun way to explore the Earth. Double-click the name to have Google Earth move to this new location.

To take a tour of your saved places, select the places you want to tour and click the Play Tour button in the bottom-right corner of the Places panel.

> **TIP** Try stopping the tour, making adjustments to saved locations. Adjust the altitude, tilt, and rotational direction to make the tour more interesting.

Pressing Ctrl+F causes a search box to appear in the bottom of the Places panel. Search for a saved place by typing search terms in this box.

Moving Around the Earth

Google Earth gives you a wide variety of tools you can use to "move around" while you explore the satellite images. This section helps you become familiar with the way to use your mouse or keyboard to navigate around the satellite image.

Using the hand that Google gave you

The mouse cursor, when placed over the satellite image appears as a hand. This means you can "grab" the image and move it in any direction you like. When you click the left mouse button you will see the fingers grab the image. In the grab position, you can move your mouse and the image moves in the direction of your mouse. This is particularly useful for making fast moves in a particular direction.

You can also grab the image and "toss it" in a particular direction. Grab the image, move it in a direction, and let the mouse button up while the mouse is still moving. This causes the image to continue moving in the direction you toss it. To stop the image from moving, simply click once on the image. This is great for viewing large sections of a map without needing to use the navigational buttons or continually grabbing and pulling the image. Be careful. You can toss too hard and the image can start moving rather rapidly.

When the mouse cursor is over an informational icon, it changes to an arrow, meaning that you can click for more information. When you right-click, the hand changes to an up and down arrow cursor. While depressing the right mouse button you can easily zoom in and out by moving the mouse up and down.

Using the navigational controls

In the upper-right corner of the satellite image, you find a number of controls floating over the image (see Figure 13.3). Placing your cursor over the compass causes hidden controls to display that allow you to move the image in straight lines, rotate the image in a 360° circle, tilt the image, and zoom in.

The up, down, left, and right arrows cause you to move in a direction that can best be described as parallel to the ground. By default, clicking the up arrow moves you in a northerly direction, the down arrow toward the south and so on. But, once you use the rotation ring, which rotates the image, the up arrow moves you in an up direction in the image, which is not necessarily associated with north. You can refer to the compass to determine which direction you are heading by using these navigational keys. To use the rotation ring, click anywhere on the compass circle and drag this ring in either direction to rotate the image. You can also use the small gear-like icon in the center of the ring to rotate the Earth in any direction by clicking on it with your mouse and pulling it in the direction you want to travel.

 **The up-, down-, left-, and right-arrow keys on your keyboard provide the same function as the controls displayed in Google Earth.**

FIGURE 13.3

Use the navigational controls to move, zoom, and tilt the image.

Tilt controls

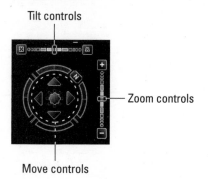

Zoom controls

Move controls

The tilt slider (horizontal slider along the top) causes the satellite image to appear as though you are looking at the image from an angle. Because Satellite imagery is taken from directly above, it is not possible to view features such as mountains or buildings in 3-D. However, there are overlays that allow you to see representations of buildings and terrain in 3-D, making the tilt feature very useful. Tilt the image in either direction using the slider. In the default view of the image, you are looking straight down. The tilt-up direction of the slider does nothing until the image is tilted down using either the slider or the tilt-down button on the right side of the slider. You can reset the tilt to directly overhead by double-clicking the tilt-up button found to the left of the tilt slider.

 **Control the tilt by pressing the Page Up (PgUP) and Page Down (PgDn) keys on your keyboard.**

The vertical slider on the right side of the Navigation tools (see Figure 13.3) consists of the zoom buttons and zoom adjustment slider. Using these buttons, you can zoom in or out. For example, clicking the + button causes the image to zoom in; click the – button to zoom out. This changes the appearance of altitude. As you zoom in, you appear to be viewing the scene from a lower altitude. You can view your apparent altitude in the status bar located along the bottom of the image.

The 411

Google Earth provides a status bar that is superimposed over the bottom of the satellite image. It contains three essential pieces of information, as shown in Figure 13.4. On the left side of the bar you can read the latitude and longitude of the location over which the mouse cursor is hovering. Move the mouse cursor and you see the latitude and longitude in the status bar change as well.

FIGURE 13.4

Information about the location you are viewing is located in the status bar at the bottom of the image.

The center of the bar displays the status of the image being streamed to your computer. This means that the images are sent to the Google Earth program running on your computer in stages. At first, before streaming has completed, you are able to view a lower-resolution image. As the data from the Google server streams to your computer, the image resolution slowly improves until it reaches 100 percent, meaning that the image you see is at its maximum resolution.

NOTE   The streaming speed depends on the speed of your Internet connection. Upgrading to Google Plus also helps with streaming speed.

The Eye alt status on the right side of the status bar shows you the apparent elevation over the Earth depending on your level of zoom. Clicking the zoom buttons or moving the zoom slider causes this value to change. It's not an exact measurement but a good approximation. The maximum distance you can zoom out is 39,353.69 miles from the Earth. The closest distance you can zoom in is around 28 feet, but the resolution of even the best image is relatively poor at that elevation. The measurement changes from miles to feet at an altitude of ten miles above the Earth.

Changing Views

You can change how you view the satellite imagery in Google Earth. Some of the things you can do are include an overview map, change the appearance of the status bar and compass on the image, optionally display latitude and longitude lines, and plan a tour.

Overview map

Google Earth has a small inset overview map that can appear above the satellite image. To launch the overview map, select Overview Map from the View menu. A red indicator square appears above a view of the entire Earth in Mercator projection rather than as a globe. As you zoom in and out, the square indicates the amount of area you are viewing. When the area is too small to represent with a box, it changes to a red indicator cross over the spot you are viewing.

You can make large changes in location by double-clicking on a location within the overview map and the satellite image changes to display the area where you clicked.

Zoom in and out of the satellite image by right-clicking in the overview map and dragging the cursor up or down. Right clicking changes the mouse cursor to an up and down arrow. Drag the cursor up to zoom out; down to zoom in.

Close the overview map by deselecting it from the View menu. You can adjust the size and various features of the overview map in the Google Earth options. This topic is covered in the section "Customizing Google Earth" later in this chapter.

Changing the display

You can cause the compass, which appears to be hovering in the upper-right corner of the satellite image, to appear and disappear. The same is true for the status bar along the bottom of the image. Select and deselect these options from the View menu. When you turn off the compass display, place your mouse cursor over the area where the compass would normally appear to reveal the navigational controls. Moving your mouse away from the compass area causes the compass and navigational controls to disappear once again.

You may want to turn these features on while finding a location, and then later turn them off when viewing your image without these features in the way. Also, if you save the image while the tools are displayed they appear in your saved image. You may want to have features, such as the status bar and compass, appear in your saved image to further describe your image. The same is true for the overview map. When the overview map appears in the display while saving an image, it is saved as part of the satellite image.

You can superimpose latitude and longitude lines over the satellite image. A display of the latitude and longitude are included over some of the lines. As you zoom in and out of the image, the latitude and longitude lines increase and decrease in accuracy resolution. For example, at lower altitudes (zoomed in) the display reads in degrees, minutes, and seconds. Zooming out the display changes to degrees and minutes and finally to just degrees. The Equator, Tropic of Cancer, Tropic of Capricorn, Arctic Circle, and Antarctic Circle lines are marked in yellow.

A small but visually appealing feature is the display of the atmosphere. When you zoom out so that you are looking at the globe you see that a blue haze, which represents the atmosphere, appears around the Earth. Zooming in and then tilting the image so that you can see the sky shows the sky as blue unless the atmosphere is turned off, in which case it appears black. Turn the atmosphere on and off in the View menu.

Applying layers

Without layers, Google Earth is little more than an interesting view of the Earth from space. Layers are data points of geographic interest. They mark locations such as roads, restaurants, hotels, borders, and more. Google Earth provides a variety of preinstalled layers along with the ability to build your own layers or include layers created by other people. Some of the preinstalled layers include:

- **Lodging:** Locate hotels, motels, inns and other places to spend the night.
- **Roads:** See highways, streets, and roads.
- **Terrain:** See terrain, like mountains and hills in 3-D.
- **Dining:** Find restaurants.
- **Borders:** See where all the national, state, and provincial borders are.
- **Buildings:** See 3-D buildings rendered in the location of the actual buildings.

Select other layers from the Layers panel in the lower-left corner of the Google Earth window by selecting the check box next to the layer name. In the Layers panel is a list of folders designated by a folder icon. You can select the folder by selecting the check box next to it, automatically selecting all the layers within the folder, or open the folder and select individual information types. For example, the Roads folder contains detailed road maps for the U.S. and additional road maps for much of Europe and Canada.

Most importantly, the Google Earth layers include Points of Interest or *POIs*. For example, the Travel and Tourism folder has a layer called Tourist Spots. Selecting this layer places little camera icons in all the locations where there are tourist POIs. Clicking on the camera icon pops up a bubble that tells you the name of the location, provides a link to more information, and also helps you plot driving directions to and from the location.

Select one or many layers. You may find that selecting too many layers crowds your display with icons and makes viewing of the satellite imagery difficult.

Customizing Google Earth

The Google Earth options allow you to customize the way you interact with Google Earth. Unlike many computer programs, where you set options once, you may find that you regularly adjust these options, particularly the 3D View and Touring options.

Select Options from the Tools menu to launch the Google Earth Options window shown in Figure 13.5. In this window, you can set features in the following tabs:

- 3D View
- Cache
- Touring
- Navigation
- General

After you set options in each of these tabs, you can click Apply Settings or Reset to Default and continue editing. If you want to save your changes and close the window, click OK. If you want to close the window without saving any changes, click Cancel.

3D View options

In the 3D View tab, you can set various options that affect the way Google Earth displays satellite imagery. Set the size of the detail area, the area where satellite imagery is displayed between small (256x256), medium (512x512), and large (1024x1024). Most graphic cards are now designed to handle colors in 32 bits. Still, you can change this setting. Set the texture colors between 16-bit and 32-bit colors and whether you want that data compressed or not. These settings are useful when using Google Earth over a lower-bandwidth Internet connection.

 **Some Macintosh displays have a problem that requires you to set the display size to small (256x256).**

Anisotropic filtering is a smoothing technique particularly useful when viewing the image when it has been tilted. Tilting causes pixels in the distance to become distorted. Using anisotropic filtering, the pixels in the distance appear smoothed. This type of filtering is very graphic intensive and therefore your graphics card must be equipped with a minimum of 32MB of graphics memory in order to use this feature. The default setting for anisotropic filtering is Off.

You can set the default size for labels and icons marking Points of Interest. You can increase and decrease the size of your placemarkers on an individual basis by editing the Labels/Icon Size configuration settings.

FIGURE 13.5

Change how Google Earth appears and functions by editing the Google Earth options.

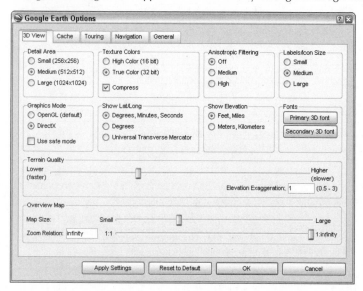

You can set the Graphics Mode between OpenGL (default) and DirectX. The only reason to select DirectX is when your graphics card and software driver do not support OpenGL. You can contact the maker of your graphics card for more information about OpenGL support. It's possible you can upgrade your graphics card driver to support OpenGL. For more information about OpenGL, see www.opengl.org.

Select options for the display of latitude and longitude information. Choose among Degrees, Minutes, and Seconds, just Degrees, or the Universal Transverse Mercator (UTM). The UTM is a coordinate system used to define points over a Mercator projection similar to the view of the earth shown in the overview map. Changing this selection changes how location information appears in the Google Earth status bar.

You can choose to display elevation in Feet, Miles or Meters, Kilometers. Also, select the primary and secondary fonts for labels and text displayed over the satellite image.

You can view terrain in 3-D by selecting the Terrain layer from the Layers panel. Set how you view the terrain by setting the terrain options. You can set options to view the terrain very smoothly, causing more data to transfer and the image to load slower. Slide the terrain slide bar to the right for more detail, or slide it to the left for less-detailed terrain images and faster load times. You can also choose to exaggerate the terrain, either positively or negatively, by setting the ratio. A 1:1 (one to one) ratio represents no change, while 2:1 represents a doubling of displayed altitudes, and .5:1 is a halving of altitudes. Positive terrain changes can show marked differences in elevation where, for example, at 1:1 you may not see the elevation change.

TIP "Flying" through mountainous terrain may appear better with a terrain ratio of lower than 1:1.

The last option in this tab is the size and zoom ratio of the overview map. Change the size of the map by sliding the slider between small and large. Set the zoom relation between 1:1 (one to one) and 1 to infinity.

Cache options

Cache is temporary computer storage space. The options in the Cache tab allow you to tell Google when to stop using the computer memory and when to start using disk cache. Using more disk cache slows performance while freeing computer memory for other purposes. The memory size you can allocate is limited to the amount of memory your computer is equipped with, and the disk cache is limited to the amount of free space you have on your hard drive.

There are buttons for clearing both the memory cache and the disk cache. When you log out from the Google Earth server you can also delete the cache file on your hard drive.

Touring options

The touring options allow you to configure how Google Earth moves through the images as you navigate to various points, whether manually or by playing a tour of selected places.

The Fly-To-Speed affects how quickly Google Earth jumps to the next position. By default it slowly flies from one point to another. By increasing this speed you can cause Google Earth to move between points much more quickly, even nearly instantaneously. Okay, not quite that fast.

Control how quickly Google Earth flies through tours. By default, the tour speed is set fairly slow. You can also set how long Google Earth pauses at each location in the tour. The default is one second. You can also control how many times the tour plays, from one time to 60 times.

Driving directions can be displayed as a fly-through. Create driving directions in the Search panel. The options for moving through the driving directions include Camera tilt angle, the camera range, and the speed. By varying these, you can appear closer to the ground to look more forward or have more of a view from above. The speed (in approximate miles per hour) gives you an idea of how long it might take you to get someplace and controls how quickly the tour moves through the directions.

TIP To create some amazing fly-throughs, increase the terrain aspect to 2:1 in 3D View. In the Touring tab, change camera view angle to 80 degrees and camera range to 175 M. Create driving directions and play the tour. You'll feel like you're driving in a car.

Navigation options

The navigation options help you control how you move through the imagery. The mouse settings control the sensitivity of your mouse and the mouse zoom direction. Remember that moving down zooms out and moving up zooms in. There are also three navigation option settings:

- Pan and Zoom (Ctrl+T)
- Flight Control (Ctrl+G)
- Click and Zoom

Select one of these options or change it using one of the speed key combinations.

General

The General settings allow you to set many of the miscellaneous Google Earth options. On the display you can choose to show tooltips or not when you mouse over certain icons. You can also choose to show Web results in an external browser, instead of using Google Earth to display Web results. This is recommended.

You can change the display language from System default to German, English, Spanish, French, Italian, or Japanese. Google Earth defaults to the language you specified when first installing the software.

Send usage statistics to Google by selecting this option. Remember that no personal identifying information is sent to Google when you elect to send usage statistics. Your privacy remains safe.

KML Error handling options configure how Google handles errors that it encounters while loading Google Earth map files (KML files). By default, it is designed to be tolerant and silently accept unknown data, and continue loading the file. You can also be prompted when an error is encountered or simply have the load fail once an error is encountered.

Select an e-mail program from the list or be prompted for which e-mail program you want to use when you are ready to send an e-mail message from within Google Earth. Lastly you have the option of disabling any on-screen advertising.

Useful Tools

The Google Earth Toolbar (shown in Figure 13.6) contains several useful tools. Access the tools discussed in this section by clicking the icons in the toolbar that appears above the satellite image detail area. When the toolbar is not visible, choose Toolbar from the View menu, or press Ctrl+Alt+T.

FIGURE 13.6

Find the toolbar above the detail area.

Add Path

Add Polygon | Add Image Overlay

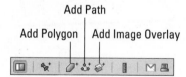

NOTE The Add Polygon and Add Path tools are only active when you purchase the Google Earth Plus version.

Add Polygon

Click the Add Polygon icon from the toolbar to begin adding interesting shapes to Google Earth. The Add Polygon window launches allowing you to name your polygon and add a description in the Description tab. Use polygons to define areas, or 3D polygons to simulate structures.

Click the Style, Color tab to define the color, width, and opacity of the lines that define your polygon. Additionally, you can determine when your polygon is filled with color, what color, and the opacity of the fill color. Try changing the opacity to less than 100 percent to see features within the polygon.

You can type the view information manually or navigate to the view where you want your polygon to appear, and click the Snapshot current view button in the View tab.

When you want your polygon to have a 3-D appearance, click the Altitude tab and move the slider from the ground position on the left toward Space, the right side. Click Extend Sides to Ground to have the polygon appear as a 3-D object from ground to your altitude setting. You can change the vertical position of the polygon above the ground by changing the drop-down from Clamped to Ground to either Relative to Ground or Absolute, and type values in the altitude box.

After you set these values, click in the satellite image detail area and begin drawing your polygon. You can grab the sides of your polygon, dragging them to new locations when the mouse pointer is placed over the line and changes to double parallel lines. You can drag the small change points to change the shape of the polygon. When you finish drawing, click OK in the Add or Edit Polygon window.

Add Path

Create a path by clicking the Add Path icon from the toolbar. Set the path name and optionally set the path description in the Description tab. The Style, Color tab allows you to set the color, thickness, and opacity of the line that shows your path.

You can manually set the view in the View tab by typing the latitude, longitude, range, heading, and for the view of the path you are creating, or simply navigate to the location, set the altitude and tilt, and then click the Snapshot current view button.

Set the Altitude of your path if you want it to appear above the ground or, like a wall, extended to the ground. This is a particularly nice feature in viewing images from an angle. It allows you to easily see the path on an angle.

Begin creating the actual path by clicking your mouse along the path over the satellite image. You can move the individual points with your mouse by clicking and dragging them to new locations. When you finish creating your path, click OK in the Add or Edit Path window.

Add Image Overlay

Image overlays are graphic images that can be placed over the surface of the satellite imagery giving additional details. The images can be mapped to the terrain or float above it and must be in one of the following formats:

- JPG
- BMP
- TIFF
- TGA
- PNG

 Overlays saved in PNG format should be modified making opaque features such as image boundaries transparent. This allows the underlying satellite imagery to show through.

The images that you use for your overlays should be aerial views, either photographic or drawn such as weather and topographical maps. Aerial and satellite photographs can also be used as overlays. Some of these overlays are created by and shared among the Google Earth community on its bulletin board. See the Google Earth Community section at the end of this chapter for more information.

To map the overlay onto a specific geographic area, the image must have north at the top of the image and use a special projection known as equirectangular projection (Plate Carrée). See Wikipedia's description of equirectangular projection for more information (http://en.wikipedia.org/wiki/Equirectangular_projection).

Overlays are given a name, like a placemark, path, or polygon. Select the path to the image you want to use as your overlay. The path can be a local path on your hard drive or a URL to a remote image.

Set the transparency by moving the slider from completely transparent on the left to completely opaque on the right. It is probably best to allow some transparency so you can see the satellite image below the overlay.

The Description, View, Altitude, and Location tabs are pretty much the same as for creating a placemark. The Refresh tab has settings that tell Google Earth when to refresh the image. Images can be refreshed based on time or change in view. The Web Mapping Service Parameters can be set by clicking WMS Parameters. See Wikipedia for more information about WMS at `http://en.wikipedia.org/wiki/Web_Map_Service`.

Once your overlay image is specified in the Link field, you can position it within the detail area using the green positioning marks that appear once you select Add Image Overlay. These marks allow you to reposition and resize the image. Grab the corner or side marks with your mouse to stretch the image to a new shape and size. The crosshair marker in the center allows you to reposition the image. The small offset triangle mark is used to rotate the image.

Save the image overlay by clicking OK in the New Image Overlay window. You can edit the image overlay by right-clicking on it in the Places tab and selecting Properties from the pop-up menu.

CROSS-REF See Chapter 33 for information about adding SketchUp 3D models to Google Earth.

Ruler

The ruler allows you to measure distances by clicking on points on the map. Click the Ruler icon to open the Ruler window. The line tab allows you to select two points on the satellite image and the distance can be read out in a number of different measures including:

- Centimeters
- Meters
- Kilometers
- Inches
- Feet
- Yards
- Miles
- Nautical Miles
- Smoots

If you're wondering what a smoot is, don't feel bad that you don't know. A smoot is a nonstandard unit of length named for Oliver Smoot who in 1958 was rolled head over heels by his Lambda Chi Alpha fraternity brothers to measure the length of the Harvard Bridge. A smoot is equal to his height, 5 feet, seven inches. Interestingly, Oliver Smoot later became chairman of the American National Standards Institute (ANSI) and president of the International Organization for Standardization (ISO). Isn't Google fun?

Send Email

You can send people e-mail about what you see or create in Google Earth. There are three ways to share this information:

- **Graphic of 3D View:** Google Earth saves a graphic image of the detailed image area and saves it as a JPG file that is automatically added as an attachment to the e-mail message that is created.
- **Snapshot of 3D View:** Rather than take a photograph, Google Earth saves all the information necessary to launch this same view in someone else's copy of Google Earth. This information is saved as an attachment to the e-mail.
- **Selected Placemark / Folder:** Send a placemark or folder to someone else so he or she can open it in Google Earth. This is great when sending party invitations. Let people create their own driving directions right to your house.

Select one of these three options and click the Email button. Depending on your e-mail settings, your selected e-mail program launches and create a new, unaddressed e-mail message containing either a graphic or the Google Earth file that allows the recipient to open and view the information in Google Earth. Add your own personal message along with the default message created by Google Earth, or just type an e-mail address and click Send.

Print

When you click the Print icon in the toolbar you are given three options based on the type of information you want to print. These are:

- **Graphic of 3D View:** Print the graphic information in the detailed satellite image area.
- **Most recent search results:** Print your most recent search results.
- **Selected Placemark in My Places:** Print the textual description information for the selected placemarks in the Places panel.

Printing continues as normal, allowing you to select and configure your printer.

 The Plus version of Google Earth allows you to print higher-resolution images.

Google Earth Community

Join the Google Earth Community. There are a large number of people all over the Earth interested in building upon the foundation of Google Earth to create imaginative and useful information. The community runs a bulletin board on the keyhole.com Web site, where it shares information and map information such as overlays and 3-D models.

Point your Web browser to `http://bbs.keyhole.com`.

After you sign up to participate (see Figure 13.7), you can share your own creations or try out some of the interesting things other people have created.

The `bbs.keyhole.com` site also hosts the KML (Keyhole Markup Language) reference for creating XML-based mapping items such as points, lines, and polygons.

FIGURE 13.7

Begin by configuring your community profile.

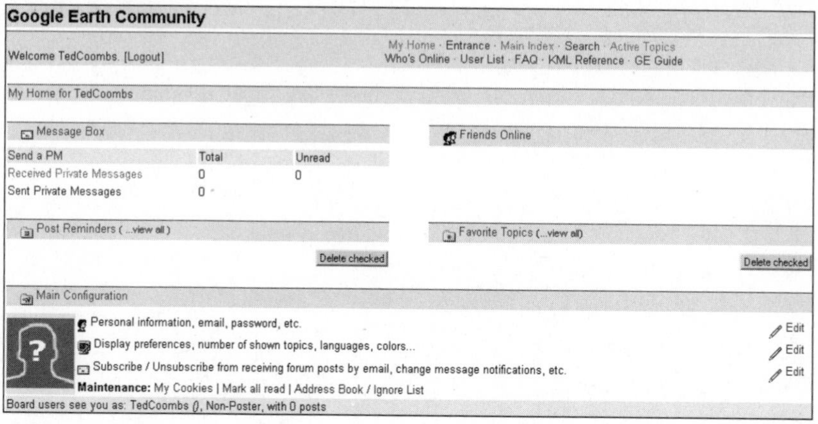

Summary

Google Earth is one of the coolest Internet applications to come along since...well, Google. It's simple to use, yet a very powerful tool for viewing satellite imagery that can show you enough detail to see the shadows people cast on the ground. Combine this high-resolution image data with other layers of information, such as road maps, business locations, terrain data, and a host of other information, and you can have hours of fun or one of the most powerful business tools of its kind.

Google Earth can be used for free, or you can pay a small license fee to use extra features that let you add polygons and trace your route manually or by importing GPS data. There are also several business versions that allow you to build applications with nearly an unlimited number of uses for geographically visualizing data. See where your customers live. Normal business data would never be able to show you that 87 percent of your customers live in valleys and at least 15 miles from the nearest road. Add this information with other business data and you learn that customers who live on hills watch Channel 9 and drive four-wheel drive vehicles and are most likely to try your product.

Most of all, Google Earth is fun and interesting. I don't know anyone who hasn't looked up his or her house on Google Earth and maybe even e-mailed me a copy of the picture. Now that you've seen what the Earth looks like, find out what's happening there by reading the next chapter about Google News.

Chapter 14

Staying Current with Google News

Google is a news service of a different sort. Technically, Google is a news aggregator. Rather than having its own reporters and gathering its own news, Google searches through the news of 4,500 other news sources and presents the best of the news to you in a form that feels like other news pages.

Explore Google News

Point your Web browser to http://news.google.com to begin viewing Google News. You can also navigate to the news page by clicking the News link on the Google search page. As mentioned earlier, Google News is an aggregator of news. This means that Google gathers news articles from different news sources and redisplays it. Not all the articles from all 4,500 news sources are displayed. When you first launch the Google News Web site you are shown the Standard News version. This version displays the top news stories from around the world. This page is automatically generated on a regular basis. You can even see how long it has been since the page was auto-generated by looking in the top-right corner of the News page, where the length of time since the last page was generated appears.

Navigating through the news

A short abstract of each news story appears with its title as a clickable hyperlink. In addition to the story brief, links to additional related stories appear beneath the abstract. Usually, the first two are links to stories and other news sources carrying a related story.

NOTE Clicking the links to related news sources will cause you to navigate away from Google News. To return to the Google News page, click the Back button in your browser.

View the full story by clicking either the title of the story or the small thumbnail image that appears with each story, as shown in Figure 14.1.

FIGURE 14.1

Click the title link or thumbnail to view the full story.

Indonesia Hit by Another Tsunami; Dozens Dead and Missing
Buzzle - **27 minutes ago**
A powerful earthquake beneath the sea has resulted in yet another massive tsunami hitting the Indonesian island of Java. The Red Cross is reporting that a tsunami in Indonesia has left at least 69 people dead and even more missing. ...
Tsunami kills 80 people in Indonesia ABC Online
Tsunami hits Indonesia's Java Scotsman
Independent Online - Reuters.uk - New York Times - The Age - **all 728 related »**

Playfuls.com

Menu surfing

Each section of Google News can be accessed using the menu along the left side of the Google News page. By default, when you first load Google News, the Top Stories menu selection is highlighted. Clicking the various menu choices reloads the page with the new selected news stories. Your choices are:

- **Top Stories:** Main news stories of the moment
- **World:** Top stories from many countries around the world
- **[Country]:** Menu selection changes based on the country you select (see News in Your Language)
- **Business:** Top business and economic stories of the day
- **Sci/Tech:** Top science and technology stories
- **Sports:** Stories about athletes, games, and sports contests
- **Entertainment:** News about movies, television, live productions, and performers
- **Health:** Top advances in medicine, drug therapies, treatments, and world health stories
- **Most Popular:** Displays the stories most selected by other readers in order from most read to least read

The menu appears while viewing any of the Google News pages. Also in the left menu are links to news alerts, news feeds, and mobile news, which are covered later in this chapter.

Top Stories

The Top Stories of the moment appear at the top of the Google News page. These stories can change as Google news auto-generates new pages. Normally, just a couple of articles are displayed in the Top Stories section. You will notice that next to the Top Stories title there is a drop-down list of countries. Changing countries often changes the language in which Google News is displayed (see News in Your Language later in this chapter).

TIP Try clicking the Refresh button in your Web browser to see if the Top Stories change. Quite often different stories will be displayed.

Remember that clicking a link to view a full story causes your browser to navigate away from Google News. To return, click your browser's Back button. It normally appears in your browser's menu bar as a left arrow.

Other news sections

By default, abstracts from the top 20 World news, Sports, U.S. (or the country you have configured), Business, Sci/Tech, Entertainment, Health, and the Most Popular stories are displayed. You can scroll down the page viewing each of the brief stories. Just like the main Google News page, each story lists the source of the story and links to related news stories. The Most Popular stories are rated by the number of people who have clicked on the abstracts to open the full text of the articles.

Each section is configurable so that you can choose to see more or fewer stories in that section. At the end of each section there are links, Show more stories, and Show fewer stories. Click these links to view Google News the way you want to see it.

News in your language

Select the country you want to view from the Top Stories drop-down list along the top of the Google News page. Selecting a new country displays headlines associated with the country you select. The world headlines often change with the country setting but may remain the same.

When selecting a new country, the language most associated with that country is used to display the Web page. In countries like India that have multiple languages but where English is the dominant language, news articles are displayed in English.

When using Internet Explorer, Google automatically senses the language your browser has set as the default language and shows you the news for that area of the world. Not only are the news articles displayed in the language you have set in your browser, Google displays different news articles that it believes will interest you based on the language you speak.

To change the language set in your Internet Explorer Web browser, follow these steps:

1. From the menu, choose Tools ➪ Internet Options.
2. In the Internet Options dialog box, click Languages, which is located along the bottom of the dialog box.
3. If the language you want to use is not displayed, click Add. Select a language and click OK.
4. When the language you want to use is listed, or you added it in step 3, click once on the language to highlight it (see Figure 14.2).
5. Click Move Up until the language you want to use is at the top of the list.
6. Click OK once in the Language Preference dialog box and again in the Internet Options dialog box to complete the language change.

CAUTION   Changing the default language changes the language for all Web pages you visit. Some Web pages are only accessible by people viewing in a particular language. For example, America Online's www.aim.com can only be viewed using the U.S. English language. Viewers using other languages are redirected.

Google does not sense the Firefox browser language setting. You can refer to the Firefox help for more information about setting the default language settings. The steps are similar to Internet Explorer except you find the language settings among the Advanced option settings.

FIGURE 14.2

Move the language you want to use for your pages to the top of the list.

At the bottom of each Google News page is a list of the different international versions of Google News. You can select an international version by clicking the link associated with the name of the country, and news is displayed in the primary language of that country.

Search Google News

A Google Search text box appears at the top of the Google News page. This allows you to search through all the articles within Google News, past and present (sorry not the future yet) and whether the news article appears displayed in your Web browser or not.

Personalize this Page

On the right side of the Google News page you will find a <u>Personalize this page</u> link, which when clicked, reloads the page with a Google News configuration page.

Requirements

There are a couple of browser settings that need to be correctly configured before you can configure and personalize Google News.

First, you must have JavaScript enabled in your Web browser. JavaScript is the scripting language that Google uses to allow editing of the configuration. The following sections provide instructions for enabling or making certain that JavaScript is already enabled in your Web browser. If you use a Web browser other than Internet Explorer or Firefox refer to the Web browser Help for instructions on enabling JavaScript.

STEPS: Enabling JavaScript in Internet Explorer

1. From the Internet Explorer menu choose Tools ⇨ Internet Options.
2. Click the Security tab in the Internet Options dialog box.
3. Click Custom Level. Scroll through the security settings until you find Scripting.
4. Under Active Scripting, select the Enable radio button.

5. Click Yes in the Warning message box.

6. Click OK in the Security window.

STEPS: Enabling JavaScript in Firefox

1. From the Firefox menu, choose Tools ➪ Options.

2. Click the Content tab.

3. Make certain the Enable JavaScript checkbox is checked; if not, click it to place a check in the box.

4. Click OK.

Enabling Cookies

It is important to have cookies enabled in your Web browser to make it possible to save the personalized Google News configuration. Cookies are small files associated with a Web site where configuration information can be saved. Enabling cookies creates information security concerns. When enabling cookies you will need to manage them. Simply erasing cookies causes you to lose your Google personalization. Using an adware and spyware checker regularly to control which cookies are saved and which are deleted is a good idea.

FIGURE 14.3

Change the way your Google News is displayed by personalizing the page.

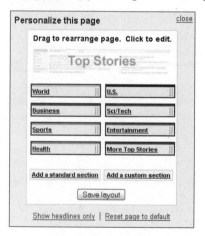

Arranging the layout

Click and drag the various sections by the vertical bars on the right side of the button to reorder how they appear when you load Google News. As you drag the item to its new position, that area is highlighted. Releasing your mouse button after dragging the section to its new location repositions it. You can drag items up and down and between left and right columns. Once you arrange the sections to how you want them to appear you can further personalize each section.

At any time while customizing your Google News page, you may log in using your Google ID and save your configuration on the Google server, rather than only on your local computer. This enables you to view your customized version of Google News on any computer whenever you log in to Google on any computer.

Customize the sections

Click on a section, such as World, in the Edit this personalized page box and you can select the edition you want to appear by choosing an edition from the drop-down list. You may also select the section by choosing from the second drop-down list. Further personalize the section by choosing how many stories you want to appear in that section. Finally, you can delete the section altogether.

 You do not need to be logged in to Google News to personalize the News page. Log in to save your configuration for customized viewing on other computers.

You can save your configuration at any time by clicking Save layout. Once you save your configuration, a message displays letting you know that "You've created your own unique, personalized version of Google News on this computer."

Adding sections

Add either additional standard, predefined sections to the Google News page or add your own custom section. Adding a standard section allows you to add back sections you might have previously deleted or create a new version of a section you have already chosen to display. The new standard section is created by first selecting the Edition; for example, if you are viewing the U.S. edition by default, perhaps you also want to see the world news from the United Kingdom. In this case you select U.K. from the edition and then select World from the Section drop-down list. You can also select how many stories you want to appear in that section.

 You are limited to the display of 20 sections. This includes the standard sections and any custom sections you create.

When you finish adding a standard section, click Add section. Your Google News page now appears as you've customized it, and the <u>Personalize this page</u> link now reads <u>Edit this personalized page</u>. To make further changes at any time click the <u>Edit this personalized page</u> link.

You can further enhance your Google News viewing by creating a custom section and adding it to Google News. Begin adding a custom section by clicking the <u>Add a custom section</u> link. The simplest way to create a custom section is to type one or more keywords, select the number of stories, and click Add section. Be aware that all of the keywords you type must appear in the stories, so adding too many keywords may result in no — or very few — stories appearing in your custom section.

Create custom sections using the advanced features to further personalize each section. Click the <u>Advanced</u> link next to the Keywords text box. The Advanced selections appear (see Figure 14.4). In addition to adding keywords, you can also select in which news sections those keywords appear. For example, when typing a name as a keyword and wanting only to see news articles about sports figures with that name, you can select Sport from the Section drop-down list.

The advanced features also allow you to select the language of your keywords. This limits stories to articles written in the language you select. Add a label for your new custom section by typing it in the Label: text box. If you do not type a label, Google creates a label based on the keywords you typed. You can then select the number of stories you want to appear or leave it at the default number of three. Click Add section to complete your configuration.

FIGURE 14.4

Create customized news sections.

 **TIP** Remember that after you add new sections you can rearrange how they appear on your Google News page.

Click Save Layout if you have changed the layout of your sections. When you finish customizing your Google News page, click the <u>Close</u> link on the Edit personalized page box.

Creating the Quick View

Each Google News article is displayed with the title, an abstract of the article, a list of the sources, and the time it was last updated. You can simplify browsing Google News by viewing only the headlines and eliminating the abstract of the article and the accompanying thumbnail. The headline of the article appears with the source of the news article and the time it was last updated. In the **Edit this personalized page** box click the <u>Show headlines only</u> link. To switch back to displaying the abstract and image click the <u>Show images and text</u> link.

NOTE Restore your settings to their default values by clicking the <u>Reset Page to Default</u> link at the bottom-right side of the <u>Edit this personalized page</u> link.

Google News Feeds

Google News Feeds allow you to use third-party computer applications called news feed readers to further aggregate news and other Internet-based information sources. You normally use a news feed reader to view the news rather than viewing the news using your Web browser. Google provides news feeds in two XML formats: RSS and ATOM. XML (eXtended Markup Language) is a way of presenting information in a standardized form through the World Wide Web. A news feed reader must support either or both of these XML formats.

To use a news feed from Google News, first find and install a news feed reader. You can Google "news feed readers" for more information or simply download and install JetBrains Omea Reader. We have found this news feed reader to be simple, powerful, and free. This is the news feed reader we use for the instructions that follow. Other news feed readers operate in a similar manner.

Download the JetBrains Omea Reader from: `www.jetbrains.com/omea/reader/`.

Once you install the news feed reader you are ready to begin adding news feeds. To use the JetBrains Omea Reader to add a Google News feed, follow these steps:

1. Navigate to the Google News page or News search result.
2. Click on either the <u>RSS</u> or <u>Atom</u> link beneath the Google News menu on the left side of the page. This loads an XML page, which may appear cryptic to you.
3. Right-click in the JetBrains Omea Reader Feeds folder and select Subscribe to Feed... from the pop-up menu. The Subscribe to Feed dialog box appears.
4. In the "Enter the address of an RSS or ATOM feed" text box, the address of the Google News feed should have been automatically added (see Figure 14.5). If not, copy the address of the news feed page from the address bar of your Web browser and paste it in this text box.
5. Click Next. This returns you to the Subscribe to Feed dialog box.
6. You can choose to have all the feeds go into the same folder or create a new folder to better organize your news feeds. Click **Next**.

NOTE Windows Vista makes this process of managing RSS feeds much easier.

FIGURE 14.5

The address of the ATOM or RSS news feed should appear.

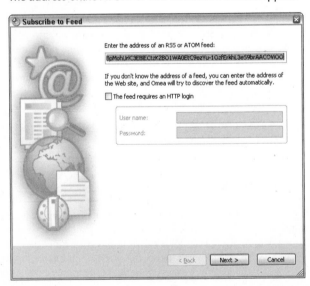

Your news feed automatically loads and news article titles appear in the top-right pane of the news feed reader (see Figure 14.6). To read the abstract, click once on the title and the abstract is loaded into the bottom pane. Clicking the title of the article in the lower pane loads the article just as it would load in a Web browser.

FIGURE 14.6

News articles appear very much like they would appear in an e-mail program.

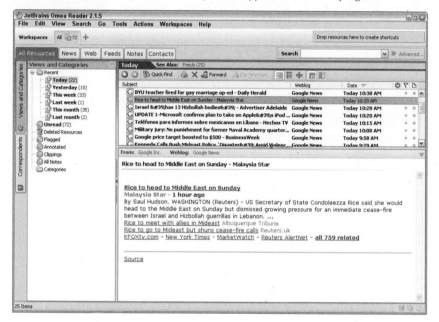

Keeping in Touch with E-mail Alerts

Quite often, the first thing a person looks at when he or she sits down at the computer is e-mail—not the day's news, Google groups, or the Web for interesting content. E-mail alerts, once just for news, now allow you to receive notification of breaking news, items of interest added to Google Groups, or items found on the Web. The alert is delivered to you as an e-mail message. This allows business professionals to respond quickly to world events as they are happening or keep abreast of group discussion topics. In general, it allows you to keep up to date with an unlimited number of topics through the aggregated Google News, through the many Google discussion groups, and through Web pages.

Setting alerts

On the Google News page (http://news.google.com), click the News Alerts link along the left side of the page. The link has a mail icon next to it. You can also access alerts directly by typing **www.google.com/alerts** into your Web browser. This launches the Google Alerts page shown in Figure 14.7. By filling in the form on this page you can create news alerts.

FIGURE 14.7

Create news alerts by filling in the form.

Setting the search terms

First, in the Search terms: text box type one or more keywords that Google can use to match in the news, groups, or the Web. Remember, the more words you type here, the more restrictive the search. You can get the most out of your searches by using the advanced search features of News, Google Groups, and Web searching. Visit the advanced search page in each of these areas and create an advanced search. Then paste it into the Alert Search Terms: text box.

Configure the type of alert

The second step is to choose a source for your alert by choosing one from the Type: drop-down list. This sets the type of query that Google performs to see if it should send you an alert or not. This search is done automatically (see the next section). The types of searches are:

- **News:** A Google News query that alerts you when there are new News articles that make it into the top ten results or your Google News search.

- **Web:** Receive alerts when your Web query finds new Web pages in the top 20 results of your search.

- **News & Web:** Get alerts when your query through the news is within the top ten results or when your search ends up in the top 20 Web search results.

- **Groups:** This is a query through Google Groups. You will receive an alert if your search through new posts since your last search has hits within the top 50 results.

At this time there is no way to combine the search through Google Groups with the other searches. You can easily create a second alert on the same keywords and effectively accomplish the same thing.

Setting the frequency

Configure how often alerts are sent to you. You can choose to see results daily (only if there are results), immediately, and once a week. Select the frequency from the How often: drop-down list. The selections are:

- **once a day:** Receive a single alert e-mail per day.
- **as-it-happens:** Get breaking news stories or alerts when new Web pages or Google Group posts appear.
- **once a week:** Saves the results and presents them all to you only once a week.

You can change the frequency or cancel your alerts at any time.

Submitting your request

The last step in configuring your request is to type the e-mail address where you want your Google Alerts delivered. Remember, if you type an e-mail address different from the one you use for your Google account you cannot use your Google account to manage these alerts. They will need to be managed by canceling the alert from the e-mail alert sent to you.

When you finish typing your e-mail address and configuring your Google Alert, click Create Alert. This sends the Alert request to Google, which then sends a verification request to the e-mail address you typed when creating the Alert.

Once you submit your request, a notification that your request has been accepted and that a verification e-mail has been sent to you. You are not finished, however. You must respond to the e-mail verification or you will not receive e-mail alerts on the topic you submitted. In the e-mail shown in Figure 14.8 you see two possible links: one to confirm and verify the alert and one to cancel. Assuming that you click the link to confirm, a new Web page appears letting you know that the Google Alert was verified. Of course, if you choose to cancel, a Web page that lets you know your alert was canceled appears.

FIGURE 14.8

Verify or cancel an alert by clicking the link sent to you in an e-mail.

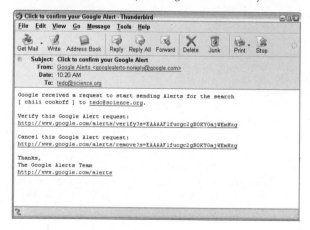

Managing Alerts

Alerts can be altered or canceled based on your changing needs. It is recommended that you sign up for and use your Google account when managing alerts. It is possible to manage alerts without an account, but it is just a little more complicated. To manage alerts without a Google account you must choose to cancel the alert by clicking the Cancel link in the alert e-mail you receive. Your only choice is to cancel the alert. Of course, you can always create a new alert with new parameters, essentially changing the alert, and canceling the old one. Still, it is simpler and recommended that you use your Google account to manage the alerts.

When using your Google account to manage alerts, you must be using the e-mail address associated with your Google account to receive alerts or Google will not associate those alerts with your account. Alerts sent to a different e-mail address will have to be managed as explained in the previous paragraph. To create a new Google account, simply click the Create an account now link when selecting to use your account to manage your alerts. Logging in to your account allows you to view all your alerts, as shown in Figure 14.9.

FIGURE 14.9

Create news alerts by filling in the form.

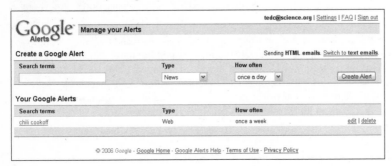

From the Web page shown in Figure 14.9 you can create news alerts by adding them in the Create a Google Alert section. The alerts you've already created appear below in the Your Google Alerts section.

Clicking the search terms, which appear as a link, allows you to see the results that Google searches to create your alert. This is an important tool when figuring out which and how many search terms to use in creating your alert. Too few words or the wrong words may give you strange results. Being able to see your results allows you to best configure your search terms.

To change an alert, click the edit link next to the alert.

Changing frequency

You may find that you need to change how often you get alerts. Perhaps you are getting inundated with e-mail alerts and want to receive them daily instead of as it happens, or perhaps only in digest form weekly. Or perhaps you are not receiving alerts often enough and need to increase the frequency in which they are sent. Select the new frequency, and your alert is updated.

Canceling alerts

There are two ways to cancel an alert. The fastest and most direct way is to click the <u>Cancel</u> link in an alert sent to you by e-mail. This is easiest particularly if you have a large number of alerts. The other way to cancel an alert is to manage your alerts by logging in to Google and managing your alerts. When managing your alerts to cancel an alert click the <u>Delete</u> link next to the alert.

Summary

Google News aggregates news from thousands of sources and presents it to you in a simple-to-read but powerful format. You can find what you need and hundreds of related articles reading Google News just the way it is, or you can personalize it by rearranging the News page, changing the language, or adding custom sections.

Reading the news is not restricted to the Web. You can install programs that accept ATOM and RSS news feeds. In many ways, these programs themselves act as aggregators of news and Usenet and other Web sources of information.

Let the computer tell you when there are important bits of news, group, or Web information that matches your interest by setting up Google Alerts. These will keep you informed without having to read all the Google Groups, Google News, and performing your own Web searches constantly. This way you never miss important information. This can form the foundation of scholarly research. Learn more about using Google for your research work using Google Scholar, which is covered in the next chapter.

Chapter 15

Researching with Google Scholar

"Stand on the shoulders of giants." This appears in bold green letters in the middle of the Google Scholar page at `http://scholar.google.com`. All research is in some way based on the work of others. The Internet, and now specifically Google Scholar, has made accessing the publication of these scientific endeavors simple. Simply searching the Web isn't always the most efficient way to do scholarly research. So, Google built a special system that provides access to content not available on the Web but instead resides in scholarly publications that have allowed their content to be indexed by Google. Google Scholar is a free service that has been shown to provide citation ability equal to other expensive services.

Searching for Papers or Books

Research is almost never done in a vacuum, unless you're an astronaut. Good research involves discovering the work of others and comparing it, contrasting it, testing it, and sometimes using it as a foundation for new research.

Scholars use a number of publication types in their research. These include

- **Peer-reviewed papers:** Papers published in journals that have scientific peers review the paper before publication
- **Theses:** Publications written in support of doctoral and masters degrees
- **Books:** Books written by scientific professionals about their research
- **Articles and abstracts:** Articles that are not peer reviewed but still contain important scientific information, and short abstracts of those articles also used in scientific research

Google Scholar creates a way to access this valuable information through academic publishers, professional societies, universities, and other scholarly organizations (Figure 15.1).

IN THIS CHAPTER

Learn how Google Scholar ranks search results

Focus your scholarly search with the Advanced Search

Understand the Google Scholar search results

Publishers, have Google Scholar index your publications

Learn some tips on Internet citation

Add a Google Scholar Search box on your Web site

FIGURE 15.1

Search through scholarly publications by typing keywords in the search box.

Ranking

The foundation of Google's search technology is its PageRank system. This is not completely applicable to the way Google Scholar ranks the information it provides. Google ranks articles by weighing the full text of each article. This probably doesn't involve a scale. Seriously, each article is ranked by a number of factors:

- Text of the article
- Author
- The publication
- Number of citations by other scholarly works

As usual, the most relevant results appear first. The text of the article must be relevant to your search in the same way the text of a Web page is relevant when doing a Google Web search. This is where it all changes. The author, who is completely unimportant in a Web search, becomes very important in a Google Scholar search. The author, based on standing in the scientific community and number of publications, helps rank the article.

In addition to the standing of the author in the scientific world, the publication is also ranked. The journals *Science* and *Nature* are ranked differently than a less scientific work such as *Scientific American*.

Searching

Searching through Google Scholar is done in a manner very similar to that of performing Web searches. Type keywords or phrases in the search box shown in Figure 15.1. To focus your search, try using either the Advanced Search discussed in the next section or the search operators listed in Table 15.1.

Using Advanced Scholar Search

To assist you in finding the right group of scholarly material, Google provides an advanced search capability. This is similar to the advanced Web search with only a few differences. The results, rather than being Web pages, represent scholarly works. That's why the advanced search page refers to articles instead of simply referring to results.

The Google Advanced Scholar Search page is divided into five sections. The first, **Find articles**, is similar to the Google Advanced Web search, except for the selection labeled "where my words occur."

FIGURE 15.2

Focus your search through articles using Advanced Scholar Search.

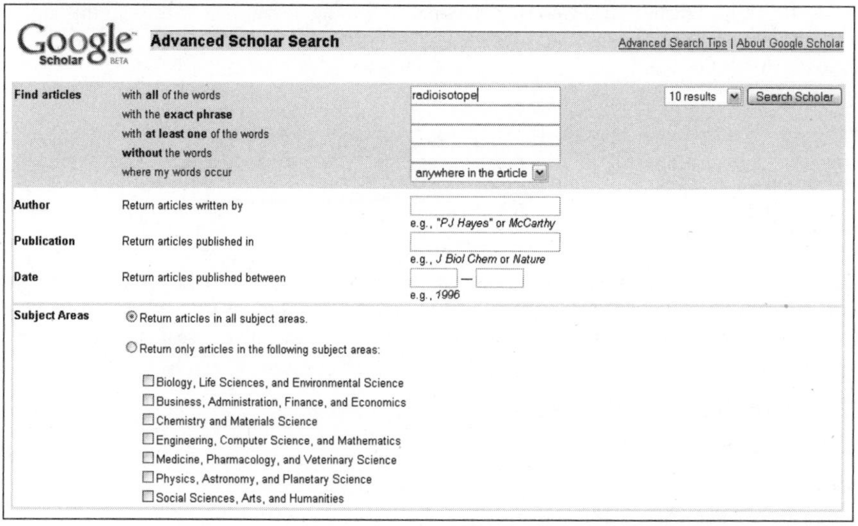

Find articles

This section allows you to search by keywords through scholarly works. The section is titled articles but many types of scholarly works and abstracts are included. Search options include the following: combinations:

- with **all** the words : Search on articles that include all of the keywords.

- with the **exact phrase:** Locate articles that include the exact phrase you typed.

- with **at least one** of the words: Find articles that contain at least one of the words in the list of keywords you typed.

- **without** the words: Exclude articles that contain keywords in this list.
- where my words occur: Locate articles that include keywords in a specific location.
    - anywhere in the article: Find articles that have keywords anywhere in the article, including abstract, title, and body of the article.
    - in the title of the article: Search on articles that specifically include your keywords or phrases in the title of the article.

Author

When you know the author's name, it helps a great deal in focusing your search. Knowing the author's name means you probably know the type of research done by the author or know of a particular article by the author. When possible, you should always try to include the author's last name to focus your search to a particular scholar.

Publication

In the "Return articles published in," section, you can limit your search to a particular scholarly publication. Focusing your search in this manner may help you find articles on a particular topic. For example, searching *Nature Genetics*, rather than simply *Nature*, helps you focus your search for publications to the field of genetics. Searching on the terms *genetic* and *engineering*, may not be enough because both those terms are also used in the field of software engineering.

Date

"The Return articles published between" option allows you to specify the range of dates in which the article was published. This helps you either search for older articles or make your search specific to articles published recently.

Subject areas

One of the best ways to find articles that are related to one another is to restrict your search to particular topics. Select one or more of the topic areas listed in the section labeled Return only articles in the following subject areas. Select the checkbox next to the area or areas you want to include in your search. The section lists the following subject areas:

- Biology, Life Sciences, Environmental Science
- Business, Administration, Finance, Economics
- Chemistry, Materials Science
- Engineering, Computer Science, Mathematics
- Medicine, Pharmacology, Veterinary Science
- Physics, Astronomy, Planetary Science
- Social Science, Arts, Humanities

Search operators

Google Scholar Search supports many of the Web Search operators. These help you limit your search when using the standard or advanced Google Scholar search features. The operators supported by Google Scholar are listed in Table 15.1.

TABLE 15.1

Google Scholar Supported Search Operators

Operator	Description
+	Words preceded by a + sign are required in the search.
-	Words preceded by a – sign are excluded from the search.
"quotes"	Words enclosed in "quotes" are treated as a phrase.
OR	Results can include either one keyword or phrase OR another.
intitle:	Returns results where the keyword is found in the document title.

Analyzing the Results

Search results in Google Scholar are a bit different from those you may be used to seeing on a Google Web search. Rather than presenting you with a link to a specific Web page, as you might expect from a Google Web Search, each Google Scholar result represents a body of work on a specific topic. This might be a single article from a book or it might include many related conference articles, journal articles, preprint articles and any other related scholarly material.

Bibliographic data

The results include bibliographic information such as the title of the publication, a list of the authors, and the source of the publication. Because the results do not always represent a single article, but may in fact represent a group of articles, the bibliographic information for the entire group of related articles is included, as well as Google's best guess at which of the articles best represents the group.

The search results list the number of articles within the group. For example, you may see a link that looks like group of 3 >>.

Clicking the link shows you a list of all three related articles within the group.

Another way to judge the importance of the article is by seeing how many other articles have cited the article in the result you are viewing. Google Scholar lists the number of citations in the result, shown as a link. Clicking the link displays a list of all the articles citing the original article.

Books

The search results may include links to books, as shown in Figure 15.3. Each book result is preceded by the word book in brackets, as in [book]. The title of the book is listed with the author, year of publication, and publisher listed in green below the book title. Google Scholar links to citations to the book in other articles and related articles.

In addition to citations and related articles, Google Scholar provides Web Search results for the book title, making it easier for you to find a copy of the book. You might even try your search using Google Books (http://books.google.com).

There is one more link provided for books, <u>Library Search</u>. Clicking this link performs a search through the WorldCat online library catalog. One of the nice features of the WorldCat catalog is that you can type your ZIP code and find a copy of the book in a library near you. It also allows you to easily find books by the same author or within the same subject.

FIGURE 15.3

Book references are labeled with [BOOK].

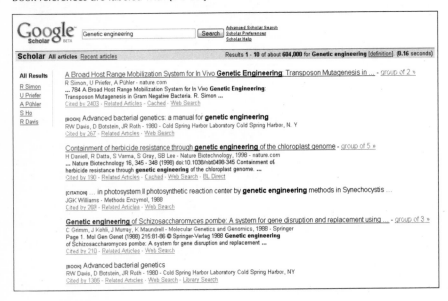

British Library Direct

One of the services provided by Google Scholar is a link to British Library Direct, when available. Clicking BL Direct takes you to a British Library page that provides additional bibliographic information and the ability to buy reprints of the article (see Figure 15.4).

British Library Direct is a free service of the British Library that allows you to search through a catalog of 20,000 journals and publications. It is not affiliated with Google, or Google Scholar. When you find the article that you want using the British Library Direct service, you can read them online for free or purchase reprints using your credit card.

You can purchase article reprints through the British Library.

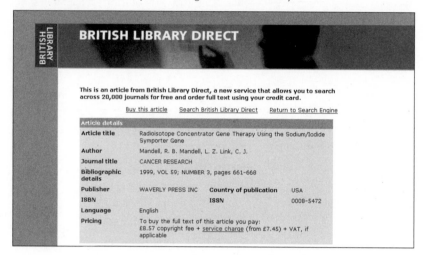

BRITISH LIBRARY DIRECT

This is an article from British Library Direct, a new service that allows you to search across 20,000 journals for free and order full text using your credit card.

Buy this article   Search British Library Direct   Return to Search Engine

Article details	
Article title	Radioisotope Concentrator Gene Therapy Using the Sodium/Iodide Symporter Gene
Author	Mandell, R. B. Mandell, L. Z. Link, C. J.
Journal title	CANCER RESEARCH
Bibliographic details	1999, VOL 59; NUMBER 3, pages 661-668
Publisher	WAVERLY PRESS INC **Country of publication** USA
ISBN	**ISSN** 0008-5472
Language	English
Pricing	To buy the full text of this article you pay: £8.57 copyright fee + service charge (from £7.45) + VAT, if applicable

Submit Your Publications

Google does not work directly with authors but with publishers of scholarly material. If you are an author of works appearing in such a journal and your articles do not appear in Google Scholar, try contacting the publisher of the journal to see if it provides content to Google Scholar.

Publishers are urged to work with Google in listing content with Google Scholar. When the articles you publish are indexed by Google Scholar, the visibility of your publication can increase and further your mission to provide scholarly publications of specific research or within broad areas of scientific research.

TIP   When publishers provide several versions of an article such as a preprint version, a published version, abstracts, and conference paper versions, article's it increases the rank increases. Doing this also improves the article's position in search results through Google Scholar.

When providing articles to Google Scholar, particularly when there are access restrictions due to copyright, it is important to have a full abstract of the article. This allows researchers to determine if the article or paper is applicable to their study and whether a reprint of the entire article should be ordered.

Google Scholar recommends that publishers of scholarly books contact Google Books for indexing of their material (see Chapter 6). For now, Google Scholar is focusing on scholarly journals only and does not index trade publications. For complete publisher assistance, visit the online publisher information page found at: scholar.google.com/intl/en/scholar/publishers.html.

Tips on Internet Citations

When writing papers, there are many guides to proper citation of an article. The articles that appear in Google Scholar actually appear in a journal or conference proceeding, and the form of citation is the same as though you had found the article searching through the print publication. The fact that you found the article or abstract searching through Google Scholar should no make no difference. For instance, you would not cite Google Scholar as the source of the information, but instead the journal in which the article will or has appeared.

Citing articles that appear on the Internet and not as part of published hardcopy journal is done differently. There are many guides to proper citation of Internet articles. Here are a few:

Columbia University Press
`www.columbia.edu/cu/cup/cgos/idx_basic.html`

International Federation of Library Associations and Institutions
`www.ifla.org/I/training/citation/citing.htm`

Modern Language Association Style Guide
`www.mla.org`

Adding Google Scholar to Your Site

The Google Web Search box has become almost ubiquitous on Internet sites. What you don't see as often is the Google Scholar Search box. Web sites that cater to researchers, scientists, students, and anyone else interested in accessing scholarly works will want to put the Google Scholar Search box on their Web page. It's quite simple. Follow these steps:

1. From the main Google Scholar page, click About Google Scholar.
2. In the list of links on the left of the About Google Scholar page, click the Add Google Scholar to your site link.
3. Type your e-mail address.
4. Select a style as shown in Figure 15.5.
5. Consent to the terms of service and click Continue.
6. Copy and paste the HTML code from the text box that appears into your Web site. The Google Scholar Search box appears after you save and publish the Web page.

FIGURE 15.5

Add your e-mail address and select the style of Google Scholar Search box you want on your site.

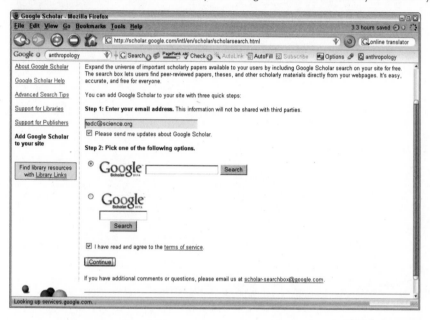

Summary

Google Scholar is for the serious researcher. Like Google Web Search, you can search through information indexed and ranked by Google to help you find the information you are looking for quickly and easily. Rather than Web sites, the results of your search are articles from scholarly publications. Publishers provide the articles for Google Scholar to index, which expands the ability of researchers to access the information they need. This increases the visibility of academic and scholarly journals, gives free access to a service that previously cost a great deal of money, and provides results in an intelligent manner.

Once you make your first million patenting a new gene or winning the Nobel Prize, you will want to invest your money wisely. The next chapter on Google Finance helps you along your way to continued financial prosperity.

Chapter 16

Managing Your Portfolio with Google Finance

oogle Finance combines information it retrieves from the Web with data that it licenses from financial data sources. The Google Finance home page provides timely financial data in an easy-to-read format. Point your browser to http://finance.google.com to get started toward your next couple million bucks.

Learn detailed information about company stocks and mutual funds, but Google Finance does not cover bond information or option quotes.

Reading the Finance Page

Google Finance homepage, http://finance.google.com, displays a summary of the U.S. stock market based on the top indices, a list of your most recently requested quotes, today's headlines, and related news (see Figure 16.1). At the top is the familiar Google Search box, but with a few twists.

Market Summary

The Market Summary is the first section displayed on the Google Finance home page. Listed in the Market Summary section are the four top U.S. market indices: the Dow Industrials, Nasdaq, S&P 500, and New York Stock Exchange (NYSE). The graph shown in Figure 16.1 tracks the Dow Jones Industrials (DJI) through its intraday trading.

To the right of each index is the current trading level of the index. The third column shows how much the index is up or down for the day, displayed in green (meaning up) or red (meaning down) with a plus or minus sign displayed before the quantity. The same value is displayed again as a percentage of the index and enclosed in parentheses.

FIGURE 16.1

See up-to-the-minute financial information on Google Finance.

Each index's name is displayed as a link. Clicking the link takes you to the detail for that index and the news about the index's performance or news that is affecting the performance of that index. Figure 16.2 shows the detail for the Dow Jones Industrial Average Index.

For each index, you can see:

- The current index price displayed in a large bold number beneath the index name
- The amount the index is up or down
- The date and time displayed as Eastern Time (either Standard or Daylight Savings Time).

The next column of information includes the index's opening price, the high price, the low price, and the volume of trading for that index. The third column of information begins with the market capitalization level, which is not applicable for any of the indexes. Below that, view the 52--week-high price, the 52-week-low price, and the average volume of trading. The fourth column does not apply to indices, only to individual companies. This is covered later in the chapter.

FIGURE 16.2

View detailed information about each of the indexes tracked in Google Finance.

Today's Headlines

The main Google Finance page displays today's financial headlines. Just like Google News, Google Finance is not a news source, but rather a news aggregator, displaying financial news from other financial news sources. Some of the financial news sources include

- Bloomberg
- New York Times
- ZDNet
- MSN Money
- BBC News
- Reuters
- Washington Post
- USA Today

Articles in the Today's Headline section are gathered from hundreds of news sources (see Figure 16.3). Similar to Google News, each article abstract appears with a link to the actual online article, a citation of where the article was printed, and how long ago the article was released.

Below each article title, which is displayed as a link, is the name of the financial news source. This could be pointing to one of the larger financial news sources or to a local newspaper article with an interesting story of financial interest.

Some articles are released in multiple sources with each of the sources listed below the article so that you can choose which news source you want to read. The first couple of additional articles are listed with the title of the article (a link to the article) and the name of the source. Additional sources are listed in green beneath these, or click the link that lists all the related articles. The link, appearing in green, tells you how many related articles you can access. For example, the link may read, all 587 related >>.

FIGURE 16.3

Read top financial stories in Today's Headlines on Google Finance.

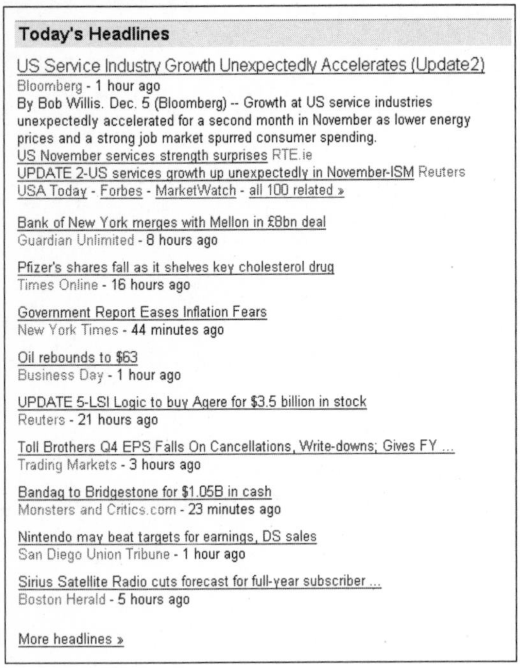

Today's Headlines

US Service Industry Growth Unexpectedly Accelerates (Update2)
Bloomberg - 1 hour ago
By Bob Willis. Dec. 5 (Bloomberg) -- Growth at US service industries unexpectedly accelerated for a second month in November as lower energy prices and a strong job market spurred consumer spending.
US November services strength surprises RTE.ie
UPDATE 2-US services growth up unexpectedly in November-ISM Reuters
USA Today - Forbes - MarketWatch - all 100 related »

Bank of New York merges with Mellon in £8bn deal
Guardian Unlimited - 8 hours ago

Pfizer's shares fall as it shelves key cholesterol drug
Times Online - 16 hours ago

Government Report Eases Inflation Fears
New York Times - 44 minutes ago

Oil rebounds to $63
Business Day - 1 hour ago

UPDATE 5-LSI Logic to buy Agere for $3.5 billion in stock
Reuters - 21 hours ago

Toll Brothers Q4 EPS Falls On Cancellations, Write-downs; Gives FY ...
Trading Markets - 3 hours ago

Bandag to Bridgestone for $1.05B in cash
Monsters and Critics.com - 23 minutes ago

Nintendo may beat targets for earnings, DS sales
San Diego Union Tribune - 1 hour ago

Sirius Satellite Radio cuts forecast for full-year subscriber ...
Boston Herald - 5 hours ago

More headlines »

Clicking the article title or news source links cause you to navigate away from Google Finance. If you do not want to navigate away from Google Finance, right-click with your mouse on the link and select the menu option that allows you to open the link in a new window. If you navigate away from Google Finance, click your browser's Back button to return to it.

Look for the More headlines >> link near the last news article to see additional financial articles.

Recent Quotes

Each time you request a quote using the Google Finance Search box (more about this in the next section), your Google Finance home page updates the list of quotes that appear in the Recent Quotes section in the upper right.

The stock symbol and company name appear as links making it easy to return to the company detail page quickly for a new quote or updated company information. Also shown is the quote for each stock and the amount changed for the day.

Related News

The Related News area is a particularly nice feature. While the top financial headlines of the day may be interesting, chances are you are interested in news articles that affect the companies in which you own stock or may be researching for a purchase or sale. The Related News section displays news articles only about companies that appear in your Recent Quotes.

The related news articles are displayed in the same fashion as those in the Today's Headlines section, and navigating to the articles works the same way. Depending on the company and how often news articles are written about it, it's possible that the news articles that appear in the Related News can be much older than those you expect to see in Today's Headlines.

Getting Quotes

The easiest way to get quotes is by typing them in the Search box at the top of the Google Finance page. You can type a stock symbol, the name of an index, or the name of a company. This Search box is quite different than the Google Web search box. As you type in the Google Finance Search box, a drop-down list appears with suggestions of what you might be looking for (see Figure 16.4). This helps for a number of different reasons: You might need information quickly and this speeds you along your way. Or if you don't know that the Nasdaq 100 Trust Shares has changed from a symbol of QQQ to QQQQ, this feature helps by showing you possible companies and their stock symbols as you type.

NOTE Stock symbols, although displayed in uppercase, are not case sensitive when you type them.

When you press Enter or click Search, the detailed page for that company appears (see "Trading Details" later in this chapter). An important thing to know is that in many cases, and depending on the stock exchange, the quote you see displayed is delayed by a specific time delay. Table 16.1 lists the various preprogrammed delays you can expect for the various exchanges and indices. Most of the indices display quotes in real time. The stock exchanges delay their quotes by 15 or 20 minutes.

TABLE 16.1

Exchange Display Delays

Exchange	Delay
American Stock Exchange	20 minutes
Canadian Venture Exchange	15 minutes
Dow Jones Index	Real time
Euronext	15 minutes
Nasdaq Indices	Real time
Nasdaq Stock Exchange	15 minutes
New York Stock Exchange	20 minutes
New York Stock Exchange Indices	Real time
Standard & Poor's Indices	Real time
Toronto Stock Exchange	15 minutes

Searching Google.com

When you do a normal Google Web search and Google recognizes an exchange ticker symbol, you automatically receive Google Finance information about the stock for that symbol. Google displays the intraday chart, the stock's high and low prices, and stock quotes from an ECN (Electronic Communication Network).

Clicking on the chart displayed in your search results causes your browser to navigate to a Google Finance page with more information about the stock in which you are interested. You also see a Google Finance link in the results. Clicking that link also takes you to Google Finance.

When you type a stock ticker symbol and you don't see a chart, and you've been able to see other charts (meaning your software is correctly configured) it usually means that the company is not trading with enough volume to generate a chart. If you've searched on a company that is no longer trading on the stock exchange, perhaps because it has gone private, it no longer displays a chart.

FIGURE 16.4

A drop--down list appears as you type in the Google Finance search box.

You can get stock quotes on your mobile device, whether it's your mobile phone, or handheld computer, through SMS. Currently, Google Finance does not offer company information through mobile services.

CROSS-REF See Chapter 28 for more information about getting quotes on your mobile device.

Trading Details

When you select a stock to review, whether you have searched in the Google Finance Search box, selected it from your Recent Quotes, or navigated to the detail from a link within Google Finance, a detailed company information page launches.

The detailed page begins with the name of the company, whether the company is public or private, its stock symbol (when it has one), and in which exchange the stock is traded. Along this same informational bar near the top of the page you also find the Add to Portfolio and Discuss symbol links. Portfolios and discussions are covered later in this chapter.

Interactive charts

A five--year performance chart appears below the index summary information just described. This is more than simply a chart. It has a special function of allowing you to see a range in the larger chart below. If you look to the right of the small chart, you will see small "grab" icons with double vertical bars (see Figure 16.5). Grabbing those with your mouse and dragging them to a new position on the chart changes the date range displayed in the chart below. You can click and drag beginning and end icons to change the range's beginning and ending dates.

FIGURE 16.5

Change the date range by dragging the begin and end dates in the five-year chart.

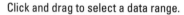

Click and drag to select a data range.

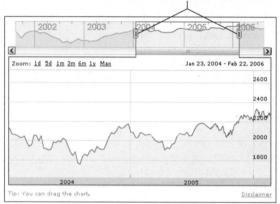

System Requirements for Google Interactive Charts

To view Google Charts there are some basic system requirements you must have.

System requirements for Interactive Charts:

- Macromedia Flash Player version 7 or greater installed (Download the latest Flash player from www.macromedia.com)
- Microsoft Windows 2000 or greater (for example, Windows Vista) or Mac OS
- Recent browser versions for Windows: IE 6.0 or greater, Firefox 1.0 or greater, or Opera 8.0 or greater
- or recent browser versions for Mac: Firefox 1.0 or greater, Safari 1.2.4 or greater
- or recent browser version for Linux: Firefox 1.0.4 or greater

NOTE **Once you properly install the right software versions, you should be able to view Google's interactive graphs.**

There is an additional way to set the date range in the chart. By default, the chart displays three trading days (Saturday, Sunday, and holidays do not appear in the chart). In the upper-left corner of the chart you see several links labeled <u>Zoom</u>. The links set the period displayed in the chart. The options are as follows:

- **1d:** One day
- **5d:** Five days (one trading week)
- **1m:** One month
- **3m:** Three months
- **6m:** Six months
- **1y:** One year
- **Max:** Five years

Clicking one of these links automatically adjusts the chart. The chart updates without reloading the Web page.

After you set your date period, you can fine-tune your chart by selecting the dates that fall in the period you want to view. When you place your mouse cursor over the chart, it turns into a hand icon, which means that you can drag the chart contents. You can not reposition the chart on the page, only move the data from left to right and back again, adjusting the dates displayed on the chart. Click the chart and drag your mouse. Continue doing this until the period you want to see appears. See the hand icon in Figure 16.6.

Charting the news

The detail page for stocks and indices contains news articles marked with a letter appearing in a small box. You can see them displayed in Figure 16.6 along the right side of the page. As you scroll through the chart, you may notice flags bearing the same letters as the news articles. These flags mark the days on which the news article may have affected the stock performance. Clicking the flag in the chart highlights the associated news article. If you click a letter that does not appear to have an associated article, the list of articles scrolls until this item appears.

When you click the letter next to a news article, that flag within the chart is highlighted. Also, as you drag the chart to different time periods, the news articles for that time period also scroll to match those marked in the chart.

FIGURE 16.6

News articles that may affect stock prices are labeled on the right and marked on the chart.

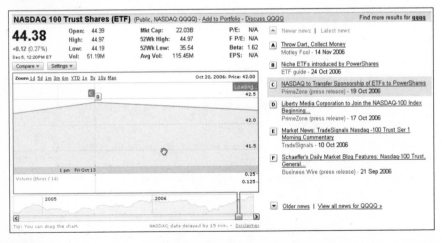

Researching company facts

The Key Stats & Ratios section of the detail page displays important company financial information related to its stock. This can include any combination of the following detail:

- Previous year's revenue.
- Net profit margin.
- Operating margin.
- Return on average assets.
- Return on average equity.
- The number of people employed in the previous year.
- The address of the main corporate office, including the phone number.
- The company Web page.
- A link from Reuters that lists additional ratios.
- When the company has additional links to important information, these are provided in the Site Links.

All of the links in this section cause you to navigate away from the Google Finance page. Some of the pages take you to company-specific Web sites, some to financial sites with additional company information, and you can even view a map courtesy of Google Maps.

Viewing the Summary

The company Summary gives you a snapshot of the company basics. It tells you what kind of business it is in. When a business has multiple locations, you learn how many locations it has. When a business owns other businesses, the summary tells you what they are. For companies that sell products, you can find out more about what kinds of products it sells and to which marketplace. It can also tell you where the company derives its revenue.

This information is truly a summary; in fact it is a summary of another summary provided by Reuters. A link to the full Reuters summary is provided at the end of the Google Finance summary so you can read additional detailed information. Simply click the More ratios from Reuters >> link.

Discover company financials

Company financials are listed in the Financials section and divided into three different sections: income statement, balance sheet, and cash flow. You can read financial data for the last quarter reported and also for the last fiscal year.

Income statement

The income statement lists the money the company made. This information consists of the company's reported total revenue, the gross profit, operating income, and net income. These figures are shown for the last reported quarter and for the previous fiscal year.

Balance sheet

The balance sheet deals with longer-term information such as the value of the company assets, both current and total. The balance sheet also shows the company's liabilities both current and total. Finally, the balance sheet also reports the company's total equity.

Cash flow

In addition to a company's income from sales and services, it is important when determining the overall financial health of a company to review its cash flow. This section of Google Finance's detailed reporting lists the company's net income/starting line, cash from operating, cash from investing, cash from financing, and the net change in cash.

Learn about the Management

It is often important to know who is at the helm of a company. The company's products or services can be excellent, the employees may be highly skilled, and there may be many customers, but the wrong management team can spell disaster for a company.

The Management section lists the company's corporate officers. Putting your mouse cursor over the name and title of the officer causes a small "card" to appear displaying the date the officer took office, his or her photo when available, and the person's age. Additional links that are also often included are:

- Reuter's bio and compensation information
- Yahoo Finance trading activity

Of course, you can also do Google searches to find additional information about many of these people.

Finding related companies

Each company tracked by Google Finance is categorized by business sector and specific business industry and specific category or categories. Find other related companies in the Related Companies section. As an example, the mythical Acme Semiconductor Co. would be categorized in the Technology sector, in the Semiconductor industry and the categories might include

- Category: Technology > Electronic Components > Semiconductors > Processor
- Category: Technology > Software > Design/Engineering > Software Development

Each of these specific categories appears in the Google Finance page as a link. Clicking one of these links launches a page showing all of the related companies in that category, along with the stock quote, change, change percentage, market capitalization, price-to-earnings ratio, annual revenue, and annual net income for each company in the list. Quickly sort on any of these company figures. Click the column heading, which appears as a link. Clicking once sorts highest to lowest; clicking again sorts lowest to highest. Viewing the companies in this fashion allows you to take a quick look at the other players in the field with a quick look at the company fundamentals.

Viewing the list of related companies also allows you to easily navigate to more specific information about each company, as the names appear as a link. Also, if there are subcategories, you can click on the subcategory and see a different list of companies. This is a great way to narrow your research.

More resources

Knowing the company financials and the people that make up the management team is not always enough to make stock purchase decisions. Google Finance provides links to other important analytical information. These may include:

- **Analyst Estimates:** Reports by industry stock analysts from TheStreet.
- **SEC Filings:** Security Exchange Commission filings through EDGAR.

- **Major Holders:** MSN Money provides a detail of how the company stock is distributed including ownership information, ownership activity and a list of some of the larger shareholders.
- **About Company:** Wikipedia, the open-source online encyclopedia provides general encyclopedic information about the company.
- **Transcripts:** Read the transcripts of stock-related conference calls at SeekingAlpha.
- **Options:** Track the sale of options, rather than the stock itself, at MarketWatch.
- **Research Reports:** Yahoo! Finance has compiled a list of research reports about the stock and provides links to them for your perusal.
- **Events:** Watch Webcasts of conferences at AOL Money & Finance.
- **Comparison Reports:** See pre-generated or custom-generated reports that compare stock performance against others in the same or different industries.

The amount of information in these resources can only be described as vast. Google Finance contains the information you need when doing much of your fundamental stock analysis.

Discussions

Anyone can join a discussion about the stocks shown in Google Finance. You can find links to a few of the discussions about the company and its stock listed in the Discussions section of the company detail page. The discussions are hosted by Google, rather than information you might find in blogs (see the next section) hosted on other sites. The Discussions section contains a link to the discussion, a brief snapshot of the discussion's text, and the name or pseudonym of the person who last posted in the discussion. To read the entire discussion, click the title link of the discussion.

The Google Finance Discussion page (see Figure 16.7) contains the full discussion transcript along with links to the profiles of the people in the discussion. To join the discussion, click the show options link next to any of the discussion posts. This causes several new links to appear that allow you to join the discussion:

- **Reply:** Reply to the group.
- **Reply to Author:** Reply only to the person posting the message.
- **Forward:** Send this post to someone else by e-mail.
- **Print:** Print the message post.
- **Individual Message:** Read only the individual message.
- **Report Abuse:** Let Google know if someone is posting nonrelated or inappropriate material.
- **Find messages by this author:** When you want to see all the other posts by this person click this link.
- **Reply with quote:** Reply to the message while quoting its content.

Before posting to the discussion, read and accept the Google Finance Discussion Groups Posting policy. After reading it, put a check in the checkbox at the bottom and click the Next step >> link. As part of the approval-to-post process, you must post your first message.

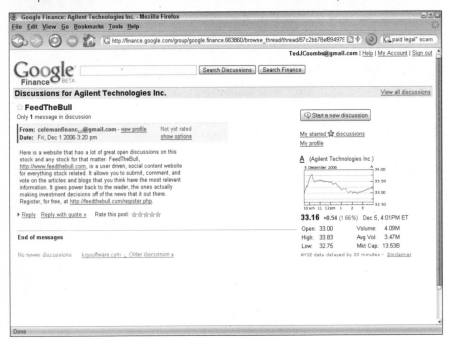

FIGURE 16.7

Participate in discussions with others about investment in various companies.

You can start a new discussion related to the company rather than join an existing discussion. Your topic should be different than the discussions currently taking place. Click Start a New Discussion to begin the new discussion thread. This launches a new page where you can fill in a new subject and text of the message, just as though you were sending an e-mail to someone. Instead, you are sending a message to the group that appears publicly. Select to have a copy of your own message sent to you by clicking the "Send me a copy of this message" checkbox below the Message text box. You can choose to preview your message by clicking Preview, or you can immediately post your message by clicking Post Message.

> **CAUTION** Discussions and blogs are merely the opinions of people, many of whom may not even be qualified to offer opinions. There are no knowledge requirements to post to these discussions. You may find wonderful information in the discussions, but be careful about the weight that you give this information.

Blog posts

Part of the company's detailed information page is a place where you can view and search through related information people have posted in their *blogs*. A blog is a weblog or Web-based journal. Clicking the More blogs >> link performs a Google Blog Search on the name of the company. The search page returns a link to the post, a notice of how long it has been since the post was made in the blog, a small snippet of the blog post, and a link to the blog's main page.

> **CROSS-REF** See Chapter 24 for more information about blogs.

When some blogs have more than one hit in the search results, only the first result appears. But a <u>More results from *Blog Name*</u> link also appears. Clicking this link shows you all the related posts from that specific blog.

Managing Your Portfolio

You can manage your portfolio within a simple-to-use interface. Next to your login name in the upper-right corner of the page you find a <u>Portfolios</u> link. Click this link to start creating your first Google Finance portfolio. By default, it is named My Portfolio. A message appears the first time telling you that "This portfolio is empty. Add a stock or a mutual fund."

Adding stocks and mutual funds

When viewing your portfolio page, you will find a text box where you can type a single or a comma-separated list of stock symbols, as shown in Figure 16.8. As you type a stock symbol, a drop-down list appears listing the name of the company associated with the symbol. This may not happen for other symbols in the list. This symbol list is the only required information you need to enter on this page. You may also choose to type the price at which you purchased your stock or mutual fund so you can easily track your trading success. Also, you can optionally type the number of shares you currently own to make managing your portfolio simpler.

When you finish adding the list of symbols and the optional price and share quantity, click Add to portfolio. At any time you can, continue adding to your portfolio by typing information in the Symbols, Price, and Shares text boxes that appear at the bottom of the portfolio listing.

NOTE The limit to the number of stocks and mutual funds you can track is 200.

Once you have items in your portfolio they are listed along with the Last Trade price and the Change in currency and percentage. When you add the optional price and share information, the portfolio also displays and calculates the Buy price, Shares (as entered by you), Investment (price x shares), Current value (shares x last trade), and Gain/Loss (Current value – Investment).

Another way to add stocks to your portfolio is when viewing the detail for a company you can quickly add it to your portfolio by clicking the <u>Add to Portfolio</u> link found next to the company name.

Adding a transaction

To add a transaction, follow these steps:

1. While viewing your portfolio click the company name or stock symbol. The detail for the company appears.

2. Click the <u>Add to Portfolio</u> link for stocks already in your portfolio and a new Add Transaction page appears.

3. In the Add Transaction page, select which portfolio you want to add the transaction to by selecting the name of the portfolio from the drop-down Portfolio list. By default, the stock symbol appears for the company you were previously viewing.

4. Optionally add values to the **Price** and **Shares** text boxes.

You can also add transactions while editing your portfolio.

FIGURE 16.8

Add one or more stocks to this page to start managing your portfolio.

Editing your portfolio

Follow these simple steps to edit your stock portfolio:

1. Click the Edit this portfolio link near the top right of the Portfolios page to begin editing a portfolio.
2. Create a new name for your portfolio and replace the default My Portfolio name. Select a new name, such as high-tech, high-risk, long term, or watch list.
3. Next to each company name you have listed in your portfolio are text boxes that allow you to add transactions by filling in the number of Shares and the Buy price.

Delete companies from your or your entire portfolio by following these steps:

1. Remove a company by putting a check in the Remove column.
2. Click Save Changes. This adds transactions that have been entered and removes any companies marked for removal.
3. Completely delete a portfolio by selecting the checkbox above the Delete This Portfolio button. This button only becomes active when the checkbox is selected. This helps to prevent accidental deletion from your profile.

Summary

This chapter explains how Google Finance is used to stay on top of the market through Google Finance news. You can perform detailed stock analyses using the many company information resources. You can read about the management team, the company performance over time, or use external services to read things such as the company's SEC postings.

In addition to gathering information, you can play an active part in the information offered by a company by using the Google Finance-hosted discussion list or reading and posting to blogs about related company financial information.

As you gather information, you can also manage your purchases in the Google Finance Portfolio. This is a private portfolio manager, and it's free. Only people who can view your Google account can view your portfolio.

Use Google Finance together with your online broker information or to track your offline brokerage account. The next chapter takes you further into ways you can communicate with others and share resources using Google Base.

Chapter 17

Google Base

Want the world to know about your chicken soup recipe? Do you have information you want posted and have no idea where to put it? Google Base is the place. Google has created a place where you can post just about any kind of information. Point your Web browser to `http://base.google.com` (see Figure 17.1). Google didn't just create a bulletin board like everyone else's. When you post things on the Google Base, you add attributes used to describe your post. This makes it easier for others searching in one of several Google search services to find your post.

Of course, like many other Google services, Google Base is free. Search Google Base or post your own items of interest.

IN THIS CHAPTER

Posting to Google Base

Learn the Google Base guidelines

Manage your posts

Searching Google Base

Understand the Google Base results

Posting to Google Base

Google Base allows you to add individual posts or upload bulk postings of all types of information, commercial or otherwise. The posting guidelines in this section guide you through creating your post and list some of the limitations you should be aware of when creating your post.

Creating a post

Click the Post an item link from any Google Base Web page. On the main page, it is located in the center of the page, as shown in Figure 17.1. A new page appears where you can choose an item type or create one of your own (see Figure 17.2).

- Events and Activities
- Recipes
- Housing
- Reference Articles
- Jobs
- Reviews
- News and Articles
- Services

- People Profiles
- Travel Packages
- Personals
- Vehicles
- Podcasts
- Wanted Ads
- Products

FIGURE 17.1

Search for stuff or post your own stuff.

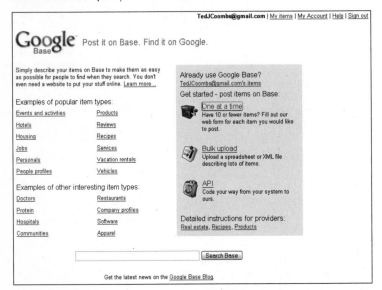

FIGURE 17.2

Select an item type or create a totally new one.

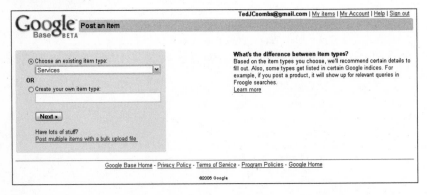

Details

Once you select a type, a form appears that enables you to describe your posting. The first thing Google Base gives you to describe your posting are attributes, which found in the Details section. These are *name-value pairs* that describe your product. A name-value pair is a descriptive attribute name, such as color, and then a value, like blue. You can use the attributes already created for you in a particular category, create new ones, or skip these altogether (not recommended). Attributes help people find you through Google by providing terms on which to search.

 **CAUTION** Creating Google Base posts without including descriptive attributes will make it very difficult for anyone to find your posting.

To add an attribute, put the descriptive attribute (name) in the box on the left and the value in the box to the right of the attribute, like this.

> Color   Blue
>
> Size Extra-large

When you want to add additional attributes, click the <u>Add another attribute...</u> link.

Labels

Labels, as shown in Figure 17.3, are different than attributes. In addition to helping people find your post, they also appear as links next to your posting. Someone searching through Google Base can click one of these labels and see all other postings with the same label. As Google Base grows, these labels will become increasingly important in narrowing a search. Therefore, you might want to do some searches through posts similar to your own to see what labels others use. That way, if someone lands on another post and clicks the label, he or she also sees your label.

TIP Posts last a limited amount of time. Use your Google Calendar account to remind you when to update your post.

FIGURE 17.3

Create attributes and labels.

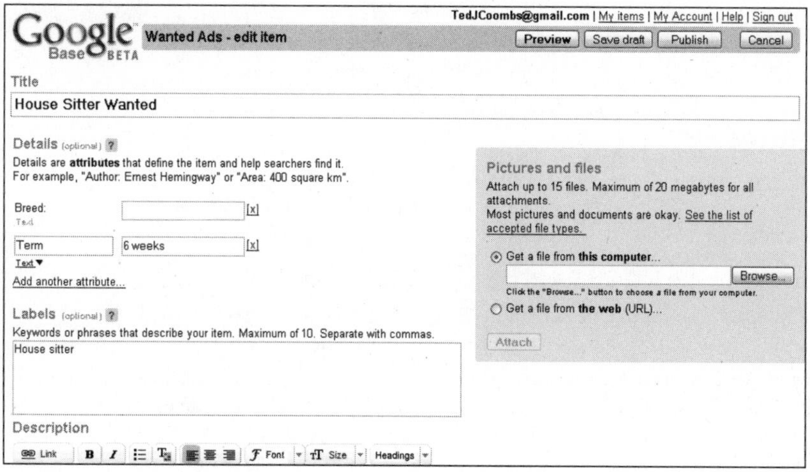

You can add up to ten labels, separated by commas in the Labels box.

Description

Create a description using the rich text editor provided by Google Base. To format your description text, you can use the following formatting features:

- Add a hyperlink
- Format text in bold
- Format text in italics
- Add a bullet list
- Change the text color
- Modify the text justification: left, center and right
- Change the font
- Set the font size between small, normal, large, and huge
- Add headings

Carefully construct your description. Remember that posts formatted so that they appear professional and appealing are going to attract more attention. If you are an HTML expert, you can switch editing to the HTML view and apply your HTML skills in creating your description.

Files

You can attach files to your posts. You can attach files found on your computer by clicking the "Get a file from this computer" radio button. Click Browse to locate the file on your hard drive or type a filename with its full path. Google Base only allows certain file types to be uploaded. For graphic files you can upload JPEG, PNG, GIF, TIF, and BMP. For publishing files, you can upload PDF, DOC, PPT, XLS, TXT, HTML, RTF, ASCII, UNICODE, and XML files.

Posting

Before publishing your post, you may want to preview it. Google Base checks for any errors, missed fields, or items that don't meet the posting guidelines (see the next section). Simply click Preview. You can save a draft of the post by clicking Save draft, a button found at the bottom of the page. This is a great way to save your work so that you can continue working on it later. Clicking Publish submits your post; soon after, it is viewable by the world. Of course, you can always choose to cancel by clicking Cancel.

Posting guidelines

You can upload information, data, text, programs, software, music, sound files, photographs, graphics, video, messages, and just about anything else that can be rendered in digital format. When posting to Google Base, there are some things you should keep in mind:

- Don't scream, which in the Internet world means don't use all capital letters.
- When you punctuate, use normal punctuation. Adding characters such as /////////==== to highlight ====\\\\\\\\\\ won't help you and is frowned upon by Google.
- When you create your posts, try to avoid unnecessary repetition. Don't repeat things and say them over and over. The posts should be specific to a topic or product. You can't just post generic phrases like "Click Here."

NOTE   Your post titles cannot include an exclamation point.

- Items must be posted in the English language. While the Google Base interface is available in English and German, the Google guidelines state that posts must be in English.

- When you intend to post adult items, they must be marked as unsuitable for minors. Keep the language clean.

URLs

When posting URLs, there are a number of guidelines you must follow:

- URLs must point to operational Web sites. When the Web site is down you must pause your post. To pause your post, select it and click Deactivate in the bar above the posted items. To resume publishing the post, select it and click Activate.

- Links cannot redirect. They must point to pages containing information about the item you post.

- Links should only be to Web pages, not to files that require external programs to view them.

- The page you land on cannot be password protected.

- When your site uses a robots.txt file to direct Web crawlers, it must allow access to the page you post a link to.

Products

- For businesses that ship products, you must be able to ship them nationwide.

- The product prices you list in the post must be displayed in U.S. dollars.

Bulk upload

To upload large numbers of postings — for example, your entire retail store inventory — you will not want to sit and add posts individually. Instead, you can upload posts in bulk form using files in one of many formats. You can include as many as 100,000 items per bulk upload. Each of these items will appear as an individual post as though you had entered them manually. Your bulk upload has a maximum of 10MB. You can contact Google if you need to upload a larger file.

Upload files in the following formats:

- **PDF:** Adobe (.pdf)
- **Excel:** Microsoft Excel (.xls)
- **Text:** Plain text (.txt)
- **HTML:** Web (.html)
- **Rich Text:** Rich Text Format (.rtf)
- **Word Perfect:** Corel Word Perfect (.wpd)
- **ASCII:** Plain text
- **Unicode:** Unicode formatted text files
- **XML:** Extended Markup Language (.xml)

Here's how to begin the bulk upload process:

1. Click either Post multiple items with a bulk upload file or the My Items link at the top of the page next to your Google user name.

2. In the My Items tab, click the Bulk upload files link (see Figure 17.4). The My Items tab changes to a list of links. The first link is Specify a bulk upload file. Clicking this link allows you to tell Google Base where to find the file containing your bulk upload information.

FIGURE 17.4

Enter the filename containing your item descriptions to be uploaded.

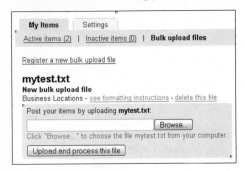

NOTE   **Your bulk upload must include items of all the same type. In other words, you can't include products and services in the same bulk upload. Your bulk upload file must be in the format for each specific type. Google Base provides templates for each category. Visit http://base.google.com/base/ types.html to download templates. Find the category, and click the link for the template.**

3. Type the filename into the File name box.

4. Select a predefined type or submit a custom type.

5. Click the Specify bulk upload file button. This file is then listed as a bulk upload file. The next step involves creating the file. Follow the instructions provided by Google Base for creating a bulk upload file. Find them here: `http://www.google.com/base/business_feed_ instructions.html`

Google Base limits

It may seem like Google Base is the last frontier and that anything goes, but that isn't exactly true. There are quite a number of limitations both legal and editorial. The editorial limits are enforced largely by the Web forms, but the legal limits are up to you to follow:

- You must be at least 18 years of age, or capable of forming a binding contract before you can upload to Google Base. Google may ask for ID.

- You can upload a total of 15 digital files of bulk upload information. The total size of all the files considered together cannot exceed 20MB.

As far as what you post on Google Base, the only restriction is that it must be legal. Google even warns that by using this service you might be exposed to material you find offensive or objectionable. Some of the things you really can't do are

- Defame other people, impersonate them, or send violent or hateful messages to them.

- Things that infringe on copyrights, patents, or trade secrets.

- No pyramid schemes or affiliate marketing programs.

- Sorry, you can't sell your body parts here, either.
- You can't transmit malware (viruses, worms, Trojans, and other destructive programs).

Other things you can't post are ads for cable descramblers, counterfeit goods, drugs and drug paraphernalia, gambling, hacking aids, miracle cures (unless your miracle cure is FDA approved), fireworks, explosives, and bulk currency (whatever that is).

International users must abide by the laws of their own country. Also, unlike many of the other Google services in many languages, Google Base is only available at this time in English and German.

Google Base Manager

Use the Google Base management page to manage your posts using the Google Base Dashboard, or manage your personal settings using the Base Settings page. Next to your login name, click the My items link. This launches a Web page with two tabs. The first tab contains information about your posts and the second tab is used for customizing your personal settings.

My items

Selecting the My Items tab (which loads by default when clicking the My items link) launches the Google Base Dashboard, displaying your links and important information about each of them.

Each item is listed with an Item title, as a link. Next to each title is an edit link. By clicking the item URL link, you can view your post as others see it. In the next column, you can easily see what type of post was created. The post status appears in the third column. Once you post, your post may not be available immediately. In Figure 17.5 you can find the status displayed in the third column of the line displaying your posted item. You may see a status listed as "Published...searchable soon." Your active posts will have a status of "Published and searchable". After a period of time set by Google Base your post expires. Your status may show that your post has expired. You can see the time your post was modified and the date it is set to expire.

Most important, you can view statistics about how many people are viewing your post. The last three columns in the Dashboard display allow you to keep track of how successful your post has been. This enables you to make modifications to your post to increase the number of people who view it. Here are the statistics and what they mean:

- **Impr.:** Impressions, which represents the number of times your post has appeared in search results.
- **Clicks:** The number of times that someone has clicked on your post when it has appeared in the search results
- **Page Views:** The total number of times that someone has viewed your post

The statistics are not real time, so don't get frustrated if your friends click on the post and the statistics don't change. Impressions and clicks are updated daily, and page view statistics are updated several times a day.

Deactivate your posting or delete it forever by clicking the buttons above the list of posts. Select the checkbox next to the post and click either Deactivate or Delete forever. If you create a draft that has not been published you can select the draft and click Publish Drafts.

FIGURE 17.5

Manage your posted items in the Google Base dashboard.

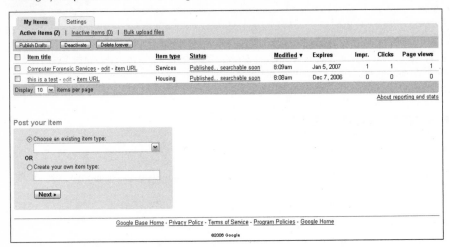

Settings

You can configure your Google Base account to make creating Google Base posts simpler. Once you sign in to your Google account point your Web browser to `http://base.google.com/base/settings`. You can also click the Settings tab in the Google Base dashboard. This launches the Base settings page as shown in Figure 17.6.

FIGURE 17.6

Configure your Google Base settings in the Google dashboard.

To configure your Google Base store follow these steps:

1. Enter a display name for your online store. This can be a nickname, store name or name of an organization.

2. Enter an optional description of your store.

3. Enter an optional link to your store's home page.

4. For sites that contain graphics or text not suitable for viewing by minors, select: This site contains content that may be unsuitable for minors.

5. Optionally configure or create an AdWords account to create keyword advertising for your product or service.

6. Configure your Contact information. By default your Gmail email address is used.

7. Optionally configure Location and deliver information.

8. Enter Payment information.

9. Set the default number of days after which an item expires. The maximum number you can enter is 31.

10. Choose to receive important notifications about your Google Base account by email.

11. Click Save Changes to complete your account modifications.

Searching Google Base

Searching Google Base is not a lot different than any other Google search: Type keywords or phrases in the Search box and then click Search Base or press the Enter key (see Figure 17.1). You may notice that there is no advanced search link for Google Base. You will learn about other ways of performing advanced searches later in this section.

Browsing categories

An easy way to view items in Google Base is to browse the categories. This type of browsing is similar to Google Directory where items are categorized, and you can view postings by category. Click one of the 20 categories listed on the Google Base page. You can even choose to view what others are searching on by clicking the links listed below Recent Searches.

Clicking each category presents all the results in that category but also displays search options based on the type of information you are viewing. Table 17.1 shows you the categories and the various search options for each category. You can also sort your results based on the type of information. Using these search options, you can focus your search through a wide variety of products, services, and information. The search options listed in Table 17.1 are likely to grow as the information stored in Google Base grows.

TABLE 17.1

Google Base Category Search and Sorting Options

Category	Search Options	Sort By
Blogs	Author, Blog type, Location, Subject, Content, Tags	Relevance Post Date
Coupons	Address, Phone, Coupon code, Expiration, Location, Diet, Ephedra Diet	Relevance Post Date
Clinical Trials	Condition, Phase, Source, Overall status	Relevance Post Date
Events and Activities	Price, Event date range, Location, Event type	Relevance Post Date Event Date Range Price
Housing	Listing type, Property type, Location, Price, Bedrooms, Bathrooms	Relevance Post Date Price Bedrooms Bathrooms
Jobs	Job function, Job type, Location	Relevance Post Date
Mobile Content	Supported devices, Phone brands, Devices, Language	Relevance Post Date
News and articles	Publish date, Author, News source, Nobel prize field, Nobel rights, Year, pages	Relevance Post Date Publish Date
Nursing home	Location, Owner has multiple homes, Service type, Councils available, Type of ownership, Number of residents, Certified number of beds	Relevance Post Date
People profiles	Gender, Age, Location, Marital Status, Sexual orientation, Interested in, Occupation	Relevance Post Date Age
Podcasts	Author, Subject, Price, Genre, Economist, Interview topic, Podcast, University	Relevance Post Date
Protein	Species, Length, Mass, Publish Date, Author, Mnemonic, Reviewed	Relevance Post Date Length Mass
Products	Price, Brand, Condition, Product Type, Author, Format, Actor	Relevance Post Date Price
Recipes	Cuisine, Main Ingredient, Course, Main Category	Relevance Post Date

Category	Search Options	Sort By
Reference Articles	Patentee address, Author, Patent title, Publication name, News source, Product type, Name of item reviewed, First named inventor, Patentee contact	Relevance Post Date
Reviews	Review type, Rating, Name of item reviewed, Reviewer type, Categories of item reviewed, Review date, Country of item reviewed, Review author	Relevance Post Date
Services	Service type, price, Location, Skill, Services offered, California coverage area, Grades, County, In business since	Relevance Post Date Price
Vehicles	Make, Model, Location, Condition, Price, Color, Year, Vehicle type, Mileage	Relevance Post Date Price
Wanted ads	Price, Agent, Bedrooms, Listing Type, City, Preferred area, Location	Relevance Post Date
Wine and food	Location, Payments, Special needs, Meals, Atmosphere, Dining, Bar info	Relevance Post Date

Using search terms

Entering a search term such as *diamond rings* results in a display like the one shown in Figure 17.7. In addition to the search results, you can view each of the categories that diamond rings may fall into. For example, as also shown in Figure 17.6 along the top of the results page are a number of different categories in which this search result is found. This is a quick way to go from reading product advertisements to reading reviews.

There are no advanced search pages for search terms because of your ability to focus your search by type of category. In the example of the diamond ring, typing the search term shows you all occurrences of the term *diamond ring* in all categories. After performing the search you can choose one of the categories that appears at the top of the page. At that time you see a new list of results that fall in that category and also give you access to the search options listed in Table 17.1. Use these to further focus your search.

Base results

Each search result appears with links to the item information. Below this link are links to information in subcategories. For example, in the case of diamond rings you might find links to Irish Wedding Rings. Clicking the link shows you all Irish wedding rings listed in Google Base. In many cases, the price is listed as a link. Clicking the link shows you all diamond rings with that price.

Each type of category presents different types of information to you. People profiles in your area, in addition to showing you the people, also shows you a map with each of the people marked on the map.

FIGURE 17.7

Search results can be sorted by relevance and most recent post.

Summary

Post almost anything you can think of to Google Base and have it searchable in many of the Google search utilities. It's a great way to post your resume, sell your car, sell many cars, post a review of the car you just bought, or learn about proteins. If your head just did that little thing it does when you read something strange, that's okay. The amount and types of information you can post to Google Base is nearly limitless. It's the ultimate catalog system and more. If you enjoy using the wonderful user interface used to create posts, you'll love using Google's Writely and Google Spreadsheet, which are covered in the next chapter.

Chapter 18

Using Google "Office"

IN THIS CHAPTER

Create word processing documents on the Web

Learn to format documents using the Google Docs document editor

Discover how to save Web-based documents to your hard drive in many different formats

Build your first Google Docs spreadsheet

Build entire applications with the power of Google Docs spreadsheet formulas

Manage your Google Docs files online

G oogle does not have a product or application called Office. That's why I've placed it in quotes. What it *does* have is Google Docs, previously known as Writely and Google Spreadsheets, two online office automation products. There is no doubt that these two products fall outside of the general goal of controlling the world's information, but they are related. After all, they are the two most common types of information-handling tools in the world. So, it still makes sense for Google to have these products.

Unlike other office-automation products common in the marketplace, these two products are Web-based and, of course, are free. One of the distinct advantages these products offer is the ease with which others can collaborate on the creation and editing of documents.

Getting Started with Google Docs

Creating word processor documents, or simply "documents" and spreadsheets is simple in this Google tool. To get started using Google Docs, point your Web browser to http://docs.google.com. From the Google Docs Web site, you can create new word processing documents, new spreadsheets, and upload existing word processing documents from many popular office automation tools such as Open Office and Microsoft Word so you can continue working on them using Google Docs products.

You can start creating new documents or send your existing documents to Google to continue editing them online. There are advantages to this strategy. One immediate advantage is the ability to share your document with others and allowing them to assist in making changes. You control who has access. Another advantage is that uploading files to Google puts them in a form of safe storage. You can never seem to back up their hard drive enough. Google takes excellent care to maintain backups, both in its equipment and its file storage. It also frees up disk space on your own computer, although with today's huge hard drives that's usually not an issue. Google Docs allows you to upload documents in Word, OpenOffice, RTF, HTML or text format.

 **If you've never heard of OpenOffice, it's worth a look. You can learn more at** www. openoffice.org.

Once you load the Google Docs Web page, the first thing you'll notice is that it has the familiar Google Search box at the top of the page. With this search box, you can search through all your word processing and spreadsheet documents online, or search the Web (see Figure 18.1). Log in to your Google account to use these applications.

FIGURE 18.1

Create new office automation documents online.

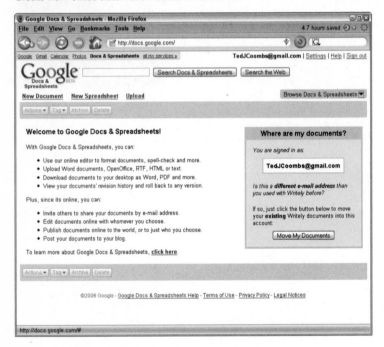

Creating a Document

Google uses the term *document* to refer specifically to a word processing document, as compared to a spreadsheet. Begin a new document by clicking the New Document link at the top of the Google Docs Web page, or when you are currently editing a document, select New from the File menu. Doing either of these launches a new, empty document.

 **You may have more than one document open at the same time.**

When you first launch the document, a new browser window opens. The document is given the temporary name of "untitled", which appears in the upper-left corner. As soon as a draft of the document is auto-saved by Google, it is given the temporary name of the first text you've typed into the document. Changing that text will not change the temporary name with the next auto-save. To rename the document you must manually choose Rename from the File menu.

Editing Documents

Begin creating your document by placing content in the large document area. Content can be text that you type or copy and paste into the document. It can also include graphics, Internet hyperlinks, tables, book-marks, separators, and special characters. Most of the time, you simply type text from your keyboard into the document. All of the same keyboard keys, such as Backspace, Delete, Shift, Page Up, and Page Down all work the same as in any other word processing program. By default, the text you type appears in the Verdana font. It's widely used and becoming the new "Times New Roman" made popular by Microsoft.

Check the spelling at any time by clicking the <u>Check Spelling</u> link at the bottom-right corner of the page. Misspelled words are highlighted in orange. You can correct the spelling and click the <u>Recheck</u> link that appears in place of the <u>Check Spelling</u> link, or click the <u>Done</u> link to remove the highlighting of any misspelled or unknown words.

As you enter text into your document, you may want to format it, remove or change formatting, or enter page breaks and special characters. These features and more are available using the toolbar displayed across the top of the document. Read the next section to learn about the toolbar.

Using the toolbar

The toolbar, located across the top of each document, contains icons representing most of the features you'll use while editing your document. If you are unsure of an icon's meaning, place your mouse over the icon without clicking and a pop-up appears that tells you the function performed by clicking the icon.

In Figure 18.2, the Edit tab toolbar icons from left to right across the top of the page are as follows:

- **Undo last edit:** Restores your last edit to its original state
- **Redo last edit:** Restores an edit that was previously undone with Undo last edit
- **Cut:** Removes selected text or image and copies it to the clipboard
- **Copy:** Copies selected text or image to the clipboard
- **Paste:** Places clipboard contents into the document at the cursor
- **Bold:** Causes new or selected text to appear in Bold
- **Italics:** Causes new or selected text to be formatted as italics
- **Underline:** Causes new or selected text to appear underlined
- **Font change:** Allows you to change the font face of new or selected text
- **Font size change:** Allows you to change the font size of new or selected text
- **Font color change:** Changes the color of new or selected text
- **Highlighter (text background change):** Changes the background color of new or selected text
- **Hyperlink:** Creates a hyperlink in the document
- **Numbered list format:** Creates a numbered list so that items are auto-numbered

- **Bullet list format:** Creates a bullet list so that each line is auto-bulleted
- **Indent less:** Moves indented text to the left one tab space
- **Indent more:** Moves indented text to the right one tab space
- **Quote:** Formats text as a quote, indenting it and placing it in a box
- **Left align text:** Aligns text along the left margin
- **Center align text:** Centers text
- **Right align text:** Aligns text along the right margin
- **Remove Formatting:** Removes formatting

FIGURE 18.2

The Edit toolbar is similar to other word processors.

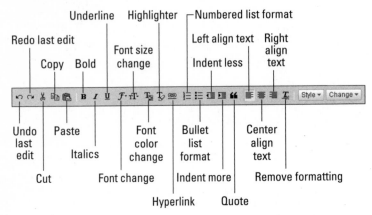

Most of the editing tools can be applied by clicking the icon and typing. Click the icon again when you no longer want that feature or formatting applied to your text. You can also select the text by first dragging across it with your mouse and then clicking the icon one time to apply that text enhancement.

To remove the formatting, you can select the formatted text and click the formatting icon of the feature you want removed, and the formatting is reversed. You can also select the formatted text and click the special Remove Formatting icon to the far right side of the toolbar to removes all formatting. For example, if the text is bold, italicized, and underlined, one click on the Remove Formatting icon returns the text to its standard, unembellished appearance.

The toolbar also contains two drop-down menus. The Style drop-down menu allows you to select preset styles to your text for fast and consistent formatting. The Change drop-down menu allows you to restore or remove blank lines and manage bookmarks.

Selecting a style

Styles are named, preconfigured formatting that you can apply to your document text. For example, if you want huge bold text to appear as a page heading or paragraph heading, you no longer need to apply both the Font Size and Bold formatting. Click anywhere in the line of text you want formatted, and then click the Style drop-down menu next to the toolbar and select a style. In this example, Header 1 (Huge) is used.

This is Header 1

You can apply styles to entire documents, paragraphs, words, or characters. Clicking anywhere in a paragraph and applying a style changes the style for the entire paragraph. Be aware that although most of the formatting you've already applied within the paragraph will be preserved, some may be changed by the new style. You can also select text by highlighting it applying the style only to the selected text.

NOTE Many word processing programs allow you to create custom styles. Google Docs documents do not support custom styles. Text formatted with a custom style appears in the Google Docs normal style, and all formatting is removed.

Google Docs offers five Paragraph formatting styles and five Page Spacing styles that control line spacing, such as single space, space and a half, double-space, and triple-space. There are also four Text formatting styles that include strikeout, superscript, subscript, and a special menu selection to remove formatting with a function identical to the Remove Formatting icon in the toolbar.

Using the document editor menu

The Google Docs document editor includes a menu consisting of a drop-down File menu and three tabs: Edit, Insert, and Revisions. The Edit tab is normally active when you edit your document. You can edit your document in the Insert tab, but the toolbar is replaced by selections you can insert into your document, such as:

- **Image:** Insert a graphic image you've uploaded.
- **Link:** Insert a clickable hyperlink.
- **Comment:** Insert a comment.
- **Table:** Insert a custom table.
- **Bookmark:** Insert a bookmark.
- **Separator:** Insert either a page break or horizontal line.
- **Special character:** Insert a nonalphabetic or foreign alphabetic character.

Here's something difficult to do in other word-processing software programs. You can review your document's revision history and roll back to a previous version. Click the Revisions tab. Your document with revisions highlighted appears. Select a revision from the drop-down list to view a previous revision of your document. This is a great feature if you carefully format your document and then suddenly, you accidentally apply formatting that affects the entire document, deleted half of the text, or turned it all blue. You can easily step backward and restore your document to its former state.

The File drop-down menu in Figure 18.3 contains selections that let you create a new document, save the current document in a number of different formats, copy the document, rename it, print it, count the number of words (useful for homework assignments), and use Find & Replace functions.

TIP You can use the familiar Windows Ctrl+S shortcut to quickly save your document.

FIGURE 18.3

The File menu is available in all the tabs.

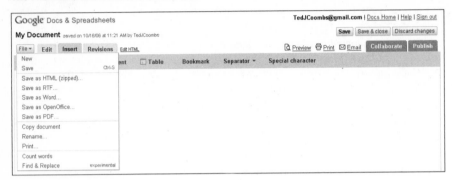

Edit HTML

The Edit HTML link is next to the Revisions tab along the top of the document. Click this link to see and edit the underlying HTML code for the document you are creating. Here is an example of the HTML code you might see:

```
this is the edit interface<br/>
<span style="COLOR:#ff6666">this is pink text<br/>
</span><span style="COLOR:#ff6666"></span>
<h1> this is huge text<br/> </h1>
```

When you finish with the HTML view, click the Back to editing the document link to return to the normal WYSIWYG (What You See Is What You Get) editor.

Preview

Preview the document as others might see it by clicking the Preview link or icon to the right of the tabs. Your document appears without the Google Docs editor interface. This is what others who view your document will see. If others are allowed to edit your document (collaborators), they can click the link that appears below the document. You can give others permission to edit your documents. You learn more about that later in the chapter.

Print

Click the Print link on the right side of the page to print your document. A copy of your document is sent to your local computer's print queue for printing. The normal printer dialog box appears allowing you to select a printer and set any print preferences before printing the document.

Email

Before you can e-mail a document, it must be shared. Clicking the Email link sends a copy of the document to one of the collaborators with whom you are sharing a document. If the document has not been shared, Google Docs prompts you to share the document first and launches the Collaborate on this document interface.

Collaborating with others

One of the great things about Google Docs is the ability to share your documents with other people without compromising the security of your own computer. You can invite collaborators to edit or merely view your document, whether it's a completed work or a work in progress.

A notice that no one else is editing the document appears in very light print at the bottom of the document. When you add others to collaborate with you, an orange bar appears at the bottom of the document containing the names of the other people who are working on your document. To add collaborators follow these steps:

1. Click the <u>Add collaborators</u> link at the bottom of the document.
2. Enter the e-mail addresses of the people you want to collaborate with in editing your document, or invite people to view your document by entering their e-mail addresses in the Invite **Viewers** box.
3. Click **Invite these people**.

When you choose to invite either a collaborator or a viewer, an e-mail message is sent to each person containing a link to the document, an invitation to view or collaborate on the document, and a personal message you can include before the e-mail is sent, as shown in Figure 18.4.

 Be aware that collaborators can invite other people to collaborate on the same document.

Collaborators can view and make changes to your document. They can also add and remove other collaborators, except for the document owner. They can also add additional viewers to the document. Viewers are people who can see the document but cannot make changes. Viewers cannot add collaborators or other viewers.

FIGURE 18.4

Send a personal message to people you invite to view or edit your document.

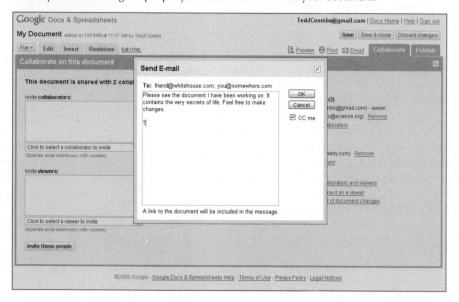

Publishing your document

Click the Publish tab on the far right of the document editor to publish a copy of the document on the Internet for anyone to view. Google gives you a unique URL that points to this document. You can then send this link to others in e-mail or create a link from another Web page — perhaps your home page — to this published document.

Next, click Publish document as shown in Figure 18.5. Your document is made available on the Web with a unique URL displayed for you. Make note of this URL because in the future, when you click Publish, your changes to this document will be published to this URL address. You can also send this link to others to view or edit your document.

FIGURE 18.5

Publish your document to the Web or post it to your blog.

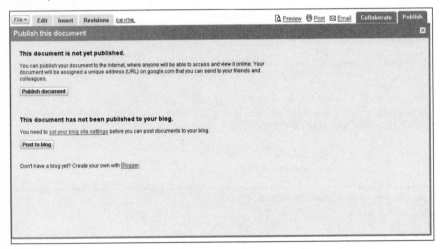

You can also publish documents directly to your blog. Click the set your blog site settings link to tell Google Docs how to post to your blog. If you don't have a blog yet, you can create one on Google's Blogger by clicking the Blogger link at the bottom of the page.

Saving the document

In the top-right corner of the Google Docs editor are three buttons: Save, Save & close, and Discard changes. These buttons allow you to immediately save changes to your document or disregard all the changes and revert to the previous saved version. The following sections describe the differences between the three options.

Save

There are four ways to save your edited document to the storage space on Google. The first is the simplest: do nothing. If you do nothing long enough, the auto-save feature automatically saves your document. If you have made changes since the last auto-save, you can roll back your changes using the Revisions tab. The next way to save changes is nearly as simple: click Save in the upper-right portion of the Google Docs editor window. The third way is to simply press Ctrl+S on your keyboard. Lastly, the only two-step process is to choose File and click Save.

To save your document to your computer in one of several formats, choose the File. The menu selections include:

- Save as HTML (Zipped)
- Save as RTF
- Save as Word
- Save as OpenOffice
- Save as PDF

Selecting one of these menu choices converts the document into the selected format and immediately begins to download this file to your local computer. Your file download is handled by your normal computer file download configuration. It may download to a default download folder, or you may be able to select a location for it to be saved.

 The auto-save feature continually saves a draft of your document. You can see the date and time of the last save in the upper-left portion of the page.

Save & close

It's midnight. The caffeine buzz has worn off, and the neon light outside your motel window flickers incessantly; it's time to sleep. While you know Google has been faithfully saving your life's work, you don't feel safe leaving it open on your laptop. Who knows when the housekeeping crew might really be spies. It's time to save the document and close it. Of course, you could just close the Web browser, but to be certain your last sparks of brilliance added in the last minute are saved, click Save & close. To be extra careful, log out of your Google account!

Discard changes

The fastest way to abandon all the edits you've just made without stepping through all the revisions is to click Discard changes. Your document reverts to its last *purposefully* saved revision. Purposefully saving means you clicked Save, Save & close, pressed Ctrl+S, or selected Save from the File menu.

Working with the context menu

Right-clicking within the document launches a context menu. All the menu selections in the context menu are availably by clicking icons in the toolbar. Sometimes it's just faster to use the context menu, rather than mousing up to the toolbar. The context menu choices are listed in Table 18.1.

TABLE 18.1

Document Context Menu Selections

Menu Choice	Action
Cut	Remove selected text or image and copy it to the clipboard.
Copy	Copy selected text or image and copy it to the clipboard.
Paste	Place clipboard contents into the document at the cursor location.
Select All	Selects all objects, such as text and graphics, highlighting it.
Insert Image	Insert an image into the document at the cursor location.
Insert Link	Insert a hyperlink into the document at the cursor location.
Insert Bookmark	Insert a bookmark into the document at the cursor location.
Insert Comment	Insert a comment into the document at the cursor location.
Insert Page break	Insert a page break into the document at the cursor location, ending one page and starting another.
Horizontal Line	Insert a graphic horizontal line the width of the page at the cursor location.
Insert Special Character	Insert a special character, such as an ascii text character, into the document at the cursor location.

Using bookmarks

You can mark blocks of text and name them, creating future links. Technically, in HTML-speak, this is an *anchor*. Bookmarks are handy ways to identify places in large documents that are referred to often, contain important quotes, need to be edited, or are just interesting enough to deserve a name of their own. Use bookmarks for creating an electronic table of contents (TOC) to your document. Clicking the TOC item takes you to that place in the document.

To create a bookmark:

1. Click the Insert tab.
2. Click Bookmark from the toolbar. This launches the Insert Bookmark dialog box where you are prompted to type a name for your new bookmark.
3. Type a bookmark name. You are also shown a list of the previously entered bookmarks. Selecting bookmarks from the list allows you to also click Remove to delete them from the document.

Use the bookmarks you create by creating links to them. When you insert a link into your document, select the Bookmark radio button from the list of items to which you can link. Type a descriptive phrase for your link — any flyover text you want — and click OK. Clicking this link causes your document to scroll to the bookmark.

NOTE Remember to remove any links to your bookmark when you remove the bookmarked text.

Crunching Numbers with Google Spreadsheet

The spreadsheet was one of the very first PC computer applications. More than 25 years ago, the first PC programmers thought that one of the most important programs they could write would be a spreadsheet. They are just as important today, and considerable functionality has been added to them since then.

To create a new spreadsheet, click the <u>New Spreadsheet</u> link from the Google Docs main page (`http://docs.google.com`). This launches a blank spreadsheet as shown in Figure 18.6. By default, you are placed in the first sheet with the Edit tab selected. You can begin adding information to the empty cells. Each spreadsheet can have more than one sheet. To add a new sheet to an existing spreadsheet, click Add Sheet in the lower-left corner of the page.

Change the order of the sheets in your spreadsheet document by first clicking on the sheet you want to move, and then selecting Move Right or Move Left. The popup menu allows you to rename or delete individual sheets.

FIGURE 18.6

Keeping your spreadsheets on Google lets you maintain them remotely.

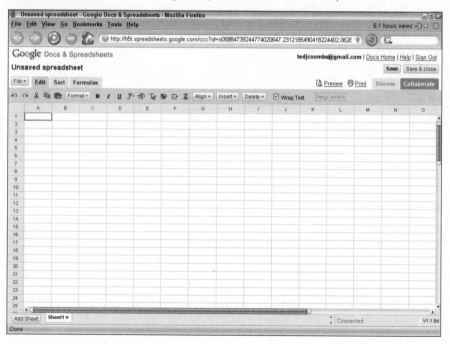

In addition to creating spreadsheets on the Google Docs site, you can also import spreadsheets in Excel (XLS), Comma Separated Value (CSV), and OpenOffice (ODS) formats.

Typing alpha (nonnumeric) text in the cell causes it to automatically align to the left of the cell. Numeric data is automatically aligned to the right. While both alpha text and numeric data can be sorted, only numeric data can be used in formulas, such as adding columns of numbers.

Using the Spreadsheet toolbar

The spreadsheet editor, like the document editor, has a toolbar along the top of the sheet as shown in Figure 18.7. The items in the toolbar, from left to right, are:

- **Undo last edit:** Restores your last edit to its original state
- **Redo last edit:** Restores an edit that was previously undone with Undo last edit
- **Cut:** Removes selected text or image and copies it to the clipboard
- **Copy:** Copies selected text or images to the clipboard
- **Paste:** Places clipboard contents into the document at the cursor
- **Format:** Formats the way numbers and dates in the cell are displayed
- **Bold:** Causes new or selected text to appear in Bold
- **Italics:** Causes new or selected text to be formatted as italics
- **Underline:** Causes new or selected text to appear underlined
- **Font change:** Allows you to change the font face of new or selected text
- **Font size change:** Allows you to change the font size of new or selected text.
- **Font color change:** Changes the color of new or selected text
- **Background Color:** Changes the background color of new or selected text
- **Borders:** Customizes cell and spreadsheet borders
- **Remove formatting:** Discards previous current formatting
- **Align:** Selects a horizontal and vertical alignment for information within a cell
- **Insert:** Inserts rows and columns
- **Delete:** Deletes a row of cells, a column of cells, or clears a selection without deleting the cells
- **Wrap text:** Selects whether to wrap text within a cell
- **Merge Across:** Merges data between sheets

Sorting

You can sort data in your sheet by selecting the columns of data (you can sort columns of information, not rows) and clicking the Sort tab. Choose whether you want data sorted from lowest to highest (ascending) (A ⇨ Z) or highest to lowest (descending) (Z ⇨ A) by clicking the corresponding button in the toolbar. Numeric data is sorted in ascending or descending order also be clicking these same buttons. Determine which column is used to sort the data by clicking on any cell in that column. You will see the Sort sheet by Column message along the top of the sheet change as you click in different columns.

To identify and freeze column headers so they are not sorted along with the data, click the Freeze header row drop-down list and select how many rows of data to freeze. You can choose from 0 rows to 5.

FIGURE 18.7

Use the toolbar items to easily edit your spreadsheet.

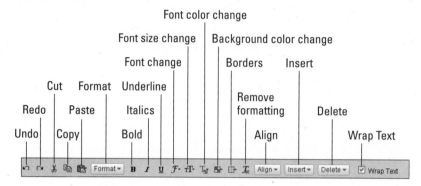

Using formulas

Like other spreadsheet programs, the Google Docs spreadsheet enables you to enter formulas that perform functions on your data. The types of functions include:

- **Math:** Perform math, trigonometry, and important functions like rounding, creating a random number, and more.
- **Financial:** Perform financial functions such as interest calculations and many more
- **Logical:** Perform Boolean logic calculations using AND, OR, IF, NOT, OR, and TRUE.
- **Date:** Perform date arithmetic and access your computer or network clock for current time and date.
- **Lookup:** Perform lookup functions on lists of textual data.
- **Statistical:** Perform the magic of statistics using these functions.
- **Text:** Manipulate text strings using these many text functions.
- **Info:** Get information about your data and calculations using these functions, most of which return a logical TRUE or FALSE.

Each formula type accepts a particular type of data. For example, the Info formula (`ISEVEN()`) can be entered into a cell preceded by the equal sign and with a value or cell address entered in the parentheses as a parameter like `=ISEVEN(7)`. The value included in the parens is evaluated to determine whether it is even. The result is TRUE or FALSE. This, of course, displays the word FALSE in the cell. This is not a text entry, but a Boolean entry that can be used in Boolean calculations using the Logical formulas.

> **TIP** Use the Info formula `ERROR.TYPE` to determine what error has occurred and display an error message.

The Text formulas operate on textual data. For example, when cell D5 contains the text "My country tis of thee" using the `LEFT()` text formula, entering the cell address and the number of characters from the left to extract `=LEFT(D5,2)` returns "My."

Click the More link to see a list of all the formulas. Selecting a formula from the Insert a Function dialog box inserts the function into the cell identified by the mouse cursor and displays the syntax of the formula in the bottom of the dialog box. For help on that formula or all formulas, click the <u>more</u> link at the bottom of the dialog box. This launches a page with a complete description of all the supported formulas.

Saving your spreadsheet

Like documents, spreadsheets are automatically saved on a regular basis. The Save button in the upper right only becomes active when an auto-save has not already taken place. Otherwise, the button is disabled and reads Automatically Saved.

To close the spreadsheet and save it at the same time, click Save & close in the upper-right corner.

Exporting to your local computer

Spreadsheets can be saved to your local hard drive by exporting the data you're your files in Google Docs. Export them as CSV, HTML, ODS, PDF, or XLS files. You can then use applications on your computer, such as Excel, Acrobat reader, or your Web browser to read or edit the files depending on the file type you've selected.

Collaborating and discussing

Invite collaborators or viewers of your spreadsheet just as described in the document section. Click the Collaborate tab (see Figure 18.8) and type the e-mail addresses of new collaborators and viewers, or select existing people from the list. Click Invite these people to launch a dialog box allowing you to personalize the e-mail that you send to your invitees.

FIGURE 18.8

Collaborate with others while building your spreadsheet.

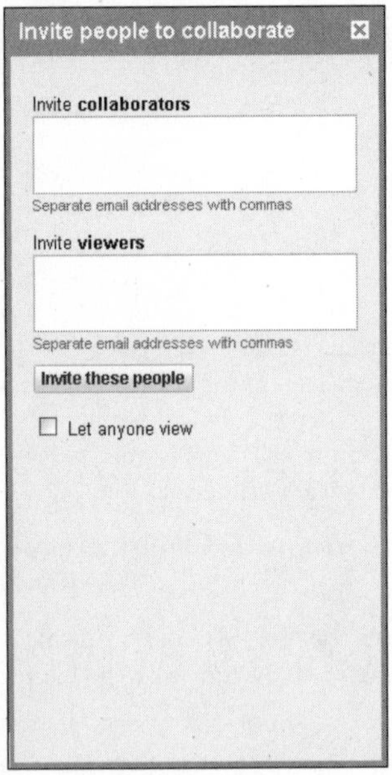

You can see a list of collaborators at the bottom of the Collaborate tab. Click the <u>Turn off</u> link to keep your invited collaborators from inviting other collaborators.

Chatting with collaborators

Chat in real time with others who edit your spreadsheet. When collaborators log in to their Google Docs account and edit your document, you see them in the list displayed in the Discuss tab. Chat with them by typing messages in the text box at the bottom of the tab and press Enter to send the message. Your conversation appears in the chat box. You can chat with several people editing the spreadsheet simultaneously.

Publishing your spreadsheet

Like documents, you can publish your spreadsheet to the Web for everyone to view. The terminology and the way you do it are slightly different, but the result is exactly the same. At the bottom of the Collaboration tab is a "Let anyone view" checkbox. Selecting this checkbox causes Google Docs to publish this sheet to the Web, giving you the URL right next to the checkbox.

Using the Google Docs File Manager

The Google Docs main page displays all of your saved documents and spreadsheets and allows you to manage them (see Figure 18.9). From this page, you can:

- Open a file for editing.
- See who the owners, collaborators, and viewers are for each file.
- See the file type identified with an icon representing either a document or spreadsheet. Save/Export the file in the corresponding supported formats.
- See when the file was last edited and by whom.
- Create new documents and spreadsheets.
- Upload documents and spreadsheets from your computer to Google Docs.
- Take actions on, tag, archive/un-archive, and delete selected files.

FIGURE 18.9

All your saved documents and spreadsheets are listed on the Google Docs main page.

Actions

You can take *actions*, which are processes such as saving and copying, on one or more selected files. Select a file in the list by clicking the checkbox next to the file icon. Click the Actions menu drop-down. The actions you can take differ between documents and spreadsheets. The only allowed actions for spreadsheets are Star and Un-star. Placing a star on a document merely calls attention to it for your sake. It does not change the file in any manner. Sometimes it's easy to place a star in front of files that need your attention or to call attention to files for collaborators.

Documents have a larger number of allowed actions. You can save the documents to your local computer by selecting Save as, and a document type. You can select Copy document, Star, Un-star, and Un-collaborate me to remove all collaborator access to this document.

Tag

You can quickly organize your documents and spreadsheets by giving them a *tag*, a descriptive word or phrase attached to the file description. Because your files are not organized into folders, tagging them is the best way of viewing all related files. For example, perhaps you are working on a proposal that involves multiple documents and spreadsheets. Label them all with the name of the proposal you are working on. This places a green link with the tag name next to each filename. Clicking on any of the links changes the file display to only files matching that tag. You can easily return to the view of all active files by clicking the Back to Active documents link at the top of the page.

To tag a file, first select a file from the list of files. Then, select New Tag from the Tag drop-down menu that appears above or below the file list. Type a new tag name or select a previously created tag name from the list, and click OK.

Creating multiple tags

Create multiple tags and apply them simultaneously by selecting Multiple Tags from the Tag menu. You are prompted to type new tag names, separated by commas. Clicking OK tags each of the selected files with all the tags you created in this step.

Removing tags

Remove tags by selecting a tagged file and clicking the Tag menu. Beneath the Remove Tag: selection is a list of tags to remove. Click the tag name and it is removed from all selected files.

Archiving old files

When you finish working with a file and no longer need to see it in your list of active files, archive it. This is not the same as deleting it. Instead, archived files no longer appear in the list of active files. Here's how you archive a file:

1. Select the file by selecting the checkbox next to the file icon. You can archive multiple files by selecting more than one file.
2. Click Archive. Files immediately disappear from your active file list.

To view archived files, click the View all link to the right of the page. All files are displayed. You can browse them by type by clicking Browse Docs & Spreadsheets. Once you click the View all link, the Archive button changes to Unarchive. Select an archived file and click Unarchive to return the file to your list of Active files.

Deleting your documents

You can delete both documents and spreadsheets in the Google Docs main page. Select the document or spreadsheet to be deleted by selecting the checkbox to the left of the file icon. Next, click Delete in the bar across the top or bottom of the page.

Deleted documents are transferred to the Deleted Docs and Spreadsheet folder. Published versions of the file also disappear. You can view the list of deleted items by clicking the Browse Docs & Spreadsheets drop-down menu and then selecting Deleted. Undelete files by selecting them from the list and clicking Undelete.

 **Files in the Trash are still available to collaborators. You may choose to remove all the collaborators when deleting a file or the file becomes unavailable when you empty the Trash.**

To permanently remove all deleted files, click Empty Trash. This button is found in the bottom bar when viewing deleted files. Permanently removed files are removed from Google Docs and no longer available for collaborative editing.

Important Information

Here is some important information about some of the limitations and requirements when using Google Docs. Each document can be up to 500KB in size. Each image you embed in a document can be up to 2MB in size.

Each spreadsheet can have up to 10,000 rows up to 256 columns with a maximum of 50,000 cells or up to 20 sheets, whichever limit is reached first.

You can import spreadsheets up to 1MB in size in either XLS or ODF format.

Supported browsers and minimum versions include:

- IE 6.0 or greater.
- Firefox 1.07. There are issues with versions 1.08. It's best to use at least the most current version, which at the time of this book is version 1.5.0.7.
- Mozilla 1.7.12 and greater.
- Netscape 7.2, 8.0.

Your browser must have cookies and JavaScript enabled to use Google Docs. Sorry, but Google Docs does not run using the Opera or Safari browsers.

Summary

Google Docs allows you to use some of the most widely used office automation tools freely on the Web. There are other free office tools, like those offered by OpenOffice, but Google Docs gives you access to instant Internet file publishing, collaboration, and communication features that are not available in other software.

Easily transfer your word processing documents and spreadsheets to Google Docs for editing, publishing, archiving, and collaboration with others. Create new documents and spreadsheets and save them in a number of popular formats, including PDF. Integrating these two popular tools with the Internet fits in well with Google's Gmail, which is discussed in the next chapter.

Part II

Communicating Google-Style

Chapter 19

Staying in Touch with Gmail

Never throw anything away! That is the goal of Gmail, Google's Web-based e-mail program. Imagine never having to erase another e-mail and later being able to simply search through all your old e-mail. There are many Web-based e-mail providers out there, but Google is adding something new to one of the most important applications to run over the Internet.

Internet communications have become more like conversations than the older idea of postal mail. Gmail organizes your e-mail as it would appear in a real-time conversation — it's more like chat than mail.

The important feature of Gmail is storage. The reason it is not necessary to delete any of your old e-mail is that it is difficult to ever fill up all the free storage space given to Gmail users. You can store files, pictures, and nearly an unlimited number of e-mail messages on the Google servers. At the time of writing of this book, users are offered 2.5 gigabytes (GB) of free storage.

Deciding to Use Gmail

Switching e-mail programs is often a big decision. E-mail has become such an important part of the way that we communicate with others that we have come to expect e-mail software to act and perform in a certain way. When checking your e-mail, you shouldn't have to think too much about the software you are using to read, respond to, and compose new e-mail messages.

When deciding to use Gmail (http://gmail.google.com) for your e-mail rather than another Web-based e-mail program, you should consider some of the features. These features can include important things such as the amount of online storage offered or the compatibility of the Web-based e-mail program with your preferred Web browser, or less important things such as the ability to customize the user interface of the Web e-mail program. Gmail's interface is currently not customizable, where Yahoo allows you to have message stationary and

MSN/Hotmail allows you to customize your interface with nine different color schemes. Yahoo and MSN/Hotmail also have drag-and-drop message interfaces where Gmail does not. But while these features are incidental, nice-to-have features, the core program is where Gmail excels.

Online storage

The amount of storage space on the server for your e-mail is an important consideration when choosing among Web-based e-mail programs. Certainly you will want an e-mail service provider that gives you plenty of storage space or you will need to begin erasing old e-mails and lose important historical information. Because Google's idea is to increase your ability to maintain historical information rather than removing old e-mail, it was important to offer more storage space. Here is a comparison of the top Web-based e-mail programs:

- **Gmail:** 2.65GB
- **MSN/Hotmail:** 2GB
- **Yahoo Mail:** 1GB

You can see from this list that a Gmail account gives you the ability to save e-mail for a very long time. Storage space is considered a technical advantage and therefore these amounts are always changing, each one trying to outdo the other. So, watch for higher storage capacities in the future.

Compatibility

Because Web-based programs rely on the features of Web browsers to make them work, it is important to select an e-mail program that works with the browser you use. For a long time, the main browser of choice was Microsoft's Internet Explorer (IE). Other browsers have gained importance as they have developed additional features. Many people are switching to Firefox for Windows, Mac and Linux installations, and some to Opera on the Macintosh.

When selecting a Web-based e-mail program, you don't want to sacrifice your choice in browsers to make the switch. This means that selecting the Web-based e-mail program that operates with your browser is important. Table 19.1 gives you the browser compatibility comparisons among the various Web-based e-mail programs.

TABLE 19.1

Browser E-mail Compatibility

E-mail Program	Compatible Web Browsers
Gmail	IE v5.5+, Firefox, Opera, Netscape, Safari
Yahoo Mail	IE v5.5+, Firefox, Opera
MSN/Hotmail	IE v6.0+ *

* Basic features will run in other browsers.

Gmail Features

The last section compares Gmail with two other popular Web-based e-mail programs. There are features that are unique to Gmail and certainly provide a strong reason to select and use Gmail for all your e-mail needs. A big feature internationally is being able to use Gmail in your own language.

In your language

Like many Google services, Gmail is available in 36 languages; 38 if you count American and the United Kingdom's English, simplified and traditional Chinese as different languages. Other languages available include Bulgarian, Catalan, Croatian, Czech, Danish, Dutch, Estonian, Finnish, French, German, Greek, Hindi, Hungarian, Icelandic, Indonesian, Italian, Japanese, Korean, Latvian, Lithuanian, Polish, Portuguese, Romanian, Russian, Serbian, Slovak, Slovenian, Spanish, Swedish, Tagalog, Thai, Turkish, Ukrainian, and Vietnamese. Gmail not only allows you to view the Gmail interface in these other languages, it also has spell-check capability in at least 30 languages.

 Google Gmail does not accept executable programs (.exe extension) as attachments.

Forwarding and POP features

The two Web-based e-mail programs that have forwarding and POP features are Gmail and Yahoo Mail. The ability to forward messages means that you can receive e-mail in your Web-based mail program and choose to automatically forward the messages to another e-mail account, perhaps a corporate account that you want to keep private.

The POP feature allows you to check and manage Gmail using a different e-mail client such as Thunderbird or Outlook. POP (Post Office Protocol) servers are e-mail servers your software contacts to retrieve e-mail.

Rich text e-mail

People have become accustomed to the ability to format their e-mail messages using rich text, the kind of text formatting found in word processing software. Gmail offers this type of formatting in Web-based e-mail. You can now use features such as font changes, color text, indenting, bullet and number lists, and more.

Never send a boring e-mail message again. E-mail written in rich text is sent as HTML, readable by most modern e-mail programs and Web-based e-mail programs.

Setting up an E-mail Account

When you decide that Gmail is the e-mail program for you, there are a few things you need to check to be certain that you are ready for a Gmail installation. After that, getting started with Gmail is quite simple.

What you need to get started

Gmail is a Web-based program, so it is not necessary to install any new software on your computer. If you can access the World Wide Web using one of the more popular Web browsers, you already have everything it takes. No other software setup is required. You need one of the following Web browsers installed on your computer to get started.

- Microsoft Internet Explorer version 5.5 or greater for use only on a Windows computer
- Netscape version 7.1 or greater
- Mozilla version 1.4 or greater
- Mozilla Firefox version 0.8 or greater
- Safari version 1.2 or greater for use only on a Macintosh computer

If you do not already have one or more of these programs installed on your computer please refer to the Resources Section of this book for more information about where to download one of these programs.

Signing up

There are presently two ways to sign up for a Gmail account. You either need an invitation to sign up for Gmail from someone that currently has a Gmail account or sign up by having Google send an invitation to your cell phone as a text message. When someone sends you an invitation, click the invitation link in the e-mail you receive. When messages come as text messages on your cell phone, you are provided an Invitation Code, which you enter on the Gmail signup page (`https://www.google.com/accounts/SmsMailSignup2`).

FIGURE 19.1

After you sign up, Gmail welcomes you with a special one-time-only welcome page.

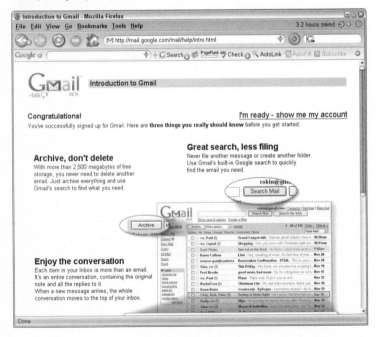

When you click the I'm ready - show me my account link displayed in Figure 19.1, the next page appears, which lets you know that you can now chat using Google Talk while using Gmail. On this page, notice an important selection for setting up the Google Talk feature within Gmail. Select between saving your chat history and not saving your chat history. If you are concerned about others discovering the content of your chats it's recommended that you select the Don't save chat history option. By default, the Save chat history option is selected. If keeping a record of your chats is important choose the Save chat history option. Remember, your chat history is indexed by the Google Desktop program when you have that installed. This easily gives you access to your chat through keyword searches from the Google Desktop software.

Speaking of easy, an easy way of accessing your Gmail account is to add Gmail to the Google Toolbar in your Web browser (see Figure 19.2).

FIGURE 19.2

Add Gmail to the Google Toolbar.

When you select your chat history save option, click Sweet! Go to my inbox >>. Your Gmail inbox appears, probably containing a couple of welcome e-mail messages from the folks at Google.

Switching to Gmail

One of the most important concerns when switching e-mail programs is maintaining your current e-mail messages and contacts. If you are like most people, contacts are very important. Rebuilding the contact list from scratch is nearly impossible, or at least time consuming and difficult. Some programs, such as Microsoft Outlook, also manage information resources like your calendar. These can be exported and many of them imported into either Gmail or some other Google service.

CROSS-REF   See Chapter 26 to learn about importing events into Google Calendar.

Import your contacts

Most e-mail programs allow you to export your contacts in CSV (Comma Separated Value) format. Some programs offer several different export formats; but when exporting so that you can import into Gmail you will want to select the CSV format. Save the exported CSV file to a place on your hard drive where you know where to find it during the import process. It is common for some e-mail programs to select the export folder for you, and then it takes forever to find the export file. Therefore, knowing where the export file is saved is an important step.

Once you have an exported file in CSV format you can begin the importing process into Gmail. Follow these steps:

1. Launch Gmail and log in to your account.
2. Look along the left side of the page, and find and click the Contacts link. This launches the Contacts page.

3. In the upper-right corner click the <u>Import</u> link. This launches the Import Contacts page in a new browser window.

4. Type the path to the exported CSV file in the File to import: text box, or click Browse and locate the file, and the path is added automatically.

5. Click Import Contacts.

When the process is complete the Import Contacts window reports how many contacts were imported into Gmail. When you are satisfied that the import is successful, click the <u>Close</u> link and the Import Contacts windows disappears. In the Contacts page, click the All Contacts tab to verify that your import is successful. You may notice that some of the information doesn't map correctly between contact programs, and some information may be wrong or missing. You may have to correct this manually by editing the contact in Gmail.

Announcing your new Gmail address

Once you import your contacts into Gmail you will want to let people know about your new e-mail address. The way to do this is to open your Contacts list and select everyone you want to notify. Here's how:

1. Launch Gmail and log in to your account.

2. Along the left side of the page locate and click the <u>Contacts</u> link.

3. Select each contact by selecting the checkbox next to the contact name. You can select all contacts by clicking the <u>All</u> link at the bottom of the <u>Contacts</u> link. You may want to send a private, individual message to each contact.

4. Click Compose. This launches the compose e-mail form.

5. Write a letter to your contacts and include your new Gmail e-mail address.

6. Click Send.

NOTE When selecting more than one contact and composing an e-mail message, all of the contact e-mail addresses are listed in the e-mail you send to everyone. This is often considered a breach of privacy, and many people would prefer not to be sent e-mail messages listing multiple people.

Add another email address to Gmail

Gmail is a great way to manage all of your email. Use the Gmail interface with more than one e-mail address. To add a new e-mail address to Gmail, just follow these steps

1. Click the <u>Settings</u> link next to your login name along the top of the page. This launches your Gmail Settings page.

2. Click the Accounts tab.

3. Below where you see your Gmail e-mail address displayed, click the <u>Add another email address</u> link. This launches a new window containing the Add another e-mail address form.

4. Type your name and the e-mail address you want to add.

5. Optionally click the <u>Specify a different "reply-to" address</u> link

6. Click Next Step >>.

Gmail will want to send a verification e-mail to be sure you are not trying to masquerade by using someone else's e-mail address (spoofing). When you receive the e-mail, type the Verification Code.

Setting Up Your Contacts

The quick way to add contacts to your Gmail contact list is by importing them from another program. Importing contacts is covered in the "Switching to Gmail" section earlier in this chapter. You can add contacts individually by clicking the <u>Contacts</u> link located on the left side of the page. In the text box that appears, type the e-mail address of your new contact. This launches the contact management form.

Creating a new contact

Click the <u>Create Contact</u> link at the top of the form to create a new contact. Fill in the name of the contact, the primary e-mail address, and any notes you want to keep about this person. You can also specify a photo for this person or choose to view a photo of his or her choosing. When you specify a photo, you need to locate it on your hard drive and upload it to the Google server. If the photo is too large, a cropping window appears above the photo. You can choose to crop this image by moving the cropping window to the area of the photo you want to display or by choosing to discard this photo and selecting another, smaller image.

To include additional contact information, such as the person's address and telephone number, click the <u>add more contact info</u> link when adding a new contact. This link appears below the person's optional display photo. Clicking this link expands the contact information.

Managing fields and sections

You can create your own contact format by choosing the information you want to add in each field. Select a label from the drop-down list. The field labels include:

- **Email:** Adds a secondary e-mail address. The primary e-mail address was already entered.
- **IM:** Include an instant messenger contact name.
- **Phone:** Telephone number.
- **Mobile:** Mobile or cell phone number.
- **Pager:** Do people still use these?
- **Fax:** It won't be long until these are a thing of the past.
- **Company:** Name of the company in which the contact is employed.
- **Title:** The contact's title within the company.
- **Other:** Add custom information.

To add additional fields, click the <u>add another field</u> link. A new field is inserted into your contact form. Select a label for the new field by choosing one from the drop-down list.

> **TIP** Once you add a field it cannot be removed. You will need to remove the section (see the following) and add the fields back.

The default sections are Personal and Work. You can choose to rename these sections simply by overwriting the current section names, or you can add new sections by clicking the <u>add section</u> link at the bottom of the contact form. The default name for the new section is Other. You can choose to keep that section title or change it by overwriting it (highlighting the word and typing over it). You can add additional fields to each new section you add.

Remove sections by simply clicking the <u>remove section</u> link in the corresponding section.

Contact management

The Contact form has three tabs, Frequently Mailed, All Contacts and Groups. The Frequently mailed tab contains a list of the people you have mailed regularly. The list contains the name of the person, their email address and a selection allowing you to manage whether each contact appears in your Quick Contacts list in the left pane of the Gmail window. The selections include: Always, Auto, Never and Block.

Import contacts into the Contact management by clicking the Import link in the upper-right portion of the Contact management tab. You can also export your contacts stored in Gmail for use in other contact management programs. Simply click the Export link and choose between Gmail CSV and Outlook CSV file formats, then click Export Contacts.

The All Contacts tab is similar to the list of contacts in the Frequently Mailed tab except that it contains a list of anyone you have either sent email to, or received email from using Gmail. It is a good idea to clean this out once in a while as it may contain contacts from people you meant to email only a single time. To create a new contact in this list, click the Create Contact link at the top of the page. Organize your contacts into groups by selecting the contacts you want to organize and selecting a group from the drop down list at the top of the page.

You can enter additional information for each contact, such as their phone number and address. To enter this information, follow these steps:

1. Log in to your Gmail account.
2. Click Contacts on the left side of the page.
3. Click the contact you want to edit.
4. Click edit contact information.
5. Type the information in each field.
6. Click Save.

Manage your groups by clicking the Groups tab. There you will see a list of your groups by group name. The details column of the list tells you how many people are in each group, and lists the names of the people in the group. Create new groups by clicking the Create Group link.

Using Gmail to Send and Receive E-mail

You can access your Gmail from any computer in the world with Internet access by pointing a Web browser to http://mail.google.com. It's best to use some of the newer Web browser versions discussed earlier in this chapter but all the basic features should be available using almost any Web browser. Launching Gmail takes you directly to your Inbox where your incoming e-mail is placed by the Gmail program.

Navigating the Inbox

Your Inbox is automatically populated with your incoming e-mail as it is received by Google's Gmail. To read your e-mail, click the Inbox link in the menu on the left of the page. Next to the Inbox link is a number in parentheses that indicates the number of unread messages in your Inbox. This number does not appear when all messages have been read (see Figure 19.3). You can select different views. Click the Gmail view at the bottom of the Gmail page to switch among:

- Standard view with chat
- Standard view without chat
- Basic HTML

Select a view by clicking the corresponding link. As the number of e-mail messages begins to grow, you may want a way to select groups of messages in your Inbox. There are special <u>Select</u> links at the top and bottom of the Inbox that, when clicked, place or remove checkmarks next to the e-mail messages that have been marked in a certain manner, either automatically by Gmail or purposefully by you. These Inbox selection links are:

- **All:** Select all the e-mail messages in the Inbox.
- **None:** Deselect all the messages in the Inbox.
- **Read:** Select all the messages that have been marked as read.
- **Unread:** Select messages that have not been read or purposefully marked as unread.
- **Starred:** Select all the messages you have marked with a star.
- **Unstarred:** Select all messages that have not been marked with a star.

Selecting groups of messages using these tools allows you to easily archive groups of messages or perform other actions on groups of messages.

Mail in other folders

When your e-mail arrives into your Gmail account, it is normally sent to your Inbox (see Figure 19.3). You may have filters that check e-mail sent to your Inbox that marks it as unsolicited (spam) and is sent to the Spam folder, or deletes the mail and send it to the Trash folder. Also, a copy of each e-mail that you compose and send is saved in the Sent Mail folder.

FIGURE 19.3

Your Inbox lists both your read and unread messages.

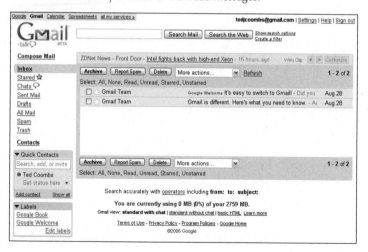

Reading e-mail

To read an individual e-mail message, click anywhere along the message display bar and the message appears. You may even see a "Loading . . ." message appear as the message is read onto your display. When the message appears on the screen, the subject appears in bold letters above the message. Inside the box that contains the message you see the address of the message sender and the date the message was sent. Gmail even calculates how long it has been since the message was sent.

Clicking the More options link displays detailed e-mail header information and a list of actions that you can take. These actions include:

- **Reply:** Send a reply to the message sender.
- **Reply to all:** Send a reply to the sender and all other recipients.
- **Forward:** Forward a copy of the message to someone else.
- **Print**: Print the message.
- **Add Sender to Contacts list:** Create a contact from the information in the e-mail message header.
- **Delete this message:** Erase the message.
- **Report phishing:** Report illegal attempts to collect information through subterfuge.
- **Show original:** Displays the message in its raw, text form.
- **Message text garbled?** Provides information for changing the text-encoding scheme in your Web browser when the message appears garbled.

You can read your message and then choose to return to the Inbox by clicking the Inbox link at the top-left corner of the message or choose to respond to the e-mail immediately by replying or forwarding the message. When you click in the text box at the bottom of the e-mail message it expands to show all the e-mail reply functions. The From field is filled in with your e-mail address but you can choose to change that by clicking the change link next to the address displayed. The To field is automatically populated with the e-mail address of the original sender. You can choose to add additional e-mail addresses to this list or add a carbon copy (Cc), blind carbon copy (Bcc), edit the Subject line, or Attach a file by clicking the links beneath the address box. You can also choose to add event information that is automagically entered into Google Calendar by clicking the Add event info link.

When replying or forwarding the message, the original message appears within the message box with a line entered by Gmail to note that, "On *some date **Sender** <sender e-mail>* wrote:.." Optionally include a note along with the message by typing at the top of the message box above the quoted message. When you finish, click Send or discard the message by clicking Discard.

 Gmail limits the size of e-mail attachments you can receive to 10MB.

Message handling

At the bottom of each e-mail message displayed in Gmail, and also displayed above and below the list of messages in the Inbox, are a number of actions you can take for each message. The first is a link to return to the Inbox without taking any actions. The second option, Archive, is shown in bold because this is what Google hopes you will do with your e-mail rather than erase it. Archiving the e-mail keeps it stored on the Google e-mail servers where it is accessible to be searched through Google Desktop. Clicking Archive quickly stores the message in the archive and returns you to the Inbox, where the message no longer appears.

Clicking Report Spam sends a message to Google, which uses this information to help filter and block future incoming spam.

The third option is to delete the message. Clicking Delete removes the message and places it in the Trash folder. You can access the Trash folder by clicking the <u>Trash</u> link in the menu to the left side of the page.

> **NOTE** E-mail messages left in either the Trash of Spam folders for more than 30 days are automatically and irretrievably erased.

Clicking the More actions... drop-down list displays additional actions that you can take. Select a checkbox on the left of the message, or click on the message to open it before selecting an action from the list. The actions you can select are:

- **Mark as unread:** Messages that have been read are automatically marked as read. You can override that by marking the message as unread for whatever reason you may find this necessary.

- **Add star:** Mark messages with a star as a visual cue that this message is important or requires your attention.

- **Apply label:** Organize your e-mail by applying labels to the messages. You can create many custom labels that can help sort your e-mail.

- **Remove label:** Remove labels from previously labeled messages. This is useful when you have filters automatically label messages and you want to manually change them. You might also have a temporary label that lets you know that an action should be taken; when the action is completed, you can change or remove the label.

Labels are a different way to organize your e-mail. Many e-mail programs allow you to organize e-mail into folders. Gmail is different. You can't add new folders as you can in other programs. Instead, Gmail allows you to add labels. You can easily limit the messages you are viewing in your Inbox to only messages with a certain label. This is a more intuitive way to manage e-mail rather than moving it between folders. It also allows you to view e-mail in the order it was received or as part of a thread.

Threading

Gmail has several different ways to organize your e-mail. The last section explained how you can use labels to organize your messages. Gmail uses another system automatically known as *threading*. Threads are groups of e-mail messages that have gone back and forth using the same subject. This is a great way to organize discussions based on topics. The messages appear in chronological order but are grouped with the subject of the messages in bold above the group.

Composing e-mail

At the very top of the menu on the left, just below the Gmail logo, is a bold <u>Compose Mail</u> link. Clicking this link launches the editor for creating a new e-mail message (see Figure 19.4).

Enter the e-mail header information

Your Gmail address is displayed in the From: field by default. If you have added and verified other e-mail addresses, you can select those from the drop-down list and your message, when sent, appears that it has been sent from the e-mail address you selected rather than from your Gmail address.

The To: field is ready to accept e-mail addresses. If you have added your contacts into Gmail these contacts appear in a drop-down list as you type in the To: field. When adding more than one e-mail address, separate them with commas. If you select an address from the list shown by Gmail, a comma is automatically added after the address.

You can add additional people to the address list as carbon copy (Cc) recipients. This does not change the message — only how it appears to be addressed. Some message filters look to see if the person is an addressee or a carbon copy recipient and filter the message accordingly.

FIGURE 19.4

Create a highly formatted or plain text e-mail message.

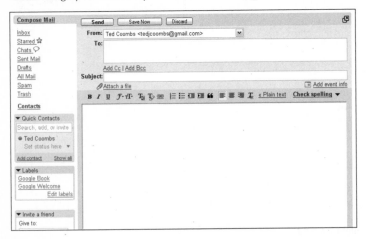

Blind carbon copy (Bcc) allows you to add recipients without having their addresses appear to other recipients of the message. This is a way to privately copy someone on a message you send.

Type a subject for your message. With today's spam filters working overtime, it's a good idea to add a subject that is more descriptive than simply, "Hi". Subject lines are not required, but many people will not read messages without subject lines out of concern for messages that contain harmful program code. These harmful messages often appear in e-mail messages without subject lines or with subjects that appear to make absolutely no sense.

Write your e-mail message

Type the message text of your e-mail in the large box. You have the choice of writing your message as plain text or formatting your message so that it appears displayed using HTML in your recipient's e-mail program. Your formatting options are (see Figure 19.5):

- **Text style:** Apply a text style by clicking the style symbol.
- **Font:** Select a font from the drop-down list.
- **Text size:** Choose Small, Normal, Large, or Huge from the drop-down list.
- **Text color:** Select a text color by clicking the color in the palette displayed as a pop-up.
- **Highlight:** Choose to highlight text by changing its background color. The default is yellow, but you can select other colors.
- **Link:** Create a hyperlink out of a valid URL.
- **Lists:** Create lists.
    - **Numbered List:** Format information in a list preceded by sequential numbers.
    - **Bullet List:** Format list information so that it is preceded with a bullet symbol.

- **Indent:** Move paragraphs of text to various levels of indenting by using either the left or right indent icons.
- **Quoted text:** The double-quote symbol does not add quotes. Rather, it precedes text with a grey vertical line to show that this is text you are quoting. This is how text appears in forwarded messages or message replies where the original text is included.
- **Justification:** Change text justification.
  - ▦ Left justification aligns text to the left of the message. This is the default.
  - ▦ Center justification aligns text to the center of the message, leaving jagged left and right margins.
  - ▦ Right justification aligns text to the right side of the message leaving a jagged left margin
- **Remove text formatting:** Click the italics T with a small red x and formatting is removed.

FIGURE 19.5

Use these toolbar options for formatting your email message.

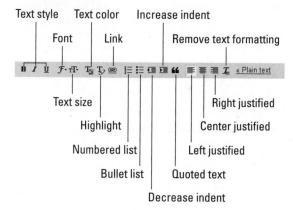

These formatting features are similar to those found in most popular word processing programs. Messages formatted using these formatting features are sent in HTML. This is the way that most e-mail programs can interpret text formatting and display the message as you formatted it.

Gmail allows you to send messages without special formatting. Send your message in plain text by clicking the << Plain text link next to the formatting icons. Clicking this link removes all the formatting icons and replaces them with a Rich formatting >> link. Clicking the Rich formatting >> link redisplays the formatting icons.

Check the spelling

When you finish writing your message you can choose to check the spelling before sending it. Clicking the Check spelling link performs a spell check on your message, marking words that it believes to be misspelled by changing the text color to red and underlining the text. You can click on the marked text to see a drop-down list of suggested spellings. The last selection in the list is Edit . . . . Select this when the suggested spellings do not include the correct spelling of the word. This puts the word in a text box where you can edit it. When you complete your spelling corrections, click the Resume editing link. Words marked as spelled incorrectly, and ignored during edits, return to their normal color and formatting when the spell-check editing is completed.

Attach a file

You can attach files to your e-mail message. Once selected from your hard drive they are specially encoded, because all e-mail is sent as text, and packaged as part of your message. Click the Attach a file link next to the paperclip icon located beneath the subject line of your message. Clicking this link causes a text box and button to appear where you can type the filename and path, or click Browse to locate the file on your hard drive. The filename and path are then stored in the text box. Click the Attach another file link if you want to attach additional files. You can also remove a file that is already attached by removing the checkmark in the box next to the filename of the attached file.

Add event info

Gmail works together with the Google Calendar. By adding event info into your e-mail message you cause two things to happen. First, if you have Google Calendar set up (see Chapter 26) it automatically adds an event into your calendar. Second, another e-mail message is sent along with the one you are composing that invites the recipient of your message to attend the event you have described. Invitations are also managed by Google Calendar.

Add the event name, the location of the event, the start date and time, and the end date and time. You can also select the All Day Event checkbox. Particularly when you have Google Calendar configured it's a good idea to click the more event options >> link. This gives you access to additional options such as whether or not the event repeats at regular intervals, such as a birthday or anniversary. You can also type a description of the event and choose in which of your calendars you want the event stored. One of the features of Google Calendar's event management is that you can invite guests to an event. You can also give permission to your guests to invite other guests.

 **See Chapter 26 for detailed information on Guest and Invitation management.**

Create and use a signature file

If you get tired of typing your name and contact information at the bottom of every e-mail message, let Gmail take the work out of it for you by including a signature file at the end of your e-mail message. You control exactly what goes in your signature.

Creating a signature file is simple enough. Click the Settings link at the top right of the page. Scroll down to the section labeled Signature:. The default setting is No Signature. To add a signature, select the radio button next to the text box and type the information you want to appear at the end of each message. Some people like to add a favorite quote or company stock symbol.

Send the message

When you are ready to send your message, click Send. You might notice next to the Send button a message telling you that a Draft of the message was autosaved, and the time it was saved. If your Internet connection is lost, hamsters chew through your computer's power cord, or some other interruption takes place, a draft of your message may have been autosaved.

Archiving messages

This chapter mentions several times that one of the Gmail features is the ability to archive messages, and that it is the philosophy of Google to keep e-mail for as long as possible so you have a searchable record. That doesn't mean you have to keep thousands of messages in your Inbox, which can be unwieldy. It's best to move messages you don't access regularly into the archive.

To archive messages stored in your Inbox, select the checkbox next to the e-mail message and click Archive either above or below the list of messages. If you later need to access a message that has been archived you can find it in the All Mail folder. This folder allows you to view all messages — those that currently appear in your Inbox and any archived messages. To archive groups of messages or multiple messages, select the checkbox next to as many messages as you want, or use the Select settings found below the Archive button. This allows you to choose messages with certain labels, messages that have or have not been read, messages that are starred, or all messages. This makes archiving large numbers of messages much more efficient.

Taking a shortcut

To easily move around in the Gmail environment, you might want to learn a few shortcut keys for actions you take regularly. For example, typing the letter "n" takes you to the next message. Typing the letter "c" tells Gmail to compose a new message. Some of the shortcuts, called *combo keys*, are activated by first pressing one key, then another. See Table 19.2 for a complete list of all the keyboard shortcuts.

TABLE 19.2

Keyboard Shortcuts

Shortcut	Description
c	Compose new message
/	Puts your mouse cursor in the search box
k	Move to the next newest conversation
j	Move to the previous (older) conversation.
n	Move to the next message.
p	Move to the previous message
o \<Enter\>	Opens or closes a conversation.
u	Refreshes the page and returns you to the list of messages and conversations.
y	Archives the currently selected message or conversation.
x	Selects a message or conversation.
s	Add or remove a "star" from the message or conversation.
!	Marks the currently selected message as spam.
r	Send a reply message to the currently selected message.
a	Send a reply to all recipients of the currently selected message.
f	Forward the currently selected message.
\<tab\>, \<Enter\>	Combo key (first press one key, then the other) Send message.
y, o	Combo key. Archive conversation and move to next one.
g, a	Combo key. Go to All Mail.
g, s	Combo key. See all Starred e-mail.
g, c	Combo key. Go to Contacts.
g, d	Combo key. Go to Drafts.
g, i	Combo key. Go to Inbox.
\<esc\>	Change the focus from the currently selected input field.

To use the keyboard shortcuts, you need to click the Settings link located at the top of the page. When the Settings page launches, make sure you are looking at the General tab. If not, click the General tab and locate the Keyboard Shortcuts section. Select the Keyboard shortcuts on radio button. This allows you to use the shortcut features.

Setting the POP and Forwarding Features

Click the Settings link at the top of the page to launch the Gmail Settings page. Click the Forwarding and Pop tab. To set up e-mail forwarding, find the Forwarding section of the Forwarding and Pop form. By default, the Disable Forwarding selection is enabled. To turn on forwarding, select Forward a copy of incoming mail to, and type a destination e-mail address in the text box provided. From the next drop-down list, select the action you want Gmail to take when forwarding your mail. Here are the choices:

- keep Gmail's copy in the Inbox
- archive Gmail's copy
- delete Gmail's copy

It's recommended that you either keep Gmail's copy in the Inbox or archive Gmail's copy. Remember that the goal of Gmail is to never require that e-mail be erased, only archived so that it can be searched and accessed at a later time.

Forwarded e-mail is simply sent on to the next e-mail address specified as the destination. It is forwarded as soon as Gmail puts it in your Inbox. You do not have to configure your other e-mail program to receive this e-mail.

When you want to forward only some of your e-mail, you can create a filter.

Creating a forwarding filter

You can filter messages based on several different types of information. For example, you can filter your messages so that only e-mail from a specific person is forwarded to you. This gives you complete control over what messages are viewed through Gmail and which are retrievable through a different e-mail client program such as Thunderbird or Outlook.

While viewing the Pop and Forwarding settings you see the Create a Filter link. Clicking this link launches the Create a Filter page. In this page, you can determine which e-mail messages are selected by Gmail for forwarding.

Set the criteria

There are six criteria that you can set for filtering messages. You can fill in one or several of the filter criteria, which include:

- **From:** Forward messages sent from a specific person or e-mail address.
- **To:** Filter on the intended recipient of the message.
- **Subject:** Forward messages that contain certain words or phrases in the e-mail subject line.
- **Has the words:** Filter on specific words or phrases in the body of the message.
- **Doesn't have:** Only forward messages that do not contain certain words.
- **Has attachments:** Only forward messages that have attachments. Checkbox only.

After typing keywords or phrases in one or more of these criteria or checking the attachments criteria, click Next Step >>. The next step is choosing an action.

Choose an action

There are five actions you can take when filtering messages. This section focuses on one of those: forwarding the message. You can also choose to filter the message where other actions take place. These actions include

- Skip the inbox (archive it)
- Star it
- Apply the label (choose label from a drop-down list)
- Forward it to *e-mail address*.
- Delete it

To continue setting up e-mail forwarding, type an e-mail address in the Forward it to: text box and select the checkbox next to this criteria. You can then either click Create Filter or first select the Also apply filter to option. This causes Gmail to evaluate e-mail currently in the Inbox. Leaving this unchecked only applies your filter to e-mail received after creating the filter.

Your new filter now appears in your filter list and can later be edited or deleted by clicking the associated links next to the filter. There is also a <u>Create new filter</u> link at the bottom of the filter list that takes you to the beginning of the filter creation process.

Setting up POP e-mail retrieval

Gmail can be accessed using an e-mail (client) program like Thunderbird or Microsoft Outlook. You can configure both Gmail to allow POP retrieval and configure your e-mail client program to retrieve messages from Gmail. Follow these steps:

1. Click the <u>Settings</u> link at the top of the Gmail page.
2. In the Settings form, click the Forwarding and POP tab.
3. In the POP Download section, select either the Enable POP for all email option or the Enable POP only for email that arrives from now on option.
4. Choose what you want to have happen to Gmail's copy of the message once it is retrieved by your e-mail client. The choices are

    archive Gmail's copy

    keep Gmail's copy in the Inbox

    delete Gmail's copy

5. Configure your e-mail client. You can find the account configuration instructions for your e-mail client program by clicking the <u>Configuration instructions</u> link in the last line of the POP download configuration form.
6. Click Save Changes.

CAUTION It's easy to get involved in setting up your e-mail client program and forget to save your changes.

Once your e-mail client is set up by adding a new POP e-mail account, you can begin receiving your Gmail right in your own e-mail client.

NOTE When using your own e-mail program to send and receive e-mail you lose many of the extra features Gmail offers when managing e-mail. You cannot use Gtalk, view pictures saved with contacts, or use your Gmail Contact information when sending and receiving e-mail. Of course, Gmail filters do not function in your other e-mail program.

Gmail Chat

One of the features that make Gmail unique when compared to other Web-based e-mail programs is the ability to chat with the people with whom you share e-mail messages. There have certainly been times when you have used your e-mail program like a chat program, sending short messages back and forth. Rather than wait for e-mail messages to hop their way to your computer, begin chatting directly. It's more efficient and more fun.

Chat requirements

In order to use Gmail chat you must have either Microsoft IE 6.0 or greater or Firefox 1.0 or greater installed on your computer. If you need to install or upgrade these programs visit www.microsoft. com/windows/ie/default.mspx. for new versions of Internet Explorer or www.mozilla.com. for new versions of Firefox.

Chat settings

To set your Gmail chat settings, click the Settings link in the upper-right corner of the page to open the Settings page. Once the Settings page loads, click the Chat tab. In this form, you can configure the way your Gmail chat program operates.

You can determine whether of not your chat transcripts are saved into you Gmail account by setting the Chat History to either:

- Save chat history in my Gmail account
- Don't save chat history in my Gmail account

In considering whether to save your chat history you must balance security with convenience. For security reasons, consider that your private chat conversations with others will be saved, and if you are using Google Desktop to index your e-mail, your chat transcripts will also be indexed and available for desktop searches. This is exactly the same reason why you might consider saving your transcripts so that you have them available for future reference.

Set the number of contacts that appear in Quick Contacts by setting the Quick Contacts Size and choosing a value (0, 5, 10, 15, 20, 40) from the drop-down list. In addition to the size, you can also set whether your Quick Contacts appear above or below the Labels box on the left side of the page. Set this value in the Quick Contacts Location field.

Set the Auto-Add Suggested Contacts to determine how contacts are added to your list of chat contacts. You have two choices:

- Automatically allow people I communicate with often to chat with me and see when I'm online.
- Only allow people I've explicitly approved to chat with me and see when I'm online.

Once again, security concerns should be your guide in choosing how people are added to your chat contacts. If you are concerned about security — and you should be — consider selecting the second option.

You can be notified of incoming chat messages with a sound by configuring the Sounds setting. To turn on the ability to be notified by sound you must have Macromedia Flash installed.

Configure your chat profile by placing the mouse over your ID in the Quick Contacts box. Adding your name allows others to see more than your Google ID. You can choose to use your real name or a name of your choosing.

Type your primary e-mail address. Your Gmail address is displayed by default. Choose to add a note about yourself by typing it in the Notes text box.

Upload a photo of yourself that appears in your chat or use the photo that your chat partners select. You can also choose to view someone's chosen photo or select one you'd rather view. You can choose to add more contact information by clicking the <u>add more contact info</u> link. The contact information you add here works exactly the same way as adding e-mail contacts as explained earlier.

To change the status that is displayed, click once on your ID in the Quick Contacts box and select a status from the list that appears. You can select one of the following status messages:

- **Available**
- **Custom Message:** Create a custom "I am available to chat" message.
- **Busy**
- **Custom Message:** Create a custom "I am busy; don't contact me right now" message.
- **Sign out of chat**

Change your status as often as you like.

Chatting

Before you can chat with someone, that person must be in the list of people you can chat with, and, of course, must have Gmail installed. Adding others to your list and inviting them to chat with you is simple.

In the Quick Contacts box on the left click the <u>Add contact</u> link. In the text box that appears, type the Gmail address of the person with whom you want to chat. Gmail processes the invitation and sends it on to the person you've invited to chat with you. Once that person accepts your invitation, a small bubble appears next to the person's Gmail ID that appears in your contact list. The bubble is green when the other person is online and able to chat with you, and gray when offline.

When you want to chat with someone who is in your list and is available, place your mouse cursor over the ID in the list and a pop-up window appears next to the entry in the list (see Figure 19.6).

Click Chat in the contact pop-up window to begin chatting. A small chat window appears within the Gmail page where you can begin sending and receiving messages. The text of your message appears above the text entry box marked with the name of the person who sent the text. Yours is marked as "me".

In the bottom of the window, you see a <u>Pop-out</u> link. Clicking that link opens a new window containing only your chat, as shown in Figure 19.7. You can always choose to restore the chat back into the Gmail window by clicking the <u>Pop-in</u> link.

FIGURE 19.6

Placing your mouse over a contact in your list expands a contact window.

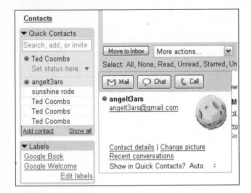

FIGURE 19.7

The chat can appear in its own window or as part of the Gmail page.

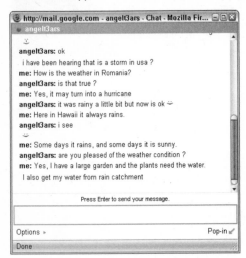

If you configure Gmail to save your chats, the full transcript appears in the Gmail Chats folder. Detailed information about the chat, including the exact time each message was sent or received appears in the chat transcript. If you are concerned that the person on the other end of the chat is saving your chat transcript and you want all or portions of it to remain private and unsaved, you can go off the record. Click the Options link at the bottom of the chat window and select the go off the record option. If you start a new conversation with the same person, this setting is not saved, so you need to go off the record each time you chat with someone and don't want the chat transcript saved. Chat transcripts, up to the time you decide to go off the record, are saved.

Searching Your E-mail

At the top of the Gmail page is the familiar Google Search box. There are two buttons, one for searching your e-mail and the button on the right for searching the Web. Click Search Options to launch a page that allows you to focus your search through your e-mail messages. The additional search options include:

- **From:** Specify from whom the e-mail was sent.
- **To:** Type in the name or email address the e-mail was sent to.
- **Subject:** Type in search terms that may appear in the subject line of the e-mail.
- **Search:** Select All Mail, Inbox, Starred, Chats, Sent Mail, Drafts, Spam, Trash, Mail & Spam & Trash, Read Mail, Unread Mail, and any labels you may have created.
- **Has the words:** Type in search terms that might appear anywhere in the e-mail.
- **Doesn't have:** Type terms that should not appear in the messages, excluding them from your search results.
- **Has attachment:** Select this option when you want your results focused to only messages that contain file attachments.
- **Date Within:** Specify a length of time, such as 1 day, and the date from which the time should start. This allows you to focus your search within a particular time period.

When you have finished entering search options and terms click Search Mail. A list of the messages matching your search will appear below.

Gmail Notifier

Google provides a special desktop program for both Windows and Mac users that notifies you when new e-mail arrives in your Gmail account. It remains invisible until mail arrives in your Gmail inbox. Then, a small window appears from the taskbar alerting you to the new message.

You can click this notification to launch Gmail and view the new message. This service is automatically installed when you install Google Desktop.

CROSS-REF See Chapter 11 for more information about installing Google Desktop.

Gmail Mobile

One of the great things about Gmail is the ability to check it while you're on the go using the Web browser on your mobile phone. First, your phone must be equipped with a Web browser. It doesn't need to use a color display, but it helps. Unlike other Web-based e-mail programs that make you search through a full-sized Web page to read your e-mail on a tiny screen, Gmail automatically adjusts its display for the phone on which you are viewing your e-mail.

Like almost all the other Google applications, Gmail mobile is free to use. Point your phone's Web browser to http://m.gmail.com. You need to know how to use your phone's Web browser because each phone works in a slightly different manner.

You can get an idea of what Gmail will look like on your mobile phone by visiting http://m.gmail.com in your regular Internet Web browser. Figure 19.8 shows how the interface is pared down with limited

Mobile Phone Requirements

Your mobile phone must meet several minimum requirements before it can be used to access Gmail. You may need to upgrade your phone's operating system or upgrade your phone to use Gmail, but it's worth it.

The phone's Web browser must be XHTML compliant. You can test your phone's XHTML compliance by using the Google test page found at `www.google.com/xhtml`. Perform a search from this page; if you are successful, then your phone is XHTML compliant.

Your mobile phone must accept cookies. No, not Girl Scout Cookies. Cookies are small files that store information on your computer and saved by Web pages. Some phones do not have the ability to save cookies, and some service providers do not allow cookies to be saved. But if your phone is cookie-capable, enable cookies on your phone. If your phone gives you a cookie error when trying to use Gmail, first check your browser's cookie setting, then try deselecting the Remember Me setting on the login page. This often solves the problem.

The mobile phone and browser your phone has installed must be able to make a secure SSL connection. This secure connection encrypts information sent and received between your phone and Gmail. This requirement is for your own security. You may need to check with your mobile phone service provider to see if your phone and your service are SSL capable.

graphics and simple text interface, perfect for most mobile browsers, particularly when bandwidth is limited, which slows your connection.

Gmail Mobile also allows you to view many kinds of attachments, including Adobe PDF files. This saves you a lot of trouble trying to transfer the files later onto you laptop or desktop just to read an attachment.

You can read your e-mail by clicking the Inbox link and selecting a message you want to read. Notice that Gmail Mobile does not show you all the various folders, such as Trash, All Mail, and Spam to limit the amount of space required to display the e-mail program on your mobile.

Clicking the Contacts link shows you a list of your Frequently Mailed contacts and then provides a search box so that you can search for other contacts from your list.

Unfortunately, many of the Gmail features available on your desktop, such as Gmail Chat, are not available using the mobile version. Some features needed to be sacrificed to create a simple interface that works on almost all Internet-ready phones and mobile devices.

FIGURE 19.8

The Gmail Mobile interface is simple and almost graphics free.

Summary

Gmail is a new experience in Web-based e-mail programs. The entire philosophy behind Gmail is different with the idea of saving e-mail messages on the Gmail server indefinitely compared with other Web-based programs that appear happier when you store nothing on their servers. Gmail integrates with other Google technologies, such as the Google Calendar and Gtalk for chatting. You can even use Google's Picasa to locate and share images located on your computer with others in e-mail.

If you've found that you really like using Gmail and want to share it with others, send them an invitation. You are given a small number of invitations to allow others to use Gmail. You can also sign up for an account using your cell phone. You can find the invitation system in the small box at the left of the screen. Type the e-mail address of your invitee and an invitation is sent. The remaining number of invitations allowed is displayed in this same box.

First, there was e-mail; then there was the Web; and soon after came Google and not long after that instant messaging. It only makes sense that all of these have come together to create Gmail.

Gmail integrates well with other Google applications such as Google Desktop. When you use Gmail with other Google applications it can easily form the heart of your Internet communications. Included in these communications should be Google's chat program, Gtalk, which is covered in the next chapter.

Chapter 20

Chatting with Google Talk

G oogle Talk is an instant messenger program that allows you to chat with friends in a buddy list. It's like many of the other instant messenger programs. See when people in your buddy list are online and when they are away. Chat with them, send them files, send your buddies e-mail, and send voice messages to them, all with Google Talk.

Setting Up Google Talk

To get started using Google Talk point your browser to http://talk.google.com (see Figure 20.1). You can choose to see the Web page in your own language by selecting from the languages in the drop-down list in the upper-right corner of the page. This also takes you to the download of Google Talk in the same language. Click Download Google Talk to install a copy of Google Talk on your computer.

NOTE When you click Download Google Talk, you automatically agree to the Terms of Service. Click the <u>Terms of Service</u> and <u>Privacy Policy</u> links above the button to read these terms and policies you are agreeing to follow.

After you download the Google Talk installation file to your computer (the file is named googletalk-setup.exe) open the file to launch the Google Talk installation program. When you agree to the terms (see the sidebar "The Terms") installation starts (see Figure 20.2).

Click Finish to complete the Google Talk setup wizard. Google Talk will then launch on your computer.

IN THIS CHAPTER

Set up the Google Talk software

Let people know when you want to chat

Configure the Google Talk client

Get the most from your chats by saving your Chat history

Learn how to easily transfer files to your friends

Use Google Talk's hands-free and enjoy talking instead of typing

FIGURE 20.1

The Google Talk download page

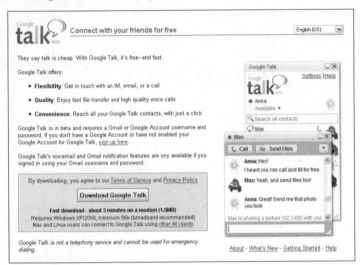

FIGURE 20.2

Google Talk client software installs after you agree to The Terms.

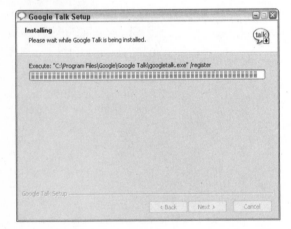

The Terms

The first thing you are asked to do, having already agreed to follow the Terms of Service and Privacy Policy by clicking the download button, is agree to the Licensing Terms, which include agreeing to the Terms of Service and Privacy Policy...again. You should read the terms yourself, but in brief it says that you can access this instant messaging service and voice calling service using any Open client, (Take that! AOL) or the Google Talk client program you just downloaded. If anything bad happens to you or your computer as a result of installing and using this client software, it's not Google's fault. You must be at least 13 years old to use the service and you can only use it for your personal use. The voice service can't be used to make regular phone calls, not even emergency ones. Use the service only for legal purposes. Google can access and turn the content of your personal communications over to law enforcement officials if asked to do so. Again, if anything bad happens, Google isn't responsible. Google owns all the intellectual property, including logos and stuff. You can't resell the service. The program updates itself automatically making your computer part of the Google army of drones. Google can stop providing the service, and you can choose to uninstall Google Talk any time you like. Google can keep all the information it collects. If anyone sues Google because you did bad things with its service, you foot the bill. The limit for filing legal actions is one year regardless of any other statute of limitations that may be in force, and if you or anyone else decides to take legal action, it all gets to happen in lovely Santa Clara, California.

Getting Started

When Google Talk launches, you are prompted to type either your Google account or Google Talk username and password. To make future Google Talk sessions simpler, you can opt to have the Google Talk client remember your password. If you are using a public computer, this process is not recommended. Deselect this option so that you must type a password even when someone already knows your username. Click Sign In and you are ready to start adding contacts.

After you log in, Google Talk loads all your Gmail contacts. For those who already have Gmail accounts, a small bubble appears next to their names. These people can begin receiving messages from you immediately.

Google loads your Gmail contacts in "Friend" order, not alphabetically. The people you e-mail the most must be your closest friends so they appear at the beginning of the Friend list. If you wonder how all your friends rate, Google tells you quickly by showing you where they all appear in the list based on the number of times you've swapped e-mail with them.

Even if you are familiar with other instant messaging programs, the Google Talk application has different features, so taking a small tour of the interface and setup is a good idea.

Look at Figure 20.3 and see that the Google Talk window lists you (me in this case) first and displays your online status. In this example, Google Talk shows I am online and available to receive Google Talk messages.

See who is online and available using the Google Talk window.

Changing status

Your online status is displayed in the Google Talk windows of people who have you in their Friends list. You can change your status, which updates your friend's display. Perhaps you're busy and don't want to be disturbed. Change your status to Busy. The status choices showing that you are available to receive messages are:

- **Available:** Hey, send me an instant message!
- **Show current music track:** Here's the music I am listening to. Send me a message.
- **Custom message:** Create a custom message telling people about your status.

When your status is busy you can still send and receive messages, but you're telling your friends you'd rather not. This is a good status to be in when having a private chat with someone and not wanting to hear from others. The status choices for busy are:

- **Busy:** Don't bother me.
- **Show current music track:** I am far too busy listening to music to be bothered. Here's the song currently playing.
- **Custom message:** Leave a custom busy message.

The last choice, Sign out, logs you off completely. This shows you as offline and unavailable to receive messages. You cannot send messages, either.

Online available status automatically changes to Idle, accompanied by an amber icon to signify when you are most likely not at your computer because you have not typed anything or moved your mouse in a while. Moving your mouse or typing changes your status back to Available.

You can easily change your online status by selecting a new status from the drop-down menu that displays your current status. You can leave available or busy custom messages by clicking on the current status, changing the status to a text box where you can type your custom message, or by selecting custom message from the drop-down menu. To change between available and busy custom messages you will need to select from the menu.

Configuring Google Talk

To change your Google Talk preferences, click the Settings link located at the top of the Google Talk window. The settings are divided into seven categories. Select a category in the list on the left and make changes to the selections in the right window.

General

The General settings allow you to change a number of important preferences. The first selection allows you to tell Google Talk whether to launch when you start Windows (log in to your account). When this option is selected, Google Talk launches each time you log in. Logging out of your account logs you off of Google Talk.

You can choose whether you want Google Talk to automatically launch Gmail when you click e-mail links. If Gmail is your primary e-mail program this makes sending e-mail messages from links much simpler. Otherwise, leave this deselected.

Control the appearance of your Friends list by selecting whether to sort your list alphabetically by name, hide your offline friends so you only see friends that are currently online, and hide the Google address book contacts that are not on your Friends list. The last choice in the friends-related selection tells Google whether to automatically add people you communicate with frequently to your Friends list. If you are uncertain or concerned about your privacy, it's better to leave this deselected.

Click Change Font to change the font face and size used throughout the Google Talk application. This is particularly important for site-impaired individuals who may need a larger font size. It's also a great way to express your personality.

Click Account Settings to launch a Web browser that allows you to change your Google account settings. The accounts page allows you to also review a list of your current services. If your list does not include all the wonderful things discussed in this book, you can quickly see what you need to add.

The Enable diagnostic logging button should not be selected unless a Google support engineer has requested that you do so. This creates a report sent to Google so that it can help diagnose problems you may be having with the Google Talk service.

Chat

There is a single choice in the Chat section having to do with how your chat history is handled. The first selection asks Google Talk to save a transcript in the Chats section of your Gmail account.

 Saving chat histories is only available to people who also have Gmail accounts.

The second selection asks Google Talk not to save your chats. You can also keep others you are chatting with from saving your chat transcripts, no matter how they have this feature set by "going off the record." This setting is explained later in the chapter.

Blocked

The Blocked setting displays a list of usernames that you have blocked for whatever reason. You can change your mind or correct an accidental block by removing them from this list. Select the name in the list and click Unblock.

Notifications

Set how you want to be notified when you receive an incoming call, an incoming chat request, when your friends come online, or when you receive e-mail in your Gmail account. For each event, you can choose the type of notification you'd like to receive. You can also turn off all notifications.

Connection

The connection settings are only important if your network requires the use of a proxy for Internet communications. You can choose to automatically detect and set firewall proxy settings or you can set them manually.

There is a special diagnostic tool for troubleshooting network connections. When asked by Google Support technicians, you can click Start Monitor.

Audio

The audio settings allow you to configure the hardware used when sending and receiving audio information from Google Talk. Audio information includes input and output hardware.

The last setting allows you to optionally share your music listening history with Google Music Trends. This helps Google track what people are listening to in order to report music trends.

Appearance

Select a chat theme from the many possible themed appearances. The selections allow you to customize the appearance of your chat window. You can elect to see chat transcripts with or without accompanying pictures or graphic icons.

Managing your Friends list

Installing Google Talk isn't much fun if you don't have anyone else to share messages with. To add friends, click +Add at the bottom of the Google Talk window. The "Invite your friends to Google talk" dialog box appears. Type their e-mail addresses in the text box. When adding more than one at a time, separate the addresses with a comma. You can also select people from your Gmail contacts, making it easier to add all your friends at the same time. Click Next to go to the next step.

Each of the friends you add needs an account to sign up. Friends in your list who do not have a Google Talk account see a message informing them they need an account to take part along with the invitation Google sends on your behalf. They are invited to sign up and download Google Talk. You can edit the default message and customize it so that people know it is from you and not just spam. Click Next after typing your custom message. Google Talk tells you that your friends have been invited, and as soon as they accept the invitation, a colored ball appears next to each name indicating online status. Click Finish. Your invited friends appear in your Friends list without a ball and with the word (invited) next to their names.

When others want to add you to their Friends list, a message appears at the top of your Friends list identifying the potential friend and asking if you want to allow your name to be added. You can say yes, no, or block this person if you never want him or her to contact you again. People can always use fake identities and create new Google accounts. So blocking is no guarantee that you won't hear from that person again.

Placing your mouse on anyone in your Friends list displays a pop-up with any custom icons or photos he or she might be using, along with that person's status and e-mail address. You can click the following buttons to interact with the person:

- Call
- Send Files
- Email
- Options
  - Chat
  - Send voicemail
  - View past chats
  - Block *friend*

Click Call to alert your friends that you'd like to chat with them. A ring sound plays on your computer and your friend's. Click Send Files to send a file. Learn more about sending files later in the chapter. Click Email to launch Gmail with a message already addressed to your friend.

If you click Options, a small drop-down menu appears. Click the down arrow in the upper-right corner to see four options. If you are not chatting, the first option is Chat. Select this option to open the chat window, which allows you to begin exchanging messages with your friends, as long as they are online. If you are already chatting, this option is "Go off the record." Learn more about this selection in later in this chapter.

Send voicemail, the second menu option, allows you leave your friend a voice message. You must have a microphone installed to use this feature. When you finish sending your message, click End Call.

Selecting the View past chats option allows you to see chats you've had in the past. Google Talk saves your chats automatically unless you specifically tell Google Talk that you don't want your chats saved. For more information about this setting see the section "Configuring Google Talk" later in this chapter. When you select View past chats, Gmail launches and displays a list of your past chats with that friend. Select one to view the entire chat transcript, including the time of day each message was sent or received.

Configure how friends appear in your Friends list by clicking View at the bottom of the window. Options include:

- **Show one page:** This option shows only a single page of friends.
- **Sort by name:** This option enables you to see your friends in alphabetical order.
- **Show pictures:** This option displays the image your friend has chosen to appear in Google Talk communications.
- **Show offline friends:** This option shows all friends, even those who have gone offline.
- **Show all address book contacts:** This option shows people in your Gmail address book, even if they have not yet been added as friends in Google Talk. This easily lets you invite them to start using Google Talk.

Search for your friends by typing all or part of their names in the search box. You can only find friends that are already part of your Google Talk Friends list or Gmail contacts list.

Chatting

Chatting begins when someone contacts you with a message, or you send someone a message. When someone sends you a message, a chat window opens where you can see the message displayed. Respond by typing in the box at the bottom of the window. Press Enter when you are ready to send your message.

If you want to initiate a chat session or simply send an instant message (technically the same thing), click a name in your Friends list and a chat window opens. Type a message and press Enter. If you friend is online, he or she receives your message.

In Figure 20.4, some of the chat messages are two lines long, and short lines so they didn't wrap around. This is what happens when someone sends more than one chat message before receiving a response. Rather than redisplay your chat name and icon for each message, as other messengers do, Google Talk neatly displays them all as a single message.

FIGURE 20.4

Chats are easier to read using Google Talk.

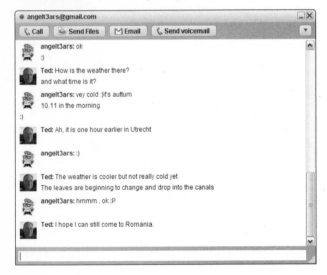

As soon as your friend goes offline, you can no longer send him or her a message. Instead, Google Talk sends you a message that `yourfriend@gmail.com` is offline and can't receive messages right now.

Maintaining a chat history

The transcripts of your chats can be saved in your Gmail account. It's often handy to go back and refer to chats for things such as phone number, driving directions, or just to reminisce about all the nice things that were said. To view past chats, put your mouse over the friend's name in your Friends list to open the pop-up window. From the drop-down menu select View past chats, which launches your Gmail account and displays all saved chats with this person. Select a chat session to view the contents. Each message also includes the time of day that messages were sent and received.

Your chat histories are treated like any other message stored in Gmail. You can archive them, delete them, star them, or anything else you can do with a Gmail message. Also, if you use Google Desktop to index all of your information, your chat histories are included in those searches.

You can select not to save chats transcripts by configuring your Chat settings. For extra privacy you can always select "Go off the record" to keep others from saving your chats in their Gmail accounts.

Going off the record

When you want your communications to remain relatively private you can take your chats off the record. While chatting with someone, click Options in the upper-right corner of the Chat window. The first selection is Go off the record.

Once this is set, it remains set for the current chat and all future chats until you choose to go back on the record. Setting this affects only chats with this friend. You have the option of saving chats or going off the record with each of your friends.

Going off the record does not guarantee that your chat transcripts are protected. In the Terms of Service, you may remember that you are allowed to access the Google Talk service using any Open application. This means that the non-Google Talk client may save chat histories to a place other than Gmail, meaning that even going off the record does not guarantee that your chat session will not be saved. Even when using the Google Talk client, the friend may choose to copy and paste your conversation from the chat window before closing it.

NOTE Remember that law enforcement officials and trusted Google employees have access to your Google Gmail account and all saved chat histories. Google Talk is for personal use only and not a way to conduct secure business communications.

Transferring Files

You can transfer any kind of file between Google Talk friends. To begin a file transfer, click Transfer File in either the message window or the pop-up that appears when you place your mouse cursor over a friend's name in your Friends list.

Locate the file to be transferred on your computer and begin the transfer. You can watch its progress as it transfers.

The file transfer is peer-to-peer, which means that rather than send files to the Google server and then down to the person you're chatting with, your computer makes a connection directly to the other person's computer. This means that there are no limits on file types or file sizes that you can send between the two computers.

When you receive files sent to you, they are stored in the Google Talk Received Files folder. When someone sends you an image, it is stored in the Received Images folder, which is found within the Google Talk Received Files folder.

Voice Chatting

Tired of typing? Google Talk allows you to carry on two-way voice chats. Click Call in any chat window to begin a new voice chat. Both you and your friend must have the right audio equipment properly installed to use this feature.

TIP Headsets equipped with a microphone work best for voice chatting. Most headset microphones are directional, eliminating much of the background noise. The earphones make your conversations easier to understand and may keep your audio chats a little more private.

Your Internet connection speed may affect the quality of your voice communications. This feature works with any connection speed but works best over DSL or faster connections.

To initiate a call, click Call, either in the Chat window or in the pop-up that appears when you mouse over a friend's name. As soon as your friend answers, your voice communication begins. An indicator, like the one shown in Figure 20.5 appears, which shows your voice levels and allows you to end the call by clicking End Call.

FIGURE 20.5

See your voice levels, end the call, or send files and e-mail messages.

You can have many voice calls connected at one time, but only one may be active. The other calls are put on hold. You cannot use this feature to access the normal telephone network, and therefore cannot use it to make emergency calls, unless it's to tell your friend that pizza has suddenly become an emergency and to hurry over with some.

Closing Google Talk

Closing the Google Talk window does not close the application. It continues to run, which is indicated by a Google Talk icon (a red M in a speech bubble) in your computer's taskbar. To re-launch the Google Talk window, double-click on the icon in the taskbar.

To close Google Talk completely so that the application no longer runs on your computer, right-click the icon and select Exit from the pop-up menu. To restart Google Talk, start the application from you computer's Start menu. Select All Programs ➪ Google Talk ➪ Google Talk.

Summary

Use Google Talk to communicate with all your friends, either by typing instant messages, carrying on complete chat sessions, using voice chat, or if you can change your status fast enough, send Morse code messages. Okay, the last thing was just a joke. Get all your friends to sign up for Google Talk, whether they have Gmail accounts or not. The Google Talk client is free and easy to use and integrates well with your Gmail account.

To communicate with other Google Talk users and to stay on top of what's new in Google Talk, try the Google Talk Blog at `http://googletalk.blogspot.com/`.

Google Talk is more than simply the Google Talk client. It's an entire Open messaging service that can be accessed by many instant message clients. For a complete list of clients accessing the service, visit `www.google.com/talk/otherclients.html`.

Finally, because Google Talk does not support video chatting you will want to read the next chapter about how to use Picasa to share pictures with your friends.

Chapter 21

Editing and Sharing Photos with Picasa2

If you check out the software installed on the average computer, you are sure to find one or more image-management programs. Depending on the hardware and peripheral devices you use with your computer, such as scanners and cameras, you are sure to have more management software of some sort. The problem with software bundled with input devices is that the program may offer limited features or may be difficult to use with images other than those created by the hardware.

Instead of relying on proprietary software, you can turn to one of many image-management programs. Image management is usually bundled with manipulation and editing software that may or may not meet your needs-the software may be too complex, or may not offer other types of output than single images.

In this chapter, you learn how to use Picasa2 as an image-management program. Available as a free download from Google, Picasa2 is ideal for general image collection, editing, distribution, and archiving needs.

Use Picasa2 for:

- **Collecting and organizing:** Configure Picasa2 to search for pictures on your hard drive when the program is started. Images are sorted into albums using a configurable naming structure.

- **Editing:** Picasa2 offers a selection of common editing functions, such as brightening images, extending a color range, and sharpening images. Other editing features let you apply effects to your images, ranging from applying soft focus to color tints.

- **Distributing:** Picasa2 lets you choose from a range of different types of output varying from simple e-mails to making collages and posters. The Web Albums feature provides an easy-to-use image upload and download system.

- **Archiving:** Easily burn images and collections to a CD or DVD for long-term storage, or copy images to a removable flash drive for easy transporting.

Picasa2 System Requirements

To use Picasa, your computer must meet these minimal requirements:

- PC with 300 MHz Pentium processor and MMX technology
- 64MB RAM (128MB recommended)
- 50MB available hard drive space (100MB recommended)
- 800 × 600 pixels, 16-bit color monitor
- Windows 2000 or XP
- Internet Explorer 5.01 or better (6.0 recommended)
- DirectX 7.0 or higher (9.0b recommended)

Getting Started with Picasa2

How many hundreds of images do you have on your hard drive? Do you know where they are and how to access them? Are they arranged in a way that makes it easy to locate them? Or are you stuck with many folders having mysterious names like DSN00393?

The simplest way to keep track of the images from Uncle Pete's birthday, the 300 snapshots of your baby's first birthday, and your class reunion is to build a uniform collection. Picasa2 offers a simple and easy-to-use method.

Scanning your computer

The first time Picasa2 opens, the program scans your entire computer or designated folders for images to include in its library.

Follow these steps to scan your computer for images:

1. **Open Picasa2.** The window shown in Figure 21.1 appears.

2. **Select one of two options for locating images on your computer based on your usual method of storing pictures:**
   - **Completely scan my computer for pictures.** Select this option if you have images scattered all over your computer, have images on more than one hard drive, or can't remember where you have stored pictures!
   - **Only scan My Documents, My Pictures, and the Desktop.** Select this option if you routinely store pictures in these folders, or use default settings for input devices, such as cameras, as the settings usually place images into named subfolders in the My Documents or My Pictures folders.

CAUTION   The complete scan option may take a long time to scan your entire system. Icons, buttons, and other small images used in installed programs may be included in the collected images.

FIGURE 21.1

Start by selecting what areas of your computer to scan for images.

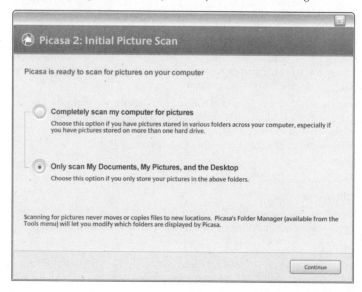

3. **Once you make your selection, click Continue.** The dialog box closes, the Picasa2 window opens, and you see the contents of your computer's folders examined and image and other files collected. Files are placed in folders according to their dates.

4. **Click OK to close the message that displays at the end of the importing process.** The number of folders and image files that have been located are listed on the message.

Collecting files

Picasa2 recognizes and catalogs a range of file types including movies, images, and RAW image data files. The file types supported include:

- **Images:** Picasa2 recognizes JPG, BMP, GIF, PNG, PSD, and TIF files
- **Movies:** Files using AVI, MPG, WMV, ASF, MOV formats
- **RAW:** Camera files supported include Nikon, Minolta, Pentax, Canon, and Kodak. Picasa2 automatically recognizes proprietary camera formats from many cameras as RAW file formats. File types include Nikon NEF, Canon CRW and CR2, Olympus ORF, Pentax PEF, Kodak DCR, Sony SRF, Minolta MRW, and Fuji RAF.

Getting Around the Program

The Picasa2 program window is composed of several sections (Figure 21.2). The main components of the program include:

- **Menus:** At the top of the program window, access commands for most program functions from the Menu items. The Menu features are summarized in Table 21.1.

- **Task buttons:** Instead of using program commands for common features, click a Task button. Select from Import, Slideshow, Timeline, and Gift CD options.

- **Library:** The Library houses the structures of folders and albums that make up your collection. By default, there are two Albums named Screensaver and Starred Photos. The rest of your images are stored in a sequence of named folders, or *collections*, either a folder you create and name to hold the images, or in folders sorted by the date the picture was taken and placed in groups of folders separated by year.

- **Lightbox:** The contents of the folder selected in the left column of the Library are shown in the Lightbox in the right column of the Library.

- **Photo Tray:** A selected image or folder is shown in the Photo Tray at the bottom of the program window along with a number of commands and output types that can be applied to the image or folder of images.

- **Scroll Bars:** Use the arrows to move the Library and Lightbox content up and down. In the Lightbox panel, click the uppermost scrollbar arrow to move up one folder at a time; click the lowermost scrollbar arrow to move down one folder at a time.

FIGURE 21.2

The Picasa2 interface is organized into a number of functional areas.

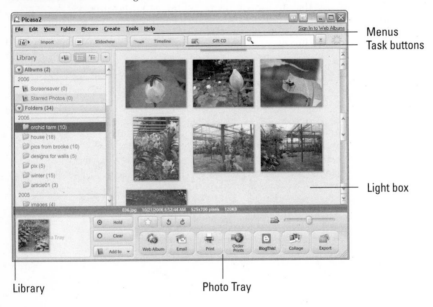

TABLE 21.1

Summary of Picasa2 Menu Contents

Menu label	Included features
File	Open, find, and save elements used in the program, including files, folders, and albums; export content using print, e-mail, and online features
Edit	Find commands for common actions, such as Cut, Copy, and Paste; includes commands for using effects and making selections
View	Show the image content in several ways, including thumbnails, Timeline, slideshow, or keywords
Folder	Specify how the images are seen, such as thumbnail sizes; specify how the thumbnails are displayed, such as black and white, or indexed color; choose a caption type for the images
Picture	Select images or folders and choose commands for batch editing, such as renaming and adjusting contrast or color
Create	Choose a product type to create from a group of images, such as a collage or a screensaver
Tools	Choose program preferences, manage and configure program features
Help	Access online Help for Picasa2, program support, and user forums

Importing Images and Other Content

You can add new content into existing folders of the Picasa2 Library or as new folders. Importing photos and video clips into Picasa2 uses the same process. Additional images can be imported into your collections from other folder or drive locations, from external media such as a CD or flash card, or directly from devices such as cameras and scanners.

You use the same method whether you are importing one file or all the images from a flash card or drive.

To import photos into Picasa2 from a camera drive, follow these steps:

1. **Click Import to display the Import screen.** The Import screen doesn't open as a separate dialog box; instead, it replaces the Picasa2 interface except the main menu.

2. **Click Select Device to open a menu.** The contents of the menu, shown in Figure 21.3, vary based on the devices you have enabled and installed on your system.

FIGURE 21.3

The listed devices depend on equipment installed on your computer.

3. **Select the device from the list.** The device's drive opens, and existing content is shown as thumbnails in the Import Tray.

4. **Preview the images on the drive by clicking the Previous and Next arrows below the Preview image, as seen in Figure 21.4.**

   If necessary, click the Rotate Clockwise or Rotate Counterclockwise buttons to rotate an image.

FIGURE 21.4

Check out the images before importing using the controls in the Preview area of the screen.

5. **Shift-click/Control-click the thumbnails to select a subset of the files to import.** The selected files' thumbnails are framed with a bounding box, as shown in Figure 21.5.

6. **Click Import Selected to import a subset, or click Import All to import the entire set of images from the drive.**

TIP   Select the Exclude Duplicates option to prevent installing two or more versions of the same image.

FIGURE 21.5

Select the images for importing from a camera's flash card.

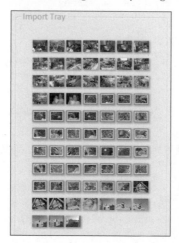

7. **On the Import All or Import [##] Item(s) dialog box that opens, choose from these settings:**

   ■ Type a name for the folder.

   ■ Click Browse and specify a location in which to store the files; select an existing folder if you want to add more pictures to it. On Windows, the default location is a folder in My Pictures.

   ■ Add additional information, such as the place, description, and a date

   ■ Choose a camera or flash card action after copying the files-leave the source files alone, perform a safe delete to remove copied pictures, or delete all pictures on the card or camera.

8. **Click Finish to close the dialog box and import the images into Picasa2.** The Import screen is replaced by the regular program interface.

 If you change your mind about importing, click Cancel to close the dialog box and return to the program window without importing any images.

 You can repeat the process of importing image files into existing folders as you work with your photo collections. Any thumbnail displayed in the Import Tray showing an X indicates an image that is already included in the Picasa2 library.

Managing Images and Folders

Unless you have established a uniform way of naming and organizing your images, you usually notice discrepancies in naming files and folders after bringing them together in the Picasa2 Library. Fortunately, Picasa2 offers a number of ways to organize your Library contents.

Specifying a Library view

Before you start rearranging the contents of your image collections, choose the Library view that is the most convenient, depending on whether you are adjusting individual images, or images and folders. Configure the view from the Library panel, or by choosing View ➪ Folder View and choosing a command.

From the Library panel, choose from these different types of views:

 ■ **Flat folders:** The default arrangement for the Library lists the folders by name according to the year the pictures are taken; selecting a folder name in the Folders list shows the thumbnails in the Thumbnail view area of the dialog (refer to Figure 21.2).

 ■ **Folder tree:** The folder tree structure condenses the content into larger groupings, which is convenient when you have a lot of images stored in a large number of folders.

 ■ **View options:** Click View Options to open a menu; select a sorting method for the Library. The default selection is Sort by Creation Date. Alternatively, choose from Sort by Recent Changes, Sort by Size, or Sort by Name.

To use the Folder Tree Structure view, follow these steps:

1. **Click Set view to show folder tree structure at the top of the Library panel to reorder the contents of the Library (see Figure 21.6).** The folders are reordered according to the highest-level folders, such as My Pictures and My Computer.

FIGURE 21.6

Locate the folder based on its location on your computer's hard drive.

2. **To open subfolders, click the small arrows to the left of a folder name.** You see the folders arranged in a nested hierarchy; all high-level folders show a folder icon, with a thumbnail showing nested contents.

3. **Click the name of the folder you want to work with to display its images in the Lightbox.** The folder's name is highlighted in the Library, and a button showing an up arrow appears.

4. **Click the up-arrow button to collapse the Folders list.** The selected folder is listed outside the collapsed hierarchy of folders (see Figure 21.7).

FIGURE 21.7

You can collapse the contents of the Library's listings.

Revising image filenames

The Picasa2 interface contains several features to readily organize the contents of your folders and files. For image files, you can:

- Rename individual images
- Rename a batch of images at one time

Renaming individual image files

To rename an individual image, follow these steps:

1. **In the Lightbox, select the image thumbnail.**
2. **Choose File ➪ Rename to open the Rename Files dialog box.**

    You can also press F2 to open the dialog box.
3. **Type a name for the file in the text field on the dialog box.** Include the date and image resolution in the file name by selecting the appropriate checkboxes shown in Figure 21.8.
4. **Click Rename to close the dialog box and change the file's name.**

FIGURE 21.8

The file's name can include date and image resolution information.

Renaming a batch of images

Instead of changing image names one by one, save some time and rename the files as a batch by following these steps:

1. **Select the folder containing the images to rename.** You can also select thumbnails if you want to change only some of the images in a folder. Shift-click to select contiguous files; Ctrl-click to select noncontiguous files.

2. **Choose Picture ⇨ Batch Edit ⇨ Rename to open the Rename Files dialog box (refer to Figure 21.8).** Type a name, and choose options to include the date and image resolution if desired.

3. **Click Rename to close the dialog box and rename the files.**

> **NOTE**   If you type a batch name, such as winter, without including date or resolution information in the name, a number suffix is included automatically to give each image a unique name, such as winter-1, winter-2, and so on.

The filename and resolution choices can be used in the Lightbox as a thumbnail caption as well as in the image's name. Choose View ⇨ Thumbnail Caption and select an option. The default choice is None; you can also choose Filename, Caption, or Resolution. Examples of these options are shown left to right in Figure 21.9.

FIGURE 21.9

Identify an image in the Lightbox using a thumbnail caption. From left to right, choose from Filename, Caption, or Resolution.

Organizing folders

Each folder contains basic information that includes its name and a date, either the date when the images within the folder were captured, or a date assigned when the folder is created. To change the folder information, double-click the folder's name in the Library panel, or choose Folder ⇨ Edit Description to open the Folder Properties dialog box, as shown in Figure 21.10. Type the changes you want to make, and click OK to close the dialog box.

Changes made to a folder's information are shown in the Lightbox below the folder's name. As you can see in Figure 21.11, the information entered for the Description is shown in the Lightbox as well.

> **TIP**   Save a few mouse clicks when adding a description. Instead of opening the Folder Properties dialog box, click Add a description below the folder's label in the Lightbox. The label is replaced by a blinking I-beam cursor. Type the description and press Enter or click off the area to finish.

All the folders listed in Picasa2 are included as folders on your hard drive, with the exception of Albums. You can rename, move, combine, or delete folders from the Library panel, just as you do on your hard drive. And, like the method used on your hard drive, you can easily move files from one folder to another.

FIGURE 21.10

You can include descriptions and location information for folders in the dialog box.

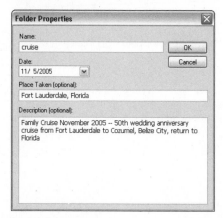

FIGURE 21.11

Folder information is shown in the Lightbox above the image thumbnails.

Moving a file

Click the thumbnail or thumbnails in the Lightbox and drag to the receiving folder. Release the mouse. Click Yes in the Confirm Move dialog box. The dialog box closes and the file is moved.

Deleting a file

Click the thumbnail or thumbnails in the Lightbox and press Delete or choose Delete from Disk from the File or shortcut menus. Click Yes in the Confirm Delete dialog box when it asks if you want to delete the file. The dialog box closes and the file is deleted.

Deleting a folder from the hard drive

Locate and select the folder in the Library and press Delete, or choose Delete from the File or shortcut menus. Click Yes in the Confirm Delete dialog box when it asks if you want to delete the file. The dialog box closes and the file is deleted. In some circumstances, an Info dialog appears that states the images can be removed but the folder can't be deleted because it contains files other than the images.

Don't worry if you delete a folder from the hard drive when you intended to delete the folder from Picasa2 instead. Files aren't permanently deleted from your system using Picasa2 commands-you'll find the folders and images in your Recycle Bin.

Deleting a folder

Choose Folder ⇨ Remove from Picasa. In the Confirm dialog box that appears, click Yes to confirm the folder's removal from the program's database.

Creating a new folder

Display the thumbnails for the images you want to separate from an existing folder. Select the file(s) in the Lightbox and choose Move to New Folder from the shortcut menu, or choose File ⇨ Move to New Folder to open the Folder Properties dialog box. Name the folder, and click OK. The dialog box closes, and the files are moved into their new folder.

Splitting a folder

Splitting a folder works similarly to creating a new folder. Right-click the thumbnail in the Lightbox that identifies where you want the list of files split and choose Split Folder Here to open the Folder Properties dialog box. Name the folder, and click OK to move the files into the new folder.

Hiding folders

You can add folders to the Hidden Folders collection in the Library. A password used to hide the contents from view within Picasa2 has no bearing on the files on your hard drive. A password can be added any time you add a folder to the Hidden Folders collection and applies to the entire collection, not just the folder in which you specified the password.

You can password-protect and hide content of selected folders. Follow these steps:

1. **Right-click the folder's name in the Library panel.** Choose Hide Folder to open the Add Password dialog.

2. **Click Yes to continue with the password process.** Open the Password Entry dialog box.

   If you don't want to use a password, click No to close the Add Password dialog box and add the folder to the Hidden Folders collection.

3. **Type a password in the field shown on Figure 21.12.** Click OK.

   The dialog box is renamed Password Verify. Retype the password and click OK again. The folder is moved to the Hidden Folders collection listed in the Library. The listing shows a red arrow to the left of the label, rather than the green arrow used with other collection listings.

FIGURE 21.12

Specify a password to use for hiding folder content.

Viewing a hidden folder

When you want to view the contents of a hidden folder, click the Hidden Folders label in the Library to open the Password Entry dialog box. Type the password and click OK. After you finish working with the files, be sure to collapse the collection's label again. Otherwise, when you close and reopen the program, the Hidden Folders are listed for display.

Viewing a folder on your hard drive

Select a folder in the Library panel and choose File ➪ Locate on Disk, Folder ➪ Locate on Disk, press Ctrl+Enter, or simply double-click the folder's name in the Lightbox. If you want to see where the folder is located, hover the mouse over the folder's icon in the Lightbox to display the folder path in a tooltip, as shown in Figure 21.13.

FIGURE 21.13

A folder's storage location can be shown in a tooltip.

Using albums

An *album* is a named grouping you create with Picasa2 that exists only within the program. The contents of the albums can be located in any number of folders on your hard drive. You can create an album to use as a storage folder when you are assembling images for a project like a collage, or want to make a slideshow, or upload them to a Web Album.

Picasa2 includes the Screensaver and Starred Photos albums that can't be renamed or deleted. When you tag an image with a star it is included automatically in the Starred Photos album. The files copied to the Screensaver album are used for a system screensaver.

Exporting Albums or Folders from Picasa2

Picasa2 offers several ways to use the contents of your folders or Albums. The commands are the same, but the menu heading changes depending on whether you select an Album or a folder in the Library. Select an album and then choose Album from the main menu, or select a folder and then choose Folder from the main menu and select one of these commands:

- Print Contact Sheet to open the Print Screen. Read about choosing settings and printing images in the section "Printing photos."

- Export as HTML Page to open the Export as HTML Page dialog box. Read about creating a Web page in the section "Creating a Web page."

- Send to Hello to open the Hello:Signup and Download home page. Hello is a separate image-sharing and chat program that requires you to create an account and download the program. Follow the online instructions.

- Create a Gift CD to open the Create a Gift CD dialog box. Read how to configure the settings and produce the CD in the section "Using a slideshow as a gift CD."

Click Create a new album on the Library panel to open the Album Properties dialog box, identical to the Folder Properties dialog box shown in Figure 21.10. Name the album and add other information as desired, and click OK to close the dialog box and add the album to the Library.

Select a thumbnail in the Lightbox and drag it to the album to which you want to add it. A new *instance*, or copy, of the image is created when you add it to an album. You can save one photo in multiple albums without having to save multiple copies of the file itself. In the Library panel shown in Figure 21.14, for example, the new album contains the same four images as the Starred Photos default album. The images are also located in their source folders.

FIGURE 21.14

The same images can be used in multiple albums.

Maintaining the Library files

When you initially set up Picasa2 on your computer, you select the folders that contain image files to include in the Library. Over time, you are sure to add more images to your computer that should be included in the Library. Fortunately, Picasa2 includes a Folder Manager used for locating and adding files.

To add content to the image database, follow these steps:

1. **Choose Tools ➪ Folder Manager to open the dialog box shown in Figure 21.15.**

2. **Locate and select the folder in the Folder List.**

3. **Select an option for the selected folder:**

   ■ Select Scan Once to check the content of the folder and import any image or video files into the Library as a single task

   ■ Select Remove from Picasa to remove a selected folder from the folder list; the folder's icon changes to the X icon

   ■ Select Scan Always to include the selected folder as one of the Watched Folders. A Watched Folder is checked for new images each time the program is opened, and is a convenient way to automatically add content to the Library.

Archiving Images

If your images are critical to a workflow or project, be sure to back them up. Follow these steps to use the backup system offered in Picasa2:

1. **Choose Tools ⇨ Backup Pictures to open the Backup your photos screen.**

2. **In Step 1 of the backup process, create a set of records.** Use the default My Backup Set or select an existing backup you have used previously. The Backup Set records where the file copies are stored, as well as which files are already stored.

3. **In Step 2 of the backup process, select the files you want to back up.** Picasa2 lists the folders and images that aren't backed up. Save time and click Select All to select all the files you haven't preserved.

4. **Click Burn to burn the backup record to a CD or DVD following your CD or DVD device procedures.**

4. **Click OK to close the Folder Manager dialog box.** Any folders marked as Scan Once are checked and new files are imported into the Library.

 **TIP** If you have different storage folders for cameras and scanners, including those folders in the Watched Folders list makes it easy to keep the Library up to date.

FIGURE 21.15

Select options to define how and when images are imported into the program.

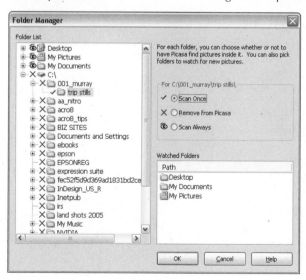

Cataloging Your Files

A major benefit of cataloging images using a system like that found in Picasa2 is the ability to search for specific files or groups of files quickly.

Tagging images with stars

In Picasa2, you can catalog images by adding a star, a keyword, or multiple keywords. Any image can include both a star and keywords.

To tag an image with a star, select the image or images in the Lightbox. In the Photo Tray, click the Add/Remove Star button, as shown in Figure 21.16.

FIGURE 21.16

Add a star to flag an image for easy access.

To locate any of the starred images, simply click the Starred Photos album in the Library to display all starred images in the Lightbox. If you have a folder containing both starred and unstarred images, click Select Starred in the Lightbox to automatically select the starred images, like the two shown in Figure 21.17.

FIGURE 21.17

Use stars as a means of selecting images in a folder.

Labeling images with keywords

Keywords are terms you use in a collection of images to describe its contents. Keywords are used to search for a specific image or images in your Library.

To add a keyword to an image, follow these steps:

1. **Select the image or images in the Lightbox.** If you are applying the same keyword to a group of images, you can select them all at once.
2. **Choose View ⇨ Keywords to open the Picasa: Keywords dialog box.**
   You can also use press Ctrl+K to open the dialog box.
3. **Type the text in the Add Keyword text field and click Add, or press Enter to move the word to the Keywords list, as shown in Figure 21.18.**
   Add more keywords to the list and click OK to close the dialog box when you finish.

FIGURE 21.18

Add keywords to describe the contents of an image.

4. **To add more keywords, select the images within the larger group and repeat Steps 2 to 4.**
   Continue selecting images and adding keywords until you define the images in the group as precisely as you require in a normal search.

 Don't worry about capitalization; Picasa2 converts all keywords to lowercase words.

You can search a large number of images quickly for a subset of images when a system of carefully designed keywords has been applied. For example, the group of 12 images shown in Figure 21.19 has an assortment of keywords applied. All images use the keywords *tropical, vacation, cruise,* and *belize.* Of that group of images, nine images include the keyword *beach;* six images include the keyword *palapa;* two images include the words *pirate* and *ship,* and one image includes the words *braid* and *beard.* When a search is performed, all images are returned using the term *tropical* while only two images are returned using the term *pirate.*

FIGURE 21.19

Keywords can be applied to a group of images at once.

Tagging an image to its location

For added interest, and a really cool addition to your image collection, tag your images to a specific location using Google Earth. The GPS (Global Positioning System) data is embedded into the photo's metadata, letting you see the photo on a rendered map in Google Earth.

CROSS-REF   Read about using Google Earth in Chapter 13.

Follow these steps to geotag an image:

1. **Select your photo or photos in Picasa2.**

2. **Choose Tools ➪ Geotag ➪ Geotag with Google Earth.** Google Earth opens, and a small Picasa2 window overlays the bottom right of the program window. You see the images you selected in the Picasa2 window, as shown in Figure 21.20.

FIGURE 21.20

The selected images are shown in an overlay window in Google Earth.

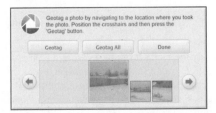

3. **Display the locale corresponding to your first image.** The locale is defined in one of two ways:

   ▪ If you previously typed information in the Place Taken field of the Picasa2 folder description (refer to Figure 21.10) the locale is shown automatically in the Google Earth program.

   ▪ If the location hasn't been identified, use the navigation tools in Google Earth to specify the locale by placing it below the large crosshairs that overlay the map, as shown in Figure 21.21.

FIGURE 21.21

Move the map into the correct location to position the locale below the crosshairs.

4. Once the correct location is identified, click Geotag on the Picasa2 window.

5. Select the next image in the Picasa2 overlay window and repeat Steps 3 and 4.

   If all the pictures use the same location, click Geotag All to set each image's locale simultaneously.

6. Click Done when you finish tagging the files to add the information to the images.

In Picasa2, thumbnails of images that are geotagged are identified by a crosshair icon in the Lightbox, such as the images seen in Figure 21.22.

FIGURE 21.22

Geotagged images display an identifying icon on their thumbnails in the Lightbox.

If you want to remove the geotag, choose Tools ⇨ Geotag ⇨ Clear Geotag info. The information is removed from the image's metadata, the icon is removed from the photo's thumbnail, and the photo is removed from Google Earth.

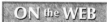 **Download Google Earth at** http://earth.google.com/downloads.html.

Viewing an image's metadata

Picasa2 lets you view an image's Exchangeable Image File Format (EXIF) metadata, which includes different types of information about the content and structure of a file. EXIF is a standard for storing interchange information in image files. Most digital cameras now use EXIF and store information such as the camera and flash settings.

You can see basic metadata for a file by selecting an image in the Lightbox and choosing Properties from the shortcut menu or the Picture menu to open the dialog box shown in Figure 21.23. The available information varies according to the type of image and the camera data attached to the file. When you geotag an image, you see the GPS information, shown as the locale's longitude and latitude, included with other EXIF metadata.

FIGURE 21.23

The image's longitude and latitude are included as part of the file's metadata.

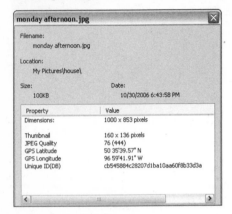

 You can also see metadata expressed in a graph showing color values and intensity called a histogram.

Searching for Files

You can scroll through the Lightbox to locate images that are included in the Library if you don't have too many images. On the other hand, looking for specific images among thousands of image files is tiresome and time consuming. Fortunately, you can use different types of search methods to quickly locate images in the Library.

Using the search features

You can use the Search function in a number of different ways to locate images in the Library. Choose View ➪ Search Options to open the Search Options, or click the arrow to the right of the Search field at the top right of the program window shown in Figure 21.24.

FIGURE 21.24

Locate images in the library using the Search Options.

Follow these steps to search the contents of your Library based on specific criteria:

1. **Click one of the buttons on the Search Options to filter the contents of your Library:**
   - **Click Starred to display only the images to which you have applied a Star.**
   - Click Movies to list only the movie files included in the Library.
   - Click Uploaded to list only the files that have been uploaded to a Web Album.

2. **To narrow the results further, filter the initial results based on a date range.** Drag the Date Range slider left to include older content, and right to include newer content.

3. **When you finish searching, click Exit Search to close the dialog box, or click Show/Hide Search Options to toggle the dialog box closed.**

   If you intend to search further, click the button selected in Step 1 to deselect it, and continue with your search.

To search for images based on keywords, follow these steps:

1. **Click the Search field to activate it.** Type a keyword or keywords. As you type, Picasa2 completes the words using text that has been typed previously, and displays the results as you add letters.

   In the example, the term **tropical** is added first, narrowing the displayed results to include the group of images shown in Figure 21.19. When the term **ship** is typed, the results are narrowed to the images shown in Figure 21.25.

FIGURE 21.25

Type keywords to narrow the search for specific images.

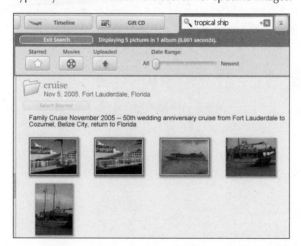

2. **Add or remove keywords as necessary to locate the images for which you are searching.**

3. **To start a new search, click the X icon that displays at the right of the text entry field as soon as you start typing a search term.**

   The contents of the search field are cleared, and you can start a new search.

4. When you finish searching, click Exit Search to close the dialog box, or click Show/Hide Search Options to toggle the dialog box closed.

Scanning visually using the Timeline

Rather than looking through folders and thumbnails in the Library and Lightbox, you can find images using the Timeline. If you can remember roughly when an image was taken, and know you took some images of a specific subject or in a specific location, you may be able to pinpoint the folder quickly in the Timeline window.

Follow these steps to look through your Library in the Timeline screen:

1. Click the Timeline task button to open the Timeline screen, as shown in Figure 21.26.

    You can also choose View ➪ Timeline, or press Ctrl+K.

Drag thumbnails to locate a folder.

FIGURE 21.26

Use the Timeline to locate images and folders visually.

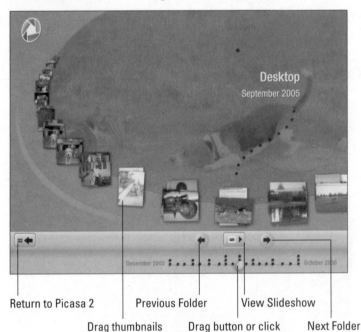

Return to Picasa 2   Previous Folder   View Slideshow

Drag thumbnails   Drag button or click   Next Folder
to locate a folder   Timeline to locate a folder

2. **Click one of the columns on the Timeline shown at the bottom right of the window.** The Timeline is dated according to the oldest and newest images in the Library.

   After you make a selection on the Timeline, the thumbnails representing the folders in the Library slide to the left to show a newer folder, or to the right to show an older folder. The folder's name and date are shown in the background, as is a grayscale version of the first image in the folder.

3. **To find other folders in the Library, choose one or more of these options:**

   ■ Click the Previous or Next buttons to show the folder older or newer than the currently selected folder.

   ■ Drag the thumbnails left to find an older folder, or right to find a newer folder than the currently selected folder.

4. **Once you locate the folder, click the Close button at the lower left of the Timeline screen to return to the Picasa2 program window.** The selected folder is active in the Lightbox.

Checking out full-screen images

Scrolling through thumbnails in the Lightbox lets you view your pictures, but reviewing images within a folder or your entire Library using a full-screen-sized image in a Slideshow offers a hands-free way to scan your pictures, change their orientation, and assign a star rating.

To start a Slideshow, click the Slideshow task button, choose View ➪ Slideshow, or press Ctrl+4 to display the Slideshow screen, as shown in Figure 21.27.

FIGURE 21.27

Use the Slideshow screen to watch and flag images in your collections.

The Slideshow screen shows the first image or a selected image in an active collection with a toolbar overlay. Move the mouse cursor away from the toolbar area to hide the toolbar; move the cursor into the toolbar area to display the toolbar again. The tools available in the Slideshow screen are described in Table 21.2.

TABLE 21.2

Slideshow screen tools

Command	Button	Explanation
 Exit Slideshow	Exit Slideshow	Click to exit the Slideshow screen and return to the program window.
 Navigate controls		Click the left arrow to reverse the playback; click the right arrow to advance to the next image; click the center arrow to play the slides automatically.
 Star	Star	Click to apply a star to the image to use for sorting and locating images.
 Rotate image	Rotate image	Click the left button to rotate the image counterclockwise; click the right button to rotate the image clockwise.
 Show captions	Show captions	Toggle the captions on or of by clicking the Captions button. The captions aren't shown if the Slideshow is using Automatic mode.
 Display Time 2 seconds	Set time	Click the (-) button to decrease the time each slide is displayed; click the (+) button to increase the time each slide is displayed. The current delay is shown in seconds.

In addition to organizing and sorting images, Picasa2 also contains features for editing, both for correcting flaws and adding some basic effects.

Editing Images

Most pictures need some degree of touch-up, whether you are capturing images of your son's soccer game or the cover of a glamour magazine. Picasa2 offers the Edit Picture screen to work with the appearance of your photos.

Follow these steps to begin editing an image:

1. **Double-click an image for editing in the Lightbox to open the Edit Picture screen.** You can also choose View ⇨ Edit View, or press Ctrl+5.

2. **A full-size image appears in the Edit Picture screen and is highlighted in the thumbnail strip at the upper right of the Edit Picture screen.**

   To view a different image from the active folder or album, click the left or right arrows at the ends of the thumbnail strip, as shown in Figure 21.28.

FIGURE 21.28

Select an image from a thumbnail strip at the top of the screen.

NOTE The Basic Fixes tab appears by default at the left of the Edit Picture screen, offering correction tasks that are applied automatically. For controlling the light in an image, click the Tuning tab and work with the sliders. Add special effects such as color tints and glows using choices on the Effects tab. Read about using each of the different sets of edit tools in the next section.

3. **Click Make a caption! below the image to activate an I-beam cursor and type a caption for the image, as shown in Figure 21.29.** Click the Caption icon at the left of the preview area to toggle the caption visible and hidden; click the Trashcan at the right of the preview area to delete the caption.

FIGURE 21.29

Add a caption to an image in the Edit Picture screen.

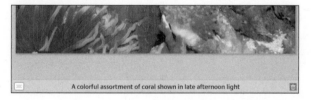

A colorful assortment of coral shown in late afternoon light

4. **Click Back To Library at the upper left to close the Edit Picture screen and return to the program interface.** You can also click Slideshow at the upper left of the Edit Picture screen to view the sequence of images in a Slideshow view.

The simplest types of edits are also the ones you use the most-isn't that convenient? It's simple for the lighting in your photos to be incorrect, the image may be crooked, or the background may be too dark.

Correcting basic image problems

In the Picture Edit screen, use one of seven tools included on the Basic Fixes tab to correct common image flaws.

Modifying the preview

Picasa2 displays your images at a size that fits on the Edit Picture screen. You can make changes to the magnification and view using the tools displayed below the preview area, as shown in Figure 21.30.

FIGURE 21.30

Use the view tools to zoom in and out of the preview for up-close repairs.

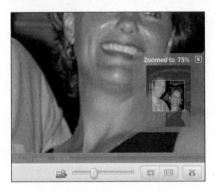

The tools include the following

- **Zoom slider:** Drag the slider to the right to increase the magnification of the image. As you drag the slider, an overlay shows you the portion of the image that is showing in the preview area.

- **Fit photo to viewing area:** Click the button to show the image at a size that fits within the Edit Picture screen's preview area.

- **Display photo at actual size:** Zooms in or out to show the image at its actual size. The entire image is shown in an overlay view with the viewed area highlighted.

- **Show/Hide Histogram and Camera Information:** Click to show a graph of the color distribution in the image. Read more about the histogram in the section "Viewing color information in a histogram." Depending on the source of the image, you also see camera data such as the focal length and ISO setting.

NOTE There is only one overlay window available. If the histogram is showing, the zoom overlay window showing the full image can't be used, and vice versa.

Applying one-click corrections

Three of the Basic Fixes tools are applied with a single mouse click. To return to the original image state, click Undo I'm Feeling Lucky. You can apply, reverse, and redo several fixes in sequence.

The one-click corrections you can perform include:

- **I'm Feeling Lucky:** Click I'm Feeling Lucky to adjust the image's color and contrast to the ideal balance based on the image's color information.
- **Auto Contrast:** Click Auto Contrast to adjust the contrast in your picture in Picasa. Click Undo Auto Contrast to reverse the contrast change.
- **Auto Color:** Click Auto Color to adjust the color levels in your picture automatically. Click Undo Auto Color to reverse the color adjustments.

Cropping an image

The Crop tool lets you remove a section of the picture that you don't want to keep. Follow these steps to crop an image:

1. **Click Crop in the Basic Fixes tab to display the Crop Photo screen, as shown in Figure 21.31.**

FIGURE 21.31

Choose the crop dimensions in the Crop Photo screen.

2. **Click one of the choices in the Crop Photo screen to use a preconfigured image size for the crop dimensions.** If you don't make a selection, the Manual option is selected by default.
3. **Drag the mouse over the image to draw a crop box, as seen in Figure 21.32.** Release the mouse and make adjustments as required.

   You can click and drag a corner of the box to proportionally resize it, drag a side of the box to resize it dimensionally, or drag the entire box to reposition it over the image.

4. **Click Preview to see how the crop appears after it is applied.**

   The image is shown cropped in the preview area, and then returns to the full-sized image again automatically.

5. **Click Apply to crop the image and return to the Basic Fixes tab.**

FIGURE 21.32

Adjust the crop box over the image until it is sized and placed correctly.

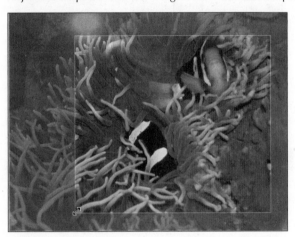

Straightening an image

It's simple to have your camera angled slightly when taking a picture. When you don't want to keep the tilted angle for effect, follow these steps to straighten your image:

1. **Click Straighten on the Basic Fixes tab to display the Straighten Picture view.**

2. **Drag the slider to align the picture (Figure 21.33).** Watch the image rotate as you move the slider; your goal is to have the content in the image align with the grid.

3. **Click Apply to make the correction and return to the Basic Fixes tab.**

Removing red eye

A common image flaw is a red eye appearance, resulting from the reflection of the camera's flash on the eye's retina. Click the Red Eye button on the Basic Fixes; then drag a rectangle around the red areas in the subject's eye. You can repeat the process for as many red eyes as you need to repair in your image. When you are finished, click Apply to modify the color and return to the Basic Fixes tab.

 Red Eye correction works only with red eyes. You can't use it to correct retinal reflections that aren't red, such as the green reflections you often find in cats' eyes.

FIGURE 21.33

Use the grid overlay to help straighten a tilted image.

Balancing the light in an image

Drag the Fill Light slider to balance the light in an image's foreground and background. In Figure 21.34, for example, the image on the left before applying the Fill Light feature; the one on the right shows the results of dragging the slider to its halfway point.

FIGURE 21.34

Use the Fill Light slider to add light to an image to balance the foreground and background. The image before using the slider is on the left; the results of using the slider appear in the image on the right.

Adjusting light and color using Tuning tools

The Tuning tab contains a number of sliders, including another Fill Light slider similar to the one just described. Use the sliders on the tab to adjust different aspects of the image's lighting and color. In addition to adjusting values using a slider, you can also use automatic light and color correction options using the buttons shown on the tab in Figure 21.35.

FIGURE 21.35

Use the sliders in the Tuning tab to make adjustments in an image's color and amount of light.

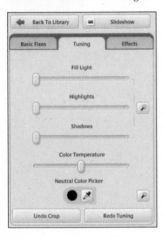

Applying the changes

To demonstrate how different options produce their effects, the tools are applied to the same image, shown in its original state in Figure 21.36. Labels on the figure identify the impact of using the sliders at a defined setting. In some effects, such as adjusting shadows, it's easy to see the difference between the before and after images. Tuning tools that didn't produce any change in the image are not shown in Figure 21.36.

NOTE   In some cases, because the figures in the book are in grayscale, it's hard to tell the difference between the original and the one with adjustments. When you experiment with making color and light adjustments yourself, display the color histogram overlay window to see how adjusting the sliders modifies the amounts of color shown in the graph.

FIGURE 21.36

The before image shows a plant urn in strong light and shadow with a definite red cast.

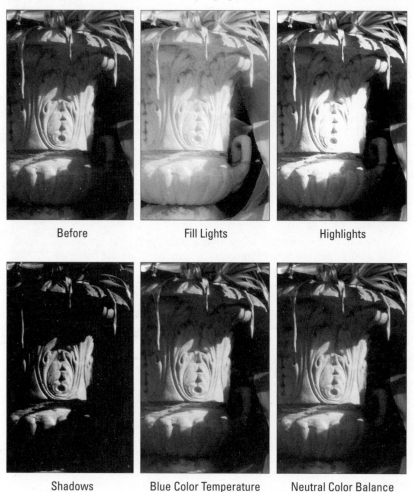

| Before | Fill Lights | Highlights |

| Shadows | Blue Color Temperature | Neutral Color Balance |

The Tuning tools include:

- **Fill Light:** Use the Fill Light slider to balance the light in the foreground and background of a picture. The example shows the effect of using 90 percent fill light.
- **Highlights:** Drag the slider to the right to add areas of brightness in the image. The example shown in Figure 21.36 uses Highlights applied at 100 percent.
- **Shadows:** Drag the slider to darken and expand dark areas of the image. The example shows Shadows applied at 100 percent.

- **Lighting auto fix:** Click the Lighting auto fix button to the right of the Highlights slider to automatically adjust and balance areas of light and dark in the image. Applying the tool to the example image had no effect as it is already balanced.

- **Color Temperature:** Drag the slider to the left to make the image cooler or bluer; drag the slider to the right to make the image warmer or redder. In the example, dragging the Color Temperature slider to the far left produces a strong blue tint to the image. Dragging the slider to the extreme right has very little effect as the original image uses a strong red cast in its color.

- **Neutral Color Picker:** Click the Neutral Color Picker and click to sample a pixel on the image that identifies an area that is considered neutral. Picasa2 balances the colors in the image against the color chosen. Instead of using a manual choice, click the Color auto fix button to the right of the Neutral Color Picker to balance the color automatically. In the example, using the Color auto fix produces a strong shift toward the blue tones, cooling the image and giving it a blue-green cast.

Viewing color information in a histogram

Camera data and color information called the RGB (Red/Green/Blue) histogram are derived from the image's data. The RGB histogram is a real-time graph that shows the intensity of colors in your picture and how they change when you make edits in Picasa2.

With an image displayed in the Edit Picture screen, click Show/Hide Histogram & Camera Information on the Photo Tray to display the histogram in an overlay window, such as the one shown in Figure 21.37. The histogram shows the color and light distributions for the image used in Figure 21.36. Although you can't identify different color bands in a grayscale image, you can see that the concentration of information is at both the lower (left) end of the color and brightness spectrum and at the upper (right) end of the color and brightness spectrum. The histogram's display identifies the high contrast settings used in the image.

FIGURE 21.37

The RGB histogram shows the distribution of color and light in an image.

Making adjustments to the color and amounts of light in the image produce visible changes in the histogram's distribution. For example, Figure 21.38 shows the same histogram as that in Figure 21.37 as it appears when the Fill Light slider is set at 90 percent in the Tuning tab (you can see the image with the Fill Light setting in Figure 21.37). Now you see that the color bands have shifted to the right, as have the brightness bands. In fact, there is no color or light pixel information in the lower range of the graph at all.

FIGURE 21.38

The histogram shows the color and light shift to the right of the graph as the amount of Fill Light is increased.

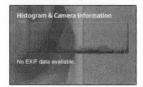

Adding interest with effects

Click the Effects tab to display a set of 12 effects that can be applied alone or in combination with other effects. Thumbnails of the image displayed in the Picture Edit screen show samples of the different effects, as seen in Figure 21.39.

FIGURE 21.39

See how an effect will appear in the thumbnails listed on the Effects tab.

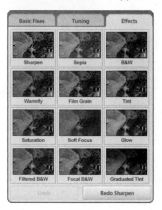

Select the effect on the Effects tab to apply it to the image shown in the preview area. For some simple effects, such as B&W, an image is either black and white or it isn't-there aren't any adjustments to make. The top five effects in the Effects tab are simple effects, indicated by the 1 shown in the bottom right of the effect button's thumbnail. The other effects open a settings tab with one or more sliders or tools to make adjustments. Effects are added in progressive layers, and you can always undo or redo the effects you make at any time.

After you choose and configure an effect, if you try to return to the Library or click another tab on the Edit Picture screen, the screen blurs and a Confirm Edit message asks if you want to apply the filter-in itself an interesting effect! Click Yes or No.

NOTE The simple effects, as well as the basic Auto Contrast, Auto Color, and I'm Feeling Lucky effects, can be applied as a batch. Choose the pictures to modify, choose Picture ➪ Batch Edit, and then select the effect to apply.

Here are the effects you can use to improve your pictures in Picasa2:

- **Sharpen:** Makes the edges of objects in your pictures crisper.
- **Sepia:** Strips the color from the image and applies a brownish red tone.
- **B&W:** Desaturates the image by removing all the color, leaving only the grayscale image.
- **Warmify:** Warms the color in an image, adding more red tones to replace blue tones; the effect is often used to improve skin tones.
- **Film Grain:** Applies a grainy film look to an image.
- **Tint:** Removes the color from the image. On the Tint tab, drag the Color Preservation slider to define how much of the original image color should remain, from 0 to 100 percent. Click the eye-dropper to show a Tint tab, and use the dropper to sample a color from the swatches or the color display to apply to the picture. In the image shown in Figure 21.40, the coral and the crab are lovely shades of magenta.

FIGURE 21.40

Select a color to use for replacing the original color in an image.

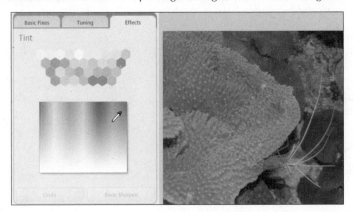

- **Saturation:** Drag the Saturation Amount slider left to remove color from the image, or right to increase the depth of color in the image.
- **Soft Focus:** The Soft Focus effect uses two sliders. Drag the Size slider to increase or decrease the size of the focus area in the image; drag the Amount slider to increase or decrease the amount of blur in the image. In Figure 21.41, you see crosshairs over the image. Drag the crosshairs to set the center point of the effect.
- **Glow:** Add a soft glow to your image by adjusting the Intensity slider to define the glow's brightness and the Radius slider to define the size of the brightened area on the image.
- **Filtered B&W:** The color is removed when the effect is applied. In the Filtered B&W tab, choose a color from the color picker that is applied like a color filter to the image. Depending on the color in the original image and the color of the filter chosen, areas of the image appear to darken or lighten.

FIGURE 21.41

The Soft Focus effect highlights an object in the image, like the crab's spines.

- **Focal B&W.** The Focal B&W effect first desaturates the image. Define the size of the colored area by dragging the Size slider; define the sharpness of the boundary of the focus area by dragging the Sharpness slider. Move the crosshairs to identify the center of the image, like the example shown in Figure 21.42.

- **Graduated Tint:** Add a gradient using a color you select from a color picker. Drag the Feather slider to adjust the sharpness or softness of the color changes; drag the Shade slider to define how much of the color is used in the gradient.

FIGURE 21.42

Highlight one area of an image in color using the Focal B&W effect.

CAUTION   Edits made in Picasa2 aren't stored in the original image. If you want to change the original, use an external editing program. Display the image in the Lightbox. Right-click and choose Open With from the shortcut menu. The list of available programs depends on your system configuration. Select the alternate editor to open and edit the image.

Saving and exporting edited images

Picasa2 doesn't save images in the same way as other common photo processing software. When an image is saved, the original version of the image is copied into a subfolder named Originals. The saved image in the folder is actually the edited copy.

Tips to keep in mind when using edited Picasa2 images:

- Edited files are saved only as JPG files at 85 percent quality, regardless of their original format.
- The original and saved copies of the image use the same size.
- Any time a change is made to an image, the Save Changes button is active on the Lightbox, as shown in Figure 21.43.

FIGURE 21.43

The Save Changes button is shown under a folder's name when edits have been made to the images in the folder.

- To save your edits to a specific location other than the default subfolder, choose File ⇨ Save As and specify the storage location.
- The edited versions of your images are used for e-mailing, slide shows, and Web Albums.
- Once your images have been edited, it's time to share them.

Distributing and Printing Your Photos

Picasa2 offers different ways to send images from within the program, which saves time and effort. For example, you can export images directly to e-mail, save them to a portable storage device, or send them to your blog.

Selecting images

You can select the images you want to distribute in a number of ways, including:

- Selecting a folder containing the images
- Adding stars to a number of images and selecting the Starred folder
- Selecting and holding images in the Photo Tray.

Selecting folders of images has been described elsewhere. To select and hold images in the Photo Tray, follow these steps:

1. **Locate and select the first image to include from the Lightbox.** A thumbnail of the image is shown in the Photo Tray holding area.

2. **Click Hold on the Photo Tray.** The thumbnail displays a small target icon at its lower-left edge, meaning it is attached to the Photo Tray.

   If you don't use the Hold feature, each time you make a selection, you replace the image currently in the holding area.

3. **Locate and select the next image from the Lightbox.** Its thumbnail is placed in the Photo Tray next to the first thumbnail.

4. **Click Hold on the Photo Tray again to store the second thumbnail.**

5. **Continue selecting and holding images until you assemble all the images you want to work with, like the set of seven thumbnails shown in Figure 21.44.**

   If you add and hold an image but then change your mind, select the thumbnail and click Clear to remove the Hold from the image and delete it from the Photo Tray.

FIGURE 21.44

Assemble and hold images to work with in the Photo Tray.

 To remove all the thumbnails you are holding in the Photo Tray, click Clear without selecting any thumbnails in advance. Click Yes in the confirmation dialog box, and the images are removed.

Distributing your photos

After you finish selecting your photos-either using the previous steps or by selecting folders-use one of the methods available from the Photo Tray to send the images.

Sending pictures by e-mail

Picasa2 automatically resizes and attaches pictures to e-mail messages at convenient sizes. The default e-mail client is Gmail. To change the e-mail settings, choose Tools ➪ Options, and click the E-Mail tab. Make your choices and click OK to close the dialog box and change the preferences.

You can choose from these options:

- Select a program from the list: You can use Outlook, Gmail, Picasa Mail, or choose each time you send pictures.

- Specify a size for sending multiple images ranging from 160px to 1024px in width.

- Choose to send individual images as their original sizes or using the specified resize width.

- Define whether to send the first frame or the entire sequence when sending a movie.

- If you use Outlook as the e-mail client, specify whether to send the images as an HTML storybook attachment.

After selecting the images you want to send, follow these steps to e-mail the images:

1. **Click Email on the Photo Tray to open the Gmail dialog box shown in Figure 21.45.**

FIGURE 21.45

Most of the information for the e-mail is added automatically in the dialog box.

2. **Type the recipient's name in the To: text box.** The Subject and body of the e-mail are already complete. Select the text and replace it if you want.

3. **Review the selected images on the dialog box.** Scroll through the set of photos to review them using the left and right arrow buttons; click Remove to the right of the arrow buttons, or Discard at the bottom of the dialog box to delete the image visible as the thumbnail.

4. **Click Send to close the dialog box and e-mail the images via the specified e-mail client.**

   Depending on how your system is configured, the e-mail message may be sent directly or open further dialog boxes with more instructions.

Transferring pictures to Blogger

If you have a blog at Blogger, use the Blog This! command to automatically transfer your selected pictures and text to your blog.

CROSS-REF   Read how to set up, customize, and maintain a blog using Blogger in Chapter 25.

Select the images to upload, and then follow these steps to transfer images to your Blogger blog:

1. **Click Blog This! on the Photo Tray to open the Picasa: Blog This! dialog box.**

2. **Follow the instructions for creating a new blog, or sign in to your account.**

3. **Select the blog where you want to display the images.**

4. **Choose a layout and an image size.** For the layout, select None, Left, Center, or Right. Specify an image size of Small, Medium, or Large.

5. **Click Save Settings to pass the content to your blog's input page.** Type the title and text for the posting and click Publish.

Back in Picasa2, the images are processed and uploaded to your blog. Check the results online, like the page shown in Figure 21.46.

FIGURE 21.46

A group of images can be sent to your Blogger blog with the click of a button in Picasa2.

Exporting to a portable device

If you want to take photos with you on a portable device, such as a removable hard drive or flash drive, you can export them in a single step. Select the images in Picasa2, and click Export on the Photo Tray to open the Export to Folder dialog box. Make the choices for export and click OK to process the files and save them.

Choose from these options:

- Specify the folder where you want to send the images. The folder can be on a hard drive or a portable drive.
- Type a name for the exported folder if you don't want to use the default folder name.
- Resize the image to a specified dimension or use the original image sizes.
- Specify the image quality, or leave the default Automatic quality option selected.
- For movie files, specify whether to export the entire movie or only the first frame.

Printing photos

Use the Picasa2 print commands for printing your images directly from the program.

Follow these steps to send a batch of images to your printer:

1. **Select the images you want to print and click Print on the Photo Tray to open the Print Screen, as shown in Figure 21.47.**

FIGURE 21.47

Print one or many images at the same time using the Picasa2 print process.

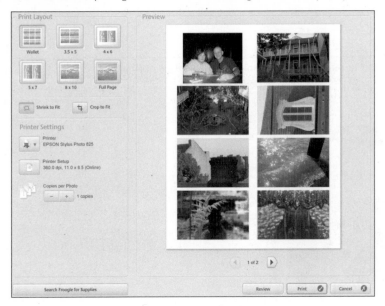

2. **Click the size for the prints in the Print Layout area.** You can only use one size of image for each printing process.
3. **Click either Shrink to Fit or Crop to Fit to size the images proportionally.**
4. **Check the printer settings.** Click Printer to open a list of printers configured for your system if you don't want to use your default printer.
5. **Click Printer Setup to open your printer's dialog boxes to configure the settings.**
6. **Change the number of copies of each photo by clicking the Copies per Photo (-) and (+) buttons.** The print settings use one copy as the default.
7. **Click the directional arrows below the Preview to view other pages if there are more images than those that fit on a single page.**
8. **Click Review to open an information dialog box that lists the names and resolutions of the images you selected.** Click OK to close the dialog box again.
9. **Click Print to send the images to your printer.**

Adjusting the Photo Tray Layout

If you want to reconfigure the task buttons on the Photo Tray, choose Tools ➪ Configure Buttons. Add, remove, and reorder buttons, and click OK to close the dialog box and revise the layout. Reopen the dialog box and click Reset to Defaults to restore the original button display, as shown in the figure.

Use the default arrangement of tasks on the Photo Tray or adjust them to suit how you work in the program.

NOTE You can change the available print sizes offered in the Print screen. Choose Tools ➪ Options and click Printing. In the Available Print Sizes section of the dialog box, click the drop-down lists and choose from a wide range of image sizes, including metric values.

While you are in the options, choose a high-quality Printer setting if you find you are changing the settings every time you print images. You can also change the print resampler quality from the default General to Extra Sharp. Click OK to close the Options dialog box.

Sending files for processing

Rather than printing images at home, many people prefer to send their photo files to an online service. You can export files directly from Picasa2 for processing by one of those services by following these steps:

1. Select the images you want to upload and click Order Prints on the Photo Tray to open the Picasa2 Prints & Products screen.

2. Choose the Location from the drop-down list if you don't live in the United States.

3. Click Choose to select the service provider you want to use for ordering prints.

4. Follow the instructions from the chosen service provider to access your account and upload areas.

Building Image Products

Use the tools and features in Picasa2 to showcase your photos in interesting ways. Some of the types of output are used on your computer while others can be shared with the rest of the world.

Producing a Web Album

A Web Album is a separate online account stored at Google that you use for loading and displaying albums of images. The first time you attempt to upload a set of images you see a dialog box asking you to register for the service.

ON the WEB To see the album created in this section, visit http://picasaweb.google.com/ donna.baker.

Follow these steps to create your Web Album:

1. **Select the images you want to use and click Web Album on the Photo Tray.** The Send [xx] photos to a Picasa Web Album dialog box opens, as shown in Figure 21.48.

Configure the appearance for the Web Album in this dialog box.

2. **Choose an option to Create a new Web album or Add to an existing Web album.**
3. Type a name for the Album Title. **The default name uses the folder's name where the selected images are located on your computer.**
4. **If you want, add information in the Description and Place Taken sections.**
5. Choose an Upload Setting. **The default setting, Optimized: Large size, fast upload (default) - 1600 pixels, is used in the example. Click the down arrow and choose Medium size, fastest upload, or Slowest upload, largest size option, if you prefer.**
6. **Choose a Visibility option.** The default is to make the album Public. If you prefer, you select Unlisted and restrict access to the album.
7. **Click OK to close the Web Album dialog box.** The Upload Manager dialog box opens, and shows the progress of the upload process.
8. **Click View Online in the Upload Manager dialog box to open your Web Album.** On the main page for the Web Albums, named My Public Gallery, click the name of the Web Album to open it, as shown in Figure 21.49.
9. **Back in Picasa2, close the Upload Manager dialog box.** In the Lightbox, images that have been uploaded to a Web Album are identified with a green arrow at the corner of the thumbnail.

FIGURE 21.49

The Web Album is accessed from your Picasa Web Albums site.

ON the WEB Picasa2 offers two Mac uploaders. Use the Picasa Web Albums Exporter for iPhoto to upload images from iPhoto. The Picasa Web Albums Uploader is a separate uploading program. Find the Mac uploaders at http://picasa.google.com/web/mac_tools.html and click Free Download. If you prefer, upload images one at a time using your Web browser.

Creating a poster

Some images are made to be very, very large. You can create a poster from within Picasa2 and specify the tiling pattern. A poster can be sized up to 1000 percent larger than the original image.

CAUTION If you intend to print a large image, make sure it is of sufficient size and resolution to print clearly-test the image to be sure.

To create a poster, follow these steps:

1. **Select the image you want to use for the poster and choose Create ⇨ Make a Poster to open the Poster Settings dialog box.**

2. Choose the Poster size from the drop-down list. **The percentage options range from 200 percent to 1000 percent.**

3. **Click the Paper size down arrow and choose either 4x6 or 8.5x11 as the paper size.**

4. To allow for overlap, click Overlap tiles.

5. Click OK to close the dialog box. **The image tiles are processed and added to the folder containing the original image, as shown in Figure 21.50.**

FIGURE 21.50

The original image of the rose at the upper left is reproduced as a set of four tiles to print as a poster.

Turning your photos into a movie

You can produce your own movies, rather than storing and sharing your images as static pictures.

Follow these steps to create and configure a movie:

1. **Select the images you want to include in the movie.**
2. **Choose Create ⇨ Movie to open the Create Movie dialog box.**
3. **Click the Delay between pictures down arrow and choose a time.** The choices range from 1 Second to 5 Seconds, or choose Just Raw Frames.
4. **Choose a Movie size.** You can select Small, Large, or Widescreen. Small is the default movie size.
5. **Click OK to close the Create Movie dialog box and open the Video Compression dialog box.** The Full Frames (Uncompressed) option is used as the default Compression setting.
6. **Click the Compression down arrow and choose either the Cinepak or Indeo codecs, as shown in Figure 21.51.**

FIGURE 21.51

Select the type of compression and how it is applied in your movie.

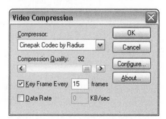

Choose from these options:

- Specify the movie quality by dragging the Compression Quality slider from 0 to 100 percent.
- Select the Key Frame option and type a number for the Key Frame Every x frames value. The default option is to use the key frame set at every 15 frames.
- Click Data Rate and type a number to specify the minimum number of KB of data that can be transmitted per second of video.
- Click Configure to open further configuration settings to specify how the codec deals with transparency, color, and so on.

7. Click OK to close the Video Compression dialog box when you have finished choosing settings. The movie is rendered and saved in your default folder location.

Using a slide show as a gift CD

If you have a large number of images to assemble, consider using a slide show. Picasa2 includes a feature to create a slide show Gift CD.

Create a Gift CD following these steps:

1. **Click the Gift CD task button below the main menu on Picasa2 to open the Create a Gift CD dialog box.**
2. **In Step 1 on the dialog box, choose folders to include in the Gift CD.**

   Also in Step 1, click the Photo Size down arrow to choose from a list of image sizes if you don't want to use the default Original Size.
3. **In Step 2 on the dialog box, type a name for the Gift CD.** The name must be 16 characters or less.
4. **If you don't want to include Picasa2 on the Gift CD, deselect the Include Picasa option.**
5. **Click Burn Disc.** Your files are processed and passed to your CD or DVD program for production.

Assembling a collage

Any number of images can be assembled as a collage-no scissors or glue are required! The collage is based on a selected group of images, and can be used as either a single image or as a screensaver.

Follow these steps to produce a collage:

1. **Select the images you want to include in the project.**
2. **Click the Collage button on the Photo Tray or choose Create ⇨ Picture Collage to open the Make Collage dialog box.**
3. **Choose the collage template.** Click the Type down arrow and choose Picture Pile, Picture Grid, Contact Sheet, or Multi-Exposure. The four types of collage are shown in Figure 21.52.

FIGURE 21.52

Choose one of four different ways to produce a collage image.

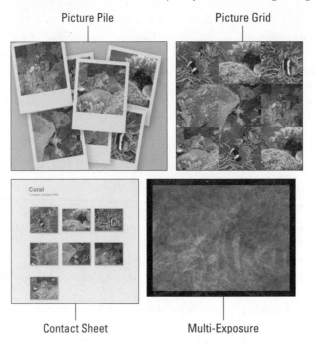

Picture Pile

Picture Grid

Contact Sheet

Multi-Exposure

NOTE If you select the Picture Pile template, you can specify a background from the Options drop-down list, and change the order of the images by clicking the individual images.

4. **Choose a storage folder from the Location drop-down list.** The options include:
   - Save as Desktop Picture
   - Current Folder
   - Screensaver Picture Folder
   - Choose a Folder, which then prompts you to locate a folder location on your hard drive.

5. **Click Create to build the collage.**

Creating a Web page

You can export any of your folders or Albums as a Web page. Using the method in Picasa2 is a convenient way to produce Web pages for your Web sites.

Follow these steps to produce a Web page:

1. **Select an Album and choose Album ➪ Export as HTML Page, or select a folder and choose Folder ➪ Export as HTML Page.**

2. **In the Export as HTML Page dialog box that opens, choose the features of the Web page.** You can choose from these options:

   ▪ Choose a size from the Export pictures at this size option, ranging from the Original Size to 320 pixels.

   ▪ Type the name for the Web page's title if you want to use a name other than the folder's or Album's name.

   ▪ Click Browse to locate a folder to store the Web page if you want to use a location other than the default location. By default, the Web page and its pictures are stored at My Documents\Picasa HTML Exports\[Album or folder name].

3. **Click Next at the bottom of the Export as HTML Page dialog box to open the Select a Web Page Template dialog box.**

4. **Select one of the seven templates from the Template Name list.** Read the short description below the list of templates, and view a preview. The choices include:

   ▪ Template 1, 2-page grey background; Template 2, 2-page black background; and Template 3, 2-page white background. These choices use different colored backgrounds, and all include two separate pages. The first page shows thumbnails linked to a full-size image shown on a separate page.

   ▪ Template 4, 1-page grey background; Template 5, 1-page black background; and Template 6, 1-page white background. These choices use different colored backgrounds, and all include a list of thumbnails at the left and a full-sized picture at the right of the page.

   ▪ XML Code. This template converts the Web page into simple XML code to be used in another page or application.

5. **Click Finish to close the dialog box and process the files.** When the Web page is created, it opens in your browser automatically, as shown in Figure 21.53.

FIGURE 21.53

The Web page shows a thumbnail index of the folder's images and adds slide-show controls above the full-sized image.

Uploading Images to an FTP Server

One new feature included as experimental in Picasa2.5 allows you to upload files from Picasa2 to your FTP server. Choose Tools ⇨ Experimental ⇨ Publish via FTP.

Required information for the upload process includes:

- The size of the image
- The title for the Web page
- The folder where the Web page and photos are to be saved
- The template to apply
- Where to display the Web page

Summary

Picasa2 is a convenient, easy-to-use, and free image-management program you can use to take care of your photos. In this chapter, you learned how to assemble images and collections using Picasa2's import features. After the images are cataloged, they can be stored and named according to your project requirements.

Picasa2 offers ways to correct common image issues such as sharpening and color, either automatically or by making manual adjustments. You can also use some special effects to enhance your image presentation.

You can distribute and share images in numerous ways, ranging from e-mail to burning CDs. Images can be printed or uploaded to a photo service. Picasa2 offers methods for producing special types of image products that you can share, such as movies, posters, and Web Albums.

Speaking of sharing, what about sharing information and insight with others? Read how to confer with a group of like-minded peers using Google Groups, coming up in the next chapter.

Chapter 22

Participating in Google Groups

Google Groups, formerly DejaNews, maintains an interface to Usenet News groups created by Google members and mailing lists. Google Groups also maintains an archive of postings to Usenet dating back to 1981, nearly from the beginning of Usenet itself. For more information about Usenet, read "Introducing Usenet" at the beginning of this chapter. Point your Web browser to `http://groups.google.com`. You don't need to have a Google account to use Google Groups, but extra features are available when you do have an account. Figure 22.1 shows how you can search through all the groups for information or find a group that interests you.

FIGURE 22.1

Search Usenet News groups using Google Groups.

Introducing Usenet

Usenet is one of the earliest Internet applications. Most people think of the Internet as just e-mail and the Web, but Usenet was around long before the World Wide Web. Usenet is based on the idea of the computer bulletin board, the way people who had computers communicated with each other before the invention of the Internet.

Bulletin board software allowed people to dial into a central computer (run by someone "running a bulletin board") and post messages. People also could download their favorite games, software, and messages sent to them by others. Some bulletin board software even allowed people to chat with one another. Usually, in the middle of the night, bulletin board programs would dial out and connect to other bulletin boards transferring messages until they eventually hopped their way to the intended recipient. This was known as *store and forward*. This method of transferring messages became the foundation of the way e-mail and Usenet groups work today. They both use the store-and-forward method for transferring messages. E-mail works by hopping a message to the intended e-mail server and stores it there until someone contacts the server and downloads the messages. This way, messages can be sent without the recipient's computer being connected to the server, which in the old days of computers, they rarely were. For this reason, you can find many parallels between the way e-mail and Usenet both operate.

Internet researchers at Duke University created a store-and-forward system for posting messages based on topics, and the topics are organized into a tree-structured hierarchy. For example, the top of one of the trees is called `sci`. No one posts directly to `sci`, but the `sci` group has subgroups, all related to science. Each subgroup is connected to its parent group name by a dot. For example, `sci.math` is a Usenet group for people interested in mathematics. Subgroups also can have subgroups. This group is for people interested in electronic design: `sci.electronics.design`. There is a catchall group named `alt`. The `alt` (alternate) group contains just about anything you can imagine: `alt.battlestar-galactica`, for example.

Messages sent to these groups are sent to Usenet News servers (technically called NNTP servers). Usenet News was the full name of the Internet application, and the servers are often simply called News servers. They never really carried breaking news as you may think of news, but they certainly contained news related to very specific topics.

You can send only text to Usenet servers. Wait! Don't throw this book into the fire just yet. Yes, you can download images, sound files, programs, and even video from Usenet groups, but they are first encoded into text, the form they take when being stored on Usenet servers. Usenet client programs, simply known as newsreaders, decode the text and change the graphics, binary programs, videos, and sound files back into their original form.

No matter what your interest may be, with tens of thousands of active groups and more than 100,000 archived groups, chances are high that you'll find what you're looking for in one of these groups. Being able to search through these groups is an amazing resource.

Google Groups is more than a Web-based interface to the Usenet News groups. It also includes groups created by Google members. Using Google Groups, you no longer need to use a separate newsreader program to view the contents of a group, post messages to the group, or even create your own group. In fact, you can't access Google's groups using a newsreader. You can only use the Web interface at http://groups.google.com.

NOTE   Google does not fully participate in Usenet. Groups created by Google users do not become part of Usenet. They remain part of Google Groups. You can't access Google-created groups using a newsreader program, and they don't appear on other NNTP servers.

You can think of Usenet as a subset of Google Groups. To truly participate fully in Usenet, you need access through a different NNTP server. Usenet service is offered by some Internet service providers. These services usually offer only a limited subset of the groups. For full access to all the groups, you can search the Web for Usenet servers and find a list of services that charge a small fee to access all the groups. You need a newsreader like the one installed in Outlook Express to access these groups.

Searching Google Groups

When Google purchased the DejaNews Web site in 2000, Google users got the ability to use Google's powerful search technology to search through Usenet News, which Google then called Google Groups. Today, you can search back through 25 years of archived groups and the more recently created groups by Google and Google members.

Figure 22.1 showed two search boxes on the Google Groups page. The top search box allows you to search for information in all the Google Groups, while the second search box allows you to locate groups, rather than information. The section "Finding a Group," later in this chapter, discusses finding Google Groups.

Type your search term or phrase in the Google Groups search box, and click Search Groups. Google does not have all the Usenet News groups as part of Google Groups. It maintains about 20,000 groups. Most of the missing groups are those that generally cater only to graphics, which are useless when doing a Google search. So, when you do your search, it looks through the 20,000 or so active Google Groups all the way back to 1981.

Using Google Group Advanced Search

The Google Group Advanced Search is accessed by clicking the <u>Advanced Groups Search</u> link next to the Google Groups search box. The Advanced Groups Search page begins the same way that all the other advanced search pages begin: focusing your keyword search. Type information into any of the Find messages section boxes to focus by keyword.

You can further focus your search by limiting your search to a single group or to groups within a specific hierarchy of groups. For example, if you want to search only the groups in the science (sci) topic, type sci.* (* is a wildcard that applies to all subgroups) into the section labeled Group.

FIGURE 22.2

Focus your search through Google Groups using Advanced Search.

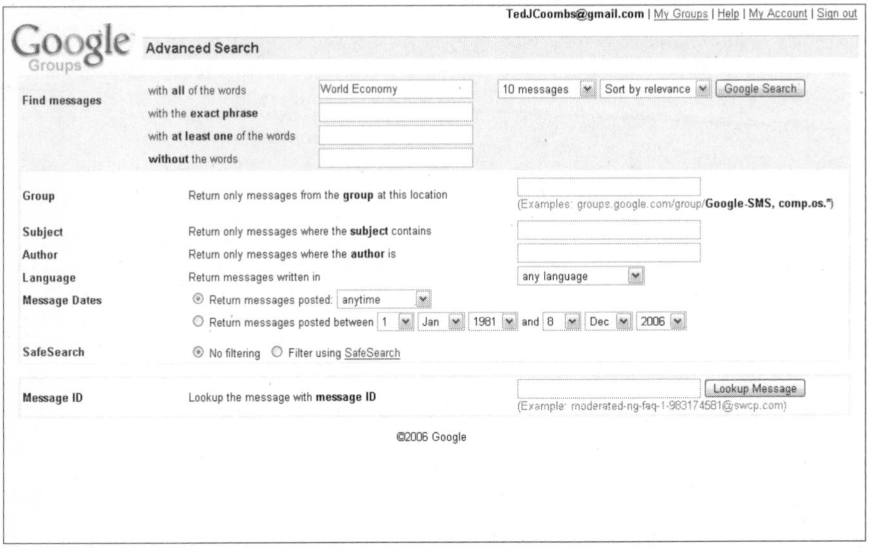

You can find messages that have your keyword in the subject, as opposed to the entire message. Type a keyword or phrase into the box in the Subject section of the Advanced Groups Search page.

You can limit your search based on author, language of the message, and message dates. You can specify message dates in two ways: manually enter a date range or select a range from the drop-down list, consisting of the following choices:

- anytime (default)
- past 24 hours
- past week
- past month
- past 3 months
- past 6 months
- past year

Remember that when you select anytime, your search may go back as far as 1981. This advanced search feature is an excellent way to limit your search to more recent postings.

The advanced search also allows you to engage the Google SafeSearch option. This limits the messages you receive to those that do not contain text with adult-oriented explicit language.

Finally, you can search for a specific message when you know the message ID. This is useful when you want to go back and read a specific message to read responses posted about the original message. Find the message ID by:

1. **Navigate to the message in Google Groups.**
2. **Click the <u>show options</u> link in the message.**
3. **Click the <u>Show original</u> link to display the unformatted version of the message.**
4. **Find the Message-ID line. The message ID looks something like this:** `Message-ID: <11656367.971544.290210@73g1000cwn.googlegroups.com>`.

Google Group search results

When your search terms match the name of a Google Group, those results appear first. Figure 22.3 shows that searching on the phrase "google groups" matched the group named Google Groups Guide. This result came first.

FIGURE 22.3

Google Group search results include groups and message postings.

The results that follow display individual message posts to various groups. The title of the message (similar to the subject of an e-mail message) appears as a link. Clicking the link displays the full content of the message. You can read a brief snippet of the message, the part of the message that includes your search term.

The last line of the result is a link to the group itself. The text that follows includes the date of the message, name or pseudonym of the person who posted the message, and how many messages can be found in the group. You also can see how many different people posted messages. For example, a group could have 100 messages with only two people posting to the group.

Reading a message

After you find a message that you want to read, whether by searching Google Groups or by browsing through the messages in the group, you can see the author's name in the From field and the date the message was posted. Clicking the Show options link reveals more information, such as the poster's e-mail address and the groups the message was posted to. It is possible to post the same message to multiple groups. Learn more on posting messages later in this chapter. Additionally, eight more links appear (see Figure 22.4):

- **Reply:** Reply to this message, and have it posted as a message to the group.
- **Reply to author:** Reply by e-mail only to the author of the message.
- **Forward:** Send a copy of this message to yourself or someone else by e-mail.
- **Print:** Print the message.
- **Individual Message:** Show only the individual message and not the list of messages.
- **Show original:** Display a raw copy of the message, unformatted, in a new window.
- **Report abuse:** Let Google know when someone is posting material that should not be posted.
- **Find messages by this author:** This handy feature allows you to see messages in all groups by the person who posted the message you are reading.

FIGURE 22.4

Read and respond to messages posted to Google Groups.

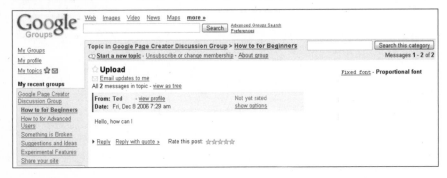

Participating in groups is very much like using e-mail, particularly Gmail, because Gmail messages are shown as threaded discussions.

Finding a Group

Instead of finding information in many groups, you may simply want to find a group that interests you. On the left side of the Google Groups home page, click the My Groups link. In the Find a group search box, type a topic and click Search for a group. The results first display topics that pertain to your search term. Next to each topic is a number in parentheses indicating the number of groups found related to that topic. The number also may represent several possible subgroups, each containing several possible groups.

Clicking any of these topics allows you to focus your search by navigating down a particular hierarchy of groups until you find the group or groups that interest you.

There may be several group topics that contain your search term. For example, searching on *Ventura* can bring up groups that focus on Ventura Publishing, a software package, or Ventura, California, and whatever else that could share the term, even Ace Ventura, Pet Detective. If you are searching for software, then you want to focus on the topics that deal with computers.

In addition to topics, the result page also displays languages that you can choose. Groups listed under this heading are in the language you select. You also can choose the level of activity the group experiences. It's not very interesting to join a group that sees one post a year, so you probably want to choose groups with higher levels of activity. The levels include:

- High
- Medium
- Low

Just like activity levels, you may want to see groups that have a certain number of members posting messages. You can select groups with higher numbers of members by selecting one of the links in the Members section showing the minimum number of members; 100+, 10-100, and less than 10.

The list of groups appears in the next section of the results page. If you are curious as to why a particular group is included, click the <u>Show matching messages from this group</u> link next to the group name and see the messages that match your search term.

Also shown in the results for each group is the following information: the category, the group language, the level of activity, the number of subscribers, and whether it is a Usenet or Google group. Some groups show that they are restricted. This means that you must get permission from the group moderator before you can participate in the group.

Joining a Group

Many groups require that you become a member of the group before you can post to the group. This is similar to moderated Usenet groups. The moderator can choose who is allowed to read or post messages to the group. In some cases, the moderator is allowed to review the messages and reject those not desirable for the group. Google Groups calls these *restricted groups*. The group owner may elect to have the group be restricted. When you must first become a member of the group you will see the following message: You cannot post messages because only members can post, and you are not currently a member.

To post to a restricted group you must first join the group. Visit the group's home page, and click <u>Join this group</u>. You may first want to click the <u>About group</u> link to learn more about the group before joining. Clicking the <u>Join this group</u> link launches the group's Join page. Here you can set the nickname that will appear in posts by you to this group and select the manner in which you receive or view messages from the group. The choices are: No Email and Abridged Email. When you have finished configuring the Join options click Join this group (see Figure 22.5).

FIGURE 22.5

Select the way you want to review postings, by abridged e-mail or no e-mail.

Starting a Group

You can participate in Google Groups in an active way by creating your own groups. Read the other groups in your topic area before creating a group so you aren't simply duplicating a group that already exists. Still, there are no restrictions to creating similar groups. Creating groups is a two-step process: Create the group, and then add members to the group.

Creating the group

You can create a group in two ways:

- From the menu on the left side of the search results page, click the <u>Create a new group</u> link.
- Complete the Start a Group section on the Google Groups home page (see Figure 22.6).

When you're ready to begin, follow these steps:

1. **Give the group a name.** Type a name into the box labeled Group name. Names must be a single word or words separated by a dash. The name you type appears in the Group e-mail address box. The name of the group automatically becomes the group's e-mail address. For example, a group named Black-Cats is given a group e-mail address of `black-cats@googlegroups.com`.

    **NOTE** The group URL cannot be edited; it is simply displayed for you. In the case of the Black-Cats group, the URL would be `http://groups.google.com/group/black-cats`.

2. **Type a description of the group.** You have 300 characters in which to provide a description of what people will find posted in this group. The group description can be the most important part of having a successful group. Take your time with this step.

FIGURE 22.6

Complete this form to create a new group.

3. **If your group contains information not suitable for children, select the This group may contain content which is only suitable for adults checkbox.**

4. **Set the access level to the group.** You can only select one of the three levels of access by selecting the radio button next to the selection:

   ■ **Public:** Anyone can read and join; members can post.

   ■ **Announcement-only:** This group is created for making announcements. It is public, but only the group owner can post.

   ■ **Restricted:** People must be invited to join the group before they can read messages or post to the group.

5. **Click Create my group.** If there are duplicate names or errors in the form, Google helps you complete the page. Look for the red message below one of the boxes on the page.

When the group is successfully created, you can begin adding group members. You will receive an e-mail message confirming that the group has been successfully created.

Adding group members

After you create your group, you can start adding members. Only members of your Google Group can post messages. This is where Google groups are different from Usenet groups, which allow anyone to post to unmoderated newsgroups.

1. **Add members by typing the name and e-mail address of the member in this format:** `first last <mymail@address.com>`. You also can simply add just the e-mail address like this: `mymail@address.com`.

2. **Add addresses, one per line, in the box provided.** When you finish adding members (and you can add more later), choose whether these people are simply added as members or invited to join the group. When you add them, they become members automatically. When you invite them, they receive an invitation via e-mail and must accept your invitation before they can begin viewing group messages.

3. **Set a default subscription type for the members joining your group.** They can change their subscription type after becoming members. These are the subscription choices:

   ■ **No email:** Read this group on the Web.

   ■ **Email:** Send each message as it arrives to the member via e-mail.

   ■ **Abridged email:** Send a brief summary of the day's messages once per day.

   ■ **Digest email:** Send an archive of the day's messages once per day via e-mail.

4. **Type a welcome message that each new member receives via e-mail after joining the group.** There is no need to type the name of the group, the group home page URL, or its e-mail address; these are sent as part of the welcome message by Google. This is a good place to describe your vision for the kinds of information you want to see posted and any restrictions you want to add.

5. **Click Done.** You have successfully created your Google Group and let prospective members know about the group.

FIGURE 22.7
_____

Type the e-mail addresses of new members in the box and configure how e-mail is delivered to them.

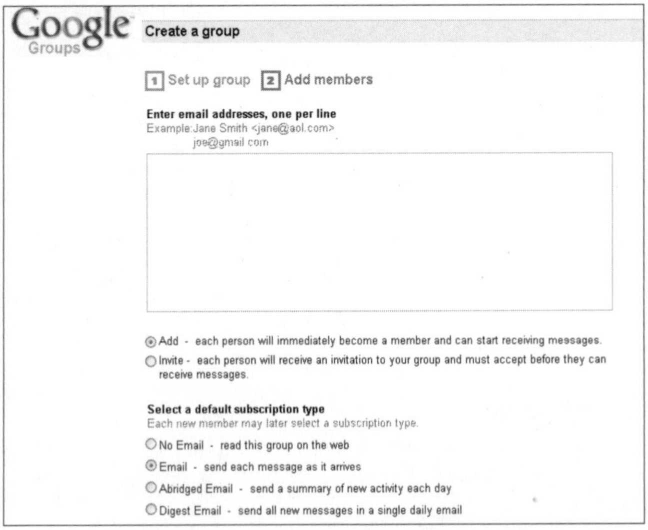

Google Groups — Create a group

[1] Set up group [2] Add members

Enter email addresses, one per line
Example:Jane Smith <jane@aol.com>
        joe@gmail.com

⦿ Add - each person will immediately become a member and can start receiving messages.
○ Invite - each person will receive an invitation to your group and must accept before they can receive messages.

Select a default subscription type
Each new member may later select a subscription type.

○ No Email - read this group on the web
⦿ Email - send each message as it arrives
○ Abridged Email - send a summary of new activity each day
○ Digest Email - send all new messages in a single daily email

---

 Your new group is accessible only through Google, not Usenet.

Managing your Google group

When you click the My Groups link on the left side of the Google Groups page (see Figure 22.8), you see the list of groups you can manage with a manage link displayed next to the group name. Clicking this link takes you to a summary page of the settings for all your groups. Select one of the areas to be managed, and click the Edit link in the upper-right corner of the section you want to edit.

FIGURE 22.8

Click the My Groups link to see a list of the groups you manage.

You have more configuration choices when managing the group than when you first created the group.

 **TIP** After creating the group, immediately edit the group settings to take advantage of the increased number of configuration settings.

In addition to changing the group description, access settings, e-mail, and group language, as a manager you also can browse the membership list by clicking the link in the Members section of the group's manage page. You also can invite or add members by clicking the Invite or Add members link in this section.

After you begin managing a group and access this page, you can see a list of your outstanding tasks. For example, you might have on your tasks list to approve messages when your list is moderated or to approve membership requests when access to your group is restricted. You see these in the Tasks section of the manage page.

It's a good idea to begin your group by posting the first message to the group. You do not have to repeat what you put in the group description. Just begin the discussion of a topic in which you think others will be interested.

Using Mailing Lists

When you create a Google Group, you create a type of mailing list. Mailing lists are composed of members who join the list. Most mailing lists allow you to receive individual messages as they are sent or to receive a digest of the messages. Google Groups actually gives you two more choices: reading your messages on the Web and receiving a summary of the messages.

There are many parallels to running a Google Group and managing an e-mail list. You can moderate the messages sent to the group, restrict access to the list, or allow anyone to *opt in* to the list. To opt in means to choose to be part of a list, unlike spam messages that make you a member and then force you to opt out to stop receiving unwanted e-mail.

> **NOTE** It is possible to create a spam list using Google Groups, but it's against the law and against Google policy.

Follow all the steps earlier in this chapter for creating a group. When you create the group, think of the group as an e-mail list rather than as a passive place to post messages, and configure the group with this in mind.

The main difference between using Google Groups as mailing lists is that most mailing list managers have special e-mail addresses where commands can be sent. Some of the commands understood by these list manager programs include the ability to unsubscribe from the list, change to receiving real-time or digest messages, and choose the message format — text or HTML. Your list members need to use their Google Groups Web interface to change their settings.

Creating Newsletters

Newsletters are a little like mailing lists with one difference: They tend to be messages sent by the group manager to the members of the group, not from the group members to all the other members of the group.

When you create a Google Group for the purposes of creating a newsletter, you should set the following restrictions:

- **Group Description:** The description of the group should clearly specify that the purpose of the group is to act as a newsletter.
- In the access settings configure the following:
  - **Who can view:** Set this to Only members can view group content.
  - **Directory Listing:** If this is a private newsletter, set this to Do not list this group.
  - **Who can join:** This is up to you. You can leave the newsletter very public or restrict access to your newsletter by changing this setting.
  - **Who can post messages:** This is the most important setting. Set this to Managers only.
  - **Message moderation:** This setting is less important because only the group manager can post messages.

You can choose to add people to your newsletter or invite them to receive it using the same procedure as adding and inviting people to your Google Group, because that's what this is.

Summary

Google Groups allows you to participate in discussions that span tens of thousands of topics. These topic groups include a great number of the Usenet groups as well as proprietary Google Groups. You can search through Usenet all the way back to 1981 or choose to read current postings.

Create your own Google group that can act like a Usenet group, an e-mail mailing list, or a newsletter. Make sure you sign up for your Google Group promotion box so you can advertise your group on your personal Web page created using Google Page Creator, which is covered in the next chapter.

Chapter 23

Creating Web Pages with Page Creator

oogle has a product still in the Google Labs that allows you to easily create graphically compelling Web pages with no previous Web page creation abilities. Most of the Google Labs products are covered in Chapter 40, but this product is being used by many people and deserves its place among all the other graduates of Google's Product Labs.

Start Your Web Page

Creating your own Web page is fun and can be very useful for communicating with friends, associates, or complete strangers around the world. Your Web page is your "home on the Internet" that people can visit to learn more about you. To get started using Google Page Creator, point your Web browser to `http://pages.google.com`.

NOTE   You need both a Google account and a Gmail account to use Page Creator.

You are asked to log in to your Google account when you visit `http://pages.google.com`. The first time you log in, select the check box in the lower left that affirms that you agree to the terms and conditions and then click I'm ready to create my pages or the I'm ready to create my pages link in the upper-right corner of the page to get started using Page Creator.

The page editor appears showing you the default page layout, as shown in Figure 23.1. This list shows the different editing features you find on the Page Creator Edit page:

- **Image**: Add a graphic to your page.
- **Link**: Add a clickable hyperlink into the page.
- **Bold**: Change text to **Bold**.
- **Italics**: Change text to *Italics*.
- **Bullet list**: Organize information into a bullet list.

- **Text color**: Change the text color.
- **Font**: Change the text font style.
- **Text size**: Make the text larger or smaller.
- **Text alignment**: Align text to the left, center, or to the right.
- **Heading** (shown in Figure 23.2): Create a large text heading.
- **Subheading** (shown in Figure 23.2): Create a medium-sized text heading.
- **Minor heading** (shown in Figure 23.2): Create a smaller-sized text heading.
- **Normal** (shown in Figure 23.2): Change the font to normal size.
- **Create a new page**: Create another page.
- **Back to Page Manager**: Return to the Page Manager.
- **Publish**: Publish your Web page so that it appears on the Web.
- **Preview**: See what your page looks like before publishing.
- **Undo | Redo**: Undo and Redo your actions.
- **Change Look**: Change the color scheme of your page.
- **Change layout**: Change the way the new Web page is organized.
- **Page title:** Create a title for your Web page.
- **Page subtitle** (optional): Create a subtitle for your Web page.
- **Page footer** (optional, appears at the bottom of your page): Add a footer to your page.

FIGURE 23.1

The Edit page is where you create or edit Web pages.

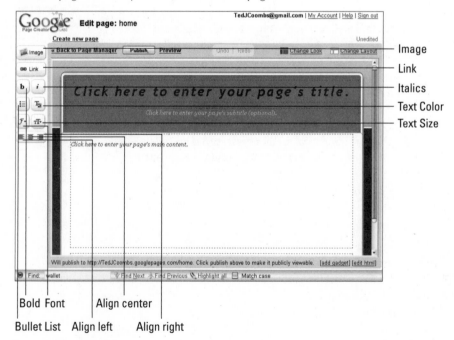

FIGURE 23.2

Begin editing in any layout you want and change it later.

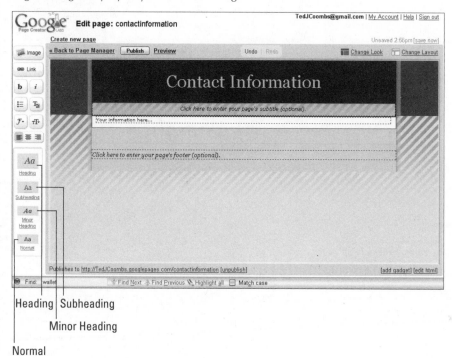

Heading | Subheading

Minor Heading

Normal

Begin creating your Web page by adding a page title. Your page title can be anything such as your name, your business name, My Home Page, or anything you want in big bold letters at the top of your Web page. Don't worry about saving your page. Google saves your page automatically every few moments. You can, however, choose to save your page immediately by clicking the save now link in the upper right of the Edit page. Google lets you know the exact time of its last auto-save.

Creating the page look and layout

You can begin creating your Web page using the default design or choose a different layout, and you can change it later if you like. It's usually best to create the page in the layout you want it published in, so you can preview it as you create it. Sometimes, changing the appearance of the page after you create it is difficult.

See Figure 23.3 to see the different layouts you can choose from. The first and default layout is great for single Web pages. But if you want to include any type of navigation between the Web pages on your site, you may want to choose any of the other layouts. For example, the second and third layouts allow you to select smaller columns on either the left or right, which are perfect for putting links to your other pages, thus creating a menu. The editor even tells you that the sidebar is a great place to link to any other pages you create.

FIGURE 23.3

Begin editing in any layout you want, but remember that you can change it later.

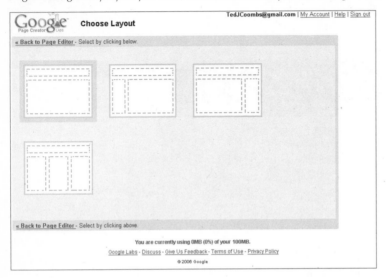

The three-column layout is great for creating online newsletters. Text you type in each column automatically wraps around, creating a "newspaper" effect.

Add gadgets

Many people have created third-party gadgets. Google has many gadgets you can add to your Web page, so visitors to your page find interesting and useful features. Click the add gadget link at the bottom of the page to add gadgets to your page. You may receive a warning like the one shown in Figure 23.4. Click **OK** to continue adding the gadget.

FIGURE 23.4

Google warns you when you are about to add gadgets not supported by Google.

Creating a Menu

On Web pages, menus are normally links to other pages. These can be pages you create on your Web site or links to other Web pages on the Internet. For example, you can create a menu of favorite sites and include links to all your favorite Web addresses.

Menus can be either horizontal (a bar across the top of the page) or vertical (listing menu items in a vertical column down one side of the page). Generally, horizontal menus are used for linking to pages on your own Web site. Vertical menus may include links to your own pages or other pages on the Web. When creating a vertical menu, choosing a layout with a sidebar on either the left or right side of the page is your best option.

To begin creating your menu, position your mouse pointer to the place you'd like the first menu item to appear and click the Link button found in the Page Creator menu on the left. Choose where you want your menu item to link — one of your pages, a file you've uploaded, another page on the Web, or an e-mail address — which is great for creating a contact menu choice.

When you select Your pages, a list of the Web pages you've created appears. Type the text you want displayed in your menu selection in the box at the top, and click OK to continue. To create the next menu item, press Enter to move to the next line, or position your mouse at the place where you want the next item to appear and add another link.

When creating a horizontal menu, do not press Enter. Most horizontal menus have a separator between the choices. You can use the vertical line (also known as the pipe) symbol (|) to separate your menu choices. After creating each link, add the | symbol (found above the \ symbol on most keyboards).

After the last menu choice in your horizontal menu, do not add a | symbol. You'll notice that horizontal menus do not allow you to add many links or long menu descriptions.

You may want to consider changing the font of the menu selections and possibly make them bold to stand out from the other text on your Web page.

FIGURE 23.5

Add one or more gadgets to your Web page to add fun and functionality.

As the warning says, many gadgets require setup. Some, like the Wikipedia search box gadget, only require that you select a language for your search box.

You can click and drag your gadget to a new location on the page. Click the gadget while editing your page, and a blue box appears below your gadget that allows you to edit the gadget's preferences or remove the gadget completely from the page. Click Edit to access the preferences, or click Remove Gadget to remove it from your page.

Adding page elements

You can add several kinds of things to your Web page using Page Creator, including text, links, and images.

To add text, simply click in the area of the page where you want text to appear and begin typing. You can format this text in a number of ways. You can click one of the text formatting buttons in the Page Creator menu, type your text, and then click the button again to turn off that formatting feature. You also can type text, highlight the text by dragging across it with your mouse, and then click the formatting button once.

The text formatting buttons include **b** for bold text and *i* for italics. You also can choose a new font for your text by clicking the *f* button and choosing a font from the list. The fonts that appear in the list are those that normally appear on all computers. When computers do not have a font that appears in the list, the text appears in the viewer's default browser text font.

Change the text color from its default black by clicking the T button that appears with a small color palette. Again, you can click the button, select a color, type the text, and then click the button again to change the font to a different color, or you can highlight text you've already typed and select a new color for it.

When you want to change the size of your text, you can click the double T button and select a font size: Small, Normal, Large, or Huge. The default size is Normal. You also can change the size of the font by identifying it as a heading, subheading, or minor heading. It's best to use heading formats for true headings rather than using them to change font sizes within a page.

Add links — clickable text that launches another page — by clicking the Link button. You are prompted to type the text you want to appear on the page and then prompted to specify the type of link you want added. These are your choices:

- **Your pages:** Web pages created using Page Creator and hosted on the `googlepages.com` site
- **Your files:** Files other than Web pages and graphics that you've uploaded to the site
- **Web address:** A Web page other than those hosted on your Google site
- **Email address:** A link that launches the viewer's e-mail program and starts an e-mail message to the address you specify

You can test the link before you add it to make certain that it actually links to another page. Links that do not work are called *dead links*. You don't want dead links on your page. Nothing makes a person move from your page faster than encountering a dead link.

You can add images to your page, whether it's a picture of your smiling face, a candid shot of your favorite pet, vacation photos, or possibly pictures of a logo and products for your business. Click Image to add an image. In the dialog box that appears, you are asked whether the image is one you uploaded previously, one you'd like to upload now, or an image that exists somewhere on the Internet that you want to appear on your page.

 When linking to images on the Internet, make certain that you are not violating someone else's copyright.

Changing your page layout

Making Web pages is a creative process, and that sometimes means changing your mind. The Undo and Redo links allow you to step backward and forward through your edits. For example, changing the font and making text bold is a two-step process. If you changed your mind, you can click the <u>Undo</u> link. Each time you click Undo, you step back to the previous edit. You can continue clicking Undo until you arrive at the point where your page was either last published or no other changes can be undone. After that, Undo is no longer active (clickable).

If you undo a change and want to change it back again, simply click the <u>Redo</u> link. Redo steps forward through your edits. Redo is active (clickable) only when you have first clicked Undo one or more times.

Follow these steps to get rid of all your changes in the fastest manner:

1. Click the <u><<Back to Page Manager</u> link at the top of the Edit page.
2. Select the page where you want all the changes discarded by selecting the check box.
3. Select Discard unpublished changes from the More actions drop-down list.

This action returns your page to its previously published (or never before published) state.

Editing your page's HTML

When you want to edit the underlying HTML code for your Web page, click the <u>Edit HTML</u> link in the lower-right portion of the Edit page. Working with HTML is not difficult, but does take a little bit of time and patience. One of the advantages is that you can add Web features that are not currently available using Page Creator, including these:

- Forms
- Frames
- Buttons
- Tables
- Script programming

Some excellent HTML tutorials are available on the Web. You can find a fairly complete, free resource at `www.w3schools.com/html/default.asp`.

Clicking the <u>Edit HTML</u> link opens a new window that displays the HTML in an editor. Follow these steps to edit the HTML of your Web page:

1. Make changes by typing HTML commands in the editor.
2. Test your changes by previewing them.
3. Click the <u>Preview</u> link/radio button in the tab found in the top-right corner of the HTML editor window. You can switch back and forth by clicking either the HTML or the Preview tabs.
4. Close the editor and switch back to the graphic version by clicking Save Changes at the bottom of the HTML editor window.
5. To exit without saving any of your changes, click Cancel. The window closes and returns you to the main Page Creator window.

Creating new pages

When you start Page Creator, you create or edit your "home" page. This is the page that people normally first see when visiting your Web site. You can create other Web pages that can appear on your site, but you can only have a single home page.

There are two places within Page Creator that allow you to create new pages. A Create new page link is at the top left of any Edit page. You also can click the Create a new page link in Page Manager.

When you create the new page from either Page Manager or from the Edit page, a text box appears asking you to type the title of the new page (see Figure 23.6). Type a title for the new page, and then click Create and Edit.

FIGURE 23.6

Enter a title for your page. Google will automatically remove spaces from your title to create a filename.

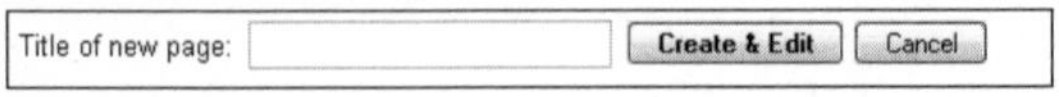

| Title of new page: | | Create & Edit | Cancel |

Your new page is created with the title filled in. The new page is in the same color scheme and layout as your home page. You can change the layout and look (color scheme) of this page without changing the layout and look of all your pages. Generally, you may want to keep the same color scheme throughout your Web site, and sometimes even the layout. Keeping the same look and feel can make a Web site easier to navigate and makes it more visually pleasing to your site's visitors. Your new page is ready for editing.

When you create new pages, you have a choice about how people navigate to the new page. If you want people to move to the new page from your home page, place a link to the new page on your home page. You can create this link in the form of a menu, but placing a link anywhere on the page works just as well.

TIP Web crawlers (programs used by search engines) index your site by starting at the home page and following all the links. Pages on your site not linked to the home page may not be indexed by Google or other search engines.

Publishing Your Web Page

As you create your Web pages in Page Creator, they are stored on the Google site in a place not viewable by Web visitors. Only after you are ready to have the world see your creation should you publish your pages, meaning that Google moves a copy of your page to a publicly available place on its servers. The address of your Web site is your Google ID, followed by a dot and googlepages.com.

Previewing your page

You do not need to publish your page to see what it looks like. You can preview the page as though it had been published. This way, any pages that you have already published on the Web site remain unchanged until you are ready to update them. This means that visitors to your page won't see your page slowly change as you edit and save changes.

To preview your page, click the Preview link found to the right of the Publish button in the blue bar along the top of the editor window. A new window opens that shows you how your new page will appear when published. An orange bar appears across the top of the previewed page telling you that this page is just a preview and has not yet been published. The page may have been published in the past, but the version you are previewing has not.

When you finish viewing the preview page, click the X in the upper-right corner of the window to close it.

How to Publish and Unpublish

When you are satisfied that your creation is ready to be made public, click Publish located at the top of the Edit page. Google makes a copy of your page and places it in your public directory. Visitors to your Web site see your new page. If you have been editing a page and have republished it by clicking Publish, visitors see your changes.

> **NOTE** When you publish your changes while someone is viewing your site, your visitor may not see your changes until he closes and restarts his Web browser. Web browsers often keep cached versions of Web pages to speed the display of pages. Normally, but not always, this cache refreshes when the browser is closed and reopened, and the browser cache is updated with your changed pages.

After you click Publish, Page Creator displays an orange bar telling you that your page has been published and contains links that let you <u>View it on the Web</u> or <u>Tell your friends</u>. View it on the Web lets you see the page as other Web visitors will see it. Tell your friends lets you send a Gmail message containing a link to your updated page to your friends so they can see your changes.

Sometimes, you may need to remove a page from your public site, but you don't want to delete the page completely from the Page Manager. You can "unpublish" a page — remove it from your public site — by clicking the [unpublish] link found at the bottom of the Edit page. The page is still available for you to edit and republish. See the nearby Note about browser caches. When you remove a page, it may appear temporarily while visitors view your site. This may continue until the visitor's browser cache is updated.

Hosting Your Web Page

When you visit a Web site, the pages are stored on a computer that is publicly accessible via the Internet. Pages are delivered by a special program called a Web server. Your Web browser, whether it is Internet Explorer, Opera, Firefox, AOL, or some other browser, contacts the Web server and asks that it deliver a particular Web page. The page is then delivered by the Web server to your browser, which loads it and displays it to you.

Each Web server has an Internet address identified in the URL. In the case of Google's Web site hosting, your pages are hosted by the Web server found at `googlepages.com`.

> **NOTE** Web servers may actually consist of many computers and Web servers to handle large traffic loads. These are known as server farms. They do not affect how visitors view your site.

Web pages for your site are stored in a particular folder located on the Web server. This folder is identified by the first part of the URL: `Yoursitename.googlepages.com`.

This directory is created by Google automatically using your Google ID. Individual pages are identified by their page names. The page names appear after `googlepages.com` and are separated by a forward slash like this: `http://yoursitename.googlepages.com/newpage`.

> **NOTE** You may notice that your home page does not display a page name in the URL. This is because a standardized default name (usually *index*) is used to name your home page. Web servers know to look for an index page when no page name is specified by the Web browser. So going to `www.somesite.com`, for example, actually loads `www.somesite.com/index`.

You don't have to be hosting your Web page on Google in order to use Page Creator. When your site is hosted by a different Web hosting service, you can create your pages using Page Creator and then copy the HTML into files that you deliver to your Web hosting service. Web hosting services vary. Some hosting services have Web-based editing capabilities, in which case, you have three choices:

- Edit the HTML of your pages made with Page Creator.
- Copy and paste the HTML from Page edit into the Web-based editor provided by your hosting service.
- Save the changes in your hosting service editor.

Some Web services require that you transfer completed files to them via some file transfer utility. Sometimes, that transfer utility is FTP (File Transfer Protocol), or you may have to use an HTML upload utility. In either case, you should copy the HTML (according to the steps listed previously) into a text file. Save the text file with the filename you want to transfer to your Web site.

Web pages normally have a file extension. File extensions used on the Web may vary depending on the technology used to create them. The file extension used mostly with HTML pages is .html or .htm. These extensions do not normally appear using the Google hosting service. For this reason, you may need to manually change any links created by Page Creator to have a file extension expected by other Web servers.

Using Page Manager

The Page Manager allows you to easily manage your entire Web site, so that you can quickly move between pages you want to edit, delete pages, lose changes, or publish pages. The Page Manager also allows you to easily create a new page on your site. To access the Page Manager, click the Page Manager link found at the top left of any Page Creator page.

Page Manager lists each of your created Web pages, as shown in Figure 23.7. If you are just starting, you may see only your home page, identified with a small "home" icon. You also can click the green page associated with the Create a new page link to create a new page and launch the Edit page.

FIGURE 23.7

Move between Web pages on your site using Page Manager.

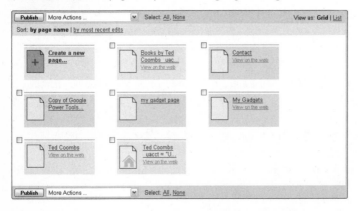

View your Web pages in Page Manager as a grid (the default) or change to a list view. To change between views, click the <u>List</u> link or <u>Grid</u> link in the upper-right corner of the Page Manager page.

The pages are listed in either page name order (alphabetical order) or by the most recently edited page first and the oldest edits last. You can easily switch between these different page orders by selecting one of the links next to Sort in the upper left of the page. Click either by page name or by most recent edits.

Page Manager actions

You can take many actions from the Page Manager. Select the page you want to take action on by selecting the check box next to the page. A shortcut for selecting all pages, particularly if you are taking advantage of all the free Web hosting and have created many pages, is to use Select All, located in the top blue bar. To deselect all the pages, click None.

After you select one or more pages, you can quickly publish them all by clicking Publish. Or you can take other actions by selecting them from the drop-down list. These are your choices:

- Tell your friends
- Discard unpublished changes
- Unpublish
- Duplicate
- Delete

When you have published new pages to your site, you may want your friends and associates to know so they can look at your updated pages. In Page Manager, select the pages you want to tell your friends about by selecting the check boxes associated with the pages you've updated. Don't click the page titles because that loads the pages into the editor. Selecting a check box launches a new Gmail message already complete with a link to the page and an announcement that your friends should see your new page. Simply add the e-mail addresses of the desired recipients.

Return pages to their unedited state by choosing to discard unpublished changes. This returns the page to the state it was in the last time it was published, even if you've chosen to save your changes while editing.

Remove a page from the publicly viewable Web site by selecting Unpublish from the drop-down list. Pages are not deleted; they are just removed from public view. The page is still viewable in Page Manager and can be republished or edited at any time.

To save time creating new pages that contain many of the same features or content, you can choose to create a new Web page by duplicating another page. Some people even create an unpublished template page that they use over and over again by using the Duplicate feature. This is particularly handy when you create menus or other complex layout features.

The Delete feature removes the page from Page Manager and any copies that exist on the public Web site. When you select this feature, the computer warns you that your actions will permanently delete the selected Web pages. If you accidentally delete a file, there is no recovering it, nada, zip, not a chance, gone forever.

TIP When unpublishing or deleting a page, remember to remove any links to it from your other pages. If you forget, users may click the link and be treated to an error message.

Other stuff

Click the Site Settings link found in the Page Manager to set some of your Web site's features, such as the text that appears in the title bar when people access your page. By default, the Site name is your Google account name.

You can see your Web site's URL for easy reference, but after you create a site, Google assigns the URL where it is published, and you can't change that.

There is an Image Upload check box. When it is selected, Google automatically optimizes the size of uploaded images, thereby reducing the download time of large images for people viewing your Web page. If you want to upload large images and not have Google optimize them, deselect this box.

NOTE Remember that large images quickly use up your allotted 100MB of storage space.

Because Page Creator is still in Google Labs, you must decide whether you want the experimental features activated. Be aware that these beta features may work with unpredictable results. When Page Creator graduates from the labs, these features will have been fully tested and the experimental features button will no longer exist.

When you click the Experimental Features button, a page appears that explains the unpredictable nature of these experimental features and asks you whether you are certain this is what you want to do. To return without enabling the experimental features, click No (sounds scary). To enable the features, click Yes (I understand what I'm getting myself into). If you click Yes, a red notice appears telling you that experimental features are enabled. The button changes to Disable experimental features. From that point on, in the Edit page you also see a notice at the top of the page reminding you that experimental features are enabled with a Send feedback link next to this notice. Google Labs wants to know when things need fixing or they would love your comments to improve their products.

If your content is not suitable for minors, you can let people know by selecting the check box under Adult Content. The terms and conditions of using the Google service state that when displaying adult content, you must check this box.

Summary

Page Creator is a simple-to-use Web page creation and editing tool. With no previous Web page creating experience, you easily can create and publish Web pages to your own free Google Web site. All you need is a Google account and something to say.

Choose from many different colors and layouts to create a compelling and professional-looking Web page the very first time. Create as many pages as you want (within the 100MB limit). Upload images and files that you can drop anywhere you like on your page.

You are not limited to the things Page Creator does for you easily; you can edit the underlying HTML. When you finish, simply publish the page with a single click of the Publish button or copy the HTML to another hosting service for display on another Web site. When you complete your Web site, Google helps you tell your friends by sending them an e-mail announcement using your Gmail account. Speaking of friends, when you have lots more to say, you might consider creating a Weblog, or *blog*, to share with your friends or everyone else in the world. The next chapter covers blogging.

Chapter 24

Introducing Blogs

oogle has created a special search page just for finding blogs. Because Google's goal is to give access to all the world's digital information, the folks at Google would have been remiss in leaving out blogs. A great deal of information, more editorial and creative than fact-based, resides in blogs around the world. This chapter introduces blogs and helps you use Google technology to find the blog that has information you want to read. Chapter 25 goes into greater depth in helping you create your own blog using the Google-owned Blogger Web site.

What Is a Blog?

Blog, a recently coined term, is a shortened version of Weblog. In fact, it has pretty much replaced the word weblog altogether. A blog is a type of online journal, usually meant for public consumption. You can think of it as a "Dear Diary" entry on a public highway billboard, except this one is on the Internet super-highway.

A blog does not require special software or a special user interface. A blog simply can be a continued posting on a Web page or a continued Google Group posting. Blogs have become popular as a way to communicate thoughts and ideas for both adults as well as young people. An entirely new Internet industry has been spawned to promote the creation and publication of blogs online. You can even find blog critics at places such as blogcritics.org.

CROSS-REF See Chapter 22 for more information on Google Groups.

IN THIS CHAPTER

Learning what blogs are and why reading them is fun and interesting

Using Blog Search to find blogs that interest you

Using Advanced Search features to better focus your blog search

Getting your blog listed in the Google Blog Search index

Searching for Blogs

Google recognizes that some of the world's information resides in blogs. Part of fulfilling its mission of providing access to this information is accomplished by the Google Blog Search (http://blogsearch.google.com).

CROSS-REF   You can find Blog Search on Google's Blogger pages, which is covered in more detail in Chapter 25.

You can search for blogs two ways in Google: You can type a keyword or phrase into the search box on the Blog Search home page and click Search Blogs, or you can choose to search the Web by clicking Search the Web also found below the search box.

NOTE   Blog Search is not limited to blogs in English or Blogger sites. Google has indexed blogs in many languages across the entire Internet.

To focus your search, you can use any of the operators found in Table 24.1 in the Blog Search text box. These operators do not work properly when used in the Google Web search.

TABLE 24.1

Blog Search Operators

Operator	Description
inblogtitle:	Finds search terms in the title of the Blog, not the individual postings
inposttitle:	Finds search terms in the posting title, not the title of the blog
inpostauthor:	Finds search terms in the name of the author of a posting to a blog
blogurl:	Finds the search terms in the URL of the blog

Use the blog search operators when typing search terms in the search box. Put the value directly next to the operator without spaces like this: **inpostauthor:"mortimer sneed"**.

NOTE   Remember that you can create search phrases by placing search terms within quotes.

Interpreting Blog Search Results

The blog search results begin by displaying the five most relevant blogs according to Google's PageRank technology. These are listed as Related Blogs. In Figure 24.1, you may notice that some of the blogs listed as Related Blogs are listed again below the Related Blogs section displaying individual postings.

The results show blog posts that contain your keyword. The posting title is displayed as a link, allowing you to navigate directly to the post. Below the title you can see when the post was published and the author's name.

You can read a short snippet of the posting and either choose to read the post by clicking the title or navigating to the blog's home page, which is listed beneath the search result. Occasionally, when a blog has multiple postings containing your keyword, an additional line appears in brackets as the bottom line of the result. It is a link that begins More results from, and it's followed by the blog title.

FIGURE 24.1

Blog search results begin with Related Blogs.

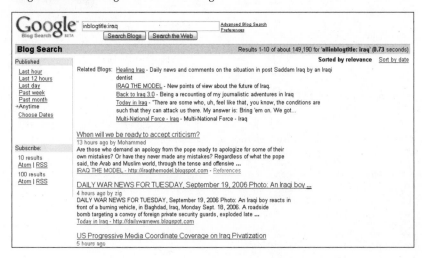

Clicking any of the results navigates you away from the Blog Search results page. To return, use your Web browser's Back button. Alternately, you can right-click the link and choose Open in New Window.

Sorting blog search results

By default, the blog search results are listed in order of relevance. You can change the ordering of the results to date order by clicking the Sort by date link in the upper-right corner of the results page. When you sort by date, the Related Blogs are no longer displayed. The date order displays the most recent post first. Return to the relevance search by clicking the Sort by relevance link.

When you click the Sort by date link or the Sort by relevance link, a new search is performed. Don't be confused when your results are not exactly the same each time you switch back.

Search results by publish date

On the left side of the Blog Search results page is a Published section containing a list of links that you can use to limit your blog search to a particular time period. These are the links in the Published section:

- **Last hour:** Limits results to posts within the last hour.
- **Last 12 hours:** Limits results to posts within the last 12 hours.
- **Last day:** Limits results to posts within the last 24 hours.
- **Past week:** Limits results to posts within the preceding seven days.
- **Past month:** Limits results to posts within the last month.
- **Anytime:** This is the default setting, with no limits by date.
- **Choose dates:** Set start and end dates to see results that fall within this date range.

Click any of these links to limit your blog search based on time and date. For most of these links, you simply click the link and a new search is performed, limiting the results to the time frame you select. You do, however, need to add begin and end dates to the date range when clicking the Choose dates link. After you type the dates, click Go.

 **NOTE** You can subscribe to your Blog Search results by selecting either the top 10 results or the top 100 results and the type of feed, either RSS or Atom.

Conducting Advanced Searches

Clicking the Advanced Blog Search link next to the search box at the top of the Blog Search page gives you access to more techniques to refine your search. You will find several options for defining your search in the two sections (see Figure 24.2).

The top section of the Advanced Blog Search page allows you to specify how Google finds blog posts using your keywords. Use one or more of the advanced search fields to focus your blog search.

FIGURE 24.2

The Advanced Blog Search assists you in focusing your blog search.

The advanced search features are similar to those in other Google advanced search pages. Limit your search using the following keyword search features:

- **With all the words:** Find posts that contain all the words and phrases in this box.
- **With the exact phrase:** Find posts that contain the exact phrase typed in this box.
- **With at least one of the words:** Locate posts that have one or more of the words you type in this box.
- **Without the words:** Exclude results that contain the words in this box.
- **With these words in the post title:** Find posts that have the search term you type in this box within its title.

Limit the number of results per page by selecting a quantity from the drop-down list located next to the Search Blogs button.

The second section of the Advanced Blog Search page includes features that allow you to focus your search to specific blogs, authors, languages, and time periods. The In blogs search features allow you to find specific blogs by the words in the blog title, rather than in the post title. If you want to ensure that posts containing your search terms are related to the blog they are posted in, this search field becomes very useful. You can be even more specific and search within a specific blog by typing the blog's URL (refer to Figure 24.2).

You may want to find postings not by blog or by posting but by author. Blog posters often post content to more than one blog and on more than one topic. You may be interested in finding anything posted by this person.

NOTE Typing an author name does not guarantee that all the posts are by the same person. Many people share the same name or pseudonym. Try to be as accurate with the author name as possible.

Similar to the time-related links listed earlier in this chapter, the Advanced Blog Search page allows you to limit the author search by time. Select one of the following from the drop-down list.

- anytime
- last hour
- last 12 hours
- last Day
- past Week
- past Month

Alternately, you can select the other date-related radio button — posts written between — and type a date range by selecting the day, month, and year from the drop-down lists. Be aware that the lists are not intelligent, so be careful that you don't type 30 February or 31 June.

You can select the language of the blogs you want to search. Select from 35 languages shown in the drop-down list, or leave the default (any language) selected.

Google allows you to turn on the SafeSearch feature. This eliminates most of the adult-oriented content from your search.

When you finish customizing your search using the advanced features, click Search Blogs in the upper-right portion of the page. If you have been too specific, you may see a results page that contains something like this: "Your search — "simple simon" inblogtitle:pie inpostauthor:mortimer — did not match any documents." In this case, try removing some of the search restrictions until you get results. In this example, you merely have to remove the author's name to get a result.

Listing Your Blog with Blog Search

When you use a mainstream blog site such as Blogger, you don't need to do any of the steps explained in this section. It is done for you. People who run their own Web site blogs find this section particularly useful.

One of the most important things about getting your blog listed in the Google Blog Search or another blog search engine is that your blog must publish a site feed in either RSS or Atom format, when you run it from your own Web site. In other words, you must set up your personal Web page so that it provides a feed.

 To create your own RSS or Atom feed, you need a feed generator. You can find free feed generator software at `www.2rss.com/software.php`.

One of the advantages of using a Weblog service is that most of them already provide either an RSS or Atom feed or both. By the way, Atom was created by software developers unhappy with RSS. So, RSS and Atom are essentially the same thing with minor differences.

 Eventually, a form is provided to let Google know about your blog. Keep watching for it.

You should consider using an update announcement service for your blog. A service that Google pays attention to is `Weblogs.com`. Weblogs.com is a free service provided by Verisign. This service, known as an infrastructure ping-server, provides information to people and to services like Google about when blogs have changed. For example, Google contacts Weblogs.com for an update of changes, and Google visits the blog sites that have changed to create a new index of the blog. Most blog services update Weblogs.com for you, but if you need to do this on your own, it's free and easy to sign up. Just make sure you have a valid RSS or Atom feed. You can validate your feed on the Weblogs.com Web site. When implementing a Weblogs ping service on your own, you need to do so on your Web page. You can find a free PHP library to implement this service on your Web site at `www.cadenhead.org/workbench/weblog-pinger/`.

After your feed is up and running and you have started using the Weblogs.com ping-server, Google can find and index your blog. If your blog has been going for a while, Google does not index the old posts. Only new posts to your blog appear in the Google Blog Search.

Summary

The type of information you normally find in a blog is largely editorial. Still, editorial information is valuable or at least entertaining. Blog Search allows you to search through thousands of blogs on almost any topic. Like other Google search tools, you can use advanced search features to focus or sort your search results.

In this chapter, you learned how blogs get added to Google's blog search index. You also learned about adding your blog to the Google index when it's run from your personal Web site rather than a Web site setup to manage blogs.

In the next chapter, you learn about Google's Blogger blog site, which surely will make you want to set up your own blog.

Chapter 25

Communicating with Blogger

logger is Google's blog site. For an introduction and background to blogs, see Chapter 24. Briefly, blogs are Weblogs, or information posted to the Web on a regular basis, like a journal or an online public diary. To make creating and publishing your blog simple, several companies have created powerful software to create and manage your blog. Google's Blogger Web site at www.blogger.com shown in Figure 25.1 does just that and more.

One of the reasons the Blogger Web site does not look like the Google sites you are used to seeing is that Google purchased Blogger in February 2003. It was already a very popular Web site, becoming extremely popular after the attacks on the World Trade Center towers in 2001. There was no need to change the look and feel of an already popular site.

FIGURE 25.1

The Blogger Web site does not look like other Google sites.

Understanding Basic Blogging

Reading the blogs that people write is easy and entertaining. Visit the Blogger main page, and you see several ways to find blogs that you may like to read in the section of the page labeled Explore blogs. Notice the rapidly scrolling list of updated blogs. This information on blogs that have been recently updated comes from a special service called Weblogs.com. Each blog, as it scrolls by, appears as a link. Clicking the name of the blog takes you directly to the blog, opening the page in a new window.

To the right of the scrolling, updated, blog list, you see BLOGS OF NOTE. You can click the blog link listed there or use the left and right arrows to the left to advance to the next or previous "blog of note." When you find a blog that interests you, click the title and the blog opens in a new window.

RANDOM BLOGS presents you with a NEXT BLOG button. Clicking this button takes you to a completely random blog. This blog does not open in a new window, but replaces the Blogger main page. You can use your browser's Back button to return to the main page.

 Random blogs may appear in any language.

Each of the features in the Explore blogs section takes you to blogs within the Blogger site. When you want to find blogs that appear anywhere on the Internet, you can use the Google Blog Search box. See Chapter 24 for detailed information on using Google Blog Search. Type a search term, and click SEARCH BLOGS. You can review the search results and find blogs that may or may not appear on the Blogger site.

Perusing the blog page

Blogs are hosted on the Blog*Spot Web site. This can be a little confusing. You may create your blog on the Blogger.com site, but the blog address actually reads `yourblogname.blogspot.com`. Blogger blogs have a blogspot.com address.

Each blog page is designed by the author of the blog. There are, however, a few things common to all the pages. These all appear in the dark blue bar across the top of the blog page.

To search through the blog you are reading, type keywords or phrases in the search box located on the left side of the top bar. Click Search this blog to start your search. You also can search through all the blogs hosted on the Blogger site by clicking SEARCH ALL BLOGS. Either of these launches a search results page that lists each location within the blog that contains your search term. Read the snippet containing the search term, and then click either the posting title to go directly to the post, or click the blog URL listed below each result snippet to go to the blog home page.

Clicking GET YOUR OWN BLOG takes you to the main Blogger page where you can start creating your own blog. You can read more about this later in the chapter.

The FLAG? button is for alerting Google to possible objectionable content. Remember that Google's SafeSearch can be used to search through blogs, and Google doesn't make it a point to censor blogs. If the blog is seriously objectionable, it may be delisted and made available only over the Web, but not removed. Only illegal and spam blogs may be reviewed for removal based on Blogger's Use Policies.

Posts

Each post on a Blogger page includes the following information:

- Post title
- Date and time of posting
- Post content (text and graphics)
- Author of the post

The content of the post is completely up to the author. Some posts are reviewed (moderated) before they appear in the blog. This is covered in more detail in the section "Managing your blog."

When you read blog postings, you can comment on them. Below each posting is a <u>POST A COMMENT</u> link. Clicking this link launches a page where you can add a comment to the post. Type your post in the text box. You can even use HTML tags when creating your comment to enhance your text or even add a link. For example, see the formatting in this fictitious comment:

```
Hah! You think <b>that's</b> bad. You should see what they wrote about
that in <a href="http://www.blogger.com/myblogpost">this guy's
blog.</a>
```

Each comment includes the identity of the comment poster. The choices are to use your Blogger identity or another identity or to post the comment anonymously. While you can read blogs without logging in, you need to log in to your Blogger account to post a comment.

Profile information

Blog authors have the choice of displaying detailed profile information about themselves. This information can include everything from their name to their astrological sign. The author of the blog has complete control over how much or how little is displayed on the blog page. Most templates are designed to display the About Me profile item. Many blog authors have at least this information available, so it doesn't appear blank in their blogs. When you create your own blog, refer to the profile information in this chapter to help you create your profile.

Logging in to Blogger

You can log in to the Blogger site using your Google account. Type your userid and password, or choose to create a new account. After you log in, you can begin creating or posting to your own blog. You may notice that after you log in to the Blogger site, your Web browser establishes a secure connection. This means that your communications to and from Blogger are encrypted and safe from prying eyes.

Creating Your Blog

To begin putting your thoughts into a blog, click the large orange CREATE YOUR BLOG NOW button on the Blogger main page. This takes you to Step 1, typing your display name and accepting the terms and conditions. The display name is what people who read your blog will see. If you don't want your actual name displayed, type your pseudonym here. After you read the Terms of Service (by clicking the blue <u>Terms of Service</u> link), check the box and click CONTINUE.

Step 2, shown in Figure 25.2, asks you to name your blog and come up with a possible URL for your blog. There are no guarantees that the URL you choose is available. You can click the <u>Check Availability</u> link to see if your proposed URL is available. If you try to type a URL that is currently taken, this error message appears: Sorry, this blog address is not available. Click CONTINUE when you finish adding your blog name and URL.

FIGURE 25.2

Create a name and URL for your blog.

The next page may appear a little confusing; it lists Step 1 as NAME BLOG and Step 2 as CHOOSE TEMPLATE. The step numbers may change at some point. The next step in creating a blog is definitely CHOOSE TEMPLATE.

In the CHOOSE TEMPLATE page, you choose a look and feel for your blog. There are a dozen different templates to choose from. Scroll down to see all the thumbnails.

Below each thumbnail, is a preview template link. Click this link to see an actual-size sample of how your blog would look using this template. One such preview is shown in Figure 25.3. Of course, the text of the preview is written in dead languages. It's just there to show you how a sample blog appears.

FIGURE 25.3

Preview the template to see what your site may look like.

After looking at each of the templates provided for you, if you just hate them all (and it's okay to hate them), you still need to select one to move on to the next step. Just pick the one you hate the least. You can change the template, or create your own after your blog creation process is complete. So, you're not stuck with your choice in this step. For more templates, you can visit `http://blogger-templates.blogspot.com`.

To easily create your own template, you can use the template creation utility found at `www.wannabegirl.org/firdamatic/`.

Adding a custom template happens after you create your blog. For now, clicking CONTINUE completes the blog creation step. Click START POSTING to move on to the next step because empty blogs are boring.

Managing Your Blog

Managing a blog isn't a huge amount of work. After you set up your profile and settle on a look and feel, the fun part begins — adding posts to the blog. You may choose to moderate the comments posted to your blog and whether other people can post there. If you've just created your first blog, you are probably staring at a screen that looks like the one in Figure 25.4.

FIGURE 25.4

Post to your blog, change the settings, or modify your template.

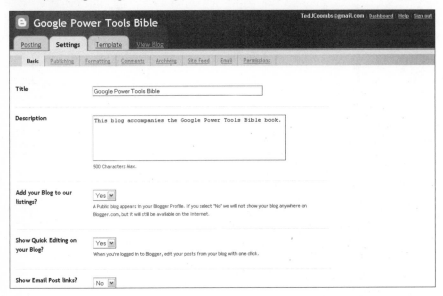

Getting started

The page shown in Figure 25.4 is the one that appears after your blog has been created. This is where all the fun happens. You can immediately begin posting to your blog by typing a post title and the content of your post. Before posting, you may want to begin by viewing and configuring your blog.

Configuring your blog

Figure 25.4 shows the Settings tab. This launches the configuration settings form. By default it starts on the Basic tab.

Entering basic settings

The title you set for your blog when you first created it appears in the Title box. You can change your blog title anytime you like.

The description box allows you to add information about your blog. Why did you start the blog? What kind of information can people expect to find in the blog? When published, this description appears below the blog's title. Don't try to write your blog in the description. You have 500 characters (including spaces and punctuation) in which to describe your blog.

Several drop-down lists ask you yes-and-no questions, including these:

- **Add your Blog to our listings? (Yes / No):** Selecting No makes your blog private. It is available on the Internet, but no public record or index of it is available through Google or Blogger.
- **Show Quick Editing on your Blog? (Yes / No):** Selecting Yes makes editing your posts simple by allowing you to edit posts right from your blog.
- **Show Email Post links? (Yes / No):** Selecting Yes allows visitors to your blog to e-mail your posts to others.

At the bottom of the Basic tab is one global configuration setting that allows you to choose to use a WYSIWYG (What-You-See-Is-What-You-Get) editor for creating your blog posts. To use this editor, set Show Compose Mode for all your Blogs to Yes.

When you finish configuring the settings in the Basic tab, click Save Settings.

Beneath the Save Settings button is a Delete This Blog button for permanently deleting the current blog.

Publishing your blog

Clicking the Publishing tab allows you to set two configuration settings: the Blog*Spot address and whether to notify Weblogs.com.

The Blog*Spot address is the URL that people can use to visit and read your blog. By default, it is set to the URL that you set up when you created the blog. Changing it is fine as long as the new URL is available. There is no availability link on this Settings page to see if the URL is available.

The second configuration setting in this tab allows you to choose whether to update Weblogs.com. Chapter 24 explains how Weblogs.com is used as a notification service for programs like Google's Blog Search. If you want your blog indexed and noticed by the maximum number of people, set this value to Yes. Click Save Settings to save any changes you make to this page. If you try to navigate away from one of the pages with unsaved changes, Blogger lets you know and allows you to save the changes.

Formatting your blog

The settings that affect the way your blog appears to others are set in the Formatting tab. Begin by determining how many posts should appear on the main page of your blog. The default is seven, but you can increase and decrease that amount. You also can change this to show a specific number of days rather than posts. Be aware that whether you set the number of posts or the number of days, the maximum number of posts that can appear on your Blogger main page is 999.

A date appears in the header of your blog posts. You can easily set the style in which this date is displayed. Choose one of 13 styles from the drop-down list to set the date style. By default, the date appears as *day of the week, month, day, year*. The other date formats are basically shorter date formats. For example, dates can appear as 9/21/2006, 9.21.2006, 20060921, 2006-09-21, and so on.

Another date setting is the Archive Index Date Format, usually appearing in the sidebar of your blog. Because these dates represent a month, week, or day of posts, rather than a single post, you can choose the way in which that date period is represented. Here are some examples:

- 09/01/2006 – 10/01/2006
- 09/2006 – 10/2006
- 09/2006
- 09.06.2006

There are 14 ways to display the archive date. Simply select it from the drop-down list.

Similar to the date options, you also can choose a timestamp display option. Choose between displaying the time in 12-hour or 24-hour format, and choose to display or not display the date with the time.

After setting the time format, you also want to select your time zone so that your posting times accurately reflect your local time. Select your time zone from the Time Zone drop-down list.

Set the blog language to one of the many languages supported by Google. Choose a language from the drop-down list.

The Encoding drop-down contains a list of various text-encoding types widely used around the world. For example, for Russian blogs, you may select one of the Cyrillic encoding types to display your blog. Universal (Unicode UTF-8), which is the default, is the most widely used.

The Convert line breaks setting affects what happens when you press Return (causing a line break) while editing your blog or when others add comments to your blog page. Selecting No causes Blogger to ignore your line breaks when displaying your blog. Because your blog is displayed using HTML, selecting Yes causes Blogger to insert the
 HTML tag. Text typed after this appears on the next line. Pressing Return more than once causes additional <br> tags to be added.

Select whether not to display the Title field on your blog page by selecting either Yes or No from the drop-down list. The default is Yes. You also can configure whether a link field is displayed. The link Field makes it easy to find links in your blog when you regularly link to other articles. In this case, the default for Show Link Field is No. If you set Show Link Field to Yes and you create your own template, include the following lines of code in your template:

```
<BlogItemURL>
 <a href="<$BlogItemURL$>">Link</a>
</BlogItemURL>
```

The Post Template preformats the post editor. This allows you to maintain a style for the appearance of your posts.

Using the Comments tab

Select the Comments tab to configure commenting in your blog. Your first selection in this tab allows you to hide the comments section of your blog page. You can hide and unhide the comments without affecting the comments that have already been written. Why hide the comments? Maybe you're trying to impress that special someone and you'd rather not have him or her read what the last special someone said about you in your blog. Select the Show or Hide radio button.

When comments are displayed in your blog, you can choose who can post comments; you have these choices:

- **Only Registered Users:** To leave a comment, the person must be logged in to Blogger.
- **Anyone:** Even the Pope can comment on your blog, if he's an avid reader.
- **Only Member of this Blog:** Members of a team blog can leave comments.

The Comments Default for Posts setting determines Blogger's behavior when creating new posts. By default, all new posts have comments turned on. If you'd rather decide which posts get comments and which don't, set this to New Posts Do Not Have Comments.

The Back Links setting lets visitors know what other blogs have linked to the post they are reading. This is to create a more interconnected experience. You can choose to hide or show them in your blog. You also can set the default for new posts, selecting either to allow back links for new posts or not to allow them by default and turn them on for individual posts.

Set the Comments Timestamp to one of the formats in the drop-down list. Then you can choose Yes or No to a series of settings:

- **Show comments in a popup window?** This opens a new browser window that allows you to read and post comments.

- **Enable comment moderation?** This lets you choose to allow all comments or approve them before publishing them.

- **Show word verification for comments?** This causes people to retype the funny graphic characters to defeat spam robots.

- **Show profile images on comments?** This allows you to get a look at who is posting comments to your blog.

The last setting in this tab is the e-mail address where you want to be notified when someone posts a comment to your blog. You can choose to type your e-mail address or leave this blank so that you are not notified.

Make sure you click Save Settings when you finish editing this settings page.

Using the Archiving tab

Blogs normally archive posts, particularly in blogs that are posted to regularly. Configure archiving by clicking the Archiving tab. The limit for the number of posts on the main page is 999. You can choose to archive your posts monthly, daily, weekly, and not at all. You may have only a small number of posts and want them to remain on the main page, so you may choose not to archive your posts. Archived posts appear in the sidebar labeled by the date formatted in the Formatting tab. Select an archive frequency by choosing from the drop-down list.

The Enable Post Pages? setting allows you to configure Blogger to display your posts on their own Web pages in addition to displaying them on your main blog page. Selecting Yes causes each post to appear on its own page. Click Save Settings.

Using the Site Feed tab

The first selection in the Site Feed tab is a link to switch to Advanced Mode. The two basic settings are Allow Blog Feed and Feed Item Footer. When you want your full posts included in the site syndication services, select Full from the drop-down list. When you want a brief (maximum of 255 characters) portion of your new post sent out as part of the site feed, select Short. When you do not want your blog included in the feed, select None from the list. The default is Full.

The Feed Item Footer appends whatever you type into the text box to the post that is sent to the feed.

 **The beta version of Blogger has this feature, but it does not append to your feed.**

Using the Email tab

Select the Email tab to set the e-mail addresses associated with your blog, and set the following items:

- **BlogSend Address:** Send your blog to this e-mail address whenever you publish your blog.
- **Mail-to-Blogger Address:** Post to your blog by e-mail using this address.

Using the Permissions tab

Clicking the Permissions tab allows you to set who can post to your blog and who can read your blog. The section of the Permissions tab labeled Blog Authors lists the people who currently have permission to post to the blog. You should appear in this section labeled as the Admin. Clicking ADD AUTHORS opens a text box where you can add the e-mail addresses of the people you want to invite to post to your blog. Type e-mail addresses separated by commas. When you finish creating your list, click INVITE. After you click this button, a list appears showing the e-mail addresses of the people you've invited to post. They are labeled as open invitations. You can then manage these invitations by inviting again or removing the invitation. The date of the invitation appears next to the e-mail address.

The Blog Readers section of this tab allows you to choose who can read your blog. You have these choices:

- **Anybody:** All people can read your blog.
- **Only people I choose:** Select the people who can read the blog.
- **Only blog authors:** Limit the blog to people you added in the first section of this tab.

When you select Only people I choose, a text box appears that allows you to add a list similar to the earlier one, where you can add e-mail addresses of the people you are inviting to read your blog. A list similar to the author's list appears with the e-mail addresses of the people you invite to read your blog. Below this list is an ADD READER button. Click this to add more people to your invitation list.

 **If you invite people to read your blog and later change to Anybody, your list of readers is saved in the event that you want to switch back to Only people I choose.**

This is the only tab that does not have a Save Settings button. These settings are saved automatically.

Using the Blogger Profile

You can tell people as much about yourself as you like, or you can choose to remain mysterious. You can tell people quite a bit about yourself by completing the profile section included in Blogger. To edit your profile, click the Dashboard link at the top right of the page next to your login name. This launches the Dashboard page shown in Figure 25.5.

In the top-right box, you find an Edit Profile link. This launches the Edit User Profile page. Table 25.1 lists the profile options with explanations.

FIGURE 25.5

Use the Dashboard page to access your profile.

TABLE 25.1

Profile Options in the Edit User Profile Page

Profile Option	Description
Share my profile	When this is selected, the items in your profile appear on your blog's main page.
Show my real name	When you select this, your first and last names, as typed in your profile, appear in your blog.
Show my email address	When this is selected, the e-mail address typed in your profile is displayed.
Show my blogs	Click the Select blogs to display link to select the blogs you want listed in your user profile page.
Username	Your username is displayed for information purposes and cannot be edited.
Email Address	This is the e-mail address that is displayed in your profile when you select Show my email address.
Display Name	This name is displayed when you are not displaying your real name.
First Name	This is your real first name or whatever you want people to call you.
Last Name	This is your last name. The first and last names appear in your blog page when you have Show my real name selected.
Photo URL	Type a URL to your photo. If you want, Google offers free photo hosting at www.hello.com.
Audio Clip URL	Post an audio file. See the section "AudioBlogger" later in this chapter for more information about how you can easily add audio to your blog.

continued

TABLE 25.1 *(continued)*

Profile Option	Description
Gender	Choose Male, Female, or other (not specified).
Birthday	Type your birthday. You can leave the year blank if you don't want people knowing how old you are. It's also a good way to dissuade identity theft.
Homepage URL	This is the URL to your personal or business Web page.
Wishlist URL	It's not quite like registering at Macy's, but you can create a wish list using Froogle and then point to it here.
IM Username	Type your instant messenger username, and select the instant messenger you use from the drop-down list. If you use more than one, select the one you prefer.
City/Town	Type the city or town you live in.
Region/State	Type the state your city or town is in.
Country	Select your country from the drop-down list.
Industry	Select the industry in which you are employed from the drop-down list.
Occupation	Type your specific occupation.
Interests	In this text box, you can add a list of your interests. Separate interests with commas.
About Me	Here is where you can wax eloquent about yourself, at least up to 1200 characters' worth.
Favorite Movies	Add a comma-separated list of your favorite movies.
Favorite Music	Add a list of your favorite genre, artist, performers, songs, albums, ripped tracks, or Hispanic Hip Hop artists.
Favorite Books	This list should start with *Google Power Users Bible,* followed by any of your other favorite books.
Random Question	Can those little red lasers really hurt your eyes? and other equally odd and random questions are asked here. Select the Give me a new question check box when you are ready for your next question.

Click Save Profile when you finish editing your profile. Your changes take effect immediately.

Going Blogger Mobile

Cell phones and other Internet-ready mobile devices have become one of the biggest leaps in communication since, well, communication. I was recently in the Netherlands and took pictures of the wonderful countryside and emailed them from my phone to my friends in Hawaii. In addition to the ability to immediately show friends what I was seeing you have the amazing ability to post these pictures and text and even audio from the phone to your blog. It's a truly amazing communications ability.

When you send text or photos from your mobile phone or handheld computer to go@blogger.com, they are automatically posted to your blog. If you don't already have a blog, one is created for you and Blogger responds to you by telling you the address of the blog so you can have others start viewing it immediately.

When Blogger creates a new blog for you, it is automatically given the title My Mobile Blog. To "claim your blog," as Blogger calls it, log in to the Web site http://go.blogger.com, as shown in Figure 25.6, and type the verification text sent to your mobile device.

FIGURE 25.6

Modify your mobile blog at Blogger on the Go.

After you log in to claim your blog, you can give it a custom template and modify it the same way you can modify any Blogger-hosted blog. Send photos or text right to the blog, as shown in Figure 25.7.

FIGURE 25.7

Instead of e-mailing photos, send them to your blog so everyone can see them.

AudioBlogger

You can leave audio posts in your blog from any phone in the world. AudioBlogger is a Listenlab service offered in partnership with Blogger that allows you to record and post audio messages to your blog completely free. To get started, visit www.audioblogger.com.

You must have a blog at www.audioblogger.com in order to leave audio posts. Create one before continuing, if you don't already have one. Follow these steps to get started posting audio messages to your blog:

1. Log in to www.audioblogger.com.

2. Type your Blogger userid and password. Your primary telephone number and pin will identify you in the future.

3. Call the U.S.-based telephone number 1-415-856-0205 (worldwide numbers soon to come). Enter your phone number and pin.

4. Create your AudioBlogger posting.

 The number you call is not toll-free. You will incur toll charges, or you will be charged for the minutes used on mobile phones. Also, the service does not work with the beta version of Blogger.

Each audio post can be 5 full minutes long. If you have some concern that the file size will be so great that people cannot download and listen to it, the good news is that the file size is about 1KB per minute that you are yacking away. So the maximum size of an audioblogger post is less than the size of most tiny graphic icons. If 5 minutes is not long enough, you can create a new post at the end of 5 minutes.

After you create an audio post, you see a link to your AudioBlogger post accompanied by an icon and time-stamp. Users can easily click the link and hear your post.

Summary

Whether you read other people's blogs on Blog*Spot or create and manage your own blog on Blogger.com, you will enjoy the clean and simple way to access Weblogs. This chapter showed you how to create your own blog, customize it, and publish it to close friends or to the world. Now, you can even post to your blog using your cell phone or mobile device. Send text and pictures to your blog, or create a new one automatically. You can even use the third-party AudioBlogger service to leave voice blog posts on your site. An entire book could be written about using all the features, writing templates, adding money-making things like Google's AdSense, and more. This chapter gave you a good overview of blogging with Blogger.

You may want to put a reminder in your Google Calendar to send a post to your blog. Learn more about Google Calendar in the next exciting chapter.

Chapter 26

Organizing Your Day with Google Calendar

Google Calendar is a free, online, shareable calendar service provided by Google. This service helps you to keep track of events in your day-to-day life. And you can share these events with your friends, business associates, or family. You also can search the Web for events that you may want to attend. This simple service can help you organize your events or important meetings in just a couple of minutes. Gone are the days when you must search through tiny scraps of paper to remind you of the day's events.

Using Your Google Calendar

The Google Calendar is feature rich and integrates well with many of the other Google programs. You can expect these features:

- Share your calendar with others across the Internet.
- Integrate your calendar with your Gmail account.
- Search the Internet for Web events you can add to your calendar.
- Create events and invite others to join you.
- Publish your events so that others can see them.
- Access your calendar by sending SMS message commands from your mobile phone.

The first step in getting started is to go to the Google Calendar page at http://calendar.google.com and sign up.

Signing up

The first time you access Google Calendar, you are prompted to sign up. Type your first and last names, and select your local time zone from the list shown in Figure 26.1. Then click Continue.

FIGURE 26.1

Signing up for Google Calendar is simple.

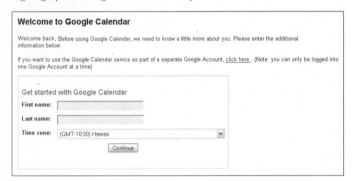

After you type your name and time zone, your first calendar appears, as shown in Figure 26.2. Today's date is automatically highlighted, and events for the day are displayed. When you first launch Google Calendar, no events appear, of course.

Scrolling through the day is possible using the toolbar to the right of the calendar.

FIGURE 26.2

At first, Google Calendar has no events.

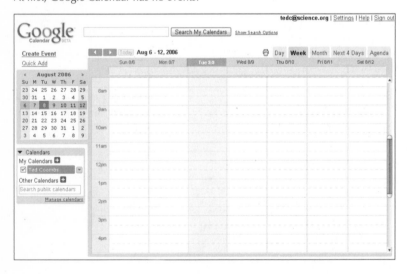

Managing Your Google Calendar

Other than knowing what day it is, the Google Calendar is pretty useless until you add *events*. Events are appointments, things to do, reminders, and anything else you may want to schedule on your calendar.

Managing events

Managing events on the Google Calendar is the most important capability. Adding, changing, synchronizing, coordinating, and deleting events makes your calendar extremely useful to you and to others with whom you may want to share your calendar.

Adding an event

You can add events to your calendar in a number of ways. They all add the same event, so use the method that you find most simple.

Clicking on the calendar

Depending on which of the calendar tabs you are viewing (Day, Week, Month, Next 4 Days), what you type and where you click may change slightly. While viewing the calendar by Day, click the time of your event. Remember, you can scroll up and down using the scroll bar on the right to see times that may not appear on the screen. A bubble appears, like the one shown in Figure 26.3.

FIGURE 26.3

Add your event information in the bubble that appears after clicking on the calendar.

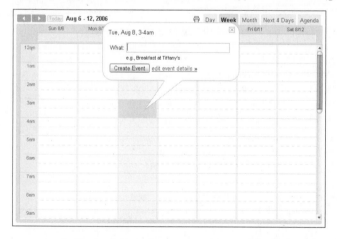

The simple and quick way to add an event is to type information about the event in the text box labeled What and click Create Event. Alternately, you can click the <u>edit event details</u> link, which opens a new window allowing you to manage the event in considerable detail (see Figure 26.4).

FIGURE 26.4

Configure the event details.

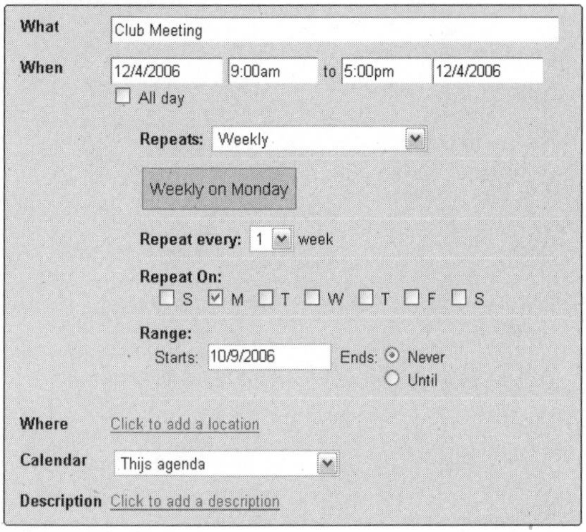

| What | Club Meeting |
| When | 12/4/2006 9:00am to 5:00pm 12/4/2006 |

☐ All day

Repeats: Weekly

Weekly on Monday

Repeat every: 1 week

Repeat On:
☐ S ☑ M ☐ T ☐ W ☐ T ☐ F ☐ S

Range:
Starts: 10/9/2006   Ends: ◉ Never
                           ○ Until

Where Click to add a location

Calendar Thijs agenda

Description Click to add a description

When viewing your calendar from the Week view, you can follow the same procedures for adding an event. In this view, you can add events for different times and days within a one-week time period. You can even add events in the past. This is particularly useful if you use Google Calendar to track your time for billing purposes or if you have other reasons for tracking your whereabouts.

Adding events in the Month view is where things change just a little. Clicking the small box that represents a single day causes an event bubble similar to the one in Figure 26.3 to appear, but it does not display the time after the date. When adding an event in this view, you have two options: You can type the time as part of the event information like this: **3PM Appointment with broker**, or click the edit event details link. This causes the edit event form to appear. When choosing the latter option, the All day check box is selected by default, expecting that you are trying to add an event that lasts all day. To add a time period for the event rather than leave it as an all-day event, deselect this box and type begin and end times.

Adding events using the Next 4 Days tab is similar to that when viewing the calendar in the Week tab. Click the time of the event, and fill in the event information in the bubble that appears.

Clicking the Create Event link

Rather than clicking on the calendar to create an event, you also can click the Create Event link found in the top left below the Google Calendar logo. Just click the Create Event link in the left column of your calendar to bring you to a page where you can type as much information as you want about your event. On this page, you also can add guests, change a reminder setting, and publish your event to other users. After you type the appropriate information and select the desired settings, click Save.

Creating an event from the Calendars menu

In the Calendars box in the left column, click the down arrow next to the appropriate calendar. Then select Create event on this calendar from the drop-down menu to launch the detailed event creation form.

Using Quick Add

Another way to add an event is by clicking the <u>Quick Add</u> link feature. Click the <u>Quick Add</u> link or press Q, and type the information for your event. You need to be specific about the information you add in this fashion.

You can type text, and Google does its best to figure out what you mean. For example, typing **noon lunch on Saturday with Michelle** in the Quick Add box creates an event on the next Saturday at 12PM with the event labeled "lunch with Michelle." The order of the words is unimportant.

When Google doesn't understand a time — for example, Google does not understand late morning — the event is created, but it appears along the top in the day's events that have no time associated with them. This is the location on the calendar where all-day events are displayed.

Inviting guests to your events

One of the powerful features of the Google Calendar is the ability to invite guests to your events. Whether it's a beach party, a business meeting, or an online seminar, you can easily invite others to attend. Google Calendar also helps you keep track of comments, responses, and RSVPs.

To invite others, edit the event details. This is the detailed event information accessible when you create the event or later when you click on the event. In the right column, you see a section titled Guests. To add guests, click the <u>+ Add Guests</u> link. In the box that appears, type the e-mail addresses of all the guests you want to attend your event. Separate e-mail addresses by commas.

You can allow your guests to do two things: You can allow the guest to invite others to the event, and you can allow your invited guest to see your guest list.

Your invited guests receive an e-mail asking them to attend. They can choose to see the event details and respond in the following ways: Yes, they are coming; No, they are not coming; or Maybe. They have the option to send a long a comment that you see when you manage your guest list. If you allow them to invite guests, they can also specify how many guests they intend to bring. Google Calendar keeps track of who has and has not responded and how many guests you can expect at your event.

Event privacy options

You may occasionally want to make an event private in a calendar you share with others. This allows you to be specific about who can see this event in a calendar where the default is that all events are viewable.

 When you create a public event in a public calendar, it must be suitable for all ages.

To set the privacy options, click the down arrow next to Options in the right column of the Event Details form. This causes the event options to appear.

Clearing events

"Clearing your calendar" takes on new meaning with Google Calendar. Now you can simply and easily remove all the events from your calendar without having to step through each day looking for events to delete. To clear all the events on your primary calendar, follow these steps:

1. Click the <u>Manage calendars</u> link at the bottom of the blue Calendars box on the left side of the Calendar page. This launches the Calendar Settings form in the Calendars tab.

2. Click the small trash can icon on the far right next to the calendar you want to clear.

3. Click Delete when asked if you are sure you want to delete all the events on this calendar.

When Google finishes clearing your calendar you are returned to the calendar page. The calendar should appear empty.

NOTE   Be patient. Google's Calendar features become available only after Google finishes deleting all events from your primary calendar.

Creating a new calendar

You may need more than one calendar. You may have one calendar that you want to share with the world, another you share with just family and friends, and a third that is completely private. You also can create a calendar for your business appointments while keeping your social calendar completely separate. Follow these steps:

1. Click the + button next to My Calendars to launch the Create New Calendar form shown in Figure 26.5.

2. Type a name for your calendar. It should be a meaningful name so you and others easily know what may be found on this calendar. You can then type a full text description of the calendar if the name isn't enough to identify it.

3. Type your location, particularly if you intend to make this calendar public and searchable. That way, people looking for events in a specific place can easily find your calendar by geographical location.

4. The time zone setting is already set to your time zone if you've set it within Google, but you can change it, if necessary. Perhaps you are going to post your vacation calendar in New Zealand and want everyone to know what time your events are scheduled in local New Zealand time, or wherever in the world you happen to be.

5. Select who you want to see this calendar. By default, the calendar is private, for your eyes only. The second choice is the most public. Share all the events with everyone. The third choice is a little more restrictive. It shares only information about your free and busy periods. It does not share the details of what you'll be doing. This is a good feature if you want people to check your calendar before trying to schedule you in a meeting, but you really don't want them to know that the time you have blocked each morning is for your Swedish massage.

6. Type the name or e-mail address of a person you want to give access for making changes and managing your calendars. Select the level of access you want to give him from the drop-down list. These are your choices:

   ▪ Make changes AND manage sharing.

   ▪ Make changes to events.

   ▪ See all event details.

   ▪ See free/busy information (no details).

7. Click Create Calendar at the bottom after you complete the form. You are returned to your primary calendar. Your new calendar appears in the list of calendars in the blue Calendars box on the left.

FIGURE 26.5

Create a new calendar by completing the details in this form.

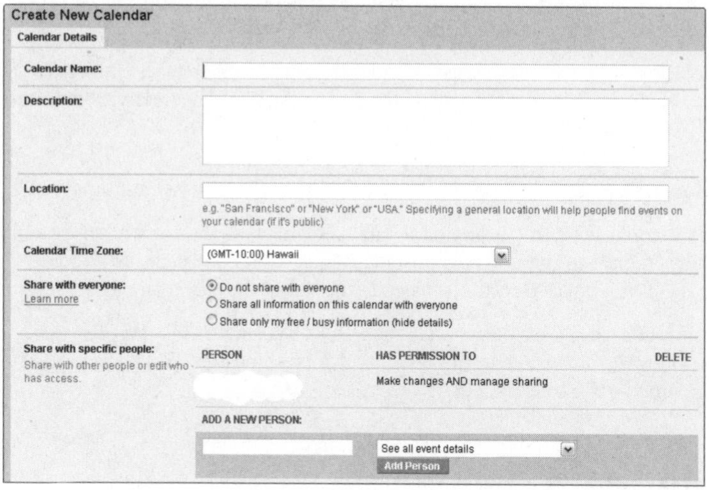

Printing and e-mailing your Google Calendar

Printing your calendar allows you to conveniently share you calendar with others who may not have access to Google Calendar, or you may just want to stuff it in your pocket for quick reference during the day. To print your calendar, click the small printer icon to the left of the calendar's view tabs. This launches a printable preview of the calendar. You may notice that the preview is in Adobe PDF with all the same controls available in Acrobat Reader. With these features, you can save, print, or e-mail a PDF version of your calendar.

To print, click the printer icon. This usually launches your printer's dialog box, where you can select which printer, if you have more than one, to send this document to and choose paper and color settings before clicking OK to print your calendar.

Navigating Google Calendar

Getting around the Google Calendar is pretty simple. The tabs along the top of the calendar allow you to see the calendar in a number of different views, including Day, Week, Month, Next 4 Days, and the Agenda view. Click a tab to change the view.

Change the day or dates you are viewing by clicking the left and right arrows in the upper-left corner of your calendar. In the Day view, clicking the arrows increments the calendar by a single day. In the Week view, the calendar advances by a week. The Month view advances by a month, and the calendar advances by four days when the Next 4 Days view is selected. In the Agenda view, the number of events that increment or decrement with the arrow keys varies by the number of events you have entered.

Notice that, as you change views by clicking the different tabs, various portions of the mini-calendar in the left column are highlighted. For example, when the Day view is selected, only a single day is highlighted in the mini-calendar. Highlighting a different number of days presents a custom view. For example, if you highlight two weeks, then two weeks are displayed in the main calendar on the right. In this example, clicking the left and right arrow keys decrement or increment the calendar by two weeks at a time.

Use the month view located in the pane to the left of the large calendar to jump to different days, months and years. Simply click on the date in the small calendar to view that day or week in the larger view on the right.

Viewing different calendars

By default, you start using Google Calendar with only a single calendar. As you create new calendars or add shared calendars, additional calendars appear in the Calendars list on the left side of the page. To choose which calendars are visible, select the check boxes next to the calendar names in the Calendars list.

More than one calendar can be visible at a time. This means that you still view a single calendar onscreen, but the events of all the calendars you select are visible in the calendar displayed on-screen. This is particularly useful when it comes to integrating public calendars.

Using Public Calendars

In addition to creating your own calendars, there are many public calendars shared on the Internet. These can include tour dates of your favorite band, public holiday calendars from many countries, sport events, club events, chili cook-offs, and whatever else you can think of.

Adding a public calendar to your list

The simplest way to add a public calendar is to click the + sign next to Other Calendars in the Calendars box on the left. Clicking + launches the Add Other Calendar form, which has four tabs:

- Search Public Calendars
- Friends' Calendars
- Holiday Calendars
- Public Calendar Address

To find a club, sports team, or other calendar, search for it by clicking Search Public Calendars and typing in the name of the club, team or other search term that might identify a public calendar. When your search results in a list of calendars, click the <u>preview</u> link and the calendar displays on-screen. If you want to include this calendar within your list of calendars, click the <u>Subscribe</u> link at the bottom right of the previewed calendar. You are prompted as to whether you want to add the calendar. If you want to add the calendar to your list, click Yes, add this calendar. To cancel click No, do not add this calendar.

To find a calendar that your friend may be sharing, click the Friends' Calendars tab and type your friend's e-mail address. If your friend has allowed you to view the calendar, you can add it to your list.

To view holiday calendars from around the world first click Other Calendars from the left sidebar. This launches the Add Other Calendar page. Scroll down through the calendars listed in the Holiday Calendars: section. Click Add Calendar next to any of these calendars that you want to include. You will never forget a holiday again!

When you know the URL of a calendar available in iCal format, you can type the address in the Public Calendar Address tab. The iCal format (RFC-2445) is an Internet standard way of publishing calendars. Several calendars, including the widely used Microsoft Outlook Calendar, publish calendars using this format.

Creating a public calendar

You can create your own public calendar. Perhaps you are part of a group, a musician, member of a sports team, or you just want to share your busy social life with everyone else. Now you can easily create a calendar that appears when people perform Google searches on topics you may have scheduled in your public calendar.

Creating a public calendar is no different from creating a calendar as shown earlier in this chapter. The key to making your calendar public is to select the Share all information on this calendar with everyone option in the form you used to create a new calendar. You are prompted, more than once, to be certain that you want to share this information with everyone, even people doing Google searches.

NOTE Your new public calendar is available through a Google Calendar search within 24 hours. Google checks to make certain the information you add is within the terms of your Google agreement.

Controlling the shared information

To change the amount of the information from your calendar that is shared with others, you can click the down arrow in the left column next to the appropriate calendar and then select Share this calendar.

Google Calendar offers you three ways to share your calendar:

- **Share all information on this calendar with everyone:** When you select this option, your calendar—along with all its public events—appears in the search results of Google Calendar. Additionally, others can view the calendar and its public events at the calendar's address or by adding the calendar to their Calendars list.

- **Share only my free / busy information (hide details):** If you select this option, your calendar information does not appear in the search results of any Google Calendar search. Additionally, only the free/busy information is visible to those who access your calendar at its address or by adding it to their Calendars list.

- **Do not share with everyone:** This option offers the most privacy. If you select this option, your calendar does not appear in the search results of any Google Calendar search and no information is accessible via the calendar's address. The calendar remains private to everyone except the people that you add in the Share with specific people section.

Adding Google Calendar to Your Web site

One of the fun things you can do with Google Calendar is to make it available from your Web site. This turns your Web site into more of a portal and gives people a reason to come back and visit your page regularly to see your updated calendar. If you run a business, club, or organization, this is a great way to display your business calendar.

To add the Google Calendar to your Web site, you need enough Web site editing skills to create a link to your Google Calendar. To create the link to your calendar, follow these steps:

1. Click the down arrow in the Calendars box on the left side of the page. This is the down arrow next to the calendar you want to place a link to on your Web site.

2. Select Calendar Settings to launch the details for that calendar.

3. Next to Calendar Address, click the blue HTML icon, which displays the URL you need to embed in your page (see Figure 26.6). If you do not need Google's help to create the HTML, skip the rest of these steps. Simply use the URL you were given in this dialog box. Click OK to finish.

4. Optionally, have Google create the HTML for you. In the dialog box that displays your URL, click the <u>configuration tool</u> link to launch the Google Embeddable Calendar Helper.

5. Add a title to your calendar. This becomes the calendar's public title.

6. Select the appropriate radio button to choose whether you want Google to display the navigation controls with the logo and title, without the logo and title, or no controls at all.

7. Choose either Month view or Agenda view; the Day and Week views are not available in this form.

8. Google places your calendar in a special frame known as an iFrame. You can choose the size of the iFrame so that it fits into a particular location on your Web site, or you can use the default size that Google selects.

9. You can select how many events for each day are shown in your calendar. This also determines the size of the calendar. If you have only one event per day, such as a concert, change to one event per day by choosing the selection from the drop-down list. You can select up to nine events per day.

10. Enter the background color of the calendar. This normally is the same background color as your Web page so the calendar maintains your site's look and feel. Enter the color as a hex color. For more information on hex colors, see the hex color chart at
www.tbi.univie.ac.at/TBI/hex_color_chart.html.

11. Click Update URL to update the URL found in the box below this form. You can preview your calendar by scrolling further down the Web page.

FIGURE 26.6

Use this address to add your calendar to your Web page.

Importing and Migrating

Most people today have some sort of electronic calendar at least partially filled in with family birthday reminders. Rather than retyping the information or calling your cousin Ed to ask him when his birthday is, again, you can import information you've exported from other calendar programs, or in some cases, you are able to simply migrate from one calendar program to the Google Calendar. You can use either iCal format, commonly used by popular calendar software programs, or comma-separated value (CSV) files to import data into the Google Calendar.

Importing events from iCal or CSV files

Before you can import a calendar file, you must first have an exported calendar. See your calendar software about exporting either iCal or CSV file format, and export the file. It is then ready to import into Google Calendar. To import events from iCal or CSV files, follow these steps:

1. Click the <u>Settings</u> link at the top of the Calendar page.
2. Click the Import Calendar tab in the Calendar Settings form.
3. Type the path to the iCal or CSV file, or click Browse and navigate to the file.
4. Select the calendar into which you want the events to be imported.
5. Click Import.

 Recurring events may be added as individual events rather than being recurring events when you import from CSV files. After importing events you need to edit any events that need to be configured as recurring events.

Migrating Outlook Calendar events to Google Calendar

To migrate your events and information from Outlook Calendar to Google Calendar, follow these steps:

 These steps are for Microsoft Outlook 2003. They may vary in later versions.

1. Launch Microsoft Outlook.
2. Choose File ➪ Import and Export to launch the Import and Export Wizard.
3. From the action list in the wizard, select Export to a file.
4. Click Next.
5. In the Export to a File dialog box, select the type of file to be exported. This should be Comma Separated Values (Windows).
6. From the folder list, select Calendar.
7. Specify a name and file location for your exported file. You can click Browse to help you locate where you are saving the file.
8. By default, Export "Appointments" from folder: Calendar is selected. You can optionally map custom fields at this time. These are special information fields where you may have stored custom information in Outlook. Click Finish.
9. Now select the date range of events you want to include in your Google Calendar. Click OK after entering start and stop dates. Your calendar is exported to the location you specified.
10. Close Microsoft Outlook, and import the exported file into Google Calendar by clicking the Import Calendar tab on the Calendar Settings form. Click Browse to navigate to the exported file. Choose the calendar to import into, and click Import.

When the import process is complete, you are notified how many events were added to your calendar.

Migrating events from Yahoo! Calendar into Google Calendar

Yahoo! Calendar is another Web-based calendar similar to Google Calendar. If you've started creating your online calendar in Yahoo! and now you want to migrate your calendar to Google to take advantage of the Google features, follow these steps:

1. Sign in to your Yahoo! account, and start your Yahoo! Calendar by clicking the Calendar tab.
2. Click the Options link in the upper-right corner of the page.
3. In the Management column of the Calendar Options, select Import/Export.
4. Select Export to Outlook to export your file as a CSV file.

After you download the file, follow the instructions in the preceding section to import your CSV file into Google Calendar.

 Google does not support Yahoo! recurring events. Instead, individual events are created. You can modify them manually using the edit features of Google Calendar.

Using Reminders and Notifications

You can receive reminders of upcoming events via your cell phone or pop-up messages on the Google Calendar Web page. Or you can choose to receive notifications of upcoming events and other Google Calendar events via e-mail messages. Select the option that bests suits your needs. To customize the reminder settings, click the Settings link at the top of your Google Calendar Web page.

Enabling Notifications

Click the Notifications tab in the Calendar Settings form to display the many notification and reminder options. First, choose when you want to be notified. You can select times between ten minutes before an event and one week before an event by choosing from Event reminders drop-down list. You can be reminded of events by e-mail, SMS, and Pop-up messages. Google reminds you of upcoming events only by pop-up. All the notifications are by e-mail or SMS only. These notifications include the following:

- **New Invitations:** This option notifies you when someone invites you to an event.
- **Changed Invitations:** This option notifies you when someone changes her mind about event details.
- **Cancelled Invitation:** This option notifies you when someone cancels an event or cancels your invitation to the event.
- **Invitation Replies:** This option notifies you when someone replies to your invitation to attend your event.
- **Daily agenda:** This option sends your agenda to you via e-mail but not via SMS.

Before you can use the SMS feature, you must first set up Google Calendar with your cell phone. Type the phone number of your cell phone, select the carrier from the drop-down list, and click Send Verification Code. When you receive the code via SMS message on your cell phone, you need to return to this page and type the verification code in the text box provided. Then click Finish Setup. The page displays a message that your phone number was successfully validated.

Disabling notifications

When you want to stop receiving Calendar e-mail notifications in your Gmail or other e-mail account, disable them by changing the settings set in the preceding section. Simply deselect the box next to the notification type, and you will stop receiving the notification. Be sure to click Save when you finish changing your notification methods.

Checking Your Google Calendar by Telephone

One of the most ubiquitous technologies in use around the world is the cell phone. Not all of them are equipped with Web browsers, but most of them allow you to send SMS text messages. This feature allows you to check your Google Calendar with your cell phone.

Sending a quick text message allows you to query your calendar. This is much better than shoving a piece of paper in your pocket.

You must first register your cell phone number in your Google Calendar account before using this service. After you log in to your Google Calendar, click Notifications on the Settings menu.

After your cell phone number is registered, send special text message commands to receive calendar information. Send the SMS text message to GVENT 48368. You can send these commands:

- **next:** Returns your next scheduled event
- **day:** Returns all scheduled events for the present day
- **nday:** Returns all your events for the following day

Remember that the calendar information is available only for events 24 hours in advance.

The GVENT 48368 feature on Google Calendar is currently only available with the U.S. mobile carriers listed in Table 26.1.

TABLE 26.1

Supported Mobile Carriers

Alltel	Nextel
AT&T	Qwest
Cellular One	Sprint
Cincinnati Bell	T-Mobile
Cingular	US Cellular
Dobson Communications	Verizon

Watch the Google Calendar site for other providers added in the future.

Summary

Calendars have become a fundamental computer tool. Meetings, anniversaries, birthdays, parties, and other events are now easily remembered. Even more difficult, particularly now where companies have become global, is the job of planning a meeting. Google Calendar makes that much simpler with its ability to send out invitations and manage user responses. There are certainly many other calendars that give you that feature, but they tend to be expensive and certainly not as globally accessible as Google. You don't need a guru systems administrator to manage what was once considered complex software. Now, Google manages it for you.

Accessibility is the key. In fact, you can even check your Google calendar by sending SMS messages through your cell phone to query your upcoming agenda. The next chapter goes much deeper into using Google applications with your mobile phone.

Part III

Going Mobile

Chapter 27

Finding Your Way with Google

Google has made its wonderful Google Maps and Keyhole Satellite data small enough to fit into your mobile phone or handheld device. You can get nearly the same functionality you would expect from your desktop or laptop computer right in your palm. Find locations, get directions, find businesses, and even see your friend's car on the satellite image. Speaking of cars, you also can save yourself lots of time sitting in traffic by finding out ahead of time what the traffic looks like along your route.

Google Maps is currently available throughout much of North America and several countries in the European Union. Google is working hard to make this service available everywhere.

Using Google Mobile Maps

Google has created a mapping application for the Java program environment that runs on many mobile phones and wireless handheld devices. People have enjoyed using Google Maps on their desktop or laptop computers, and that same service is now available for the small displays typical of cell phones. As with most of Google's services, this one also is free.

To begin using Google's Mobile Maps, visit www.google.com/gmm from your mobile device's Web browser. The Google Maps application begins installing automatically. After the installation is complete, you can access Google Maps by selecting it from your mobile device's list of applications.

After Google Maps launches on your mobile device, you can click the right button on your device to select the menu. These options appear on-screen and are shown in Figure 27.1:

1 Find Business

2 Find Location

3 Directions

4 Satellite View

5 Clear Map

6 Zoom

7 Help

Show Traffic

0 Quit

Select one of these Google Maps menu options by pressing the number or symbol on your mobile device keypad. The first three selections and Help launch a pop-up dialog box that assists you with these features. Choosing Satellite View, Clear Map, Zoom, and Show Traffic does not display a dialog box.

FIGURE 27.1

Select a map feature from the menu.

NOTE This service does not currently work with Nextel, T-Mobile USA, or some Verizon phones. See www.google.com/gmm/devices.html for updates on supported wireless services.

Finding a Place

Before you can use most of the map features, you need to find a location on the map. First, find a location by pressing the number 2. Type an address, and a new map loads, displaying your destination. By default, your destination displays as a map, as shown in Figure 27.2.

TIP If your display appears as a satellite image, your location is still noted but may be difficult to navigate. Select menu item 4 to toggle between Map view and Satellite view.

FIGURE 27.2

Type an address to view a location.

You can type your location in many different ways, as specific or as general as you like. For example, typing a ZIP code shows you a map centered in the middle of that ZIP code. Additionally, you can type a street address to see a specific home or business. Type a country name to view an entire country.

When you type the street address, you should include the city and state, or at least the ZIP code because there are many 123 Main Streets in the world. If you do type only 123 Main Street, then you must select the specific location from the list of locations by pressing the numbers 1 through 9 on your mobile device keypad. Only the first nine results can be displayed. So if you were looking for a location in Ohio, you would be disappointed because the first nine locations displayed in Google Maps for 123 Main Street are in the United Kingdom.

NOTE Google Maps are not case sensitive, so 123 main street works fine.

After you locate the address on the map, a balloon appears over the location with the address and the option to press the number 1 for options. These are your options:

- Directions to here
- Directions from here
- Save as favorite

Select Directions to here to get driving directions from another location to this location. You are prompted to type the starting location. Select Directions from here to see directions from this point to another location. In this case, you are prompted for an end location. You can find more information about driving directions later in this chapter.

The third option is to save this location as one of your favorites. Favorite locations are saved for easy access later when you need the address to see a map or to see directions to or from your favorite location.

After your location is saved as a favorite, it changes color and appears with a star. You can press the * key on your mobile device at any time to view your favorites.

Sometimes, the balloon displayed on the map blocks important information. You can make the balloon disappear by pressing option 5 from the menu, Clear Map.

TIP Save time when frequently mapping the same location by selecting it from the Recent Searches list or by adding it to your favorites.

Using the Map Interface

You can easily view a smaller portion of the map in finer detail (zoom in) and see great portions of the map in less detail (zoom out) by using the keys on your mobile device.

To zoom in and see maps in greater detail, press the center button on your phone or the equivalent of the center button on your mobile device. Zoom out using the *soft key* on your phone, or the left button beneath the word Zoom. A soft key is a key immediately below the cell phone display window, performing the function currently listed on the cell phone display screen.

NOTE Zooming in too far eventually gives you an error telling you that no data is available. Zoom out to again view your map.

You can zoom in either Map view or Satellite view. Zooming in Satellite view allows you to spot landmarks that may help you find your way. When you zoom in or out, a rectangle appears momentarily on the map showing you the area you will see when the new map loads.

Drag the map using the up, down, right, and left arrow keys on your phone. This is a simple way to move around the map. Dragging the map — moving it north, south, east, and west — using the arrow keys is similar to grabbing it with a mouse on the computer-version of Google Maps.

Locating Services

Need gas? Find gas stations or any other type of business by pressing 1 from the Google Maps menu. A pop-up appears that prompts you to type the category of service you are looking for in the next screen. You must press the right OK soft key to type the service in the text box, as shown in Figure 27.3.

FIGURE 27.3

Find services by typing the category of service in the text box.

A map appears that shows you the services you searched for, each appearing on the map marked with a small number. You can press the number of the marked location on your mobile device keypad to see information about the service, including its address and phone number. By default, the phone number is highlighted so you can press to call. Not having to dial the number is a great feature.

TIP You probably should not use Google Maps while you drive. Use your navigator, co-pilot, or whatever you call the person in the passenger seat. If you are driving alone, pull over and use the service while parked.

From the information box, you can select from these choices:

- Directions to here
- Directions from here
- Save as a favorite

Some of the pop-up boxes have Address and Details tabs. The Address tab contains the information normally displayed in the information box when no tabs are displayed. See the Details tab by pressing the right arrow on your mobile device; it toggles to the Address tab using the left arrow. The Details tab contains links to additional information, such as `Citysearch.com`, where you can view online city guide and Yellow Pages information. Additional information regarding the service may be displayed as text, rather than as a link. For example, for restaurants you may find the average meal price, and for coffee shops, you may see that Wi-Fi hotspots are available.

NOTE
Google Maps does not use GPS technology (the satellite Global Positioning System) to find locations on the map. You need to find your own location and track your progress using the arrow keys on your mobile device.

Getting Driving Directions

One of the best reasons for using online maps is to get driving directions from one location to another. Google Maps offers this same important feature in its mobile application. After bringing up the Google Maps menu, press 3 from the menu. In the pop-up that appears on your mobile device, type the address of the starting location. After you enter the starting address, another pop-up asks you for the end address. The route is traced, and Google Maps displays the following information:

- **Distance:** In miles
- **Time:** Driving time in days, hours, and minutes
- **Traffic delay:** The typical delay you can expect when driving from your starting location to the end location

Press the number 3 on your device to begin viewing the directions. You also can choose to save this route in your favorites, which saves you from having to enter begin and end locations in the future. The driving directions appear as bullets above the map for each turn you will make. They are displayed one at a time so that you can read them easily on a small screen.

To return to the information screen or the previous directive, press 1 on your device. To advance to the next directive, press 3. You can continue pressing 3 until you finally arrive at your location.

Getting Information on Live Traffic

One of the very cool things about Google Maps on your mobile device is the ability to check the real-time traffic delays along your route. From the Google Maps menu, select the last option or press # on your mobile phone keyboard. You also can select the Show Traffic menu option. The map changes to show the current traffic situation in the area you have mapped, using color coding. Of course, this works only on mobile devices with color displays. Otherwise, it looks like the image in Figure 27.4.

FIGURE 27.4

You can see the flow of traffic graphically anywhere.

Traffic moving along at normal speeds is shown in green. When traffic is slowing, it appears in yellow. And when traffic on the road turns into a parking lot, roads appear in red on the map.

TIP If you have previously mapped locations or services, the information boxes or balloons may hide the traffic information. You may want to press menu option 5, Clear Map, before selecting to view the traffic. Also, if you drive the same way every day, try saving your location as a favorite.

Google Maps does not have an alternate route selection, so you need to drag the map until you find your own alternate routes. Just a reminder: Don't check Google Maps while you're driving, particularly if you are also drinking coffee.

Using Mobile GMaps

GMaps is a free third-party product found at www.mgmaps.com. It displays Google Maps as well as maps from other online map providers, as shown in Figure 27.5.

The GMaps product has support for Mobile WikiMapia, KML files (Keyhole Markup Language used by Google Earth — Keyhole is the name of the satellite that takes those great satellite images), subway maps for the world's large metropolitan subway systems, and GPS tracking through Navizon and APRS systems.

FIGURE 27.5

The GMaps service supports GPS-enabled phones.

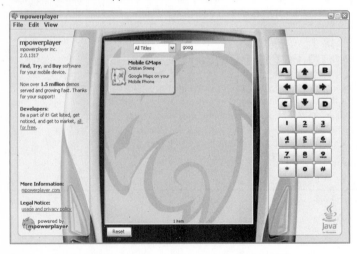

To use GMaps, your mobile device must be Java J2ME-enabled. Of course, your device must also be Internet or WAP-enabled.

To download GMaps, point your mobile device Web browser to http://wap.mgmaps.com. Select the Download here link. After you install GMaps, you can begin using it to locate your current position and track your progress along the way.

Summary

Google Maps on a mobile device is a great timesaver and convenient way to locate businesses, get driving directions, or show your friends a satellite view of the hidden reef that has become your favorite secret surfing location. The interface is simple and not unlike Google Maps on the Web. Best of all, it's free. Also free is the downloadable Tip Sheet from `www.google.com/gmm/tip_sheet.pdf`.

Google Maps is not the only service that Google has configured for mobile devices. Learn about many of your favorite Google applications squashed to fit on your mobile device in the next breathtaking chapter.

Chapter 28

Using Google Mobile

The world's information is at your fingertips when you have access to Google on your mobile phone or handheld device. In Chapter 27, you learned about finding directions using Google Maps on your mobile device. This chapter shows you that you can do even much more with mobile access to Google applications.

Many people have grown to rely on Google services, such as Gmail (see Chapter 19), searching the Web (see Chapter 1), Google Maps (see Chapter 27), and Blogger (see Chapter 25). These services are now available through your mobile device, whether it's a cell phone or handheld computer. Learn how to use and configure these mobile services in this chapter.

NOTE When this chapter refers to mobile devices, it means small devices such as cell phones, handheld computers, and PDAs. Yes, laptops with wireless modems are also wireless devices, but they do not require the special display technologies discussed in this chapter.

Web Searching

Google Web Search is great for settling arguments, finding an airline, comparing prices, and about a million other things that are all best when you have mobile access. You can use four formats for searching the Web with Google on your mobile device, depending on the technology it supports. The technologies are called XHTML, iMode, WML, and PDA. XHTML, iMode, and PDA can be used to access any of the 8 billion Web pages indexed by Google. WML is more limited, and Google provides a special search just to find pages created to fit mobile displays. The PDA (Personal Digital Assistant) interface is identical to that of XHTML.

XHTML search

To access the familiar Google Web search using XHTML (see the About XHTML sidebar nearby), point your mobile Web browser to `www.google.com/xhtml`. A Google Web search box appears, as shown in Figure 28.1. Type your search terms in the box. Then highlight the Google Search button, and click the button using the keys on your mobile device.

FIGURE 28.1

Type your query into the XHTML Google search box. This image is a simulation.

NOTE If you are using a PDA, simply follow the directions for XHTML with one exception: To access the PDA interface, use `www.google.com/pda`.

Google displays ten results per page. This small number of results makes it possible to easily view them on smaller displays. It may take you a little longer to page through many results. To access the results, use the keys or thumbwheel on your mobile device that allows you to scroll through Web page elements, such as links and text boxes. Find the result you want to view, highlight it, and click Enter on your device.

About XHTML

XHTML, or eXtensible Hypertext Markup Language, can be thought of as the intersection of XML, a markup language created to support the growing amount of data on the Internet, and HTML, the markup language used to graphically create most Web pages. This combination is a stricter form of HTML used more for the transfer of data, a function of its origins in XML. It has abilities that HTML does not have, such as the ability to support scalable vector graphics. On mobile devices, the ability to scale bitmap graphics larger and smaller is very limited. Scalable vector graphics, an XML standard, allows for clear zoom-in and zoom-out capability of text, raster graphics, and vector graphic shapes.

XHTML, thought of as the future of Web publishing, is supported in Web browsers such as Firefox and Opera and in a limited way currently by Internet Explorer. Many mobile devices now support XHTML because of its superior ability to present legible graphics on small devices.

By default, your search is through all Web pages indexed by Google. Be aware that even though Google does its best to reformat the Web pages so they are viewable on small displays, the page may not be viewable in your phone or handheld.

Setting XHTML search preferences

You can set a couple preferences for your mobile search using the XHTML interface. Point your XHTML-compatible device to www.google.com/xhtml/preferences. Here you find two preference settings: language and Google's SafeSearch, as shown in Figure 28.2.

FIGURE 28.2

Change language and SafeSearch settings in the Preferences.

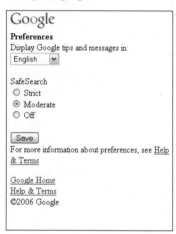

The interface display language is different from the languages you can use to search the Web. The display language is used to display the Google search page. To change the display language for Google tips and messages, select a language from the drop-down list. These are the choices:

- Dutch
- English
- French
- German
- Russian

Set the SafeSearch level to eliminate or include results that may contain adult content. By default, this setting is set to Moderate. Switch between Strict, Moderate, and Off by scrolling to the level of your choice and selecting it with the Enter key on your device.

When you finish setting your preferences, scroll to the Save button and click it with the Enter key. Your preferences are saved, and you are returned to the search page.

WML search

WML (Wireless Markup Language), like XHTML, is based on XML. WML pages are supported on devices that use the Wireless Application Protocol (WAP). It is still supported by many mobile devices, but it's quickly being replaced by XHTML. If your phone or device does not support XHTML or iMode (see the next section), try using Google's support for WML by pointing your mobile Web browser to www.google.com/wml. Type your search terms, and click the Web button.

Because of its limitations, WML search results only display five search results per page. Move from page to page by highlighting and selecting the Next link at the bottom of the page.

The older WML technology does not allow most Web pages to be displayed easily or correctly on the smaller mobile screens, so Google provides the ability to limit your search to only Web pages that are formatted for the display of WML pages. To see a list of WAP-compatible pages, click the Mobile Web button rather than the Web button after typing your search terms.

I-Mode search

Different from XHTML or WML, I-Mode (iMode) is a wireless communications technology developed by NTT DoCoMo that is very popular in Japan and gaining popularity throughout the world. Google has created a Web search page specifically for iMode-compatible devices. To perform a Web search using iMode technology, point your mobile Web browser to www.google.com/imode.

Use the same search techniques described in the preceding section on XHTML searching. Many mobile devices have a special I-Mode key to turn on this technology. If your device supports iMode, you may want to use this to search through Google.

> **TIP** You can change to a different language by appending a two-letter language code to the end of the URL used to access your search. Append ?hl= followed by the two-letter language code. For example, use www.google.com/imode?hl=fr to switch to French. Visit www.w3.org/WAI/ER/IG/ert/iso639.htm for a full list of two-letter language codes. This also works for XHTML.

Set the iMode preferences, language, and SafeSearch by pointing your browser to www.google.com/imode/preferences. See the section "Setting XHTML search preferences" for more information on setting the iMode preferences.

Searching Images

When you absolutely need to know if the person sitting in the back of the room is a famous TV star, do a Google Image Search right on your cell phone. For devices that support XHTML and iMode, you have the ability to search for an image just as you might from your desktop or laptop computer. Pointing your mobile Web browser to either www.google.com/xhtml or www.google.com/imode, you can enter a search term, as shown in Figure 28.1, scroll down to Images, press the Enter key on your device, and click the Search button. This selects the Images radio button; click the Search button to have Google find some images.

The search results appear, showing from one to three images per page depending on the display capabilities of your device. Each image appears with a number next to it. You can choose to view this image on its Web page by pressing the number on your device keypad or by scrolling to the image and pressing the device's Enter key. Google then displays the page containing the image.

To continue to the next image, you can scroll down to the Next link and select it. To perform a new search, scroll down to the search box at the bottom of the page.

Finding Local Listings

A fast way to find businesses or services in your area is to use the Local Listings search found on the Google Web search page. Just as with the image search, you can point your mobile Web browser to either the XHTML or iMode search page. Type the category of business you are looking for in the search box, scroll down to Local Listings, select it, and press the Search button.

After you press the Search button, Google prompts you for a location, as shown in Figure 28.3. Type a city, state, or other location in the Where box. For example, type Los Alamos NM. A comma is not required. Google is smart enough to know that NM in this example is the abbreviation for New Mexico.

FIGURE 28.3

Find the taco you've been craving by searching Local Listings.

The results for your search appear with the name of the business, the address, the phone number, and the distance from the location you typed. The more specific the location you type, such as a complete street address, the more specific the distance to the business.

As with Google Maps, the local listing includes a link to the business phone number so you can highlight the phone number and click to call. Clicking the name of the business launches a Google Map of the location and allows you to get driving directions. See Chapter 27 for more information on Google Maps and driving directions.

Searching the Mobile Web

Some mobile Web browsers are compatible only with Web pages that have been designed for small screens using WAP (Wireless Application Protocol). Google allows you to do searches through just the pages that are WAP-compatible. You can perform this search by pointing your mobile browser to www.google.com/wml or by selecting Mobile Web from either the XHTML or iMode search pages.

The results appear with a link to the WAP-compatible Web page along with a short snippet from the page. Scroll to the link and press Enter on your device to view the page, or scroll to the Next link and press Enter to see more results.

Mobile Gmailing

One of the exciting things Google has added is the ability to use Gmail on a mobile device. From the XHTML search page, click the <u>Gmail</u> link. Gmail is currently available only using XHTML. When you sign in, your Gmail inbox automatically appears for you, as shown in Figure 28.4.

FIGURE 28.4

Access all the features of Gmail from your mobile device.

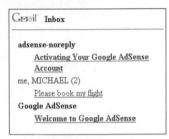

You need to sign up for a Gmail account using a nonmobile Internet account before you can use it on your mobile device.

Reading your mobile Gmail

Scroll down to the e-mail message you want to read and click on it by pressing the mobile device Enter key. An e-mail "header" appears listing the sender's name, the name of the recipient, the date the message was received, and the subject of the message. If there are attachments, they are listed in the header as links. Scroll to them, select the one you want to view, and click it with the Enter key.

Your mobile device must have an application that allows it to view files other than most standard image types. For example, if someone sends you an Excel spreadsheet, your mobile device needs Excel or a program that allows you to view Excel spreadsheets before you can view an Excel spreadsheet attachment.

One of the features of Gmail is to show you e-mail as threaded messages, so when an e-mail message has replies, you can view those as a list of message links. Selecting and clicking one of these links causes the message to appear, including the header described earlier.

The body of the message appears below the e-mail header. You may need to scroll to see the entire message. When you finish reading your message, you can choose to respond to the message using the standard Gmail message options.

Using the message options

You may need to scroll further below the body of the message to view the Gmail message options, which appear beneath the text of the message. To move to the next message, simply click Next conversation. To respond to the e-mail you are viewing, select one of the Gmail options by clicking the number listed before the option or by scrolling with your mobile device and pressing Enter. These are your options:

1. **Reply:** Reply to this message by sending a return message to the sender only.
2. **Reply to all:** Reply to this message by sending a return message to the sender and all other recipients of the message.

3. **Forward:** Send a copy of this message to a new recipient.

4. **Archive:** Create an archive of this message.

5. **Mark unread:** Mark this message as though it has never been read.

6. **Add star:** Add a star to this message to mark it.

7. **Trash message:** Send this message to the trash.

8. **Compose Mail:** Create a new e-mail message.

10. **Inbox:** View your inbox.

Two additional selections appear below the numbered menu. These are Contacts, which allows you to view your list of contacts, and more views, which allows you to select other Gmail folders and labels.

By selecting the more views option, you are presented with a list of folders that can be included in the list that appears on the main Gmail page when viewing it in your mobile device. It is wise to include only those folders you view on a regular basis to limit the amount of space used by the list of folder options.

Searching your Gmail

At the bottom of the list of options, a Google search box appears that allows you to search your e-mail. Type a search term in the search box, and click Search Mail. Your search results appear listed as links. Scroll to the message containing your search term, and press Enter on your mobile device. You see the number of search results listed. You may need to continue to the next page of messages. Because they are listed from newest to oldest, click the Older link to continue to the next page of older messages. This link changes to Newer after you continue to the next page, allowing you to return to the previous page of messages.

 **For more information about Gmail and its features, see Chapter 19.**

Mobile News

Google News gathers news stories from thousands of news sources and updates Google News viewers as the stories are reported. There is no need to be out of touch with the news simply because you are not sitting in front of your computer. Use your mobile device to read Google News.

Point your mobile Web browser to `www.google.com/xhtml`. From the XHTML search page, scroll down to and click the News link. This launches Google News (XHTML version), as shown in Figure 28.5.

Below the Google News search box are links to the Top Stories. To save space on your mobile device, the news "headline" is displayed without the normal Google News snippet of the article. You can still see the name of the news source and find a link to the related articles.

Scroll to the news story that interests you, and click it by pressing Enter on your mobile device. Clicking a news story causes you to navigate away from the Google News site. Each of the news sources for Google News provides an XHTML interface to its stories. Each news source appears formatted in a slightly different way and provides different options for things like moving to the next page of an article or reading other stories. You need to use your mobile Web browser's Back button or option to return to Google News on your mobile device or start over by typing `www.google.com/xhtml` and selecting News. Remember that Google News is updated constantly, so the information that appears may be different each time you launch Google News.

FIGURE 28.5

View Google News on your mobile device.

To see all the Top Stories, scroll to the last link in the Top Stories section of Google News and click the <u>All Top Stories</u> link. This launches a page listing the top ten stories along with a link to return to Google News.

Under the Top Stories section, you see a list of the various news sections, including these:

- U.S.
- World
- Entertainment
- Sports
- Sci/Tech
- Business
- Health

You can click any of these sections, or you also may see all the sections expanded to show the top news stories in each section by clicking the <u>+ Expand Sections</u> link located just above the list of sections. When you want to collapse the sections, scroll through each of the sections until you reach the <u>– Collapse Sections</u> link. Clicking this link returns Google News to its default appearance, showing only the Top Stories with links to each section.

Selecting one of the sections, such as U.S. or World, presents you with a list of the top ten stories in that section. You can return to the Google News main page by clicking the <u>Back to Google News</u> link at the bottom.

Of course, you can search the news using the search box found on each Google News page. Remember that, when reading stories, you are no longer on the Google News site, so the search box does not appear.

Typing a search term and clicking Search News returns a list of all current news articles containing your search term. You see links to ten news articles (with sources and links to related articles) per page. When there are more than ten results, you can move to the second page by clicking the <u>Next</u> link found at the bottom of the page. Move between pages by clicking the <u>Prev</u> and <u>Next</u> links.

 Some mobile device browsers support HTML and do not need to use the XHTML interface. These devices can simply use the Google News interface at `http://news.google.com`.

For more information about Google News, see Chapter 14.

Configuring Mobile Home Pages

You'll love setting up your own Google Mobile home page because you can design your own home page to access the information that is really important to you. Similar to Google Desktop, you can see the weather, check stock prices, see movie showtimes, and, of course, keep up with breaking news right on your mobile device.

Setting up your home page

You can create a personalized home page for your mobile device that gives you access to the latest news, the weather, how-to information, and other items that Google provides, as shown in Figure 28.6. It's a great start page to have on your phone.

 You can view the same personalized home page on your desktop or laptop computer, but some items may not be visible on a mobile device.

FIGURE 28.6

Your mobile device should have its own Google home page.

To set up your Google home page, you need to use either a laptop or desktop computer with Internet access. You can't use your mobile device to configure your home page. To get started, point your Web browser to www.google.com/ig/cp.

Several things are found on the Google Homepage Personalization page that you can add by clicking the +Add to my phone button found next to the item. Use the graphic mobile phone, shown in Figure 28.7, to configure the position of items on your home page. Items such as the New York Times news page are available, or you can click Add next to items in the New Stuff box. Some of these items are available on mobile devices but not on cell phones. These items are identified with the warning that they are not available on phones.

As you add items, you see them added to the graphic phone like the one shown in Figure 28.7. After they appear in the phone, you can reposition them by dragging and dropping them using your mouse or other pointing device. Remember that you must use your computer to configure your home page.

FIGURE 28.7

Personalize access to Google services by creating a mobile Google home page.

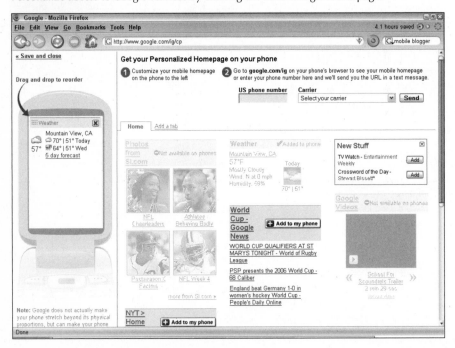

When you finish customizing your home page, you can point your mobile Web browser to http://google.com/ig, or in the Personalization page, you can type your mobile phone number, select your provider from the drop-down list, and click Send. A URL is sent to your phone for accessing your personalized home page.

Visit the Google Co-op Directory to find other sources of content that you can add to your home page. You can select from these items:

- Latest
- Lifestyle
- Health
- Information
- News
- Travel

Find the third-party provider of services that interest you, and click Subscribe below the logo. After you subscribe to the service, the button below the logo changes to Unsubscribe.

Partner with Google Mobile

Google has created many partnership programs discussed in this book, and Google Mobile is no exception. The number of people accessing the Internet using their mobile phones and other devices is growing rapidly. More than ever, your site must be accessible to mobile users, and helping people find your mobile Web site is one of Google's goals. You can partner with Google by adding Mobile Web Search to your site and making sure that Google indexes your mobile Web page.

Adding Google Mobile Web Search

You can add Google Search to your mobile Web site by signing up for Google Mobile and using the free copy-and-paste search service. Visit `www.google.com/mobile/partner.html`, and click Sign up for Google Mobile. Fill in the registration form, telling Google about your Web site. When you finish, click Submit.

 You can sign up for Google Mobile several times if you have more than one site.

Your mobile Web site must be compatible with one of the following mobile technologies:

- XHTML
- WML
- iMode
- PDA devices (standard HTML formatted for smaller displays)

Indexing your mobile Web page

A mobile Web page is one that has been formatted using one of the wireless technologies discussed throughout this chapter. At the very least, if you use HTML, it should be formatted for small displays. Create an account with Google Sitemaps to add your mobile Web page.

Creating a mobile site map

A site map is an XML page that lists information about your Web site. There are many reasons to create a site map. One reason may be that your site does not have pages that are easily found by Google's Web crawler. A site map helps the crawler better index your site. The same is true for mobile Web pages.

The easiest way to create a mobile site map in the Sitemap protocol is to use the Sitemap generator script. This is an open source script downloadable from SOURCEFORGE.net. The URL is rather lengthy. You can type this or point your browser to www.sourceforge.net and search on google-sitemap_gen. Here is the URL: http://sourceforge.net/project/showfiles.php?group_id=137793&package_id=153422.

Your Web site must be running Python 2.2 or higher to use the Sitemap generator script. Webmasters must know how to transfer files to their site and run scripts.

You also can manually create a site map using the Sitemap XML protocol. You should be familiar with creating well-formed XML pages. See full instructions for creating a site map here: https://www.google.com/webmasters/sitemaps/docs/en/protocol.html.

Please note that this site requires you to log in first.

Adding your site map

Point your Web browser to www.google.com/webmasters/sitemaps. Add your mobile Web site to the list of sites that you manage. Your site then appears in a list of managed sites. In the Sitemaps list column, click the Add a Sitemap link. This launches the Add Sitemap page where you should choose a type from the drop-down list. There are only two selections. The first one is for adding a sitemap that describes a regular Web page. Choose the second option, Add Mobile Sitemap from the list. New form selections appear based on which selection you choose. After you create a site map using one of the techniques described in the preceding section, upload it to your Web site. Type the URL of the site map in "Step 3. My Sitemap URL is."

Finally, select the markup language used by your mobile Web site from the drop-down list, and click Add Mobile Sitemap.

Finding out what's new

Stay on top of what's new in Google Mobile technology by signing up for notifications of new Google products. Point your Web browser or mobile or desktop computer to www.google.com/mobile/submit_email.html, type your e-mail address, and click Submit.

You also can stay up to date by reading Google's official blog at googleblog.blogspot.com.

Mobile Markup Languages

Mobile devices, because of their small screens, have required a rethinking about the way information, particularly graphic information, is displayed on the small screens. The first tendency, in early mobile markup language implementations, was to leave out the graphics, or only include very small graphics. There are now more advanced solutions that allow full4 Web pages to scale down for viewing on a small screen. Here is an overview of the markup languages used to create Web pages viewable on small screens.

XHTML (WAP 2.0)

XHTML is the successor to HTML and technically the reformulation of HTML 4.0 within the strict formatting of XML pages. The reason for this reformulation of HTML is due to the number of devices now used to access the Internet. HTML is a "loosey-goosey" markup language that requires a fairly heavy-duty *parser* — a special translation program — to correctly display HTML. Mobile devices just don't have the horsepower or resources to properly parse HTML, so switching to the very strict format of XML reduces the overhead necessary to properly display HTML.

WAP 2.0 is the latest version of the Wireless Application Protocol, the technology used by many mobile devices to provide Internet access. WAP acts as a gateway for XHTML content onto the mobile devices. Someday, WAP will be replaced by WIP (Wireless Internet Protocol), considered to be a true Internet protocol.

The official Web site for XHTML is www.w3.org/TR/xhtml1/.

WML (WAP 1.2)

Wireless Markup Language (WML) is an XML-based language used for displaying mobile Web pages. It is considered an older technology and is largely being replaced by XHTML. WML was the first language to be understood by wireless "micro-browsers," which were created to conform to the WML 1.1 DTD (Document Type Definition).

The official Web site for WML is www.wapforum.com.

cHTML (iMode)

Japanese-based NTT DoCoMo decided to create a competing technology to WAP called i-Mode. I-Mode, or commonly iMode, uses *cHTML*, compact HTML, as its markup language to create Web pages for small mobile devices. cHTML is a significantly smaller subset of HTML, thus cutting down on the need to parse the full version of HTML tags. cHTML does not support common HTML features such as JPG image support, tables, image maps, multiple fonts and font styles, background colors and images, frames, and style sheets. Basically, it supports two colors, usually black and white. While still used largely in Japan, cHTML is being replaced by the more widely used XHTML.

The official Web sites for cHTML (in Japanese) are www.access.co.jp/ and (in English) www.access.co.jp/english/index.html.

Summary

Google has created a portal to the world's information. With Google Mobile, you have access to this same information on your handheld wireless device. Search the Web using several wireless technologies. Check your Gmail account right from your phone. Reading the news and checking the weather are among the things you can set up on your own mobile Web page.

There are many Google applications available from your mobile device, even blogging. A blog, when created from a mobile device, is affectionately called a moblog (pronounced m_ blog) for mobile blog. You can find more information about Blogger Mobile in Chapter 25.

There's more to mobile computing than e-mail and the Web. You can use Google to send SMS text messages. Find out more about Google SMS in Chapter 29.

Part IV

Google-izing Your Computer

Chapter 29

Messaging with Google

oogle SMS (Short Message Service) is designed for people on the go. You can send text messages to Google to get information on many topics. Unlike other Google searches, the SMS service is meant to provide quick information for someone who needs info quickly, such as "Where is the movie playing?," "Where can I get gas?," "How did that game end?," or "How do I get there?"

Getting Started

You can send SMS text messages to the five-digit U.S. shortcode 46645 or GOOGL on your keypad. Receiving a return message can take some time, possibly up to a minute. Be aware that although Google provides this service at no charge, your cell phone provider may charge for both outgoing and incoming text messages. Some providers have unlimited messaging plans, while others allow a certain number of messages, both outgoing and incoming, and still others charge per message.

Sending a text message

Most cell phones today are capable of sending and receiving SMS text messages. This includes phones that are not Internet-capable. SMS does not use the Internet to transfer text messages so your phone does not need to have a Web browser or Internet capabilities.

You access the messaging application on your cell phone using the number 46645. For the text of the message, enter your query to Google. The queries are formatted in a particular manner, depending on the type of query you are sending. The various queries are explained throughout the rest of this chapter.

 Make sure your cell phone is not set up to add signatures to text messages. The signature cannot be understood and causes an error, meaning you won't get your response.

The messages you send to Google are not case-sensitive, so don't worry about capitalizing things like business, people, or place names. Also, don't use any punctuation. You absolutely can't use the following characters when sending text messages to Google: [ ] \ ^ _ { } ~ ` | .

You also will find that the period has a special meaning, used optionally in formatting a local listings query. So unless you are using it for that purpose, don't use a period, either.

Query results

The results you receive from Google depend entirely on the type of query you send. If your query is very specific, you may get a single result, hopefully the one you want. If not, try changing your query. You receive a maximum of three results no matter how broad your query is. So if you are looking for Smith or Jones in Chicago, you may have trouble without a first name. Even then, your query may not appear in the top three results. Your query then needs to become much more specific. Each query type returns different results explained throughout the chapter.

Sometimes results are too large to fit into a single text message. This message length size is a limit of the SMS service. To overcome this limit, Google splits the results into several messages numbering them as they are sent, numbered 1 of n, where n is the total number of SMS messages that comprise the entire Google text message. For long results, such as driving directions, this means that the result could exceed the maximum number of result messages sent by Google, which is seven. In that case, your result is incomplete. Try sending a query again from a place further along your route to get the rest of the directions.

Finding Local Listings

When you need a hospital or you're just suffering from hunger pain, you can find the right place to go using the Local Listings SMS. Find almost any type of business in a specific area or neighborhood. After you send your local listing query, Google returns a message, shown in Figure 29.1, with the following:

- Business name
- Business address
- Business telephone number
- Distance from your location
- General geographic direction (N, E, W, S, NW, SW, NE, and so on)

 Currently, this service is limited to businesses within the United States and Canada.

To get a business listing, begin by entering the type of business you are looking for. This can be very general (like hospital) or specific (like St Francis); refer to Figure 29.1. Enter your Local Listing query like this:

business type . your location

When entering a business name or category, you can enter as much or as little of the name as you want. For example, enter thai, or thai restaurant. They both work exactly the same. Notice in the example above that there is a period between the business type and your location. This period is optional, but it helps Google know when you are finished typing the business and when you have started typing a location. For this reason, don't use periods. In the example of st francis, don't type st. francis, because it will confuse Google.

Find listings for hospitals, restaurants, and any other type of business.

```
Local Listings:
St Francis Medical Center
140 Rainbow Dr
Hilo, HI 96720
808-935-8733
11.9 mi, NW
```

When you enter your location, you can simply use a ZIP code, or type the city and the two-letter state code, as in these examples:

- coffee. 90250
- hospital. hilo hi
- gas 70504
- pizza albuquerque nm
- starbucks northampton ma

Don't worry about getting the query wrong. If it is formatted incorrectly, you either get a message from Google telling you that it is unable to find your request, or if it is formatted very badly, you may not receive a return message at all. If you don't receive a response to your query within two or three minutes, try reformatting and resending your query.

Getting Driving Directions

Google loves telling you where to go. You can get driving directions in a number of Google services, so it only makes sense get directions through SMS when you're on the go. Format your driving directions by first typing your starting location, the word *to*, and then your destination. It should look like this:

starting location to *destination*

The start location or destination can include the following (but don't type the + sign):

- *Street address + ZIP code*
- *Street address + city + state*
- *City + state*

- *City*
- *State*
- *ZIP code*
- *Three-letter airport code*

Here are some examples of queries:

- 123 main milwaukee wi to 225 oak st paul mn (very specific query)
- milwaukee wi to st paul mn (less specific)
- california to new york (This works, but there are too many directions to fit in the seven-message limit. See Figure 29.2.)
- 90250 to 90210
- lax to sfo

FIGURE 29.2

Your driving directions may exceed the seven-message limit.

Directions:
Distance: 2852 mi (about
1 day 16 hours) 36 steps.
Sorry, the requested
route is too long. You
may want to get it online
at http://
maps.google.com.

The detailed driving directions include the total number of steps necessary to arrive at your destination, the estimated distance, and the estimated travel time. Each step is numbered and includes the distance you must travel along each route. When directions or turns are included, they are abbreviated to shorten the message. You can find a list of the driving direction abbreviations used by Google in Table 29.1.

TABLE 29.1

Driving Direction Abbreviations

Abbreviation	Description
N	Go north
S	Go south
E	Go east
W	Go west
L	Turn left
R	Turn right
Cont.	Continue

Finding Movie Showtimes

Because going to the movies is often one of those spur-of-the-moment ideas you have while you're out somewhere, you need access to movie listings. That's how MovieFone was invented. But why waste cell phone minutes listening to endless descriptions of each movie. Now you can get the results you want quickly and right to the point. See which movies are currently playing in your area, as shown in Figure 29.3.

FIGURE 29.3

Typing films and a ZIP code returns all the movie showtimes in or near that ZIP code.

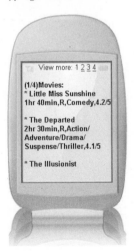

You can use Google SMS to find movie showtimes, theater locations, and information such as the running time, MPA rating, movie genre, and critics' ratings.

To find movies and theater listings, send a text message to Google using one of the following formats (but don't type the + sign):

- *movie name* + *location*
- movie: *movie name* + *location*
- movie: theaters + *location*
- movie: showtimes + *location*
- movie: movies + *location*
- movie: films + *location*
- *movie name* (displays only information about the movie)
- theaters + *location*
- films + *location*

> **NOTE** When typing only the movie name and location, Google may not understand the movie name and may return a business listing instead. If that happens, try typing movie: first.

The location can be entered as simply a ZIP code, or a city and state. If you enter a city name, you must also enter a state. Here are some example queries:

- little miss sunshine los angeles ca
- movie: little miss sunshine los angeles ca
- movie: theaters 90210
- movie: showtimes 96760
- movie: movies phoenix az
- movie: films cleveland oh
- harry potter retirement of doom
- theaters myrtle beach fl
- films honolulu hi

Remember that the film you are looking for must be playing in a theater near you or the query will not return a result. Before checking the movies, you may want to see what the weather is going to be like. See the next section.

Getting Weather Conditions

You can use Google SMS to get the latest weather conditions and four-day forecast for a particular location within the United States. Simply send an SMS text message to Google with the word weather (or weather:) followed by your location. The location can be entered as a ZIP code or city and state combination. You can use these formats:

- weather 47408
- weather kurtistown hi

> **TIP** Use the shortcut "W" or "WX" rather than typing the word weather to find the weather conditions in a particular location.

The results shown in Figure 29.4 include the following information:

- Location name
- Current temperature measured in Fahrenheit
- Visibility
- Humidity
- Four-day forecast including temperature range and chance of precipitation

---

FIGURE 29.4

Google tells you that there's always a chance of rain in Hawaii.

Weather:
Kurtistown,HI
75F,Clear
Wind:E 6mph
Hum:89%
F:71-84F,Chance of Rain
Sa:70-84F,Chance of Rain
Su:68-83F,Chance of Rain
M:67-82F,Chance of Rain

Converting Measurements

When you write to your mom in Indiana and want to tell her how hot it was in Marbella, Spain, on the beach, you probably want to convert the temperature from Celsius to Fahrenheit. The most important word to remember when sending conversion text messages to Google is *in*. For example, type **27 C in F** or change it the other way, **80 F in C**. See what the results look like in Figure 29.5.

Try converting from one currency to another. If you're in Europe trying to convert to Euros from dollars, the math can have you going crazy. If you can multiply by 0.78486775 in your head, you may not need the currency converter. But you may just want to give your head a rest, send Google a quick text message, and let it do the work.

Here are some other conversions that Google can do for you:

- cooking (example: tablespoons in cups)
- weight (example: 1 ton in troy ounces)(example: .5 ounces in carats)
- length (example: .5 inches in millimeters)
- distance (example: 5 miles in kilometers)
- area (example: 1 acre in square feet)(example: 1 acre in hectares)

- pressure (example: 100 psi in bars)
- power (example: 1 kilowatt in horsepower)
- speed (example: 100 mph in kph)
- angles (example: 1 radian in degrees)
- astronomical (example: 1 light year in kilometers)
- time (example: 1 day in milliseconds)

FIGURE 29.5

Convert temperature, weight, distance, and many other things.

Google Calculator:
80 degrees Fahrenheit =
26.6666667 degrees
Celsius

The format for sending a conversion is: *amount + measure* in *converted measure*

I'm sorry to tell you this, but there are just some things that Google SMS won't convert. You have to use some of the online calculators to convert shakes into milliseconds or man-years into dog-years.

Translating Words

Google SMS could put those little handheld translator companies out of business. Not really, because SMS works only in the U.S. But, there are still many times when you need to translate English into another language. Use the Google SMS translator when you need to translate words or phrases from English into another language, as shown in Figure 29.6. For now, the list includes English into these languages:

- Italian
- German
- Spanish
- French
- Portuguese

FIGURE 29.6

You never know when you might want cauliflower tacos.

Google Translation: 'cauliflower' in English means 'coliflor' in Spanish.

The format for submitting a translation query is:

translate *word/s in English* in/into *language*

 **You can use the shortcut "T" rather than type the entire word *translate*.**

Here are a couple of examples:

- translate sea into french
- translate wonderful in portuguese

You also can translate phrases such as:

- translate life is wonderful in italian
- translate you ate my goldfish into spanish (The answer is: comiste me goldfish)

Getting Stock Quotes

Sending Google SMS text messages is a sure sign of success. Another one is sending Google text messages to check on your stock portfolio. To receive stock and mutual fund information using Google SMS, send the stock or mutual fund ticker symbol.

Your result includes the most recent exchange and ECN quote for this stock (delayed), along with its volume, average volume, opening price, the day's range, and the current market capitalization, as shown in Figure 29.7. The stock or mutual fund must be traded on a U.S. exchange. Generally, Google does not return quotes for stocks listed in the "pink sheets."

FIGURE 29.7

Send a ticker symbol to Google SMS to stay on top of stock and mutual fund trading.

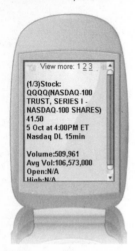

Send only a single stock ticker symbol per text message. Google does not understand multiple ticker symbols.

You can use these formats for sending a text message to request stock and mutual fund information:

- *ticker symbol*
- stock *ticker symbol*

Use the word *stock* when the ticker symbol is not clearly understood by Google SMS.

Engaging in a Little Q&A

Want to settle a bet, answer a question that has been bugging you, or impress someone with the amazing range of your knowledge? Send text messages to Google on almost any topic.

You can get the answers to lots of questions over a very broad array of topics. You can find out who wrote certain books or who invented certain things. There is no guarantee that Google knows the answers. Tests of Q&A revealed huge holes in Google's ability to answer things. For example, Google knew the inventor of television, but not of radio. Google knew the author of *To Kill a Mockingbird*, but not the author of any of the Harry Potter books. You can learn things such as the population of cities or countries, the gross domestic product (GDP) of various nations, and all sorts of other trivia (see Figure 29.8).

Here are some sample queries:

- GDP of Netherlands
- mass of the moon
- author to kill a mockingbird

There is no exact format for creating a Q&A query. Basically, phrase it as what you want to know about a certain topic: *question + topic*. If Google does not understand your question, you may get a suggestion in return or a message telling you the reason Google can't answer your question.

FIGURE 29.8

Send text messages to Google to find things such as the GDP of the Netherlands.

Q&A:
Netherlands
GDP: $ 481,100,000,000
Source: www.cia.gov/cia/
publications/factbook/
rankorder/2001rank.html

Shopping with Froogle SMS

Imagine standing in a store, trying to figure out whether to buy something, and having the power of Froogle in your hand. You no longer need to wonder if you are getting a good deal. Simply send SMS messages to Froogle using Google SMS to search the prices of millions of products indexed by Froogle. You can compare prices or simply find products (see Figure 29.9).

 The results are not ads. These are the same results you get by using Froogle on the Web.

Format your Froogle text messages like this:

- froogle *product*
- price *product*
- *product* prices

 You can use the shortcut "F" or "f" (for Froogle) to find product prices.

The *product* in your text message can take many different forms. It can include a product name, such as MP3 player; or a brand name, such as Singer sewing machine. Searching for a book won't require you to type in the entire title, possibly giving you the wrong results. You can simply type in the 10-digit ISBN of the book, and Froogle lets you comparison shop for the book. Most online booksellers include the ISBN of books they sell. You might first want to find the ISBN at an online store, then perform a comparison search.

You also can use Froogle to query products and prices by typing in the 8- or 12-digit number found beneath and represented by the bar code on the product, known as the UPC (Universal Product Code). Just find the bar code on the product, type the number into a Froogle text message, and find prices across the Internet.

FIGURE 29.9

Find prices on almost anything you can think of through Froogle SMS text messages.

Here are a few examples of Froogle searches using text messages to Google SMS:

- froogle dvd player
- f dvd player
- price dvd player
- dvd player prices
- 0470097120 (the ISBN of this book)
- price 0470097120
- 018208252145 (UPC code for a pastry blender)
- f 018208252145
- price 018208252145

Your search may result in multiple "pages" requiring you to view several text messages. Remember that Froogle returns only the top three results using Google SMS.

Getting Definitions

If someone calls you duplicitous and you don't know whether to smile or feel hurt, pull out your phone and pretend to call someone, but type a quick text message to Google SMS. Use Google SMS to find definitions for a word or phrase the same way you use the Google search box to look up the meanings of words. Don't worry about spelling the word correctly. We all have relied on Google to correct our spelling of difficult words, and Google SMS is no different. Type the word incorrectly, and if you are even close with your spelling, Google suggests the correct spelling, and performs the lookup, and returns your result.

Format your text message query like this:

define *word or phrase*

Your results appear as shown in Figure 29.10. Yes, you can be upset. Duplicitous is not a nice thing to call someone.

FIGURE 29.10

Define words and phrases by sending a message to Google SMS.

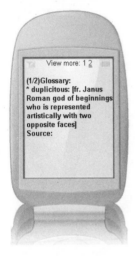

 You can use the shortcut "D" rather than type the entire word define.

Getting the Latest Updates on Sports

You never need to wonder how that game turned out or how it is going. Google SMS can give you real-time basketball, football, baseball, and hockey scores and schedules by simply typing a team name.

The results as shown in Figure 29.11 give you the score of the current or last game played, the score of the most recent game prior to the current game, and the schedule for the next game.

To see sports scores, your sport must be in season. Google SMS currently allows you to query for scores from the NFL, NHL, NBA, MLB, and NCAA. Notice that these sample queries simply consist of the team name or the team name preceded by the name of the city:

- eagles
- sharks
- dodgers
- los angeles dodgers

FIGURE 29.11

Get nearly real-time sports scores by sending Google a sports query.

Remember to send your text message to the short code 46645 or GOOGL on most keypads. You might be wondering how it is that Google knows that eagles and sharks are team names and that you are not asking a question about eagles, or sharks. When these words are not accompanied by a question, such as *How long do sharks live?* Google assumes these are names.

Finding More Useful Information

Google continues to find new information and new ways to get it to you. You can use Google SMS for a few other things to help you through your daily information needs.

Getting ZIP codes

When you need to know what city is associated with a particular ZIP code, send an SMS message to Google SMS that simply includes the ZIP code and nothing else. The result, such as the one shown in Figure 29.12, is the ZIP code and the city with that ZIP code.

Some cities, like Los Angeles, have many ZIP codes. Google SMS does not distinguish between different neighborhoods. So typing 90001 and 90002 both return Los Angeles as the city.

The format for entering a ZIP code is:

99999

 Google SMS understands only five-digit ZIP codes.

FIGURE 29.12

Send a ZIP code to Google SMS to find which city it represents.

Getting area codes

When you see a telephone number on your caller-id and you want to know where the call originated, ask Google SMS. Type the area code as a text message, and Google returns the city associated with the area code. For queries in larger cities, the area code query, unlike the ZIP code query, usually returns a specific part of a city when the city has more than one area code. The results are displayed as shown in Figure 29.13. Enter the query like this:

999

Of course, the three digits must represent a valid area code. The first *9* can be any number from 2 to 9 and the second and third *9s* can be any number from 0 to 9. For example, 111 returns a message that Google did not find any results.

NOTE The first area code was 201 for New Jersey, created in 1951.

FIGURE 29.13

Let your fingers do the walking by sending a text message with an area code to Google SMS.

202: area code for Washington, DC.

Using the calculator

People rarely carry calculators anymore. Are they doing the math in their heads like the old days? No, they are sending messages to Google SMS, which can act like a powerful scientific calculator. This is the same powerful calculator you have access to using the Google Search Box. Type almost any mathematic equation, and Google returns an answer.

Queries can be anything from simple math like 2 + 2 to trigonometry or scientific equations using constants. The results appear as a text message, as shown in Figure 29.14.

Type your equation with or without an equal sign, and Google returns a result. Here are some of the ways you can use Google calculator through Google SMS or any Google Search Box:

- *percentage* % of *total*   Example: 19 % of 200   Answer 19 % of 200 = 38
- *base* **power*   Example: 10**2   Answer 10**2 = 100

 NOTE   When using Google calculator in a Web browser, you can use the ^ symbol, but not when sending messages to Google SMS.

You can create complex expressions by using parentheses to enclose parts of your expression. Parentheses are evaluated according to the rules of algebra; in other words, the parts of the expression enclosed in parentheses are evaluated before evaluating the entire expression.

(2 + 5) * (5/6)

Also, when expressions enclosed in parentheses appear embedded in larger expressions, the innermost expression is evaluated first. For example, in the following expression, 6 * 7 is evaluated first and then added to 5, and finally, the result is multiplied by 29.

(29 * (5 + (6 * 7)))

FIGURE 29.14

Look for answers to simple or complex equations and have the results appear on your phone.

Google Calculator:
19% of 200 = 38

Constants

Constants are values represented by a term, letter, or abbreviation. For example, the letter c represents the speed of light. Avogadro's number, 6.0221415×10^{23}, is represented by the entire phrase, Avogadro's number. Here are some of the constants understood by Google SMS.

- Avogadro's number 6.0221415×10^{23}
- c   Speed of light
- e   Base of the natural system of logarithms
- gamma   Euler's constant
- pi   3.14159265 used to calculate the circumference of a circle

TIP You must use valid numeric entries for the trigonometric functions, or Google cannot recognize your entry as a calculator function. For example, arcsin requires a decimal value.

Google can also give you these values:

- cosine
- tan
- cotangent
- sec (secant)
- csc (cosecant)

Inverse functions

According to Answers.com, an inverse function is a function whose relation is such that their composite is the identity function. It is often found by changing dependent and independent variables. Google includes the following inverse functions:

- arcsin
- arcos

425

- arctan
- sinh
- cosh
- tanh
- csch
- arcsinh
- arccsch
- Many others

Logarithms

`Answers.com` defines logarithms as: The power to which a base, such as 10, must be raised to produce a given number. The calculator handles the following logarithm functions.

- ln
- logarithm base e
- log logarithm base 10
- log logarithm base 2

Others

The following two functions, exp and the factorial function are also useful for scientific calculations:

- exp exponential function
- ! factorial

This is not a complete tutorial on using the calculator, but it should be enough to get you started.

Summary

Google SMS is an incredibly powerful way to access information through Google by using your phone or mobile device's SMS text message system. This is a great way to use Google when your device does not have normal Internet access. Get local business listings, driving directions, movie showtimes, and weather forecasts; convert from one measure to another; translate from English to several other languages; get stock quotes; ask questions with snippet answers; comparison shop; and get sports scores. You also can use Google SMS to find ZIP code and area code locations or use it as a high-powered calculator.

You probably can't remember all the cool stuff Google SMS can do, so you can download wallet-sized tip sheets from `www.google.com/sms/tips.pdf`. Print several of them, and post them on your car's dashboard, your bulletin board at work, or wherever you think you may need quick help.

Remember, it's simple and all you really need to remember is GOOGL. With all the power of Google in your cell phone, you hardly need a desktop computer. But when you do, there is so much more you can do with Google. Learn about installing the Google Pack in the next chapter.

Chapter 30

Getting to Know the Google Pack

The Google Pack is an electronic package of essential Google software. It includes software programs written by Google to enhance your desktop, customize Microsoft's Internet Explorer with the Google Toolbar, and Google's image software tool, Picasa. Also included are several software tools provided by Google partner companies, including these:

- Mozilla Firefox with Google Toolbar
- Norton Antivirus 2005 Special Edition
- Ad-Aware SE Personal
- Adobe Reader 7

You also can choose to download and install optional programs not included in the Google Pack by default. When this book was being written, the optional software package was GalleryPlayer HD Images, a group of high-definition photos and artwork that you can use as screensaver images or to customize the image on your computer desktop. You also can print them and use them for your child's origami project. See, Google thinks of everything!

> **TIP** Cut printed pictures square for use in origami projects.

IN THIS CHAPTER

Getting to know Google Updater

Finding your current update or download status

Seeing what Google software you have installed

Setting your Google Updater preferences

Learning more about Google Gadgets and Plug-ins

Downloading and Installing the Google Pack

To download and get started installing the Google Pack software, go to http://pack.google.com, as shown in Figure 30.1. Click Download Google Pack. You must agree to the license agreement before the software is downloaded using the Google Updater program. If you've already installed the Google Pack, this page displays and allows you to download any additional software that has been made available since you last installed the Google Pack.

> **NOTE** The software is for personal, noncommercial use only.

FIGURE 30.1

Click Download Google Pack to Googleize your computer.

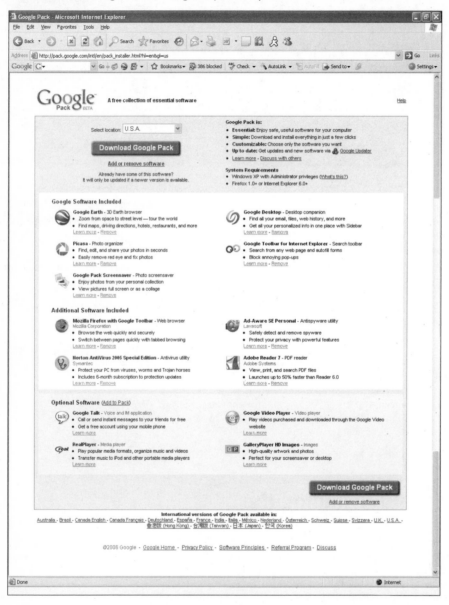

With the Google Pack, you will receive essential Google software to give you access to the world's and your own information stored on your computer.

Google Updater

The Google Updater program is the application that Google uses to download and install all the programs in the Google Pack. Google Updater includes these features, among others:

- It monitors your Google Pack installation status.
- It runs installed Google Pack software.
- It uninstalls Google Pack Software.
- It remains in your taskbar and informs you of updates as they become available.

The Google Updater application automatically starts when you log in to your Windows account. The application runs in the background, but a Google Updater window can be launched by double-clicking the multicolored ball icon in your computer's taskbar, as shown in Figure 30.2.

FIGURE 30.2

Launch the Google Updater program from the taskbar.

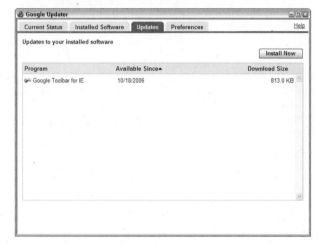

Current status

Google Updater can display the current status of Google Pack software installed on your system or its installation. Launch the Google Updater application from the taskbar, and click the Current Status tab. This tab allows you to see potential downloads and downloaded software that needs to be installed and to check the current status of any programs being downloaded or installed while you watch.

Downloads

The Downloads section of the Current Status tab displays a list of all the software that is available for download. When no new software is available, a message tells you that there is Nothing to download. You also can click the Get more software link in this section to navigate to the Google Pack page and see a list of optional software.

Installs

The section to the right of the Current Status tab lists any Google Pack software that has been downloaded to the computer and is awaiting installation. Because most of the software is installed immediately, this should rarely have any entries. But if there are, you can see which programs still need to be installed.

Status

You can see a live status report on the download and installation of programs. The box at the bottom of the Current Status tab shows you the program name, the current installation or download status, and the program's download size in bytes.

Installed software

Clicking the Installed Software tab of the Google Updater program allows you to see a list of the software installed or detected by the Google Updater program. This program does not detect all the software on your hard drive, only those it was designed to manage.

From this list you can select, run, get help, and uninstall software. Clicking the Run link next to the program name launches the application. Clicking the Help link loads a Web page with support information applicable to the selected product. You can see the date the application was installed on your computer and the size of the installed program. This can be handy if you want to verify that the software you installed is genuine. It's not a perfect way to tell, but it's at least one indication. Click the Uninstall link to remove any of these installed applications.

When you want to see any recent activity with regard to updates or recent installs, click the Recent Activity link in the bottom of this tab. This launches the Recent Activity window displaying a list of any Google Pack programs that have been installed or updated recently, the current version, which action took place, and the date on which it happened. After reviewing this list, you can clear it by clicking Clear History Now. Click Close to close the window and return to the Google Updater program main screen.

To launch the Google Pack home page to see what new software is available, click the Get more software link in the top-right corner of this tab.

Updates

The Updates tab displays a list of updates to currently installed Google Pack programs that have not yet been installed. The list contains any downloaded updates that have occurred and not been installed. You can see the date the update became available. Click the small arrow in this column to sort updates chronologically from newest to oldest or oldest to newest.

Select the program name to see a small description, and when you are ready to install it, click Install Now in the upper-right portion of this tab. This takes you to the Status tab. The Status changes to Updating, and the progress of each installation appears in a progress bar in the top left of the tab. When installing multiple updates, you can watch your progress through these updates by watching the Installs progress bar in the upper right. When the updates are installed, the Status changes to Updated. Returning to the Updates tab should show you that all the updates you requested no longer appear in the list.

Set Google Updater preferences

Click the Preferences tab to configure Google Updater. The Preferences tab is organized into five different types of configuration settings.

You can set the following preferences:

- **Notifications:** Select whether you want to be notified about new software by selecting or deselecting the check box.
- **Updates:** Choose whether to automatically update your software, be notified of updates before installing them, or let you check for updates on your own.
- **Connection Settings:** Set manual proxy settings for computers protected behind firewalls.
- **System Tray:** Choose to display the Google Updater icon in the system tray or only when there are updates.
- **Other:** Allow Google to collect anonymous statistics to improve the services it offers you.

TIP For security reasons, you should choose to be notified of any updates before allowing them to be installed on your computer. It's a small hassle to put up with to be a little safer. Of course, you can trust Google, but you may not be able to trust people who manage to hack the Google Updater program. It can happen.

When you finish making changes to the preferences, click Save Preferences. A bar appears across the top of the tab telling you that your preferences are saved. To exit Google Updater, click the small red X in the upper-right corner of the window.

Google Pack Screensaver

One of the enjoyable little extras you get with the Google Pack is the Google Pack Screensaver. When your computer is idle, the screensaver displays to your screen pictures it finds on your hard drive.

To configure the Google Pack Screensaver, follow these steps:

1. Choose Start ⇨ Control Panel.
2. Double-click Display.
3. Click the Screen Saver tab.
4. Select Google Pack Screensaver from the Screen saver drop-down list, as shown in Figure 30.3.
5. Click Settings. This launches the Google Pack Screensaver configuration window.
6. Set the Visual and Picture Folder Settings described next.
7. Set the Visual settings for the Google Pack Screensaver by selecting how you want images to appear on the screen when the screensaver is active. The choices are
   - **Collage:** Displays many images (size-reduced) in a random collage
   - **Wipe:** Shows full-screen images in a wipe from left to right across the screen
   - **Crossfade:** Shows full-screen images as they fade onto the screen

FIGURE 30.3

Configure the Google Pack Screensaver in your Display Properties settings.

8. Set how often you want new images to appear on-screen. The default is 2 seconds. You can increase or decrease this number by using the slider shown in Figure 30.4. The Preview window allows you to see how the screensaver will appear when it's active.

FIGURE 30.4

Set the display type and speed of the display.

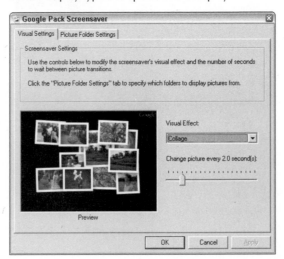

The Picture Folder setting is important. It determines where images are selected from for viewing. Click the Picture Folder Settings tab to configure this setting. By default, the Google Pack Screensaver program selects images from your My Pictures folder and any subfolders.

 Only images saved in the JPEG format are displayed.

You can select any subfolders not already selected by selecting the check box. Deselect check boxes from any folders you want the Google Pack screensaver to ignore. For example, you may not want "business design images" displayed for just anyone to see.

Add new folders by clicking Add Folder. A dialog box appears that allows you to browse to the folder you want to include. Select the folder, and it appears in your list with the check boxes already selected. Deselect any subfolders you do not want to include.

To make selecting and deselecting all the check boxes simple, click Check All or Uncheck All. When you finish making changes, click Apply and continue with configuring the screensaver, or click OK to save your changes and close this window.

In the Screensaver Display Properties window, you can click Preview to see a full-screen preview of your selections. After watching the show, you may want to make changes to the selections displayed on-screen.

Google Gadgets and Plug-ins

Everyone has become gadget-happy. There are Yahoo! Gadgets, Google Gadgets and now Vista Gadgets (Vista is the code name for the Microsoft Windows version after XP). Essentially, they are all the same with minor differences. Google Gadgets tend to be more web-centric than the Vista gadgets. You can certainly take advantage of all the different gadgets. To get you started, Google Pack comes with several Gadgets included in the download. Chapter 11, Personalizing Google Desktop, has additional information about installing and using the Google Gadgets.

NOTE **Vista gadgets will soon run on Windows XP once updates for XP are made available.**

You can find hundreds of additional Google Gadgets at `http://desktop.google.com/plugins/ sidebar/`.

You'll see the Google Featured Gadgets displayed across the top of this Web page. You also can choose to sort hundreds of others by popularity (based on the number of user downloads), by date (when they were added), and by name, in case you know the name of the Gadget and want to find it quickly.

Click the Next link to see additional pages of Gadgets. The Gadgets are organized by category. Choose from one of the following Gadget categories:

- All
- News
- Tools
- Communication
- Finance
- Fun & Games

- Google
- Sports
- Lifestyle
- Technology

Select one of these categories from the column on the left and view the Gadgets in this category. For example, clicking the Lifestyle category link displays Gadgets for viewing your daily horoscope, seeing the local weather, or assisting you in a job search.

Clicking the Gadget launches a page with more information about the Gadgets, such as the company or person who authored the Gadget, the size in bytes, what type of license it is offered under, the version number and the release date. You can learn even more by clicking the Learn more link or join in discussions about the Gadget by clicking the Discuss this gadget link, which launches the Google Group associated with this Gadget.

When you're ready, click Download gadget to begin the download. You are asked to confirm that you want the Gadget installed, as shown in Figure 30.5.

FIGURE 30.5

Confirm that you want to install the Gadget once your download is complete.

Some Gadgets require that you set preferences before they can be used. For example, you may need to set the month and day of your birth before using one of the horoscope Gadgets. Some Gadgets are not authored or controlled by Google. You may be giving out personal information to a third party.

When your Gadget is installed you can begin using it with Google Desktop.

 **Consider using Gadgets on your Google Page Creator Web page. Click the add gadget link in the bottom corner of the Web page edit screen.**

Summary

Download Google Pack when you want to install all the latest personal Google software on your computer. Get some of the latest Open software offered by Google partners or important desktop protection tools. Open software is written by programmers that believe that the source code to software should be shared "openly" and that software should not be proprietary. Open software is generally free to download and use. Developers make money offering services such as support or products such as user manuals.

The Google Updater helps you manage all your Google Pack software by watching for updates; managing your downloads and installs; and providing a place where you can run, get help, or uninstall your downloaded programs.

One of the great add-ons for the Firefox and Internet Explorer browsers is the Google Toolbar. The next chapter helps you manage this great search feature.

Chapter 31

Managing the Google Toolbar

The Google Toolbar has become an important addition to the two most popular Web browsers, Internet Explorer and Firefox. There are different toolbars for Internet Explorer and Firefox. The features of the two toolbars are not the same, and this chapter helps you learn about those differences. But whether you use the Toolbar for IE or for Firefox, installing the Toolbar in your browser will make your Internet life easier.

Pointing your Web browser to http://toolbar.google.com takes you to a different start page depending on which browser you use to access the site. Your browser is automatically detected and the appropriate page appears.

Installing Toolbar for IE

Using Internet Explorer, point your Web browser to http://toolbar.google.com and click Download Google Toolbar, as shown in Figure 31.1. There also are links to the Enterprise version of the Toolbar, which is discussed in Chapter 37. This download is for Internet Explorer version 6 or greater and those using Windows Vista, Windows XP, or Windows 2000 operating system. For users of Windows 98 or Windows Me, click the Download Previous Version link.

> **NOTE** Click the Firefox version link to download the Firefox version even if you are using IE. The Firefox page also has a link to the IE Google Toolbar page.

Clicking Download Google Toolbar starts the immediate download of the GoogleToolbarInstaller.exe file. You can choose to run this program or save it to your hard drive to run later. You may receive a security warning similar to the one shown in Figure 31.2. Click Run.

IN THIS CHAPTER

Learn to install Google Toolbar for both Internet Explorer and Firefox

Discover the features that make your Web surfing more productive

Customize the Toolbar with your personal preferences

FIGURE 31.1

Learn about and download Google Toolbar for Internet Explorer.

FIGURE 31.2

Internet Explorer may display a warning.

The installer, shown in Figure 31.3, appears and gives you three installation options:

- Set Google as the default search in Internet Explorer and notify me of changes
- Help Google improve the Toolbar by sending us usage statistics
- Close all Internet Explorer windows to ensure a conflict-free installation

The first setting determines whether you want Google set as your default search. If the answer is yes, select the check box. The Toolbar also tells you if some other search program tries to change this setting, possibly without your knowledge. This keeps viruses and other sneaky programs from making settings to your computer without your knowledge.

The second setting sends anonymous usage statistics to Google about how the Toolbar is being used. Google does not use this feature to collect personal information about you.

The third option is an installation-only option, asking if the installer can close all open Internet Explorer windows to avoid any program conflicts. If you have important pages open you should save or complete your work before continuing the installation. It's recommended that you allow the installer to close any open IE windows, including the one you used to download the Toolbar.

Read the license agreement, and if you agree click Agree & Continue. The next page asks that you read it carefully as it is not the usual yada yada. For Google's PageRank technology to work, information about the pages you visit must be sent to Google. Once again, no personally identifying information is sent to Google. Your privacy is important to the people at Google.

You must choose to either enable or disable PageRank before you can continue. Click Finish to complete the installation. A Web page appears in IE letting you know that your toolbar has been installed. It should appear along the top of your IE Web browser. If for some reason it does not appear, try choosing View ➪ Toolbars and selecting Google, or if your menu is not visible you can right-click on the IE toolbar and select Google from the pop-up menu. In the event that Google does not appear in either menu, try restarting your Web browser, and if that doesn't work restart your computer. If it still does not appear, try downloading and reinstalling the Toolbar.

FIGURE 31.3

Set install options and agree to the license terms.

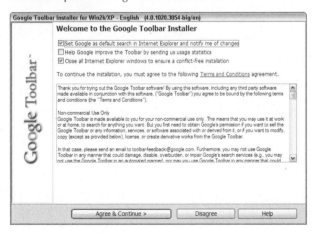

Installing the Toolbar for Firefox

The process for installing Google Toolbar for Firefox is similar to installing the Toolbar for IE. Click Download Google Toolbar to get started. The requirements for installing the Toolbar for Firefox are that you must be running Firefox 1.5 or greater and one of the following operating systems:

- Windows Vista
- Windows XP
- Windows 2000 SP3+
- Mac OS X 10.2+
- Red Hat Linux 8.0+

There are no installation options for the Firefox Installation. You are simply asked to agree to the license terms by clicking Agree and Install. When the installation is complete, close all Firefox windows and restart them to view the Google Toolbar.

If you click Agree and Install and your installation does not start, it's possible that Firefox is blocking the Toolbar installation. You'll know because Firefox displays a message that the installation is blocked. To unblock the installation, follow these steps:

1. Click Edit Option on the right side of the Firefox block message.
2. In the box that asks for Address of Web site, type **toolbar.google.com** and click Allow.
3. Click OK to continue the installation.

In the event that you must unblock the installation, you are asked to click Agree and Install again.

Using the Google Toolbar

Both Google Toolbar for IE and the one for Firefox have the familiar Google search box. Typing your search term in this box allows you to quickly search Google without visiting a Web page, such as Google's main search page. The Google Toolbar for IE also includes the ability to add custom buttons that, when configured, allow you to launch all types of Web pages in a single click from your toolbar.

The results of the Google search are displayed in the normal Google results Web page. If you are currently viewing a Web page, it is replaced with your search results unless you configure the Toolbar to open a new tab.

The small vertical line, with left and right arrows on either side found to the right of the search box, can be clicked and dragged with your mouse and moved left or right, making the Google search box larger or smaller. This does not affect the amount of text that can be typed in the box, only the amount of text you can see without scrolling.

NOTE   When you increase the size of the search box some Toolbar icons may no longer fit. A small arrow appears on the right side of the Toolbar, which signifies that more icons can be seen by clicking this arrow.

The next icon in the Toolbar allows you to search Google News for articles. Clicking the small newspaper icon causes the Toolbar to search for the terms you typed into the search box. The Google News page launches with the results of your search.

The PageRank icon displays the ranking given to the Web page you are viewing based on the calculations made by Google's PageRank technology. When no PageRank information exists for a page, the icon displays a blank white line.

Spell-check the information you type into a Web page. For example, if you want to check the spelling of your Blogger posts or things you are putting on your Google Pages Web page, click the Spell Check icon.

CAUTION   Information you type into Web forms is sent to Google for spell checking. Make sure you understand the privacy implications of using this feature.

Clicking the AutoLink button on the Toolbar causes Google to search for any postal mailing addresses, shipping information, or other types of items where Google can provide extra information and turns the display of that information into a hyperlink. You can click the hyperlink and get, for example, a Google Map displaying the location of an address or tracking information on shipped packages.

Automatically fill in Web forms with your saved, personal information by clicking the AutoFill button. The Google Toolbar does its best to figure out what form fields match corresponding saved personal information. Google relies on the form field names used by the Web page author. So, when field names are fname for first name, or city, these are easily recognized by Google. When the field names are unintelligible, such as nm1 or cty, Google will have less luck placing the right information in these fields.

When Web pages provide an Atom or RSS feed you can subscribe to the contents of the page by clicking the buttons or links setup by the site's creator to enable this feature. For example, news.google.com has both RSS and Atom links on the left panel of the page. You are then able to view the contents of this Web page in Google Reader (`www.google.com/reader`) or other feed reader programs.

You can toggle whether you want your search terms highlighted in a Web page by clicking the Highlight button. It is sometimes easier to locate information within a Web page when the search term you use is highlighted within the page. Multiple search terms are highlighted in different colors making it easy to distinguish them. Once you locate the information, having the words highlighted can be annoying. Click the Highlight button again and the highlighting disappears.

Your last search terms are saved in the Toolbar, making it easy to find them again in the same or different Web pages. In the Firefox version of the Toolbar, the words are displayed in the Toolbar itself. In the IE version, you must click the down arrow on the search box and select the search terms from the drop-down menu.

There is also a button only on the IE Toolbar for adding or accessing Google Bookmarks. But instead of putting this topic in the IE-Only Options, it is included here because you can still use Google Bookmarks with Firefox and other Web browsers. It's just made simpler in the IE version of the Toolbar by having a button. See the additional steps later in this section for adding Bookmarks to the Firefox version.

In the IE Toolbar, you find a blue star. Clicking that star launches a window where you can log in to your Google account, enabling you to access Google Bookmarks. Clicking the Bookmarks button then allows you to:

- Bookmark the current page (see Figure 31.4)
- Manage your bookmarks
- Launch a Web page from the list of bookmarks
- Refresh the list of bookmarks from your stored bookmarks
- Import your IE favorites into Google Bookmarks, enabling you to access all your bookmarked "favorite" pages from any computer by simply logging into your Google Bookmark page

From that point on, use Google Bookmarks to bookmark a page rather than setting a bookmark in IE. You also have Google Bookmark functionality using other browsers; it is just handled differently.

FIGURE 31.4

Create bookmarks you can access from any computer using Internet Explorer by logging in to your Google account.

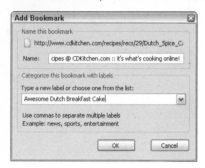

Using Firefox, or other Web browsers, follow these steps to add Google Bookmark functionality:

1. Point your browser to www.google.com/bookmarks. The first time you go there, you see a Google Bookmark button. Click and drag it to your browser's bookmark menu, adding Google Bookmark to your list of favorites.

2. Next time you want to bookmark a page, add it to your Google Bookmarks by selecting Google Bookmarks from your browser's bookmarks/favorites list. A bookmark window like the one shown in Figure 31.5 appears.

3. The name and destination are added to the bookmark window automatically; you need to add a label and optional description and then click Save.

FIGURE 31.5

Save your bookmark information to Google so you can access it from anywhere.

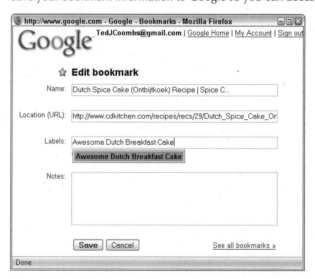

Once bookmarks have been saved to your Google Bookmark account, they can be accessed in two ways: in IE using the Bookmarks button or by logging in to Google Bookmarks (`www.google.com/bookmarks`) and clicking the link to your bookmarked Web destination (see Figure 31.6).

The Google Bookmarks page also allows you to sort your bookmarks by title, label, or date. And, of course, you can search through your bookmarks using the search boxes located at the top and bottom of the page.

FIGURE 31.6

Use the Google Bookmarks page from non-IE browsers.

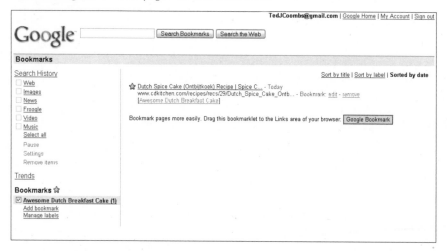

You can add new bookmarks from the Google Bookmarks page by clicking the <u>Add bookmark</u> link in the left column. The <u>Manage labels</u> link allows you to remove bookmarks and rename them.

IE-only options

There are options available in the Internet Explorer version of the Google Toolbar that are not available in the Firefox version. One of these is the Google Earth button, which simply takes you to the Google Earth home page. It does not launch Google Earth on your computer.

Click Search your own computer to launch the Google Desktop search page. If you have Google Desktop installed and indexing your content, you can click this button to access the search page. This is particularly useful when you don't have Google Desktop docked to the side of your screen.

CROSS-REF See Chapter 11 for more information about Google Desktop.

In Figure 31.7 you see a button you won't see on other installations of the Google Toolbar. It's actually a very tiny image of the author. Clicking that little custom button launches the author's home page. You can create custom buttons and install them here or load other people's custom buttons to enhance your Toolbar.

FIGURE 31.7

The Google Toolbar for IE includes the ability to have custom buttons.

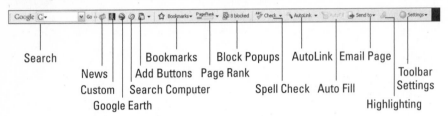

The Blocked button allows you to block or unblock pop-ups for a particular Web page. When you visit a Web site where you want the pop-ups to appear, click the Blocked button and it changes to "Popups ok." From that point on, pop-ups are allowed for that site only.

Toolbar Options

Customize the Google Toolbar to personalize it for your own use. The IE and Firefox versions of the Toolbar have different options and thus launch different option windows. If you use both browsers, you need to set the options for each of your browsers. Setting them for one browser type does not affect the settings for the other.

In the Internet Explorer version of the Toolbar click the Settings icon and select Options from the menu. This launches the Toolbar Options window, as shown in Figure 31.8.

The Google Toolbar for IE allows you to set Features, Buttons, and More by selecting the applicable tab in the Toolbar Options window. In the Features tab, you can customize the Search Box, Bookmarks, SpellCheck, Translate, AutoFill, AutoLink, and SendTo settings.

The Buttons tab allows you to choose which buttons appear on your toolbar by selecting or deselecting them. This is also the place where you can add custom buttons. Download custom buttons from the Google Toolbar Custom Button Gallery found at `toolbar.google.com/buttons`.

For information on creating custom buttons, see `toolbar.google.com/buttons/apis/howto_guide.html`.

Once you've downloaded a button from the gallery, or created your own custom button, save the custom button code to your hard drive, then click Add, selecting the custom button you want added. The new button will then appear in your Toolbar.

The More tab allows you to select a number of various Toolbar features and additional buttons not included in the Buttons tab.

FIGURE 31.8

When using IE, customize the Toolbar in the Toolbar Options window.

In the Firefox version of the Toolbar, clicking the Options button launches the Google Toolbar Options window, as shown in Figure 31.9.

The Firefox version of the Google Toolbar allows you to customize settings in the Browsing, Search, and More tabs. In the Browsing tab, select which navigation features you want to appear in the Toolbar and set the Safe Browsing settings.

Also in the Browsing tab, you can select and configure a number of various productivity tools such as SpellCheck, WordTranslator, AutoFill, AutoLink, Subscribe, and Send with Gmail. The AutoFill settings are particularly important because AutoFill will not work unless you add your personal information.

The Search tab has settings that allow you to configure the Toolbar search box settings, add custom search buttons, and add Google Search buttons for searching through sites such as Froogle, Google Groups, and more.

The More tab has a variety of settings and options, including the ability to switch between icons only, icons with text, or text only. You can also create your own custom Toolbar layout.

FIGURE 31.9

When using Firefox, customize the Toolbar in the Google Toolbar Options window.

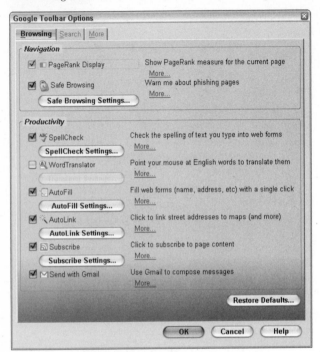

Summary

The Google Toolbar is one of the easiest of all the Google applications to integrate with the way you already access the Internet. Rather than creating a new way to do things, it enhances what you already do. You no longer need to go to the Google home page to do a Google search — you can use the search box in the Toolbar. Use the buttons on the Toolbar to quickly access commonly used Google features, or create custom buttons when using Internet Explorer to access anything you want. Visit the Google Toolbar Gallery to find all the buttons you can possibly imagine to customize your Google Toolbar.

Chapter 32

Creating 3-D Models with SketchUp

Pop quiz: What do you put on the Goggle Earth view of your street?

Answer: A 3-D model of your house, of course.

It may seem like a far-fetched idea, but you can do it using SketchUp. SketchUp is a full-featured program that allows you to create models of anything from teapots to tankers, sundials to skyscrapers. Google offers SketchUp in both a free version-used in this chapter-as well as a Professional version.

There are several integral stages to 3-D modeling that are covered very briefly in this whirlwind introduction to the program. You see how to draw a model, and how to manipulate and view it in this chapter. In the following chapter, read more about using 3-D models built in SketchUp.

Getting Started

When you open SketchUp, a Tip of the Day dialog box appears like the example shown in Figure 32.1. Click Previous Tip or Next Tip to read the tips. From the Tip of the Day dialog box, click one of the links to access online resources and the SketchUp sites. Close the dialog box to get into the program itself.

> **TIP** If you prefer, deselect the Show tips on startup check box at the lower left of the dialog box. You can access the online resources through the Help menu in the program.

The SketchUp interface uses two windows, as shown in Figure 32.2. The program window is used to build and manage your models, and the Instructor is a secondary window that provides instruction and guidance for each tool that you select in the program. Both windows can be resized.

FIGURE 32.1

Read the Tip of the Day to get acquainted with program features and access other resources.

The Instructor window floats above the program window, regardless of which window is active. To collapse the Instructor window, click anywhere on the upper bar of the window. If you click the Close button at the upper right of the Instructor window, choose Window ➪ Instructor to reopen it.

Viewing menus

The default organization of the SketchUp window is shown in Figure 32.2. The program includes several main menu items, described briefly in Table 32.1.

TABLE 32.1

Menu Groups in SketchUp

Heading	Contains
File	Open, Save, Import/Export, and Print commands are located in the File menu.
Edit	In addition to the usual types of Edit commands, such as Cut/Copy/Paste, find specific types of editing, such as Make Component and Make Group.
View	Find the toolbars in the View menu, as well as a number of different ways to view the model.
Camera	Specify how the model is viewed based on different perspectives, zooms, and camera positions.
Draw	Find commands for drawing basic elements such as rectangles, polygons, and lines in the Draw menu.

Heading	Contains
Tools	Find tools, including many found on the Getting Started toolbar, in the Tools menu.
Window	Open information dialog boxes, browse and edit materials, open the Instructor dialog box, and the preferences using commands in the Window menu.
Google	Find commands for viewing and getting models online.
Help	Find commands to open SketchUp and Ruby help, as well as a number of online sources. Reopen the Tip of the Day dialog box, and view the Quick Reference card.

FIGURE 32.2

Build the model in the program window, and read about the tools as you use them in the Instructor.

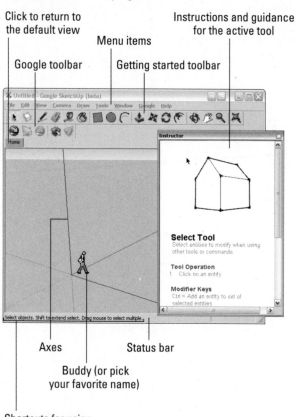

Click to return to the default view

Menu items

Instructions and guidance for the active tool

Google toolbar

Getting started toolbar

Axes

Status bar

Buddy (or pick your favorite name)

Shortcuts for using the active tool

Looking at the tools

Two toolbars are displayed in SketchUp when you open the program, including the Getting Started and Google toolbars. The Getting Started toolbar combines tools from a number of toolbars to give you the basic tools needed to start and edit a drawing. The Google Toolbar offers several commands for accessing and downloading online information. The contents of the Getting Started toolbar are listed in Table 32.2.

TABLE 32.2

Tools on the Getting Started Toolbar

	Name of Tool	Purpose
	Select	Use for selecting one or more objects that are then modified by other tools or commands
	Make Component	Combines two or more objects into a single unit that is a named, separate object
	Line	Use to draw lines or edges of objects
	Eraser	Use to erase objects one at a time
	Tape Measure	Use for measuring distance, scaling a model, or creating construction guidelines for placing objects
	Paint Bucket	Use for creating and selecting materials and colors, and then applying them to entities
	Rectangle	Use to draw a rectangular Face entity
	Circle	Use to draw a circular Face entity
	Arc	Use to draw an Arc entity
	Push/Pull	Use to either add or remove volume from a model by pushing or pulling Face entities
	Move	Use to move, copy, or stretch entities
	Rotate	Use to rotate, stretch, distort, or copy entities along a curved path
	Offset	Use to create copies of lines that are at a uniform distance from the original lines
	Orbit	Use to rotate the camera around the model
	Pan	Use to move the camera view vertically or horizontally
	Zoom	Use to move the camera view inward toward you, or outward away from you
	Zoom Extents	Use to fill the view to a distance where the entity is centered in the drawing window at a magnification that shows the entire content

Designing in Three Dimensions

You are familiar with working in two axes on a computer screen. To represent a third dimension, another axis simulates an object moving toward you or away from you-coming out of the ground or moving underground is another way to describe the movement.

Examining coordinates

SketchUp uses a standard 3-D coordinate system of three axes called X, Y, and Z, as shown in Figure 32.3. Keep these ideas in mind as you learn to move around in 3-D space in SketchUp:

- Each axis can have both negative and positive values. In the program, the positive directions are shown as solid lines, while the negative directions are shown as dotted lines.

- Each axis uses a different color. Although you can't see different colors in the figure, in the program the X axis is green, the Y axis is red, and the Z axis is blue.

- The point at which all three axes intersect is called the *origin*.

- The *ground plane* refers to the plane at which the X axis (green) and Y axis (red) lines run.

FIGURE 32.3

SketchUp uses a standard 3-D coordinate system, identifying positions on three axes.

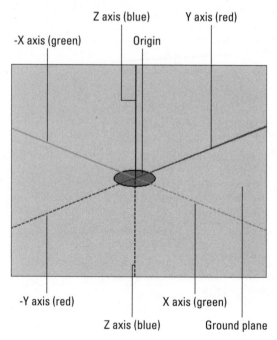

Understanding entities

The simplest object you work with in SketchUp is a line, or *edge*. Lines are combined to form *faces*. Models are composed of edges, faces, and other objects or *entities*. The entities available for building a SketchUp model include:

- **Line:** A line, or edge, is straight and forms the connection between two points.
- **Face:** Faces are created automatically when three or more lines or edges on the same plane form a closed shape. Faces have a front side and a back side. SketchUp puts the front side of all faces on the outside of models.
- **Arc:** An arc entity is a combination of several line segments connected to form the curvature of the arc. The combined lines act as a single entity. An arc is drawn with the Arc tool.
- **Curve:** A curve entity is drawn with the Freehand tool. It is made up of several line segments connected together that act as a single line. A curve may be *closed*, meaning it begins and ends at the same point, or *open*, beginning and ending at different points like the examples shown in Figure 32.4. Both open and closed curves have lines, but only the closed curve has a face as well.

FIGURE 32.4

A curve may be closed (left) or open (right).

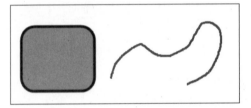

- **Polygon:** Use the Polygon tool to draw a polygon entity. Polygons are made up of a radius and three or more sides.
- **Rectangle, Circle:** These entities are composed of several lines or edges using specific geometric relationships.
- **3D polyline:** A 3-D polyline entity is like a curve in that it is made up of a number of lines that act as one but doesn't affect a model's geometry. A tracing of an imported drawing or hatched lines used to decorate a model are examples of a 3-D polyline.
- **Group:** Group entities are two or more entities of different types that are combined to make it simpler to perform operations like copying or moving.
- **Component:** Component entities are like groups in that they can be created from two or more entities of different types. A component is a named entity that you can reuse in any model, such as the window shown in Figure 32.5.

FIGURE 32.5

A component is made up of different objects and can be saved in a library and reused, like the window.

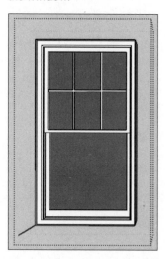

■ **Construction line and Construction point.** Use a Construction line or point entity as a drawing guide, such as the distance between the benches shown in Figure 32.6. Unlike other entities, a construction line or point is temporary, and can be hidden or erased. Construction lines and points are drawn with the Tape Measure tool. Choose Edit ➪ Construction Geometry and choose Hide, Unhide, and Erase to manipulate the construction lines or points in a drawing.

FIGURE 32.6

You can specify length or distance using a construction line.

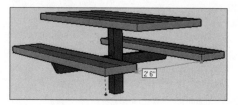

■ **Dimension:** A dimension entity is a notation on a model that indicates the length or radius of an edge, such as the height of the shrub shown in Figure 32.7. The values shown move and update automatically as you make changes. Add Dimension entities to a model using the Dimension tool.

FIGURE 32.7

Add the dimensions of an object, like the height of the shrub, on the model for reference.

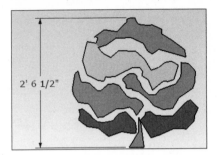

2' 6 1/2"

- **Surface:** A curved surface, like the roundness of a cylinder, is made up of a number of faces. The higher the number of faces, the greater the appearance of a smooth, curved surface. The faces combined to create the smooth appearance are surface entities (see Figure 32.8).

FIGURE 32.8

A curved surface is actually made up of many faces to create the smooth appearance.

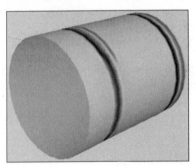

- **Image:** An Image entity is a type of group made up of a face with an applied bitmap. An Image entity can be manipulated, such as scaled or rotated, but not made nonrectangular. Add an image by choosing File ⇨ Import ⇨ 2D Graphic, and selecting the image.

 **TIP** SketchUp can use JPEG, PNG, BMP, TIFF, and TGA image formats.

- **Text:** Text entities are used to add annotations to a model. Text can be used as Leader Text, which has leader lines and is attached to a face, like the upper label in Figure 32.9, or Screen Text, which remains fixed at a specific location, like the lower label in Figure 32.9.

FIGURE 32.9

Text can be applied using a leader line or added as a flat label to a model.

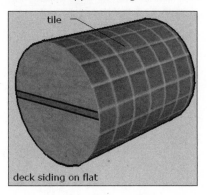

Drawing Objects

Take the time to understand how the coordinate system works in SketchUp. An internal program feature called the *inference engine* uses the program's coordinates to help you draw accurately by identifying probable points you will add to the object. Nearly all objects can be created in SketchUp using the Line tool and the program's inference engine.

Drawing in three dimensions

A drawing in SketchUp starts out as a 2-D object built by drawing and joining lines. SketchUp assists you to make the lines that create the 3-D object.

Follow these steps to draw a simple cube:

1. Click Home on the upper left of the drawing area to orient the screen showing the origin of the three axes in the center.

The Home tab defines a page view for the model, and is a default page. Additional pages can be added to the model to produce a TourGuide slide show

CROSS-REF Read about creating a slide show in Chapter 33.

2. Click the Line tool on the Getting Started toolbar. Click and drag along one axis as shown in Figure 32.10. Release the mouse to finish the line segment.

3. Move the tool upward, perpendicular to the Y axis green line and click and drag to add the second edge. Drag left parallel to the X axis red line to add the third edge, shown in the center image in Figure 32.10.

4. Draw the fourth edge along the Y axis green line to complete the shape at the start point. Double-click the mouse to complete the shape. The closed shape is automatically filled, indicating it has a face, shown in the right image in Figure 32.10.

FIGURE 32.10

Draw the first edge along an existing axis line (left), continue adding edges using lines parallel to the axis lines (center), and complete the shape to create an object with a closed edge and one face (right).

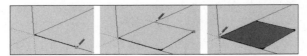

5. Draw up or down in the direction of the Z axis blue line to start drawing in 3-D space. Click to place the endpoint and finish the line, shown in the left image in Figure 32.11.

6. Draw the next point, watching for the prompts as you move the Line tool. Drag to close the side, and add the second face, such as the example shown at the right in Figure 32.11.

FIGURE 32.11

Draw the first edge along an existing axis line (left), and continue adding edges using lines parallel to the axis lines (center)

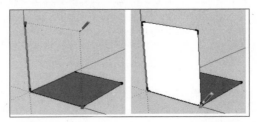

7. Choose View ⇨ X-ray to make the faces added to the drawing semitransparent, as shown in Figure 32.12. You can also rotate the image or start drawing from the back toward the front.

FIGURE 32.12

Using the X-ray view lets you see into and behind the cube to finish constructing it accurately.

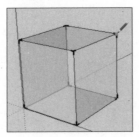

8. Continue adding lines and closing faces of the object. The final 3-D cube is shown in Figure 32.12.

Specifying precise measurements

You don't have to guess or estimate the size of an element as you draw. Instead, use the value control box (VCB) at the bottom right of the program window on the status bar. The VCB displays dimensional information as you draw.

There are different ways to use the VCB depending on your preferred way to work. Follow these steps to use precise values for drawing:

1. Click the Drawing or Modification tool you want to use from the toolbars or menus. When the tool is selected, the VCB displays a cursor for typing.

2. Choose a method for drawing and assigning the value:

   ■ **Use the Drawing or Modification tool and then type the value in the VCB.**

   ■ Type the value in the VCB, such as 10" shown in Figure 32.13, and then drag the Drawing or Modification tool on the drawing.

3. Press Enter/Return to commit the value to the drawing.

4. Repeat typing the value and committing it to the drawing as necessary.

FIGURE 32.13

Type precise measurements for an object as you add it to your model.

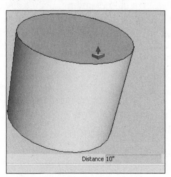

After you finish with the tool and select another tool in SketchUp, you can't return to the VCB to redefine the object's measurement. Whether the program is using the measurements you specify or not, the program converts the value to its default system. For example, typing a value in centimeters is changed to feet and inches automatically if you use the default program system.

NOTE The default unit of measure for your models is the Architectural format. To change to a different format, such as Decimal or Engineering, choose Window ➪ Model Info, and click the Units heading to display the settings. Choose the format, precision, and characteristics for angles in the dialog box.

Drawing automatically

Instead of drawing lines and connecting points yourself, let the SketchUp inference engine feature assist you in drawing accurately. As you draw lines, the inference engine infers points from other points in your model. For example, if you draw a cube, the program reads where your cursor is currently located, determines what points are in the area, and shows you the options as you draw.

You see the points that are identified as different color indicators and pop-up tooltips. Carefully watch for the changes in the color of lines and points on the model and read the tooltips to build your model. Figure 32.14 shows several examples of how the inference engine suggests drawing cues.

FIGURE 32.14

Watch carefully as you draw to see how SketchUp offers suggestions for where your next line can be located or placed.

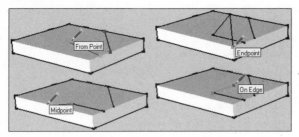

Modifying a Shape's Geometry

Whether you have modeled a cube or a spaceship, SketchUp defines anything you draw as geometry. There are a number of 3-D drawing techniques that can be applied to the geometry using tools in SketchUp. Most of the tools are based on the fact that you can add more faces and edges to existing geometry and then make changes based on those additions.

Dividing and healing

One SketchUp feature that makes modeling objects simple to do is the ability to divide an object's structure, and then remove the dividing lines and restore the original if desired. The only tool required is the Line tool. SketchUp refers to the addition of extra edges and faces as *dividing*.

A complete cube drawn in SketchUp is shown in Figure 32.14. To add additional lines and faces, follow these steps:

1. Click the Line tool on the Getting Started toolbar.
2. Drag from an edge along one of the cube's faces across the face. The inference engine shows you probable points, such as the midpoint.
3. Release the mouse when you place the line as desired. Continue adding other lines as desired.
4. Check the model shown in Figure 32.15. The front is split horizontally, and the face to the right is split vertically.
5. To remove a dividing edge, click the Select tool on the Getting Started toolbar and then click the edge to select it, such as the vertical line shown in Figure 32.16. Press Delete to remove the line and heal the face of the cube.

Using the Line tool to add extra edges divides only the faces on a cube, but doesn't cut through the cube to make separate objects.

FIGURE 32.15

You can easily add lines to create divided faces on a model.

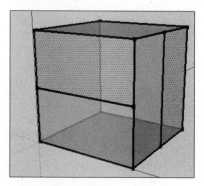

FIGURE 32.16

Remove edge lines to heal the face of the cube, returning it to its former state as a single face.

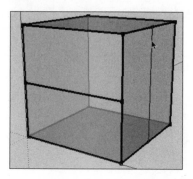

Extruding sections

Extrusion is a method of changing the geometry of an object by increasing or decreasing the dimensions in one plane or axis. The previous section that explains how to add lines to make a square into a cube is one example of an extrusion.

The Push/Pull tool on the Getting Started toolbar is an extrusion tool. Starting from a simple shape such as a 2-D square or circle, you can easily push or pull the shape into a 3-D cube or cylinder, like the examples show in Figure 32.17.

FIGURE 32.17

Use the Push/Pull tool to change a 2-D square to a 3-D cube (left) or a 2-D circle to a 3-D cylinder (right).

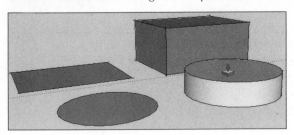

Using the Push/Pull tool isn't restricted to a simple shape.

To use the Push/Pull tool to convert a shape from a simple cube to a more complex staircase object, follow these steps:

1. Click the Push/Pull tool on the Getting Started toolbar, and click one of the faces on the cube. The selected face shows an overlay of dots indicating it is active.

2. Drag to increase the size of a section of the cube.

3. Repeat the selecting and dragging of the cube's faces.

4. Make adjustments as necessary by clicking an extruded face with the Push/Pull tool and dragging. The finished staircase is shown at the right of Figure 32.18. Where the original cube shown at the left of the figure has four faces specified, on the plane there are now four steps in the staircase.

FIGURE 32.18

Use the Push/Pull tool to modify the faces on a cube (left) to a staircase configuration (right).

Working with sticky geometry

You can modify the geometry of an object by manipulating a face or edge, as shown in the previous examples using the Push/Pull tool. The SketchUp geometry is called *sticky geometry*, as moving an edge or face causes the objects attached to the edge or face to move as well.

Other tools can be used for modifying faces and edges on an object, and can be applied individually or in a sequence. Here's an example using a variety of tools in sequence to create a finished model of a birdbath, complete with a base, column, and basin.

Drawing the base elements

The object begins with a simple rectangle, and then the Push/Pull and Offset tools are used to build the beginning of the structure.

1. Click the Rectangle tool and draw the starting square.

2. Use the Select tool to select the entire rectangle.

3. Use the Push/Pull tool to drag upward, completing the base of the object. In the example, the base is 4 feet square and 5 inches thick.

4. Click the Offset tool and drag it over the surface of the cube. As you drag, a rectangle is drawn using the same proportions as the original and centered over the original. Drag up/down and in/out to resize the new rectangle, as shown in the example in Figure 32.19.

FIGURE 32.19

Add the second rectangle proportional to the first and centered over the first using the Offset tool.

5. Click the Push/Pull tool, and move it over the new rectangle. When you see the dotted lines that indicate the new rectangle is selected, drag upward to add a box shape on top of the original, as seen in Figure 32.20.

FIGURE 32.20

Drag the second shape to form a box on top of the original base shape.

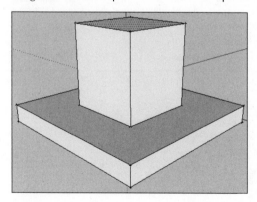

Rotating the top box

The next stage is to rotate the top of the rectangle to create a twisted, multisided effect for the top box. Although the tools can be used regardless of the view you show in the program window, it's simpler to organize what you see to make the tools easier to understand and to use.

The example model is drawn using the default SketchUp positioning. To view the object from the top down, choose Camera ⇨ Standard ⇨ Top. The modified view shows the tops of the concentric boxes.

> **NOTE**   Depending on how you place the object initially, using the Top view may or may not show you the object directly.

To rotate the top box numerically, follow these steps:

1. Click the Rotate tool on the Getting Started toolbar, and move it over the objects on the screen. The tool displays a protractor, shown in Figure 32.21.

FIGURE 32.21

It's easy to understand how the Rotate tool functions when you view it directly.

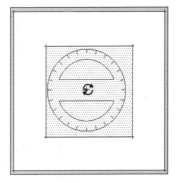

2. Move the tool over the center of the upper box, viewed as the smaller square in the model when seen from the top. Click and drag with the tool to identify the object to which the tool is applied.

3. Type an angle for the rotation in the VCB and press Enter/Return. The example is rotated 345 degrees. The top view now shows some shallow triangle shapes on each side of the inner rectangle, as seen in the left image in Figure 32.22.

FIGURE 32.22

After the rotation is applied, it's difficult to see the effect from the Top view (left), but easily seen in the default view (right).

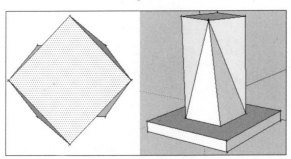

TIP You can type a value in the VCB or drag on the screen to rotate the protractor to the amount of rotation you want to add to the object, and click again to set the amount of rotation.

4. Reset the view to the default by clicking Home on the upper left of the program window below the toolbars. The sides of the upper box are now angled, resulting from rotating the top surface. Read the sidebar "Folding the Model" for more information.

Finishing the model

Even though the vertical faces of the column of the birdbath are now pairs of triangles, the top face is still a flat rectangle, and the rest of the model is built from the top face.

The finished birdbath model is shown in Figure 32.23.

FIGURE 32.23

The birdbath is a simple model that you can create using a few tools.

The final steps to complete the basic model include:

- Selecting the upper face of the top shape.
- Using the Offset tool to draw a square centered over the top shape and larger than the twisted column.
- Using the Rotate tool to reverse the rotation for the new square. The square is placed over the twisted column, but is not in alignment with the base. Setting the Rotation value to -345 degrees

---

Folding the Model

One of the basic rules in SketchUp is that a face must remain planar, or parallel, to a plane at all times. Rotating a face on an object causes warping. SketchUp automatically twists and folds the faces of the object to make sure you aren't violating the rules. The example shown in the chapter is typical of the way the program compensates for rotation. Each face of the box, originally a rectangle, is split into a pair of triangles that allow the top to rotate without violating the planar face rule.

makes the new square drawn with the Offset tool match the orientation of the original base of the object.

- Using the Push/Pull tool to pull up the sides of the birdbath's basin, leaving the basin space the size of the column.

If you want the basin of the birdbath to be larger or smaller than the column's dimensions, use the Offset tool to add one more square between the column and the square that defines the birdbath's margins.

NOTE   If you want to resize any of the objects, select the object and choose Tools ➪ Scale to open the Scale tool. Move the mouse over any of the resize anchors to read the tooltips offered by the inference engine, and drag any of the resize anchors to change the scale.

Combining and moving objects

SketchUp helps you build complex geometry using a set of four processes that include:

- Intersecting two forms
- Defining new edges where the objects intersect
- Redefining the geometry
- Deleting extra lines and faces from the combined geometry

The birdbath model can be developed into a postmodern sculptural object using more tools and program commands.

Follow these steps to add some cutout details to the model:

1. Click the Rectangle tool on the Getting Started toolbar, and draw a rectangle on the screen. Click the Push/Pull tool, and extrude the rectangle to make a box.

2. Click the Select tool to drag a marquee around the box to select all its elements.

3. Click the Move tool on the Getting Started toolbar. The Move tool repositions an edge, face, or an entire object depending on the selection. In the example, the Move tool affects the entire box as it is entirely selected.

4. Drag the block from its drawing location on the screen to intersect with the column of the birdbath. Release the mouse once the block is positioned as shown in Image A in Figure 32.24.

   The front face of the box is protruding through the face of the birdbath's column. Notice that areas that intersect don't display edges.

5. Choose Edit ➪ Intersect with Model. The geometry of the block intersects with the geometry of the column of the birdbath. On the model, the areas of intersection now show edges, as seen in Image B in Figure 32.24.

6. Click the Eraser tool on the Getting Started toolbar and click faces and edges in the intersected areas to remove them, as shown in Image C in Figure 32.24. New faces and edges are shown within the structure based on the intersected areas.

7. Add more cutouts to change the geometry as desired. In the final model, shown in Image D in Figure 32.24, another block has been used to cut out another area of the column.

NOTE   Several other drawing and manipulation tools are also available. Please experiment with the tools, and refer to the SketchUp Help files and tutorials for more information.

Mirror Images

Many objects have mirrored halves. That is, a table has a left and a right half, as does a television. Instead of drawing the complete object, draw one half and create a group. Then copy and paste the group to the model. Right-click/Control-click to open the shortcut menu and choose Flip Along. Select the direction or axis in which you want the object to flip. Position the second half to match the first.

FIGURE 32.24

Use other program tools to make cutouts in the original model.

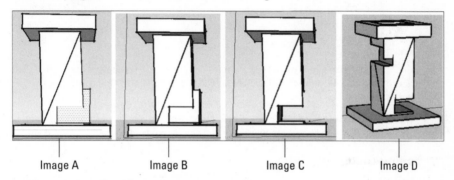

Image A   Image B   Image C   Image D

Creating Groups and Components

Selecting the faces and edges of an object over and over can be tiresome and can lead to inaccuracy if you forget one edge or face. Instead of selecting the elements each time you need to work with them, create a group. If you want to have an object that can be reused, create a component instead.

To help you get organized, make groups within groups, components within groups, groups within components, and so on.

Working with a group

Groups are entities that hold other entities. For example, a polygon representing a flower petal is made up of one edge for each line used to draw the group and its face.

Creating a group

Follow these steps to create a group:

1. Click the Select tool on the Getting Started toolbar.
2. Drag a marquee around the content you want to include in the group.
3. Choose Edit ➪ Make Group or choose Make Group from the shortcut menu. As shown in Figure 32.25, the group is shown with a bounding box identifying its components.

FIGURE 32.25

The grouped content displays a bounding box.

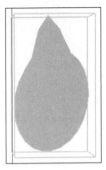

Exploding a group

To ungroup a group and return it to its component elements you have to explode it. Select the group you want to explode with the Select tool. Then choose Edit ➪ Group ➪ Explode, or choose Explode from the shortcut menu.

CAUTION   Be sure to check the exploded group. Sometimes, if an element is placed next to other geometry, it may become joined to the external element when the group is exploded.

Editing content in a group

The contents in a grouped object can be edited within the context of the group. The flower petal shown in Figure 32.26 is composed of two groups. The smaller shape is nested within the larger shape. Double-click the group to open it in a group editing view. A group is open for editing when it is surrounded by a bounding box; other objects on the screen turn gray.

FIGURE 32.26

A group open for editing displays a bounding box and other content is grayed out.

Make the edits as required, and choose Edit ➪ Close Group to exit the editing mode or choose Close Group from the shortcut menu.

Applying Ruby Scripting

You can extend the functionality of the program and add components automatically using macros scripted with Ruby. Scripts can be downloaded from the SketchUp Ruby Forum online. Copy the script into the SketchUp Plugins folder in the SketchUp installation directory (Windows). For MacOS X, copy the script into the Macintosh HD\Library\Application Support\Google SketchUp\Plugins folder.

If you want to write your own scripts, choose Window ➪ Ruby Console to open a dialog box for writing Ruby commands and methods. Learn more about Ruby and find tutorials and help guides at www.ruby-doc.org.

Building component objects

If you design an object that you intend to use numerous times in your current project or think you will reuse in another project, build a Component object. Components are stored in the Component Browser. For some objects, such as a flower petal, the placement isn't critical as you can and often do move the petals into a number of positions.

 For some components, orientation is critical. For example, a door or window should be oriented to be parallel with structures such as walls and not cut through them.

To create a component, follow these steps:

1. Click the Select tool on the Getting Started toolbar, and drag a selection marquee around the objects you want to include in the component. The two objects that make up a flower petal are shown selected with their respective grouped bounding boxes in Figure 32.27.

FIGURE 32.27

Select the objects to combine into a component.

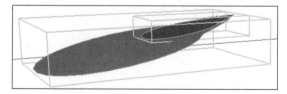

2. Click the Make Component button on the Getting Started toolbar, or choose Edit ➪ Make Component. The Create Component dialog box appears.

3. Type information about the component as required, as shown in Figure 32.28. As a minimum, the component must have a name and may include other settings including:

   ▪ Click the Glue to down arrow and choose an option from the drop-down list to define faces where the component can be placed. The choices include None, which is the default, as well as Any, Horizontal, Vertical, or Sloped.

   ▪ If the component axis shown at the edge of the object isn't oriented correctly, click Set gluing plane to activate a set of axes. Click the component where you want to set the origin for the component.

4. Click Create. The dialog box closes, and the multiple groups are replaced by a single component object.

FIGURE 32.28

Specify alignment characteristics for the component if necessary.

Using components and groups

Components are similar to groups in many ways, but very different in two important ways.

A component is created once and stored on your computer once. It doesn't matter whether you use one flower petal or one hundred; the same amount of information is stored as a single component definition. Using instances requires fewer memory and processing resources than pasting copies of groups as the component definition is stored only once.

A copy of the component placed into a model is called an *instance*. Editing an instance makes the same edits to the component definition and changes all other instances of the component. In a group, on the other hand, each copy is an individual object unrelated to any others.

Managing components

When it's time to add an instance of the component into the model, choose Window ➪ Components to open the Components dialog box, your model library. Click the down arrow, and choose In Model from the drop-down list. The components used in the model you are working with are listed in the dialog box, as shown in Figure 32.29. Click the thumbnail for the component you want to insert and drag your mouse over the program window. You see a copy of the component; click to place the object where you want it located.

NOTE   SketchUp offers a collection of components you can experiment with as you learn to use the program. In the Components dialog box, click the down arrow and choose Components from the drop-down list. The Sampler folder display appears in the dialog box. Double-click the Sampler folder to open it and display thumbnails in the Components dialog box.

FIGURE 32.29

Locate the new component stored in your component library.

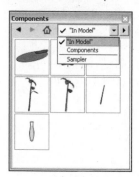

To check the component's information and make changes, choose Window ⇨ Entity Info to open the Entity Info dialog box, as shown in Figure 32.30. You see the default Layer0 defined at the top of the dialog box, as well as a label stating that four instances of the component have been used in the model. The Definition tab displays the information entered in the Create Component dialog box (refer to Figure 32.28). Click the Statistics tab to view a list of the component's geometry, including edges, faces, groups, and so on.

FIGURE 32.30

Adjust or modify the information about a component in the Entity Info dialog box.

Organizing with Layers

When building a large model, or one using a large number of complex objects, you can use layers to keep track of what you are working with. Each SketchUp drawing includes one layer named Layer0 by default. All objects you add to the drawing are placed on Layer0 automatically.

Each layer in a SketchUp drawing is a named attribute. The geometry of one layer isn't separate from the geometry on another layer if the object assigned to one layer shares a face or edge with an object assigned to another layer.

Understanding Camera Views

One of the most difficult concepts to grasp when working in 3-D is defining your point of view. SketchUp, like many 3-D modeling programs, uses a camera analogy to represent your view of the model.

By default, you look directly down at the ground from the sky, which isn't a usual way of looking at things! However, the camera angles to the view of the ground because many SketchUp models begin on the ground, represented as the X and Y, or red and green axes, such as the example shown in the left of Figure 32.31.

To produce the sense of modeling in three dimensions, you have to rotate the 3-D space to show the third dimension, which is visible in the right example in Figure 32.31.

FIGURE 32.31

Viewing the screen from the top down doesn't show any detail (left) while rotating the view to include a three-dimensional projection shows Buddy and his backpack (right).

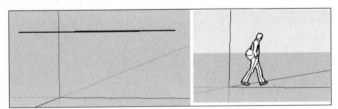

Adjusting the camera position manually

To assist you in positioning and viewing your model, SketchUp offers two toolbars. The most common Camera tools are included on the Getting Started toolbar, as well as on the Camera toolbar. You can see the icons for the tools in Table 32.3.

CROSS-REF   Read about another set of Camera tools used for creating a walkthrough in Chapter 33.

The tools you use regularly for placing the camera include the following:

- **Orbit tool:** Click the Orbit tool from either the Getting Started or Camera toolbars, or choose Camera ➪ Orbit. Move the cursor in any direction to rotate the camera around the center of the drawing.

- **Pan tool:** Click the Pan tool from either the Getting Started or Camera toolbars, or choose Camera ⇨ Pan. Click and drag the tool in any direction to pan the image, moving the camera either horizontally or vertically.

- **Zoom tool:** Click the Zoom tool from either the Getting Started or Camera toolbars, or choose Camera ⇨ Zoom. Click and drag the tool upward to zoom in, moving the camera closer to the model, such as the image in the left of Figure 32.32; click and drag the tool downward to zoom out, moving the camera away from the model, such as the image at the right in Figure 32.32.

FIGURE 32.32

Zoom in on the action using the Zoom tool (left) or move the camera away from the model, making it appear to grow smaller and farther away (right).

Using standard camera views

Instead of using the tools and changing positions manually, you can use a set of standard views to check out your model. The icons for the views, their display characteristics, and the location of an image example are shown in Table 32.3.

TABLE 32.3

Using Standard Views

Looks Like	View Name	Shows	Example Location
	Iso	Shows a standard 3/4 view of the model	Upper left, Figure 32.33
	Top	Shows the top of the model	Upper middle, Figure 32.33
	Front	Shows the front of the model	Upper right, Figure 32.33
	Right	Shows the right side of the model	Lower left, Figure 32.33

continued

TABLE 32.3   *(continued)*

Looks Like	View Name	Shows	Example Location
	Back	Shows the back of the model	Lower middle, Figure 32.33
	Left		Shows the left side of the model Lower right, Figure 32.33

FIGURE 32.33

Instead of trying to position and reposition a model in a location you have used previously, select one of six standard views to work with your models.

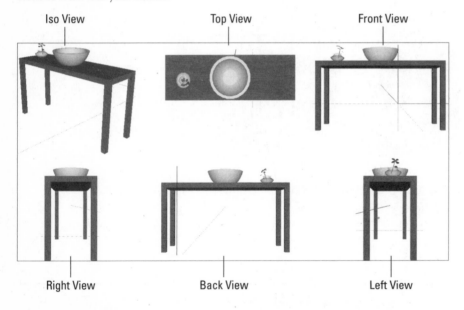

Iso View   Top View   Front View

Right View   Back View   Left View

NOTE   Content in a model can be shown in axonometric or perspective projections. An axonometric perspective shows a view of the model where lines appear parallel in both three-dimensional and two-dimensional space. Perspective projections show a distortion based on the vanishing point of the lines in the distance at the horizon. SketchUp uses a perspective view as its default.

Summary

This chapter introduced you to the 3-D world. Google SketchUp allows you to draw fairly sophisticated three-dimensional objects, buildings, and other entities. You saw how SketchUp defines three-dimensional space, and how to draw and specify measurements in that space.

The basis for modeling in SketchUp is a line and the inference engine, the feature in SketchUp that tracks the movement of your line and associates it with points, axes, and other objects in the area, helping you to draw more accurately and much more quickly than working on your own.

Once a shape is constructed, its geometry can be manipulated in many ways by using a variety of manipulation tools. For example, additional lines can be added to the face of an object and then extruded using the Push/Pull tool to form a complex structure. The geometry in SketchUp is said to be sticky, allowing the points, edges, and faces of an object to move along with anything that is being manipulated. Once perfected, objects can be combined into groups or stored as components for future use.

The Camera view in SketchUp can be adjusted in a number of ways, using standard views or working with tools that manipulate the view manually. Moving a camera around your model shows its structure, and points out the fact that a model would look much more realistic with some texture and shadow. Fortunately, all you have to do is turn the page. Up next, another chapter on SketchUp.

Chapter 33

Using 3-D Models

In the previous chapter, you saw how Google SketchUp can be used to create 3-D models. You learned how to create an object in 3-D space, and how to modify it and view it.

This chapter picks up where the last one leaves off. Now that your model is drawn, it's time to add some realism. SketchUp offers a number of ways to configure the appearance of the object and its material, which is called rendering.

The surfaces of objects aren't flat gray as the default material in SketchUp implies. Choose from hundreds of available textures and color them as you want. If that's not enough, you can edit existing materials or create your own. Once a material is added to an object, transform it further to fit the object's configuration. As a final realistic touch, see how to use shadows and simulate the time of day and year.

Once the models are finished, explore different ways to view the model. Take a walk through the model, or create different page views to bring it together as a TourGuide slide show. If your model is intended for use at a particular location, work with both SketchUp and Google Earth to build a model designed for a particular location on the planet. If your models aren't enough to keep you going, explore models in the 3D Warehouse that you can download for inspiration.

Adding Realism to a Model

One of the most interesting aspects of 3-D modeling is the art of applying textures and materials to surfaces of objects. With just a few tools, your model can appear quite realistic.

Before configuring the textures, look through the rendering settings to see how the objects in your model will be visualized.

Changing the render appearance

Rendering refers to the process of converting the mathematical information in a drawing into an image of differing levels of quality and detail. Rendering can be defined by the way the faces of the model are treated, as well as how the edges are displayed.

To change the way the model is displayed, choose options from the View ➪ Rendering menu, the Rendering toolbar, or in the Display Settings dialog box, as shown in Figure 33.01. The Display Settings dialog box is a convenient way to set the appearance of your model, rather than using various toolbars and menu commands to set the mode. Also, having the settings collected in one dialog box lets you toggle different effects and settings on and off to see how they affect your model.

FIGURE 33.1

Choose a display type and specify other display options such as edges and profiles in the Display Settings dialog box.

In the Display Settings dialog box, you can specify the following:

- **Rendering mode:** Choose one of the modes from the buttons at the top of the dialog box. See the different modes later in this section.

- **Edge Effects:** Choose an effect and modify its depth as you view the model. You can see the Edge effects later in the section.

- **Edge Color:** Specify the colors for the edges of the model entities. The default is All same. Click the Edge Color down arrow and choose By material from the drop-down list to use an edge that is colored the same as your model's objects. If you are working with a geometric model, choose By axis to color the edges red, blue, or green according to which axis an edge lies along.

- **Face rendering:** You can select the Use sun for shading option to apply default sunlight, or select Enable transparency to use transparent materials, which is described in the Choosing Materials section. Finally, click the Quality down arrow and choose an option from the drop-down list for the display. You can choose Faster, Medium, or Nicer. The Faster display shows the least detail, but renders the quickest, while the Nicer display shows the most detail, but requires more rendering time. Medium shows some detail.

Applying a rendering mode

The model seen in Figure 33.2 shows the same potted plant using the available rendering modes. The modes are as follows:

- **Wireframe:** This mode shows the model as its structural lines. You can't see the faces, nor can you use tools such as the Push/Pull tool on a rendered model. Use Wireframe when you want to work with the simple structure of your models as it uses the least time to render the model's image on-screen.

- **Hidden Line:** This mode shows the model's edges and faces, and is another way to work with the structure of the model without taking rendering time. Hidden Line mode is also good for printing a sketch of your model.

- **Shaded:** This mode shows faces in the model reflecting a light source. You see the color applied to the faces in response to the light. If your model doesn't have color applied, the default colors are displayed.

- **Shaded With Textures:** This mode shows both the applied color and an applied texture as they appear reflecting the light source.

- **X-Ray:** This mode can be used in conjunction with other modes. Applying the X-Ray mode adds a global transparency to the model, showing all faces. You don't see shadow cast by model faces in X-Ray mode.

- **Monochrome:** This mode is available from the View ⇨ Rendering menu. Using Monochrome mode displays the model in the default program color and shows default shading.

FIGURE 33.2

Choose different methods of displaying your model based on the detail you want to see.

Wireframe   Hidden Line   Shaded

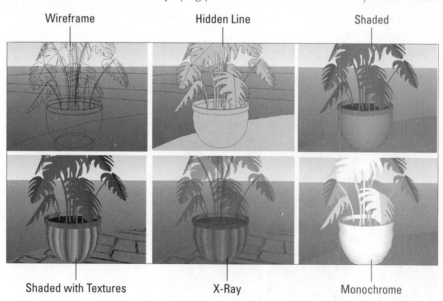

Shaded with Textures   X-Ray   Monochrome

Showing object edges

The Edge effects can add an edgy effect to your drawing, so to speak, making it appear sketch-like or look like a technical drawing, rather than simply rendered, such as the image shown in Figure 33.3. Choose the different effects from the Display Settings dialog box, or from the View ➪ Rendering menu.

FIGURE 33.3

The "before" image of the model shows a chair sitting on a patio with a tree in the background.

To apply any of the edges, follow these steps:

1. Select the check box to specify whether to show Edges, Profiles, or both.
2. Specify a depth for Profiles or leave the default value. All values are shown in pixels.
3. Click to select the Edge Effect you want to use, and specify a depth in pixels as necessary.
4. Toggle different options on and off to view the effects in combination.

The different edge displays are shown in Figure 33.4. They are applied using the sun for shading, and rendered at the Nicer quality setting. All effects use the default pixel values, with the exception of the Extension effect, which uses 10 pixels to show in the figure.

FIGURE 33.4

Choose from a number of different effects to display the edges of your model.

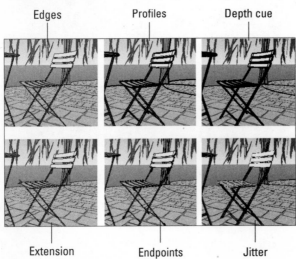

The edge options you can apply to your drawing include:

- **Edges:** If you intend to use any edge effects, you must select the Edges check box. Edges follow the lines used in the model and are evenly applied throughout the model. In the figure, you see the edges of the chair and the tree are identified with a simple line.

- **Profiles:** The Profiles option produces a heavier line that emphasizes the outlines of the major objects in the model. In the figure, for example, the Profiles show the detail at the right edge of the chair's back.

- **Depth cue:** Simulate the appearance of perspective using the Depth cue effect, with a heavier line closest to you and thinner lines farther away. The depth cue value specifies the size of the area closest to you in the model. In the example, the lines on the chair are heavier than those used on the tree or patio edges.

- **Extension:** The Extension effect extends the lines past their endpoints, creating a technical sketch appearance, such as at the edges of the boards making up the chair's seat and back. The length specified for the effect is the distance of the extension.

- **Endpoints:** Instead of creating a sketched effect, use the Endpoints effect to highlight the tips of the edges. The area where two edges intersect appear as heavier lines, such as the ends of the chair's legs, based on the value entered for the effect in pixels.

- **Jitter:** The Jitter effect produces a pencil sketch appearance. Sketching by hand uses multiple lines that are often offset slightly. Jitter is either added or it isn't — you don't specify a depth.

 The Jitter added to a model has no effect on the drawing of the model. The inference engine takes its cue from the edges and faces in the model, not from an effect applied to the object's appearance.

Choosing and applying materials

Real life has color and texture, and so too can your models in SketchUp. Use the Paint Bucket tool to apply the color and texture, select paint materials from the Material Browser, and create your own material in the Material Editor.

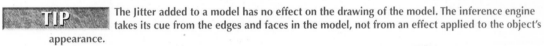 In order to see the materials applied to a model, you must be using the Shaded or Shaded With Textures rendering options, described in the section "Applying a rendering mode" earlier in the chapter.

Applying material to an object's face

SketchUp offers many default library files containing materials ranging from tile to roof shingles to grass. There are many different rules, keystroke combinations, and processes to consider when applying color to your model. Please refer to the SketchUp help files or online resources for more information.

Follow these steps to apply a material or color to an object:

1. Click the Paint Bucket tool from the Getting Started toolbar, the Principal toolbar, or choose Tools ➪ Paint Bucket; you can also choose Window ➪ Material Browser. The Materials dialog box appears, and shows the last color or texture applied.

2. Click the Library tab on the Materials dialog box and choose an option. You can also click the directional arrows to the right of the Library drop-down arrow to flip through the library choices. The selected material appears in the swatch at the upper left of the dialog box, as shown in Figure 33.5.

FIGURE 33.5

Select the material to use for painting faces in your model from the Materials dialog box. The post assembly for the mailbox is painted with a cherry wood color and texture.

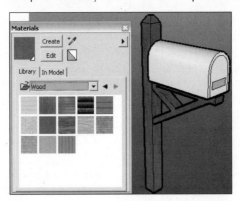

3. Move the tool over the model and click to paint the faces of the object with color.

TIP If the face of an object included in a Group or Component has already been painted, the face won't accept the new color. In order to recolor, you have to explode the Group or Component and apply the default color, shown as the swatch to the right of the Edit button in the Materials dialog box.

Creating a new material

Instead of using one of the materials in the existing libraries, create your own. In this example, see how to change the default cherry wood material used to fill the mailbox post to a new wood color and texture.

Follow these steps to create a new material from an existing material:

1. Click Create at the top of the Materials dialog box to open the Mix New Material To Paint With dialog box, as shown in Figure 33.6.

FIGURE 33.6

Develop custom materials in the dialog box based on existing material swatches or new materials.

2. Specify the starting material in the upper-left swatch of the dialog and change if necessary. The original material shown is the cherry wood material.

   Click the eyedropper, and move it over the model to sample a texture from the model if you want.

3. Click the text field at the upper left of the dialog box, and type a name for the new material if you plan to add it to the library.

   A new material is named according to the existing material; the example is named <Wood-cherry>1 by default. The new example material is named Wood-walnut.

4. Select or create the color for the new material at the upper right of the dialog box. The example uses a rich dark brown. Choose from several different methods to derive the color, including:

   - Choose a color model from the drop-down list; in the example RGB color is used. Click and drag the sliders, or type values in the RGB fields to define the color.

   - You can also click the eyedropper to sample an existing color on the model.

   - Click the Match Color button at the upper right of the dialog box to open the library to locate and select a color from an existing material.

5. Specify the texture map and its characteristics. The Use texture image option already is selected in the example as it starts from an existing texture, which is named in the field. Choose other options for the texture image including:

   - Click the Folder button to open the Choose Image dialog box. Locate and select the image to use for the texture on your hard drive. Click Open to insert the file into the new material and close the Choose Image dialog box.

   - Click the Lock/Unlock Aspect Ratio button to allow different values for the width and height as in the example.

   - Type measurements in the horizontal and vertical aspect ratio fields to change the measurements for the repeat of the texture's pattern.

   - Click Reset Color to revert to the original color used by the material on which you are basing the custom material.

   - Select the Colorize option to force all colors to use the same Hue if there are discrepancies in the color, which doesn't apply in the example.

6. Define the opacity for the material. The default is 100 percent, meaning there is no transparency in the object, and is the value used for the new material. Click the color bar to specify an opacity level, or type a value in the field.

7. Click Add and then Close to close the Mix New Material To Paint With dialog box. In the Materials dialog box, the new material is added to the In Model tab's thumbnails, as shown in Figure 33.7.

8. Right-click/Control-click the color swatch to display a shortcut menu and choose Add to Library. The new material, Wood-walnut, is included in the Wood library folder.

9. Continue working with the Materials dialog box, or close it. When you perform another operation, a dialog box appears stating there are changes made to the default library, and do you want to save them. Click Yes.

FIGURE 33.7

The new material is added to the thumbnail list of other materials used in the model.

NOTE You can pare down the number of swatches showing in the Materials dialog box on the In Model tab. Click the arrow at the upper right of the dialog box (shown in Figure 33.5) and choose Purge Unused. Anything you may have experimented with but decided against using is removed from the thumbnails list.

Editing an existing material

You don't have to start from scratch, nor do you have to save anything that you have customized. If you find an appropriate material in one of the default Library files and apply it to your model, you can make changes to update its appearance automatically.

Follow these steps to edit an existing material:

1. Choose Window ➪ Materials Browser to open the Materials dialog box.
2. Click In Model to display thumbnails of the materials currently applied to your model.
3. Select the thumbnail of the material you want to modify, and click Edit to open the Edit Material dialog box.
4. Make the changes as desired. The dialog box is identical to the one shown in Figure 33.6 and discussed in the previous set of steps.
5. Click Close to return to the Materials dialog box, and close the Edit Material dialog box. Reapply the edited material to your model.

Changing the default colors

Rather than using the default program colors, you can change them in a model to suit your tastes. For example, the figures showing the garden model use a grass color as the default for the ground, rather than the default gray-beige color.

To change the default colors for your model, follow these steps:

1. Choose Window ➪ Model Info to open the Model Info dialog box. Choose Colors from the column at the left of the dialog box to display the options.
2. Select the Background options to use as the defaults. You can choose Sky, Ground, and to Show ground from below. Drag the slider to adjust the transparency of the ground if you want.
3. Click the color swatch for any color you want to change in the program, either for the geometry or for the background. The Choose Color dialog box appears, as shown in Figure 33.8.

FIGURE 33.8

Choose specific colors for different aspects of your model in the Choose Color dialog box.

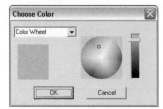

4. Click the upper-left down arrow, and choose a color model from the drop-down list. The default is Color Wheel.

5. Click a location on the Color Wheel (or other model if chosen) to specify a color.

6. Drag the slider at the right of the dialog box to select a lighter or darker version of the color. The selected saturation is seen in the swatch at the left in the dialog box.

7. Make other changes as desired and click OK to close the dialog box and set the color.

NOTE Depending on what you are building, the default colors for the background and sky may not be detailed enough. For example, a model of a house may be enhanced by showing it in its location or using actual views outside windows that you could see during a walkthrough. Use a vertical plane such as a rectangle, and apply a photo of the location on the face.

Editing a texture on an object

You aren't restricted to using an object at the configured size. If you are applying a material to anything having a flat face, like a cube, you can adjust the appearance of the material on the face.

An example is shown in Figure 33.9. In the figure, the left cube is colored with a solid color. The center cube has a texture applied, which is intended to be used as a label for the object. There are two copies of the image tiled on the front face, as well as the left and top faces. Look at the right figure — the label on the front of the box shows a single label. The material wasn't changed in its settings; instead, it was changed on the object itself.

FIGURE 33.9

Adjust the texture on the face of an object to change the appearance.

Decide how and why you need to change a texture. If you want the object changed uniformly, change its dimensions in the Edit Material dialog box. If you decide you want to change it on one face, as in the example, follow these steps to make the changes:

1. Apply the material using a texture image as described in earlier steps.

2. Right-click/Control-click the object and choose Texture ⇨ Position to open a positioning screen overlaying the image, as shown in Figure 33.10.

FIGURE 33.10

Choose specific colors for different aspects of your model in the dialog box.

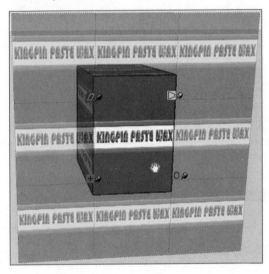

3. Click and drag using the appropriate corner tool to reconfigure the object. Click the pin and move it in any direction to readjust the point at which the effect is applied; click again to anchor the pin to the grid.

From the upper right, the tools in clockwork order are:

- **Distort:** Click the tool and then drag in any direction to change the configuration of the surface.

- **Scale/Rotate:** Click the tool and then drag inward or outward to the center of the object to change the scale; drag up or down to rotate the texture.

- **Move:** Click the tool and drag to move the texture horizontally or vertically.

- **Scale/Shear:** Click the tool and drag inward or outward to the center of the object to change the scale, drag diagonally or vertically to change the angle of the geometry.

4. Click off the grid area to close the tool.

Applying shadows

The final feature in applying a realistic appearance to your models is using shadows. The shadows can be cast based on the time of day and year. Shadows don't have to be applied and reapplied when you make changes. Fortunately, the shadows update themselves automatically when you change the structure of the model or adjust the camera's view.

The two types of shadows you can apply in the program are ground and face shadows. Shadows are configured for the entire model, not for a selected object.

Ground shadows are based on a flattened set of the model's faces and placed on the background based on the angle of the sun. Figure 33.11 shows the impact of applying shadow to a model's appearance. In the figure, the upper image shows the model without a shadow; the center image shows the model using a ground shadow.

In three-dimensional space, objects cast shadows on other objects, as well as on the ground. Use the Face shadows in SketchUp to add more realism to your project. Again, like the ground shadow, the angles are based on the location of the sun. The same model using both ground and face shadows is shown at the bottom of Figure 33.11

FIGURE 33.11

The basic model (top) shows more realism when ground shadow is added (center). Adding face shadows (bottom) casts a shadow from one object to another, as you see on the fence post.

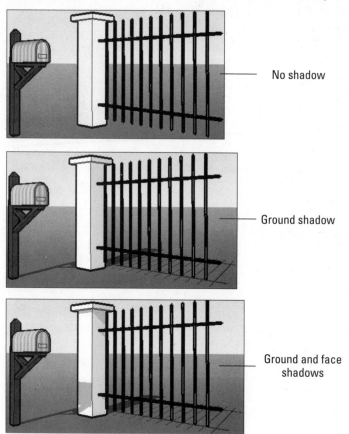

No shadow

Ground shadow

Ground and face shadows

If you want to configure the shadow settings, choose Window ⇨ Shadow Settings to open the Shadow Settings dialog box.

TIP If you don't want to make any changes to the shadow, choose View ⇨ Shadows to apply the existing shadow settings.

You can make these selections in the Shadow Settings dialog box, as shown in Figure 33.12:

- Select Display shadows to show or hide shadow in the model.
- Specify a time and date.
- Drag the Light and Dark sliders to specify how much intensity is used in the shadow.
- Select the shadows to display. Select On faces, On ground, or From edges; faces and ground shadows are realistic in appearance, the From edges shadow casts shadow only from the lines that make up the margins objects.

FIGURE 33.12

Customize the settings for the intensity and type of shadow for your model.

CAUTION Face shadows require a lot of processing power and will slow down the redraw speed when used in a large model.

Demonstrating and Exporting Models

After working hard to learn the program and build a model, be sure to take advantage of the demonstration and presentation options SketchUp offers. You can set different views and then save the appearance as a page, which can be used for an animated tour of your model.

Here are some different presentation methods to consider:

- Add information such as dimensions and labels, which is described in the section "Understanding entities."
- Show the interior of an object using a section cut effect, which is described in the sidebar "Showing a Cross-Section."
- Create a walkthrough showing the details of your model from varying perspectives at eye level.
- Design a TourGuide tour that shows an animated tour of the model.

Showing a Cross-Section

Splitting open a model can be an effective way to demonstrate some aspect of its appearance or function, such as showing the inside of a building or cross-sections of a piece of equipment.

You use the section cut effect to both display the interior of an object and to allow you to work inside an object: A model of an avocado is more realistic if its pit shows when it is split open.

The highlighted edges that display on the model after intersecting the geometry using a section plane are called *section slices*. Section slices are dynamic objects in that as you move the section plane through the model you can capture a number of slices.

- Print the model.
- Export the model as images.
- Using the model with Google Earth.

Conducting a walkthrough

A *walkthrough* is a process you design using some of the Camera tools. While it isn't necessarily an export or demonstration option, it serves much the same purpose. That is, it shows you the contents of your model in some way. A walkthrough is intended to simulate walking through the model as if it were in the real world. To accomplish the proper perspective, SketchUp lets you adjust your point of view to use a specific height and angle to the model.

Use the Walkthrough toolbar as a convenient way to define your view. Choose View ➪ Toolbars ➪ Walkthrough to open the toolbar. There are three tools, including:

- **Position Camera:** Use the Position Camera tool to set the camera at eye level to simulate looking and moving through a model at life size.

- **Walk:** Use the Walk tool to simulate walking around and through your model.

- **Look Around:** Use the Look Around tool to pivot the camera around a specific point, as you would if you were standing inside a room and turning around.

To create a walkthrough, follow these steps:

1. Click the Position Camera tool and click a point on your model. In Figure 33.13 the tool is placed on the patio close to the water feature at the default height of 5 feet, 6 inches.

2. To change the level of the point of view, type a different height in the VCB. The camera zooms into the specified location, and the tool changes to the Look Around tool automatically.

3. Click and drag the Look Around tool to rotate the view around you. In Figure 33.14, the view shows the table and chairs on the patio through the tree branches from a location just in front of the water fountain.

FIGURE 33.13

The location for the camera's viewing level is based on where the tool is applied; in this case, close to the water feature.

FIGURE 33.14

The Look Around tool shows the view of the garden from the height of an average person.

4. When you are ready to move on, click the Walk tool and click a location where you Want to travel next. Drag the tool to walk through the model. In Figure 33.15, the walk has returned to the patio fountain.

NOTE There are multiple ways to control the walkthrough process. Read the Help files, or experiment by pressing Shift, Alt, or Ctrl while moving the cursor closer or farther away from the crosshairs.

FIGURE 33.15

Drag the Walk tool, shown as the pair of shoes to the right of the fountain, to move the model.

Presenting a TourGuide tour

You can produce a TourGuide tour that works much like a slide show presentation in SketchUp. The tour is made up of different pages of your model showing different perspectives, details, section cuts, and so on.

Follow these steps to produce a TourGuide tour:

1. Choose View ➪ TourGuide ➪ Settings to open the Model Info dialog box displaying the TourGuide tab, as shown in Figure 33.16. Click Enable page transitions to include a transition between slides. Click the up or down arrows to change the time in seconds.

FIGURE 33.16

Specify whether to use page delays and transitions in your TourGuide tour.

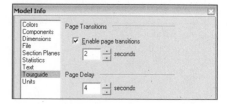

2. Type a value for the Page Delay or click the up or down arrows to change the time in seconds. Close the dialog box.

3. Choose Window ⇨ Pages to open the Pages dialog box, as shown in Figure 33.17. The model includes one default view called Home that is shown at the upper left of the model, below the toolbars.

Add and configure pages in the dialog box to include in your slide show.

4. Move the view of the model to display what you want to see in a page. You can make any sorts of modifications such as changing shadow, rendering mode, time of day, and so on.

5. Type a name for the page in the Name field, and add some detail in the Description field if you want. The new page is added to the list at the top of the dialog box.

6. Select the Properties to save to include in the model's page from the check boxes at the bottom of the dialog box.

7. Continue adding pages as desired. When you finish, check the sequence of the pages at the top of the Pages dialog box, and click the up or down arrows to move a selected page in the order.

8. Deselect the Include in slideshow check box for any slides you want to omit from the slide show.

9. Close the dialog box.

You can check through the pages you have defined from the program window. Each new page is tabbed at the top of the model's view, as shown in Figure 33.18. Click a tab to display the view in the program window.

Each new page added to the model is tabbed on the program window.

When you want to play your slide show, choose View ⇨ TourGuide ⇨ Play Slideshow. The Slideshow controls open, as shown in Figure 33.19. Your slide show plays according to the settings you specify. Click Stop to stop the show.

 **You can't export the slide show from the free version of SketchUp, but you can configure and export the slide show in a number of ways in SketchUp Professional.**

FIGURE 33.19

Use the controls to play your TourGuide slide show.

Exporting and printing your model

The free version of SketchUp includes a number of different export options. One is the ability to export shots of the model in different image formats. Your model could become a cover for a CD containing drawings and other elements from the model, either prepared in SketchUp or exported from SketchUp and manipulated in other programs.

Exporting model views

You can export many different views from your model as images in several formats. To export images from your model, follow these steps:

1. Position the model in the program window as you desire. The exported image includes only what is shown in the program window.
2. Choose File ➪ Export ➪ 2D Graphics to open the Export 2D Graphics dialog box. The file uses the model's name and the PNG image format as defaults.
3. Name the image file as desired. Click the Export type down arrow and choose another image format from the drop-down list if you want. You can export as JPG, TIF, or BMP, as well as PNG.
4. Click Export to process the image and save it.

Printing a model

In the free version of SketchUp, you print your model as it exists. If you are using SketchUp Professional, you can specify Print to Scale and span across pages options to let you print a large drawing from a standard printer. You can also specify other settings such as the quality of the image output.

To print a model, follow these steps:

1. Choose File ➪ Print Setup to choose your printer's paper size.
2. Choose File ➪ Print to open your printer's dialog box. Change settings as desired.
3. Click Print to close the dialog box and send the model to your printer.

Integrating SketchUp Models and Google Earth

For added realism and the chance to tinker with another intriguing program, you can use material from both Google Earth and SketchUp to create and test models, and to upload a finished model to a specific location.

CROSS-REF   **Refer to Chapter 13 for a discussion of Google Earth.**

SketchUp conveniently includes the Google Toolbar that includes several commands for working with the two programs. The toolbar and its contents are listed in Table 33.1.

TABLE 33.1

Tools for Working with Google Earth

Looks Like	Name of Tool	Used For
	Get Current View	Download an image of the current view shown in Google Earth to use for placing a model
	Toggle Terrain	Show alternate 2-D and 3-D versions of the current view for creating and placing your model
	Place Model	Place a temporary version of your model on the current view in Google Earth
	Get Models	Access the 3D Warehouse repository of models
	Share Model	Upload a completed model to share via the 3D Warehouse

Configuring Google Earth

To make the model work in an online location in Google Earth, you need to work with both programs. Before you start in SketchUp, open Google Earth and follow these steps to optimize settings for capturing a terrain image:

1. Choose Tools ➪ Options to open the Google Earth Options dialog box. The 3D View tab is shown by default, as seen in Figure 33.20.

2. In the Detail Area, select the Large (1024 x 1024) radio button. You must have the largest detail area possible for a good terrain image.

3. In the Terrain Quality section, type a value of **1** in the Elevation Exaggeration field. Drag the Quality slider to the Higher end, depending on the speed of your Internet connection.

FIGURE 33.20

Configure settings in Google Earth before capturing a terrain image.

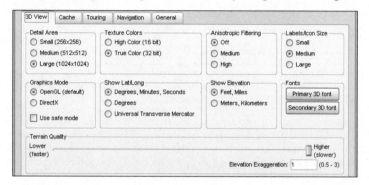

4. Click OK to close the dialog box and apply the settings to the map area in Google Earth.

5. In the Layers sidebar, toggle the Terrain Layer to visible. If the sidebar is hidden, choose Tools ⇨ Sidebar to display it at the left of the program window, as shown in Figure 33.21. The terrain image for modeling in SketchUp uses a specific layer included with the terrain image, which is described in the next section.

FIGURE 33.21

The Terrain layer has to be enabled in order to capture the terrain image correctly.

6. Using the Google Earth tools, display the location in the program window where you want your model to appear.

Creating and testing a model

After the view is set in Google Earth, switch to SketchUp. Whether you close Google Earth depends on your modeling workflow and Internet connection.

Creating the model

Follow these steps to create your model using a Google Earth view as a terrain map:

1. Click Get Current View to get an image of the current view from Google Earth. This image contains the location information needed to properly place the model at the correct location in Google Earth.

NOTE When you view your imported map image in SketchUp, if the map image appears solid black, change one of the graphics mode options. In Google Earth, choose Tools ⇨ Options to open the Google Earth Options dialog box, as shown in Figure 33.20. Select the Direct X option instead of Open GL in the Graphics Mode area of the dialog box. Close the dialog box, and restart Google Earth to change the graphics engine. Recapture the image.

2. Create your model on top of the 2-D image, and move it to the appropriate location on the map, such as in the example in Figure 33.22.

FIGURE 33.22

Move your model to the desired location on the map.

3. Click the Toggle Terrain button on the Google Toolbar to toggle to the 3-D image. Reposition the model to conform to the terrain in the 3-D image if you are using terrain with a lot of elevation differences.

4. If the appearance of the map is distracting, select the map on the drawing and choose Windows ⇨ Material Browser to open the Materials dialog box. Click the In Model tab and select the map, which is added to the textures when imported into the model. Click Edit to open the Edit Material dialog box, and drag the Opacity slider left to decrease the map transparency. Click Close to exit the Edit Material dialog box and close the Materials dialog box.

5. Click the Place Model button on the Google Toolbar to place the model in Google Earth. SketchUp creates a temporary file of your model and places the model in Google Earth at the proper location. As you can see in Figure 33.23, the model is listed in the Temporary Places in the Places list in the sidebar.

FIGURE 33.23

Check out the placement of the model on Google Earth using the Place Model command in SketchUp.

If you decide you don't have enough models or want to look for inspiration, SketchUp offers the 3D Warehouse.

Checking out the 3D Warehouse

The 3D Warehouse is an online storage site containing hundreds of different models. Anyone may search and download models, but to submit your own, you need to log in using your Google Account.

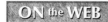 **Find models of buildings, furniture, plants, and so on contributed by SketchUp users from around the world at** http://sketchup.google.com/3dwarehouse/.

The 3D Warehouse models are freely available for you to share, use, and even display on your own Web site.

Follow these steps to locate and download a model:

1. In SketchUp, choose Google ➪ Get Models or click the Get Models button on the Google toolbar to open the 3D Warehouse in a browser window.

2. Find the model you want to work with. You can:
   - Scroll through the list on the opening page of the 3D Warehouse browser window and choose a category from either the Popular, Recent, or Google Picks sections.
   - Search for a model based on its name, description, location, type, or other term.

3. Select a model in the search returns displayed in the browser window to open a window with more information on the selected model, such as in the example shown in Figure 33.24.

   The information includes a description, the keyword tags associated with the model, its location on a map, and a preview of the model.

4. Click Edit with Google SketchUp to open a dialog box asking if you want to load the model directly into your Google SketchUp model. Click Yes to load the model into the current model open in SketchUp; click No to save the model to your hard drive.

   If you click No, locate and select the folder in which you want to save the model in the Save As dialog box, and click Save.

FIGURE 33.24

Read about the models before you download them in the search results window.

5. If you click Yes, the model is downloaded and placed. Depending on the conditions attached to the current model and the one you are downloading, you may have additional dialog boxes to specify where the model is placed:

■ If both the open model and the model being downloaded have specified locations on Google Earth, a message asks if you want to place the model yourself. Click No to have the model sited at its Google Earth location; click Yes to place the model on the program window.

■ If your model doesn't have a location and the downloaded model has a location, it is placed on the ground plane centered at the origin point with green=north, red=west, and blue=up.

■ If the model is an object, such as a bumblebee or a teapot, the model is selected automatically on the ground plane and the Move tool is active.

 If you load the model directly into SketchUp it is treated as an inserted object. Any pages or different views of the model are not displayed, nor is any screen text if it was included with the model.

Tapping into Additional Resources

The community surrounding SketchUp is growing as the program and its accompanying features grow. Here are a few sources of information and interaction for you to learn more:

- **http://earth.google.com/intl/en/3d.html:** Download and install the 3D Warehouse Network link, a KMZ file used by Google Earth. After you download the file and open Google Earth, you see house-shaped markers indicating the locations of 3-D models, as shown in Figure 33.25.

FIGURE 33.25

Markers indicate the placement of 3-D models on the map.

- **http://sketchup.google.com/components.html:** You don't have to reinvent the wheel. Rather than starting a model from scratch, Google offers literally hundreds of components that can be added to your models. In addition to the libraries that are installed with the program, download libraries of objects ranging from Transportation to Architecture in both Windows and Mac OS X versions.

- **www.sketchup.com/training:** Some people prefer to learn in a classroom situation. Visit this site to see a list of training courses available in your area.

- **http://download.sketchup.com/OnlineDoc/gsu_win/GoogleSketchUpHelp.htm:** A standard type of Help file system, including Contents, Index, and a Search frame, is available from this site. The Help files include both SketchUp and SketchUp Pro 5.

- **http://sketchup.google.com/tutorials.html:** If you want to see how something is constructed in SketchUp, visit this site for a list of videos. The set of seven SketchUp videos includes three quick-start videos, a video showing how to use the 3D Warehouse, and three videos on applying textures.

- **http://sketchup.google.com/examples.html:** To inspire you as you make your way into the world of 3-D modeling, this site contains a number of georeferenced models for a number of famous buildings, such as the Eiffel Tower. You can also view a number of nongeoreferenced models.

■ **http://download.sketchup.com/GSU/pdfs/QuickReferenceCard.pdf:** Be sure to download and print a copy of the reference sheet you access at this site. You can find a key to the toolbar icons, mouse buttons, and combinations using tools, some of which are shown in Figure 33.26. If you are working in SketchUp, choose Help ➪ Quick Reference Card to open the document.

FIGURE 33.26

Keep the Quick Reference Card close at hand as you learn the program.

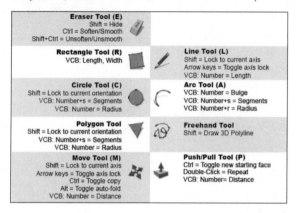

■ **http://groups.google.com/group/sketchup:** Share your expertise and pick up pointers, advice, and troubleshoot problems at the Google SketchUp Help group. You must become a member of the group to post messages.

CROSS-REF   Read about Google Groups in Chapter 22.

Summary

This chapter carried on with a look at Google SketchUp. As you have seen, it is a substantial program, especially for free software!

In this chapter, you saw how to add realism to your model using different types of material that simulate anything from pansies to glass to rusty metal. In addition to using preconfigured materials, you saw how to edit materials from the libraries, how to create and add a new material, and how to adjust a material once it is placed on your model.

In the latter part of the chapter, you learned that SketchUp includes several ways to export content from a model, including printing pages and creating a TourGuide slide show. You saw how Google Earth and SketchUp work together to identify locations and to incorporate that data into a model for placing it on the map. Upload models to the SketchUp 3D Warehouse, where you can also find and download hundreds of different models to incorporate into your projects.

And now for something completely different: In the next chapter, dive into the world of online commerce and take a look at Google AdWords.

Part V

Google and the Enterprise

Chapter 34

Increasing Web Traffic with AdWords

If you search Google, you've seen the sponsored links that appear above and beside your query results. People actually click those links and visit the sponsored sites. That's how your business and Google make money. It's a great partnership.

When your business depends on people finding you on the Internet, there is no better tool than using Google AdWords to advertise your site. You pay Google each time someone clicks your link to land on your Web page. The rest is up to your Web site to compel visitors to buy your products or use your services.

This chapter helps you create an advertising campaign using Google AdWords, teaches you how to use the tools Google provides to select keywords people will use to find your site, helps you plan the financial side of advertising with Google, assists you in ad creation, and helps you read the reports to see how well your campaign worked.

As in any ad campaign, there is no guarantee that it won't need some tweaking along the way to improve performance. Google's AdWords provides immediate feedback on your campaign's performance and allows you to make ad hoc changes to drive more traffic to your Web site.

Taking Your First Steps

Your first steps have nothing to do with computers, Google, or the Internet. They have to do with your business and how people find you. You also need to create an advertising budget for your business or at least carve out part of your existing ad budget for Google advertising. It also doesn't hurt to figure out how you're going to know if your ad campaign is successful so you're not just throwing away money on Google advertising just because you think Google is a cool company.

Because this is the first chapter that talks about how Google makes money, you should know that taking your money for no good reason goes against the Google

Code of Conduct and Google's informal motto of "Don't be evil." If you want to know whether Google is the kind of company you want to invest your money in, in the hopes of making money yourself, perhaps it would be a good idea to read the Google Code of Conduct, which can be found at `http://investor.google.com/conduct.html`.

After you do your homework and decide that Google AdWords is the right place to spend your money and you have an idea about how much money that is, take the next step and point your Web browser to `http://adwords.google.com` (see Figure 34.1).

FIGURE 34.1

Get started by signing up for an AdWords account.

Click Sign up now. A new page launches, and you're given the choice of signing up for the Starter Edition for single product or service offerings with simplified options, or the Standard Edition with the full range of AdWords features and functionality. This chapter discusses the Standard Edition. You can find the information you need in this chapter to help you explore the Starter Edition if that is the edition you select. Table 34.1 compares the various options between the two editions.

TABLE 34.1

Starter versus Standard AdWord Account Comparison

AdWords Feature	Starter Edition	Standard Edition
Simplified signup	Yes	No
Single product, single set of keywords	Yes	Yes
Multiple products, ad campaigns, and sets of keywords	No	Yes
Single-page reporting	Yes	No
Advanced and custom reporting	No	Yes
Single-target customers	Yes	Yes
Multiple-target customers	No	Yes
Advanced cost control	No	Yes
Advanced planning tools such as conversion tracking	No	Yes
Site targeting	No	Yes

After you select either the Starter or Standard edition, click Continue. You are now ready to begin creating your first ad campaign in Google AdWords.

Targeting customers

You first want to target your customers by the languages they speak. People who live in other locations around the world search Google in their own languages. When you want your ad to appear in Google searches by users within those countries, specify the language associated with those countries. Select languages from the What language(s) do your customers speak? drop-down list. You can select multiple languages from the list by Ctrl-clicking or Command-clicking the selection with your mouse.

Continue targeting your customers by specifying their geographic locations. You can select from three possible area sizes:

- **Countries and territories:** Your ads appear in the countries and territories you specify.
- **Regions and cities:** Your ads appear in the region or cities you specify.
- **Customized:** Your ads appear in browsers of people searching within a specific distance from your business.

Select an area, and click Continue. The next page that appears depends on the previous area selection.

When you select Countries and territories, you are asked to select the specific countries from a list. Click Add to move them into a list of selected countries.

When you select Regions and cities, first select the country of interest from the drop-down list. The available areas box below the drop-down is populated with specific regions for the country you select. You can select regions only from a single country. Selecting a new country clears any regions you may have previously selected.

When you select Customized, you are asked to specify the location of your business, either by typing a physical address or by pointing out its position on a map for this purpose provided by Google. Move the map pointer by dragging the map. The pointer stays in the middle. Then you are asked to define an area by specifying the number of miles from your business that defines the area in which you want your ads to appear. (You also can specify your area in kilometers by clicking the change to kilometers link.) If you happen to know the latitude and longitude of your business, you are welcome to enter it here. If you're curious about what your latitude and longitude might be, type your physical address and click the Map this location link. Then click Select a point on the map. You see your latitude and longitude displayed.

> **NOTE**   Identifying the location of a Web searcher is not an exact science. Google recommends specifying a custom area at least 20 miles or 35 kilometers from your business location.

You must first click the Map this location link before specifying the custom area. The maximum size of your custom area is 500 miles.

Creating an ad

The Web form shown in Figure 34.2 is one that should make you sit back and scratch your head. What you put in this simple little form can mean the complete success or abject failure of your ad campaign. Okay, here's the good news. If your ad campaign fails and no one clicks your sponsored ad, it won't cost you a nickel. Still, the point is to have people clicking your ad to see what's in store for them on your Web page.

> **TIP**   Advanced Web developers know how to use the "referrer" to know when visitors land on their Web site from a Google search. They can then customize the Web site for the Google visitor.

FIGURE 34.2

What goes in this form could spell instant success for your business.

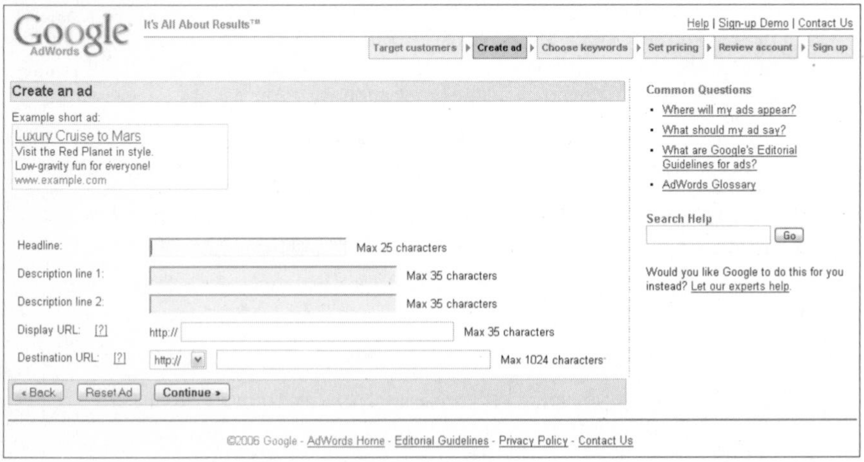

The first thing you must create is the headline for your ad. This is what appears in bold letters and attracts the attention of the Google searcher. What you place here is very important. A poor headline can mean poor performance for your ad; no pressure or anything. So, rather than a generic "Discount Sporting Goods," think about your specialty and what people are going to buy over the Internet. Remember that you can change this later, so you might consider a seasonal ad, "Surfboards — Kitesurf Gear." You have only 25 characters to work with. If you're the kind of person who makes up personalized license plates in your head for fun, you'll do fine.

You get two more description lines, 35 characters each. They appear in normal text below the headline. Here you can go into a little more detail, amplifying what you put in the headline. The description lines are a good place for "Sports gear guaranteed low price" and on the second description line, "Free shipping w/in continental US." Certainly you can come up with better ad material than this, but you get the idea. Give people a reason to click your ad. If you get stumped and you need some inspiration, do Google searches on various keywords associated with your business and see what other people have written. You need to research keywords that identify your business anyway.

Type a Web address in Display URL. This is a URL identifying your site. It does not have to be the URL of the actual page on which the Google searcher lands. You can put www.sportinggoodsforless.com here while the actual page the user lands on is www.sportinggoodsforless.com/surfcatalog.htm. Specify the actual destination in the Destination URL field. Your display URL can be only 35 characters long, while the actual destination URL can be 1024 characters long (a small book). Notice that your destination URL also can be a secure site by selecting HTTPS:// from the drop-down list. Of course, your site must actually have a secure page that uses an HTTPS connection. For more information about HTTPS, visit http://en.wikipedia.org/wiki/Https.

As you type your ad, you can watch it take shape in the example ad shown in the upper-left portion of the Create an ad page.

Choosing keywords

Creating a compelling ad that people want to click for more information is important, but you also want to make certain that your ad actually appears when people do Google searches looking for your kind of business. This happens by selecting the right keywords to associate with your ad. After creating your ad, the next step in the Google AdWords wizard is to type keywords. Naturally, the keywords you type here should be directly related to your service or merchandise.

Your keywords can be single words or entire phrases. Don't make your phrases too long or they become so specific that the chance of someone typing the exact phrase becomes slight. Type one word or phrase per line in the box provided on the Choose keywords page.

> **TIP** Choose keywords that are general enough to have your ad displayed but not so general that they appear too often. You don't want people who are not truly looking for your service clicking to see your Web page.

Google helps you think of keywords by providing a service that displays all the related keywords you might consider using. To use this service, type a keyword in the Want more? box, and click Search. A list of additional possible keyword selections appears. Click Add next to the selection to add it to your list.

Type up to 20 keywords, one per line. When you finish, click Continue to move to pricing.

Later, you can edit important keyword options using the tools in your online AdWords account or in the AdWords Editor software discussed later in this chapter. One of the parameters you want to set for each keyword is match type. This determines how closely you want the match to be between your keywords and those used in a search. These are the choices:

- **Broad:** This choice returns the highest and least selective number of matches.
- **Phrase:** This choice matches when the entire phrase matches.
- **Exact:** The keyword must be an exact match to the one typed by the Google searcher.

You also can set the maximum Cost Per Click (CPC) for each individual keyword. This allows you much greater flexibility than setting one CPC for all keywords in your campaign. The next section discusses how to set the pricing.

Set the pricing

We're not talking about the pricing of your goods and services to your customer; it's the price you agree to pay to Google for displaying your linked ads and having visitors land on your Web page. There is no set fee. You can set your own prices, limits, and budget. This is a topic you want to play close attention to. Mistakes here can be costly, but done correctly, Google's AdWords can be a very cost-effective way of driving potential business to your site.

Set the currency

The first selection in the next wizard page asks you to choose a currency. This is usually not a big choice, but make certain you make the right choice because you can't change this at a later date. Google usually sets the currency to your computer's actual location by default, but you can change this by selecting a different currency from the list.

Set your budget

You set your daily budget. There is no minimum spending requirement. Tell Google how much you want to spend on average per day. The amount you spend is completely up to you. When you reach your daily average limit, your ad stops displaying for that day. Your budget controls how many times people can view or click your ad.

Your budget is something you can control, raising it and lowering it as often as you like. At first, you may want to set it just a little high to see what kind of new traffic your site receives. If you find that your ad is very successful and you experience new cash flow, you may want to maintain this level or even raise it.

Google charges a nominal one-time activation fee. Other than the fees you agree to pay for clicks on your ad, you will not expect to pay additional fees or hidden costs.

Set the maximum Cost Per Click

Setting the Cost Per Click affects your position in the list of sponsored ads that appear. This setting allows you to compete for the "top spot" against your business competitors. This particular setting is a ceiling or maximum amount you want to pay per click. Your actual amount could be lower, as explained later. You can quickly do the math, thinking about your daily budget divided by the maximum CPC to figure out the minimum number of times per day someone might be able to view your ad.

Google doesn't make you guess; it provides tools to help you make this critical decision. Would you like to know what it would cost to appear at the top of the list given the keywords you entered? Warning: You may want to be sitting down when you see the number. Click the Want to purchase the most clicks possible? link to see what Google estimates as your suggested budget and Cost Per Click.

A more useful tool is the traffic estimator, which shows you a list of your keywords, their predicted status, the estimated average CPC, the estimated ad position, the estimated number of clicks per day you might expect to receive, and a calculation of your cost per day. These estimates are all based on the costs and click-through rates of current Google AdWords customers.

Review your selections

When you finish configuring your initial ad campaign, Google displays a summary of the things you entered so you can double-check your entries before continuing. You can edit many of these selections right from this page. Here is a list of the items for your review:

- Campaign name
- Languages
- Locations
- Currency
- Daily budget
- Ad group name
- Your ad
- Keyword list
- Maximum CPC

Google asks if you would want extra help. Select either or both of the following options for more assistance. They are selected by default. So if you do not want extra assistance, you need to deselect these by clicking in the check box to remove the check mark.

- Send me personalized ideas for improving my ad performance.
- Send me AdWords newsletters with tips, surveys, and best practices.

Google asks a question similar to one you might consider putting on your own Web page. How did you hear about Google AdWords? Answering this helps Google figure out its own advertising policy. Create a small form on your own Web page that asks the question "How did you hear about us?" And, of course, put Google in the list of ways people used to land on your site. This helps you figure out how many of the people who click your ad filled out your form or purchased your product.

Signing up

In the next step, you actually create your AdWords account. Up to this point, you've been creating a potential account but have not actually signed up. Signing up is simple. Follow these steps:

1. Choose to use your current Google account or tell Google that you do not use the other Google services.

2. If you want to use your current Google account for AdWords, you can select I'd like to use my existing Google account for AdWords. Because most of the Google services do not involve money or your personal financial information, you may want to set up a different login and password just for AdWords. For security reasons, this is recommended.

3. To set up a new login and password for this account only, select I'd like to choose a new login name and password just for AdWords.

4. Click Continue, and Google begins creating your AdWords account. When your account setup is complete, a new page appears alerting you to the fact that your account has been created, but you're not finished.

> **NOTE** Your ad will not run until you give Google your billing information.

5. Click the Sign into your AdWords account link to continue to the next step (detailed in the following section).

Managing AdWords

After setting up your initial ad, you are presented with the primary AdWords management page. Notice in Figure 34.3 that two messages in large boxes appear at the top of the page. This is the location that Google AdWords will post any important messages concerning your ads or your account. The initial messages tell you that your account has not been activated yet, and the second message tells you about the AdWords Editor. You can learn more about the AdWords Editor later in this chapter. Here is an easy-to-view look at how an AdWords account is organized:

Account: You can have only a single AdWords account.

Campaign(s): Each account can have multiple ad campaigns.

Ad Group(s): Each ad campaign can have several ad groups.

Keywords: Each ad group can have one or more keywords.

Managing Your Campaigns

Good campaign management is the key to getting results from your AdWords account. From the Campaign Management tab, you can select a campaign to edit or see information about each of your campaigns. View the following about each of your campaigns:

- Current status of your campaigns
- Budget for each of your campaigns
- Number of clicks and impressions for each campaign
- Statistics such as the CTR (Click Through Ratio) and Avg. CPC (Average Cost Per Click)
- Your actual cost for each campaign

When viewing the information about your campaigns, similar to that shown in Figure 34.3, you can select the time period from which the statistics are compiled. Two radio buttons are located above the statistics. One button allows you to select a present period from a drop-down list ranging from today through all time. Of course, that means from the time you first started your AdWords account. You also can select the radio button that allows you to specify a date range by typing begin and end dates. Click Go after specifying your date range. Selecting a period from the drop-down list automatically adjusts the campaign statistics for the newly specified date range.

FIGURE 34.3

When you first create your campaign, it appears in the list of All Campaigns.

In addition to viewing statistics about a campaign, you can edit your campaign or create new campaigns.

Editing a campaign

Each of the campaigns listed in the Campaign Management tab appears as a link. Clicking the campaign name launches a list of Ad Groups, displayed as links, for that campaign. An Ad Group is a group of keywords. To see the keywords associated with a particular Ad Group, click the Ad Group name. Three tabs are displayed, each giving you specific information about your ad group.

The Summary tab displays an overall look at how your ad group is performing. You can see performance in the Google + Search Network. These are the results of your ad group in Google search pages and on Google partner search pages. You also can see its performance in the Content network or impressions on relevant Google partner Web sites.

The Keywords tab presents information about all the keywords within the ad group. Each keyword is listed along with its status; your current bid (maximum CPC); the number of clicks, impressions, and the click-through ratio; average CPC; cost; and the average position among the ads when the ad was displayed. This gives you a good idea of how well a particular keyword is working for you. You can see the cost associated with the keyword, see how often it was displayed, and compare that to the number of times people clicked the ad. Low click-through ratios can mean that the ad may not be of interest to people searching on that particular keyword. Consider either removing the keyword or changing the wording of the ad to make it more applicable to people searching on the keyword performing poorly.

The Ad Variations tab allows you to view and manage your display ads. You can change your ad's content, see performance statistics, and choose to create a new ad.

Creating a new campaign

To begin creating a new ad campaign, you must first select the type of campaign you want to create. Choose between keyword-targeted and site-targeted campaigns. Your ad may appear the same, but how and when it appears and how you are charged are very different.

Keyword-targeted ads can appear in Google search pages and on other Web sites within the Google network. You can tell Google where you want your ads to appear. Your ads appear when someone uses keywords to perform a search that matches the keywords you specified for your ad campaign.

Site-targeted ads appear on specific Web sites within the Google network that you specify. Your ad appears each time someone visits the site, and you are charged based on how many times your ad is viewed, rather than by how many times someone clicks your ad. This is an important distinction between keyword-targeted ads and site-targeted ads.

The steps for creating a keyword-targeted ad are the same as when you first set up your AdWords account: targeting the customer, choosing keywords, setting the price, reviewing your campaign, and saving it.

Creating a site-targeted ad begins by configuring the ad for your target customer. Creating a site-targeted ad campaign differs from the keyword-targeted ad in the next step where you select the sites on which you want your ad to appear. You can select sites based on these characteristics:

- **Category:** Select sites based on the category of site such as animals, home & garden, lifestyles, recreation, or one of the other many categories listed. After you select a category, a list of sites appears. Click Add to select a site location for your ad. You easily can see what type of ad formats each site accepts and what your expected impression rate might be.

- **Topic:** Describe the topic of your targeted site by typing topic keywords. This is not exactly like keyword-targeted ads, but similar in idea. A list of sites containing your specified keywords appears, allowing you to select all or specific Web sites.

- **List URLs:** Specify Web sites that are already part of the Google network (hosting Google ads on their Web pages). You can type a URL to see if it is part of the network. This is the most specific way to specify where your ad appears.

You can try each method of selecting Web sites to host your ad until you find the method that offers you the best selection of sites. When you finish selecting Web sites (they appear in the Selected Sites column on the right), click Continue.

The next step is to type your daily budget. Remember that you are charged based on impressions, not clicks on your ad. Impressions are the number of times someone views your ad. Type the maximum amount you are willing to pay per impression. This affects your position in the list of ads placed by your competitors. Clicking Continue again allows you to review your ad, the list of Web sites on which your ad will appear, and the pricing you set up. You can then choose to create another Ad Group for this campaign or simply save your campaign. After your account is set up with Google, your ad begins appearing on your selected sites.

Tools

Google AdWords provides you with a number of tools for creating, editing, customizing, and tracking your ad's performance. These are some of the tools you can use while creating or modifying your ad:

- **Keyword tool:** This tool allows you to add new keywords, view performance, and view important details such as advertising competition and search volume.

- **Negative Keyword tool:** This tool allows you to specify keywords that indicate you do not want your ad displayed when these keywords are included in the user's search. This can save you lots of money by eliminating unwanted clicks on your ad.

- **Traffic Estimator tool:** This is another keyword tool that helps you determine how well a particular keyword will perform for you. It is an invaluable tool when selecting keywords.

- **Site Exclusion tool:** This tool lets you designate sites in the Google network on which you do not want your site-targeted ad to appear. For example, you may not want your ad appearing on your competitor's Web site, or maybe you do.

When determining the performance of your ad campaign, Google AdWords provides several other important tools, including these:

- **Ads Diagnostic tool:** This tool lets you know if your ads are appearing for a particular search. It helps you adjust keywords or your CPC bid.

- **Disapproved Ads tool:** This tool informs you of the reasons some of your ads may not have been approved. For example, certain keywords and phrases are disallowed.

- **My Change History tool:** This tool lets you see all the changes you've made to your account over the last three months. This helps you see things you've tried and measure performance against your efforts. It's a great tool for improving your ad strategy.

- **Conversion Tracking tool:** Find out how many of the people that click your ad actually buy your product or use your services. This is covered in more detail in the next section.

When an ad is working for you and you are pleased with its performance, it may not require any tweaking. But you may want to play with it from time to time to see if you can improve its performance, or you may want to create new ads that supplement the ones that are already working for you. These tools assist you in focusing and managing that ad's performance.

Conversion tracking

Conversions occur when someone clicks your ad, visits your Web site, and then possibly buys a product, reads something you wrote, or took some other action that you consider a successful visit to your Web site. Google has a special process by which it can drop a cookie on the user's machine. You tell Google which page visit is considered a success — for example, an online receipt for a purchase the visitor makes on your site or the "congratulations, you've signed up for my newsletter" page. When this page is reached, Google tallies a successful conversion. Conversions help you decide if your ad is attracting the people who will buy your product or use your service.

You have two tracking options:

- AdWords campaign tracking of existing campaigns
- Cross channel tracking of campaigns using other providers

To get started, you must have an ad already approved and running in Google AdWords. Choose from Google's two conversion tracking products: basic and custom. The basic conversion tracking product allows you to quickly and easily start using conversion tracking. As the name suggests, you get basic number of clicks compared to how many successes you had.

The customized conversion tracking option gives you greater flexibility. This option allows you to select one of the four types of conversion tracking:

- Purchase or sale tracking
- Lead tracking
- Signup tracking
- Page view tracking

To begin conversion-tracking setup, set the format and background color of the small box that appears on your conversion confirmation page. The conversion confirmation page is the one that says, "Thanks for buying my product." Next, set the language and security level of your page.

For custom tracking, you can assign a conversion value, either a constant or a variable. Use a constant when you have a set value that you will receive from the conversion. For example, everyone who views your site's video product pays $5. Your constant would then be $5. Variables include things like purchase prices of many different products. You need to know how to find that price in your Web site's shopping cart to use variable conversion value tracking.

When you finish configuring your conversion tracking, copy the HTML that Google creates for you and paste it into the Web page you consider the "success" or conversion confirmation page.

NOTE You must be able to edit the HTML on your conversion confirmation page.

Visit your conversion confirmation page to see that the Google Sites text box appears there. Then visit the conversion statistics page (in about an hour) to see that your test conversion has been tracked.

NOTE Conversions can take up to an hour to appear in your conversion statistics.

You can choose to view standard conversion tracking reports, such as the conversion ratio, or select custom reports to receive additional metrics, such as your cost of conversion. You can find conversion tracking right down to the keyword level.

Google AdWords Editor

When installing the Google AdWords Editor, you can make the application available to everyone or "Just me." For security reasons, select Just me. Remember that editing your AdWords can affect the amount of money you need to pay Google.

When you finish your AdWords Editor installation, you can launch it from your Start menu. Choose Programs ➪ Google AdWords Editor ➪ AdWords Editor, as shown in Figure 34.4.

When you first launch the AdWords Editor program, you are prompted to type your account information so the editor software can communicate with your existing Google Ad Worlds account. The Add New AdWords account dialog box appears and requests the e-mail address and password you configured to access your AdWords account. Remember that this may be different from your Google account. After you add your login information in the dialog box, it closes and the AdWords Editor downloads your AdWord campaign information.

FIGURE 34.4

Manage your AdWords account using the AdWords Editor application.

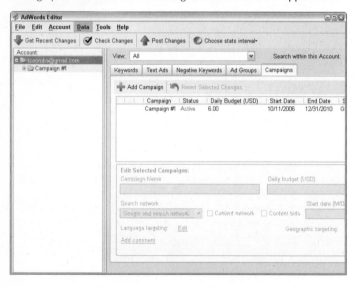

The AdWords Editor main window has five tabs: Keywords, Text Ads, Negative Keywords, Ad Groups, and Campaigns.

Edit and add keywords in the Keywords tab. Change the text of the keyword. Select the Match Type, Broad, Phrase, or Exact, the maximum cost per click, and the destination URL. Setting the destination URL for each keyword gives you the greatest flexibility in determining on which page people land when they click your ad. By default, there is one destination URL per ad. Consider how you might construct your Web site to take advantage of this ability to target specific customers.

You can add a comment for each keyword by clicking the Comment link.

The <u>Advanced Max CPC Changes</u> link launches a window that allows you to set how your Cost Per Click bids are handled. You can choose to increase and decrease them by percent or by actual monetary amounts. You can raise inactive keywords to their minimum CPC levels to reactivate them, or you can remove the keyword-specific CPC and return to the Ad Group's maximum CPC level set when you created the Ad Group. You also can set additional maximum and minimum CPC constraints in this window.

Take finer control over your destination URL by launching the Advanced URL Changes window. Here, you can set the specific URL for the keyword and add text to an existing URL, such as a directory name or URL parameter. And you can remove certain URL parameters that you do not want associated with this keyword.

Add and edit existing text ads (see the section "Creating an Ad" for more information on creating text ads). You also can add a comment for your ad, replace text in an ad for faster editing, and make advanced URL changes as discussed previously for keywords.

Add special keywords, known as negative keywords, in the Negative Keywords tab. Negative keywords are those that when matched, keep your ad from displaying. For example, if you are selling puppies, but you never sell Yorkshire terrier puppies, your negative keyword may be Yorkshire terrier. That way, if someone types Yorkshire terrier puppies into a Google search box, your ad does not appear.

In the Ad Groups tab, you can add new ad groups and do these additional things:

- Change the Maximum CPC
- Change the Maximum Content CPC
- Change the status of the ad group among Active, Paused, or Deleted

The Campaigns tab has features that allow you to add a new ad campaign, change the name of the campaign, set the daily budget, set the status, select the search network, set content bids, and set start and end dates for ad campaigns with time constraints, such as seasonal ads or sale ads. Set the language and geographic location of your target customers and add a comment.

When you finish modifying keywords, ads, ad groups, and campaigns, click the Post Changes menu icon along the top of the main window. Your changes are transferred to your AdWords account.

Creating an Ad

There was a time when the only type of ad you could place in Google was a text ad. That is no longer true; now, you can place full multimedia presentations within the Google network, or you can choose to stick with the tried-and-true text ad. In a wireless world, your ad also can appear on mobile devices and cell phones. Here are the types of ads you can create:

- Text
- Image
- Mobile text
- Local business
- Video

Most of the parameters for creating ads are the same. You definitely need a destination URL for any type of ad so that, after viewing your ad, the user can click it and purchase or experience your site's offering.

Creating a text ad

The steps for creating a text ad are the same as the steps you took when first setting up your account. To create the text ad, type the following information:

- Headline
- Description line 1
- Description line 2
- Display URL
- Destination URL

Click Save Ad when you finish creating your ad.

Creating an image ad

Image ads are exactly what they sound like: graphic images rather than boring old text. The advantage of graphic image ads is that they are eye-catching. The disadvantage is that you can say so much more in a text ad. You need to decide how best to attract people to your ad: content or pizzazz. Your image ads can be formatted in the styles listed in Table 34.2.

TABLE 34.2

Image Ad Styles

Shape	Style
468 x 60	Banner
728 x 90	Leaderboard
200 x 200	Small Square
250 x 250	Square
300 x 250	Inline
336 x 280	Large Rectangle
120 x 600	Skyscraper
160 x 600	Wide Skyscraper

The image you select for your ad can be a maximum of 50KB in size. Display ads must be in one of these file types: JPEG, GIF, PNG, or SWF.

> **TIP** Make sure to use a good-quality graphics editor to create your image. Poor-quality images do not attract people to your Web site.

Browse your computer to find the image you want to upload for your ad. Type a name for the image. This should be a descriptive name that makes viewing its performance in reports simple. Like text ads, the display ads also have a display URL and an actual destination URL. Type these two URLs. Google also asks for your permission (by clicking the check box) to adjust any of your image ads to an appropriate size. Click Save Ad when you finish creating your ad.

Creating a mobile text ad

If you want your ads to appear on cell phones and other mobile devices when someone does a search that matches your selected keywords, create a mobile text ad. It's similar to creating normal text ads, except that due to size constraints you are limited to only 18 characters in the headline and a single description line, also only 18 characters long.

You can choose how people respond to your ad. You can link them to your business via your phone number, making it simple to call you rather than read about you on the Web. This is great for services such as towing where you want them to call you immediately. You can link your ad to a mobile Web page (a Web page designed for viewing on a small display) or both of these options.

When linking to a mobile Web page, type the display URL, the one they see, and an actual destination URL. You are limited to only 20 characters for the display URL and 200 characters for a destination URL. Remember that your destination URL must point to a Web page designed to appear on mobile devices and designed using a mobile protocol. Specify the mobile protocol used to create your mobile Web page from this list: WML, XHTML, CHTML, and PDA-compliant.

Finally, you can specify which mobile carriers display your ad. Your choices are: All carriers and select specific carriers from the list. You may want to select specific carriers if you are selling mobile goods and services designed for specific carriers. Click Save Ad to complete your mobile ad creation.

Creating a local business ad

Local business ads are listed in Google Maps business listings for a particular area. They appear on the map with a distinctive location marker. You must first be listed in the Google Maps business listings. To add your business to the local listings, point your Web browser to `www.google.com/local/add`.

Your local business listing can include your location, your phone number and contact person, a description of your business, your hours of operation, and payment methods. Adding your local business listing is free. You should consider adding your listing even if you are not going to run a local business ad.

To create a local business ad, you only need to type your business name and its location. Google looks in its local business listings to find your entry. Make sure you correctly type your full address or Google Maps does not correctly display your ad.

Creating a video ad

When a video ad first appears on a Web page, it appears as a static image until someone clicks it. Then your video begins playing. You must supply both the initial static image and the video. Your video ad should conform to one of the styles listed in Table 34.3.

TABLE 34.3

Video Ad Styles

Shape	Style
300 x 225	Inline Rectangle
336 x 252	Large Rectangle
200 x 175	Small Square
250 x 225	Square

Select the static image you want to appear initially from your computer. You can use the Browse button to locate it on your computer. Then select a video you want to use in your video ad.

Type the display and destination URLs in the text boxes provided. The display URL can be 35 characters long and the destination URL 1,024 characters. Finally, create a name for your ad. This is how the ad will appear in your reports. Click Save Ad when you finish creating your video ad.

Viewing Reports

To view reports of your ad campaign's performance, click the Reports tab when you log in to your AdWords account. If it's your first time in the Reports tab, you'll want to first create a report by clicking the <u>Create a Report now</u> link.

The Create Report page contains everything you need to create powerful custom reports. Begin by selecting the type of report you want to create from these choices:

- **Keyword Performance:** See how each of your keywords is performing.
- **Ad Performance:** See reports on the overall performance of all your ads.
- **URL Performance:** See performance based on the destination URLs you've specified in your ads.
- **Ad Group Performance:** View performance at the Ad Group level rather than at the campaign level.
- **Campaign Performance:** See reports on the performance of all your Ad Campaigns.
- **Account Performance:** See the performance of your entire AdWords account.

After you select the type of report you want to create, you must select the type of report based on time. For example, you may create a summary report, or daily, weekly, monthly, quarterly, or yearly reports.

Specify a date range by either selecting a range from the drop-down list or by typing a range with begin and end dates. Typing your own range is particularly important when specifying your company's fiscal year, which may begin and end midyear.

Select which of your campaigns you want included in the report—all or selections from a list of campaigns. After you select which campaigns, you have the choice of altering which columns appear in the report and filtering the report. You can filter based on a number of criteria such as whether the ads are content- or search-type ads, whether keywords are active or have some other status, the level of keyword matching you've set up, a particular keyword, the level of average position ads have maintained, clicks, cost, average Cost Per Click (CPC), Click Through Ratio (CTR), and number of impressions.

After you finish building your report, you need to give it a meaningful name. It's probably not a good idea to give it a name such as Report #1 or My AdWords Report. Give the report a meaningful name, such as Fiscal Year Performance – All Campaigns.

Select whether this report you are creating is a template from which you can create future reports, possibly specifying different date ranges or selecting different ad campaigns. Then tell Google how often you want the report run; these are your choices:

- Every day
- Every Monday
- First day of every month

You can choose to be notified by e-mail when the report runs or even receive the report via e-mail. When receiving a report via e-mail, you need to select the format in which it is sent to you. You can choose formats that easily allow you to include them in spreadsheets, such as CSV files, or you can send them out to company-wide reader programs that expect an XML format or for easy viewing in HTML. Click Create Report to create your report or template.

In addition to viewing your reports in e-mail, you also can click the Reports tab to view reports that have been run. Click the Report Center link in the Reports tab to view existing reports.

CROSS-REF Learn more about how to analyze your ad's performance using Google Analytics in Chapter 36.

My Account

You may be wondering why the My Account section comes at the end of the chapter. It was important for you to understand how AdWords works and all the tools Google provides for creating and managing your ad before you enter your financial information and launch your ad campaign. You could have just as easily typed your text ad, blindly added a few keywords, turned over your credit card number, and been done with things. But you don't need to rush into spending money when there are so many tools to help you maximize your success for each dollar you spend.

There are four sections in the My Account tab. Billing Summary gives you a quick look at your recent billing. Billing Preferences is where you set up your billing arrangements with Google. Access is where you can add or edit the list of users who have access to your AdWords account. And the AdWords Account Preferences section is where you can set some basic information about how you access and view your AdWords account.

Setting your billing preferences

The Billing Preferences section is where you type your billing style, form of payment, billing address, any backup payment details, and any promotional codes you may have received to start an AdWords account.

The billing payment types allowed are based on your currency and billing location. Normally, you need to enter your credit card information. When you enter a credit card, this activates Post-Pay billing, which means that when you receive clicks or impressions, your credit card is debited.

Type your credit card information in the Primary Payment Details section. There are a large number of credit card types accepted by Google. You also can add backup payment details. This is important in case your trip to Rome causes your credit card to hit its upper limit and you don't want your ads to stop running. You can specify a backup credit card that is billed automatically when charges to your primary card are declined.

NOTE Entering your payment options automatically starts your ad display.

Finally, redeem any Google coupons by typing the promotional code and clicking Redeem.

Setting access privileges

By default, your Google AdWords account ID is the only one authorized to access your AdWords account. When you want others to have access to your account, click the Invite other users link. You are then prompted to type a list of names and e-mail addresses for the invited people. Click Continue to continue, or click the Invite more users link to add additional users.

After adding the list of users, Google asks you to format the personalized message that will be sent by e-mail to the people you are inviting. They must accept your invitation before they can have access to your account. The last section allows you to monitor your awaited invitation responses.

Setting up your account preferences

Your AdWords account preferences allow you set some basic information about your account and your business. You can change which of your Google accounts you will use to access your AdWords account. When you first set up your account, you had the choice of using your existing Google account or selecting a new userid and password to access just the AdWords account. This is where you can change that information.

Set your language and notification options. These are your options:

- **Display Language:** This is the language in which your AdWords account pages are displayed, not your ads.
- **Disapproved ads email notification:** Tell Google if you want to be notified by e-mail when your ads are disapproved so you can take immediate action.
- **Account performance suggestions:** Decide if you want Google to send you suggestions in e-mail on improving your ad performance.
- **Newsletters:** Opt in or out of receiving the Google AdWords newsletter in e-mail.
- **Google Market Research:** Choose whether you want to participate in Google market surveys or product tests.
- **Special Offers:** Tell Google whether you want to receive special AdWords promotional offers.

Click Save Changes to save your language and notification option selections.

There are a few more settings you can modify in the account preferences. Set the time zone of your location. Select your business type in the About Your Business section. When running pharmaceutical ads, you need to enter your PharmacyChecker ID.

The Tracking section allows you to turn auto-tagging on or off. Auto-tagging is turned on by default and allows Google to create performance reports and analyses using Google Analytics by adding a URL parameter called glcid into the URL used to access your Web site.

 Some Web sites do not allow arbitrary URL parameters such as the glcid. In that case, you need to turn auto-tagging off.

It's recommended that you keep auto-tagging turned on unless it is critical that it be turned off. Without auto-tagging, you can't receive important tracking statistics on your ad performance.

Finally, click the printer-friendly document link to view/print the Google AdWords Terms and Conditions.

Summary

When world consumers go to Google to find information, you want to make sure they find you when they are looking for whatever it is you're selling, whether it's a service or a product. Pay Google as little or as much as you want, and experience what many have already experienced: growth in their business.

Use the many tools that Google AdWords provides to update your ad campaigns, track their performance, see when ads have been disallowed, view performance against competitors, and suggest and create new keywords.

Entire books are being written about Google AdWords. This chapter gives you the essential information on launching ad campaigns and discovering the Google tools that help you manage those campaigns and track their performance. You can learn more about partnering with Google and becoming part of the Google network in the next chapter.

Chapter 35

Making Cents with AdSense

dSense is a Google program that lets you earn money by hosting Google ads on your Web site, 24/7, nonstop, all day, all night, 365 days a year. You've probably seen the "Ads by Google" boxes on Web sites. Whenever you see these, the owners of these Web sites are making money from these ads. For sites that generate a lot of traffic, it can be a substantial amount of money. There are tricks for improving the visibility of these ads so that people have a higher tendency to click the ads, which generates the money. Depending on the type of ad, simply the ad does not always generate income. The idea is that these ads drive people to advertiser's Web sites. It is simple to get started in this program, and within a couple of months you could be receiving your first check from Google.

Applying for an Account

To get started, you'll need an AdSense account. This is separate from your Google account. Google will need much more information so that they can pay you. First, point your Web browser to `www.google.com/adsense`. The first part of the AdSense application asks you about your Web site. First, type the URL of your site, and then enter the display language of your site by selecting a language from the drop-down list. At this point, don't worry that you have several Web sites you'd like to host ads on. Google needs one to get started. You can use your AdSense account for as many Web sites as you like.

NOTE When you're not certain if you have an AdSense account, try logging in with your Google account. If you do not have an AdSense account Google asks if you want to create one.

Next, you must complete the form that gives Google your contact information, including the following information:

- **Account type:** Individual or business. Select the business option only if your business has 20 or more employees; all others should select individual.

- **Country or Territory:** Select your country or territory from the drop-down list.

- **Payee name:** This is your name or the name of your business if you select business in the account type. Checks are made out in this name. This should be your full name and should not include initials.

- **Address:** Type your full mailing address. This is where the check is mailed, so it should be complete and correct. Fill in Address 1, optional Address 2, City, State, and Zip Code. The country should be the one you selected in Country or Territory. Your address cannot be a P.O. Box.

- **Phone:** Type your phone number including area code and country code when outside the United States. The fax field is optional.

- **Email preference:** Choose whether you want Google to send you service announcements regarding AdSense.

- **Products:** Select AdSense for content, AdSense for search, or both.

- **Agree to the AdSense policies:** Basically, you can't put AdSense units on porn sites or "Click this ad" pages. You agree not to cheat Google by clicking the ads to earn money. You agree that you can accept checks under the payee name you entered and that you have read and you consent to the AdSense Program Policies.

When you finish filling in the form, click Submit Information. Your information is transmitted securely (encrypted) to Google.

When your account is accepted and you are ready to log in to your account, you can begin creating ad units to appear on your Web page (and start making money). Begin by clicking the AdSense Setup tab, as shown in Figure 35.1.

FIGURE 35.1

Get started by selecting the type of AdSense unit you want to install on your site.

In the AdSense Setup tab, you can install one of three types of products. An AdSense product is the small display, similar to the three shown in Figure 35.1, that can appear on your Web page. Some products pay money simply when someone views the ad displayed. These are called impressions, and you are paid based on the number of people who view certain types of ad units on your page.

Configuring AdSense for Content

AdSense for content has two types of services: ad units and link units. With ad units, you can select to receive text and image ads, text ads only, or both. Link units display a list of topic links relevant to your site's content that the viewer can click to view related ads.

Selecting a format

Your first step is to select the format. There are three horizontal formats, three vertical formats, and six square formats to choose from. See the section "Customizing the Appearance" later in this chapter, for format recommendations.

Choosing a color palette

Now it's time to select a color palette, or you can create your own. Creating your own is simple. If you know the exact six-character hexadecimal color, you can type it in the text box next to the # sign or simply click in the color box and select a color. You can watch the sample ad unit on the left as you scroll over the colors. You also can select from the list of preconfigured AdSense palettes. And you can choose to have multiple palettes rotate.

To use a rotating palette, select Use multiple palettes and then select one to four palettes from the list of AdSense palettes that appears. To select more than one palette, Ctrl-click or Command-click with your mouse. Your selections appear on the left.

Specifying a placeholder

You can choose what to display when no relevant ads are available. These are your choices:

- Show public service ads
- Show non-Google ads from another URL
- Fill space with a solid color

The default behavior is to have Google fill the space with a public service advertisement. You also can choose to fill the space with an image or a Web page.

 **Be sure that images selected for display in the Google AdSense ad unit match in size and dimension.**

To fill the ad unit with a static image, type the full URL that points to the image you want displayed. All users see is a pretty picture, but they can't click it.

Filling the ad unit with a clickable image takes a little more work. You can use the same image, but it must first be placed on a Web page that you host on your site. When you create your Web page, you must do these important things:

- Enclose your image tag `<img>` in an anchor tag `<a href></a>` to make your image clickable and act as a link.
- Add `target = "_top"`.

519

Here is an example:

```
<a href="http://www.mypage.com/myad.html" target="_top"><img
src="http://www.mypage.com/mypic.gif"><a/>
```

This example displays an image that, when clicked, loads a new Web page containing any content you might think of.

Use absolute URLs when creating your clickable Web page. Absolute URLs are full URLs (http://www.something.com/graphic.gif) rather than partial URLs (/graphic.gif).

Selecting a tracking channel

When you have created channels, you may select a channel from the list by clicking the add link next to the channel name. You also may choose to create a new channel by clicking the Add new channel link below the ad unit. You also may select the Manage channels link to configure your channels for better tracking of your AdSense ad units.

 **You can select up to five custom channels to track performance in areas such as page position.**

Click Continue to see the AdSense code that Google creates for you based on your configuration. Copy and paste this code into your Web page in the location where you want the ads to appear.

Adding a link unit

Another way to display AdSense for content is by using the Link unit. These units display topic links rather than display ads. Viewers of your Web site can see several topics related to your site's content and can click the topic to see ads related to their topic choices.

When you are given the choice between creating an Ad unit or a Link unit, select Link unit when you want your viewers to have the ability to "drill down" and find ads related to a specific topic.

The steps for creating a Link unit are the same as for creating an Ad unit. Select a format from the drop-down list. Then select or create a color scheme, viewing the sample on the left. Finally, choose what to display if there are no relevant ads, and then click Continue to view the code you copy into your Web site's HTML code.

Adding AdSense for Search

AdSense for Search is a way to make money when visitors to your site perform Web and site searches from a search box on your site. Begin to create an AdSense for Search box from your AdSense account by clicking the AdSense Setup tab and then clicking the AdSense for search link.

You must first select a search type from these choices:

- Google WebSearch
- Google WebSearch + SiteSearch

The Google WebSearch presents visitors to your site with a Google Search box where they can do Web searches as they would from the Google main search page. With Google WebSearch + SiteSearch you can provide Web search and site searching of three additional sites that you specify.

After you select Google WebSearch, additional options appear. A sample search box is displayed so you can watch how your configuration changes will appear. You can set the following:

- **Logo type:** This displays the Google logo above the search box or Google Search in the button.
- **Search button:** Choose to have the search button below the search box changing the shape of the box.
- **Background color:** Set the background color to white, black, or gray.
- **Length of text box:** Configure the number of characters displayable in the text box. This does not limit the user to the number of characters that can be typed.

In addition to hosting the search box on your site, you can tailor the results to favor topics related to your site's content. Select the Site-favored search check box. Set additional configuration items such as your site's language. Set the language of the search box by selecting a language from the drop-down list.

The configuration setting offers three choices:

- **Open search results page:** This allows you to see your results in the same window, thereby having users navigate away from your Web site.
- **See the results in a new Google window:** This still takes users from your site, but it leaves your site open in the original window.
- **Open results within my own site:** This option is optimal, but takes a little more work.

The steps for setting this up are covered in the next section.

The last configuration option is to set your site's encoding. Select an encoding type from the list. If you are unsure, the most generic type of encoding is found last in the list, Unicode (UTF-8). Click Continue to proceed to the next page.

On the next wizard page, you are asked to configure how the AdSense search results page will appear. You can configure the following search page items:

- Upload your logo, which will appear on the top of the search results page.
- Specify where your logo, when clicked, takes the visitor.
- Set the color palette to a Google palette, or create one yourself.
- Choose the country or territory so that Google can use the correct domain when specifying search results.
- Turn SafeSearch on to limit the searcher's ability to see adult or offensive content. This is particularly important if your site is geared toward children.
- Specify a tracking channel so you can better track your results.

> **TIP** If you want people to use the search box, don't make it too difficult to find by having it blend in with your site too well.

After you set these configuration settings, click Continue to move on to the next page. Here, you can view the code you need to copy into your Web page at the place you want the search box to appear.

Displaying AdSense search results on your site

Before you can implement AdSense for search so that the results appear on your site, you need to prepare the Web page where visitors who click the ads will see the results.

Create a new Web page on your site where viewers of AdSense for search will view the results. Make note of the URL of this new page because you will need it during the AdSense setup. This new page will be referred to in the setup steps as the "results page," but you can call it anything you want.

Log in to your AdSense account, and follow these steps:

1. Click the AdSense Setup tab.

2. Select AdSense for search as the product.

3. In the first step of the setup, scroll down to More options and click the option button marked Open results within my own site.

4. Type the URL of the results page you created earlier.

5. Configure the appearance of your search box and results.

6. Copy the code found in the text box labeled Your search box code, and paste it into the HTML source of the page where you want the AdSense search box displayed. This is not the results page.

7. Copy the code found in the text box labeled Your search results code, and paste it into the HTML source of the results page.

8. Save both of your Web pages.

TIP   People who have hosted both AdSense for content and AdSense for search note that the revenue stream is significantly lower for AdSense for search.

Referrals

When you want to make extra cash beyond all the money you're already making by hosting the Google network ads, you also can place referral buttons on your page to refer people to products and services.

Log in to your AdSense account, and click the AdSense Setup tab. Click the Referrals link. You will see a list of products Google would like you to refer your Web site visitors to. These include:

- Google AdSense
- Google AdWords
- Firefox plus Google Toolbar
- Google Pack
- Picasa

Select the product you want to refer from the list by clicking the icon or the option button. Click Continue.

1. One of the choices you must make is labeled: Show referrals in. Select a language from the drop-down list.

2. Select the style of referral ad. Table 35.1 lists the various referral styles.

TABLE 35.1

Referral Ad Styles

Style	Shape
Text	Horizontal text as link
110 x 32	Small horizontal button
120 x 60	Tall horizontal button
180 x 60	Wide and tall button
480 x 60	Banner button
125 x 125	Square button
120 x 240	Large vertical button

3. Select a channel, or choose to create a new channel. Click Continue. Your AdSense Referral code appears in the text box. You can copy and paste this code into any Web page that complies with the Google program policies. See how it looks in Figure 35.2.

FIGURE 35.2

Place a referral where it will be seen so people will click on it.

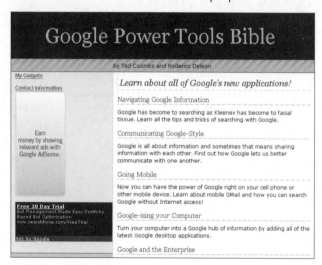

Using Channels

AdSense channels are designed to help you find out where AdSense is earning you the most money. The AdSense channels give you a deeper level of reporting than the standard AdSense revenue reporting. The following information is tracked for each channel:

- Impressions
- CTR (Click Through Rate)
- CPM (Cost Per Thousand Impressions)
- Earning Statistics for a particular channel

There are two kinds of channels: URL Channels and Custom Channels. URL Channels are for domains, subdomains, and page-specific reporting. With a URL channel, you can learn which of your URLs, pages, or resources are earning the most money. Custom channels, on the other hand, are designed for much finer detail, including ad placement or a particular ad unit.

Creating a URL channel is easy. After you log in to your AdSense account, click the Channels link, type a name for your channel, and click OK.

To create a Custom Channel, click the AdSense Setup tab, click the Channels link, and then click Add new custom channel.

Customizing the Appearance

Your goal in hosting an AdSense unit is to make as much money as possible by having people clicking in the AdSense unit, which earns you money. You will want to customize it for optimal performance.

Choosing an appearance format

Google experts say that the wider ad formats tend to outperform the taller ones. This is because people tend to absorb more text visually in a longer text stream. Google recommends these three formats most often:

- 336x280 large rectangle
- 300x250 inline rectangle
- 160x600 wide skyscraper

You want visitors to your site to see the ad, so selecting a color palette that blends in with the color scheme of your site is not the best idea. This can confuse the visitor into thinking it is part of your site and create "ad blindness."

Using themed ad units

Drawing attention to an ad on your page involves change and color recognition. Google can change the look of the ads on your site based on certain holiday periods, thereby creating *themed ads* or ads that are decorated to commemorate certain local and worldwide holidays. The holiday period decoration selected for display on your page is geographically chosen based on the IP address of your Web site. For example, red, white, and blue themes may accompany Fourth of July ads for sites within the United States.

To set up themed ad units, follow these steps:

1. Click the My Account tab.
2. Edit the Add type preferences.
3. Select Enable themed ad units when available.
4. Save your changes.

Selecting a background color

Selecting a background color can help overcome ad blindness. When the area behind your AdSense ad has a light background, consider ad backgrounds that complement or blend with the background. For example, choosing a color used to highlight other portions of your page might make a good background color. For ads that have dark backgrounds behind them, choose a contrasting, lighter color. It doesn't have to be white and can be a complementing color, but it should just be lighter than the dark background.

You may consider changing the background color from time to time to draw the attention of frequent visitors to your site. You can rotate the background colors among four different colors by selecting Use multiple palettes and selecting four of the preconfigured color palettes in the AdSense ad setup.

Selecting a location

Consider moving your ad from time to time so that frequent visitors to your site are drawn to the ad. Static locations can cause the frequent visitor to overlook the ad. One thing to keep in mind is that you don't want visitors to your site to scroll down in order to see the Google ad unit. Position the ad unit, text unit, or referral so that it always appears on the upper portion of your page.

Optimizing Your Web Site

For best click-through results, you want to optimize your Web site. Remember that you can't host AdSense units on pages that entice or tell the visitors to click the ads. You can, however, position the ad, highlight the ad, set colors and borders, and add graphics such that the user's attention is drawn to the ad. Google AdSense ads are designed to complement your site's content, not be the focus of the content.

Excited about AdSense and want to host as many ads as possible? Great idea! You can have multiple ads on a single page, but within limits. You can have a total of three ad units + two search boxes + one link unit + four referrals.

Managing Your Account

Managing your Google AdSense account is important if you want to continue receiving revenue from the ads that appear on your Web site. To manage your account, sign in to AdSense and click the My Account tab.

To see a quick summary of how much Google has paid you for your efforts, click the Payment History link located in the bar across the top of the tab. To notify Google of your tax information, click the Tax Information link, also located in the bar at the top of the tab. Here, you can fill out a W-9 form or select from a number of other forms, particularly when you or your business is not located in the United States or not subject to IRS tax collection.

Your account settings include these options:

- **Login information:** Change your Google account information outside of the AdSense account management page.
- **Language and Contact Preferences:** These are important if you want to receive additional information.
- **Payee Information:** This is important when you want to get paid. This is the address where payments can be sent unless you select EFT in the Payment Details section.
- **Payment Details:** Choose how you want to receive payment — in check form or by electronic funds transfer (EFT).
- **Payment Holding:** Select to have Google hold your payments until you want them released. This can help you with tax considerations, or perhaps you're on vacation and don't want checks for millions of dollars sitting in your unopened mail.
- **Ad Type Preference:** Select whether you want text and image ads or both, and whether to enable themed ads.
- **Onsite Advertiser Sign-Up:** Allow visitors to your site to sign up to be advertisers.
- **Property Info:** See a display of your currently created ad types, search boxes, and referrals.

Managing your information is one important task you should keep up on. Consider using Google Calendar to schedule a time to check up on your account settings and to read the Google AdSense Reports.

Reviewing AdSense Reports

Not many things are as much fun as reading reports about money that your Web site is making for you without any effort on your part. Log in to your AdSense account as many times as you like to see current reports.

Click the Reports tab if it does not appear by default after logging in. The first thing you see is Today's Earnings followed by the amount of your earnings for the current day, displayed in the currency you selected when you set up your account. When you first click the Reports tab, you are viewing the Overview.

Overview

In the Overview, below Today's Earnings, you find a link for viewing your payment history. Click the View payment history link to see all the payments for the date range you specify. Clicking this link takes you to the My Accounts tab. You need to click the Reports tab to continue viewing the report.

Select the period for which you want to see your earnings. You have these choices:

- today
- yesterday
- last 7 days
- this month (supply *month name*)
- last month (supply *month name*)
- all time (from the time you first signed up for AdSense, not from time of the Big Bang, which is currently in scientific dispute)

In the boxes below the period selection, you see the detail for each of the ad types, including AdSense for content, AdSense for search, and Referrals. Here, you can view how many page impressions, clicks CTR, your page's eCPM (effective CPM), signups, conversions, and your earnings. These totals should adjust based on the period you choose to view.

In the Quick Reports section, you can view reports by clicking the link of the report description. There are four AdSense for content reports and three AdSense for search reports. Click the link, or click the small <u>csv</u> link to receive the report in comma-separated-value format suitable for uploading into spreadsheets and other reporting tools.

Advanced Reports

To create and view advanced AdSense reports, click the <u>Advanced Reports</u> link in the Reports tab. Creating a custom report simply requires you to answer a few questions about the report you want to create. Fill in the following form fields:

- **Choose product:** Select which AdSense product you want to report on — AdSense for content, AdSense for search, or Referrals.
- **Choose a date range:** Select today, or specify begin and end dates.
- **Show data by:** Report by Web page, by ad unit type, or by individual ad.
- **Show:** Aggregate all the data together, or break it out by channel.

Click Show Report to view your custom report.

Report Manager

Manage all your custom reports in the Report Manager. The <u>Report Manager</u> link is found along the top bar of the Reports tab. Custom reports are created by saving advanced reports with a report name.

Select the custom report name from the list, and set its frequency. These are your choices for setting the frequency with which the report runs:

- **Never:** Never automatically run the report.
- **Daily:** Run the report every day.
- **Send to:** Send the report to the recipient whose e-mail address is listed here. You can click the <u>edit addresses</u> link to quickly add a new recipient address.
- **Format:** Choose from CSV or CSV–Excel format.

Click Save Changes, or choose to delete the selected report by clicking Delete checked reports.

Site Diagnostics

When you manage many Web sites and ad locations, you'll want to use the Site Diagnostics tool. As Google crawls through Web sites in order to display relevant ads, it may find problems or issues and it may block your page. The crawl report includes the following information:

- The blocked URL
- The reason it was blocked
- The date of the last crawl attempt
- The number of failed attempts

Two of the biggest reasons for site blocking are when the crawler fails to find the URL and when a `robots.txt` file blocks the crawler. Fix either or both of these issues to correct your site's problem.

Summary

Google has created an excellent partner program for hosting ads on your Web page and paying you for it. Google, a multibillion-dollar company, makes most of its money from ad revenue. You can share in that revenue by becoming a serious AdSense user. This chapter showed you how to create and configure AdSense for content, AdSense for search, and Referral ad units. Get them on your Web page now so the AdSense reporting shows you an increase in your net worth, almost immediately. To stay on top of the AdSense program, participate in both the AdSense Blog and the AdSense Forum. To get a much better picture of your Web site and its earning potential, the best tool is Google Analytics, which is covered in the next chapter.

Chapter 36

Making Decisions with Google Analytics

The best way to know what's happening on your Web site is to analyze the information Google makes available to you through the Google Analytics product. You can learn important information about how people are using your Web site and see what pages they visit and for how long and what they are doing on those pages. You no longer have to rely on endless Web server log files and meaningless hit counters.

Google purchased an expensive product in 2005 and, like so many other of its products, made it freely available. With Google Analytics, you can find out how well your AdWords are working to bring people to your site.

CROSS-REF   See Chapter 34 for more about AdWords.

IN THIS CHAPTER

Creating a Google Analytics account

Configuring your Web site for analysis

Setting goals to achieve

Focusing your Analytics data using filters

Seeing the Analytics results

Understanding the Basics

By adding a small amount of Javascript code to each of the Web pages you want analyzed, Google can track statistics about visits to those Web pages. The statistics are stored on the Google Analytics site indefinitely for your analysis using the Google Analytics tools. The following information is sent to Google about the page visit:

- The IP address of the computer visiting your page, which is important for information about the geographic location of the user

- The Web browser the visitor is using: Internet Explorer, Firefox, Opera, AOL, and so on

- The page request history, made possible by a cookie on the visitor's site and telling you how long the visitor was on each page and the path he took through your site

Imagine being able to know how many of the visitors to your site used the Firefox browser. This can help Web developers decide which technologies are best used to display content. Each browser has advantages and deficiencies. Now you can take advantage of that knowledge in planning future technology decisions.

Knowing the geographic location patterns of your site's visitors tells you whether your AdWords targets are working. When you purchase AdWords ads in Google Search, you can specify geographic locations. If you specify St. Louis but most of your visitors are from Nashville, you may have some issues to deal with. Perhaps you could take advantage of the Tennessee interest in your site and switch your advertising. Remember, it's always easier to take something that is already working and make it work better than it is to take something not working and make it work.

It's important to know the path the user takes through your site. You need to find out if people who purchase your products leave after visiting the Thank You page and whether they ever return, and you want to find out the time duration between visits to your site. Are people visiting every day? Do they wait six months between visits? Find out how well your attempt to get people to continue using your site after shopping is working. Learn which paths people take from your home page. You may be surprised to learn that people are landing on pages other than your home page as their first page. Often articles and important information indexed in Google causes people to visit your site. You want to know if this informational page leads them to visit the rest of your site. Answer these questions and many others by using the powerful Analytics reporting tools. But first, you need to sign up.

Signing Up for Google Analytics

Point your Web browser to `www.google.com/analytics`, and click the <u>Sign Up</u> link, as shown in Figure 36.1. If you are not already signed in to your Google Account, you are prompted to do so. This launches a short page of information where Google tells you that to improve the return on your investment, it wants to help you bring more of the visitors you really want to your Web site.

FIGURE 36.1

Get started with Google Analytics by clicking the <u>Sign Up</u> link.

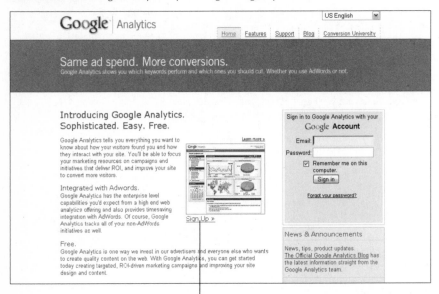

Click here to sign up

The next step is to again click Sign Up, which launches the New Account Setup Wizard. Begin by typing the URL of your Web site, the name of the account, your country or territory, and the time zone of your site.

NOTE Google tracks only the first 5 million visitors to your site unless you have an active AdWords account. In that case, Google Analytics tracks an unlimited number of visitors.

Enter the time zone of the location of your Web server. This may be different than your location. The reason for entering the Web server's time zone and not your own (unless they are the same) is that you'll want to know what times of day people are visiting your site. If your visitors all arrive at approximately the same time, you may want to consider ways to distribute the Web server load during that peak time. You don't want the visitor experience to be one of a slow-loading site. You also can see what times of day people are visiting from different geographic locations. For sites with worldwide appeal, you can see when visitors from around the globe are checking out your site.

The next step in the setup wizard asks you to type your last and first names, your phone number, and your country or territory selected from a drop-down list. Clicking Continue brings you to the page where you must read and agree to the terms and conditions by selecting the check box. Click Create New Account when you are ready.

You are then presented with the Javascript code that you need to copy and paste into the HTML of each of the Web pages you want to track. Paste this code just before the end of the page, right before the </BODY> tag. It should appear as the last thing in the Web page.

You can check the status of your code installation by logging in to Google Analytics and clicking Check Status found on the Analytics Settings page. This validates the Javascript found in the pages installed on your site. After your pages have been verified, you see a notice at the top of the Analytics Settings page that tells you that Analytics has been successfully installed and it is waiting for data.

Now, be patient. Your Google Analytics reports are updated every 24 hours. So you can't instantly see reports after adding your Javascript code. Check back in 24 hours.

Managing Web Site Profiles

You can have many Web site profiles. When you first start out adding Analytics to a single site, one profile appears in the Profile Manager. If you add Analytics tracking for more than one domain, click the Add Website Profile link at the top left of the Website Profiles box and follow these steps:

1. Select Add a profile for a new domain.
2. Type the URL of the new domain. Do not type individual subdirectory names.
3. Enter the country in which the Web server is located.
4. Enter the time zone of your Web server.
5. Click Finish.

After you finish adding the new domain, you see it listed in the Website Profiles box, as shown in Figure 36.2.

You can add a profile for either a new or an existing domain name. You may want to create additional profiles for existing domain names in order to specify different goals and provide different filtering. There is more on goals and filtering to come.

FIGURE 36.2

You can track multiple domains using Analytics.

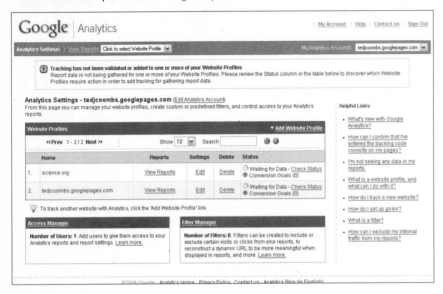

Web site status

Each profile has a status listed in the Website Profiles box. After you install your Javascript for a profile, the status should read Waiting for Data. Check the status of the profile. You will find one of the status messages listed below:

- **Waiting for Data:** A new installation is waiting to receive data.
- **Tracking Not Installed:** The tracking code cannot be detected.
- **Receiving Data:** A healthy installation is sending data to Analytics.
- **Tracking Unknown:** There is an unknown reason why Analytics is not receiving data. Perhaps the Javascript was incorrectly installed.

For additional information about troubleshooting sites that don't send data, visit the Analytics Help center at www.google.com/support/analytics/.

Editing and deleting profiles

Click the Edit link next to the profile name to edit important profile features. You are redirected to the Profile Settings page, the top portion of which displays information about the URL.

Most importantly, when you edit the profile, you can set conversion goals. You can set up to four goals for each profile. The goals are labeled G1 through G4. You can see in the table a column labeled Active Goal that tells you which goals are off and which are on.

Reaching the goal

Goals are reached when someone lands on a particular page, for example, the Thank you for shopping my business page or a checkout page. On non-e-commerce Web sites, the goal page might be when someone visits the page that explains your services or displays a list of your products. When you set up a goal, the first step is to type the URL of the goal page. Then you give the goal a meaningful name such as Purchase or Ad View. Select whether the goal is active by selecting the option button. You may want to create goals that you turn on and off depending on seasonal changes in your Web site. You can then optionally define one or more *funnels*.

Creating the funnel

Funnels are lists of URLs that a visitor to your site travels along to reach your destination page. This helps you determine when and where people fall out of the funnel on their way to the goal. A good example of a Web site that has this type of funnel is the Kelly Blue Book site at www.kbb.com. To see the current value of a new or used car, you must take several steps in defining the vehicle make, model, condition, features, and so on. If your site uses a number of steps like this to reach its ultimate goal, you may want to create a tracking funnel so you can see where people lose interest or where ads placed on pages pull users away from the goal.

When you edit a goal, you find a section labeled Define Funnel (optional). You can define up to ten steps to reach your goal. More than ten steps is probably excessive, and you should consider combining steps. Type the URL of the page that defines the first step, and then give it a friendly name by which you can refer to it later, for example, LOGIN. You can then tell Google if this is a required step by selecting the Required step check box. For example, if you require someone to log in before he can take the next step, then perhaps the page he reaches after a successful login defines the first step, so you would select Required step.

After someone logs in, he may enter the funnel toward the goal. For example, a funnel may define a wizard that someone uses to define a product or service. The goal might be the purchase of the product or service or a request for more information.

Continue adding URLs that define steps toward the goal, giving each step a friendly name. When you complete the list of URLs, you can establish these additional settings:

- **Case sensitive:** URLs typed by the user must conform to a specific uppercase or lowercase, or they are not considered in the funnel. This keeps users from typing URLs to enter the funnel and having it appear as though they entered the funnel.

- **Match Type:** Use one of these match types:
  - Exact Match
  - Head Match
  - Regular Expression Match

- **Goal value:** Set a fixed value for reaching the goal. You also can set a variable value for use with shopping carts. When tracking e-commerce values, leave the Goal value blank.

Save your funnel, and it appears listed below your goals. You can create several funnels for tracking different paths through your Web site.

Tracking E-Commerce

Using Google Analytics to track your e-commerce transactions can provide an extremely powerful reporting tool to your Web-based business. Detailed financial history can be tracked against Web site performance and geography. For example, you can find out what area of the country is spending most of the money on your site and which of your pages interests your customers the most.

Enabling e-commerce tracking on your site is a two-step process. To begin, follow these steps:

1. Log in to your Analytics account.
2. Find the profile you want to track, and click the <u>Edit</u> link.
3. On the Profile Settings page, click the <u>edit</u> link along the top of the Main Website Profile information.
4. Select Yes next to E-Commerce Website. You may notice that in the Available Reports section the E-Commerce Analysis report is selected.
5. Click the Save Changes button.

You have completed the first step. To continue, you must be able to edit your e-commerce Web pages so that you can include special Javascript tracking code into the receipt page. The simplest way to add this code is to place the following into the HTML of your receipt Web page.

> **TIP**   Your receipt may be generated by scripts and may not appear as a separate Web page. If that is the case, you need to edit the script that generates the receipt to write this code into the body of the receipt page.

```
<script src="http://www.google-analytics.com/urchin.js"
type="text/javascript">
</script>
<script type="text/javascript">
 _uacct="UA-xxxx-x";
 urchinTracker();
</script>
```

The _uacct="UA-xxxx-x" in the preceding code needs to be replaced with your actual Analytics account number. You can find this in the tracking script that you added to each of your pages. You aren't finished editing the HTML code, however. You next need to add an invisible form.

Next, somewhere in the receipt below the tracking code, the following lines need to be written by your engine. Everything in italics should be replaced by actual values, as described in the Parameter Reference that follows.

```
<form style="display:none;" name="utmform">
<textarea id="utmtrans">UTM:T|order-id|affiliation|
total amt|tax amt|shipping amt|city|state|country UTM:I|order-
id|product id/sku|product name|category|price|
quantity </textarea>
</form>
```

The form is made invisible by setting the display parameter to none. The invisible form is then named utmform.

The form is written in a single textarea tag and begins with a single transaction line, starting with UTM:T. The *order-id* is your company's identification for this order. You also can set an optional partner affiliation field. If you don't set this, you still need to leave this place blank like this: ||.

Type the *total amt* of the transaction, making certain not to use commas in the number. Type the *tax amt* and *shipping amt*. These may be zero based on whether you are charging tax or shipping. Type the *city*, *state*, and *country* associated with this order. Google does not need an exact address, only a general location for geographical tracking. These parameters should all appear on a single line in your text area. This ends the transaction line portion. You should now enter as many line transactions UTM:I as you have items in the transaction, one per line.

For each item line, type the *order-id,* which should match the *order-id* in the transaction line. Next, type the *product id/sku*. This is your company's product identification or stock keeping unit. Follow this with the actual text name of the product, Rubbon Hair Gel, for example. Type a category for your product if it has one. Type the unit *price* and the *quantity* ordered.

> **NOTE** Make certain to close your `<textarea>` tag with `</textarea>`.

After the form is submitted, you must take one additional step in the next page, calling a special function that records the transaction. This is called the `utmSetTrans` function. You can set this function in two different ways. The simplest is placing a call to this function in the `<body>` tag of the Web page loaded after the form submission. It should look like this:

```
<body onLoad="javascript:__utmSetTrans()">
```

Another way you can call the `utmSetTrans` function is by creating a separate Javascript tag making certain it is called after the form:

```
<script language="text/javascript">
__utmSetTrans();
< /script>
```

This completes the setup necessary for e-commerce tracking. It's a little complex, and if you are not comfortable with script programming, you may need to enlist assistance in this step. It's worth it for the value you receive from Analytics.

Creating and Applying Filters

You can apply filters to profiles to help narrow the area of analysis to specific areas of your Web site, include otherwise excluded matching clicks, or make dynamic URLs more meaningful in Analytics reports. In the Analytics Setting section, find the subsection labeled Filters Applied to Profile. Click the + Add Filter link along the top bar of this section to get started.

In the Add Filter to Profile page, begin by selecting whether to apply a new filter or an existing filter to your profile by selecting one of the option buttons.

Follow these steps to begin creating a new filter:

1. Select Add New Filter for Profile.

2. Type a meaningful name for your filter in the Filter Name box. Create a name that explains your filter and remember that you can use it later to filter other profiles.

3. Select the type of filter you want to create. These are the Filter type choices:

   ▪ Exclude all traffic from a domain

   ▪ Exclude all traffic from an IP address

   ▪ Include only traffic to a subdirectory

   ▪ Custom filter

4. Specify a domain name as a *regular expression*. Regular expressions are phrases containing special characters that build *matches*. Matches are simply when two separate phrases somehow match each other. The special characters included in a regular expression are called *wild cards*.

Wild cards are named for the special cards like the Joker in playing-card games. When you say, "Deuces are wild." you are saying that all the 2 cards can represent any card you want them to represent. For example, *.JPG represents all filenames ending in .jpg. The * is a wild card used to represent all possibilities. So, `myfile*.JPG` is a regular expression that matches when filenames begin with `myfile`, followed by all possibilities, and ends with `.JPG`. There are several other characters used by Analytics to build regular expressions. They are explained in Table 36.1.

NOTE   It has been said that, "Regular expressions are a means by which IT people confuse non-IT people."

An important character you must know about when building filters is the escape character — the forward slash. You must use the escape character / to specify periods ("dots") in a domain name, or IP address. For example, `www/.mydomain/.com` or `192/.168/.120/.151`. You must use the escape character to identify the literal period because the dot has a special meaning in regular expressions. It means "match any other single character."

The domain name or IP address you type in this form represents the domain from which you want data included or excluded. Remember to use the escape character to escape periods. This is required.

TABLE 36.1

Wild Cards for Regular Filter Expressions

Character	Description
.	Match to any other single character
*	Match to zero or more of the previous items
+	Match to one or more of the previous items
?	Match to zero or one of the previous items
()	Designate contents of parentheses as an item
[]	Match to an item in this list
-	Creates a range in a list
|	Logical OR match if *this* matches OR *that* matches
&	Logical AND match only if *this* matches AND *that* matches
^	Anchor character — match all to the beginning
$	Anchor character — match all to the end
/	Escape character used to include literal character such as the . (dot) in a domain name

Entire books have been written about building regular expressions. It takes some work to become comfortable creating these expressions. Be patient and experiment creating your filter expressions. One of the common filter expressions you may want to create is one that filters out all the hits from your own domain. Hits from your own domain may not accurately represent true traffic patterns to your site or may include testing data.

For more information about regular expressions, you can read the Wikipedia page at `http://en.wikipedia.org/wiki/Regular_expressions`.

Creating include and exclude filters

Include and exclude filters are used to focus your report by excluding unwanted user visits to your site, or *hits*, from your report. The names of the filters, include and exclude, are a little confusing because both are used to narrow the number of hits in a report by excluding data from the report, but how they work to accomplish this is different.

When patterns match in an exclude filter, the hit is ignored (not included in the report). An include filter tells Google which hits to keep. Patterns that match are included in the report and those not matching are ignored. You can't mix and match expression types. You either use exclude filters or include filters.

You can create exclude filters using a single expression with multiple pattern matches, or you can create several exclude expressions. When several patterns are used in a single expression, they are grouped together using the logical OR, found in Table 36.1. Only one of the patterns in the expression needs to match in an exclude filter expression for the hit to be excluded.

Building include filters works the same way, creating a single expression with multiple pattern matches or creating several include expressions. This is where the similarity stops. Unlike exclude expressions, all the patterns in an include expression must match to be included. Otherwise, the hit is ignored.

Building search and replace filters

Search and replace filters are used to replace information gathered by Analytics, such as part numbers or meaningless directory names, with text that will be meaningful in a report. For example, if you run an e-commerce site and you track part numbers, replace part number *x123* with **Barber Chair, black**.

Using advanced filters

Analytics allows you to combine fields of information into a single field so that they are more informative. You can do this using advanced filters. Advanced filters put two or more fields, or parts of fields, together using *constructor expressions*. Constructor expressions are regular expressions that take information from two extracted fields and create a single field.

Analytics Reporting

So far, this chapter has been about preparing Analytics to create reports. After the tracking code is in your page, Google is tracking statistics, and you have set up any desired goals, funnels, and filters, then you are ready to view your reports.

After you've logged in to your Analytics account, select a domain from the drop-down list and click the <u>View Reports</u> link located in the top orange bar. There are three "dashboards" depending on your role within your company. You can view data of interest to executives by selecting the Executive dashboard. View reports of interest to the marketing department by selecting Marketer from the drop-down list. For reports of interest to the Webmaster, select the Webmaster dashboard from the list.

Most of the reports described in this section require a date range. Select a date range for any of your reports by using the calendar found in the left column of the View Reports page.

Executive reports

The Executive reports include many of the summary reports from the other areas and give a good idea of the general performance of the Web site. This section lists each of the reports with a brief explanation.

Executive Overview

The Executive Overview, of immediate interest to executives and the Web designer, displays four panels. The Visits and Pageviews panel plots visits and page views by day. The Visits by New and Returning panel shows a 3D pie chart of new visits to your site compared to returning visits. The Geo Map Overlay displays a graphic representation of where most of your visitors are located throughout the world. The lower-right panel, Visits by Source, displays a 3D pie chart of how visitors end up on your site, directly or by some referring Web site.

Conversion Summary

The Conversion Summary report, measuring the effectiveness of your Web site, is most useful once you set goals. See the section "Reaching the Goal" later in this chapter. This report shows you visit results over a specified time period. See whether visits to your site have increased or decreased over the period. Also, find out how many visits resulted in conversions (reached specified goals). You can graphically see the increase or decrease represented by green and red arrows, respectively, and an actual percentage. It looks a little like a typical stock market report.

This report tracks both changes in visits to your site by goal as well as the actual conversion rate of each goal.

Marketing Summary

The Marketing Summary report tracks the effectiveness of your company's online marketing efforts. This report is similar to the Conversion Summary, but it adds an additional layer of information: the way in which people land on your site. This is broken into three categories. The first category displays visits and goal visits for the top five sources of visitors to your site. The second category tracks the top five keywords used to search, find, and ultimately visit your site. The third category tracks the effectiveness of your top five campaigns.

Visitors can end up on your site in a number of ways. Direct visitors type the URL of your site into their Web browsers, or if you're lucky, select it from the browser's favorites list. They do not first visit search engines or other sites with links to your page. Referral visitors end up on your site because they clicked a link from a non-ad-related link. Consider these as "freebies." You paid no cost to get these people on your site. Then there are people who visit your site because of your campaigns. There are two types of campaign visitors: those tagged with campaign variables and those not tagged. This report can help you determine the financial effectiveness of your AdWords campaigns.

Content Summary

The Content Summary shows the effectiveness of your Web site in attracting and maintaining user visits. You can track the effectiveness of several variables based on percentage increase or decrease over a specified time period.

See the number of visits to your top five entrances (pages people first visit when coming to your site) as well as the number of people who bounce ("Hmmm, not interesting, I'm outta here.") and immediately leave your site from the entrance page.

The statistics for your top five exit pages also are shown in this report. An exit page is the one where people generally leave your site. See the increase or decrease in exits from these pages and the number of overall pageviews compared to the number of pageviews where people exited. It is very helpful to see where people are leaving your site.

The number of visits to your top five content pages also displays the approximate length of time people spend on those pages. This is calculated from the time the page is loaded until the next page is loaded. It's approximate because some people might go to lunch while visiting a site, come back, and then continue to the next page. The only way this may change is if your site has session tracking and automatically logs a user out after a certain amount of idle time.

Find out if people are actually reading your content or simply hopping through your pages toward some goal. Find out what content visitors find interesting and whether more or fewer people are visiting those content pages over time. If you are running an online magazine, this is a great way to find out which authors or articles are most popular.

Site Overlay

The Site Overlay report, shown in Figure 36.3, displays your Web site and allows you to navigate through it page by page. As you move through the pages, you can view updated statistics on traffic to the page and conversion rates.

FIGURE 36.3

Navigate from page to page within your site using the Site Overlay.

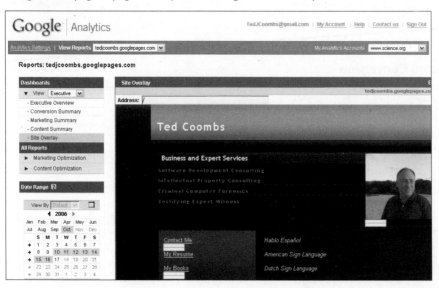

View the number of clicks on the page, the number of clicks compared to the number of clicks over a period of time, the number of clicks you've defined as a goal, and an average score given to links most commonly visited just prior to clicking a goal link that leads to a high-value conversion.

Marketer reports

The reports of interest to people involved in marketing a site are included in this section. These reports show trends in Web site success as compared to your marketing efforts. Find out things like trends in cost per click, your keyword successes, or how well people manage to stay in funnels as defined by marketing goals. The Marketer Overview and Site Overlay reports are the same as those found in the Executive dashboard.

All CPC Analysis

This report shows you which of your marketing programs are most effective in driving traffic to your site. You can view this report as either a pie chart or a bar chart, providing statistics all the way down to the keyword level.

The CPC Analysis report shows you the number of times your ad was displayed, the number of times the ad was clicked, the number of goals reached after an ad was clicked, the cost of the ad, and the revenue earned as a result of the ad. You also can review statistics such as the click-through rate, the conversion rate, average cost per click, the revenue broken into the revenue for each click (this can be different for e-commerce-enabled tracking), and your overall return on investment — in other words, the bottom line.

For AdWords customers, this is the most comprehensive and useful report for determining ad effectiveness.

CPC vs Organic Conversion

The CPC vs Organic Conversion report tells you the value of your cost per click (paid ads) compared to the value of other ways in which people reach your site, such as links, non-paid advertising such as articles written about your product or company, and search engine results that did not originate from paid ads.

This report also allows you to see which keywords were used in each of the search engines allowing you to optimize the keywords in your AdWords account for maximum effectiveness.

Overall Keyword Conversion

The Overall Keyword Conversion report shows the cost effectiveness of your keywords by showing you which keywords result in page visits, how many pages were viewed for each site visit, how many visits were converted into goals reached, and the average value of each keyword per visit based on whether they were keywords from paid ads or keywords from unpaid marketing efforts. Free is good, particularly when you make money.

Keyword Considerations

Learn how your organic keywords are doing in terms of their conversion rate using the Keyword Considerations report. See the total number of visits to your site due to someone ending up on your site using non-paid keywords. See the average number of pageviews as a result of these visits. Most importantly, find out what percentage of the visits due to organic keywords result in goals and, if applicable, the average revenue.

One of the decisions you need to make in the future is whether to complement the use of organic keyword success by also using these keywords in paid advertising. It's not completely clear whether the cost benefit of leaving alone what is working for free or whether to pour a little money into ads that use these keywords to see if your profits can be maximized. It takes some experimentation. This report helps you get started giving you the knowledge to get started in that research.

Campaign Conversion

This report complements the one you can view using your AdWords account. It tells you which of your ad campaigns are resulting in the highest number of visits, pageviews, goals achieved, and revenue. These are broken out into separate statistics so you can see which campaigns result in a high number of visits (curiosity factor) and which ones actually result in completed goals or revenue. They are not necessarily the same. For example, one keyword may be interesting and exciting causing someone to want to see your page (example: snow report), while another brings the buyer actually interested in purchasing your products (example: discount snowboards).

Conversion Summary

The Conversion Summary report is a simple report that shows you quickly whether your visits and conversion rates for each defined goal increased, decreased, or remained static over the time period you specify in the date range. The statistics are displayed in green up and red down arrows, as well as actual values and percentages.

Defined Funnel Navigation

For each funnel you defined earlier, the Defined Funnel Navigation report shows the entrance points along these funnels. For more information about defining funnels, see the section "Creating the funnel" earlier in this chapter. This report displays the number of visitors still remaining along each of the steps. It then displays the number of people who left the page and went somewhere else (outside the funnel). Most important, it tells you where they went and when they left. It's possible that you may need to remove ads along your funnel that lead to distractions that cause visitors to exit the funnel. Consider removing some site navigation features, making it more difficult to leave. Consider using technologies such as Ajax that allow you to update the Web page information without launching a new page or reloading the current page. Consider reducing the number of steps to reach the goal, eliminating steps that lose people.

There are many strategies for keeping a visitor moving through the funnel toward a defined goal. This report helps you determine how effective the funnel is and where its weak points are so that it can be improved.

Entrance Bounce Rates

Learn how effective your site is at keeping visitors, depending on their first reactions. People can enter your site on different pages depending on how they were driven to your site. For example, search engines may direct them to a content page where someone typing the URL may first visit your home page. The Entrance Bounce Rates report shows you how well these different pages are at retaining visitors and how many of the visitors leave immediately.

This report helps you with things such as keyword optimization. Are your keywords relevant to your site? Nonrelevant keywords can lead to high bounce rates. Are some of your Web pages ugly or unreadable? Try to keep your entire Web site appearance professional, and provide easy navigation from every content page making it possible to continue navigating through your site from any page. Orphaned pages, those with no navigation, may lose visitors while also having high entrance statistics.

Webmaster reports

Many of the reports within the Webmaster dashboard also are included in the Executive and Marketer dashboards. The Webmaster Overview is the same overview as the Executive and Marketer overview, providing a quick look at important site statistics. The Defined Funnel Navigation and Entrance Bounce Rate reports are the same as those discussed in the Marketer dashboard section. The Content Summary also can be found in the Executive dashboard.

Goal Tracking

The Goal Tracking report is a simple plot of goal conversions over time. This report quickly tells the Webmaster how effective the site content is over time. Perhaps the site content has become stale and no longer draws site visitors. Consider ways to update content on a more frequent basis or how to make it more dynamic. This report also helps Webmasters determine whether navigational changes to the site have increased or decreased goal conversion. This report and the Defined Funnel Navigation report are excellent tools to assist the Webmaster in defining site navigation.

Content by Titles

Some Web sites have different pages with the same title. This often occurs when pages are delivered from content stored in databases, where the page is a template and the content is included from data queried from the database. The Content by Titles report shows the relative popularity of pages based on their titles, aggregating pages with the same title, as defined in the HTML `<title>` tag.

Web Design Parameters

The Web Design Parameters section of reports includes information valuable to the developer. It's important to know what software and versions, equipment, and network speeds people use to visit your site. The Web Design Parameter reports include this information:

- Browser versions
- Platform versions
- Browser and platform combos
- Screen resolutions
- Screen colors
- Languages
- Java enabled
- Flash version
- Connection speed
- Hostnames

Armed with the information in this section, Webmasters can refine the graphic design and technologies they use to increase user satisfaction and efficiency.

Summary

Google Analytics has been called Web reporting on steroids. It's actually much more than simple Web reporting. Analytics allows you to define goals you hope your visitors will reach, whether that is to purchase a product, see a demo, read an article, or see an ad. You also can define the paths along which visitors reach those goals and track visitor progress through those funnels. Analytics helps you learn about the effectiveness of your ad and marketing campaigns. Find out whether your ads are working and which people are buying products through organic keywords rather than ads. Discover your customers' locations, when they buy, and how much they buy.

Analytics allows you to tailor the data viewed in reports by creating filters based on regular expressions. You can set up an e-commerce site so that Analytics provides detailed feedback on your sales and marketing successes.

Chapter 37

Creating a Google Enterprise

Google does lots of things well, especially creating an enterprise. In a short amount of time, Google has taken its search technology and leveraged itself onto *Fortune 500*'s 2006 list of fastest-growing companies. Google has managed to grow quickly by partnering with millions of other businesses of all sizes. Information is "King in the World" on Google Enterprise, and Google has made no secret that it hopes to be a portal to the world's information.

Most people know Google through its end-user tools, primarily the Google Search box, and a smaller number through services such as Gmail and Google Talk. In a continuing effort to bring its innovation to the world, Google has taken some of its most successful tools and turned them into Enterprise products, including Google Desktop for Enterprise, Google Maps for Enterprise, and important business tools such as Google Trends that helps you see what direction your interests are going on the Internet based on the massive amount of data Google collects about search trends.

Visit the Google Enterprise home page at www.google.com/enterprise/, and you might think that Google's solution for the enterprise is hardware-based. This is partially true, and Google's hardware is discussed in detail in the next chapter. This chapter covers some of the enterprise-level software solutions you'll want to incorporate into your small, medium, or large business, creating your own Google Enterprise.

Adopting Google Desktop Enterprise

Google Desktop, when used in a business environment, is a good productivity tool. The normal Google Desktop is for personal use only. To implement Google Desktop and take advantage of Enterprise-level installation and management features, you need to install Google Desktop for Enterprise.

You can find Google Desktop for Enterprise at http://desktop.google.com/en/enterprise.

NOTE Google offers a premium support package that assists administrators with enterprise deployment of Google Desktop for Enterprise.

Like any good enterprise-quality software product, Google Desktop for Enterprise allows system administrators to control user features and preferences across the entire domain. Because Google Desktop provides such a wide variety of features and functions, administrators also have the ability to control things such as document retention, the encryption of user data, and search indexes.

Google Desktop for Enterprise uses Group Policy to manage its global preference options, indexing options, and integration with the Google Search Appliance or Google Mini, which are hardware devices discussed in Chapter 38. For more information about Group Policy, see the sidebar "Microsoft Group Policy Refresher."

Setting Google Desktop preferences

When setting the preferences, the system administrator can control many important features, including what types of files are indexed. This is particularly important when information security is of great concern. For example, one of the things you can choose to turn off for the entire enterprise is the ability to index secure Web pages. The administrator also can control gadgets by disallow them, silently install them, or create a gadget "whitelist" to allow only certain approved gadgets.

When you are ready to push your Google Desktop policy out to the users, follow these steps:

1. Create a Group Policy Object (GPO).
2. Edit the GPO in either your Group Policy Management Console or the Active Directory Management Console.
3. Apply the GPO to the entire domain or to specific Organizational Units (OUs).

Installing Google Desktop

You can install Google Desktop on computers throughout your business in several ways. You can have users install Google Desktop on their own, controlling the features they can configure through Group Policy. You also can push out or publish the application to the end users using Group Policy Software Installation, and you can use the Microsoft System Center Configuration Manager. When you use the System Center Configuration Manager, installations are done only when the user activates the Google Desktop icon.

Adding Google Toolbar for Enterprise

Windows Domain administrators can install and configure Google Toolbar across their entire enterprise. Chapter 31 explains how useful the Google Toolbar is for personal use. Using it as a business tool can give your users quick access to important corporate information and business applications. Installing the Enterprise version allows you to do these things:

- Define Enterprise-wide policies
- Decide which buttons and features users can access
- Create and install custom buttons

Most large enterprises still use Microsoft Internet Explorer as their supported Web browser. Google Toolbar for Enterprise works only with Internet Explorer. Perhaps in the future, more enterprises will adopt Firefox as the supported Web browser.

 Chapter 39 has more information about creating custom buttons.

Getting started

Google Toolbar for Enterprise uses Microsoft Group Policy, which is an infrastructure for managing users and computers in an Active Directory environment. Follow these steps to begin using the Google Toolbar for Enterprise:

1. Download the Google Toolbar for Enterprise at
   www.google.com/tools/toolbar/T4/enterprise/.

2. Click Download Google Toolbar for Enterprise, and save the download to the company domain controller. The download consists of a Zip archive file containing four files: an Admin guide, a Google Toolbar Administrative template, the installer program, and a readme file.

3. Import the administrative template (GoogleToobar.adm) into your Group Policy editor. You will be able to see these categories:

   ■ **Preferences:** Set any or all of the preferences. Preferences left unconfigured are set by the user.

   ■ **Enterprise Integration:** This determines if you allow the Google Toolbar to auto-update from Google.

   ■ **Custom buttons:** Add custom buttons to Google Toolbar; if policy dictates, keep the user from adding custom buttons.

   ■ **Popup Whitelist:** Control which sites are allowed to have pop-ups. By default, no pop-ups are allowed.

Now you can create custom toolbar buttons for searching your company's intranet (local network) or create a link to corporate payroll and benefit systems or to the company policy manual. You also can create buttons to start important intranet applications such as a company Customer Relationship Management (CRM) system. Creating the buttons is very easy. You create a small XML file and, if you want, a custom button icon. See Chapter 39 for details.

Pushing policy

After you create the policy for the Google Toolbar for Enterprise, you will want to push this policy to the end users. Follow these steps:

1. Create a Group Policy Object (GPO).

2. Edit the GPO in either your Group Policy Management Console or the Active Directory Management Console.

3. Apply the GPO to the entire domain or to specific Organizational Units (OUs).

You can edit and update this policy by changing the GPO and pushing it to the users.

Installation

You can install the actual Google Toolbar on user machines in two ways. For smaller organizations, having the end users themselves install Google Toolbar may be fine. You may even have a support person who goes around to all the machines and installs the toolbar.

The second way, and possibly the only way for a larger enterprise, is to push the application out to the end users using Group Policy Software Installation or using the Microsoft System Center Configuration Manager, formerly System Management Server (SMS).

Microsoft Group Policy Refresher

Group Policy allows you to manage configurations for many users and groups managed across a computer domain that can possibly include many networks. Group Policy is stored in an object known as a GPO (Group Policy Object). Group Policy Objects exist in a domain that can be linked to sites, domains, and organizational units (OUs), all Active Directory containers. Group Policy Objects are edited in either the Group Policy Management Console or the Active Directory Management Console.

Group Policy objects are broken into two parts: one part exists in the Active Directory while the other part is stored on individual domain controllers in the Sysvol folder. The settings within the Group Policy Objects are then evaluated by the target hosts using the Group Policy engine.

Using Google Maps for Enterprise

Your business can license Google Maps for use in Web site and stand-alone applications. Your application programmers can integrate corporate data into Google Maps to perform instant display of customer locations, equipment failure hotspots, corporate locations, and any other way corporate data can be integrated into your business.

To get started with Google Maps for Enterprise point your Web browser to www.google.com/enterprise/maps/.

Google Maps for Enterprise uses the Google Maps API to customize control over the map interface. With this API, you can give the user as much or as little control as you want over the map. You can plot important locations and have pop-ups display even more information. Chapter 39 provides more information about using the Google Maps API.

While the Google Maps API is free for public Web sites, Google Maps for Enterprise is not. Paying for the Enterprise version of Google Maps gives businesses user telephone support and the ability to include Google Maps into nonpublic sites and applications — something you can't do with the free version. Also, some day Google will display advertising on Google Maps, and the Enterprise version will have the ability to disable these ads.

NOTE   While Google provides maps of the entire world, Google Maps for Enterprise is licensed only in the U.S. and Canada.

For Google Maps for Enterprise questions and licensing information, fill out the form found at http://services.google.com/enterprise/gme.

Tracking Trends with Google

When you want to know what the world is searching for, check out Google Trends. Point your browser to www.google.com/trends and get ready to say, "WOW." This lesser-known Google tool is not technically an Enterprise tool, because there is no installation or specific Enterprise control. But, as a business tool for your enterprise, it is indispensable. Figure 37.1 shows you the trend for searches on the keyword *forensics*. The trend shows a gradual decline in searches on this term since its peak in 2004. This could be due to the popularity of the TV show *CSI: Crime Scene Investigation*. Interestingly, checking trends for searches on the keyword *csi* shows a low in early 2004 and a slight increase into 2005 and holding stable in 2006. Who would have known?

FIGURE 37.1

Track trends for keyword terms, and compare them to news stories.

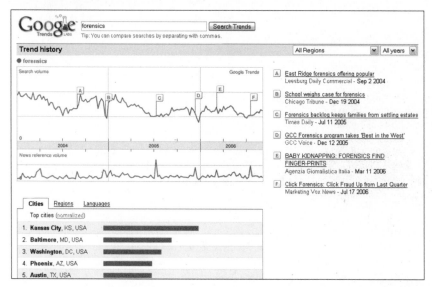

Directly below the chart is a smaller graph showing the frequency with which the search terms appeared in news articles for the same period. This gives you an idea of public interest and searching patterns compared to the amount of press the topic was receiving. The two graphs do not always correspond with one another. You can have fun figuring out why.

Below the chart is a tabbed display showing the top cities where Google searches were initiated on the keyword you typed into the Trends search box. See a bar chart comparing search volume in the top cities.

Launch the Regions tab by clicking the <u>Regions</u> link. This displays search volume in the top ten regions. Click the <u>Languages</u> link to see search volumes by language. It is likely that there will be fewer than ten languages listed.

Notice that the charts are often marked with small lettered boxes. These correspond to news events on specific days. See the corresponding news event marked with the same letter on the right. Click the news story to read it.

Advanced trending

Create comparison trends by typing more than one keyword into the search box, separated by commas. You can type up to a maximum of five terms. To type phrases, don't put them in quotes, as in other search boxes. Instead, enclose the phrases in parentheses like this (*my search phrase*). Clicking Search Trends creates a new chart, displaying each trend in a different color. A color key appears above the chart making it easy to see which line belongs to which keyword.

You can exclude searches that contain certain terms from the volume calculations by including the term you want excluded, preceded with a minus (–) sign. For example, the term *google –earth* shows search volumes for Google, but not for Google Earth.

To maintain the order of your search terms, enclose them in quotes. This restricts results to searches that were done with terms in the same order as you typed them.

 When using any advanced search features, only the volume graph is shown. No news is included.

You can expand the scope of your search by typing multiple keywords separated with the pipe | symbol, normally located over the Enter key. The | symbol means "or." This comparison allows you to see results based on searches that contain either one search term or the other, expanding the potential number of searches in your search.

Further customize your trend by selecting a particular region for your search. By default, All Regions is displayed. Choose a new region (actually a specific country) from the drop-down list above and to the right of the chart.

Select a time period for your chart by clicking the drop-down list on the far right above the chart. By default, charts display all time periods beginning in 2004. Notice that the trend becomes more detailed as you track trends across individual years and months. This may be useful in plotting the sale of stocks and securities based on specific news stories.

Using trend data

The trend data is an approximation, not exact numbers. Google uses the term *propensity* to describe what the data describes. This is most likely the reason that the y-axis of the chart never has exact numbers. Comparison charts, for example, show relationships in trends and never exact value differences. Users show a propensity to search on a particular term differently over time. That's what these charts show.

 The data is aggregated from millions of searches with no personal information included, so your private information is safe.

You can use the Google Trends data and chart images freely as long as you properly attribute Google when you do. You may want to join the others interested in Google Trends data in the Google Labs Trends group at `groups.google.com/group/Google-Labs-Trends`.

Summary

Many of the tools discussed in this book are offered freely by Google for your personal use. Google has created expanded versions of these tools for use in enterprises, both large and small. Some of the enterprise solutions are free, and some, like Google Maps for Enterprise, charge license fees. System administrators will find the Google applications easy to administer across tens, hundreds, or even thousands of desktops.

Google Trends is a great application of particular interest to business owners curious about user interest over time in particular topics based on their Google searches. You may find this of particular interest should you enroll in Google AdWords.

Enterprise tools like Google Desktop also integrate well with the powerful Google hardware, which is discussed in the next chapter.

Chapter 38

Introducing Enterprise Hardware

nformation. We are all deluged with information on a minute-by-minute basis. Dealing with information has become a fact of life, and one we must learn to handle efficiently to be competitive in today's business world. The key is rapid access to the right information. It's no longer enough simply to have access to all the information, a major goal of the 1990s IT professional. It's now important that we can put our fingertips on very specific bits of information without spending hours looking for it. Enter Google.

While businesses often use information found on the Web, and mostly through Google Web search, the information they use most on a daily basis resides in files throughout their own enterprises. Through a combination of hardware and software solutions, Google provides rapid access to business information in medium and large enterprises. Most small businesses and organizations won't require the power offered by this solution. But enterprises the size of universities and libraries may.

To get started toward faster access to business information, check out the Google Enterprise page for more information about its hardware/software business solutions at www.google.com/enterprise.

Compared to the salary of a person working to manage your business information, the Google hardware is very cost effective. For example, the Google OneBox for Enterprise, with capabilities of indexing and managing access to 500,000 documents, starts at about the same as the person's annual salary. You also can pick up a Google Mini, good for 50,000 documents at a much lower price.

Learning how to use Google Search Appliance to your company's advantage

Discovering the features of the Google OneBox

Seeing how Google Mini can solve data access in smaller enterprises

Comparing the Google OneBox Search Appliance with Google Mini

Finding out how to participate in the Google Enterprise Partner Program

Managing the Google Search Appliance

The Google OneBox for Enterprise, shown in Figure 38.1, gives you access to data in 220 file formats and 109 languages, no matter where it's located throughout your enterprise. This includes data residing in databases, on Web servers, and in business information applications such as Customer Relationship Management (CRM) and Enterprise Resource Planning (ERP) systems. That's why it's called OneBox. Using "one box," you can type search queries for a wide variety of business information.

To understand the advantage of the Google approach to information retrieval, first think back to how information in a business was previously retrieved. Databases were queried using complex SQL (Structured Query Language) statements, or report writer software was employed to create endless ad hoc reports, sometimes to retrieve a single bit of information. There were no effective means to search stored documents unless they were stored in a managed data warehouse program that normally required regular system administration. The Google advantage is the ability to index documents in a wide variety of information storage mechanisms and the means for retrieving data in a unified manner, with zero end-user training. It takes no more skill to search through all your business data than it does to use the Google Web search box found at Google.com.

FIGURE 38.1

Install the Google Search Appliance for access to large enterprise data sources.

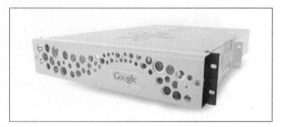

These are some of the other features Google is famous for that assist you in retrieving enterprise information:

- **Spelling suggestions:** When you type a misspelled word, Google suggests the correct spelling. Because Google has indexed your business information, this works even with your business-specific terms.

- **Relevant results:** The true power of Google searching is based on Google's PageRank technology. Your search might result in thousands of possible business documents. Google helps you find the right information by suggesting the most relevant results first. Enterprise results also can be grouped based on where the information resides.

The Enterprise version provides even more services such as the ability to view a document without having the original application installed on your computer.

How it works

In the same way that Google Web Crawlers index billions of Web pages across the Internet, crawlers find their way through your business information, creating a master index of all your documents. Because many business documents contain sensitive data, the Google OneBox has an effective security management system that allows access to data only through secure permissions. Follow these steps to make a typical query:

1. The user (person who wants information) types a query into a search box provided on an internal company Web page. This is similar to the familiar Google Search box at Google.com. Instead, this box is customized with your company information.

2. The user's query is analyzed to determine if a particular OneBox module has the relevant information.

3. A secure HTTPS (encrypted) GET request is sent to the relevant OneBox provider (information source). Security information is sent along with the request to determine if the user has permission to access the requested document. The communications are encrypted so that sensitive company data is not transferred openly across the network.

4. Results are sent back from the provider to the OneBox in XML format.

5. The XML is formatted into HTML by the XSL template located on the OneBox.

6. The results are displayed to the user in familiar Google results format.

Results are displayed using relevant snippets of the document that contain your keyword. Also, keywords are highlighted within the page to make finding the relevant information simpler.

Integrating Enterprise applications

One of the features of the OneBox search appliance over the lower-end Google Mini is its ability to integrate with your enterprise applications. The Google Search Appliance uses the REST-based API with a fully documented SDK for integration with enterprise applications. You create small programs called *OneBox modules* to access data. A OneBox module defines a type of search, the keyword used to invoke the search, how the information is obtained, and how it is returned to the user making the query. It also defines any security requirements for access to the data. You can write as many OneBox modules as you like. For example, LDAP, a form of hierarchical storage, is used to store a great deal of corporate information, particularly employee contact information. A OneBox module is written to access employee contact information in human resource systems. Remember, access to information in the Search Appliance can be restricted based on user permissions.

See many examples of enterprise applications in the OneBox Gallery at http://code.google.com/enterprise/oneboxgallery.html.

You also can access the full OneBox for Enterprise Developer's Guide at http://code.google.com/enterprise/documentation/oneboxguide.html.

Managing the device

Management of the Google OneBox for Enterprise can be handled from any place on the planet where there is Internet access and can be managed in 16 languages. The administrator also can easily monitor the health (running status) of the equipment due to its SNMP (Simple Network Management Protocol) compliance. If something does go wrong, you can activate remote diagnostics so Google support can help you analyze the problem. While administration of the OneBox is simple, it also is powerful. The administrator can do simple things such as define synonyms for corporate terms so they appear as alternate suggestions when the user types a keyword. The administrator also can manage user access to information, see usage statistics, and monitor the health of the OneBox.

Managing accounts

You can manage user access, security, and permissions to the OneBox using a Web interface, and you can restrict access to documents based on custom security restrictions that you set.

Creating OneBox modules

Creating a OneBox module involves creating a trigger, selecting the provider, and formatting the output of the results. The OneBox can process queries all the time, when specific keywords are encountered, or when the query matches a regular expression.

There are two types of OneBox providers: internal and external. An internal provider returns information within the OneBox collection of information. An external provider is designed to retrieve real-time data from external applications such as databases, CRM systems, and other business applications.

Performing system analyses

You can view reports of user queries to help optimize the performance or your information system. This helps you quickly determine where the data is coming from, problems with access to information, errors that are encountered, and problematic servers. You can track system usage by the hour or by the day or track the use of certain custom features.

Introducing Google Mini

The Google Mini is a smaller version of the Google OneBox appliance, as shown in Figure 38.2. It's still fast and powerful. It's very easy to administer. Turn it on, point it at your data, put a search box in the Google Toolbar for Enterprise or on an internal or even public Web page, and you're done.

FIGURE 38.2

Use the Google Mini when you have fewer documents and no databases to index.

Google Mini can crawl through documents on your public Web server, your intranet Web site, and corporate file systems, and can recognize more than 200 file types.

Google Mini features

The administrative interface is simple. Using the Web interface, you specify where in your enterprise the documents reside using URLs. Because the Mini does not have document-level security like the OneBox Search Appliance, you need to control access to certain sensitive data by keeping the Mini from crawling into certain directories. You can run more than one Mini in your organization and allow different levels of access to sensitive information.

The Mini crawls through your data and organizes the information into collections. You can tell the Mini to crawl continuously through your data, regularly updating the index. It automatically senses and crawls dynamic data more often than static data (data that does not change very often, or ever.)

There is a graphic interface for creating the look of your result pages. Using this interface, you can customize the user experience when searching your business data. You also can use the advanced interface for further customization.

The Mini has a keymatch feature that lets you assign particular pages or documents to certain keywords. In this way, you can assure that searches such as "annual report" get right to the correct documents.

You also can assist the user searching your system by defining your own synonyms. When a user begins typing a particular keyword into the search box, your recommended synonyms are shown as suggestions.

Like the OneBox Search Appliance, the Google Mini also has reports that help you better manage your device and access to your company data. Find out what the top queries have been and see error reports that tell you when there are problems accessing your data.

Selecting a Mini

The Mini has versions starting at its minimum capability of 50,000 documents. There are different versions in incremental document-handling capabilities. The next levels are 100,000, 200,000, and 300,000. When you need to handle more than 300,000 documents or you need access to enterprise applications and databases, you need the OneBox Search Appliance.

Choosing between OneBox and Mini

Your business needs and budget likely will help you choose which search appliance you need in your company. Table 38.1 shows you some of the advantages that the Google Search Appliance has over the Mini. Basically, if you need to search through large numbers of documents, business applications, and databases, then save your pennies for the Search Appliance because the Mini just doesn't have that kind of horsepower.

TABLE 38.1

Search Appliance versus Mini

Feature Description	Google Mini	Google Search Appliance
Document capability	300,000 maximum	30 million maximum
Secure content access control through permissions	No	Yes
Integration with enterprise applications	No	Yes
Relational database query support	No	Yes
External metadata indexing	No	Yes
Device SNMP monitoring	No	Yes
Supports RAID disks	No	Yes
Clustered redundancy	No	Yes

Google Enterprise Partner Program

Enterprises large enough to need search appliances like either the OneBox for Enterprise or Google Mini also may need expert assistance in installation, integration, custom support, training, and custom programming expertise. The Google Enterprise Partner Program is a group of third-party companies that provide these services. A directory of the current partners and the services they offer can be found at www.google.com/enterprise/gep/directory.html.

You also can become a partner by applying at www.google.com/enterprise/gep/overview.html.

 You may notice in the overview document that there is a sizeable membership fee for participating as a partner in the Google Enterprise Partner Program.

Google Enterprise Blog

The subtitle of the Google Enterprise Blog is: A blog about enterprise information, search, and the users that live there. If this sounds like you, then definitely join the blog found at http://googleenterprise.blogspot.com/.

This blog has information about administration and using all the Google Search Appliance hardware and software tools.

Summary

This chapter began by stating that access to information would give your company a competitive advantage. Getting access to information stored in many forms throughout your enterprise has never been simpler. No more endless report writer reports, training in SQL for accessing databases, scratching your head about how to access LDAP data, or figuring out how to query through hundreds of different data types. The Google Search Appliance can do this and more. For smaller applications, for searching through company documents and Web data, install the Google Mini.

Integrate the Enterprise software tools discussed in Chapter 37 with these hardware devices for greater business data access. Learn how to further enhance your business access to data and integrate Google technology into your enterprise in the next chapter.

Part VI

Exploring Google Innovation

Chapter 39

Exploring the Future of Google

Number 10 of Google's "Ten things Google has found to be true" is "Great just isn't good enough." If that's not incentive enough to drive innovation, nothing is. Google's goal of building a better search engine led it to learn, listen, and pay attention to the user. And from that, to innovate. The folks at Google have come a long way since building the best search engine, and Google innovation now includes communications in the form of e-mail, chatting, and blogging; entertainment like Google Videos, News, Mapping, and Web publishing; and office automation tools such as Google Docs. I would be remiss in leaving out everyone's favorite, Google Earth.

Part of the Google goal of not being evil sets the tone and direction for its software development and interaction with users. This chapter explores some of the ways Google works with software developers and partner companies to continue innovation. This chapter introduces many of the Google programming technologies that allow you to integrate your Web site or Internet-ready application with Google services and applications.

Find Google's Ten things at www.google.com/corporate/tenthings.html.

NOTE This chapter is geared toward the more advanced Web developer and software programmer.

IN THIS CHAPTER

Learning how to enhance your Web site using Google Maps, Webmaster tools, and the Google AJAX Search code

Reaching Google users by creating clever Google Gadgets and by enhancing the Google Toolbar with your custom button

Integrating Google into your Web and desktop applications

Searching through public Open Source code to find useful code for your applications

Software Development

Google has taken every precaution to remain a principled software development company devoted to the cause of ethical behavior and Open software development. Part of its efforts to maintain this way of doing business is to create a set of software development principles and participate fully in allowing others access to its code and by developing software development APIs to simplify interacting with Google programs.

Principles

Google worries about what it perceives to be evil trends in software development and has therefore created a set of broad software development principles. Google means to follow these principles in its own software development and hopes that others in the software industry will adopt them out of ethical concern for the end user. In brief, these principles are:

- Software should not trick you into installing it.
- When you install software, it should tell you its purpose or function, and if it makes money through ads, you should know that, too.
- Software should be easy to delete or disable.
- Software should not make secret changes to other installed programs, and the software user interface should not try to trick you.
- You should be asked before a software product can collect and transmit personal information.
- Software applications that meet these guidelines should not be bundled with software that does not.

You can join the software "Neighborhood Watch" by visiting www.stopbadware.org, the Web site for an independent group formed to fight malicious software.

Enhancing Your Web Site

Get started enhancing your Web site with the tools and application programming interfaces (API) found at http://code.google.com. Build Web services, create full applications that talk to Google services, and interact with your users by building gadgets or custom Google Toolbar buttons (my personal favorite).

Google Maps API

Your Web site can use the power of Google Maps to show people how to find you, the way to the family picnic, or your favorite historic sites. The Google Maps API lets you use JavaScript to embed a Google map right in your own Web page. You can additionally customize the map using markers, polylines, and shadowed information windows.

You need a key to get started. You can apply for your key at www.google.com/apis/maps/. Click the Sign up for a Google Maps API key link at the top of the page.

Each key you sign up for is good only for a single directory on your site. This means that if you have a directory at www.mysite.com/contact, then this key is good for all pages found in the contact directory. If you have a second directory that needs the Google Maps API, such as www.mysite.com/birdmigrations, then you need a second key.

There are no limits to the number of requests your site can make to Google Maps for a map display, but there is a limit to the number of geocode (address location) requests to 50,000 requests per day.

You'll be happy to know that the Google Maps API does not include advertising. Along the same lines, Google does not allow you to charge others to view these maps. If you have an application for the maps and want to charge, check out Chapter 37.

After you sign up for your API key, Google provides a sample Web page to get started. Figure 39.1 shows you the sample, modified to show the Orchidland area on the Big Island of Hawaii. If you are unsure of your latitude and longitude, try using Google Earth. The API uses a different format for latitude and longitude than the values Google Earth displays. The U.S. government to the rescue! Point your Web browser here: www.fcc.gov/mb/audio/bickel/DDDMMSS-decimal.html.

The FCC has a simple converter you can use. Here is the sample code used to generate Figure 39.1:

```
<!DOCTYPE html PUBLIC "-//W3C//DTD XHTML 1.0 Strict//EN"
  "http://www.w3.org/TR/xhtml1/DTD/xhtml1-strict.dtd">
<html xmlns="http://www.w3.org/1999/xhtml">
  <head>
    <meta http-equiv="content-type" content="text/html; charset=utf-
8"/>
    <title>Map to our house on Oliana Street</title>
    <script

src="http://maps.google.com/maps?file=api&amp;v=2&amp;key=ABQIA...
QChi6Cg"
      type="text/javascript"></script>
    <script type="text/javascript">

    //<![CDATA[

    function load() {
      if (GBrowserIsCompatible()) {
        var map = new GMap2(document.getElementById("map"));
        map.setCenter(new GLatLng(19.58277, -155.0395), 13);
        map.addOverlay(new GMarker(19.58277, -155.0395));
      }
    }

    //]]>
    </script>
  </head>
  <body onload="load()" onunload="GUnload()">
    <div id="map" style="width: 500px; height: 300px"></div>
  </body>
```

NOTE The key in the previous example was modified for security reasons. Your key will be much longer.

FIGURE 39.1

Modify the sample code to get started with maps quickly.

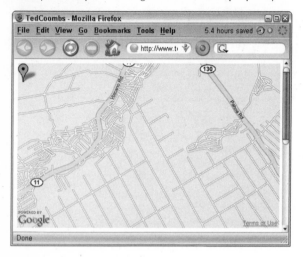

Google Webmaster Tools

Google's Webmaster Central is a hub of information for Web developers. There are links to the Site Status Wizard to learn whether your site has been indexed. There is a link to the Webmaster tools, commonly known as Sitemaps. You can also learn more about submitting information to Google Base and the Book Search. Most important, you can stay on top of current Google developer information by subscribing to the Google blog for Webmasters and join the Google Group for Webmasters. You also may find the Webmaster help center useful. To find Webmaster Central, point your Web browser to www.google.com/webmasters/.

When you use Google's Sitemap tool, you can add a list of your Web sites and use the Google Webmaster tools. Log in to your Google account and navigate to www.google.com/webmasters/sitemaps/siteoverview.

In the upper-right corner of this Web page, you see a + Tools link, where you can do these things:

- Download data for all your sites
- Report spam in the Google Index
- Submit a reinclusion request

Additionally, you can see crawl stats, query stats, page analysis, and index stats by clicking the Statistics tab. If your site is having problems getting indexed, click the Diagnostics tab for help in determining the probable cause of indexing problems. There could be problems with a robots.txt file or any number of other problems.

Google Web Toolkit

If you've seen the pages where portions of the page update without reloading the entire page, like Google Maps, you're looking at an application written in AJAX, sort of Javascript on steroids. The Google Web Toolkit lets you build powerful front ends to your Web site using the Java programming language and the

Google Web Toolkit framework. Then the Google Web Toolkit (GWT) compiler converts the Java classes into Javascript and HTML.

When developing your application in Java, you use the GWT user interface components known as *widgets*. Combine the widgets on traditional Java panels. Here is sample button code that launches a window alert:

```java
public class MyButton implements EntryPoint {
  public void onModuleLoad() {
    Button btn = new Button("I am a button", new ClickListener() {
      public void onClick(Widget sender) {
        Window.alert("I have been clicked");
      }
    });
    RootPanel.get().add(btn);
  }
}
```

There are two modes in which your Google Web Toolkit application can run: Hosted mode and Web mode. Hosted mode applications are run as Java and use the Java Virtual Machine. Web mode applications are converted to Javascript using the GWT compiler and run strictly as Javascript and HTML; no Java is included in the page.

For more information and detailed instructions on using the GWT, visit code.google.com/ webtoolkit/overview.html.

Google AJAX search API

Now that you know a little about AJAX, you'll be happy to know that Google has made it easier to build applications on top of the Google Search technology. The Google AJAX search API also helps you add dynamic search boxes for Google Web, Video, News, Maps, and Blog search results.

As with the Google Maps API, you need to have Google generate a key. Point your Web browser to http://code.google.com/apis/ajaxsearch/.

Click the Sign up for a Google AJAX Search API key link. Agree to the license agreement, and type the URL that will host the AJAX Search code. Then click Generate API Key. Also like the Google Maps API, Google provides you a sample page, with the results shown in Figure 39.2:

```html
<!DOCTYPE html PUBLIC "-
//W3C//DTD XHTML 1.0 Strict//EN" "http://www.w3.org/TR/xhtml1/DTD/xhtml
1-strict.dtd">
<html xmlns="http://www.w3.org/1999/xhtml">
  <head>
    <meta http-equiv="content-type" content="text/html; charset=utf-
8"/>
    <title>My Google AJAX Search API Application</title>
    <link href="http://www.google.com/uds/css/gsearch.css" type="text/c
ss" rel="stylesheet"/>
    <script src="http://www.google.com/uds/api?file=uds.js&amp;v=1.0&am
p;key=ABQdaX_wm1K-
Q6KdSr5G7WhQDZiGdv9tL82_8S5e2Pd_QChi6Cg" type="text/javascript"></scrip
t>
    <script language="Javascript" type="text/javascript">
    //<![CDATA[
```

561

```
function OnLoad() {
    // Create a search control
    var searchControl = new GSearchControl();

    // Add in a full set of searchers
    var localSearch = new GlocalSearch();
    searchControl.addSearcher(localSearch);
    searchControl.addSearcher(new GwebSearch());
    searchControl.addSearcher(new GvideoSearch());
    searchControl.addSearcher(new GblogSearch());

    // Set the Local Search center point
    localSearch.setCenterPoint("New York, NY");

    // Tell the searcher to draw itself and tell it where to attach
    searchControl.draw(document.getElementById("searchcontrol"));

    // Execute an initial search
    searchControl.execute("Google");
}

//]]>
</script>
</head>
<body onload="OnLoad()">
    <div id="searchcontrol"/>
</body>
</html>
```

NOTE   The key in the code above has been abbreviated for security reasons. Google will create this same sample for you with a key that works on your own Web site.

FIGURE 39.2

Place the dynamic Google Search anywhere on your Web page.

You will find the complete documentation for this API at `http://code.google.com/apis/ajaxsearch/documentation/`.

Reaching Google Users

One quick way to reach Google users is to write Google Gadgets that they can use on their home pages or their Google Desktops. It's a fun and simple way to interact with others. Another simple thing you can do is to create custom buttons for the Google Toolbar. Create fun buttons that point to your home page and trade them with your friends.

Write your own Google Gadgets

You can write two types of Google Gadgets: Universal Gadgets and Desktop Gadgets. The Universal Gadget sounds like the perfect tool for any toolbox. Though it's up to you to build one, the Universal Gadget can be plopped onto any Google Home page (`http://pages.google.com`), Google Desktop, Blogger blogs, or even your Web page hosted somewhere other than GooglePages.

The Desktop Gadget works with Google Desktop and can run on your desktop after you install Google Desktop. Read more about personalizing Google Desktop in Chapter 11.

Building Universal Google Gadgets is fairly simple compared to the other API technologies in this chapter. You won't have to download anything, and there are no API libraries to learn about. You can write a Google Gadget using simple HTML, or if you want to get fancy, you can use Javascript. One downside to a Universal Gadget is that you must be online for it to work. If you need a gadget that works offline, try a Desktop Gadget.

The Desktop Gadget has a bit more flexibility. Even though it works only with Google Desktop, it runs even when you are not connected to the Internet. Google Desktop Gadgets also can interact with other desktop applications. For example, have your gadget interact when someone starts writing an e-mail message. Your gadget could create boilerplate e-mail messages for you. You can write Desktop Gadgets using Javascript, as with the Universal Gadget, or the C and C++ programming languages, as well as the newer Microsoft .NET languages, C#, and VB.Net. You need to download the software developer's kit (SDK) in order to develop Desktop Gadgets.

To get started developing Desktop Gadgets download the SDK at `desktop.google.com/developer.html`.

Google Toolbar API

You can create custom buttons that can be added to the Google Toolbar. These buttons can have custom navigation, search, send, and update capabilities. Custom buttons can be represented as an icon, a drop-down list of icons, or text strings, any of which can be updated by an RSS feed. A custom button can have a tooltip when the mouse hovers over it and an optional title that appears next to the button. This is particularly useful for drop-down buttons.

To make your button functional, you can save important preferences in an XML file. These preferences include such things as a URL you want to have the user navigate to when the button is clicked and URLs that include search parameters or text parameters that send important parameters to the Web site. You also can include an update URL where updates to the button can be obtained.

To create and install a custom button, first create an XML file that defines the button's important information:

```
<?xml version="1.0" encoding="utf-8"?>
<custombuttons xmlns="http://toolbar.google.com/custombuttons/">
  <button>
    <site>http://www.tedcoombs.com</site>
  </button>
</custombuttons>
```

You can create custom icons for your new button in a number of different graphic formats. Before you can use it in the Google Toolbar, it needs to be converted to Base 64 ASCII text. Base 64 what? Luckily, this Web site can do that for you: www.motobit.com/util/base64-decoder-encoder.asp.

Simply browse for your file on your computer, and the file is uploaded and encoded for you. Copy and paste the text it creates into your XML file surrounded by an <icon> element like this:

```
<icon mode="base64" type="image/x-icon">
/9j/4AAQSkZJRgABAgEAtAC0AAD/4QOuRXhpZgAATU0AKgAAAAgABwESAAMAAA
ABAAEAAAEaAAUAAAABAAAAYgEbAAUAAAABAAAAagEoAAMAAAABAAIAAAExAAIAAAAc
gEyAAIAAAAUAAAAhodpAAQAAAABAAAAnAAAA
</icon>
```

In reality, the text between the begin and end <icon> elements will be much greater than the sample above. To do this quickly and easily, take your favorite picture. Open it in a program like Photoshop. Shrink the image down to 16x16 pixels, and save it. Then upload it into the encoder, copy the text into your XML file with icon elements, and you're golden.

 The custom button feature currently works only with Internet Explorer.

Integrating with Google

You can build powerful applications that manage Google services such as AdWords. You no longer need to use the AdWords Web management interface. You can build your own application that makes calls into the AdWords service. The Google Data API takes ATOM and RSS to the next level. Find out how to use the GData protocol to create enhanced syndication applications. Create powerful e-commerce applications using the Google Checkout API.

Google AdWords API

The Google AdWords API provides nine basic services that allow you to build powerful AdWords maintenance applications. To get started using the AdWords API, you must first sign up to receive a special token that is included in each of your AdWords API calls to identify you. To receive your token, point your Web browser to www.google.com/apis/adwords/.

Sign in to the AdWords API center, or sign up by clicking the links in the blue box in the upper-right corner of the AdWords API page.

Your applications can do everything from creating new AdWords accounts to listing the performance of certain keywords. The messaging technology used is XML-based technology known as SOAP. Using the AdWords API, you build Web service clients that provide the following services:

- **Account Service:** Create and modify Google AdWords accounts.
- **Campaign Service:** Create, list, and modify your campaigns including setting the campaign name, its daily budget, and the end date.
- **AdGroup Service:** Create and list ad groups, associate ad groups with a campaign, and perform related actions.
- **Keyword Service:** Access, modify, and create keywords in an AdGroup.
- **Criterion Service:** Create and modify keyword and Web site targeting criteria. You can get the keywords for a keyword-targeted campaign or the Web sites for site-targeted campaigns.
- **Keyword Tool Service:** Generate keywords based on a seed keyword or on the words found on a specific Web page or Web site.
- **Creative Service:** This lets you create and modify creatives and associate them with an ad group.
- **Traffic Estimator Service:** This lets you estimate data, such as the cost per click (CPC), click-through rate (CTR), and average position of your ads.
- **Report Service:** Get reports on ad impressions, clicks, and click-through rate.
- **Info Service:** This provides basic data regarding the AdWords API usage.

NOTE   All the AdWords API calls are sent encrypted using SSL for security purposes.

Visit the AdWords API blog at `http://adwordsapi.blogspot.com`.

Google Data API

The Google Data API, more commonly called GData, is an XML protocol based on, and extending, the Atom 1.0 and RSS 2.0 syndication protocols. If you need to refresh your memory, you can find more information about ATOM and RSS in Chapter 14.

GData extends these two syndication protocols in a number of ways. For example, neither the ATOM nor the RSS protocol has query ability, while the GData protocol allows queries to be sent. It just wouldn't be Google without search capability.

The GData protocol also allows for authentication, updates, and something known as *optimistic concurrency*. For those familiar with database updating, this is similar to transactions. It makes certain that if one person is changing information, and another person changes the information before the first person does, any updates based on the old information are denied.

The authentication preferred by Google when using the GData protocol is known as Authentication for Installed Applications, a Google-specific authentication mechanism. Third-party front-end applications to a GData service should use an authentication mechanism known as Account Authentication Proxy for Web-based Applications.

Session state (the current state of all application variables) is managed in two ways by Google: one through the use of cookies, and the other by sending a query parameter in the URL. It's recommended that your GData application support one of these two methods of maintaining the session state. Your application still works if you don't maintain session state, but two round trips to the server are required, which is less efficient.

For the full GData documentation, visit `http://code.google.com/apis/gdata/protocol.html`.

Google Checkout API

Integrate Google Checkout into your e-commerce Web site to enable customers to easily check out by paying with their credit cards. Your account is automatically updated with their purchases.

Your E-commerce checkout pages host a Google Checkout button. Users click this button, and they see a signup or sign-in page. When users already have a Google account set up with their payment information, they can simply sign in and continue with their checkout. New users can easily sign up. What your users see is shown in Figure 39.3.

FIGURE 39.3

Sign up for a Google Checkout account for easy checkout at Google-enabled sites.

The shopper on your site then sees his order detail and can click Place your order now. When checkout is complete, he is thanked for his order and an e-mail copy of the receipt is sent.

You must first sign up for a Google Merchant account. By doing this, you ask Google to process credit card transactions on your behalf, and this is not a free service. As of the writing of this book, you can discount your fees to Google by using an AdWords account; otherwise, each transaction is a percentage of the total sale plus a small per-transaction fee. After logging in to Google, find the current rate at `https://checkout.google.com/seller/fees.html`.

Signing up for the account is easy. Type a little information about your business Web site, your policies regarding refunds, and your financial information. After you sign up for your Google Merchant account, and are approved, you receive a Merchant ID and a Merchant Key. These are used to identify your transactions and allow you to communicate with Google.

After you have a Google Merchant account, the first step is to begin integrating the Checkout API XML into your shopping cart code. The second step is including a Web service that sends and receives XML messages.

NOTE Google Checkout works with AdWords by displaying a special Google Checkout icon in your ad, letting people know that you want them to spend money on your site (and you use Google Checkout).

Get all the technical documentation for using and integrating the Google Checkout API at `http://code .google.com/apis/checkout/developer/index.html`.

Google Talk XMPP and Jingle

When you want to create your own client application that talks to the Google Talk service, you need to understand the XMPP protocol in order to program the new client application. The Google Talk service uses an open communications protocol known as the eXtensible Messaging and Presence Protocol. In 1999, Jeremie Miller announced the existence of Jabber, which was an open technology for instant messaging and presence. This later formalized as (IETF) RFC 3920 – RFC 3923. Google has extended XMPP for its own purposes, and documentation for those extensions can be found at `http://code.google.com/ apis/talk/jep_extensions/extensions.html`.

The features in this protocol include:

- Instant messaging
- Presence (anybody home?)
- Media negotiation
- Whiteboarding
- Collaboration
- Lightweight middleware
- Content syndication
- Generalized XML delivery

Google Talk also uses a set of XMPP extensions called Jingle. These extensions allow for the creation and maintenance of peer-to-peer communications between clients. This is useful for functionality such as peer-to-peer file sharing or video chatting. When writing your application in C++, a set of C++ components called Libjingle is provided by Google. Use these components to implement Google's version of Jingle and Jingle Audio for voice communications. Download Libjingle from SourceForge at `http://sourceforge .net/projects/libjingle/`.

NOTE Libjingle components are offered free under a BSD license agreement.

For more information about XMPP, visit `www.xmpp.org`.

Google Code Search

Google Code Search is not an API or a protocol, but because this chapter is primarily for programmers and Web developers, the Google Code Search is of particular interest. Search through public source code by launching Google Code Search at `www.google.com/codesearch`, shown in Figure 39.4.

Search through public Open Source code using Google Code Search.

Search using the Code Search box by typing regular expressions, search strings, special search operators, or a combination of these three. The operators are included in Table 39.1.

Google Code Search Operators

Operator	Description
file: *regexp*	Search in files matching the regular expression (*regexp*). For example, file:*jin.c*.
package: *regexp*	Search in packages identified by the regular expression. For example, package:perl MyFile.
lang: *regexp*	Search only for code written in a particular programming language. For example, lang:"c++".
license: *regexp*	Search only for code protected by a particular type of license. For example, license:gpl.

Figure 39.5 shows the result of a very broad search for all public source code covered under the GPL license. The result includes a code snippet, a link to identical code found in other sources, a link to the actual source code archive, and a link to the license agreement. When the same code is found in several places within a single code source, you see a link to the other locations by clicking the More from link.

FIGURE 39.5

See code snippets and links to the license agreements.

Summary

This chapter provided an introduction into the many ways to interface with, integrate, talk to, and otherwise use Google technologies in your Web and desktop applications. You can create your own Google Talk client or use the Google Checkout in your e-commerce Web applications. Google has attempted to make interfacing with its technologies as simple as possible by creating programming APIs and by using standard open protocols. For additional information on these and other Open Source projects or just to see a list of Open Source programming projects at Google, visit `http://code.google.com/projects.html`. With this foundation for innovation, it's no wonder that the Google Laboratories are full of upcoming and interesting projects, which are discussed in the next and final chapter.

Chapter 40

Graduating from the Product Labs

Google tools and products don't spring forth fully-developed and ready to use. Instead, they are incubated and carefully nurtured in a development laboratory. In this final chapter, you can see some of the products currently sporting Google Labs status. Some are ready for moving into the full application world, while others are in differing states of development.

One of the neatest products for space buffs is Google Mars. Similar to Google Earth, the Google Mars product shows you in-depth maps and details of the red planet.

Google is working on some mobile Web technologies such as Google Transit for finding maps, and Google Ride Finder for finding buses and subway schedules and stops.

To enhance your browsing experience, look for Notebook and Google Web Accelerator, two tools designed to make your use of Web content easier to manage.

As you might expect, several different search features are in the works, both for browsing and for providing service to people browsing your site.

ON the WEB Check out the projects and programs in development at
http://labs.google.com/.

Applying Map Information

One segment of the work being done in Google Labs is the extension of mapping products. As explained in Chapter 13, Google Earth is a feature-rich Web application that lets you work with addressing, georeferenced coordinates, 3-D models, and more.

CROSS-REF Read about using Google Earth in Chapter 13. Check out 3-D modeling using Google SketchUp in Chapters 32 and 33.

Three projects currently in development are Google Mars, Google Transit, and Ride Finder. Google Mars is similar in design to Google Earth, although it isn't as developed and there's no way to plot your next vacation itinerary! Google Transit and Ride Finder are projects utilizing Google Map technology. As with other Google Labs products, the scope of both the Transit and Ride Finder programs is limited to specific locations. As the applications develop and feedback indicates the direction in which to take the products, they are sure to expand in their scope and coverage.

First stop — the red planet.

Google Mars

Google Mars is a fascinating Web destination. From the Google Mars site at `www.google.com/mars` you can view the Martian landscape composed of three types of image data.

At the top right of the map, click one of the choices shown in Figure 40.1 that include the following:

- **Elevation:** The default view is a shaded relief map in bright ice-cream colors. The color coding is shown in an Elevation key overlaying the lower left of the map, letting you estimate the height.

- **Visible:** The visible view is composed of images taken by a digital camera. Along with the terrain, the images also show clouds and dust, just as you would have in your own camera shots.

- **Infrared:** The sharpest images are those captured in infrared because clouds and dust are transparent to the camera. The infrared map view shows tan-colored patches that indicate an area where a high-resolution mosaic image has been constructed using the infrared data.

FIGURE 40.1

Three different map choices are based on three imaging processes.

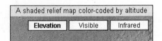

You don't see the planet's surface in true color. Mars is a dusty reddish-beige color, as you probably know from the images published from the Mars landing vehicles. The maps shown on Google Mars are grayscale images that show contrast in surface details more clearly than images in color.

Getting around the planet

Click Search the top of the Google Mars browser window to search by predefined categories, or type text in the Search field and click Search.

For example, suppose you are looking for one of the rovers that have been exploring Mars. You can type **rover** in the Search field, or if you can't remember the name, click the <u>Spacecraft</u> link, as shown in Figure 40.2.

FIGURE 40.2

Type a search term, or click one of the predefined search links.

The search results are listed in a column at the left of the map. Click a result link to see the balloon showing information and a pin on the appropriate map location. The example in Figure 40.3 shows the location where the Mars Pathfinder Rover worked for three months a decade ago. Click the image of the spacecraft or other object that displays in the pop-up to view further information.

FIGURE 40.3

Points of interest on the map display pop-up balloons that link to further pages of information.

Maneuvering around Mars

Google Mars offers a set of navigation tools for moving around the screen, as shown in Figure 40.4. Use the directional arrows at the top of the navigation tools to pan around the map view; click the center to return to a previous view. Drag the lower slider upward toward the (+) to zoom into the map, and drag the slider downward toward the (–) to zoom out of the map.

Use the navigation tools to move and zoom in and out of the map.

Google Mars displays the Elevation view as the default image type. Although less detailed than the Infrared view, the color represents differences in altitude on Mars quite distinctly. To help with distinguishing an extremely high mountaintop from a plain, the view displays a color key at the lower left of the map window, showing the differences in elevation. Figure 40.5 shows an area at approximately 21 km above ground level and an area at about 4 km below ground level.

Viewing Mars in color using the Elevation view

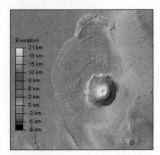

Viewing high resolution imagery

In the Elevation and Visible map options, you can zoom in as far as the navigation tool allows. Not so with the Infrared map. Zooming in too far produces a tiled image displaying the message shown in Figure 40.6.

The Infrared view doesn't support extreme magnification.

No imagery available at this zoom level. Try zooming out or click _here_ to center on a high-resolution insert.

Click the link in the image to display one of the close-up areas. As explained earlier, the Infrared view shows blocks of tan-colored surface, which indicates that a high-resolution image overlays that area of the map. An example of the high-resolution image and its neighboring image are shown in Figure 40.7.

FIGURE 40.7

You can see a number of close-up views of different points of interest in high detail, like the lower part of the figure.

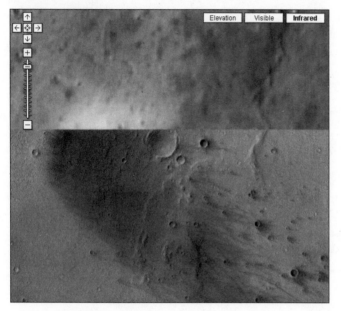

Into the future

You can't use Google Earth and its tools to examine Mars, although that is the plan for the future. Of course, you won't be placing any images of your backyard on Alba Tholus using Picasa2 or viewing 3-D fly-through movies to the park in the Galle Crater Dunes anytime soon.

To see a fly-through on Mars built using the data that makes up Google Mars maps, check out themis.asu.edu/valles_video and select your viewer from several options. The scenes are built by the JPL (Jet Propulsion Laboratory) and make up a four-minute movie. The animated overlay shown in Figure 40.8 gives you a sense of proportion when you view the movie.

Image Sources

The different types of images are generated by different NASA systems. The Elevation and Visible view images are both captured by the Mars Global Surveyor spacecraft. The Elevation maps are built from data from the Mars Orbiter Laser Altimeter (MOLA), and the Visible images were taken by the Mars Orbiter Camera (MOC).

Infrared images were taken by the Thermal Emission Imaging System (THEMIS) on NASA's Mars Odyssey spacecraft. THEMIS is one of the projects administered by Arizona State University; read more about the projects at www.themis.asu.edu.

FIGURE 40.8

For a taste of things to come, check out the fly-through of Mars's largest canyon.

Developing an itinerary with Google Transit

Instead of calling a cab, sitting in traffic, or missing your bus to the shopping mall again, some communities can now use Google Transit Trip Planner. Check out the service at www.google.com/transit. At the time of this writing, there are eight areas involved in the program, including Tampa, Honolulu, Eugene, Portland, Pittsburgh, and Seattle.

In areas where the service is available, simply type the information for your travel needs and receive the most efficient itinerary. The Google Transit Trip Planner functions in much the same way as Google Maps, although the directions returned are public transportation options instead of directions for driving.

CROSS-REF Read about Google Maps in Chapter 12.

Suppose you are in Portland, Oregon, for a few days and decide to take in a Trailblazers game. To find the most efficient route from your hotel to the game and arrive in time for the opening tip-off, follow these steps:

1. Open Google Transit at www.google.com/transit. You can use a combination of the street address, city/town name, or intersection for the search.

2. Type the Start address and the End address, as shown in Figure 40.9. If you have the addresses in the wrong field, click the double-headed arrow between the address fields to switch the addresses. Switch the addresses if you are looking for a return trip as well.

FIGURE 40.9

Specify addresses and time for travel in the respective fields to search for public transportation.

3. Select either Depart at or Arrive by, and type the date and time in the respective fields.

4. Click Get Directions to perform the search.

The search returns appear in the browser window. As you can see in Figure 40.10, the directions for walking and public transport are listed in sequence. Click any of the links in the returns to change the data, such as change the addresses, edit the times, or review reverse directions. You also can map the numbered points in the directions.

FIGURE 40.10

The most convenient route to your destination is shown on a map along with a list of interim stops and costs.

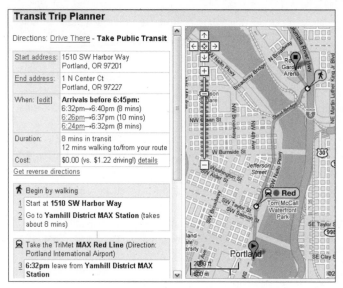

Browser Requirements

Google Transit supports a number of browsers, including these:

- Firefox 0.8 (Windows, Mac, Linux)
- IE 6.0 (Windows)
- Mozilla 1.4 (Windows, Mac, Linux)
- Netscape 7.1 (Windows, Mac, Linux)
- Opera 8.02 (Windows, Mac, Linux)
- Safari 1.2.4 (Mac)

One interesting feature of the Transit Trip Planner is a comparison of the cost of driving versus taking public transportation. In the example, driving cost is estimated at $1.22, while the route planned costs $0.00. The trip cost is based on the average mileage for the shortest route between the endpoints multiplied by the IRS business cost allowance for mileage of $.445 per mile.

If you decide to drive to the game after all, click the Drive There link at the top of the browser window to see a list of driving directions courtesy of Google Maps.

Hitching a ride with Google Ride Finder

You can watch little icons representing taxis and shuttles stuck in traffic using Google Ride Finder. Although that may not be the most scintillating event to watch, the very fact that you can watch it is remarkable.

Ride Finder offers a real-time view of the positions of public vehicles for hire in a number of U.S. cities, ranging from Austin, Texas, to Washington, D.C.

Suppose you are working late and decide that you want to take a taxi home from the office. Rather than calling the service and waiting in the lobby, follow these steps to check out the location of vehicles in Ride Finder:

1. Open the Ride Finder program at `http://labs.google.com/ridefinder`. The product opens in a browser window containing three parts: a Search field for typing a location, a map showing pins in locations that are tracked, and a list of cities linked to the map.

2. Select the city in which you are traveling by clicking the pin on the map, clicking the link in the list, or typing the name in the Search field and clicking Search.

3. Zoom into the map using the navigation tool at the upper left of the map, and position the area in which you are looking for transportation. The example in Figure 40.11 shows the collection of shuttles available at the Baltimore-Washington International Airport.

4. Click the Update Vehicle Locations link on the page below the map to see a trend in movement of vehicles — or nonmovement in the case of a traffic snarl.

FIGURE 40.11

View a snapshot of transportation services in a particular location that can be updated in real time.

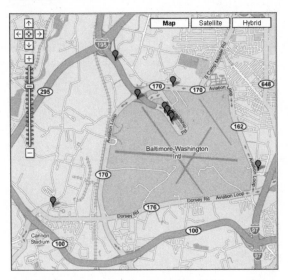

Making Browsing Easier

Some Google Labs tools are designed to make browsing and searching simpler and more targeted. The Web Accelerator, for example, uses a number of methods for increasing the speed of page loading. After you find your speedy results, check out Google Notebook for storing snippets of information and other data for future reference.

CROSS-REF Read about other desktop and browser enhancements such as Google Desktop in Chapter 11, the Google Pack in Chapter 30, and the Google Toolbar in Chapter 31.

Google Web Accelerator

Google Web Accelerator uses Google's computer network to make pages load faster and shows you how much time you have saved. The Web Accelerator is a download, and there's nothing to do manually once it is installed. Download the file from http://webaccelerator.google.com.

CAUTION The Web Accelerator doesn't make an appreciable difference in downloading pages for dial-up users, nor does it speed up HTTPS pages for security reasons. Finally, don't expect to speed up large downloads like streaming video or MP3 files.

Saving time

The Web Accelerator tool works in several ways, including these:

- Sending page requests through dedicated Web Accelerator traffic servers
- Storing copies of frequently used pages for quick access

- Scanning for and downloading updates to Web pages rather than the entire page
- Compressing data before downloading to your computer
- Prefetching pages in advance
- Managing your Internet connection's function to reduce delays

The list of actions appears to infringe on your personal security, and it does to some extent in order for the tool to work — for example, prefetching pages that you haven't asked for. In order for the Web Accelerator tool to work, it must create a cache on your hard drive, and it works in many ways like your ISP.

When you restart your browser after installation, you find a small toolbar added to the interface, as shown in Figure 40.12. The toolbar uses a speedometer icon to indicate that it is active, and it displays the amount of time that has been saved since the tool was installed or the cache cleared.

FIGURE 40.12

The Web Accelerator increases your browsing speed using a variety of methods.

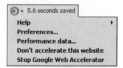

Managing settings

Change the way the Web Accelerator works on specific sites or in general. Click the down arrow on the Web Accelerator toolbar to open the drop-down menu, and then do any of these things:

- Choose Don't Accelerate this Website to exclude the page you are viewing from the tool's function. When you view a page that is excluded, the speedometer icon is shown in grayscale.
- Choose Stop Google Web Accelerator to prevent the tool from operating. When you stop the program, the icon appears as a pale gray circle without its speedometer indicator.
- Choose Performance Data from the menu, or click the time indicator shown on the tool to open a Web page showing the data from your Web Accelerator cache. You can reset the counter on this page.
- Choose Preferences to open the Preferences in a Web page. You can specify how pages are cached, whether to use prefetching, and the list of sites to exclude from the tool's operation. Select Clear History in the preferences to clear the Web Accelerator cache.

> **NOTE**   At the time of this writing, Google Web Accelerator was designed for automatic installation on Firefox 1.0 and Internet Explorer 5.5 and newer browsers. For other Windows browsers, the HTTP connections must be configured manually.

You can find the Web Accelerator in Internet Explorer by choosing View ➪ Toolbars ➪ Google Web Accelerator. In Firefox, choose Tools ➪ Extensions to find the toolbar listed in the Extensions dialog box.

Google Notebook

Many times, Web browsing is done for a specific purpose, such as searching for information on a particular topic or researching products before purchasing. Organizing the information you gather as you conduct your research can be difficult, and sometimes you don't have the information when you need it.

Installing the extension

Google Notebook is designed to make researching and organizing information simpler as well as portable. Google Notebook is a browser extension that you download and install before use.

Follow these steps to install and open Google Notebook:

1. Log in to your Google Account. In order to use Google Notebook, you must have a Google Accounts username and password.

2. Open the page at www.google.com/notebook.

3. Read the Terms of Service information, and click Agree and Download if you are using Firefox. For Internet Explorer, click the appropriate link on the page to locate and download the extension.

4. Close and reopen your browser to install the extension. When it is active, you see an icon and Open Notebook displayed at the lower-right edge of the browser window on the status bar.

5. To open the mini Google Notebook window, click Open Notebook on the status bar, as shown in Figure 40.13.

FIGURE 40.13

Install Google Notebook as a single icon on the status bar at the bottom of the browser window.

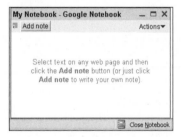

Adding content

You can add content to the Notebook, referred to as clippings, in two ways:

- Right-click the text, image, or link you want to clip, and choose Note this (Google Notebook).
- When using Google for searches, right-click the link, image, or other search result and choose Note this (Google Notebook).

Organizing results

The mini Google Notebook window that pops up from the status bar is handy for storing clips as you capture them, but it's not designed for organizing your clippings. Instead, use the full-page view. Either click the Actions button on the mini Google Notebook window and choose Go to full page view, or log in through www.google.com/notebook.

In full-page view, you can organize the clippings, add notes and comments, use section headings, and so on. Some of the common actions are shown in Figure 40.14 and include these:

- **Rename the notebook:** By default, a notebook is named My Notebook. To change the name, click the Actions down arrow at the upper right of the browser window and choose Rename this Notebook from the drop-down list. In the field that opens, type the new name and press Enter.

- **Use section headings:** By default, all contents are collected into one group. To add a section, click the first listing you want to appear under the section heading. Then click the Actions down arrow, and choose Add section heading from the drop-down list. Type a name for the heading, and click off the field to add the heading.

- **Reorganize content:** Drag a clipping from one heading to another, as shown in Figure 40.14.

FIGURE 40.14

Organizing clips into sections is a convenient way to keep track of your information.

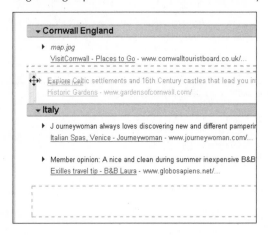

- **Delete content:** Select a note or section on the Notebook page, and click <u>Delete</u> when the link appears at the upper-right edge of the note. If you have multiple notebooks, select the notebook. Click the Actions down arrow, and choose Delete this notebook from the drop-down menu.

After you are working in the browser, the mini Google Notebook displays a list of your notebooks. Open the mini Google Notebook, and click Actions. Choose Show Notebook list to open the set of notebooks you are storing, as shown in Figure 40.15. Click a notebook's name to list its contents.

Google Dashboard Widgets

Google makes several widgets specifically for the Mac OS X user. Dashboard is an interface used to display widgets—small applications that you use for specific functions or tasks like the temperature, joke of the day, stock tracking, dictionaries, and so on. The Google widgets include Blogger, Gmail, and a Search History function.

FIGURE 40.15

Access the contents and add more clips to specific notebooks in the mini Google Notebook available on the browser window.

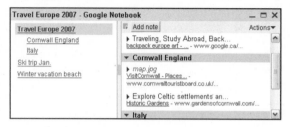

 Read about different ways to share and annotate your Notebook in the Google Notebook Help files.

Improving Specialized Searching

Two up-and-coming offerings from Google Labs are designed to enrich the material accessible to your site's users by offering specialized types of search options. Related Links offers links to information related to your content. Google Co-op lets you configure and host your own search engine.

Related Links

A Related Links unit is included on your Web site to provide links to information targeted to your site's content — hence the product name. Visitors can access content including video, news, pages, and searches.

 Related Links doesn't generate revenue for your site, and it isn't related to AdSense. You don't need to be an AdSense publisher to use Related Links.

The Related Links program is located at www.google.com/relatedlinks. Follow these steps to produce a Related Links product for your Web site:

1. On the main page for the Related Links product, read the Terms of Service and click Get Related Links to open the formatting options.

2. Choose the features you want to display in the Related Links unit:

   ■ **Specify a size:** Sizes range from a leaderboard that can hold three types of links to a small rectangle that can display two links.

   ■ **Select the link type:** Choose from Searches, News, Videos, and Web Pages. You can choose two or three, depending on the size of the link selected. Specify which link type to use as the default as well.

   ■ **Choose a color palette:** Click one of the color options, and view the color preview, as shown in Figure 40.16.

FIGURE 40.16

Choose the settings for the Related Links, including a default color palette.

3. Click the code within the code box at the bottom of the browser window to automatically select it.

4. Copy the code, and paste it into your Web page. If you want, customize the colors and size of the object to match your site's color scheme and layout.

If you want to add more links using different configurations, follow the steps again and make alternate choices, or configure the code yourself if you are comfortable working with JavaScript.

Some Related Links may not display as you anticipate for a number of reasons. Common reasons for display issues include a site that doesn't allow JavaScript, content that doesn't relate to available materials, or a site that doesn't comply with the program's guidelines. As shown in Figure 40.17, another reason that a Related Links block may not display content is when the page is new and hasn't yet been crawled.

FIGURE 40.17

A Related Links object on the Web page may not display as you expect for a number of reasons.

```
Design items for catalogs that combine images, links, and
backgrounds


              [                    ] [ Google Search ]
```

Customizing search engines with Google Co-op

One product recently released into the Google Labs is Google Co-op. With Google Co-op, you can create a custom search engine for your Web site. Unlike the Related Search tool, you can generate income for your site using the custom search in conjunction with AdSense for search.

Google Co-op offers three options for customizing searches, both from the user and the Webmaster perspectives:

- Create your own search engine.

- Use subscribed links to integrate your information into user's search results.

- Label sites with topics to improve the quality of Web searches in general. Contributors sign up to contribute to a topic area, and then search for sites to include as their favorites. Refer to www.google.com/coop/topics/ for information and a link to the current topic list.

Designing a custom search engine

To create the engine, follow these steps:

1. Open the Custom Search Engine page at www.google.com/coop/cse/overview.

2. Click Create a Search Engine to open the first page of the wizard. On this page, type a name for your search engine, a description, and keywords. List the sites to search, or use your own site.

NOTE If you haven't logged on to your Google account, the logon window opens first; log in and then continue.

3. Click to accept the Terms of Service, and then click Next to view the next screen.

4. Type search terms into the text field, and click Search. Results appear in a window.

   To make changes to the contents of your engine and consequently the likely search results, click back to Step 1 to make changes and repeat Step 3. Continue modifying your search engine's content as necessary.

5. Click Finish. Your search engine is ready for further use. For example, you can do these things:

   ■ Add it to the Google home page, as shown in Figure 40.18.

   ■ Download and use the code to include an Add to Google button on your Web site to allow users to include your search engine on their Google home page. The code for the button is available from the Search Engine's control panel.

FIGURE 40.18

You can use a custom search engine in a number of ways, including a custom Search Console on your Google home page.

ON the WEB Go to www.google.com/coop/cse/examples/Latest to view and experiment with some featured search engines.

Building Subscribed Links

A Subscribed Link is used to provide customized information that is displayed as part of a user's search results, such as the example shown in Figure 40.19.

FIGURE 40.19

Subscribed Links are included as part of a user's search results.

The Future of Accessible Searching

Google Labs is working on a product that is designed for those who work with screen readers and other assistive devices. Accessible Search is built on the same technology as Google Co-op and is designed to customize search results based on specialized interests. The Accessible Search tool first searches for the best results as in any search and then evaluates the pages for accessible markup. In particular, the pages are scanned for those likely to render well without viewing images, those that degrade gracefully, and those that are accessible with keyboard navigation, defined by the structure of the HTML.

The W3C standards and guidelines, such as Web Content Access Guidelines, are used as the benchmark for evaluating a page.

A Subscribed Link can be generated in three ways:

- **Use a basic link:** A basic link is built through a wizard interface. Although it is the simplest type of link to build, it also is the least flexible.

- **Upload a feed file:** Upload a data file from your disk to the Google servers in XML, RSS, or TSV formats. The uploaded file method is best for content that changes infrequently.

- **Submit a feed file URL:** For data that is updated regularly, specify the URL for a feed file that can be in XML, RSS, or TSV file formats. The file is recrawled and reflects the changes in your data in the Subscribed Link output.

Refer to the Google Co-op Web site for more information and instruction on designing and using the feed files.

Froogle on the move

Sometimes, you may come across what seems to be a bargain on an item for which you hadn't been searching and hadn't researched. To find out if you have a real bargain in your hands, check out the product via your mobile phone or device and Froogle.

CROSS-REF   Read Chapter 8 for information about Froogle and Chapter 28 for Google Mobile.

You can use Froogle Mobile if your phone or device supports Wireless Markup Language (WML), an XML-based language that was developed for wireless applications and that complies with Wireless Application Protocol (WAP 1.2).

To check out competing prices for your bargain product online, follow these steps:

1. Load Froogle on your phone's browser from http://wml.froogle.com.
2. Type the search term in the field, and click Search Froogle.
3. Check the results using the phone's keypad arrows; sort by price or best match using the links at the bottom of the search results.
4. Proceed with your bargain purchase, or say "Thank you for your time" and leave the premises.

Searching tidbits

A few more products developing in the Google Labs are designed for searching. Some are fairly obvious in their function, while seeing how others are put to use will be interesting. These are some of the products to watch:

- **Google Glossary:** You won't see anything loaded into your browser or download anything to use Google Glossary. Instead, redefine how you search for content using definitions. You can search for words, phrases, and acronyms. In the browser window, type "define [*term*]" and click Search. Your search returns list dictionary links and definitions.

- **Google Suggest:** Open the Google Suggest browser from the Google Labs listing, at `http://labs.google.com`. As you search, suggested keywords are added and change as the entered text changes, such as in the example shown in Figure 40.20. Google Suggest is available in English and Japanese.

FIGURE 40.20

Google Suggest completes terms as you type, according to the related result.

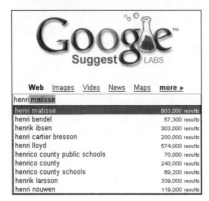

- **Google Sets:** Open the Google Sets browser from the Google Labs listing at `http://labs.google.com`. Type the names of some items in the fields, and click either Large Set or Small Set (15 items or fewer) to generate a set of terms that likely are extensions to the terms you typed in the example set. It is an interesting experiment.

Mining for Data

One product direction emerging from Google Labs scans the millions upon millions of searches and offers trends based on specific terms. Two products currently in the lab are Google Trends and Google Music Trends.

Google Trends

What's new and interesting in consumer electronics? Or fishing poles? Or steamer trunks? Find out using Google Trends, a feature that automatically reviews aggregate data and calculates trends based on a percentage. That is, how many searches have looked for the terms you typed compared to the total number of searches conducted in a specific time period? The results are based on a sample of the total number of searches conducted and displayed as a search-volume graph, as shown in Figure 40.21.

FIGURE 40.21

The returns are shown as linear graphs and identify the percentage of all searches that included your search terms.

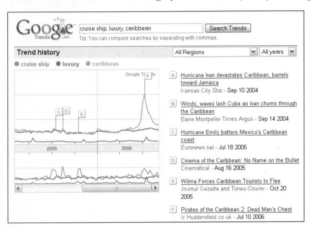

The graph also displays a news-reference graph that shows the number of times your search terms appeared in Google News stores. Spikes in volume result in a news story from the time of the spike. The story is automatically selected from Google News. Below the news reference graph are listed the top cities, regions, and languages for the first search term you used.

 If you use search operators in your search terms, the news-reference graph isn't displayed.

Use these rules and tips when using Google Trends:

- Compare up to five terms separated by commas.
- Include and exclude search terms using common search operators, such as (–) to exclude returns containing a particular term.
- Find an exact term by enclosing your search results in quotation marks.
- Restrict your returns to a specific time frame or region by choosing options from the drop-down boxes in the upper-right corner of the results page.
- The results shown by city are ranked by a search ratio, as shown in Figure 40.22. A sample of all searches in the listed cities is compared to the number of searches conducted for your first search term. The Regions and Languages searches work in the same way as the Cities searches.

FIGURE 40.22

Filter the returns from your search by time frame or region.

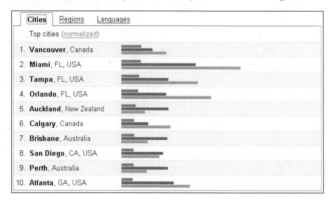

**CAUTION** Check the Terms of Use for the Trends features. The results from both Google Trends and Google Music Trends are free for you to use, but they must be attributed to Google.

Google Music Trends

Google Music Trends is a way to examine global tastes in music, at least among those using Google Talk. Music Trends is a voting system whereby each time you share your music status online through a music engine, you are voting for the music you are playing. The larger the pool of participants, logically, the more accurately the musical tastes are profiled.

CROSS-REF Music Trends is a feature of Google Talk, the subject of Chapter 20.

Setting up the tracking

To participate in Google Music Trends, you must configure several settings and tools, including these:

- Download and install Google Talk, available at www.google.com/talk.
- Indicate that you have one of the supported music players, including iTunes, Winamp, Windows Media Player, or Yahoo Music Engine.
- Opt in to the Music Trends system. On Google Talk, click Settings to open the Settings dialog box, and click Audio in the column at the left of the dialog box. In the Audio settings, select Share music listening history with Google Music Trends.
- Share your music status in Google Talk. Click the Status down arrow, and choose Show Current Music Track from the Available or Busy section, as shown in Figure 40.23.

The music status is automatically updated each time your player starts a new song. When the music stops, the status displays the default Available or Busy message. Change the status to an Available or Busy message to stop contributing data to the Music Trends results.

NOTE Opting in to Music Trends enables Personalized Search in Google to include your music history with your Search History along with Web, video, image, and other searches.

FIGURE 40.23

Activate music tracking from the Google Talk Status menu.

Viewing the results

The Google Music Trends results are updated every night. At the time of this writing, Music Trends are shown for ten countries. Votes from participants not living in one of the listed countries are included in the All Countries grand totals.

View the results at `www.google.com/trends/music`. From the results page, you can do these things:

■ Click a song's title or artist to open the entries in Google's Music Search, a service providing links to online music stores where you can buy the track or album.

■ Filter the trend results. Click the Genre down arrow, and choose an option from the available list. Not all countries filter by genre. Click the Country down arrow, and choose a country from the drop-down list. You can also filter by both country and genre, as shown in Figure 40.24.

FIGURE 40.24

Filter the Google Music Trends results by country and genre.

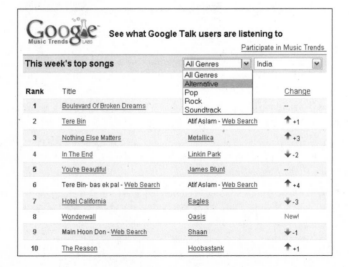

Summary

In this final chapter, you've literally been all over the map. Starting on a distant planet, you saw how Google Mars is developing as a repository of information and imagery. From outer space to urban space, Google Transit and Google Ride Finder are two applications under development that are aimed at making getting around your part of the world simpler. Although restricted to a number of specific markets at the present time, the data and user feedback being collected will help expand the service over time and make it a useful tool.

Searching and browsing for information isn't an easy task! Some of the new products in the Google Labs are designed to make your browsing experiences easier. To keep track of search results and notes for future reference, Google Notebook offers a replacement for the multiple stickies stuck around your monitor or all over your bulletin board.

Specialized searches are a Google specialty, and they continue to develop. Related Links is a tool you can add to your Web site that offers sophisticated options for visitors to your site for further investigation. Accessible Search generates filtered search results listing Web sites that are likely to be used by users working with screen readers and other assistive devices, based on Google Co-op technology. Google Co-op offers means to develop your own custom search engines.

And what is to be done with all that data? Google offers two types of trend tracking described in this chapter. Evaluate trends in searching sorted by categories such as city and date, and track music trends for a specific group using Google Music Trends.

Index